PRAISE FROM OUR READERS

Mastering Access 97

"I read this book from cover to cover and found each page loaded with very practical information and explicit examples. I commend the authors for their ability to communicate otherwise very technical detail in understandable 'user friendly' language. I highly recommend this book."

Jim Shannon, Montana

Mastering FrontPage 98

"Best of the 9 FrontPage 98 books I own. Sybex does it again! I have been reading computer books for the last 10 years and Sybex has been a great publisher—putting out excellent books. After reading 3/4 of the book so far, I know that the publisher and the authors take pride in their product. It's a wonderful book!"

Mike Perry, New Jersey

"This is THE book for mastering FrontPage 98! I skimmed through 4 other books before deciding to buy this one. Every other book seemed like a larger version of the weak documentation that comes with the software. This book provided the insight on advanced subjects necessary for administering a web. A must buy for FrontPage users."

Richard Hartsell, Utah

Mastering Windows 98

"The first book I've read that does what it says it will do! I learned more about Windows 98 in the first one hundred pages of this book than in all of the previous books I had read. My copy lies, dog-eared, beside my computer as a constantly ready source of easy to understand information. It really does show you how to Master Windows 98."

Steven Dean, Arizona

SYBEX

www.sybex.com

MASTERING™

MICROSOFT® PROJECT 2000

Gini Courter
Annette Marquis

SYBEX®

San Francisco • Paris • Düsseldorf • Soest • London

Associate Publisher: Cheryl Applewood
Contracts and Licensing Manager: Kristine O'Callaghan
Acquisitions & Developmental Editor: Sherry Bonelli
Editor: Nancy Sixsmith
Project Editors: Donna Crossman, Lisa Duran
Technical Editor: Acey James Bunch
Book Designers: Patrick Dintino, Catalin Dulfu,
Franz Baumhackl
Graphic Illustrator: Tony Jonick
Electronic Publishing Specialist: Franz Baumhackl
Project Team Leader: Shannon Murphy
Proofreaders: Jennifer Campbell, Molly Glover,
Patrick J. Peterson
Indexer: Matthew Spence
Cover Designer: Design Site
Cover Illustrator/Photographer: Sergie Loobkoff,
Design Site

Library of Congress Card Number: 99-69456
ISBN: 0-7821-2656-1

Manufactured in the United States of America

10 9 8 7 6 5 4

SYBEX is a registered trademark of SYBEX Inc.

Mastering is a trademark of SYBEX Inc.

Screen reproductions produced with FullShot 99.
FullShot 99 © 1991–1999 Inbit Incorporated. All rights
reserved. FullShot is a trademark of Inbit Incorporated.

Screen reproductions produced with Collage Complete.
Collage Complete is a trademark of Inner Media Inc.

Internet screen shot(s) using Microsoft Internet Explorer 5
reprinted by permission from Microsoft Corporation.

TRADEMARKS: SYBEX has attempted throughout this
book to distinguish proprietary trademarks from descriptive terms by following the capitalization style used by
the manufacturer.

To Charlotte, who continues

to stick by us through it all.

You are the best!

ACKNOWLEDGMENTS

This book about project management also served double-duty as a case study in project management. Some tasks went as planned and some went completely awry. Every project provides "opportunities for learning" if you're open to the experience. During the course of creating this book, we learned and relearned lessons about scheduling and resource allocation that come only when you are managing a real live project. We can't say enough about the team we had to work with to pull off this ambitious enterprise. It took the entire project team—the incredible group at Sybex and the skilled employees at our company, TRIAD Consulting—to steer this project to a successful conclusion.

Sherry Bonelli, our phenomenal acquisitions and developmental editor, hung in there with us even through the dismal days, and for that we are eternally grateful. She is a noble champion, a great cheerleader, and a caring but pragmatic editor who also knows where to shop for truffles online (www.godiva.com). We can't imagine working with anyone else. Thanks, Sherry, for everything.

Donna Crossman was a wonderful project editor, providing just enough pressure to keep things flowing, even when the flow was only a trickle. This was our first experience working with Donna and we appreciated her good humor and encouragement throughout the first part of the project. Initially, Lisa Duran was only pinch-hitting to get us through the holidays, but she loved this book so much that she ended up taking over the project. You both had challenges placed before you, and you handled them with grace and style. Editor Nancy Sixsmith was very helpful in tightening up our text, fixing our grammatical errors, and making us sound much more coherent than we were on our own. We also appreciate the help of our tech editor, Acey James Bunch, who made sure we stayed technically accurate while describing work with a complex product. Thank you, Donna, Lisa, Nancy, and Acey for all your contributions.

We also want to thank our Sybex production team: Shannon Murphy, project team leader; Franz Baumhackl, electronic publishing specialist; and Jennifer Campbell, Molly Glover, and Patrick J. Peterson, proofreaders. We write words—they make them attractive and get the pages out to the printer on time. We appreciate the incredibly fast turnaround and all the hard work by our production team.

Finally, we have to extend our heartfelt thanks to network administrator Sharon Roberts for getting the Project Central Server installed and running, despite the challenges presented by largely undocumented beta software. With deep gratitude, we thank the TRIAD team—Sharon, Karla Browning, James Howe, Angie Okonski—and Lauren Works for stepping up to the plate and hitting a grand slam. The crowd goes wild. The authors cheer. The book is completed. Thank you all.

CONTENTS AT A GLANCE

TABLE OF CONTENTS

PART II • CREATING A PROJECT FROM START TO FINISH

PART IV • EVALUATING AND ANALYZING PROJECT DATA

INTRODUCTION

In today's fast-paced, production-oriented work environment, managing one project after another, and often juggling several at once is a way of life for many middle managers. Project management is a complex field to which some people dedicate their careers. A professionally trained project manager may have a graduate degree in project management and be certified as a Project Management Professional (PMP). However, more and more job descriptions include elements of project management, whether or not project management appears in your title, job description, or training. If you are ever responsible for coordinating a variety of tasks that must be completed within a specific timeframe for a set amount of money, you are a project manager and we wrote this book for you. We've included background about quality project management, especially as it applies to small and medium-sized projects. This book does not focus on projects such as sending a probe to Mars or building a skyscraper. Instead, we focused on the projects that millions of project managers like you are involved with every day: developing a software product, publishing a newsletter, establishing a new office in another city, or implementing a training program. These projects of the workaday world might not involve a multi-million- or billion-dollar budget, but they must still be managed effectively. Careers are advanced or stalled based on our success in managing projects of every size.

If you're a professional project manager, we hope that this book helps you find the best ways to utilize the tools offered with Microsoft Project 2000. If you're an experienced project manager, you may want to forego the appetizers and skip to the main course, beginning in Chapter 4. Refer to the section called "Using this Book," later in this Introduction, to see what chapters you might find most interesting.

 NOTE If you are interested in finding out about what it takes to be certified as a project manager, you should check out the Project Management Institute at www.pmi.org. This is how PMI defines itself: "Since its founding in 1969, Project Management Institute (PMI®) has grown to be the organization of choice for project management professionalism. With over 50,000 members worldwide, PMI® is the leading nonprofit professional association in the area of Project Management. PMI establishes Project Management standards, provides seminars, educational programs and professional certification that more and more organizations desire for their project leaders."

Using This Book

Mastering Microsoft Project 2000 was written to help demystify the process of managing a project with PC software. This is not always an easy proposition. Microsoft Project gives the appearance of being an enhanced task manager. You can make lists of tasks and then assign them to individual resources and resource teams. You can assign costs to tasks and to resources so you can track budgets and expenses. However, Microsoft Project's primary mission is not to help you create task lists. First and foremost, Project is designed to schedule projects. Project 2000 calculates project schedules based on the estimates you provide for variables such as task duration, assigned resources, effort, and start and finish constraints. If you don't understand the way Microsoft Project calculates schedules, you cannot use Project effectively to manage your projects. When you grasp the concepts that underlie the schedule calculations, Project not only helps you manage your projects, but it also identifies over- and underallocated resources, estimates cost overruns, and helps you make informed managerial decisions to get the project completed successfully.

Throughout this book, we make every attempt to help you understand these project management concepts, specifically as they relate to Microsoft Project 2000, so you can apply the concepts to the features you need to use. We discuss general project management concepts in Chapters 1–3. Other project management topics are interspersed through the chapters when we introduce specific Project features. If you are new to project management, we recommend that you read Chapters 1–3, and then follow Chapters 5–12 through developing the project plan and into tracking project progress. You could skip from there to Chapters 17, 18, and 20 to learn how to report on and close a project. If you have trouble understanding specific features, you may want to review the general concepts information to help put the features into perspective.

If you are an experienced project manager who has used previous versions of Microsoft Project, the chapters stand on their own, so feel free to skip around to the topics you need most to get your project underway.

 NOTE Project 2000 is based on the Office 2000 software model, and was designed for increased interaction with Office 2000. Sybex publishes a Mastering book for each Microsoft Office 2000 application. If you need additional information about Office 2000 software or features, consult the Sybex Mastering book for the application you want to know more about.

Throughout the chapters, you will find sidebars—brief boxed discussions that call your attention to related topics. "Mastering the Opportunities" sidebars describe techniques you can use to apply Project 2000 in a specific setting. "Mastering Troubleshooting" sidebars focus on common mistakes or problems that users encounter, and suggest strategies to get around them. You'll also find Tips, Notes, and Warnings scattered throughout the book to highlight additional information you'll find useful.

 To focus on new features being introduced or greatly improved in Project 2000, look for the symbol shown here.

This book is divided into five parts, each of which focuses on specific skills related to project management. Part I gets you started in project management and Microsoft Project 2000. Part II is the main course, from opening to closing a project in Microsoft Project 2000. Part III covers how to manage multiple projects, assess risks in a project, and work effectively with a project team. In Part IV, you'll learn how to evaluate what's going on in a project, respond to problems that could affect the project's outcome, and use importing, exporting, and reporting tools to make the most of project data. Part V gives you the skills you need to customize and automate Project to meet your specific needs.

Part I: Introducing Microsoft Project 2000

The first three chapters in Part I introduce Microsoft Project 2000 and provide an overview of project management. You'll learn about project management concepts, such as the project triangle and the project cycle. If you are an experienced project manager and you are raring to go, you'll find Chapter 4 particularly helpful; it's a complete overview of how to use Project from start to finish. If you are new to this arena, Chapter 4 lets you see the complete picture so you'll have a better idea of where you are going as you move forward and develop your project plan.

Part II: Creating a Project from Start to Finish

Part II is the longest section of the book because it covers the nuts and bolts of working with Project: from building a new project to preparing your project for publication, tracking progress, and making management decisions. In Part II, you'll learn how to enter and schedule tasks, define and assign resources and costs, identify over- and underallocations, and control scope creep. You'll also learn about using earned value analysis to analyze costs and variances. This part also discusses how quality standards affect projects and how you can assess your project for quality.

Part III: Juggling and Managing Projects

Part III introduces a method of creating estimates and analyzing risk in projects: PERT (Performance Evaluation and Review Technique). In complex projects or projects with unfamiliar tasks, PERT is used to more accurately estimate the project schedule.

Very few projects are completed in a vacuum, and most project managers have more than a few irons in the fire. In Part III, you'll also learn how to share resources and tasks among multiple projects and how to communicate project information to members of the team. Chapter 16 introduces Microsoft's new and improved Web-based project communication product: Microsoft Project Central. Sold separately, Project Central integrates with Microsoft Project for full-featured, team-based communication about your projects.

Part IV: Evaluating and Analyzing Project Data

Getting data in and out of Microsoft Project is always a challenge. In Part IV, we'll show you how to create views and reports that include the information you want to see represented. Chapter 19 is an exhaustive review of importing and exporting methods that you can use to move Project data back and forth between other database and spreadsheet products for analysis and reporting.

Part V: Customizing and Automating Project 2000

Chapter 21 begins with a discussion of customizing the Project 2000 environment to suit your needs, including customizing toolbars, setting options, creating and using templates, and working with the Organizer—Project's tool for copying and moving Project forms and objects. In Chapter 22, you'll create and use macros in Project. Chapter 23 focuses on customizing Project fields and creating custom forms for your use in Project. In Chapters 24 and 25, you'll see how to use Visual Basic for Applications and the Project object model to create custom applications in Project. And finally, Chapter 26 gives you what you need to know to install and administer Microsoft Project Central.

Conventions Used in This Book

Throughout this book, you will find references to the Standard and Formatting toolbars. The Standard and Formatting toolbars are the two toolbars most commonly displayed in various Office applications, as shown here.

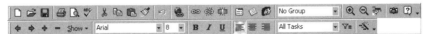

When you launch Microsoft Project, the Standard and Formatting toolbars are set to share one row, and are referred to collectively as the personal toolbar. The personal toolbar is a new feature of Office 2000 that displays the buttons you use most commonly on one toolbar row. As you add additional buttons, less-frequently-used buttons are removed.

Buttons displayed on the Personal toolbar still "belong" to either the Standard or Formatting toolbar. In this book, you will see figures and graphics that display the Personal toolbar option and others that show the more traditional two-toolbar display. In either case, the text refers to the native location of the button, i.e., the Standard or Formatting toolbar. To turn off personal toolbars, choose View ➢ Toolbars ➢ Customize, and clear the Standard And Formatting Toolbar Share One Row checkbox on the Options tab of the Customize dialog box. We also recommend turning off the personalized menus by clearing the Menus Show Recently Used Commands First checkbox.

We also used a couple of typographic variations that you've probably seen in other computer books:

- **Boldface type** shows any text you would type into Office dialog boxes.

- *Italicized type* is used for new terms, placeholders, and emphasis.

- This `special font` represents programming instructions, URLs, Excel formulas, HTML or Visual Basic code, directories, path names, and filenames.

We'd Love to Hear from You!

We hope this book provides you with the skills you need to master Microsoft Project 2000. We would love to hear what you think. We always enjoy hearing from our readers and are especially interested in hearing about your experiences and accomplishments with Project 2000.

Gini Courter and Annette Marquis

c/o Sybex, Inc.

1151 Marina Village Parkway

Alameda, CA 94501

E-mail: `authors@triadconsulting.com`

PART I

Introducing Microsoft Project 2000

LEARN TO:

- *Manage Project 2000 Basics*

- *Understand Projects*

- *Understand Project Management Tasks*

- *Use Project 2000 Quickstart*

CHAPTER <u>1</u>

Project 2000 Basics

I f you're browsing this book, you probably have more than a casual interest in projects and project management. You may have managed scores of projects, or you may be starting on your first project as a team member or project manager. Perhaps you already use Microsoft Project or its competitors, and want to know about the new features of this version of the most widely used project-management software. Whether you're launching your first or fifty-first project, Microsoft Project 2000 can improve the probability that your project will be a success. Before we examine Project 2000, however, we'll spend a few pages on a quick but pragmatic review of project fundamentals.

What Is a Project?

It's estimated that half of our work life is spent on routine, repetitive tasks: processing time cards, filling out sales orders, picking up passengers, and delivering parcels. Projects account for the other half of the work done in organizations. A *project* is a job that has a beginning and an end (time), a specified outcome (scope) at a stated level of quality (performance), and a budget (costs). Here are a few examples of projects:

- Moving your company's offices to a new location
- Developing a new software application
- Creating a policy manual
- Remodeling a room in your home
- Developing an intranet
- Preparing for accreditation or certification
- Revamping a training program
- Starting a new business
- Auditing your organization's software or accounting systems

The four project parameters—time, scope, performance, and costs—are related. This relationship is often expressed as a formula $[C=f(P,T,S)]$, which indicates that a project's cost is a function of a project's time, scope, and performance. One definition of project management is efficiently using resources to complete a project as designed, on time, at the desired level of performance, and within budget. These project parameters are also called *constraints*.

At any point in time, you can control only three of the four parameters because when one of the project parameters changes, at least one other parameter must change in response. Imagine, for example, that you're adding a deck to your home. The planned deck is an incredibly tasteful 200-square-foot redwood deck with built-in benches and a small yet attractive planter. A few months ago, your contractor said that she can build the deck for a total cost of $2,500 with three weeks' notice. There's only one problem: the deck needs to be completed in the next ten days. You already sent out the invitations for your inaugural deck barbeque, but neglected to contact the contractor. The project time changed, so performance, scope, or costs must also change. The contractor's possibilities are limited, as follows:

- Performance: "We have an additional crew that hasn't built a deck before, but they've got some extra time on their hands, so we can assign them to help."

- Scope: "We can't build the benches in time, and the deck won't be stained or treated."

- Costs: "We can build the deck as planned, but it will cost an extra $750. I'll have to pay overtime and rush ship the redwood."

It's usually easy to know when a project's time criteria change. The project manager (in our example, the contractor) is notified that work must be completed sooner, or could finish later. Changes in scope, on the other hand, can sneak into a project as managers, customers, and team members request seemingly minor enhancements. *Scope creep*—unplanned changes in project scope—is understandable. The project manager and team members want to create a product that people use. Fulfilling requests for minor changes is relatively easy and will certainly please the requestor. The cumulative effect of these small changes, though, can significantly extend the project timeline and costs. Experienced project managers have a formal process for reviewing and approving changes to the project. The process is communicated to everyone involved with the project to stave off scope creep.

Understanding the Project Cycle

The *project cycle* broadly describes the stages that a project typically goes through from beginning to completion. There are as many descriptions of the project cycle as there are project-management experts. Here are the stages of a six-stage project cycle that is used in a number of different disciplines:

- Problem Identification
- Definition
- Project Design
- Development
- Implementation
- Evaluation

Whether a product cycle has six stages, or four or ten, the sequence is the same. Each stage has different activities that may require different skills. The project team is the human resource assigned to the project. Some projects are short-lived, lasting for a matter of months. Other projects span years, team members leave, and new members are added, but the scope and budget for the project remain unchanged.

Problem Identification

In the problem identification stage, also referred to as the *concept stage* or *needs stage*, the project is just a thought. Someone realizes there is a problem in search of a solution or an opportunity that the organization can take advantage of. For example, the Customer Service department reports that half of their calls about software X are user questions about installation. The urge, of course, is to immediately search for a solution. One solution is to rewrite the relevant portion of the user guide, but is it the best solution or even an appropriate solution? To answer this question, you need to have a better understanding of the problem.

Definition

In the definition stage, a person or group of people accurately describes the problem (or, more positively, the challenge or opportunity) that the project is attempting to solve. In our Customer Service example, there are a number of possible problem definitions:

- The Customer Service department gets too many calls about installation.
- The installation program is too difficult for customers to use.
- The installation program doesn't work well on all computers.
- The instructions for the installation routine are incorrect or hard to follow.
- Customers often purchase the wrong software for their computer because the software packages aren't labeled clearly.

Each of these problems has one or more solutions, but the solutions are different.

The definition stage is often neglected, which helps explain why some projects fail. The definition of the problem determines the solutions that the project team will examine and eventually choose to implement. If you're focused on rewriting the installation program, you won't spend a lot of time looking at the product packaging. An often-heard complaint during the project definition stage is "We all know what the problem is, so why are we wasting time talking about it? Let's get to work!" The challenge of the definition stage is to take the time to thoroughly describe the problem, beginning with the naïve question: What is the problem we're trying to solve?

 NOTE In the past decade, the trend in project management has been to study and define the problem and its solution from the customer's point of view. For example: Customers should be able to easily install and use the correct version of software X.

When the problem definition is complete, check it out with people outside the project team. This is a good time to talk to the person or department who initially identified the problem. When a problem involves customers, some organizations survey customers to help gauge the accuracy of the definition.

When the definition is accurate, the team can begin identifying potential solutions. Brainstorming possible strategies that address the problem is a good way to begin. Then, each strategy needs to be quickly assessed to estimate the time and resources involved. As you'll see in later chapters, you can use Microsoft Project 2000 to assess strategies. You'll eliminate some strategies in this analysis because they're cost-prohibitive, require resources your organization can't hire or contract, or would take too long to complete. For the remaining strategies, you'll complete a risk assessment. Ask what can go wrong and how your team could respond if the worst happened. Use the risk assessment to eliminate high-risk strategies and identify risky aspects of acceptable strategies. Choose the best strategy from those with a level of risk that's acceptable in your organization, and begin designing a project to implement the strategy. Before you begin, check again to make sure that the selected strategy will solve the problem you defined.

Project Design

In the design stage, it's finally time to put the pedal to the metal and complete a number of tasks. In order to do this, you must

- define the project's objectives,
- finalize the project scope,
- identify project activities,
- break each activity into logical components,
- assign resources, and
- create estimates for time and costs.

This is the "go/no go" point of the project. The outcome of the design stage is a project budget and timeline. If costs are prohibitive, if the timeline can't be met, or if the outcome is not desirable, a decision may be made to scrap the project. On the other hand, if a realistic solution can be attained in a cost-effective and timely manner, the project may very well get the "go ahead."

Project design is critical because the parameters you set or accept during design determine what victory—the successful completion of the project—will look like. Project objectives should be well-defined products or services, often called *deliverables*. Design serves two purposes: It provides a clear vision for the members of the project team and helps fend off scope creep as the project progresses. The finished design includes a list of deliverables with completion dates.

NOTE In some organizations, the design stage includes pressure to trim the timeline or budget in ways that potentially compromise the project. In the book *Death March: Managing "Mission Impossible" Projects*, software project manager Edward Yourdon defines a *death march* as a project in which at least one of the four parameters exceeds the norm by at least 50 percent. A two-year project is optimistically scheduled for completion in 12 months or less, the staff or budget for a project is cut in half, or the features and performance requirements are twice what can reasonably be completed during the life of the project. When one of the parameters is off by 50 percent or more, the likelihood of project failure is at least 50 percent. As the project deadline approaches, members of the project team do triage by lowering performance standards, abandoning project objectives, or incurring increased costs to complete the project within at least one of the specified parameters—activities—that should have occurred in the design stage.

Near the end of the design stage, circulate a project proposal that describes the project in detail so that project team members and managers are all aware of the project's scope, costs, performance standards, and timelines. You can print some of the reports you need for the project proposal from Project 2000. Other parts of the document may be created in Word, PowerPoint, Excel, or other applications.

Have the project's customers and other stakeholders sign a letter of agreement or project charter that indicates their approval for the project design, budget, and timeline. In most organizations, this is done for internal customers (the department or people the project is being done for) as well as external clients. Use the final budget and timeline information to update your project information in Project 2000 before moving into the next stage of the project.

Development

In the development stage, you expend resources according to the project plan to complete the activities specified in the project design. If the project outcome is a new product, manufacturing tools up and the product begins rolling off the assembly line. In the software industry, interface specialists begin designing the interface, and then programmers start writing code. In the publishing industry, authors write, editors edit, and desktop publishers lay out pages. In an organization that creates new curricula, trainers design and write the curricular modules.

Quality assurance and communication skills are vital to measure performance and to communicate the status of the project tasks in the development stage. As tasks are partially or wholly completed or revised, you update your project file in Microsoft Project. Project 2000 will help you manage development by providing accurate comparisons of actual performance and resource use to the project plan, budget, and timeline.

Implementation

Implementation involves field-testing and measurement. Products are used by focus groups, software is sent to beta testers, and new courses are tested on a limited basis. Based on feedback, products may be modified or re-engineered, and services or service delivery might be redesigned.

NOTE There is a tendency to rip through this stage with great speed, particularly if the project involves a product. In the computer industry, in particular, the conventional wisdom is that it's better to release an adequate software version or microcomputer processor on time than to release a drastically improved version of the same product six months late.

Evaluation

In the final stage of a project, members of the project team review the project. Using project reports and their personal experiences with the project, team members decide what worked well and identify areas for improvement. Even when a project is incredibly successful, it can be difficult to conduct a good evaluation—the project is over, you already held the victory party, and team members have been assigned to their next projects. Do it anyway. Solid, thoughtful project evaluations can provide a foundation for the organization's success in future projects.

NOTE If you want more information on project management strategies and practices, we recommend *The Project Manager's Desk Reference,* by James P. Lewis (McGraw Hill, 1999, ISBN 0-07-13-4750-X) and *Project Management for the 21st Century,* by Bennet P. Lientz and Kathryn P. Rea (Academic Pr., 1998, ISBN 0-12-449966-X). For insight on project management in high tech industries, see Edward Yourdon's *Death March* (Prentice Hall, 1999, ISBN 0-13-748310-4), mentioned earlier in this chapter.

Project Management and Software

At the heart of every project is a project manager, the person responsible for ensuring that a project is completed on time, within budget, and at the specified level of quality. Project-management software is a set of tools that support the core tasks of project management: planning, scheduling, and control. The first project-management software tools were developed in the late 1960s for mainframe computers. In the 1970s and 1980s, new microcomputer project management packages were released in a continual stream. By the early 1990s, there were more than 100 software-management packages on the market. Early packages focused on scheduling people and equipment, and managing costs.

There are still a number of project-management software packages, but only a handful are widely used. Project 2000 is the newest version of Microsoft's market-dominating project-management software. As you'll see in the chapters that follow, Project 2000 supports many aspects of project management: scheduling, budgeting, tracking, analysis, reporting, and communication. With Project 2000, you can manage multiple projects, share resources between projects, import and export project data, and create reports to analyze and communicate project objectives and progress.

What's New in Project 2000

If you're a Project user, you will be pleased with a number of new and improved features in this version. The team that created Project 2000 focused on Web components, increased flexibility, and greater ease of use. They also added software features that users of prior versions of Project requested, and made Project easier to use with the Office 2000 applications.

Web-based Workgroup Features

Project 2000 expands the workgroup features that originally appeared in Project 98. With Microsoft Project Central 2000 and Microsoft Internet Information Server, members of your project team can view project data by using Internet Explorer or another browser. Information for the project is stored in a database (SQL Server, Oracle, or MSDE—which is a light version of SQL Server). You enable the project's Web features by simply entering the URL for your Web server. Users log into the server and see a personalized home page for the project like the page shown in Figure 1.1.

From the personal home page, users can switch to other views, including time sheets, task lists, and charts. Project Central 2000's Web features make it easy to communicate information about the project to all members of the project team, no matter where they're physically located.

Even without Project Central, if your Web server has the Office or FrontPage server extensions loaded, you can easily save a project to your corporate intranet or to another Web site. And you can use the email workgroup features to communicate by using Microsoft Outlook or another email program.

 NOTE One license of Project Central is included with Microsoft Projec. purchase additional licenses separately. For more information visit the Micr at www.microsoft.com/office/project.

FIGURE 1.1

Use Microsoft Project Central 2000 to increase communication between team members through the use of the Web.

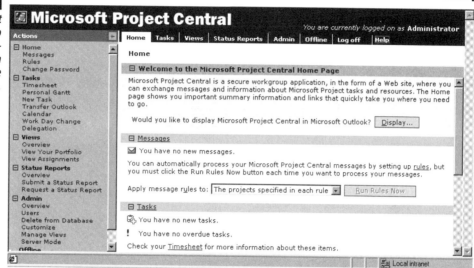

Increased Flexibility

Project 2000 has a number of subtle enhancements that make it more responsive to user needs. For example, in Project 2000, you determine the format for WBS (Work Breakdown Structure) numbering, so you can set activities as ordinal numbers and subactivities as decimal numbers (1, 1.1, 1.2, 2, 2.1, 2.2, and so on.). Project assigns codes based on the format, and ensures that each code is unique. Like Office 2000, Project 2000 supports language packs to display application features in the language you select.

Improvements in Tasks and Scheduling   If you've ever had second thoughts after locking down a project baseline, you'll appreciate Project 2000's Clear Baseline feature. You can clear the baseline for the entire project or a selection.

Months have been added to the list of duration units, so you can enter **2mon** as a length of time rather than **60days**. Tasks can have different base calendars, so a project can reflect time for factory retooling, scheduled maintenance, and other adjustments that are task- rather than resource-dependent. Project 2000 has a greater range of values for prioritizing tasks: 1 to 1000 rather than the 10-step scale used in Project 98. You can assign a priority to an entire project to improve resource leveling between projects that share a resource pool.

Tasks have another new attribute: deadline dates. Deadline dates are different from constraints; deadlines don't affect the project schedule calculation, but they provide needed information for management control of the project. Assign deadline dates to critical tasks, and you can quickly view the tasks that were not finished before the deadline.

The PERT Chart view has been remodeled and renamed. The new Network Diagram view (see Figure 1.2) supports filters. The diagram is expandable and collapsible, so you can hide or display subtasks.

FIGURE 1.2

The Network Diagram view replaces the PERT Chart view.

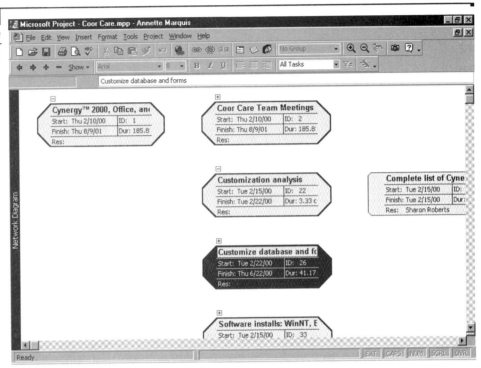

Programming and Customization   Prior versions of Project let you store custom fields. In Project 2000, you can manipulate the data in custom fields and create calculated fields by using many of the same functions you use in Excel (see Figure 1.3). Customization doesn't stop with custom fields. You can customize the forms that you use to enter data about project tasks and the people who work on them. When you customize a form, you can use list box controls for more accurate data entry.

Project 98 provided good support for Visual Basic for Applications (VBA), increasing Project's viability as a development platform. For Project 2000, Microsoft has exposed even more project objects, which results in increased programmability. You can use VBA to program Project 2000, but you also take advantage of this added flexibility when you load COM objects that extend the functionality of Project 2000. If you need more customization than the custom fields and forms included in Project 2000 provide, you can create user forms and project level variables in VBA.

FIGURE 1.3

With Project 2000, you can create calculated fields.

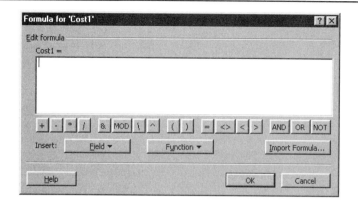

Ease of Use

Many of the new features in this category provide functionality that users take for granted in other Microsoft desktop applications. For example, the fill handle works as it has in numerous versions of Excel. Click a cell in Project to edit in the cell as you would in an Excel worksheet, or use the row height adjustment tool to set the height of an individual row. Project 2000 is a Single Document Interface (SDI) application; you can open multiple projects and switch between them by using the buttons on the Windows taskbar.

As in the Office applications, you can specify a default Save path (finally!), rather than switching folders each time you start a new session of Project or save a file. There's also an AutoSave option as there is in Word and Excel 2000.

Accessibility   There are two improvements in this version of Project that address accessibility. Project 2000 relies directly on the display settings in the Windows Control Panel, which results in improved support for the high-contrast display settings. Project supports Microsoft Active Accessibility (MSAA), so third-party accessibility programs such as text readers, and voice-input and speech-recognition software can be configured to work with Project.

What's Next

In the next chapter, we'll walk through the design stage of a project to learn about Project 2000 components like activities and resources in more detail. Chapter 3, "Understanding Project Management Tasks," focuses on project management tasks used in the development stage.

CHAPTER 2

Understanding Projects

When you have completed the problem identification and definition stages (see Chapter 1, "Project 2000 Basics"), you're ready to begin designing your project. In this chapter, we'll use a training project scenario to illustrate project design.

Scenario

Train2K, Inc. is a software training company. Train2K has ten trainers; most of the company's training is conducted within 200 miles of its Georgia office. One of Train2K's clients, XYZ Corporation, is creating software templates and applications for use throughout the company to replace manual paper-based forms. Many of the 120 employees at four branch offices (Detroit, Kansas City, San Francisco, and Dallas) will not use the software templates and applications; they will continue to use the paper-based forms that XYZ wants to phase out.

Problem Identification and Definition

In their first meeting about the training project, the Train2K and XYZ Corporation managers examined the problem and created the following definition:

It is difficult for branch office employees to embrace the software tools developed at corporate headquarters in Atlanta. The problem isn't software or hardware—it's training. There are frequent training opportunities for Atlanta-based staff that focus on the skills that XYZ employees are expected to have. Compared to employees at headquarters, branch office employees receive less training, and the training they receive from local companies is less focused.

XYZ managers talked to their corporate help desk and branch office employees, who agreed with the problem definition.

Project Objectives and Deliverables

At the second meeting, XYZ and Train2K managers agree on a plan. Training will be held near each branch office. Each branch office employee will be encouraged to attend a total of 20 hours of training in Windows, Word, and Excel—just like the training provided at the Atlanta offices. Employees will take a pretest and a posttest, to be developed by Train2K. Pretest results will be used to schedule employees for classes. Posttest results will be used to measure training effectiveness. The Train2K managers have agreed to create a training proposal for XYZ Corporation and implement the training proposal, if it is accepted.

Project Constraints

All training must be completed by the end of the budget year, three months away. Train2K maintains a trainer to trainee ratio of 1:12 or fewer in applications courses.

Analyzing Project Activities

A *project* includes a series of activities. To analyze project activities, begin by creating a comprehensive sequential list of the major activities that the project deliverables require. Some of the major activities for the XYZ Branch Office Training project (which will quickly be shortened to the "XYZ-BOT project") are shown in Table 2.1.

TABLE 2.1: BOT PROJECT ACTIVITIES

1. Develop proposal.
2. Get approval for project.
3. Develop pretest.
4. Set training schedule for each branch office.
5. Make trainer travel arrangements.
6. Reserve training facilities.
7. Pretest branch employees.
8. Prepare course materials.
9. Deliver training at each office.
10. Posttest branch employees.
11. Evaluate the project.

Just as the only way to eat an elephant is one bite at a time, the only way to confidently determine the resources and costs for a project is to separate the project activities into bite-sized pieces. Work Breakdown Structure, or WBS, is a method for analyzing activities. With WBS, you break each activity into subactivities and *work packages* (the lower-level activities that are required to complete the activity), create estimates for the work packages, and roll up the costs into the subactivities and activities. In the Work Breakdown Structure, the total program for the enterprise is the highest level of the structure. The XYZ-BOT project and other Train2K projects are at the second level—the project level. Activities, subactivities, and work packages follow at levels 3, 4, and 5, as shown in Figure 2.1.

 NOTE Although it's convenient to think about activities in the order they will most likely occur, the Work Breakdown Structure is not designed to show the sequence of activities or the relationships between activities. You'll use Calendar and Gantt Chart reports from Microsoft Project to illustrate the activity schedule, sequence, and linkages.

FIGURE 2.1

The WBS structure organizes activities within a project.

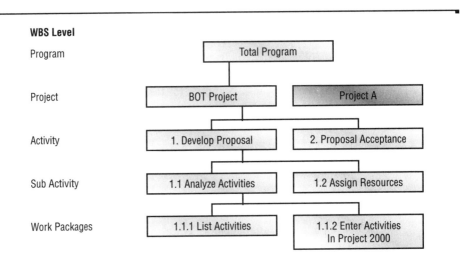

FIGURE 2.1

The WBS structure organizes activities within a project.

Break each activity down into its logical work packages. Here's one way to break down activity 8, Prepare Course Materials:

8	Prepare course materials
8.1	Modify course materials
8.1.1	Identify current materials
8.1.2	Compare current materials to XYZ skill list
8.1.3	Prepare list of modifications
8.1.4	Edit materials
8.2	Publish materials
8.3	Print materials
8.3.1	Duplicate materials
8.3.2	Bind materials
8.4	Ship materials to sites
8.4.1	Package materials
8.4.2	Address packages
8.4.3	Schedule delivery

The breakdown doesn't need to have the same level of detail for each activity. For example, subactivity 8.2 has no work packages, but 8.3 has two.

NOTE Many organizations assign project numbers and have a WBS numbering standard. More complex projects require more WBS levels; ten or twelve WBS levels are common, particularly in durable goods manufacturing.

Ideally, a work package is small enough that you can hand the package to a person or team for completion, and the assignees will understand the work included in the package. Each work package can be further broken down into one or more tasks. Work package 8.2, for example, may require a series of steps that include identifying artwork, design and layout, desktop publishing, and printing. The best source for information about tasks (and the time that each task is estimated to take) is usually the department, person, or vendor who performs the task.

The XYZ-BOT project involves shipping materials to the XYZ client sites—an easy enough task that could probably be completed in less than an hour by anyone who can fill out a shipping form. (Imagine a project that includes a direct mailing to XYZ Company's 3500 current customers!) The project manager (PM) at XYZ Company hasn't done many bulk mailings, so she talks to the manager of the shipping department (SM). The project manager's purpose is not to become an expert on shipping, but to understand direct mailing processes in her organization. See the following dialogue:

Project Manager (PM): My project involves a direct mailing to our current customers. I need to know what's involved so I can create the budget and schedule.

Shipping Manager (SM): How many pieces?

PM: Between 3500 and 4000.

SM: What kind of pieces?

PM: Eight-and-a-half by eleven-inch catalogs. We think they'll be about 40 pages total.

SM: Are we using envelopes or addressing directly on the catalog?

PM: I'm planning on envelopes.

SM: Simple enough. It will take us a day to get the mailing out. We'll bill the costs back to your department. I can send you an estimate next week.

Although you may now have a sense of what's required to plan for the mailing, overlooked activities that "crop up" later can delay the project and increase costs. In our example, what activities has the shipping manager included in the estimate of one day? What activities are not included, but are critical to the completion of the mailing? The project manager needs to ask questions to identify process inputs: in this example, the activities that are completed outside the shipping department that the shipping manager doesn't reflect in his estimate. Consider the following dialogue:

PM: I know we need to provide the catalogs, but what else do you expect me to provide? Do I need to provide the envelopes?

SM: Oh, you need us to stuff them, too? We can order envelopes, but we'll need extra time to put your catalogs in the envelopes, and we need a week's lead time to guarantee that the envelopes will get here. Normally, I contract assembly work to a local vendor. If we do it, it's done manually. They can turn around 5000 pieces pretty quickly, but we need to get in their schedule.

PM: And where do you get the address labels?

SM: From you. You might want to talk to Customer Service to see whether they can provide them for you.

You and the shipping manager now have a much better idea of what's expected. You can create a project plan that includes these activities, although you'll still need to conduct some additional research to find out about obtaining labels. A numbered list is a common way to present activities, subactivities, and work packages. In this stage of the project, don't hesitate to provide information in a variety of formats to enhance communication about the activities that the project encompasses, and participate in the planning process. The list is one communication tool, but some people find a flowchart or workflow diagram more accessible. You can create flowcharts like the one shown in Figure 2.2 by using the Drawing tools in Word or Excel.

FIGURE 2.2

You can create simple flowcharts by using the Office drawing tools.

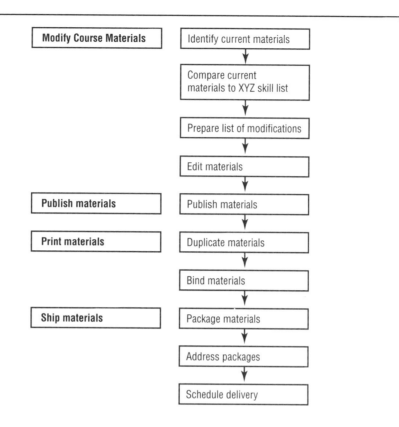

The workflow diagram shown in Figure 2.3 was created by using a popular business diagramming software product called Visio.

 NOTE Visio is a product of Visio Corporation, which was recently purchased by Microsoft Corporation. You can find out more about Visio by visiting www.visio.com.

A workflow diagram helps project partici- pants to envision the steps in a project.

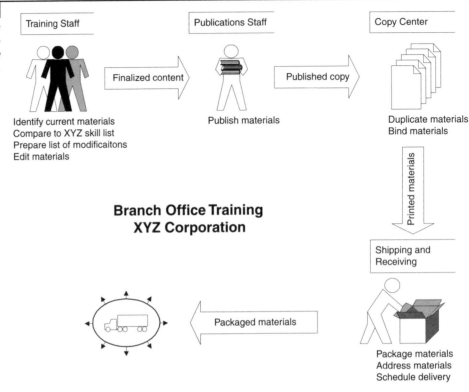

These diagrams aren't a replacement for the charts and reports you'll create later in Project 2000. Rather, they are tools to communicate with stakeholders and resource people while you're gathering information for design and development. As you'll see in Chapter 4, "Project 2000 Quickstart," activities, subactivities, and work packages can be pasted or imported from another application such as Excel or created directly in Microsoft Project 2000. Figure 2.4 shows a list of the project activities listed previously in Microsoft Project 2000's Gantt Chart view, which you'll be using in Chapter 4.

 NOTE Figure 2.3 also includes information about the project's human resources, which we'll discuss later in this chapter.

 NOTE Stakeholders are any people who have an interest in the project including proj- ect team members, clients, funders, contractors, customers, and other interested parties.

PART

I

Introducing Microsoft
Project 2000

FIGURE 2.4

You can use the Gantt Chart view to view and enter activity information about the project.

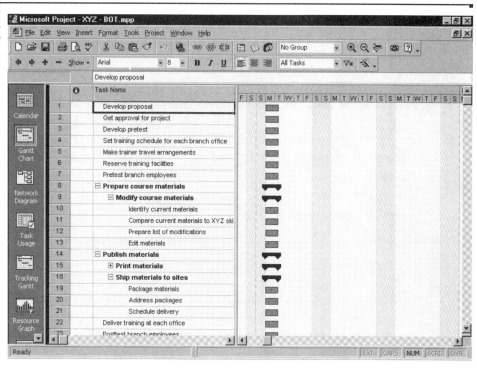

Identifying Tasks and Times

After you identify the project activities and break them down into work packages, it's time to determine the resources required for each package. This is the breakdown for activity 7, Pretest Branch Employees:

7.1	Communicate the pretest requirements to employees
7.2	Post the pretest on the intranet
7.2.1	Create welcome page
7.2.2	Create the pretest results database
7.2.3	Post and test Web pages
7.3	Follow up with employees
7.3.1	Check to see who has completed the test
7.3.2	Email reminders to employees who have not completed the test
7.3.3	Email supervisors with completion information
7.4	Evaluate the results
7.5	Communicate the results to XYZ Corporation

Subactivity 7.2 includes three work packages. According to the Train2K Web master, work package 7.2.3 (Post and Test Web Pages) involves four separate tasks. The tasks and the Web master's estimates of the hours of work required for each task are shown in Table 2.2.

TABLE 2.2: POST AND TEST WEB PAGES

Task	Est Work Required
Apply templates, post, and test static pages	3 hours
Post pretest pages	2 hours
Test links to results database	2 hours
Create hyperlinks from home page	1 hour

Make sure that the estimates (such as those shown in Table 2.2) are estimated work hours: the number of hours it will take one person to complete the task, rather than the number of hours it will take a crew of four to complete the task. As you'll see in Chapters 7 ("Entering Project Tasks") and 8 ("Scheduling and Linking Project Tasks"), there are a variety of ways to enter activity, work package, and task information in Project 2000. You can use the Gantt Chart view shown in Figure 2.4, enter information in a task sheet, or use the Task Information dialog box shown in Figure 2.5.

FIGURE 2.5

Enter information about a task in the Task Information dialog box.

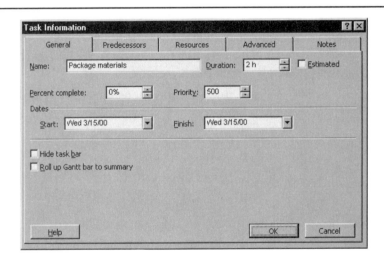

The exhaustive list of activities, subactivities, work packages, and tasks is the final definition of the scope of the project. When you're convinced that the list is complete, move on to the remaining aspects of the project: costs, performance, and timeline.

Estimating Project Costs

In Project 2000, you assign activity costs indirectly. Costs are assigned to *resources*. Examples of resources include the following:

- Employees at their hourly rate or prorated salaried rate, optionally including employee benefits
- Contractors
- Temporary employees
- Equipment at a lease rate or calculated periodic cost
- Facilities

Begin by creating a *resource pool* that includes the project resources. Resources from the pool are assigned to tasks, and the cost of a task is the cost of the resource multiplied by the amount of the resource used to complete the task.

If your colleagues use Project, you can use resources from a pool in another Microsoft Project file. This is more than a convenience—if the projects share staff, using a common resource pool helps ensure that staff members aren't accidentally overworked.

You'll learn about defining and using resources in Chapter 9, "Defining Resources" and more about shared resource pools in Chapter 14, "Sharing Resources and Tasks among Multiple Projects." After tasks, resources and costs, and resource assignments are entered, you can quickly and easily create the project budget.

Developing the Project Schedule

A project *schedule* includes the sequence of activities, the relationships between the activities, and the timing of each activity. There are two major tools used to schedule projects: Gantt Charts and networks, including PERT and CPM. Henry Gantt invented the chart that bears his name to present the sequence and time required for a project's activities. A simple Gantt Chart that illustrates some of the BOT project activities is shown in Figure 2.6.

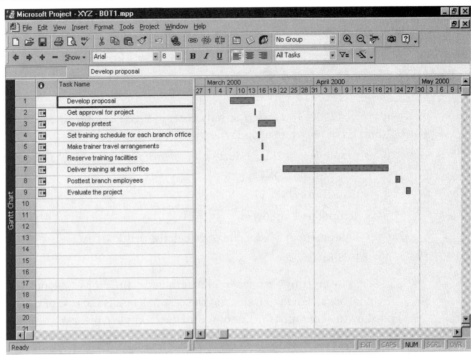

What the traditional Gantt Chart can't show is the relationship between activities. Some activities aren't related at all. The pretest (refer to Figure 2.6) can be developed at the same time that travel arrangements are being made. (Unrelated activities are also called *parallel activities*.) Other activities can't begin until another activity is partially or wholly completed. Activities that must occur before the current activity are its *predecessors*, and an activity and its predecessors are related in *series*. The relationship between activities directly influences the project timeline. Materials must be published before they can be duplicated, and they must be duplicated before they can be shipped. Thus, publishing and duplicating are predecessors of shipping. If the materials aren't published at the time specified in the project schedule, duplicating and shipping might be delayed.

Project 2000 uses a modified Gantt Chart that includes links to show activity relationships. The Gantt Chart shown in Figure 2.6 is shown with links in Figure 2.7. The link lines clearly indicate series and parallel relationships between the activities.

Although Project's linking feature handles the shortcomings of the traditional Gantt Chart, two other methods were created to schedule projects long before the creation of Microsoft Project (or microcomputers).

FIGURE 2.7

*Project 2000's
modified Gantt Chart
shows activities and
relationships.*

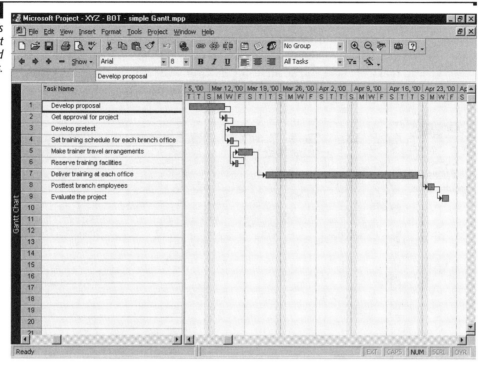

PERT (an acronym for *Program Evaluation and Review Technique*) and *CPM (Critical Path Method)* are network-scheduling methods. PERT was created by the U.S. Navy to manage an ambitious project: building the first nuclear submarine. At nearly the same time, CPM was developed by Remington Rand Corporation's J.E. Kelly and M.R. Walker of DuPont Corporation to manage maintenance projects in chemical-manufacturing facilities. PERT is more mechanistic because it was designed with an emphasis on using mathematics to manage uncertainty. CPM was designed for a very certain environment. Over the past three decades, the two methods have been modified through continued use and are now quite similar.

Both PERT and CPM use *network diagrams* (also called *precedence diagrams*) to represent the relationships between activities. Each activity is represented by a node on the diagram.

One advantage of using Project 2000 is evident when you begin to schedule activities: Gantt Charts and network diagrams are easily created by simply switching to a different view. A Project 2000 network diagram for the first four tasks in the Gantt Chart (refer to Figure 2.7) is shown in Figure 2.8.

Simple projects can be easily scheduled and managed with Gantt Charts. In Chapter 8, we'll show you how to use Gantt Charts to schedule a project. For more complex projects or projects with a great number of unknowns, we recommend PERT. PERT is more than a diagram; it's a method to manage project uncertainty, and is a useful tool whenever you do anything innovative or risky. For more details on using PERT in a variety of environments, see Appendix A, "Setting Quality Standards."

FIGURE 2.8

A network diagram is another way to view tasks and relationships.

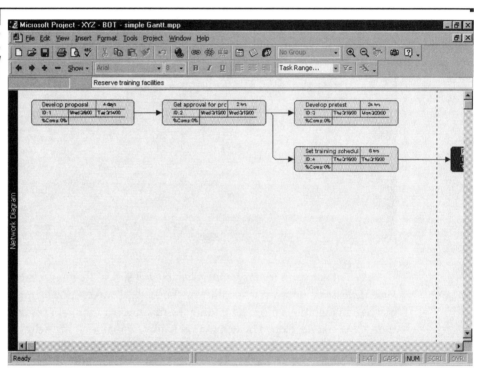

Determining Performance Standards

When we typically think of performance, we think of attributes such as efficiency and effectiveness. In project management, performance has a more specific meaning: the quality of the activities performed. Examples of quality measurement include the following:

- Measurements of the customers' perception of quality
- Manufacturing: rejected parts as a percentage of all parts produced

- Machining: machine hours within prescribed limits as a percentage of all machine hours (statistical process control)
- Education: percentage of graduates who pass a standardized competency test
- Medicine: percentage of patients who respond positively to a course of treatment
- Software engineering: lines of error-free code as a percentage of all lines of code

In the XYZ-BOT project, we could use a number of different measures. For example, we could have trainees fill out an evaluation form at the end of the class. We already have a posttest in place that serves as one measure of training quality. The goal of the XYZ-BOT project, however, is increased trainee software proficiency so trainees can use specific templates and applications. So, we need to measure training transfer—differences in employee performance with the software after training. If every trainee shows marked improvement in the posttest but still can't use the templates created at corporate headquarters, the project is a failure. (It may be a project *design* failure rather than faulty implementation, but it's still a failure.)

Large companies require quality certification for approved vendors. If you work for a large organization, you're probably familiar with the quality measurements and methods used in your company, or have quality specialists on staff who can help you determine appropriate standards for activities in your project.

If your organization doesn't have standard agreements or measurements in place, work with the project's customers and stakeholders to determine the appropriate quality standards that you can communicate to project participants, including employees and vendors. You'll find more information about quality standards and measurements in Chapter 13, "Assessing and Managing Risks."

Communicating Project Information

One of a project manager's principal tasks is communication. Project managers are responsible for communication between all members of the project team, including vendors, customers, and stakeholders. Project 2000's TeamAssign feature (see Figure 2.9) integrates with Microsoft Outlook and Exchange Server, so you can easily assign activities to teams or individuals. Team members automatically communicate the status of tasks simply by updating tasks in Outlook. Chapter 15, "Communicating Project Information," is dedicated to using these tools and others for excellent project communication.

Project 2000's new Web client, Project Central, was created to enhance communication with onsite teams members through the corporate intranet, and with offsite team members and vendors on an extranet. Chapter 16, "Team Project Management with

Project Central 2000," is dedicated to working with Project Central; and Chapter 26, "Installing and Administering Project Central 2000," helps system administrators and senior project managers with Project Central administration.

FIGURE 2.9

The Team Assign form is used to assign activities or tasks.

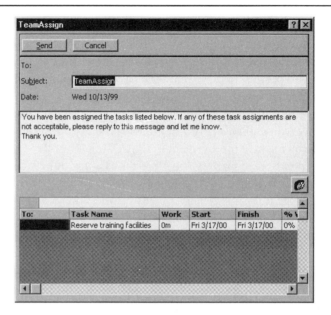

Managing Project Security

The final design consideration is project security. The Manhattan Project (the project that built the first atomic bomb) is at one end of the security spectrum. At the other end of the spectrum is the project to plan the company picnic. Somewhere in between are projects to determine the feasibility of acquiring another firm, sell a manufacturing facility, or launch a new product line. Before you can manage project security, you need to know how secure the project needs to be. You probably won't need to purchase retina-scanning equipment to secure access to the company picnic project files, for example.

Include a statement about security (even if the statement is "Discuss this project with anyone you wish") in the project design. The statement should clearly delineate which project information is confidential, and who is entitled to access or discuss confidential information or files. You may want to have project staff members sign a non-disclosure agreement, indicating that they have read the security statement and understand it.

(Sample non-disclosure agreements, created in Word, are available on the Sybex Web site: www.sybex.com.) You can attach the agreements and any other files to the Microsoft Project 2000 file you create.

What's Next

This chapter provided an overview of project design. In Chapter 3, "Understanding Project Management Tasks," we'll broadly examine the project manager's tasks after the project enters the implementation stage. If you're an experienced project manager, feel free to jump to Chapter 4, "Project 2000 Quickstart."

PART

Introducing Microsoft Project 2000

CHAPTER **3**

Understanding Project Management Tasks

n Chapter 2, "Understanding Projects," we used the Branch Office Training (BOT) project to discuss the components of project design. The BOT project, as outlined in this chapter, has been approved. Tasks and task durations have been entered in Project 2000. Resources have been assigned, a budget prepared and adopted, and the project schedule finalized. The Microsoft Project 2000 Gantt Chart for the BOT project is shown in Figure 3.1.

FIGURE 3.1

Project 2000's Gantt Chart view of the BOT project

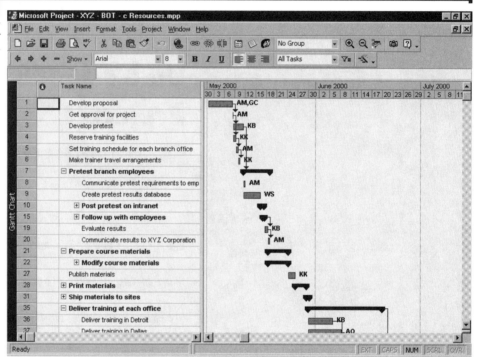

As the implementation phase begins, the project manager's focus changes from planning and design to monitoring and tracking. Six primary responsibilities fall directly on the shoulders of the project manager:

- Supervising and encouraging members of the project team
- Discerning the current status of project work
- Comparing the current status to the project schedule
- Assessing project quality
- Resolving problems and implementing opportunities
- Reporting to team members and stakeholders

Project team members are involved in specific tasks, whereas the project manager is responsible for all project tasks. Monitoring and tracking project activities help the project manager see the entire expanse of the project in a way that no task-oriented team member can. Successful monitoring and tracking help the manager quickly address problems and take advantage of opportunities to improve performance.

When a well-designed project succeeds, these tasks have been performed well, or at least well enough to keep the project on track. When a well-designed project fails during implementation, one or more of these tasks have been ignored or given short shrift. It's important to note that the assessment, analysis, and one-to-one communication skills required in this stage of the project life cycle are often different from the skills that were required to design, develop, and promote the project.

Monitoring Project Progress

You monitor a project by systematically and intentionally collecting data about the status of each project task. Data can be collected in several ways:

- During project team meetings
- In one-on-one discussions with team members
- Electronically by using email
- From team members' written reports
- As a result of correspondence or meetings with project vendors and suppliers
- From support departments, such as purchasing and receiving

It's easier to monitor progress when status reports are standardized. Project 2000 has two tools for collecting project status reports. Project Central is used to exchange messages using an intranet- or Internet-based Web. If all your team members have access to a relatively current email system, use email. Project 2000's email workgroup features (which include TeamAssign, TeamStatus, and TeamUpdate) provide a consistent format for status reports. If you need information that isn't included in the TeamStatus form, shown in Figure 3.2, you can customize the form by adding fields (see Chapter 23, "Customizing Fields and Forms"). Data from Project's workgroup tools are automatically entered in your project plan.

P Microsoft Project Central must be purchased separately; it is not included with the
 version of Microsoft Project 2000. See Chapter 16, "Team Project Management with
 t Central 2000," and Chapter 26, "Installing and Administering Project Central 2000,"
 rmation on configuring and using Project Central.

FIGURE 3.2

*Use the TeamStatus
form to request status
reports from team
members.*

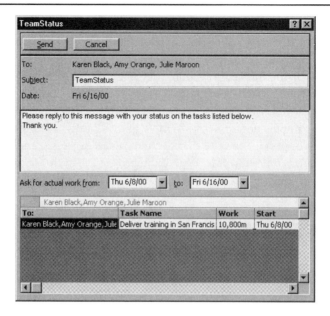

If team members don't have access to MAPI-compliant email, the company's intranet, or the World Wide Web, you can collect data manually. You may also choose manual data collection for a small project with a limited number of team members. Because you need to enter the data in your Project 2000 file, a standardized format is still important. Decide which data you want to collect and how frequently you want to collect it. Don't collect data more frequently than you can enter and analyze it.

Choose a collection method: verbal or written reports at weekly meetings, telephone interviews, or faxable forms are all useful methods. When you provide a format for team members to use, you increase the probability that you'll receive useful data that can be easily entered in Project 2000. Design your forms so they are easy for your team members to complete.

 NOTE Even if you use Project Central or workgroup email tools, you'll still need to manually update tasks that aren't assigned to human resources.

Analyzing Project Variances

Before you begin tracking project progress, you should save a project baseline. A *baseline* is a "locked-down" version of the project plan that isn't affected by status updates, so it's a powerful tool for spotting discrepancies between actual work and scheduled work. After you receive status reports on project tasks and update the actual schedule (automatically or manually), you can compare the schedule to the baseline to identify potential problems. If the project scope changes or external factors require you to change the project schedule (for example, a hurricane or a labor strike), you can adjust the baseline. In Project 2000, you can also store up to ten interim plans that you can compare to the baseline or actual work completed.

Project 2000 includes tools for earned value analysis, also called BCWP (Budgeted Cost of Work Performed) analysis. *Earned value analysis* measures key performance indicators and compares them to the baseline. The gap, or *variance*, between the baseline and actual performance indicates whether the project is being implemented as planned. *Cost variance* is the difference between a task's planned cost and its actual cost. *Schedule variance* is the difference between the actual progress and the scheduled progress of a task. You can use these variances to calculate useful ratios that indicate project performance. For more information on earned value analysis, see Chapter 12, "Tracking Project Progress."

Managing Project Schedules

If a project is running as scheduled, schedule management is an easy task. When tasks are completed ahead of schedule, you'll probably breathe a sigh of relief and move on to other management activities. Problem projects are the projects in which critical tasks start to slip. For a visual representation of project performance against the schedule, you can add progress lines to the Gantt Chart to show the percentage of each task completed as of a specific date, as shown in Figure 3.3. When a task's progress line's peak is pointed to the left, the task is behind schedule. Peaks that point to the right indicate tasks that are ahead of schedule.

Earned value analysis and progress lines help you identify the performance gap; closing the gap is the job of the project manager. If other tasks are being completed ahead of schedule, you may be able to reallocate resources and get the project back on track. With Project 2000, you can easily move resources between tasks. Alternatively, you can adjust one of the four project parameters:

- Time: extend the project finish date
- Scope: eliminate or alter project activities
- Costs: throw overtime at the problem task
- Performance: lower standards

You'll find information on all of Project's schedule-management tools in Chapter 12.

FIGURE 3.3

Progress lines identify tasks that are ahead of or behind the baseline.

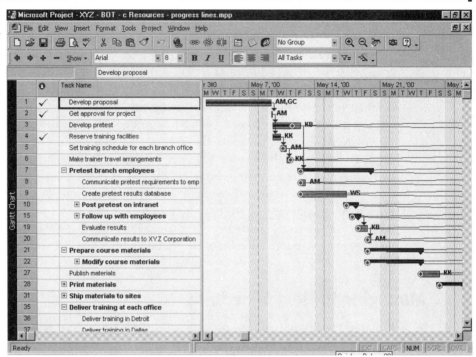

 TIP Effective schedule management begins prior to the implementation stage, during project design and development. In other words, it's better to change the schedule before the project starts. It lessens stress and makes you look better as a project manager. See Chapter 13, "Assessing and Managing Risks," for information on PERT and other tools to help estimate and manage project risk.

Managing Resources

Throughout the project, the project manager needs to analyze resource usage. If some tasks aren't progressing according to schedule, you'll be forced to examine your resource utilization, but there are other reasons to review the way your project plan uses resources:

- Resources that you free up can be used in other projects that share the same resource pool.
- Increased resource use by other higher-priority projects lowers the resource availability for your project.

- Resources can be moved from low-risk or less-critical tasks to critical tasks within a project.
- Idle resources cost money.

With Project 2000, you can view assignments for all resources or for specific work groups. You can quickly view resources with available time, and then assign them to tasks that are falling behind schedule.

Overallocated resources increase the risk that a project will fall behind schedule, so Project includes several tools for identifying and leveling or reassigning over- and under-allocated resources. In the Resource Usage table, shown in Figure 3.4, it's hard not to notice that Amy Orange is overcommitted on May 16th. Her name is bold (and shows red onscreen). She's currently scheduled to work 15 hours (900 minutes) in what is normally an eight-hour workday. If she doesn't work a 15-hour day, one or more tasks will not be completed as scheduled. May 16th is in the second week of the project, so we probably want to shift some resources or risk burning out our employees before the project really picks up steam.

FIGURE 3.4

The Resource Usage table highlights over-allocated resources and unassigned tasks.

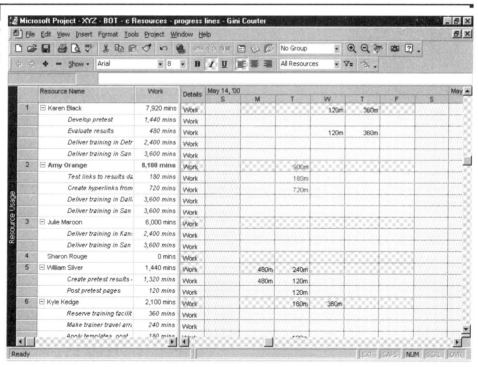

Resource management is a common and continuous project management task, and Project 2000 includes views, tables, charts, and reports to help you with these critical tasks. You'll find information to help you with resource management in Project 2000 in three chapters of this book: Chapter 9, "Defining Project Resources and Costs," Chapter 10, "Assigning and Scheduling Resources and Costs," and Chapter 11, "Preparing Your Project for Publication."

Managing Costs

Costs are one of the most difficult aspects of a project to manage and control. Some costs are external. For example, when vendors raise prices, you may not be able to locate other acceptable vendors without sacrificing time or quality. Earned value analysis (see "Managing Project Schedules," earlier in this chapter) identifies cost variances, but identification does not provide a solution. When actual costs exceed the project plan, you need to decide how to keep the total costs under control. You can adjust the total project cost, scope, performance, or schedule—the choice depends on which parameter is most critical to the project's stakeholders.

With Project 2000, you can model changes in project parameters and then make recommendations for project changes. Adjust one of the project parameters and observe the effect on the other parameters, including cost, to see whether the tradeoffs are acceptable. For more information on cost management and control, see Chapter 12.

Managing Project Scope

During project implementation, you may need to increase or decrease the scope of the project. When scope increases, one of the other project parameters also needs to change. As the project manager, you may not have the authority to reject any and all requests to change project scope, but you can set the ground rules for decisions about scope changes. This should be done when the project proposal is accepted. See Chapter 11 for information on managing expectations about project scope.

Project Reporting

Project managers communicate information about project status and progress to members of the project team, managers, and stakeholders. Unless your project is simple enough to be easily understood by people who aren't intimately involved with project tasks, you'll want to create different reports for each audience.

Creating Reports for the Project Team

Team members want access to information that will help them participate successfully in the project. As the project manager, you can encourage communication between individuals and groups working on the project, but you need to provide project-wide reports that meet the team members' needs for connection with the entire project. Gantt Charts that show completed tasks or include progress lines (refer to Figure 3.3), bar charts that show the percentage of work completed, and project calendars and timelines are all effective ways to communicate information within the team. (Thank-you notes and congratulatory emails are good tools, too.)

Creating Reports for Other Managers

Company managers need project summaries and timelines, variance reports, and written communications about your management of the project. Managerial reports should include the following:

- Current progress of the project work, including variances and indices
- Major activities or milestones completed in the reporting period
- Major activities scheduled for the next reporting period
- Problems and opportunities handled in the reporting period
- Your risk assessment for critical tasks in the next reporting period

If your company doesn't have a standard format for project reports, create one and use it consistently at regular reporting intervals. A report can be periodic (monthly or quarterly reports), time-dependent (end-of-year reporting), and/or related to major project milestones.

Creating Reports for Stakeholders

Stakeholder reports often come in only two forms: press releases with a timeline or Gantt Chart attached or reams of paper that discourage close examination (the "bury-them-with-data" approach). Project managers often view stakeholders as a potential source of scope creep, rather than as valued customers whose needs must be met for the success of the project. Both views are accurate. Create reports for stakeholders that communicate the information they need, based on their level of participation in the project.

You can create reports for all three audiences using the reporting tools in Microsoft Project 2000 and Microsoft Word. See Chapter 17, "Using Views to Evaluate Data," and Chapter 18, "Using Reports to Analyze Data," for detailed information about reporting in Project.

What's Next

In Chapter 2, "Understanding Projects," and this chapter, we examined project definition, design, development, implementation, and the tasks required for project managers. Now, it's time to get to work. In Chapter 4, "Project 2000 Quickstart," we'll look at using Project 2000 to launch and manage the BOT project. Beginning with Chapter 5, "Working in Project 2000," you'll find detailed information on each aspect of project management.

CHAPTER 4

Project 2000 Quickstart

Now that we've covered the basics of project design and management, you're ready to begin entering information for your project. The next twenty-two chapters cover project management in great detail. This chapter is a quick overview of how to use Microsoft Project 2000 to build, manage, and close a project. We'll use the XYZ-BOT (Branch Office Training) project outlined in Chapters 2 and 3 as our sample project, but if you have a project that you're ready to sink your teeth into, locate your design documents and get ready. That black smoke pouring out of your computer isn't just your imagination—it's coming from the place where the rubber meets the road.

Building a Project

The first time you launch Microsoft Project 2000 from the Windows Programs menu (Start ➤ Programs ➤ Microsoft Project), Project opens a new project in Gantt Chart view, as shown in Figure 4.1. The timeline in the right pane displays dates, beginning today.

NOTE If the Microsoft Project Help screen opens on startup, you can choose to turn the Help screen off so it does not open every time you launch Project. Clear the Display Help At Startup checkbox on the Help screen, or choose Tools ➤ Options and clear the Display Help On Startup checkbox on the General tab.

FIGURE 4.1

To allow for more viewing area onscreen, we have turned off the View bar on the left side of the screen for the remaining figures in this chapter and many in subsequent chapters. To turn off the View bar, choose View ➤ View Bar from the menu.

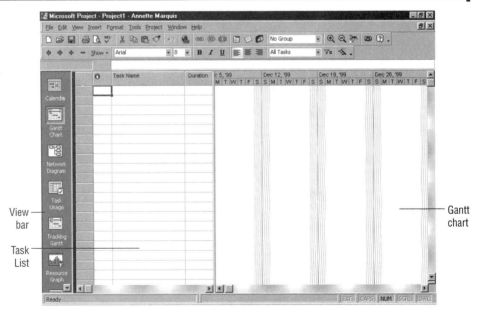

Defining the Project

There are three activities you should complete before you begin entering individual project tasks: setting file properties, entering project working times, and adding project properties. You can do these activities in any order, but they must be completed prior to other tasks. Although the first one, setting properties for your project file, is optional, you may already be in the habit of doing this when you start a file in other applications. Choose File ➢ Properties from the menu to open the Properties dialog box shown here. Make sure that you're listed as the Author. Enter a few keywords and a summary if you wish. You'll find detailed information on file properties in Chapter 6, "Building a New Project."

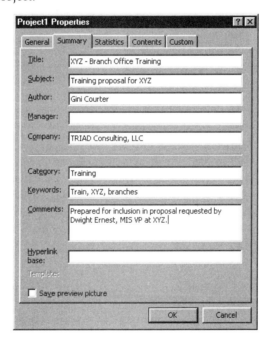

Establishing Working Times

The second activity is setting the options and working times in the standard calendar that all other calendars use as a default. Choose Tools ➢ Change Working Time to open the Change Working Time dialog box, shown in Figure 4.2. Make sure that Standard (Project Calendar) is selected in the For drop-down list.

The default work times are 8 a.m. to noon and 1 p.m. until 5 p.m., Monday through Friday, fifty two weeks of the year—eight working hours every day with a nonworking hour for lunch. If this calendar doesn't reflect the working hours for human and non-human resources you'll assign to your project tasks, now is the time to change it.

Set working days in the Change Working Time dialog box.

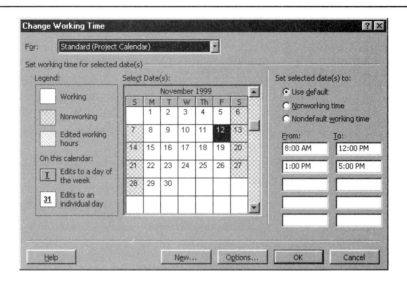

 WARNING Establishing working times in the project's calendar is not an optional activity. If you fail to set working times before entering tasks, there are no flashing warnings complete with audible signals—but there should be. Calendar settings affect every aspect of the project, and changes to the base working times later in the project cycle aren't fully reflected in tasks that have already been assigned resources.

Click to select an individual day; click the header buttons at the top of the calendar control to select every day in the column. Set selected days as working or nonworking by using the option buttons on the right side of the calendar control. If your organization gives the entire staff Christmas day off, make December 25 a nonworking day. Project won't schedule tasks on that day, so you won't find yourself acting like Scrooge, explaining that your project could have been completed on time were it not for Christmas.

Type times in the From and To boxes to indicate working hours for the selected days. Changing the working times doesn't necessarily change the working hours in a day. Working from 9 a.m. until noon and then from 12:30 p.m. until 5:30 p.m. still yields an eight-hour workday. Some offices, however, work ten-hour days or seven-hour days. If you change the number of working hours from the default eight hours, you also need to change the Hours Per Day and Hours Per Week calendar options. Click the Options button in the Change Working Times dialog box to jump to the Calendar tab in the Options dialog box (see Figure 4.3).

FIGURE 4.3

*Change the number
of hours in a day or
week in the Options
dialog box.*

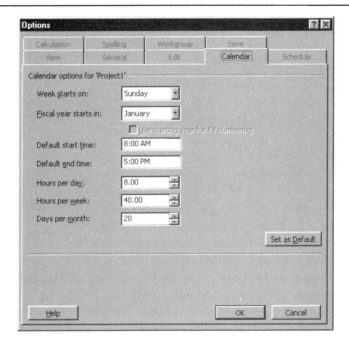

You want to make sure that the Calendar options are in sync with your calendars. The Hours Per Day option determines how Project 2000 converts durations. If Hours Per Day is 8, then 2 days is converted to 16 hours. When Hours Per Day is set to 10, Project converts 2 days to 20 hours. Hours Per Week and Days Per Month are also used to convert durations.

 NOTE You'll find more information on calendars and calendar options in the section "Defining the Project Calendar" in Chapter 6.

After you set working and nonworking days, and change the calendar options (if necessary), close both dialog boxes.

Setting Project Properties

Choose Project ➤ Project Information to open the Project Information dialog box, shown in Figure 4.4. There are three information settings you'll want to affirm or change: task scheduling method, priority, and calendar.

Set your project's task scheduling method, priority, and default calendar in the Project Information dialog box.

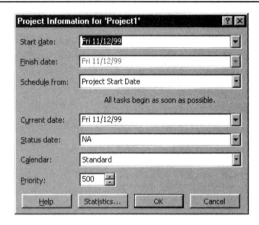

A project can be scheduled from the start date until its completion, or it can be scheduled backward from the finish date. For example, you can start scheduling tasks on June 1 and schedule forward, or start on December 1 and schedule backward, but you can't set both dates. Project Start Date is the default scheduling point. Project 2000 schedules all tasks to begin as soon as possible. When you choose Project Finish Date from the Schedule From drop-down list, tasks are scheduled to begin as late as possible. Use the calendar control to set the Start Date or Finish Date.

Select the calendar you used for working times from the Calendar drop-down list (refer to Figure 4.4) so it will be used as the project calendar.

The Priority setting is used to establish this project's priority, relative to other projects that use the same resource pool. The default is 500; priority values range from 0 to 1000. If your project is the most important project on the table right now, choose a higher number.

Planning Project Activities

For this phase of project creation, you need your list of project tasks, resource references such as an employee directory and/or materials list, and the estimated costs for resources.

Entering the Task List

Enter your project tasks roughly in order (although you can drag and drop tasks to rearrange them later) in Project 2000's Gantt Chart view. To enter a task, either click in the Task Name textbox and enter the task's name, or double-click in the Task Name textbox to open a Task Information dialog box, shown in Figure 4.5. Enter the task name on the General tab.

FIGURE 4.5

*Enter task information
in the Task Information
dialog box.*

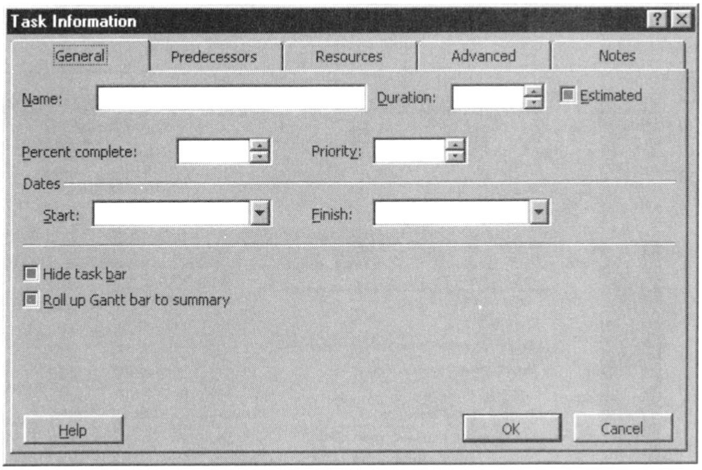

If you are entering tasks directly in Gantt Chart view, you can adjust the Gantt Chart task columns, as you would with columns in Excel or Access, by pointing to the right edge of the column header button. The pointer changes to a column adjustment tool. Drag to the right to widen the column, or double-click to have Project size the column to fit the contents. Drag the vertical gray bar between the task columns and the Gantt Chart to display additional columns of task information.

Task Name	Duration
Develop proposal	4 days

 NOTE If you created your list of tasks in another application, you may be able to import them. See Chapter 19, "Importing and Exporting Project Data," for information on importing and exporting in Project 2000.

  Outlining Tasks Some project managers begin by entering all the lower-level tasks first; others enter summary tasks, and then insert the subtasks and work packages. Use the Indent and Outdent buttons on the Formatting toolbar to indent selected lower-level tasks in relationship to the higher-level summary tasks. Tasks are displayed in the Gantt chart with blue bars, whereas summary tasks are represented by a black bar with black triangular terminators. Figure 4.6 shows a project Gantt with summary tasks and lower-level tasks.

 NOTE For more about work packages, see the section "Analyzing Project Activities" in Chapter 2, "Understanding Projects."

FIGURE 4.6

Use the Indent and Outdent buttons to outline tasks and subtasks.

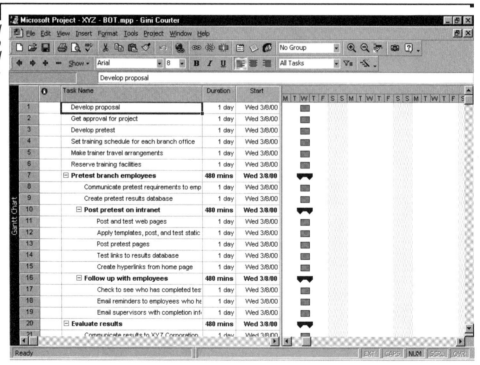

 TIP The Task Information dialog box has a Notes tab, which you will use a lot, beginning in the project design phase. The Notes tab is the ideal place to record customer specifications, quality measurements, and general information related to a task. You can also attach related documents such as Word documents or Excel spreadsheets that support the task in some way.

Entering Task Durations   Duration is the result of the formula work divided by assigned units, where work is the time required to complete the task and assigned units are the resources you apply to the task. With the exception of milestones, discussed as follows, every task has a *duration*: the number of days or hours that resources will be employed on the task.

 NOTE Duration and its relationship to resource assignments and task type is Project's black box—the unknown area where project managers report having the greatest difficulty. You'll find a wealth of information on task duration in Chapter 9, "Defining Project Resources and Costs," and more about resource assignments in Chapter 10, "Assigning and Scheduling Resources and Costs."

Project 2000's default duration is an estimate of one day. You know it's an estimate because Project appends a question mark to the duration. You can enter durations in minutes (m), hours (h), days (d), weeks (w), or months (mo). Type a number and then enter the abbreviation for the time unit in the duration column of the Gantt Chart: **4h** for 4 hours, **5d** for 5 days. If the duration still needs fine-tuning, type a question mark after the time unit abbreviation, or enable the Estimated checkbox in the Task Information dialog box. You can't enter durations for summary tasks; Project calculates summary duration from the durations of the summary task's subtasks. As you set task durations, Project 2000 redraws the bars in the Gantt Chart to reflect task duration, as shown in Figure 4.7.

FIGURE 4.7

Enter task durations in the Gantt Chart view.

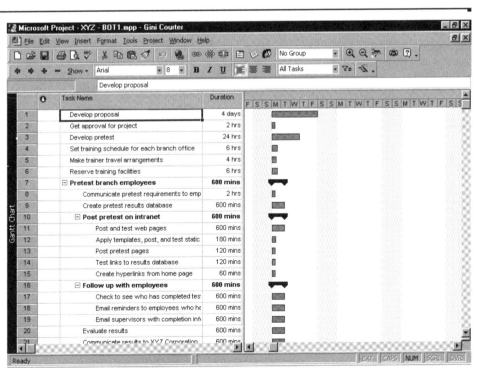

A milestone is a significant event in your project. Enter milestones as you would other tasks. Mark the task as a milestone by setting the task duration to 0, either in the third column of the Gantt Chart view or in the Duration textbox in the Task Information dialog box. Or, mark the task as a milestone by selecting the Mark Task As Milestone checkbox on the Advanced tab of the Task Information dialog box.

NOTE For information on outlining, project phases, and task duration, see Chapter 7, "Entering Project Tasks."

Setting Task Relationships   If there's a dependency between two or more tasks, you need to reflect it in your project file. The links between tasks are the heart of project scheduling. There are four types of links in Project 2000:

- Finish-to-Start (the default): Task A must be finished before Task B can start.
- Start-to-Start: Task A must start before Task B can start.
- Finish-to-Finish: Task A must finish before Task B finishes.
- Start-to-Finish: Task A must be started before Task B can be completed.

You can set task relationships by linking tasks as you go along; or wait until you've entered all the tasks and outlined subtasks, and work packages before linking tasks. We recommend waiting, particularly if you're creating the project file during the project design phase for use in the Project Summary. It's chaotic enough already—you don't need to have extra practice removing and adding links as new tasks get added to your list.

To link tasks, hold Ctrl and select the tasks you want to link, in order. Hold Shift, and click to select consecutive tasks. For example, choose the Post To Intranet task and then the Follow-up task. Click the Link Tasks button on the Standard toolbar. (If you choose Follow-up with Employees first, the link indicates that you will follow up before you post the test.) As you add links, the Gantt Chart task bars adjust along the timeline to create the project schedule. Indented subtasks are already related to their summary tasks, so they can't be linked, but you can link subtasks within and between summary tasks. Figure 4.8 shows linked tasks in the XYZ-BOT project file.

To unlink previously linked tasks, select the linked tasks and then click the Unlink Tasks button on the Standard toolbar.

FIGURE 4.8

*Links create the
project schedule.*

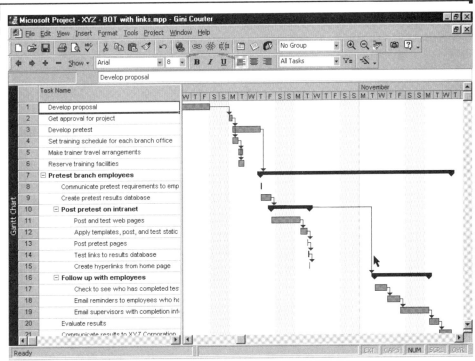

A link can be modified to build in some lag. For example, after we post our branch
training pretest on the intranet, employees need a few days to take the test before we
begin nagging them about it. We'll link the Post Pretest and Follow-up tasks Finish-to-
Start, and then add four days of lag to the schedule by double-clicking the link line in
the Gantt Chart and setting the lag value in the Task Dependency dialog box:

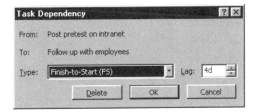

This is a great time to save your project file. Choose File ➤ Save from the menu.
You are asked whether you want to save the file with or without a baseline. Save the
file without a baseline for now—you'll save the baseline after the project schedule has
been approved.

NOTE For more information on dependency and linking see Chapter 8, "Scheduling and Linking Project Tasks."

Entering Resource Information

Resources are the people, materials, and equipment assigned to project tasks. Project 2000 lets you assign resources "on the fly" by entering resource names on the Resources tab of the Task Information dialog box or in the sixth column of the Gantt Chart's task grid. This is both a blessing and a curse because every typo or name version becomes an accidental "new" resource. Andy and Andie, Rich and Richard, James and Jim become different resources, even if they're the same people. When you enter resources in Project's Resource sheet and choose them from the drop-down lists in various columns and dialog boxes, you're less likely to introduce error. Choose View ➤ Resource Sheet to open your project's resource sheet, or double-click in any cell of the resource sheet to open a Resource Information dialog box.

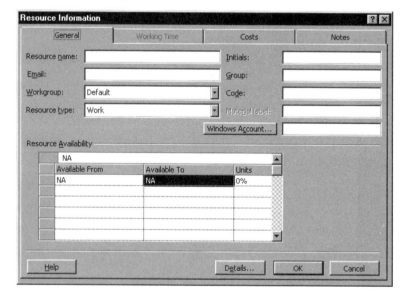

Enter the following for each resource: resource name, type (work or material), material label (for example tons, feet, or cubic yards), initials (displayed in Gantt Charts and reports), maximum units (percentage or value), standard and overtime rates, cost per use, accrual method, base calendar, and an optional resource code you can use later for sorting and grouping. If you don't know the names of all your resources, enter placeholders (**Programmer 1**, **Trainer A**, **Trainer B**), and change the names later.

TIP People, equipment, and other resources that have a time-based (hourly, daily, or monthly) cost are work resources; raw goods and consumables used by the unit are materials.

If a resource is available less than 100% of the time, be sure to adjust the maximum units percentage because it affects the project schedule. (With the possible exception of contract and production employees, human resources aren't available 100% of the time. There are emails to answer, telephone calls to return, and committee meetings to attend that are unrelated to the project.) The Resource Information dialog box has additional fields, including the range of available dates for a resource. Our resource sheet is shown in Figure 4.9.

FIGURE 4.9

Add resources in the project's Resource Sheet.

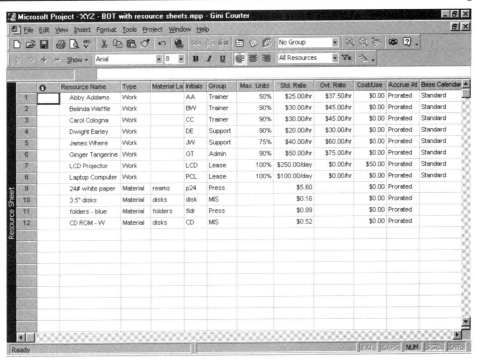

 NOTE You can add resources from an Outlook address book, import them from another application, or use resources from another Project file. See Chapter 9 for detailed information about resources.

Assigning Resources to Tasks

Project 2000 offers a variety of ways to assign resources—enough different ways, in fact, to become confusing. We'll concentrate on two methods. Switch back to the Gantt Chart view (View ➤ Gantt Chart), and select a task. You can do this in two ways. The first is to double-click the task to open the Task Information dialog box, click the Resources tab, and choose resources from the drop-down list:

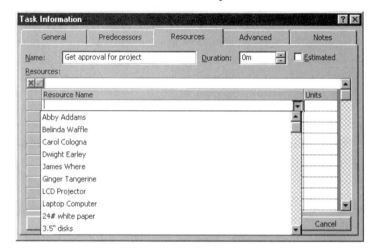

 You can also click the Resources button on the Standard toolbar to open the Assign Resources dialog box, shown here:

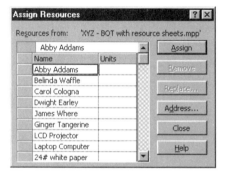

Shift-click, or hold Ctrl and click to select resources for the task, and then click the Assign button to assign the resources to the task. Each resource is assigned fully to the task. If a resource is assigned at less than 100%, its maximum units in the resource sheet is less than 100%. If you want to have the resource work half-time on the task, change the percentage in the Units Assigned column.

When you assign materials, enter the number of units required in the Units Assigned column. Project adds the materials label from the Resource Sheet (see Figure 4.9).

The Assign Resources dialog box remains open so you can move back to the grid, select one or more tasks in the task grid, and assign resources. Work through the task list, assigning resources to all tasks. *Don't* assign resources to summary tasks. As you assign resources, the resource names are displayed at the right end of the task bar, as shown in Figure 4.10.

FIGURE 4.10

Assigned resource names appear in the Gantt Chart.

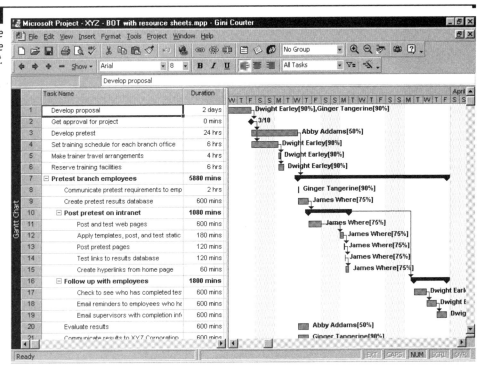

 TIP You can easily change the Gantt Chart settings to display initials, group names, or more information other than the default. See Chapter 17, "Using Views to Evaluate Data," for information about modifying views.

Estimating Project Costs

There are two types of costs associated with a project or a project task: variable costs and fixed costs. The variable costs should already be accounted for in the hourly costs, overtime costs, and per-use costs of work resources and materials assigned to tasks. You can add fixed costs to specific tasks.

TIP Use the Notes tab of the Task Information dialog box to record information about cost components.

Until now, we've worked in the Gantt Chart's Entry Table. The Cost Table provides useful information about the cost of each project task. In Gantt Chart view, choose View ➤ Table ➤ Cost to display the Cost Table. Drag the vertical split bar that runs between the table and the Gantt Chart to display all the columns of the Cost Table, as shown in Figure 4.11.

FIGURE 4.11

The Cost Table shows fixed and variable costs for each task.

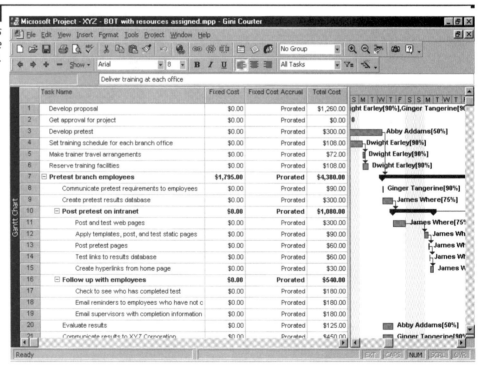

Enter the fixed cost associated with a specific task or summary task in the Fixed Cost column. Our project includes a few fixed costs. We'll add the airline ticket costs to each site to the Deliver Training task for that site. (It doesn't matter how many hours of training occur at the site; it costs a set amount for a round-trip ticket.) We're also purchasing authorware software to create the pretest. The software costs $1,795, so we'll attach this fixed cost to the pretest. Our fixed and variable costs are shown in Figure 4.11.

PART

I

Introducing Microsoft
Project 2000

 TIP If you want to enter fixed costs for the entire project, display the project summary task. Choose Tools ➢ Options from the menu to display the Options dialog box. Click the View tab. Enable the Project Summary Task checkbox, and then click OK. The project summary task is displayed as the first task in the table.

Optimizing the Plan

Optimizing the project plan means adjusting resources, costs, and the schedule while maintaining the quality standards specified in the project plan. The relationship between resources, budget, and timeline means that you're looking for an ideal balance between the three that accurately reflects your organization's priorities for the project.

 TIP Optimization relies on the accuracy of the task, cost, and resource information you've already entered. See Chapter 13, "Assessing and Managing Risks," for methods to accurately estimate task duration and cost.

Optimizing Resources

 You've assigned and scheduled resources. To optimize resources, first find out whether any of the resources are overallocated. Choose View ➢ Resource Sheet. Overallocated resources stick out—they're red and bold, and a leveling icon appears in the Information column. If you point to the icon, a screen tip appears with a leveling setting (for example, Day By Day) to select when leveling this resource. (See "Using the Leveling Feature," later in this section.) If you have overallocated resources, you *level* the resources by

- delaying a task until the assigned resource can complete it
- delaying part of the task by splitting the task
- assigning additional resources to the task

Project 2000 can automatically level resources to avoid overallocation and optimize resources. Project takes a number of factors into account when leveling. However, Project 2000 levels resources by delaying or splitting tasks—it doesn't add resources.

Delaying tasks extends the project schedule; adding resources increases costs unless the added resources were underallocated. There is another possibility, of course: you can incur overtime to complete the project. We don't recommend starting a project with scheduled overtime. There's ample evidence that the typical rush project with extended periods of overtime has high hidden costs, including lowered employee morale and product quality.

 TIP Project's bias is to optimize resources and costs while adjusting the timeline. This may not be the appropriate solution for your project, so you may prefer to optimize resources yourself. Project 2000 provides all the information you need to level resources. See Chapter 11, "Preparing Your Project for Publication," for detailed information on leveling tasks individually and using automatic leveling.

Using the Leveling Feature   Before using Project's leveling feature, there are two settings you should adjust for the absolutely critical tasks: constraints and priority. Set constraints on the Advanced tab of the Task Information dialog box, shown in Figure 4.12. Choose the Constraint type, and then set a Constraint date. Tasks, like projects, have a priority setting between 0 and 1000. Tasks with lower values are leveled before tasks with a higher priority. Don't spend a lot of time worrying about the difference between 500 and 550. If a task must be started or finished by a particular date, constrain it and then set its priority to 1000. Save a copy of the unleveled project file before proceeding. You might also want to choose Project ➤ Project Information to check the scheduled finish date for the project before resource optimization.

FIGURE 4.12

Constrain critical tasks before using automatic leveling.

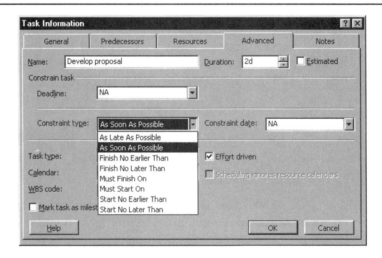

Choose Tools ➤ Resource Leveling to open the Resource Leveling dialog box, shown in Figure 4.13. Use this dialog box to set how Project 2000 should level resources. With

Automatic Leveling Calculation enabled, Project will adjust tasks as soon as you assign a resource that creates an overallocation. For now, leave this option on the default setting, Manual, so that leveling occurs when you open this dialog box and click the Level Now button.

PART

I

Introducing Microsoft
Project 2000

FIGURE 4.13

Set options and adjust tasks for overallocated resources in the Resource Leveling dialog box.

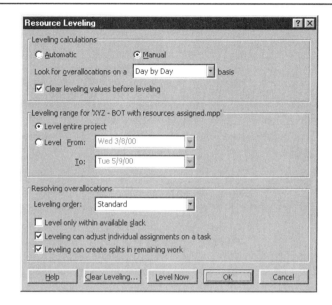

In the Look For Overallocations drop-down list, choose the time period that Project should examine to spot an overallocation. If, for example, you check overallocations on a week-by-week basis, a person can be scheduled to work sixteen hours two days in a row. If you check on a day-by-day basis, the person is overallocated on both sixteen-hour days, so the tasks on those days would be adjusted. After you set the time period, click the Level Now button, and Project examines overallocated resources and the tasks causing overallocation, and then adjusts the tasks to optimize the resources.

 TIP If you allocated a resource to a summary task and one of its subtasks, leveling pauses and you are prompted to stop leveling or skip this task. Note the summary task with the resource assigned, stop leveling, and then remove the assignment and start leveling again.

Leveling takes only a few seconds. Choose View ➤ More Views ➤ Leveling Gantt, shown in Figure 4.14, to see the changes made by leveling.

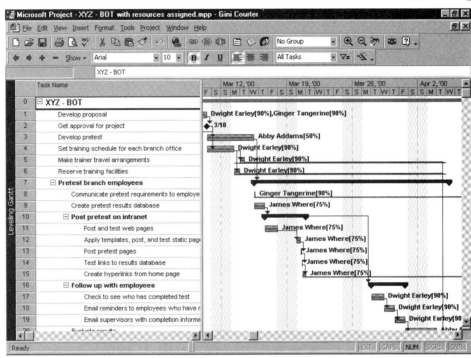

Optimizing the Project Schedule

You optimize the schedule to ensure that the project will be completed in an acceptable timeframe. Don't worry about optimizing unless the schedule runs longer than desired. Choose Project ➤ Project Information to see the current project Finish Date. If you need to adjust the project to finish on time, here are a few strategies:

- Start earlier: Change the project Start Date in the Project Information dialog box (Project ➤ Project Information).

- Change one or more calendars: If you're going to be working Saturdays or longer hours on the weekdays, adjust the calendar accordingly (Tools ➤ Change Working Time).

- Do less: Get a stakeholder agreement to limit on project scope by eliminating deliverables or cutting the project into phases, one or more of which will be completed by the desired finish date.

- Decrease quality: Adopt lower-quality standards or looser measurements, but only after reviewing Bonus Chapter A, "Setting Quality Standards," on the Downloads page of the Sybex Web site (http://www.Sybex.com).

In every project, there are tasks that require more attention because failure to complete them on time affects the project completion date. These tasks are in the critical path. To view the critical tasks in your project, make sure that you're in Gantt Chart view, and then choose Critical from the Filter drop-down list on the Formatting toolbar:

Project hides all non-critical tasks. The remaining critical tasks are the tasks that should draw your attention during the project or those that you should focus on optimizing to affect the timeline now. For example, you can do the following:

- Review tasks to identify and eliminate optional tasks.
- Make sure that task constraints, especially Start After constraints, are necessary.
- Break down critical tasks into work packages that you can assign to separate resources.
- Review and remove unnecessary links on the critical path.
- Add resources to critical tasks.

After you make one or more of the adjustments listed earlier, return to the Resource Sheet to make sure that you haven't accidentally introduced an overallocation. If you have, you can do the following:

- Assign additional resources.
- Replace one resource with another.
- Adjust the amount of time that a resource is available for a task.

After you've made changes, level the resources again and then check to make sure the project finish date is still acceptable.

Optimizing the Project Budget

Optimizing the budget is a very popular pastime. Project costs affect the bottom line for your department and the entire organization. To find out what your project, as designed, is estimated to cost, choose Project ➢ Project Information to open the Project Information dialog box. Click the Statistics button in the dialog box to open the Project Statistics dialog box, shown in Figure 4.15. This dialog box shows the vital statistics for the project, including the total cost, actual cost-to-date, and amounts remaining in the project budget.

FIGURE 4.15

The Project Statistics dialog box contains a wealth of summary information for planning and management.

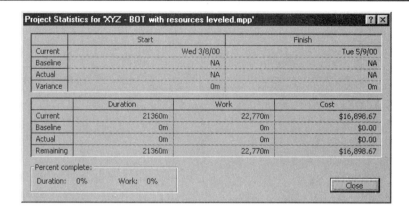

Here are some strategies to pursue when the total project costs need to be lowered:

- Replace expensive resources with less-expensive resources.
- Eliminate overtime.
- Reduce project scope by eliminating deliverables or project phases.
- Adopt lower-quality standards.

Communicating the Project Plan

We leveled resources and determined that the timeline and cost are acceptable. Now, it's time to distribute the project plan to stakeholders and workgroup members. Before we waste too many trees, though, we often ask for feedback from potential workgroup members or other project managers in our organization. To send the entire project file to another Project 2000 user, choose File ➤ Send To ➤ Mail Recipient (As Attachment). Project will fire up your email client and open a message with the project file attached. Address the message, add some explanatory text, and click Send. The attached file is a copy, so you'll have to incorporate user suggestions into your original project file.

After all feedback is incorporated, you can print views and reports from Project 2000 to communicate the project essentials to shareholders, managers, and workgroup members. In our project, we'll print the Calendar and Resource Sheet views, three versions of the Gantt Chart, the Resource Usage Workload, the Project Budget, and the Top Level Task reports to distribute to appropriate stakeholders.

 NOTE You'll want to print views and reports that are easy for the recipients to understand. Examine the views and reports in Chapter 17 and Chapter 18, "Using Reports to Analyze Data," to find those that best meet your stakeholders' information requirements. If you need to fine-tune your documents, these chapters include instructions on customizing views and reports.

Printing Views

To print the Gantt Chart or any other view, first use the View menu to display the view. Choose the data you want to display by selecting a table (View ➤ Table), and then adjust the columns and position the timeline. The Gantt Chart prints with the timescale displayed. You may want to print a more condensed timescale, either because your project spans a number of months or the audience for the printout needs only summary data. To change the timescale, right-click the timescale at the top of the chart and choose Timescale from the shortcut menu, or choose Format ➤ Timescale from the menu. In the Timescale dialog box, shown in Figure 4.16, set the Major and Minor scales (for example, weeks and days, days and hours, months and days). Check the preview in the dialog box as you change scales and set other display options. Click the Nonworking Time tab to change the way weekends and holidays are displayed in the view.

FIGURE 4.16

Adjust the timescale in the Timescale dialog box.

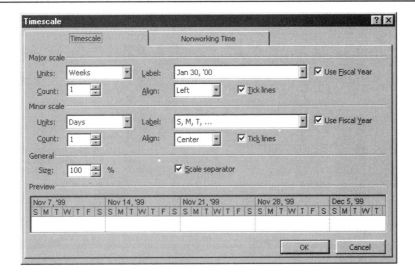

TIP   Right-click an empty area of the Gantt Chart and choose Bar Styles from the shortcut menu to change the text displayed in the Gantt Chart.

Click the Print button on the Standard toolbar to print the view as it appears. To set a range of dates or print multiple copies, choose File ➤ Print from the Menu bar to open the Print dialog box.

We want to print filtered versions of the Gantt Chart so that each group can see their tasks in isolation. To filter the Gantt, choose Resource Group from the Filter drop-down list on the formatting toolbar:

Type the name of the group (from the Resource Sheet) that you want to display. The Gantt Chart will include only tasks for this group, as shown in Figure 4.17. Choose All Tasks from the Filter list to remove the filter.

FIGURE 4.17

A filtered Gantt Chart lets a group view its tasks.

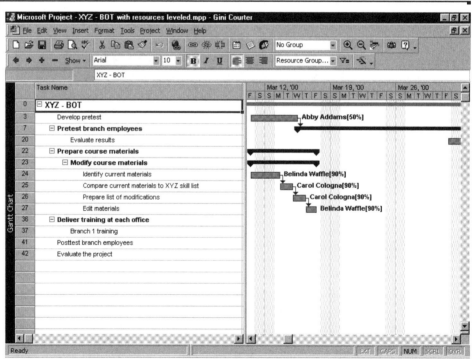

 TIP Choose View ➢ Header and Footer to change the header and footer text in a view or report.

You can easily print a Gantt Chart that shows only major tasks. Choose the level of task you want to display from the Show menu on the Formatting toolbar before printing the view:

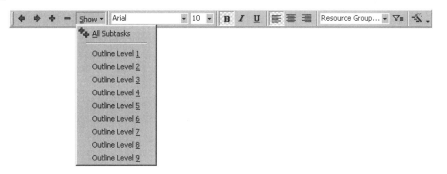

Printing Reports

With Project 2000, you can print reports about every aspect of your project. As with printed views, you can change reports by using tables and filters. To print a report, choose View ➤ Reports to open the Reports dialog box:

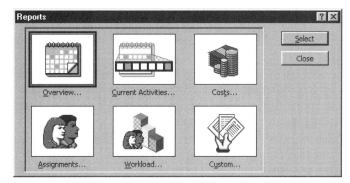

Double-click the category of report you want to print (in this case, Workload) to see the reports included in the category:

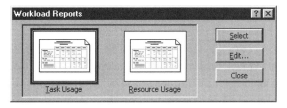

Double-click a report, such as the Resource Usage report, and Project opens it in the Print Preview window, as shown in Figure 4.18. Click the Print button to print the report, or click the Close button to discard the report and return to the dialog box.

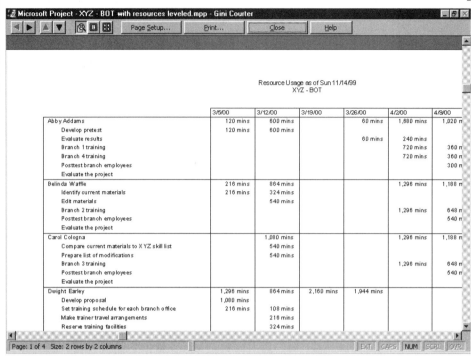

FIGURE 4.18

The Resource Usage report, showing each resource's weekly tasks, is only one of many useful reports for planning and management.

The views and reports are the core of the final project proposal. We'll also revise the project summary that we created earlier in Microsoft Word, with references to each of the printed Project icons and reports to round out the printed documentation.

The project documentation isn't limited to paper-based communications. If we still need to "sell" this project, or want to garner some enthusiasm and support, we'll create a PowerPoint presentation that shows the project goals, deliverables, timeline, and costs.

Tracking and Managing a Project

Your project's been approved, so it's time to get started. But before you do, it's also time to save a project baseline. The baseline is a snapshot of the planned project. As the project moves into development, you'll update the project file with actual costs, hours worked, and completion information, which you'll compare to the baseline. Choose File ➢ Save and leave the default baseline option selected when prompted. If you checked the Don't Ask Me About This Again checkbox earlier, you won't be

prompted to save a baseline. Choose Tools ➤ Tracking ➤ Save Baseline to open the
Save Baseline dialog box and click OK to save a baseline:

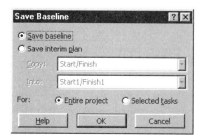

Setting Up Project Communication

Project communication includes data collection and information reporting. There are
three ways to collect data: manually, by email, or over the Internet or an intranet using
Project Central. (Project Central is Project 2000's new Web-based client/server system
for communicating project information.) Data-collection tasks are the same, regardless
of the collection method. Using email or the Web as your primary collection method,
however, means that workgroup members' status reports automatically update the Project 2000 file. With manual collection, the project manager has to enter information
in Project. Project 2000's workgroup features provide outstanding support for email
communications using Microsoft Outlook or another MAPI-compliant email system.
Project Central handles data collection and some information reporting, freeing your
time for other project management tasks.

All our workgroup members (also known as *resources*) use Outlook as their email client,
so we'll use email to communicate and collect data for project management. (The project
manager must have Project 2000, as well as Outlook, but team members only need to
have Outlook.) We'll handle all our task assignments and data collection from Project's
workgroup menu:

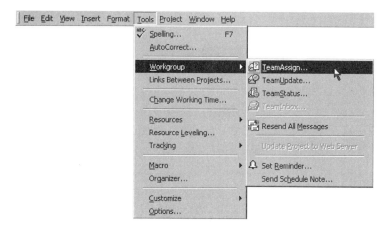

NOTE It's easy to set up Project's TeamAssign features. You'll find instructions for setting up workgroup members to use TeamAssign in Chapter 15, "Communicating Project Information."

Assigning Project Tasks

Workgroup members can use the workgroup features to report on tasks that are assigned to them using the workgroup features. To assign all the tasks in the project or one task, switch to Gantt Chart view, select a single task, and then choose Tools ➤ Workgroup ➤ TeamAssign. A dialog box appears, asking if you want to assign all tasks or the single selected task:

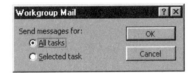

Choose an option and click OK to open the TeamAssign dialog box, shown in Figure 4.19. If you want to assign more than one but not all project tasks, select the tasks, and then choose Tools ➤ Workgroup ➤ TeamAssign. With two or more tasks selected, Project assigns only the selected tasks.

FIGURE 4.19

Use the TeamAssign feature to assign tasks to resources.

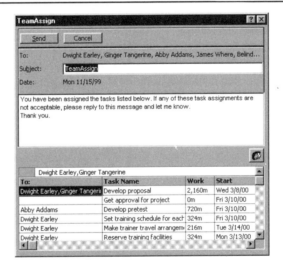

Change the subject line if you wish, and edit the text in the message. When you're assigning tasks at the beginning of the project, you might want to let team members know how often and when you'll ask for status reports on the tasks they've accepted: for example, every week on Thursday. Click Send to send the task assignments to the workgroup members. A message box appears, reminding you that recipients must have the workgroup-messaging features installed from the Project 2000 CD (see Chapter 15). Click OK to send the messages. A message box appears briefly as each recipient's Team-Assign message is created:

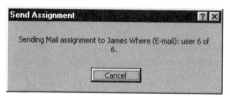

 In the Resource Sheet, an icon in the Indicator column indicates that the workgroup member hasn't responded to the message. For a visual overview of the status of all task assignments, open the Gantt Chart and switch to the Usage table (View ➤ Table ➤ Usage).

When team members receive the TeamAssign message, they can click the Reply button and accept or reject individual task assignments, and send comments about individual assignments or a message about all assignments. When a team member accepts an assignment, the task is automatically added to their Tasks folder in Outlook. (This is another good reason to assign your project tasks using TeamAssign.) Responses from workgroup members are delivered to your Inbox in Outlook. Open the message, and the Project Messaging Service starts:

When the response opens, review the contents. To update the Project file with the accepted assignments, click the Update Project button.

Updating Task Status

Workgroup members send progress reports in response to your request for an update. In Gantt Chart view, select one or more tasks and choose Tools ➤ Workgroup ➤ Team-Status to open a TeamStatus form, much like the TeamAssign form. Set the beginning and ending dates for the status report. Click Send to send the request for a status report to the team members assigned to the selected tasks.

The TeamStatus message has a grid in which the assignee can enter hours worked on the task(s) each day and the time remaining on the task, as shown in Figure 4.20. When you receive their response, review the contents and then click Update Project to update the actual work and remaining work in the project file for the tasks included in the TeamStatus report.

FIGURE 4.20

TeamStatus reports include hours worked each day during the reporting period you selected.

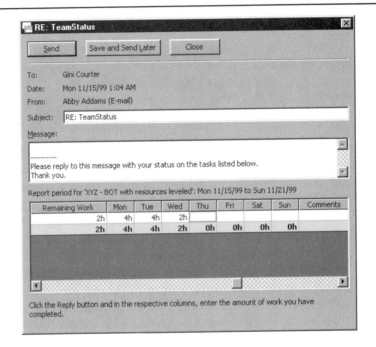

 TIP You can customize the TeamStatus form to request specific information from workgroup members. See Chapter 15 for information on customizing Project's workgroup features.

Creating Additional Reports

Project's workgroup features handle reporting from workgroup members to the project manager. The project manager still needs to create reports for external consumption by stakeholders and managers. There are several reports commonly used for external reporting, including Current Activity Reports (Tasks In Progress, Tasks Completed, and

Slipping Tasks), and Cost Reports (Cash Flow and Overbudget Tasks). Current Gantt Charts show the percentage of each task completed as a dark bar within the task bar. The reports you include depend on the audience. Gantt Charts are user-friendly and popular with stakeholders. Managers often require a budget comparison report (either Overbudget Tasks or the Gantt Chart with the Cost table, which shows budget and variance). You can access Project's predesigned reports and create custom reports by choosing Reports from the View menu. For more about creating reports, see Chapter 18, "Using Reports to Analyze Data."

Managing Project Scope

Scope management begins with the project definition and continues through the entire project. With soft products such as software and the first round of a multi-year training program, project managers can divert requests for additional features or functionality by saying "I'll include that in our recommendations for the next project." The "wait until the next version" message is harder to sell when your major project deliverable is a new building or cruise ship.

Whether your project deliverables are soft goods, services, or durable goods, the project manager needs to create and clearly communicate a process for collecting, evaluating, and accepting recommended additions or modifications to the project plan. We widely circulate a change form (see Chapter 11), and make sure that team members route all suggested changes through the project manager, preferably by email with a copy to the group or individual suggesting the change. Change requests are evaluated by the project manager or assigned team members to determine whether the change falls within the current scope, as defined in the project definition. If they are not, the project manager determines the following:

- The cost to implement the request
- The amount of delay, if any, if the request is implemented
- Other areas of the project impacted by implementing the request

Requests that increase the budget, extend the timeline, or redefine or delay one or more deliverables must be approved in writing, by the individual or group authorizing the project, before the project file is modified to reflect the change. After the project file is modified, we use TeamUpdate (see Figure 4.21) to inform workgroup members of the change. As with TeamAssign, team members can provide immediate feedback on the proposed schedule changes. The authorized change request is included in the next periodic report to stakeholders and managers.

FIGURE 4.21

Use TeamUpdate to notify team members of project changes.

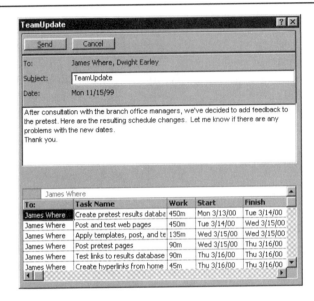

Managing the Project Schedule and Costs

With frequent updates from workgroup members of actual work performed and their estimates of work remaining, you have the information you need to manage the project schedule and costs. The mantra for this management task is "catch it early." Request status reports frequently at the beginning of the implementation phase. Relatively small amounts of unnoticed slippage early in the project can create large delays later.

After you receive responses to TeamStatus requests and update your project file, check the Project Statistics to see whether the project is still on schedule and within budget. Choose Project ➤ Project Information. Change the Status Date to the date you want to view project statistics for, and then click the Statistics button to view the current statistics, as shown in Figure 4.22.

FIGURE 4.22

Check the Project Statistics to see whether your Finish Date varies from the baseline.

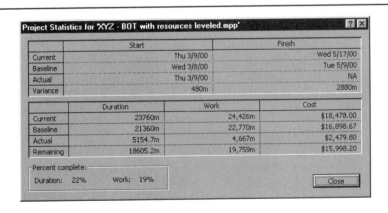

The statistics in Figure 4.22 show that the project started a day late and is projected to finish eight days behind schedule. Review the critical tasks (see "Optimizing the Plan," earlier in this chapter) to see why the project is scheduled to finish late. Get approval for the delay, or follow the optimization strategies discussed earlier in the chapter to get the project back on track. Our critical path analysis (see Figure 4.23) traces the delay to one task: Identify Current Materials. The task should have been completed a week ago, and hasn't been started yet. We discussed this with Belinda, and found that the training director hasn't responded to her request for the curriculum map. (At this point, we're all agreed that "Obtain Curriculum Map" should have been a separate task!) Abby agreed to help Belinda review the materials without the map (assigning additional resources). They will have the task completed today. We'll assign additional resources to the Prepare List of Modifications and Edit Materials tasks to make up the rest of the delay.

FIGURE 4.23

Filtering the Gantt Chart for Critical Tasks reveals why the project is behind schedule.

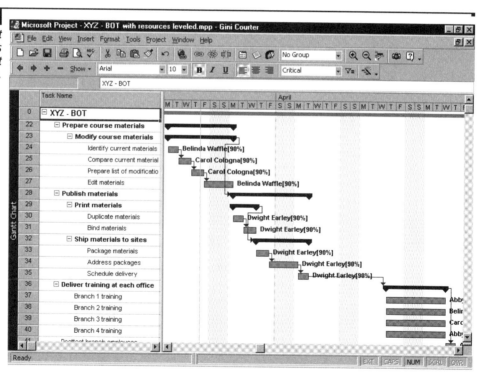

Another tool used in schedule management highlights tasks that are incomplete or behind schedule. In the Tracking Gantt (View ➢ Tracking Gantt), bars representing the baseline Gantt Chart are shown in gray, and the percentage of each task completed is displayed at the end of the task bar, as shown in Figure 4.24. The Gantt Chart filtered for critical tasks helps identify problems that affect the project timeline, but the Tracking Gantt shows you all the problem tasks, even if their delay doesn't affect the deadline.

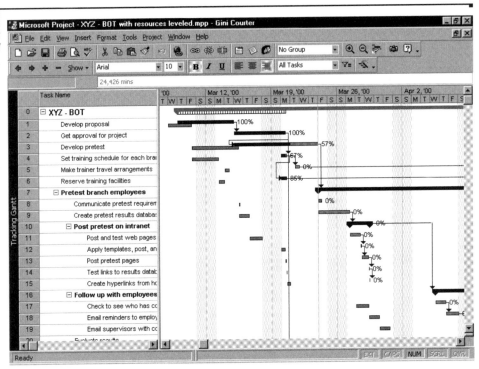

FIGURE 4.24

The Tracking Gantt shows the baseline and actual performance.

We'll want to know, for example, why the pretest preparation is seriously behind schedule in Figure 4.24. When materials preparation gets back on schedule, the pretest needs to be ready to post on the Web site. If it is not, the project won't be completed on time (but at least we'll have different people to point our fingers at!).

Managing Project Resources

Adding resources can result in overallocation. Schedule changes can also lead to overallocation, as tasks from one week slip into a week when the resource is already committed to other tasks. Use the Resource Sheet to locate overallocated resources, and use the optimization strategies listed earlier in this chapter to resolve overallocation.

After changing the task assignments, we switched to the Resource Sheet to check for overallocations. Abby and Dwight are now overallocated, as shown in Figure 4.25.

We checked Abby's Resource Graph (View ➢ Resource Graph), shown in Figure 4.26, and found that the overallocation is due to the additional tasks we assigned. Dwight's overallocation is due to slippage on the pretest.

FIGURE 4.25

*Check for over-
allocated resources in
the Resource Sheet.*

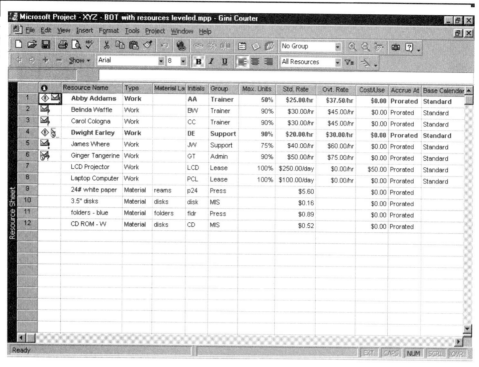

FIGURE 4.26

*Use the Resource Graph
to view overallocations
for a specific resource.*

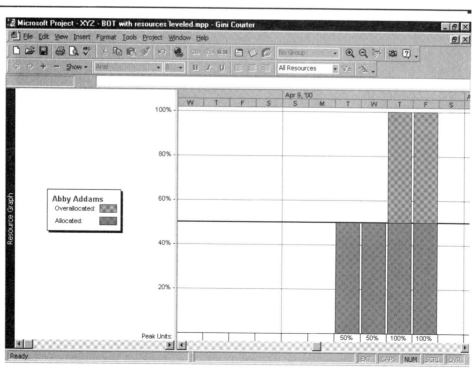

Both employees are willing to work overtime one day. We saved the project, and then leveled resources and checked the proposed Finish Date in the Project Statistics dialog box. The cost of overtime is minor. Without eight hours of overtime, we can't finish the project by the original finish date. This amount of overtime falls within the project manager's discretion, so we authorized the overtime and reverted to the file we saved before leveling.

Now, we'll use TeamAssign to assign Abby's additional tasks, and use TeamUpdate to inform workgroup members of the schedule changes. The Indicators column on the Resource Sheet or Gantt Chart view (see Figure 4.27) shows which tasks and resources need updates. To send all the updates at once, select any task and choose Tools ➤ Workgroup ➤ TeamUpdate, and then select All Project Tasks in the dialog box.

FIGURE 4.27

Indicator icons show tasks that have changed.

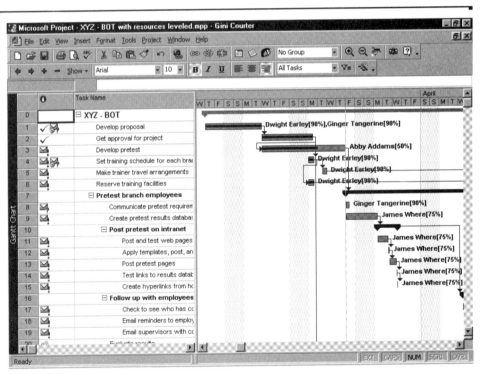

You'll repeat the project management tasks until the project is completed. Each day, week, or month, the project manager requests status reports; updates the project; checks the finish date and budget; and manages the schedule, costs, and project resources. At some point, however, the project will be finished. The last task of the project manager is closing the project.

Closing the Project

At the conclusion of the project, the project manager schedules a meeting called a *post-implementation review*, *project review*, or *postmortem*. The purpose of the session is to gather and summarize project information for a number of potential users: stakeholders, organizational managers, the project team, and other project managers. Solid, well-documented information about the project provides a basis for success for future projects, and is included in the final project report.

In many organizations, a lessons-learned brainstorming session is used to elicit ideas that can be useful in other projects. Lessons can be positive experiences or techniques that should be repeated, as well as procedures that need to be buried in the deepest hole the organization can locate.

In addition to a summary of the postmortem, the final project report should minimally include the following reports and views:

- Reports: Project Summary, Milestones, Budget, Overbudget Tasks, Overbudget Resources
- Views: Tracking Gantt, Gantt Chart with Variance Table

Your final report will include other information dictated by the type of project. The XYZ-Branch Office Training Project final report, for example, will include pretest and post-test results, trainee and trainer evaluations of each course, and recommendations for future training. The electronic version of each final report includes a copy of the Project 2000 project file.

What's Next

In this chapter, we built, managed, and closed a project in record time. But Project 2000, like project management itself, is in the details. In the next six chapters, we'll build a project piece by piece, taking time for the seemingly trivial distinctions that directly affect project success.

Chapter 5, "Working in Project 2000," focuses on working efficiently in Project 2000. In Chapter 6, you'll learn about the intricacies of project calendars. Chapters 7 and 8 cover creating, constraining, outlining, and linking tasks. In Chapters 9 and 10, we explain resources, resource assignment, costs, and the task triangle: work, units, and duration. In Chapter 11, we optimize and publish the project plan.

PART II

Creating a Project from Start to Finish

LEARN TO:

- *Work in Project 2000*

- *Build a New Project*

- *Enter Project Tasks*

- *Schedule and Link Project Tasks*

- *Define Project Resources and Costs*

- *Assign and Schedule Resources and Costs*

- *Prepare Your Project for Publication*

CHAPTER <u>5</u>

Working in Project 2000

Microsoft Project 2000 is a multifaceted and full-featured program. However, its complexity is simplified by its familiarity. When you first open Microsoft Project, you are bound to notice the similarities between Project and other Microsoft productivity products. If you are already familiar with any of the Microsoft Office applications, you'll have no trouble when navigating Project. And if you find yourself needing help along the way, Project places a wide variety of help at your fingertips.

Exploring the Project 2000 Application Window

Project 2000 is somewhat of a hybrid of Microsoft Outlook and Excel, with a carryover of features from Project 98. Even if you're using Project for the first time, it won't take long to find your way around. Figure 5.1 shows the Project application window. At the top, you'll see the customary Title bar and Menu bar. This is followed by the new personalized toolbars introduced in Microsoft Office 2000 (for more about personalized toolbars, see "Working with Personalized Menus and Toolbars," later in this chapter).

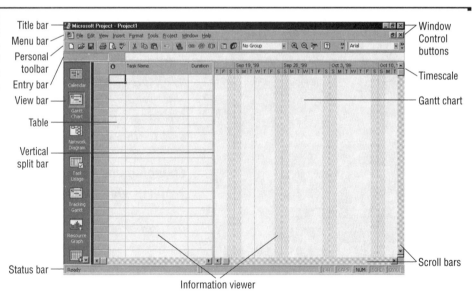

FIGURE 5.1

The Project 2000 Application Window has a number of features found in Microsoft Office applications.

The bar underneath the toolbars is the Entry bar. Similar to Excel's Formula bar, the Entry bar is used to enter and edit text. On the left side of the application window is the View bar. Baring a close resemblance to the Outlook bar, the View bar allows you to switch between Project's many views.

The Information Viewer or project worksheet, which is located in the main part of the application window, displays different information depending on the view you choose. The default view is the Gantt Chart view. In this view, you see a task list on the left and a graphic image of a Gantt Chart on the right. If you are new to Gantt Charts, don't be too intimidated. As you work through this book, you'll have plenty of opportunity to see them in operation.

 The Vertical Split bar divides the two sides of the Information Viewer. You can point to the Vertical Split bar and drag it in either direction with the two-header resize arrow to see more of one side of the Viewer or another.

At the bottom of the application window is a Status bar and a horizontal scroll bar for each side of the Information Viewer. The Status bar is a great place to find out if you have the Num Lock, Caps Lock, Scroll Lock, and Insert/Overtype keys turned on. And coming full circle, you'll find the vertical scroll bar on the right side of the application window.

Opening More than One Project

 Project 2000 employs a new paradigm for managing open windows, called SDI or *Single Document Interface*. First introduced in Microsoft Outlook 97, SDI essentially means that each document window operates independently of the application. The biggest advantage of SDI is that every open project appears on the Windows taskbar; each appears with the appropriate application icon. This makes it much easier to switch between projects without having to access the Window menu to see what's open.

 When you want to close one project and leave Project 2000 running, click the Close button on the second row (Menu bar) of the Window control buttons, as shown here.

 WARNING Unlike the SDI in Word 2000, clicking the Close button on the Title bar in Project closes the Project application and any open projects.

Working with Personalized Menus and Toolbars

When you start any new application, we always recommend that you take a few minutes to familiarize yourself with the menu and toolbar options. This is an excellent way to find those features you are already familiar with and those that are new to this

PART

II

Creating a Project
from Start to Finish

application. If you've worked in Office, you probably recognize a number of toolbar buttons; as a result, you have a clear idea of what those options can do for you.

However, if you haven't used Office 2000 yet, you are in for a bit of a surprise. When you first click a menu, only a portion of the menu appears and displays the most commonly used features (as shown on the left in Figure 5.2). The rest of the menu is hidden. To expand the menu to see all of the available choices, as shown on the right in Figure 5.2, you have to hover over the open menu for about five seconds or click the double arrows at the bottom of the menu.

FIGURE 5.2

The menu on the left displays commonly used menu items, and the menu on the right is expanded to show all menu choices.

Similarly, only some of the toolbar buttons are immediately available. The traditional Standard and Formatting toolbars share one row, as shown in Figure 5.3, and only the most commonly used buttons are displayed.

FIGURE 5.3

The Standard and Formatting toolbars share one row, and only the most commonly used buttons are available.

You can distinguish where one toolbar ends and another begins by the double right arrows and the vertical selection bar.

The double right arrows indicate that there are more buttons available. Click the More Buttons button at the end of any toolbar to see the additional button choices.

To use one of the buttons listed on the More Buttons menu, click it just as you would on any toolbar. The tool becomes active and the button moves to the visible toolbar. In the process, it displaces another button to the More Buttons menu. Project determines what button to replace, based on whether or not you have used the button in the past and whether it is generally a commonly used button.

 NOTE For more about creating custom toolbars, see Chapter 21, "Customizing Project 2000."

If you find the Personalized menubars and toolbars feature disconcerting and want to work in a more predictable environment, you can turn these features completely off by following these steps:

1. Right-click any toolbar or Menu bar, and Choose Customize from the shortcut menu that opens; or choose View ➤ Toolbars and choose Customize.

2. Click the Options tab if it is not already visible.

3. Clear the first two checkboxes: Standard and Formatting Toolbars Share One Row and Menus Show Recently Used Commands First.

4. Click Close.

The Standard and Formatting toolbars appear on separate rows and when you click a menu, all options are visible.

PART

II

Creating a Project
from Start to Finish

NOTE Throughout the remainder of this book, the Personalized Menu and Toolbars feature is turned off in all screen pictures.

Changing Views

Views allow you to examine and work with a project from all different angles, focusing on the information that is important to you at any given time. But views in Project are not just ways to see the same data. Views come in several varieties: some are used to enter data; some are used to analyze data. Some views combine different types of data to help you make decisions about the project's status.

Project views can generally be categorized into two primary types: Task views and Resource views. *Task views* include views in which the focus is on entering and reviewing task information: tasks, duration, start dates, finish dates, predecessors, and other similar information. *Resource views* include views related to assigning and tracking the use of human resources, materials, and equipment used to complete the project. A resource can be an individual, a company, a department within a company, a team, a piece of equipment, a room, or any other resource you need for the project.

 Many of Project's predefined views are available on the View bar. Use the scroll buttons at the top and bottom of the View bar to scroll through the available views. There, you'll find five commonly used tasks views and three resource views.

Task Views

Calendar view is a familiar way to look at tasks. Project displays a traditional monthly calendar, with tasks represented by bars spanning the days on which they are scheduled.

Gantt Chart view is the default view. In Gantt Chart view, you can work with task information in both text and bar graphics format: entering new tasks, establishing relationships between tasks, and assigning personnel and resources to tasks.

 Network Diagram view, shown in Figure 5.4, displays the project's tasks in a flowchart. A box or node represents each task and includes several data elements such as duration, start and finish dates, and percent completed.

Task Usage view focuses on how much work each resource has completed over time. In this view, you can also compare actual work and costs to budgeted work and cost.

Tracking Gantt view is similar to the traditional Gantt Chart view, but it compares baseline start and finished dates to scheduled start and finish dates, or to the percentage of the work that has already been completed.

FIGURE 5.4

Network Diagram view displays the project in a flowchart, showing relationships between tasks and other critical information about each task.

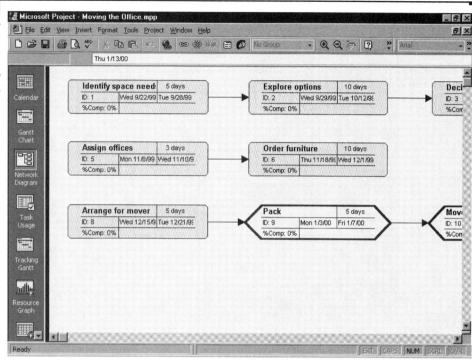

Resource Views

Resource Graph view offers a graphical representation of the way resources, work, and costs of resources are allocated over time.

Resource Sheet view provides a summary of information about resources in a spreadsheet format. In this view, you can enter and review information about payment rates.

Resource Usage View, shown in Figure 5.5, groups tasks by resources; and displays the amount of work, work allocation, and work availability for each resource.

Additional views are available on the View bar by clicking the More Views button.

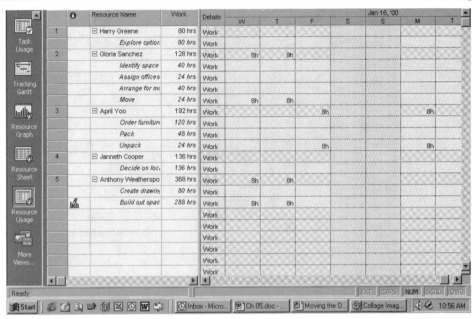

Resource Usage view organizes tasks underneath each resource, so you can easily see when someone is committed and how long they will be involved in specific tasks.

This opens the More Views dialog box, shown here. All of the views can be modified to display different data fields and to include filters to focus on just the information you want to see. For more about creating custom views, refer to Chapter 17, "Using Views to Evaluate Data."

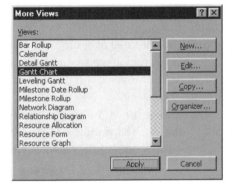

Applying Tables to Views

In addition to Project's views, each view has a number of tables to choose from that display different fields of data. For example, the default view is Gantt Chart view and the default table is the Entry table. In the Entry table you have fields (columns) such as Duration, Start, and Finish. If you apply the Cost table to the Gantt Chart view, the fields change to Fixed Cost, Fixed Cost Accrual, and Total Cost. You can change tables by choosing Table from the View menu and selecting a table from the menu.

 NOTE As you work through the chapters in this book, you will have the opportunity to work with many of Project's views and tables, so don't worry if they are a bit overwhelming right now.

Getting Help in Project 2000

Although this book is an excellent resource for your Microsoft Project questions, we recognize that we can't put everything you need to know about Project in a single book. As experienced trainers, we also know that it is sometimes necessary to hear the same thing from a different perspective before it will sink in. Whether you are new to Project, new to project management or an old pro at both, you can find something of value in the Project help files.

Project puts six types of help at your disposal:

- The Office Assistant
- Contents and Index
- Getting Started
- What's This?
- Office on the Web
- Detect and Repair

The Office Assistant

You've probably already encountered the ever-so-helpful Office Assistant.

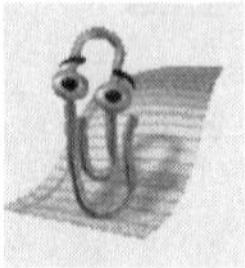

The *Office Assistant* is Microsoft's "social interface" for Project 2000 and other members of the Office family. Modified significantly from Office 97, the Office Assistant is now a separate application called an agent, which, like SDI windows, operates independently of the open application. The Office Assistant crosses all applications, and provides help for specific features of each application. You can choose from several Assistants from the Assistant Options. Each has its own "personality."

The Assistant offers help the first time you work with a feature and if you have difficulty with a task. Sometimes the offer is subtle: In Figure 5.6, the light bulb over Rocky, one of the characters you can select, means that you can click the Assistant to receive a tip that could save you time and energy.

FIGURE 5.6

The light bulb is a clue that the Assistant has something to say.

Other offers of help are a bit more intrusive. If, for example, you open a wizard, the Office Assistant pops up to ask if you'd like help with the feature.

After you've worked with Project 2000 for a few days, you might decide that you'd like a little less help from your eager assistant. To change the Assistant's options, click on the Assistant, choose Options to open the Office Assistant dialog box, and then click the Options tab to display the Options page, shown in Figure 5.7.

When you're ready to go it alone, you can turn off the Assistant by unchecking the Use the Office Assistant checkbox. If you are not quite ready for total abandonment, clear the other checkboxes to reduce the frequency with which the assistant volunteers help.

If you start to get lonely, click the Microsoft Project Help button or choose Help ➢ Show the Office Assistant to invite the Assistant back into your office.

 TIP For help with any dialog box in Office 2000, click the dialog box Help button (the button with the question mark), and then click on the item you want help with.

FIGURE 5.7

The Office Assistant dialog box lets you adjust the amount of support you get from the Assistant.

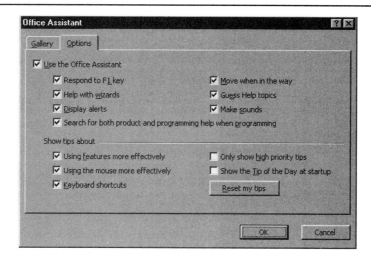

Contents and Index

The Contents and Index choice available on the Help menu is the Web-style help system that gives you options for Contents, Answer Wizard, and Index. The Contents page is shown in Figure 5.8.

FIGURE 5.8

The Contents page of Help has a table of contents of all of the available Help files.

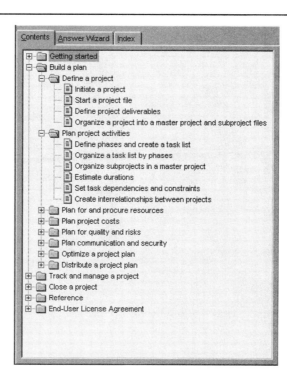

PART

II

Creating a Project from Start to Finish

To find help about a particular subject, click the plus button to expand the listings.

In Figure 5.8, the contents of several of the folders are expanded. Notice that the second folder, "Build a Plan," contains a number of subfolders. Expand the subfolders to see the actual Help topics. You can also point to the window divider and drag it to see all the contents.

 The sheet of paper icon designates individual Help topics. Click the topic you are interested in to display it on the right of the window. Figure 5.9 shows the steps for Estimated Durations. Click the hyperlinks to review the instructions for each step.

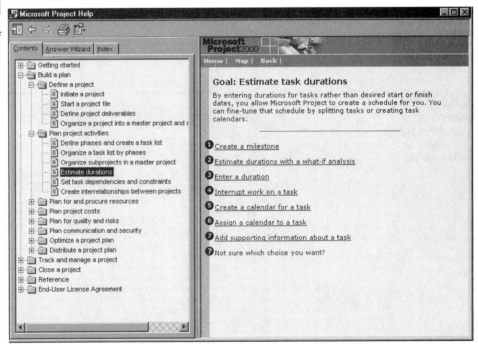

Click any word that appears in blue to read a definition of that term. Follow the See Also links to find out more about a particular topic. At the top of the Help Topic frame, shown in Figure 5.9, there are several navigation buttons. Click Home to return to the Welcome screen and click Back to return to the previous topic.

The Map option opens a Project Map in a separate window, shown in Figure 5.10. The Project Map outlines how to create and manage a project. Click any topic on the left to see the steps outlined on the right. Clicking a topic on the right takes you to that Help topic in the main Help window. If you like following the Project map, click Map again to return to the Map window.

FIGURE 5.10

The Project Map outlines how to create and manage a project.

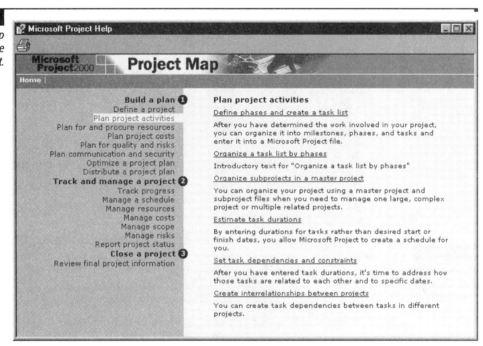

PART

II

Creating a Project from Start to Finish

Using the Answer Wizard and the Index

Help in the Answer Wizard (shown in Figure 5.11) is the same as the Office Assistant's help, except it has a slightly different format. Enter a question in the What Would You Like to Do box, and choose from a list of related topics.

The Index is organized by key words. You can enter a keyword in the Type Keywords box or choose a keyword from the supplied list. Click the Search button to search for the help topics that contain that keyword. Enter multiple keywords, as shown in Figure 5.12, to narrow your search.

FIGURE 5.11

Use the Answer Wizard
to find help for specific
questions.

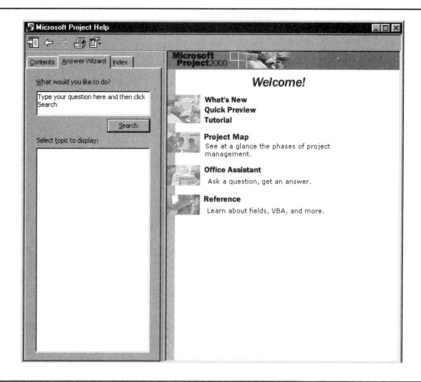

FIGURE 5.12

To narrow a keyword
search, enter multiple
words before searching.

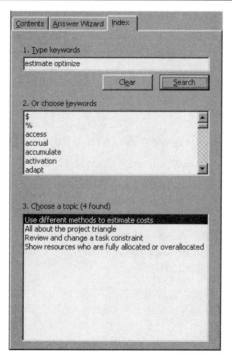

NOTE If you deactivate the Office Assistant and then click the Help button on the Standard toolbar, Contents and Index opens on the Answer Wizard tab. When you finish with Help, click the Close button to close it.

Getting Started

For people who are new to Microsoft Project and to project management, Project includes three Getting Started options on the Help menu. Choose Getting Started, and then choose between Quick Preview, Tutorial, and Project Map.

Quick Preview, shown in Figure 5.13, is a visual overview of project management and the tools Microsoft Project has to help you create and manage a project.

FIGURE 5.13

Quick Preview provides an overview of what project management is all about.

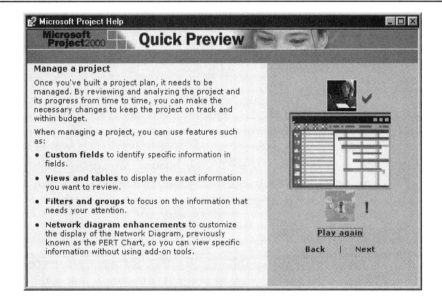

PART

II

Creating a Project from Start to Finish

The Tutorial is a step-by-step look at creating a project. The Basics section, shown in Figure 5.14, is designed to acquaint you with Microsoft Project and project management concepts. In the second section, Create Your Plan, you can actually walk through the process of creating a plan. Of course, this book covers each of these topics in more detail than is allowed in the tutorial. However, the tutorial is a helpful tool if you want to review a particular skill or approach it from a different angle.

The Project Map option on the Getting Started menu takes you to the same map that is accessible from the Contents and Index Help selection.

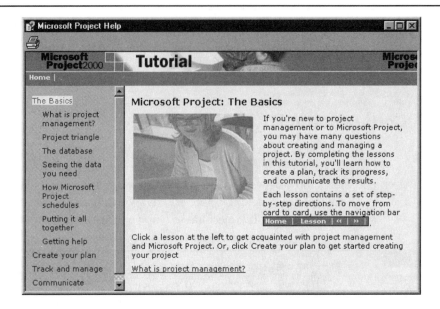

What's This?

What's This? is available throughout Microsoft Office. When you choose What's This? from the Help menu, the pointer changes to a pointer with a question mark. Click any option onscreen to get a pop-up description of that feature. You can also use this option to open a menu and find out about a menu option. What's This? is good for only one description before it automatically turns off. To turn it off manually, choose Help ➤ What's This? again.

Office on the Web

If you choose Office on the Web from the Help menu, Microsoft Internet Explorer launches and you are whisked away to the Project section of the Microsoft Office Update Web site. There, you can find informative articles, updates, and other downloads to assist you when working with Project. This site is updated regularly so it's worth checking once a month or so to see what's new.

Using Detect and Repair

Although you find Detect and Repair on the Help menu, this option offers a different kind of help. Introduced as part of Office 2000, Detect and Repair identifies corrupted or missing Project program files, and automatically repairs them for you. Project generally warns you when it's a good idea to run Detect and Repair, but if Project starts acting quirky, it might be worth giving it a try. To run Detect and Repair, you must have access to the installation disks or file location.

Opening an Existing File

If you want to open a previously saved project file, you can open it by clicking the Open Document button located on the Standard toolbar or by choosing File ➤ Open from the File menu. Each of these methods brings you to the Open dialog box. The Open dialog box is used in all Microsoft applications and is new to the 2000 versions of Office products. If you spend the time to learn what it has to offer, it can end up saving you a lot of time in Microsoft Project and other Microsoft applications. This section will take you through the Open dialog box in detail to ensure that you have an understanding of the most frequently used capabilities of the Open dialog box.

Using the File Open Dialog Box

The File Open dialog box enables you to perform many different functions. Although the main function of the Open dialog box is to open files, you can also rename files, create folders, find files, print files, and move files.

The Open dialog box, as shown in Figure 5.15, contains several different buttons and graphics. When the Open dialog box first opens, it opens up to a default directory. This default directory is set as the file location for your project files. If this is incorrect, go to Tools ➤ Options and click on the Save tab to change the file location of your projects.

FIGURE 5.15

The Open dialog box enables you to perform many file functions.

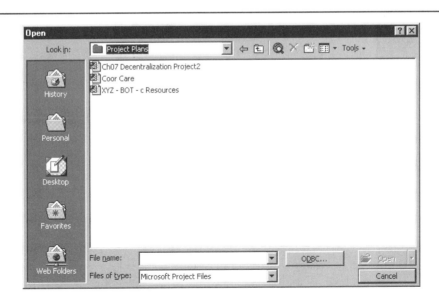

To open an existing file, it is necessary to first locate the file. The following information will help you determine the best method for finding or locating your files. File locations can vary based on whether your project plans are stored on your hard drive or stored out on a corporate server or Web application. Microsoft Project 2000 supports the file types listed in Table 5.1.

TABLE 5.1: PROJECT 2000 FILE TYPES	
Extension	**File Type**
.mpp	Microsoft Project documents
.mpt	Microsoft Project templates
.mpw	Microsoft Project workspaces
.mpd	Microsoft Project databases
.mpx	Microsoft Project Exchange files

Navigating with the Places Bar

The Places bar, located on the left side and shown in Figure 5.16, contains five different folders or areas that you can easily navigate to by clicking on the graphical icon. Depending on where your files are stored, you may find the Places Bar to be a quick way to locate your project files.

FIGURE 5.16

The Places bar on the Open dialog box

Click History to see your most recently used folders and files. Personal takes you to your Personal folder in Windows (c:\windows\personal) or Windows NT (c:\winnt\profiles\[loginName]\Personal). Clicking on Desktop takes you to your computer desktop, where it shows My Computer, Network Neighborhood, and My Briefcase. Click Favorites to see those folders and files you have placed in your Favorites folder.

This folder is also located under the Windows folder (c:\windows\favorites and in Windows NT C:\WinNT\profiles\[loginName]\favorites). The last option, Web Folders, is for documents and projects posted to a shared folder through your corporate intranet.

Once you locate the file you want to open, double-click it or click the Open button to open the file.

Using the Toolbar

The toolbar on the Open dialog box, shown in Figure 5.17, helps you manage files and folders. The Look In drop-down list allows you to see all the drives and folders available on your system. If you know exactly where your file is located, this allows you to go to the file location, select the file, and open it by either double-clicking it or pressing the Open button located on the Open File dialog box.

FIGURE 5.17

The Open dialog box toolbar helps you find the files you are looking for.

Table 5.2 shows each button and how it can help you find files.

TABLE 5.2: TOOLBAR BUTTONS ON THE OPEN DIALOG BOX

Button	Description
⇐	If you are searching through folders, you can go back to your last location by pressing the Back button.
🔼	Use the Up One Level button to move up one folder level.
🔍	Use the Search the Web button to find the file on a Web site.
✕	Click the Delete button when you want to delete the file or folder you currently have selected.
📁	Create a new folder to help you organize files.
▦	Use the Views button to switch between List, Details, Preview, Properties, and Preview views, and to arrange icons in List view.
Tools ▾	Click the Tools button to access the Find, Delete, Rename, Print, Add to Favorites, Map Network Drives, and Properties options.

PART

II

Creating a Project
from Start to Finish

Managing Files from the Open Dialog Box

The Open dialog box allows you to organize your files on-the-fly rather than having to go to Explorer or My Computer to perform file management functions.

Moving and Copying Files   Follow these steps to copy or move a file:

1. Select the file you want to copy in the Open dialog box.

2. Right-click and choose Copy to copy the file, or select Cut to move from the shortcut menu.

3. Select the Folder you want to copy or move the file to. (Note: it must be a folder—you cannot copy a file into another file. If you notice that the Paste command is not available, you probably have a file instead of a folder selected.)

4. Right-click and choose Paste from the shortcut menu.

Deleting Files   In the Open dialog box, you can delete a folder or file in three different ways. Select the file or folder you want to delete and then choose one of these ways to delete it:

• Press the Delete key on the keyboard.

• Right-click to access the shortcut menu and select Delete.

• Press the Delete button located on the Open toolbar.

A confirmation box appears, asking you if you are certain you want to delete the file. Verify that you definitely want to perform the deletion, or press No to cancel the deletion.

If you try to delete a file that is currently open, the following error message will display. This error message alerts you to the fact that the file is open and cannot be deleted:

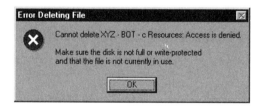

Creating Folders   To create a folder to move or copy files into, follow these steps:

1. Open the folder you want to serve as the parent folder to your new folder.

2. Click the Create New Folder button on the toolbar.

3. Confirm the location of the new folder by looking at the file path on the New Folder dialog box (see Figure 5.18).

4. Enter the name for the new folder.

5. Click OK.

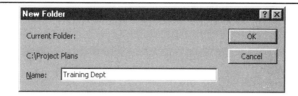

Opening Files

After you have located the project file you want to open, select it and then use one of the following three methods to open the file:

- Double-click the file.
- Right-click and select Open from the shortcut menu.
- Click the Open button on the Open toolbar.

Opening a File as Read-Only By opening a file as read-only, you protect the original from any changes you make to the project. If you decide to save the file with the changes, Project forces you to give the read-only file a new name.

To open a file as read-only, follow these steps in the Open dialog box:

1. Select the file you want to open.
2. Click the down arrow on the Open button and choose Open as Read-Only.

Opening as a Copy Sometimes, you may want to open a file as a copy rather than working on the original (if you want to create a new project based on a previous project plan, for example). To open a file as a copy from the Open dialog box:

1. Select the file you want to open as a copy.
2. Click the down arrow on the Open button and choose Open as Copy.

Opening a Password-protected File Some project files are protected so that only specific individuals have access to modify the project plan. Project prompts you to enter the password when you attempt to open the file. If you don't know the password, you are out of luck. If the password was applied with a Read-Only recommendation (see "Saving Project Files," later in this chapter), Project displays the following message to give you the option of opening it read-only.

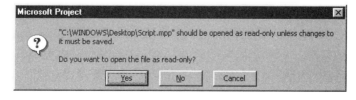

Saving Project Files

In this section, we'll talk about how to properly save your project files. Projects can be saved with or without a baseline. The first time that you save a project file, Project's PlanningWizard asks you if you want to save it with or without a baseline (see Figure 5.19). After you save a project with a baseline, the PlanningWizard no longer prompts you with this question again.

FIGURE 5.19

The PlanningWizard prompts you to save a project with a baseline.

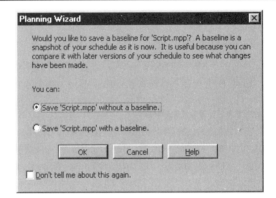

 NOTE The PlanningWizard is a Help tool that appears at various times to give you general advice about using Project, advice about errors, and advice about scheduling. You can turn off the PlanningWizard on the General tab of the Options dialog box (Tools ➤ Options).

Using the Save As Dialog Box

The first time you save a project, the Save As dialog box appears. This dialog box is where you identify where you want the file saved and what the file name will be. Similar to the Open dialog box, the Save As dialog box allows you to perform many functions other than just saving files. To save a new Project file, follow these steps:

1. Select File ➤ Save As from the File menu or click the Save button on the Standard toolbar.

2. Use the Save In drop-down list to locate where you want to save the file.

3. Type in the desired file name in the File Name field.

4. Click on the Save button.

The PlanningWizard prompts you to decide whether you want to save the project with a baseline. Baselines are project estimates that help you track how you are doing. Ideally, you should save a project with a baseline after you have entered the project plan and before the actual project begins. To learn more about saving with a baseline, refer to Chapter 11, "Preparing Your Project for Publication."

 NOTE If you are unsure how to navigate through the Save As dialog box, refer to the previous section, "Using the File Open Dialog Box." The options that are available in the Save As dialog box are similar to those in the Open dialog box.

Using the Auto Save Option

If you do not always remember to save your project files, you can have Project automatically save your project files at regular intervals. You can find the Auto Save option on the Save tab in of the Options dialog box (Tools ➤ Options), shown in Figure 5.20. You can decide how often you want the project to be saved and whether you want to save just the active project or all open project files. You can also specify whether or not you want to be prompted before it saves.

PART

II

Creating a Project
from Start to Finish

FIGURE 5.20

The Auto Save option can be set up to save your project automatically.

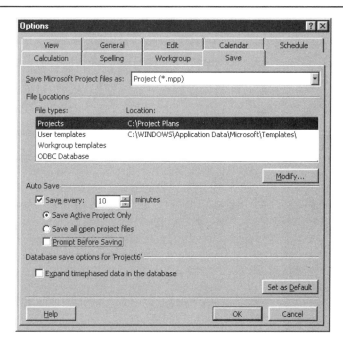

NOTE The AutoSave feature in Project is not the same as AutoRecovery in Microsoft Word. Project's AutoSave is a true save, not just an emergency recovery save in the event of a crash.

Printing in Project

Part of managing a project is being able to communicate project information effectively. Many times, this is accomplished through printing and distributing specific project reports. You can print formal reports and you can print views. For more information about printing reports, see Chapter 18, "Using Reports to Analyze Data," and for more about setting up and printing views, see Chapter 17.

Using Print Preview

 Print Preview allows you to preview before printing. Click the Print Preview button on the Standard toolbar or choose File ➤ Print Preview to display the Print Preview screen, shown in Figure 5.21.

FIGURE 5.21

Print Preview gives you a clear picture of what the printed document will look like.

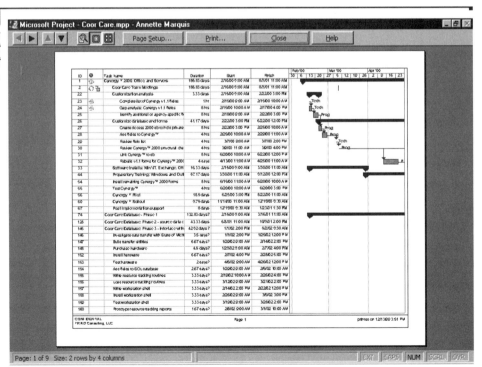

Use the Print Preview toolbar, located at the top of the Print Preview screen, to navigate through the document.

Table 5.3 describes the buttons on the Print Preview toolbar.

TABLE 5.3: PRINT PREVIEW TOOLBAR	
Button	**Description**
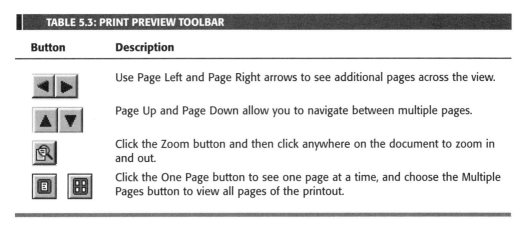	Use Page Left and Page Right arrows to see additional pages across the view.
	Page Up and Page Down allow you to navigate between multiple pages.
	Click the Zoom button and then click anywhere on the document to zoom in and out.
	Click the One Page button to see one page at a time, and choose the Multiple Pages button to view all pages of the printout.

If you want to change the page orientation, margins, headers and footers, legend, or view, click the Page Setup button. When you are ready to go to the Print dialog box, click the Print button. To close out of Print Preview and return to the project, click the Close button. If you need additional assistance to use Print Preview, click the Help button.

Changing Page Setup Options

Page Setup options allow you to do the following:

- Change the page orientation
- Adjust the scaling to a percentage or force it to fit on one page
- Adjust page and margin settings
- Add headers and footers
- Add legends
- Set view options

You can access the Page Setup dialog box from Print Preview or by Choosing File ➤ Page Setup.

PART

II

Creating a Project
from Start to Finish

Adding Headers, Footers, and Legends

Headers, footers and legends are useful to show project information such as project name, date, page numbers, and keys or legends. Headers and footers appear on every page, and you can specify if you want a legend to appear on every page or on its own individual legend page.

To enter a header, footer, or legend, click one of the alignment tabs shown in Figure 5.22, and enter the text you want to appear.

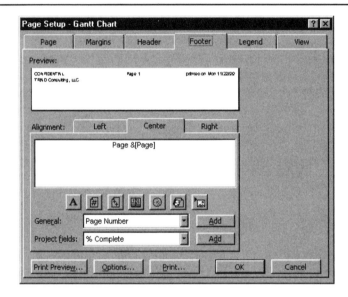

FIGURE 5.22

Use the Header, Footer, and Legend tabs to set up text that repeats on every page of the printed documents.

To enter Fields such as Page Numbers, Number of Pages, Current Date, Current Time, File Name, or Picture, click the corresponding button on the toolbar underneath the text box. You can also select fields from the General and Project fields drop-down lists. Select the field you want to add and click the Add button located next to each list.

When working with the settings on the legend page, you need to specify whether you want the legend to print on every page or on a legend page, which prints at the end of the project file. You can also specify the width of the legend page and set the font style, size, and color.

Sending the File to the Printer

After the project file is set up the way you like, it's time to send it to the printer. Although printing is rather straightforward, there are a couple of settings you should be aware of.

To print a project file, follow these steps:

1. Choose File ≻ Print.

2. Set the Print Range to print certain pages or accept the default of All.

3. Indicate the number of copies you want printed.

4. Set the Timescale to print information for only certain dates, or accept the default of All.

5. Choose OK.

TIP Using the Print button on the Standard toolbar automatically sends one copy of whatever is visible on the screen to the printer. Be careful with this because it bypasses the Print dialog box. Be sure that the print range and timescale default of All is what you want, otherwise, you will have to reprint your project file.

Closing Project Files

To close a project file, click File ≻ Close, or click the Close button in the Project file window. Each open file needs to be saved and closed individually.

What's Next

Now that you know your way around Microsoft Project, it's time to begin defining a project. In Chapter 6, "Building a New Project," you'll learn how to set up project information, enter project properties, and define project calendars.

PART

II

Creating a Project from Start to Finish

CHAPTER **6**

Building a New Project

The single most important phase in project management is the project definition phase. If this is done well, the project has the best chance of success. In Chapter 1, "Project 2000 Basics," Chapter 2, "Understanding Projects," and Chapter 3, "Understanding Project Management Tasks," you learned about the project cycle, project components, and project management tasks. You are now ready to build a project. Although Microsoft Project is an excellent place to track project activities, other Office tools such as Word, Excel, and PowerPoint can be used to develop the documentation that defines the project objectives, assumptions, constraints and scope. Each of these documents can then be attached or linked to your project, so you can readily access them while you are tracking a project's progress.

Throughout this book, we use several sample projects to guide you through your work with Project. For example, in the Decentralization project, the computer consulting company you work for decided to decentralize its offices and open a satellite office in a community close to several clients. You were assigned to be the project manager to oversee the decentralization. Your job is to identify and assess space needs, locate suitable lease space, work with the management company to draw up plans and build out the new space, purchase new furniture and equipment, hire office staff, set up communication systems and computer networks, develop a marketing plan, and organize and complete the relocation. You have been asked to start the project right after the first of the year, and complete it within the first six months of the new year. It is hoped that the office can be operational before the end of the second quarter.

The goals of the *Decentralization project* are as follows:

- To become more accessible to your clients and improve customer satisfaction by establishing a satellite office within a thirty mile radius of our major mid-state clients

- To have an aesthetically pleasing office in which you can hold meetings and entertain clients

- To develop five new clients in the tricounty area surrounding the new office within the first year after the decentralization

To accomplish these goals, you will have to accomplish a significant number of tasks. Although you will be able to complete some of the tasks yourself, your primary role as project manager is to identify the internal and external resources needed to complete the project. You may need an architect, for example, to draw plans for the office space. You may use carpenters and other skilled workers to build out the space. An internal committee may be given the responsibility to decide on furniture and equipment purchases. The marketing department may develop the marketing plan. In Chapter 7, "Entering Project Tasks," and Chapter 8, "Scheduling and Linking Project Tasks," we'll list the tasks and divide them into phases to make the project more manageable. Each phase will include a milestone to mark the completion of the phase. In Chapter 9, "Defining Project Resources and Costs," we'll enter resources and costs associated with the project; in Chapter 10, "Assigning and Scheduling Resources and Costs," we'll schedule the resources and forecast the costs related to the project.

 NOTE Although you may not have been responsible for moving an entire office, chances are that you have been involved in some sort of move in your personal or professional life. Those experiences should help you relate to many of the tasks involved in moving an office.

Before you begin listing and organizing project tasks, you will want to enter general parameters for the project (the start or finish date, for example) and set up the project calendar. By completing these preliminary activities, Project will know how to calculate schedules, and you'll end up with a project plan that meets your expectations.

Setting Project Information

 When you are ready to start entering information about a new project, click the New button on the Standard toolbar or choose File ➤ New and click OK to open a Blank Project template. Project opens a Project Information dialog box, shown in Figure 6.1, in which you can enter details about the project.

PART

II

Creating a Project
from Start to Finish

FIGURE 6.1

The Project Information dialog box sets up key information about a project.

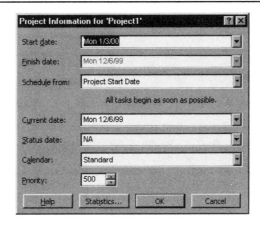

TIP If you just opened Project and already have a Blank Project template open, choose Project ➤ Project Information to access the Project Information dialog box.

The Project Information dialog box identifies key dates and calendars that are used to track project status.

Establishing Start and Finish Dates

Project has two ways to calculate project dates: It can calculate from a specified start date or from a finish date. If you know when a project can begin, choose the Start Date option. As you enter tasks into the project, Project calculates the finish date of the project based on the start date.

Scheduling Forward from the Start Date

The *Decentralization project* is scheduled to start the week of January 3, 2000 (refer to Figure 6.1). When you select Project Start Date in the Schedule From field, the Start Date field is active and the Finish Date field is dimmed. Because no tasks were entered, the Finish Date corresponds to the Current Date. When you enter all the tasks required to complete the move, Project will tell you the projected Finish Date.

Scheduling Backward from the Finish Date

If, instead of a start date, you are given a finish date when the project should be completed, you can choose Project Finish Date in the Schedule From field shown in Figure 6.2. When you enter all the tasks for the project, Project calculates when you have to start the project to complete it on time, and assigns the As Late As Possible constraint to each task. If, for example, you were told that the office move must be completed by June 30, 2000 and you can start any time after the first of the year, Project would calculate the start date of each task to begin as late as possible to still be completed on time. For more about constraints, see Chapter 7.

 TIP If you choose to schedule from the finish date, you should enter all the tasks for the project at one time. Adding tasks to the project will affect all the start dates of linked tasks, potentially changing the entire project.

FIGURE 6.2

*In this example, the
project is scheduled
from the project finish
date, so all tasks will
be scheduled to begin
as late as possible.*

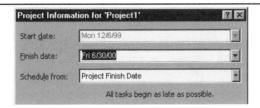

 WARNING Scheduling a project from a finish date or changing a project to schedule from a finish date affects leveling delays and leveling splits. For more information about leveling, see Chapter 11, "Preparing Your Project for Publication."

Setting the Current Date and the Status Date

The Current Date field in the Project Information dialog box automatically defaults to today's date. In most cases, you do not need to change this date. However, Project uses the current date to calculate variances, such as in the Earned Value table, that help you track the costs of work performed. If you want Project to use a different current date in its calculations, you can change the date in the Current Date field by typing a date or clicking the down arrow to open the date navigator.

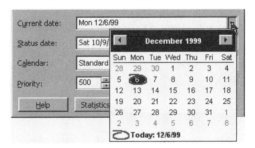

 NOTE A variance is any deviation from the plan. For more about how to calculate variance reports such as an Earned-Value Analysis, see Chapter 12, "Tracking Project Progress."

Project uses the current date to calculate variances unless there is a date in the Status Date field. If you want to calculate reports from a specified date (for example, the last day of a fiscal year), you can enter a date in the Status Date field. You can change this date at any time during the course of a project to use a different status date.

NOTE   Changing the current date in the Project Information dialog box does not affect the date that Project uses when you insert a date field into a header or footer or into other reports. This date is based on the system date. You must insert the Project Current Date field into the report to show a different current date.

Selecting a Project Calendar

The project calendar is an essential tool in managing a project. The project calendar is used by Project to calculate how long a project will take to complete. Project provides three default calendars:

- Standard is the workday calendar that is set by default to 8 a.m. to 5 p.m., Monday through Friday.
- Night Shift covers the hours from 11 p.m. to 8 a.m., Monday through Saturday.
- 24 Hours includes hours around the clock, seven days a week.

Choose the calendar that most closely mirrors the schedule that work will take place toward the completion of the project. The project calendar can be changed at any time to reflect the actual working hours of people and other resources on the project (for more about defining the project calendar, see "Defining the Project Calendar," later in this chapter).

Priority

The priority of the project is a subjective ranking of how important this project is when compared to other projects. You can choose a number between 0 and 1000 to rank its relative importance. Using a priority is important when you track multiple projects that share the same resource pool. Higher-priority projects receive first consideration when allocating resources to a project (for more about resource allocation, see Chapter 9 and Chapter 14, "Sharing Resources and Tasks among Multiple Projects").

Statistics

When a project moves into full swing, click the Statistics button on the Project Information dialog box to take a quick look at the way things are going. The data available in this dialog box is view-only—you cannot change any data here.

Figure 6.3 shows the Project Statistics dialog box.

FIGURE 6.3

The Project Statistics dialog box shows critical information about a project at a glance.

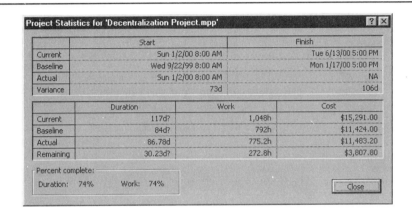

Project statistics include current, baseline, actual, and variance information about the project's start and finish dates; and current, baseline, actual, and remaining information about the duration, work hours, and costs. You can also easily see the percent complete for duration and work. These percentages tell you how far along you are in the project.

 NOTE Don't worry if you don't know what all these statistics mean yet—you'll see them in action in upcoming chapters.

Click Close to close the Project Statistics window and the Project Information dialog box.

Defining the Project Calendar

Project uses several different types of calendars to reflect when resources are available to work on a project. All projects that you create are assigned a calendar by Project. The project calendar reflects the general working hours for the project. The calendar contains the number of hours per day that will be spent on the project and the days of the week when the work will occur. In the project calendar, you can exclude holidays and other days in which no work will be done, and set realistic expectations of how much time will be devoted to the project. If you have a wide variation of how much time will be available from different resources, you can create additional calendars that can be assigned to specific tasks and particular resources.

Setting the Standard Calendar

The standard calendar is set for a 40-hour week: Monday through Friday, from 8:00 a.m. to 5:00 p.m., with one hour for lunch. No holidays are represented in the Standard calendar. If this does not represent your standard schedule, you can change the settings for the standard calendar or any of the calendars used in Project. To change the calendar settings, click Tools ➤ Change Working Time. This opens the Change Working Time dialog box, shown in Figure 6.4.

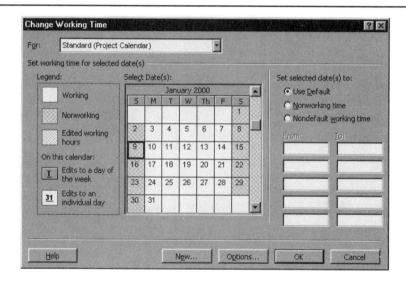

The Change Working Time dialog box displays the calendar you chose in the Project Information dialog box. We selected the Standard calendar, so it is the calendar that displays in Figure 6.4. Days that appear in the calendar in white are default working days. Days that are shaded are nonworking days.

In the calendar in Figure 6.4, Monday through Friday are working days, and Saturday and Sunday are nonworking days.

Before you change the working times for particular dates, let's review the default working hours for the Standard calendar.

Changing the Default Calendar Options

To change the default working hours for the standard calendar, click the Options button in the Change Working Time dialog box. This opens the Calendar page of the Options dialog box, shown in Figure 6.5.

FIGURE 6.5

On the Calendar page of the Options dialog box, you can change the default working hours of the Standard calendar.

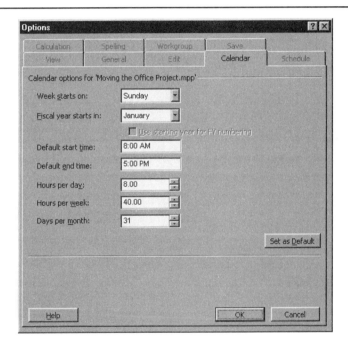

In the Calendar options, you can change the day the week starts on and the month the fiscal year starts in. If the fiscal year starts in any month besides January and thereby extends over two years, you can designate how you want Project to refer to the year. Click the Use Starting Year for FY Numbering checkbox if you want Project to label the year using the starting year. Clear the checkbox if you want Project to use the ending year as the year label.

If your default workday differs from the 8 a.m. to 5 p.m. day displayed here, enter new start and end times in the appropriate boxes.

PART

II

Creating a Project
from Start to Finish

Defining Days, Weeks, and Months The most important Calendar options are the options that determine how you define a workday, week, and month. Microsoft Project makes all of its duration and other time calculations based on minutes, and then uses the values entered in the Calendar options to convert the minutes into day, week, and month units.

Because of this, it is vitally important that you tell Project how to define these time intervals. Enter the hours available per day, the hours available per week, and the days available per month for the typical resource that will be involved with the project.

Although you can change these values after you enter tasks into a project, the changes you make here will also change task durations. For example, let's say you set the Days Per Month to **31** and the Hours Per Week to **40**. If you schedule a task with a duration of two months that begins June 9, Project will set the Finish date to September 4, three calendar months away. This is because two months is equivalent to 62 days in this scenario, and 62 days at five days per week results in 12.4 weeks, or just about three calendar months.

If you meant for the duration to be two calendar months, then the days per month must reflect the actual number of work days per month, which in this case is only 20 (eight hours per day and 40 hours per week).

Setting the Working Times as the Default If you plan to use the same Calendar settings in future projects, you can set the options as the default Calendar settings by clicking the Set as Default button on the Calendar options page (see Figure 6.5).

When you finish setting Calendar options, click the OK button to save the changes and return to the Set Working Times dialog box.

 NOTE The Options dialog box contains other options that you may want to review before starting a new project, such as the time unit Project uses when estimating duration. For more about customizing the Project environment, see Chapter 21, "Customizing Project 2000."

Changing Working Times

Now that you have set the default working times for the project and defined days, weeks, and months, you can change the working times for selected dates and for days of the week in the Change Working Time dialog box. You can change selected dates from the default working time to nonworking time or to nondefault working time. If, for example, your organization does not work on Martin Luther King Day, you could mark that day as nonworking time. Or, if your organization is open on Saturday mornings, you could select Saturdays and include hours for that day.

 WARNING Make sure that the total number of hours your organization works in a typical week corresponds to the number of hours per week and hours per day in the Calendar Options. Refer to "Setting the Default Calendar Options," earlier in this chapter.

Selecting Dates

To change the working times for any of the dates, you must first select the dates you want to change (see Table 6.1).

TABLE 6.1: SELECT DATES IN THE WORKING TIME CALENDAR

To Select	Action
A single date	Click the date.
Multiple dates	Hold Ctrl and click each date.
Consecutive dates	Click the first date and hold the Shift key before clicking the last date in the sequence.
Day of the week	Click the column header for that day.

PART

II

Creating a Project
from Start to Finish

 TIP You can select multiple days of the week by holding Ctrl and clicking the column headers, or dragging across column headers to select consecutive days.

Editing the Calendar

To change a date to a nonworking date, select the date and click the Nonworking time option.

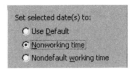

Project shades the date in the Calendar and underlines it to indicate that it deviates from the default calendar. January 17 is marked as a nonworking time in Figure 6.6.

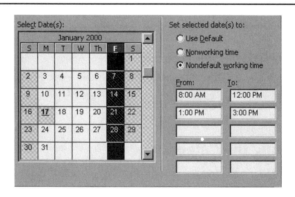

You can also change the work schedule for a particular day of the week. To change the working hours of a day of the week, select the day by clicking the day header to select the entire column, and click the Nondefault Working Time option. Enter the scheduled working time in the From and To fields, as shown in Figure 6.7. If times are already entered in the From and To boxes, you can delete them by dragging over them to select them and pressing Delete or entering a new time. Pressing Tab to move between the From and To fields automatically selects the contents.

When you have entered new times, Project designates the edited working hours with a lightly shaded pattern.

TIP To enter a work shift that extends beyond midnight, you must enter the time up to midnight (e.g., 11 p.m. to 12 a.m.) on one day and the time after midnight on the next day.

Restoring the Default Working Times

If you want to change any of the calendar dates back to the default working times, select the dates and choose the Use Default option on the Change Working Time dialog box. Note, however, that you may have changed the default for a particular day (for example, making Saturday a working day), and the Use Default option changes the particular date back to the new default for that weekday, not to the original default for that day. To change an entire weekday back to the original default, select the day column and choose Use Default.

Changing Other Calendars

After you make all the desired changes to the Standard calendar, you can edit the Nightshift or 24 Hour calendars in the same way by choosing them from the drop-down list at the top of the Change Working Time dialog box. If the calendar you need is drastically different from the Standard calendar or if you need to apply a special calendar to specific resources, you can create additional calendars.

PART

II

Creating a Project
from Start to Finish

MASTERING TROUBLESHOOTING

Mastering Time Formats

Project accepts time entered using the 12-hour or the 24-hour clock. If you use the 24-hour format, enter the time as **8:00**, **13:00**, **16:00**, and so on. If you use the 12-hour format, you should enter **a.m.** or **p.m.** after the time to ensure that Project interprets the time correctly. Project assumes that the time you enter is after the Default Starting Time on the Calendar tab of the Options dialog box, and chooses the first occurrence of that time after the Starting Time. So, if you enter **10:00**, for example, it assumes 10:00 a.m. If you meant p.m., you must designate it as such.

It's not necessary to enter the minutes if the time is on the hour. Project interprets **5 pm**, **5 p.m.**, **5:00 pm**, and **5:00 p.m.** in the same way.

Creating Additional Calendars

As you plan the project, you may already know that a resource you plan to use does not work in the schedule laid out in the standard calendar. With Project, you can create additional calendars, and you can apply the appropriate calendar to them when you assign these resources to the project (see Chapter 9). If you don't yet know the work schedules of all of the resources involved with the project, you can create the additional calendars as you discover them.

To create an additional calendar, follow these steps:

1. Click the Tools menu, choose Change Working Time, and then click the New button in the Change Working Time dialog box.

2. Enter a name for the Calendar in the Create New Base Calendar dialog box, shown in Figure 6.8.

3. Choose Create a New Base Calendar if you want to start with a blank calendar that uses the default working times set on the Calendar tab of the Options dialog box.

   OR

   Choose the Make a Copy of Calendar option if you want to use an existing calendar as the basis for the new calendar. From the drop-down list, select the calendar you want to base the new one on.

4. Click OK to start working on the new calendar. If you made changes to the calendar you were working on, Project prompts you to save those changes before moving on to the new calendar. Click Yes to save the changes to the previous calendar or No to discard them.

5. Edit the calendar, as described in "Changing Working Times," earlier in this chapter.

FIGURE 6.8

You can create a new calendar based on an existing calendar, or start from scratch with a new base calendar.

After you edit the new calendar, Project saves it automatically when you click OK to close the Change Working Time dialog box, or it prompts you to save it if you create another new calendar.

NOTE For information about how to delete calendars, how to copy calendars from one project to another, and how to make a calendar the default calendar for future projects, see Chapter 21.

Printing Calendars

Project includes a standard report that prints the details of each of the active calendars in a project. You'll learn more about printing and customizing reports in Chapter 18, "Using Reports to Analyze Data." However, if you want to review the data you entered in the calendars, here are the steps to creating a Working Days report:

1. Choose View ➣ Reports to open the Reports dialog box shown in Figure 6.9.
2. Choose Overview and click the Select button, or double-click Overview.
3. Click Working Days and click the Select button to display the report in Print Preview, as shown in Figure 6.10.
4. Click the Print button to print the report. Each active calendar in the project prints on a separate page.
5. Click Close to close Print Preview, and click Close again to close the Reports dialog box.

PART

II

Creating a Project
from Start to Finish

FIGURE 6.9

Choosing Overview in the Reports dialog box gives you access to the Working Days report.

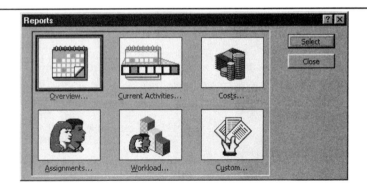

The printed reports show the standard hours for each day and then displays a list of exceptions, such as holidays and other days that do not follow the default working hours.

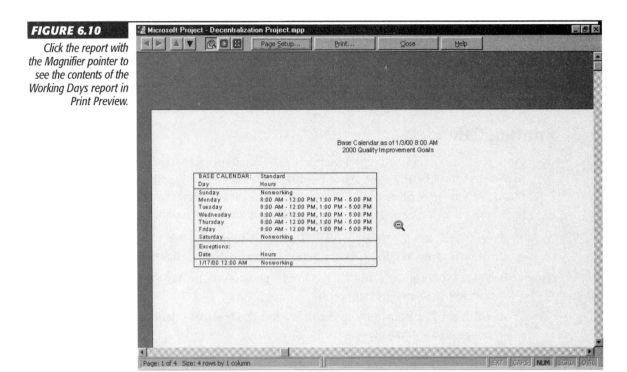

Setting Project Properties

As with any document, the Properties sheet provides information about the document, such as when it was created, modified, and last accessed. You can access the Properties sheet for a project by choosing File ➤ Properties. The properties sheet opens to the Summary tab.

Using the Summary Tab

You can use the Summary tab to enter additional information about the project, as shown in Figure 6.11.

To enter text in any of the data fields, click in the text box and type the information you want to add. Press Tab to move on to the next text box.

Some of the other data fields can be added to the headers and footers in project reports: Title, Subject, Author, Manager, and Company. The Category, Keywords, and Comments fields can be helpful when you need to search for the project on a local or network drive.

PART

II

Creating a Project
from Start to Finish

FIGURE 6.11

*Use the Summary tab
to enter additional
information about
the project.*

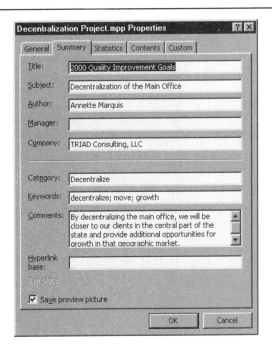

In the Hyperlink Base text box, you can enter the path or URL that you want to use for all hyperlinks to documents with the same base address that you insert into the project. You can enter a Web address or a file path on a local or network drive.

If the project is based on a template, the template name is listed in the Template field.

Click the Save Picture Preview checkbox if you want to make a preview of the current project view available in the Open dialog box.

Viewing the General, Statistics, and Contents Tabs

The General tab, shown in Figure 6.12, provides file location, file size, and other file-related information.

The Statistics tab shows similar information, but also includes the number of times the file has been saved (Revision Number) and the number of minutes the file has been open for changes since it was created (Total Editing Time).

The Contents tab, shown in Figure 6.13, provides relevant information about the project, including start and finish dates, duration, work, cost, percent complete, and percent work complete. Although it looks as if you can edit this information, this tab is also read-only.

FIGURE 6.12

The General tab displays information about the project file.

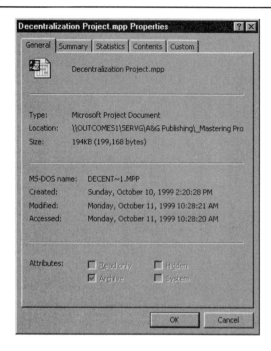

FIGURE 6.13

The Contents tab displays summary information about the project.

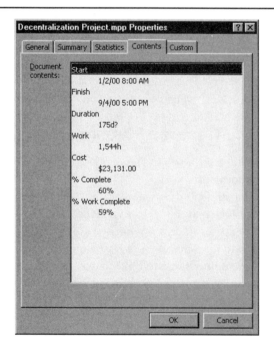

Customizing the Properties

Click the Custom tab (refer to Figure 6.13) to display a variety of predefined properties about the project. The properties displayed here can be removed, and additional properties can be added to make this sheet reflect the data you want to see. These properties can be linked to actual data in the project or can reflect data that you enter manually. Linked properties are designated by the link icon, which is shown on all the properties listed in Figure 6.14.

FIGURE 6.14

Use the Custom tab to add custom properties that you want to monitor for a project.

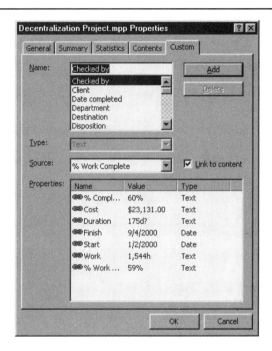

PART

II

Creating a Project
from Start to Finish

Click any of the properties in the Properties box to see the source of the data. For example, the % Complete property is linked to the % Complete field in the project. When changes are made to the project that affect the % Complete, the property is updated automatically.

To create a Custom property for the project, follow these steps:

1. Choose File ➤ Properties to open the Custom dialog box.

2. From the Custom tab of the Properties dialog box, select a property from the Name drop-down list, or type a property name in the Name text box. You could, for example, add a Reviewed By or Date Approved property. The value of these properties would not be linked to project data, but could be entered manually to track the status of a project.

3. If you want the property linked to an existing field in the project, click the Link To Content checkbox and select the source from the Source drop-down list.

> OR

If you do not want the property linked to an existing field in the project, clear the Link To Content checkbox and select a property type from the Type list. You can choose between Text, Date, Number; and Yes or No. Choose the type that most closely matches the expected value in the property.

4. If you choose Text, Date, or Number, enter a value in the Value text box. For example, if you entered Date Approved as the property, you would enter the date the project was approved in the Value text box. If you choose the Yes or No option, you can use the Yes or No buttons that appear in the Value box.

5. Click the Add button to add the new property to the list.

Deleting a Property

If you want to delete a property from the list, select the property in the Name column of the Properties list (the box on the bottom of the tab), and click the Delete button. If you change your mind, you can add the property back to the display at any time by following the previous steps for creating a custom property.

Modifying a Property

To modify an existing property, follow these steps:

1. Select the Property name in the Properties list to move the name and value to the appropriate text boxes at the top of the dialog box.

2. Make the desired changes to the Type, Source, or Linking of the property. The Add button changes to a Modify button.

3. Click Modify to accept the changes.

When you finish the project Properties, click OK to save the changes you made, or Cancel to close the dialog box without saving the changes.

What's Next

In this chapter, you learned how to set up Project before you begin entering project tasks and other information. In Chapter 7, "Entering Project Tasks," you'll enter tasks and milestones, use the outlining features, and explore some of Project's views and printing tasks.

CHAPTER **7**

Entering
Project Tasks

You prepared all the preliminary material for your project, outlined the project goals, and identified how you'll measure project success. Now, you are ready to begin entering tasks. In this chapter, you'll learn how to enter tasks and set task durations. You'll learn how to use Project's outlining features to create summary tasks and subtasks, and how to move tasks around to group them in the most logical order. After the initial project planning, creating a solid task list is the most critical step in being able to use Microsoft Project to help you effectively manage a project.

Planning Project Tasks

In planning the tasks that make up a project's definition, you can adopt one of two generally accepted approaches to creating a task list. With the first method, called *top-down*, you create a list of the major tasks or phases of the project that you need to complete for the project to be a success. Using the office decentralization project outlined on the first page in Chapter 6, "Building a New Project," as an example, we can include the following major tasks in the portion of the project related to finding a new location and moving into office space there:

- Find suitable lease space
- Design space
- Build out space
- Decorate suite
- Move

Accomplishing any one of these tasks would require a number of additional steps or subtasks. Any task that has subtasks related to it is called a *summary task*. In the top-down approach, you list all the summary tasks, and then break down each of these tasks into its logical subtasks. For example, the subtasks related to finding suitable lease space include the following:

- Identify space needs
- Contact a realtor to identify potential available properties
- Tour properties
- Make an offer on a property that meets specifications
- Negotiate a lease
- Sign a lease

Even some of these tasks, such as Identify Space Needs, have a series of smaller tasks related to them. To identify space needs, you might do the following:

- Develop a list of potential criteria (based on goals of the decentralization project)
- Solicit input to prioritize criteria
- Finalize a criteria list

Therefore, the Identify Space Needs task also becomes a summary task with a list of subtasks. By listing the major tasks first, you can break down each task into manageable, bite-sized pieces. You may even look at this list of subtasks and decide to break them down even further. At some point, the tasks become too small to be valuable from a tracking and management perspective. Using Solicit Input to Prioritize Criteria as an example, suppose you decide to hold a series of meetings with staff members to get their input by using a multiple voting technique to prioritize the criteria list. You might list Set Up Meeting Room as one of the subtasks. Would you also include Arrange Chairs, Set Up Flip Chart, and Buy Markers as subtasks? If the person to whom you eventually assign this task has never set up a meeting room before, providing this level of specificity might be valuable. After a time, however, you may find that you are spending more time documenting the status of project tasks than managing the project itself. You might be better off giving a description of the task to the person responsible for setting up the meeting room that outlines the specifications for the room, but keeping the task at the level of Set Up Meeting Room. In fact, depending on the project and your needs for detail as project manager, even this task may be too specific. The key is to find a level of detail that shows you are making progress without losing the big picture.

 TIP Break down project tasks into smaller pieces in those areas that run the greatest risk of holding up the rest of the project or interfering with the project's success. You can then more easily determine where the trouble spots are, and work to solve them.

The second method of creating a task list uses a *bottom-up* approach. In this method, you list all the lower-level tasks of the project, usually organizing them in chronological order. You then insert summary tasks to group related tasks together. The bottom-up approach works best with smaller projects in which you are already familiar with the task details and just want to organize the tasks in some sort of logical order.

Whichever method you use, keep these things in mind:

- Every task should have clear completion criteria. For every task, you should be able to answer the question, "How will I know when this task is completed?"

- Break down tasks that have long durations compared with the total project. This makes it easier to assign resources and estimate completion dates.

- If you are uncertain about how a task will be accomplished, break it down into subtasks until it becomes clear.

Types of Tasks

A project usually consists of four major types of tasks:

- Summary tasks are tasks that contain subtasks. Microsoft Project automatically summarizes the durations and costs related to subtasks into the summary task.

- Subtasks are smaller tasks that roll up into a summary task.

- Recurring tasks are tasks that occur at regular intervals during the course of the project—a project review meeting, for example.

- Milestones are tasks that usually have no duration and mark the completion of a significant phase of the project. Move Completed might be an example of a milestone in the office space example used earlier.

When you create a task list, you should consider what type each task is, and be sure to include recurring tasks and milestones to make the list complete.

Entering Tasks in Gantt Chart View

The Gantt Chart view is the default view in Microsoft Project. This view, shown in Figure 7.1, consists of a task list on the left pane of the window and a Gantt Chart in the right pane.

 NOTE If the Gantt Chart view is not the current view, click the Gantt Chart button on the View bar.

Use the horizontal scroll bars at the bottom of each pane to scroll to additional information. If you scroll the task list, you see additional columns in the task list. The Start, Finish, Predecessors, and Resource Names fields, shown in Figure 7.2, become visible.

FIGURE 7.1

The Gantt Chart view shows the tasks list and the Gantt Chart timescale.

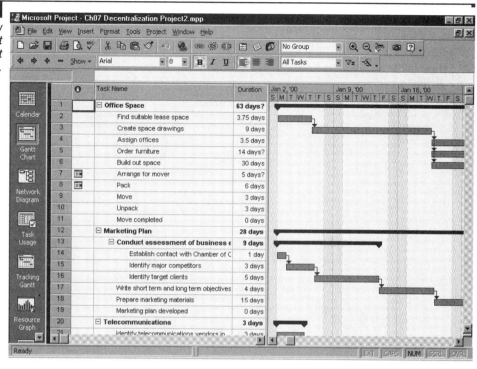

FIGURE 7.2

Scroll the task list horizontally to see additional task-related fields.

	Start	Finish	Predecessors	Resource
1	**1/3/00 8:00 AM**	**3/29/00 5:00 PM**		
2	1/3/00 8:00 AM	1/6/00 3:00 PM		
3	1/6/00 3:00 PM	1/19/00 3:00 PM	2	
4	1/19/00 3:00 PM	1/25/00 10:00 AM	3	
5	1/19/00 3:00 PM	2/8/00 3:00 PM	3	
6	1/19/00 3:00 PM	3/1/00 3:00 PM	3	
7	2/21/00 8:00 AM	2/25/00 5:00 PM		
8	3/14/00 8:00 AM	3/21/00 5:00 PM		
9	3/22/00 8:00 AM	3/24/00 5:00 PM	8,6	
10	3/27/00 8:00 AM	3/29/00 5:00 PM	9	
11	3/29/00 5:00 PM	3/29/00 5:00 PM	10	
12	**1/3/00 8:00 AM**	**2/9/00 5:00 PM**		
13	**1/3/00 8:00 AM**	1/13/00 5:00 PM		
14	1/3/00 8:00 AM	1/3/00 5:00 PM		
15	1/4/00 8:00 AM	1/6/00 5:00 PM	14	
16	1/7/00 8:00 AM	1/13/00 5:00 PM	15	
17	1/14/00 8:00 AM	1/19/00 5:00 PM	16	
18	1/20/00 8:00 AM	2/9/00 5:00 PM	17	
19	2/9/00 5:00 PM	2/9/00 5:00 PM	18	
20	**1/3/00 8:00 AM**	**1/5/00 5:00 PM**		
21	1/3/00 8:00 AM	1/5/00 5:00 PM		

PART

II

Creating a Project
from Start to Finish

You can also drag the vertical split bar to change the size of the panes. Point to the vertical split bar; when the pointer changes to a two-header arrow, as you can see in Figure 7.3, drag to the left or right.

FIGURE 7.3

Point to and drag the vertical split bar to change the width of the individual panes.

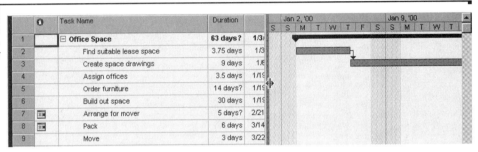

Use the horizontal scroll bar on the timescale to move to future or past dates in the Gantt Chart. By default, the Gantt Chart displays the Project Start date you entered in the Project Information dialog box (Project ➤ Project Information) as the leftmost date.

Entering Tasks

To enter a task, click in the first cell of the task table and type the task. Press Enter to move to the next row. Project automatically assigns an estimated duration of one day and creates a bar on the Gantt Chart representing the task.

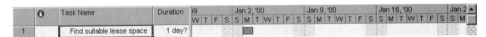

You can tell that the duration is estimated because it has a question mark after it. You can enter task durations as you go along, or enter all the tasks and then come back and assign durations. For the purposes of this chapter, we'll focus on tasks first and then discuss durations later in this section.

Enter additional tasks in the same way: type the task and press Enter. Don't worry at this point about the different types of tasks because you can convert a task to a summary task, subtask, milestone, or recurring task after you enter the list.

Adding More Details about a Task

In the task list itself, the amount of detail you can include in a task description is pretty limited. However, those limitations are removed when you click the Task Information button on the Standard toolbar or double-click a task to open the Task Information dialog box, shown in Figure 7.4.

PART

II

Creating a Project
from Start to Finish

FIGURE 7.4

Enter details about a task in the Task Information dialog box.

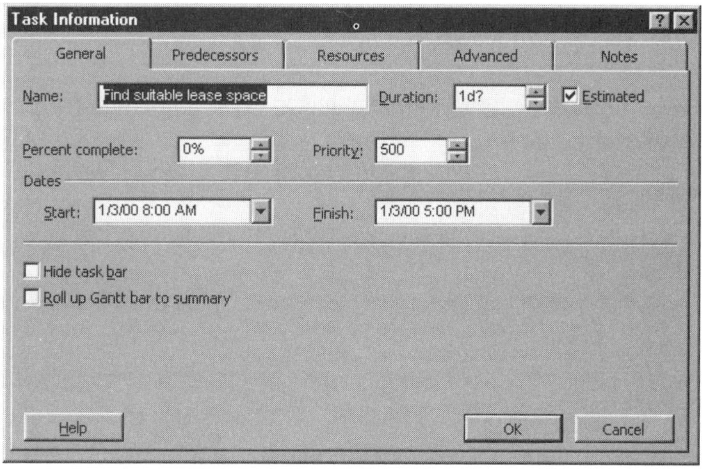

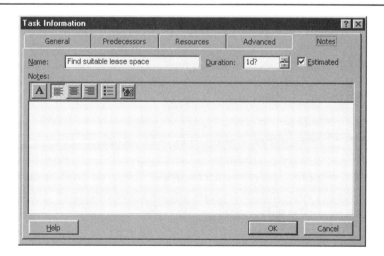

The Task Information dialog box consists of five tabs: General, Predecessors, Resource, Advanced, and Notes. You will enter and view additional information about tasks in this dialog box as you progress through the project's creation. For now, focus on the last tab called Notes. As you can see in Figure 7.5, the Notes tab is an open text box, in which you can enter text and insert objects.

FIGURE 7.5

Use the Notes tab to insert text and enter objects.

Here, you can enter a more thorough task description, identify issues and concerns related to the task, and attach documents that were created to support the task. For example, if a task is related to creating a marketing plan, you could attach the marketing plan document and workbook to the task. In the Notes text box, you have access to only a few formatting options, as shown in Table 7.1.

TABLE 7.1: FORMATTING OPTIONS AVAILABLE ON THE NOTES TAB	
Button	**Description**
	Use the Font button to open the Font dialog box to change font attributes.
	Align the text on the Left, Center, or Right.
	Apply bullet characters to lists.
	Insert documents and objects created in other applications.

If you want notes that are formatted more extensively, you can create a document in Word, and copy and paste it in (right-click in the text box to choose Paste).

Attaching a Document to a Task   To attach a document, such as a Word document or Excel spreadsheet, to a task, follow these steps:

1. Click the Insert Object button on the Notes tab of the Task Information dialog box to open the Insert Object dialog box shown in Figure 7.6. It may take a few seconds to load, so be patient.

2. When the Insert Object dialog box opens, choose whether you want to create a new object or create an object from file.

3. If you choose to create a new object, scroll through the Object Type list, and select the type of object you want to create. Click OK to launch the application that creates that object type, and create the object. For example, if you choose to create a new Microsoft Word document, Project launches Word and you can create the document. Close the application to return to the Insert Object dialog box.

   OR

   If you choose to insert an existing object, click Create from File and enter the file path where the object is saved. Click the Browse button if you want to explore for the object. Click the Link checkbox if you want to link to the object. Linking ensures that any changes you make to the original document are reflected in the linked document.

4. Click the Display as Icon checkbox if you want to insert an icon to represent the object instead of the object itself. Click the Change Icon button if you want to select a different icon for the object.

5. Click OK to close the Insert Object dialog box and insert the object.

WARNING If you link an object to a Project task, and then move or delete the object, Project won't be able to find it. As a result, Project does not respond when you double-click the object's icon to open it.

FIGURE 7.6

Use the Insert Object dialog box to insert objects created in other applications.

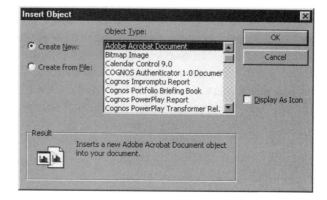

Figure 7.7 shows an icon representing an Excel workbook. Because it was not linked to the workbook, it is only named Worksheet. An object must be linked to the original in order to display the object's file name.

FIGURE 7.7

An Excel worksheet inserted into the Note

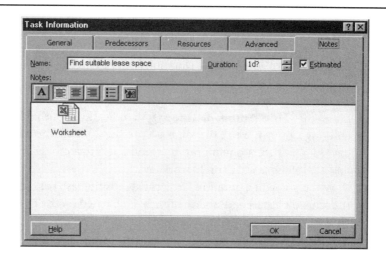

After you finish entering Notes about the task, click OK to close the Task Information dialog box.

PART

II

Creating a Project from Start to Finish

Assigning Task Durations

Duration is the total span of time you expect it will take to complete a task. In most cases, durations are estimates because you generally can't predict exactly how long a task will take. Although you can use your previous experience and the experience of others to make predictions, when it comes down to it, you will often use your best educated guess. You also must consider that the duration of the task can be directly tied to the resource and the number of resources assigned to the task. If the task is to paint an office, one resource might take two hours and another might take two days, based on their painting skills. If you assign two people to the task, they could split the painting and finish it in even less time. Microsoft Project calculates duration by counting the amount of active working time between the scheduled start and finish of the task. When you assign resources (see Chapter 9, "Defining Project Resources and Costs"), you can revisit duration and make refinements to the project estimates.

 NOTE For a more systematic method of assessing duration by using PERT estimates, see Chapter 13, "Assessing and Managing Risks."

How Calendar Settings Affect Duration By default, Project assigns one day to each task. The definition of one day is based on the number of hours per day setting on the Calendar tab of the Options dialog box (Tools ➤ Options ➤ Calendar). If this is set to the default eight hours, a duration of two-and-a-half days is equivalent to 20 hours. If the task starts on Thursday and the default Standard calendar shows that Saturday is not a workday, then Project would set the task's completion to noon on Monday (assuming that the workday starts at 8 a.m.)

 Entering Duration Units Durations can be entered as minutes, hours, days, weeks, or months. Project accepts abbreviations or the full word. For example, you can enter **1h**, **1hr**, or **1hour** (no space is required). Because 1m is equivalent to 1 minute, you must enter **1mo**, **1mon**, or **1month** to indicate a month. However, remember that entering a month is not the same as entering 20 days, the standard number of workdays in a month. A one-month duration refers to a month of workdays, so it could take six calendar weeks or 30 workdays.

When you edit a duration, Project extends the task bar on the Gantt Chart to show the scheduled start date and the finish date, based on the new duration.

If you are unsure about the actual time it will take to complete a task, enter a question mark after the duration. Project marks this as an estimated duration.

TIP To change the view options for the way Project displays time units, choose Tools ➤ Options and click the Edit tab. For more about setting View options, see Chapter 17, "Using Views to Evaluate Data."

Applying Elapsed Duration *Elapsed duration* is a type of duration that you can use when the activity or task continues around the clock, irrespective of the workday hours. A ship that is carrying parts to a manufacturing plant does not typically stop sailing at the end of the workday. If the trip takes 10 hours to sail from one port to another, the duration can be entered as elapsed time. Figure 7.8 shows the difference between a 10-hour duration and a 10-hour elapsed duration. To enter an elapsed duration, type the letter **e** before the time unit (**10ehrs**, for example).

FIGURE 7.8

A 10-hour trip entered as a standard duration and an elapsed duration

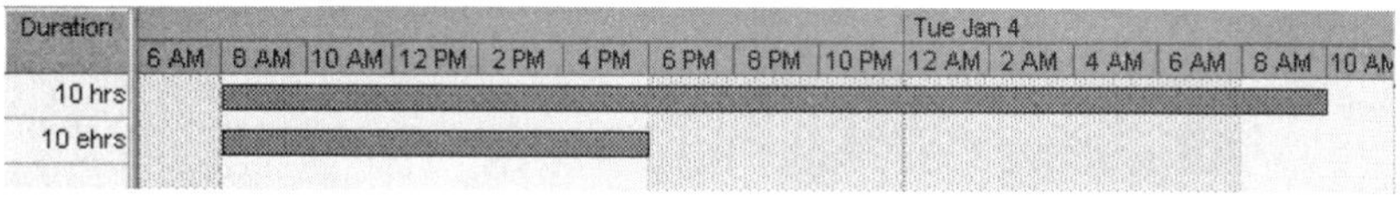

Duration	6 AM	8 AM	10 AM	12 PM	2 PM	4 PM	6 PM	8 PM	10 PM	Tue Jan 4 12 AM	2 AM	4 AM	6 AM	8 AM	10 AM
10 hrs															
10 ehrs															

Editing Tasks

After you enter a task list, chances are you will want to make some changes in it. You can edit text in a cell, adjust columns and rows, move and copy tasks, and insert and delete tasks.

Editing Text

Editing text in Gantt Chart view is most easily accomplished using the Entry bar. The Entry bar is the bar above the task list that displays entries you make to cells in the table. When you are entering or editing text, a Cancel button (X) and an Enter button (red check) appear in the Entry bar.

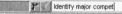

To edit in the Entry bar, follow these steps:

1. Click the cell you want to edit.

2. Point to the contents in the Entry bar so the pointer changes to an I-beam.

3. Click the I-beam where you want to edit.

4. When you finish editing, click the Enter button (or press Enter) to accept the changes, or click the Cancel button to cancel the changes.

PART

II

Creating a Project from Start to Finish

To move or copy an entry in a cell, click the cell to select it, and click the Cut or Copy button on the Standard toolbar. Move to the new location and click Paste.

To delete an entry, click the cell to select it, right-click, and choose Clear Contents from the shortcut menu.

Undoing Mistakes

When you change your mind, Project gives you a chance to undo your last action. Click the Undo button or choose Edit ➤ Undo.

When you click Undo, the button changes to a Redo button. If you want to reverse the last undo, click Redo or choose Edit ➤ Redo.

WARNING   Unlike Word or other Microsoft Office applications, which allow you to "undo" multiple mistakes, you can only Undo or Redo the last action in Project.

Adjusting Columns and Rows

If a numeric or date column is too narrow for you to see its contents, Project displays pound signs (#) in place of the actual contents. You can resize any column by pointing to the column head divider, and double-clicking or manually dragging left or right.

	Task Name	Duration	Start	Finish
1	⊟ Office Space	#######	#######	3/29/00 5:00 PM
2	Find suitable	#######	#######	1/6/00 3:00 PM
3	Create spac	9 days	#######	1/19/00 3:00 PM

If a text column is too narrow, you can resize the column or let it automatically wrap by increasing the row height. You can resize a row by pointing to the row divider and dragging up or down.

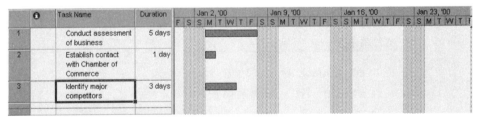

NOTE   Double-clicking a row divider opens the Task Information dialog box; it does not adjust row height.

Moving and Copying Tasks

Being able to change the order of tasks is essential to effectively organizing a project. In Project, you can move and copy tasks by using the traditional cut/copy and paste, or drag and drop.

To move or copy a task, follow these steps:

1. Select the entire task by clicking the ID number for the task.

2. Click the Cut or Copy button. If you click Cut, the task should be removed from the list.

3. Click in the row where you want the task to appear.

4. Click the Paste button.

To drag and drop a task, follow these steps:

1. Select the entire task by clicking the row header (ID number) for the task.

2. Point to the row header, or the top or bottom border of the selected area, with the arrowhead pointer.

3. Drag the mouse and when the shadowed I-beam appears just below where you want the task to appear, release the mouse button.

You can select multiple consecutive rows by dragging over the row headers with the four-headed cross. To select rows that are not consecutive, hold down the Ctrl key while clicking the row headers. You cannot drag and drop multiple nonconsecutive rows. You must cut and paste to move them. When you paste nonconsecutive rows into a new location, the rows become consecutive.

Inserting and Deleting Tasks

To insert a row, select the row below where you want the new row by clicking the row number choose Insert ➤ New Task, or right-click and choose New Task from the shortcut menu. If you want to insert multiple rows, select the number of rows you want to insert by clicking the first row number and dragging to select additional rows.

To delete entire tasks, select the row or rows you want to delete, and choose Edit ➤ Delete Task or press the Delete key on the keyboard.

You can also choose Edit ➤ Clear to delete tasks or parts of tasks. The Clear menu, shown here, has options for clearing formats, contents, notes, hyperlinks, or the entire task.

PART

II

Creating a Project
from Start to Finish

Using the Outlining Features

To organize the tasks of a project into summary tasks and subtasks, Project uses outlining. Outlining has several advantages; you can

- Create multiple levels of subtasks that all roll up into a summary task
- Collapse and expand summary tasks so that you can focus on specific phases of the project
- Move, copy, or delete entire groups of tasks.
- Apply WBS (Work Breakdown Structure) numbering (see Chapter 2, "Understanding Projects," for more about WBS)

Outlining is not a feature you have to turn on—it is already active when you launch Project. The Outlining tools occupy the space on the left end of the Formatting toolbar

The major activities related to outlining involve demoting (indenting) and promoting (outdenting) tasks to create summary tasks and subtasks. You can have multiple levels of subtasks. When you demote a task to a subtask, the task above it becomes a summary task. You can no longer edit the data related to that task. As a summary task, it derives its values from its subtasks. The Start Date, for example, is determined by the earliest Start Date of any of its subtasks. Its Finish Date is the latest Finish Date of its subtasks. The duration of a summary task is the total of all its subtasks' durations.

Creating Subtasks

To enter a new subtask, enter the task in a blank cell in the Task Name column and click the Indent button on the Outlining toolbar. In addition to indenting the new task, it automatically changes the task above it to a summary task. A summary task, such as the one shown in Figure 7.9, is outdented to the left cell border, it is bold, and it has a Collapse (Hide Subtasks) button (-) in front of it. The task bar in the Gantt Chart changes to a solid black bar with start and finish markers.

FIGURE 7.9

By indenting the second task, the first task automatically becomes a summary task.

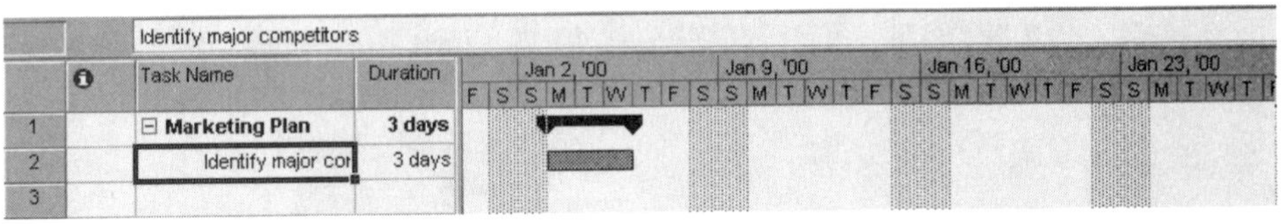

	ⓘ	Task Name	Duration	Jan 2, '00	Jan 9, '00	Jan 16, '00	Jan 23, '00
				F S S M T W T F	S S M T W T F	S S M T W T F	S S M T W T F
1		⊟ **Marketing Plan**	**3 days**				
2		Identify major cor	3 days				
3							

Identify major competitors

The next task you enter is entered as a subtask. If it is not a subtask, click the Outdent button on the Outlining toolbar. If the new task is a subtask of the first subtask (a third-level task), click the Indent button again. This indents the new task even further and makes the second task a summary task, as you can see in Figure 7.10.

FIGURE 7.10

Indenting the third task makes the second task a summary task.

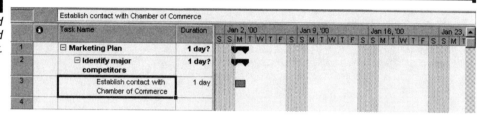

In Figure 7.9, the Identify Major Competitors task has a duration of three days, as does its Marketing Plan summary task. Because there is only one subtask, the summary task assumes the duration of the subtask. In Figure 7.10, notice that the durations for both these tasks have changed to one day. The third task, Establish Contact with Chamber of Commerce, has a duration of one day, so both the immediate summary task and the first-level summary task assumed that duration. As more tasks and subtasks are added, the duration for both summary tasks will change, as you can see in Figure 7.11.

PART

II

Creating a Project from Start to Finish

FIGURE 7.11

As more subtasks are added, the durations for the summary tasks increase.

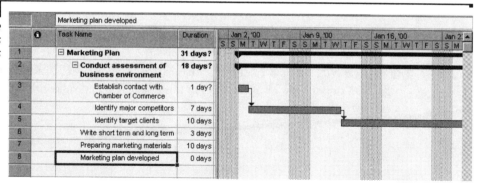

Showing and Hiding Outline Levels   One of the advantages of using outlining is that you can hide outline levels and then show them again as you want to focus on a particular task group. When you create a summary task, a Hide Subtasks button is added to the task. Click the button next to the task or click the Hide Subtasks button on the Formatting toolbar to hide all the subtasks under the summary task.

When the subtasks are hidden, as they are in Figure 7.12, you can focus your attention on the major areas of the project. The button next to the task changes to a plus symbol. Clicking it again or clicking the Show Subtasks button shows the subtasks again.

FIGURE 7.12

With the subtasks hidden, the major sections of the project become the focus of attention.

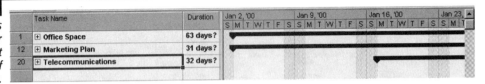

You can also use the Show menu to display the outline levels that you want to see and to show all the tasks without having to go through each one to display the subtasks. Click the Show button to access the menu of choices.

Displaying WBS Numbering

If you use WBS (Work Breakdown Structure) to define project tasks and work packages, you can display a WBS column in the task table. To display the WBS numbering column, follow these steps:

1. Click in the column to the right of where you want the new column to appear.

2. Click the Insert menu and choose Column.

3. Select WBS from the Field Name drop-down list in the Column Definition dialog box that opens.

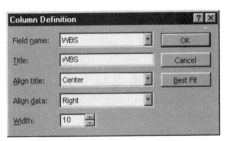

4. Enter a Title for the new column, such as **WBS**.

5. Make any desired modifications to the title alignment, data alignment, and width.

6. Click OK to insert the column.

Defining the WBS Coding Schema   Project's default WBS coding schema is 1, 1.1, 1.2, 2, 2.1, and so on. To change this coding definition, follow these steps:

1. Choose Project ➢ WBS ➢ Define Code.

2. In the WBS Code Definition dialog box, enter the Project Code Prefix if you would like to use one.

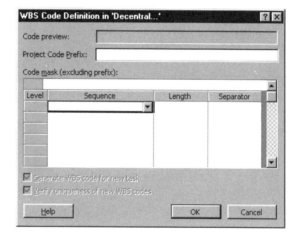

3. Enter a Code Mask (excluding prefix), if desired.

4. Click in the Sequence field to choose a sequence from the drop-down list.

5. Click in the Length field, and select a length or choose Any.

6. Click in the Separator field and choose a separator.

7. Repeat Steps 4 through 6 for each additional level you want to define. If you do not define additional levels, Project applies the first-level definition to subsequent levels by using the indicated separator.

8. Check to see that the first checkbox is checked if you want Project to generate a WBS code for each new task.

9. Check to see that the second checkbox is checked if you want Project to verify the uniqueness of each WBS code.

10. Click OK to apply the new coding definition to the WBS column.

PART

II

Creating a Project
from Start to Finish

NOTE For a more detailed understanding of WBS, refer to Chapter 2, "Understanding Projects."

Entering Milestones

Earlier in this chapter, we defined milestones as tasks that usually have no duration and mark the completion of a significant phase of the project. To create a milestone, reduce the duration of the task to **0**. Project immediately converts the task to a milestone by changing the task bar in the Gantt Chart to a black diamond with the date above it. In Figure 7.13, Marketing plan developed shows an example of a milestone—the plan shows it being completed by February 14.

FIGURE 7.13

Marketing plan developed is an example of a milestone.

12	⊟ **Marketing Plan**	**31 days?**
13	⊟ **Conduct assessment of business e**	**18 days?**
14	Establish contact with Chamber of C	1 day?
15	Identify major competitors	7 days
16	Identify target clients	10 days
17	Write short term and long term objectives	3 days
18	Preparing marketing materials	10 days
19	Marketing plan developed	0 days

2/14

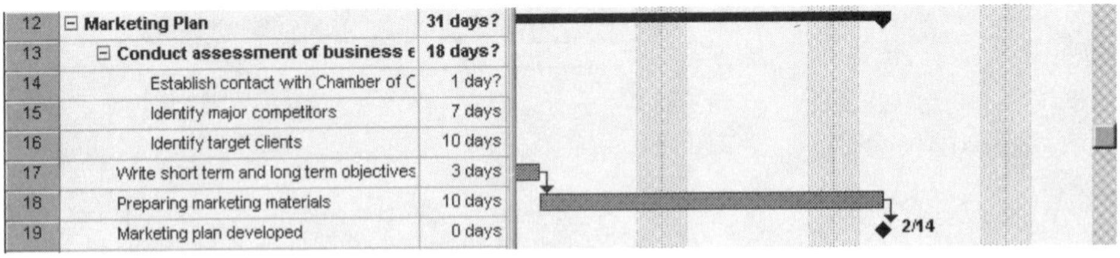

NOTE Although milestones do not typically have durations, you can create a milestone that has a duration of more than 0 days by clicking the Task Information button on the Standard toolbar and then clicking the Advanced tab. In the Duration box, enter the task duration, and then select the Mark Task as Milestone check box.

Entering Recurring Tasks

When planning a project, it is not uncommon to plan for tasks that recur throughout the life of the project. A project review meeting is the most obvious example. If a task occurs more than once during the life of the project but does not occur at regular intervals, then you need to enter the task multiple times. However, if a task does recur at regular intervals, you can enter the task once and Project can show it as a recurring task.

To enter a recurring task, follow these steps:

1. Click in the row where you want the recurring task to appear.

2. Choose Insert ➤ Recurring Task (Project inserts a row for you so there is no need to insert a blank row first).

3. Enter a Task Name in the Recurring Task Information dialog box that appears (see Figure 7.14).

4. Enter a duration and recurrence pattern for one occurrence of the task. The Project Review meeting shown in Figure 7.14 will be held for one hour every Thursday. Depending on whether you choose Daily, Weekly, Monthly, or Yearly, you have different options for the recurrence pattern. See Figure 7.15 for the choice available in each pattern.

5. Enter a date in the Start field for Range of Recurrence. If the task is an event, such as a meeting, enter the start time also.

6. Indicate whether you want the task to end after a specific number of occurrences or by a certain date.

7. Assign a calendar for scheduling the task, if you want. If you don't assign a calendar, Project uses the default Standard calendar.

8. Click OK to set the recurrence pattern.

PART

II

Creating a Project
from Start to Finish

FIGURE 7.14

Enter information about the recurring task in the Recurring Task Information dialog box.

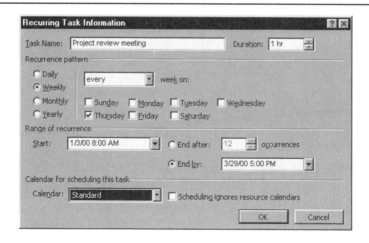

FIGURE 7.15

Choose a recurrence pattern that best meets your needs.

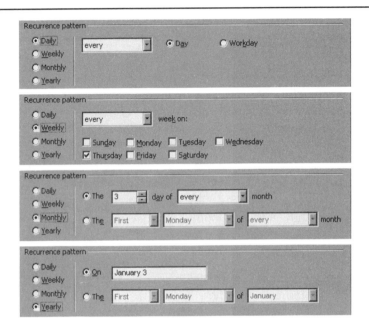

Project enters the task as a summary task with multiple subtasks that represent each occurrence of the task. It differs from a normal summary task, however, as you can see in Figure 7.16. Each occurrence of the task is represented by a single blue bar in the Gantt Chart rather than by a solid black line.

FIGURE 7.16

A recurring task is represented by individual bars on the Gantt Chart.

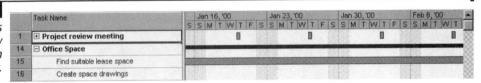

Revising the Recurrence Pattern

To revise the recurrence pattern, double-click the major summary task to reopen the Recurring Task Information dialog box. Make the changes and click OK. Every occurrence of the task is changed.

Making Changes to Individual Occurrences

You can edit individual occurrences of the task. For example, suppose that the Project Review needs to occur on Friday during one week because of a conflict, but the other meetings are scheduled to stay on Thursday. To make changes to an individual task, follow these steps:

1. Click the Show Subtasks button on the summary task to view each task occurrence.

2. Double-click any of the subtasks to open the Task Information dialog box for that occurrence.

3. Make any changes you want to make to the recurrence pattern or range of recurrence.

4. Click OK to save the changes.

 WARNING If you change an individual occurrence of a recurring task and then revise the recurrence pattern for the summary task, the individual changes are lost.

Entering Tasks in Different Views

The additional views that are available in Project provide options for looking at the project's information in different ways and for accessing fields that are not readily available in Gantt Chart view. Although Gantt Chart view is the default Project view, it is not the only view in which you can enter tasks. Several other views, such as the Task Sheet view shown in Figure 7.17, focus on tasks and can be used to enter and edit tasks. Many of these views are most valuable when you have linked tasks and are assigning resources.

To access the predefined views, Choose View ➤ More Views and choose a view from the Views list. For a detailed description of each of the major views and how to use them most effectively refer to Chapter 17, "Using Views to Evaluate Data."

PART

II

Creating a Project
from Start to Finish

FIGURE 7.17

You can use the Task Sheet View as an alternative to Gantt Chart view to enter task information.

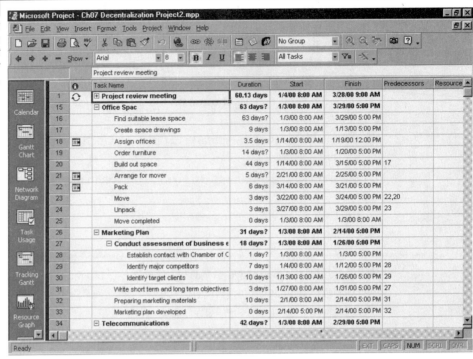

A Quick Look at Spelling

Project 2000 shares its spelling features with other Microsoft Office 2000 applications. If you are familiar with how to correct spelling in Word or PowerPoint, you already know how to check your spelling in Project.

 NOTE Project does not have the Check Spelling As You Type feature or grammar feature found in Microsoft Word.

Correcting Spelling Errors

 To use Spelling in Project, click the Spelling button on the Standard toolbar. Project reviews all the text in the project, flags possible misspelled words, and opens the Spelling dialog box shown in Figure 7.18.

FIGURE 7.18

se the Spelling dialog
ox to find misspelled
words.

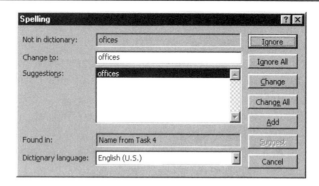

When the Spelling feature finds a word that is not in one of its dictionaries, you have a number of ways of dealing with it. You can choose the following:

Ignore this occurrence of the word.

Ignore All occurrences of the word in this document.

Add the word to the Custom dictionary so Project/Office recognizes it the next time you use it.

Change the word by choosing one of the suggested corrections or editing the word manually.

Change All occurrences of the word in this document by choosing one of the suggested corrections or editing the word manually.

AutoCorrect the word (after choosing or entering a correction) and add it to the AutoCorrect dictionary (see "Automatic Fixes for Common Errors," later in this chapter).

Because Project checks the spelling of words even in fields that are not currently visible, it identifies where the word was found to help give you a context for the word. The word found in Figure 7.18 was found in the Name field from Task 15.

 TIP All the Office 2000 applications share a user dictionary with Project, so words you add in one application are ignored in others.

Checking Words in Other Languages

If the text you are entering in Project is traditional Spanish, French, or Canadian French; or if you speak English from the UK, Canada, or Australia, you can switch the spelling dictionary to reflect that language. To change the language dictionary, follow these steps:

1. Click the Spelling button on the Standard toolbar.

2. When the Spelling dialog box opens, select the language you want to use from the Dictionary Language drop-down list (you must have at least one misspelled word for the dialog box to open).

3. Project warns you that you must restart the spelling checker for the dictionary to take effect. Click the Close button to the Cancel button to close the Spelling dialog box.

4. If the language you selected was not previously installed, Project's Install on Demand feature runs. You must have access to the program files from the CD-ROM or network installation path. As long as Project can find the install.msi file, it installs the alternative dictionaries.

5. Rerun Spelling by click the Spelling button or choosing Tools ➤ Spelling to check the spelling in the new language.

 NOTE Installing language dictionaries does not change the language that Project uses in its menus and dialog boxes. To change the program to another language you must install the Language Settings Tool and the Microsoft Office 2000 language pack.

MASTERING TROUBLESHOOTING

Editing the User Dictionary

When you choose Add from the list of Spelling choices, the identified word is added to the default user dictionary. The next time you type that word, Project recognizes it and ignores it. If you work in a field with lots of specialized terminology, you can save time and trouble by editing the dictionary directly. The user dictionary is shared by all of the Microsoft Office 2000 applications so you must be in one of the Office applications to edit it directly. To access the dictionary and add new words or edit existing words, follow these steps:

1. Switch to Microsoft Word and choose Tools ➤ Options. Click the Spelling and Grammar tab.

2. Click Dictionaries to open the Custom Dictionaries dialog box.

3. Select the dictionary you want to open and choose Edit. This opens a document that contains any words already in the dictionary. If none have been added, the document is blank.

Continued

MASTERING TROUBLESHOOTING CONTINUED

4. Type individual words, pressing Enter after each word.

5. Edit or delete misspelled words.

6. When you finish adding or editing words, close and save the document in *.dic format. You will be prompted twice about file formats; click Yes both times.

Even though you added them through Word, all of the words you entered should now pass a spelling check in Project with flying colors.

Automatic Fixes for Common Errors

Project 2000 shares another feature with Office 2000: AutoCorrect. With AutoCorrect, you can build your own list of common misspellings. When Project encounters one of those words, it automatically fixes it for you. Some misspelled words, such as "adn" and "teh," are already in the list. As you correct misspelled words, you can add them to the AutoCorrect list. AutoCorrect is one of the options in the Spelling dialog box. You can also access it from Tools ➤ AutoCorrect.

AutoCorrect maintains a dictionary of commonly misspelled and mistyped words; when you mistype one, AutoCorrect fixes it automatically. AutoCorrect is also the feature that changes :) to a smiley face ☺ and (c) to the copyright symbol ©.

Because some of the AutoCorrect changes can be a bit disconcerting, you have the option of turning these features on and off as desired. Figure 7.19 shows the AutoCorrect dialog box; you can access it by clicking Tools ➤ AutoCorrect.

To add a word or phrase to the AutoCorrect dictionary, you can either select the text in the document, or enter the words in the Replace and With text boxes in the AutoCorrect dialog box. If you select text in your document and open the AutoCorrect dialog box, the text appears in the With text box. You have the option of saving this AutoCorrect entry as plain or formatted text. Text that you enter directly in the Replace and With text boxes can appear only as plain text.

NOTE AutoCorrect is case-sensitive. If text appears in the Replace column in uppercase, it must be typed in uppercase for AutoCorrect to replace it.

Although AutoCorrect is typically used to correct single words, you can use it to insert entire paragraphs or even longer segments of formatted text. Just be careful to use a "Replace" word that you don't typically type. Every time you type this word, the text will be replaced with the AutoCorrect entry.

FIGURE 7.19

AutoCorrect options automatically correct common typing mistakes.

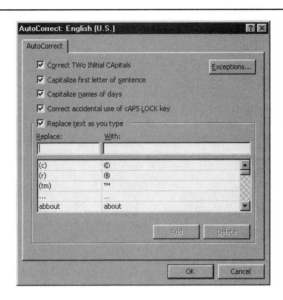

Using AutoCorrect to Shortcut Data Entry

AutoCorrect is designed to prevent typing and spelling errors, but it is also valuable as a shortcut tool. You can enter words that you type regularly into your AutoCorrect list to save yourself time and keystrokes—long company names, for example, or legal or medical terminology. Just enter a code that you will recognize, such as USA, and AutoCorrect expands it for you into United States of America. However, if you think you will ever want to use the abbreviation without expanding it, enter a slash (/) or some other character in front of the abbreviation (**/USA**). Then, you can choose whether to have AutoCorrect supply the long form (by typing **/USA**) or use the abbreviation (by typing **USA** without the slash). If you want the actual characters to appear in your document rather than the AutoCorrect symbol, type the characters—for example, type **(c)**. As soon as the symbol appears (©), press the Backspace key. This replaces the symbol with the original characters. This only works on symbols, however. It doesn't change text back to the typed text.

What's Next

Now that you know the basics of entering tasks, you are ready to begin creating a project schedule by linking tasks together that must be completed in succession. In Chapter 8, "Scheduling and Linking Project Tasks," you'll learn how to create task relationships, allow for task delays and overlaps, split tasks, and set task constraints.

CHAPTER 8

Scheduling and Linking Project Tasks

I f you use Project only to enter tasks and task durations, as described in Chapter 7, "Entering Project Tasks," you could just as easily use Word or Excel to create tasks lists. Both Word and Excel provide tools for creating lists and make it easy to resequence and sort lists. However, Microsoft Project is more than a list creator. The real power of Project lies in its capability to calculate schedules based on task relationships and resource assignments. In Chapter 9, "Defining Project Resources and Costs," and Chapter 10, "Assigning and Scheduling Resources and Costs," you'll learn about allocating resources and costs. In this chapter, you'll learn how to use scheduling to show relationships between tasks, identify which task must come before another, and see how the completion or start of one task affects the others.

Creating a Project Schedule

In its simplest form, a project schedule is a list of tasks with their respective due dates. In its most developed form, a project schedule is a dynamic tool that defines not only what needs to be completed and when, but also how the project tasks impact upon one another. For a project to be successful, it generally must be completed as defined, within the estimated time, and within budget. So what happens when one task cannot be completed on schedule? What impact does that have on the completion of subsequent tasks? How does that affect the costs related to the project? Will the resources assigned to the project be sitting around with nothing to do while they wait for a task to be completed? What happens if a task is completed early? Can the next task begin or must it wait until a prescribed date or time? Unless you, as project manager, can answer these questions, the success of the project is at risk. Microsoft Project can help you answer these questions long before something outside of your control impacts the project plan, and can prepare you for any possible contingency.

Identifying Predecessor and Successor Tasks

Linking tasks is Project's way of showing you how tasks are related to each other. By linking tasks, Project can make the necessary adjustments to the schedule whenever there are changes that affect the start or completion of other tasks. No matter how invested you are in a schedule, you can't move an office if the moving van doesn't arrive; you can't train new staff if they haven't been hired yet. By linking tasks, you create a project schedule that is realistic and logical, updates automatically when tasks are delayed or completed ahead of schedule, and provides you with a clear plan of the resource needs at various points throughout the project.

When tasks are linked, the task that must be started or completed first is called the *predecessor* and the task that depends on the predecessor is called the *successor*. In Figure 8.1, it's clear that before the architectural drawings can be completed, suitable office space must be found. Before offices can be assigned, the drawings must be completed, and before furniture can be ordered, the offices must be assigned. If all these tasks are completed at the same time or in a different order, the drawings won't fit the space, too much furniture might be ordered, and people might be assigned to offices that didn't even exist. The sequencing of the tasks is essential to each task's successful outcome and one task is clearly dependent on the other. The arrow between tasks shown in Figure 8.1 plainly shows the dependency relationship. The arrow points to the dependent, or successor, task. In this example, Task 3 is a successor of 2, Task 4 is a successor of 3, and Task 5 is a successor of 4.

FIGURE 8.1

These linked tasks are dependent on each other and must be completed in order.

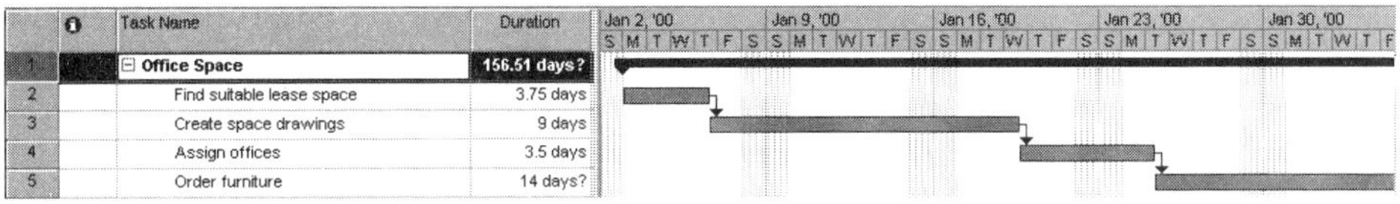

When these tasks are actually underway, the relationships might not be as clear. Figure 8.2 shows the comparison of actual Start and Finish Dates with the Baseline, or planned Start and Finish. In Figure 8.2, you can see that Task 2, Find suitable office space, took a day longer than planned to complete. As a result, Task 3, Create space drawings, which is dependent on Task 2, could not start on schedule. Task 3's start was delayed by several days. Because the task started behind schedule, it was decided that as soon as a general sketch of the office was laid out, offices could be assigned (Task 4), and furniture could be ordered (Task 5). This decision actually benefited by the project by putting it about four days ahead of schedule.

FIGURE 8.2

Comparing the planned schedule with the actual completion shows how linked tasks are affected when the schedule changes.

Although not every task in a project may have a predecessor or successor, defining those that do can help develop a realistic schedule and keep the project on track.

Using Different Types of Relationships

Defining task relationships is not always as straightforward as the terms *predecessor* and *successor* suggest. The most common type of relationship, referred to a finish-to-start relationship, is a relationship in which one task, the successor, can't start until the predecessor is completed. However, not all relationships fit this pattern. With Microsoft Project, you can define four different types of relationships between tasks.

Finish-to-Start (FS)

A *finish-to-start* relationship is the default relationship in Project, and it is the most common type of dependency. In a finish-to-start dependency, one task cannot start until another task finishes. For example, you cannot distribute new office furniture until the furniture arrives from the vendor. Figure 8.3 shows a typical finish-to-start dependency.

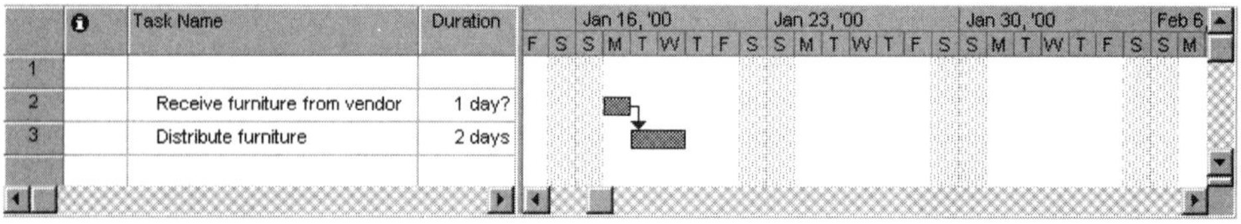

FIGURE 8.3

The most common type of a relationship is a finish-to-start relationship.

	ⓘ	Task Name	Duration	Jan 16, '00	Jan 23, '00	Jan 30, '00	Feb 6
1							
2		Receive furniture from vendor	1 day?				
3		Distribute furniture	2 days				

Start-to-Start (SS)

A *start-to-start* dependency is a dependency in which one task cannot start until another task starts. In this type of dependency, the successor task may be able to start immediately or soon after the predecessor starts, rather than waiting until the predecessor task finishes. To use an everyday example of a start-to-start relationship, baking holiday cookies is an obvious predecessor to decorating the cookies. However, you don't need to wait until all of the cookies are baked to begin decorating. By adding *lead time* to the decorating task, you can start the decorating as soon as the first batch comes out of the oven and cools a bit.

NOTE For more about lead time, see "Allowing for Task Delays and Overlaps," later in this chapter.

Figure 8.4 demonstrates a start-to-start relationship in the Office Decentralization project. One of the groups of tasks in this project is related to hiring staff for the new office. In this example, as soon as the people responsible for hiring begin reviewing resumes, they can schedule interviews with likely candidates. A day of lead time allows the interview team to contact the candidates and set up the interviews.

FIGURE 8.4

In a start-to-start relationship, the successor can't start until the predecessor has started.

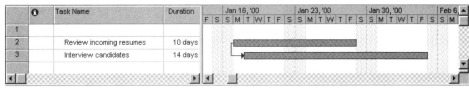

Finish-to-Finish (FF)

When a *finish-to-finish* dependency is established, one task cannot finish until another task finishes. In this type of dependency, start dates are irrelevant to the relationship. What matters is that the predecessor finishes before or at the same time as the successor. Let's say, for example, that two interview teams are responsible for interviewing and coming up with a list of hiring recommendations. The team that hires sales staff must finish before the office hiring team finishes to make sure that appropriate office staff is hired to meet the needs of the sales managers.

In Figure 8.5, the task of interviewing was divided into two separate tasks: interviewing sales staff and interviewing office staff. Each task has a start-to-start relationship with reviewing resumes. In addition, the two interviewing tasks have a finish-to-finish relationship with each other. Interviewing the sales staff must be completed first, so it is the predecessor task. Interviewing the office staff cannot be completed until the sales staff interviews are complete, so interviewing the office staff is the successor task.

FIGURE 8.5

In a finish-to finish relationship, one task cannot finish until another task finishes.

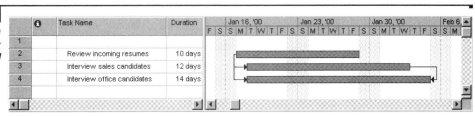

Start-to-Finish (SF)

The last type of dependency is a *start-to-finish* dependency. In this type of relationship, the finish date of one task is dependent on the start date of the other task. For example, if painting the new office space is scheduled to start in the afternoon of March 26, the paint should be delivered freshly mixed in the morning of March 26. If the mixing is completed too soon before the painting begins, it may have to be remixed on-site. If the painting is delayed because the painters are held up on another job, the paint should not be delivered. Figure 8.6 shows the start-to-finish relationship between these two tasks.

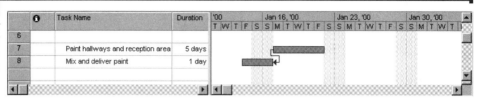

FIGURE 8.6

A task that cannot finish until another task is started is in a start-to-finish relationship.

Although the mixing of the paint occurs first chronologically, the process of mixing and delivering the paint is dependent on the start date of the painting. So, in this instance, painting is viewed as the predecessor and mixing is the successor.

TIP To decide which task is the predecessor and which is the successor, ask yourself this question: If the start or finish date of a task changes, will it affect the scheduling of the other task? The scheduling of a successor (dependent) task is always affected when the scheduling of its predecessor changes.

Establishing Links

You can enter links between tasks when you enter tasks into Project, or you can wait until you have all the tasks entered and then go back and establish links. Whichever method you choose, you want to establish links before assigning resources and costs to a project. Links are important for determining the required timeline of a project, which, in turn, impacts decisions about resources and subsequent costs.

Project 2000 offers a variety of methods of linking tasks. You can link tasks by using the following:

- Toolbar or menu commands
- Task Information dialog box or task tables
- Drag and drop with the mouse

Some of these methods depend on the view you are in and the order in which you select tasks for linking.

Linking Tasks by Using Toolbar or Menu Commands

The easiest way to create a finish-to-start link is to use the Link Tasks toolbar button. To create a link using the Link Tasks button, follow these steps:

1. Select the tasks you want to link. You can link two tasks at a time or an entire series of tasks. If you select tasks by dragging, the tasks with lower ID numbers are set as the predecessor tasks and the tasks with higher ID numbers are successors. If you want to select noncontiguous tasks or if you want to designate a task with a higher ID number as a predecessor, select tasks by holding Ctrl while you click the tasks in order.

2. Click the Link Tasks button on the Standard toolbar to create the links.

Figure 8.7 shows the links created by dragging Tasks 2, 3, and 4. Figure 8.8 shows the links created by selecting Tasks 4, 3, and 2 using the Ctrl key.

FIGURE 8.7

These links were created by dragging to select the tasks.

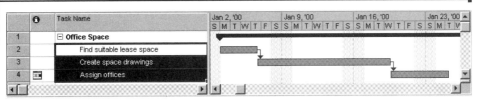

FIGURE 8.8

These links were created by using Ctrl to select the tasks in reverse order: 4, 3, 2.

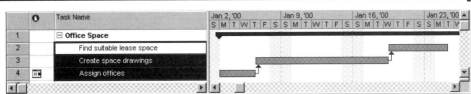

If you prefer, you can also links tasks by selecting the tasks you want to link and choosing Edit ➢ Link Tasks or pressing Ctrl+F2.

All of the links created using the menu or toolbar are finish-to-start links with no lag or lead time. If you want to create other types of links, you must use one of the task forms, described in the next section, to enter or edit linking information.

Linking Tasks by Using Forms and Tables

If you want to create a finish-to-start, start-to-start, or finish-to-finish link, or if you want to enter lag or lead time between tasks, you have the option to create or edit links using one of these methods:

- Task Entry table
- Task Information dialog box
- Task Form view

Linking Tasks by Using the Task Entry Table

The Task Entry table you use to enter tasks can also be used to create relationships between tasks. The Predecessor field is available by using the horizontal scroll bars at the bottom of the Task list or by dragging the vertical split bar to make more columns visible, as shown in Figure 8.9.

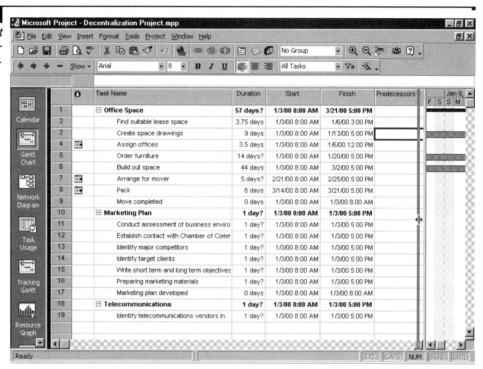

To create a simple finish-to-start relationship with no lag or lead time, follow these steps:

1. Select the Predecessor field of the successor (dependent) task by clicking in the field.

2. Enter the ID number of the predecessor task.

 3. Press Enter and click outside of the field, or click the Enter button on the Entry bar to create the link.

 TIP Project tables work similarly to spreadsheets in Excel. To select a cell in one of Project's tables, all you have to do is click the cell.

If you want to create a different type of relationship, enter the task ID number, followed by the abbreviation for the relationship type:

FS   Finish-to-Start

SS   Start-to-Start

SF   Start-to-Finish

FF   Finish-to-Finish

For example, to create a start-to-finish relationship between Tasks 2 and 3, enter **2SF** in the Predecessor field, as shown here.

	Task Name	Duration	Start	Finish	Predecessors	Resc
	✕ ✓ 2SF					
1	⊟ **Office Space**	**57 days?**	**1/3/00 8:00 AM**	**3/21/00 5:00 PM**		
2	Find suitable lease space	3.75 days	1/3/00 8:00 AM	1/6/00 3:00 PM		
3	Order furniture	14 days?	1/3/00 8:00 AM	1/20/00 5:00 PM	2SF	
4	Build out space	44 days	1/3/00 8:00 AM	3/2/00 5:00 PM		

To enter multiple predecessors, separate the predecessor information with a comma. For example, enter **2FS,4FS**. When you have finished creating relationships, you can drag the vertical split bar back to the left to display the relationships in the Gantt Chart.

NOTE See "Allowing for Task Delays and Overlaps," later in this chapter to see how to include lag and lead time in the Task Entry table.

Linking Tasks by Using the Task Information Dialog Box

The Task Information dialog box is the main vehicle for viewing and entering all of the details about a task. To enter predecessors for a task, you want to open the Task Information dialog box for the successor or dependent task. You can access the Task Information dialog box by using one of these methods:

- Double-click a task
- Click the Task Information button on the Standard toolbar
- Choose Project ➢ Task Information

The Task Information dialog box has five tabs. In Chapter 7, we introduced the General and Notes tabs (see "Adding More Details About a Task" in Chapter 7). To enter predecessors in the Task Information dialog box, follow these steps:

1. Open the Task Information dialog box for the successor (dependent) task.

2. Click the Predecessors tab to display the page shown in Figure 8.10.

PART

II

Creating a Project
from Start to Finish

3. Select the ID field and enter the number of the task. Project displays the number in the Entry bar.

OR

3. Select the Task Name field and click the down arrow to open the Task list. Select the predecessor task from the list.

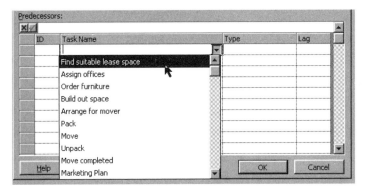

4. To accept the entry, click the green check mark in the Entry bar, press Enter, or press the tab key. Click the red X in the Entry bar to cancel the entry.

Project enters the ID and Task Name, defines the type as Finish-to-Start, and enters **0d lag**.

5. To change the link type, select the Type field and click the down arrow to choose from the list of types.

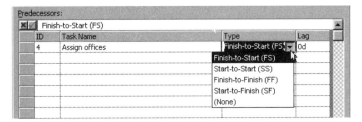

6. Select the Lag field and use the spin box arrows to increase or decrease the amount of lag or lead time. Positive numbers represent lag time and negative numbers represent lead time.

7. Repeat Steps 3–6 if you would like to enter additional predecessors for this task.

8. Click OK to create the links and close the Task Information dialog box.

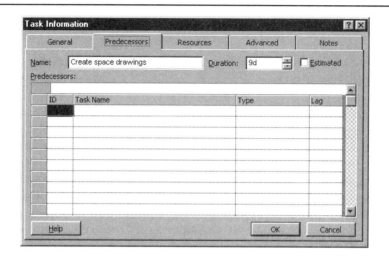

 NOTE For more about lag and lead time, see "Allowing for Task Delays and Overlaps," later in this chapter.

Linking Tasks by Using the Task Form View

The Task Form view is an alternative view available that allows you to see the Task Entry table, the Gantt Chart, and a Task form displaying additional information about the tasks. The Task form, shown in Figure 8.11, appears at the bottom of the window. To activate the Task form view, choose Windows ➤ Split from the menu.

As you can see in Figure 8.11, the Task Form view displays resources and predecessors by default. To change the display to focus on predecessors and successors, right-click anywhere in the Task form. Figure 8.12 shows you the menu of display choices. Choose Predecessors & Successors from the list.

PART

II

Creating a Project
from Start to Finish

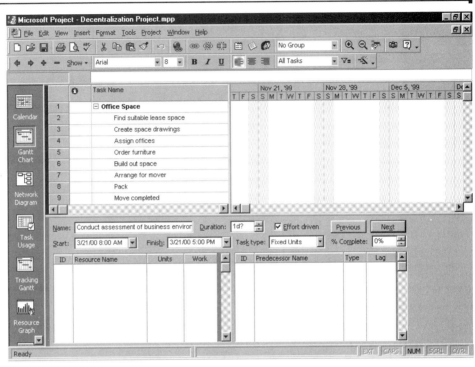

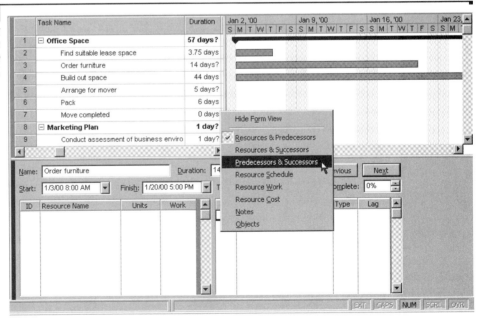

Creating Predecessors   To create predecessor tasks, follow these steps:

1. In the Task Entry table, click the task for which you want to set a predecessor, or click the Previous or Next buttons on the Task form to move to the desired task.

2. Select the task ID number field or the Predecessor Name field to identify the predecessor task. If you cannot see the ID number, you can use the vertical scroll bar in the Task Entry table to locate the correct task. You can also choose the task directly from the Predecessor Name field list. Click the down arrow in the Predecessor Name field to access the list.

3. Click the OK button on the Task form to accept the entry. When you click OK, Project fills in the task name if you enter the ID number and the ID number if you enter a task name. (Although you can wait to click OK until after you complete Steps 4 and 5, Project won't fill in the missing ID or task name until you click OK.)

4. If you want to change the type of the relationship from the default finish-to-start relationship, select the Type field and click the down arrow to open the Type list. Select a type from the list.

5. To enter lag or lead time, select the Lag field and use the spin box arrows to enter a positive or negative value.

6. Repeat Steps 2–5 to enter additional predecessors.

7. Click OK on the Task form again to save the changes.

 NOTE As soon as you begin entering predecessor or successor information, the Previous and Next buttons change to OK and Cancel buttons. They stay that way until you click OK or Cancel, or until you select another task in the Task list in the Task Entry table.

Creating Successors   To create successor tasks, follow the steps for creating predecessors, but use the right side of the Task form. Figure 8.13 shows a predecessor and two successor tasks to Task 4.

 NOTE Effort-driven tasks and Task types, two fields available on the Task form, are discussed in Chapter 9. The % Complete field is reviewed in Chapter 12, "Tracking Project Progress."

PART

II

Creating a Project
from Start to Finish

FIGURE 8.13

Predecessor and successor tasks displayed in Task Form view.

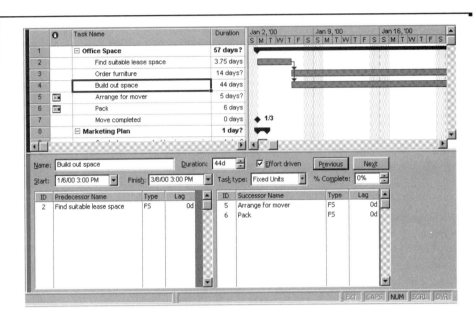

Closing the Task Form   When you finish entering relationships, you can turn off Task Form view by choose Window ➤ Remove Split from the menu. You can also remove a split by dragging the horizontal split bar down to the status bar at the bottom of the window, as shown in Figure 8.14.

FIGURE 8.14

To close the Task form, drag the horizontal split bar down to the status bar.

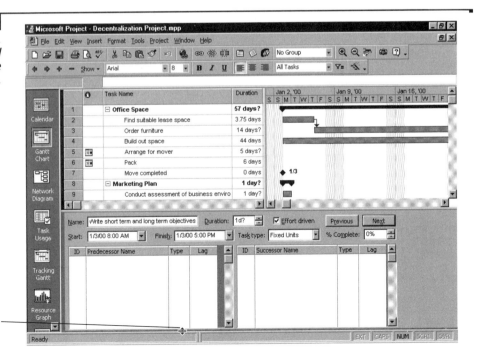

Dragging horizontal split bar

Linking Tasks Using Drag-and-Drop

One of the easiest way to link tasks when you can see both the predecessor and the successor task in the Gantt Chart or Calendar view is to use drag-and-drop with the mouse. You have to be careful when you use drag-and-drop to make sure you are linking tasks, but once you get the hang of it, it's a quick way to create finish-to-start relationships with no lag or lead time.

To use the mouse to link tasks, follow these steps:

1. Point to the predecessor task. When you point to the center of the task in the Gantt Chart, the pointer changes to a four-headed arrow.

   In the Calendar view, use the standard arrow pointer.

2. Drag the task and drop it on the successor task. As soon as you start dragging, the pointer changes to a chain link pointer shape.

 WARNING Be sure to drag the chain link pointer—with any other pointer shape, you could be moving the task, or changing the task's duration or % complete.

MASTERING TROUBLESHOOTING

Locating a Taskbar on the Gantt Chart

You may have already discovered that selecting a task in the task list does not display the corresponding taskbar in the Gantt Chart. Although you can use the horizontal scroll bar at the bottom of the Gantt Chart to locate a specific taskbar, this is a tedious process in a project that extends over many months. To quickly jump to a taskbar, select the task in the task list and click the Go To Selected Task button on the Standard toolbar.

This immediately moves the Gantt Chart to the start of the selected task.

PART

II

Creating a Project from Start to Finish

Modifying Task Relationships

In even the best-laid plans, there comes a time when you need to change the relationship between tasks. This could be as drastic as completely unlinking tasks or as simple as changing the relationship type. Project offers a number of ways to change established relationships.

Unlinking Tasks

 The easiest way to unlink a task is to select a task and click the Unlink Tasks button on the Standard toolbar. This immediately removes all predecessor and successor links related to this task. If you want to remove only one link, select the predecessor and successor tasks and click the Unlink Tasks button.

You can also delete links using the menu by selecting the links and choosing Edit ➤ Unlink Tasks.

Modifying Links with the Task Dependency Dialog Box

In the Task Dependency dialog box, you can change the type of a relationship and modify the lag or lead time. To access the Task Dependency dialog box, double-click the connecting line between two tasks.

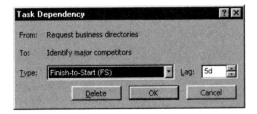

To change the relationship type, click the down arrow on the Type field to open the Type list. Select the Type from the drop-down list. If you choose None as the relationship type, the link is removed. You can also remove the link by clicking the Delete button. Click OK to close the dialog box.

Using Forms and Tables to Modify Links

After you establish links, you can also modify them in the Task Information dialog box, the Task Entry table, and the Task form.

To modify links in the Task Information dialog box, follow these steps:

1. Double-click the task to open the dialog box.

2. Click the Predecessors tab.

3. Select the field you want to edit.

4. Enter the modified information by selecting it from a drop-down list or typing in the field.

5. Click OK to close the dialog box and save the changes.

To modify information in the Task Entry table, follow these steps:

1. Drag the vertical split bar to the right to display the Predecessors field.

2. Select the cell you want to edit. The pointer changes to an I-beam.

3. Click the cell again with the I-beam pointer to switch to Edit mode. The flashing insertion point appears.

4. Make any desired changes.

5. Press Enter or select another cell to enter the changes.

 WARNING Do not attempt to remove a link by selecting a cell in the Predecessors column and pressing Delete. This removes the entire task, not just the link. To remove a link, switch to Edit mode (see Step 3 in the previous set of steps), select the entry, and press Delete.

To modify information in the Task form, follow these steps:

1. Choose Windows ➤ Split Screen to activate the Task form at the bottom of the window.

2. Check to see that the Task form is displaying Resources & Predecessors, Resource & Successors, or Predecessors & Successors. If one of these views is not the current view, right-click on the form and choose one from the menu that opens.

3. Select the field you want to edit.

4. Enter the modified information by selecting it from a drop-down list or typing in the field.

5. Click the OK button on the Task form to accept the change.

6. Close the Task form by choosing Windows ➤ Remove Split.

MASTERING TROUBLESHOOTING

Editing in the Entry Bar

Project gives you two ways to edit the entries in a cell. You can select the cell and switch to Edit mode by clicking again in the cell, or you can select the cell and click in the Entry bar. The Entry bar is the bar at the top of the task list in the Task Entry table. You can also find an Entry bar in the Task form view and in the Task Information dialog box. The Entry bar becomes active only when a cell is selected and Project is in Edit mode. To switch to Edit mode, click in the Entry bar.

	Duration	Start	Finish	Predecessors	Resource Names
17					
18	10 days	1/3/00 8:00 AM	1/14/00 5:00 PM		
19	8 days	1/10/00 8:00 AM	1/19/00 5:00 PM	18FS-50%	
20					

✗ ✓ 18FS-50%

Continued ▮▶

PART

II

Creating a Project
from Start to Finish

Using Autolink to Repair Broken Links

When you move, delete, or insert a task, Project automatically repairs the broken links created by the changes. In Figure 8.15, the first set of tasks is linked. In the second set, the middle task, "Interview sales candidates," was deleted with Autolink on. The link was automatically re-created between Task 2 and Task 4. In the third set, the middle task was deleted with the Autolink feature off. The link was broken between the two tasks.

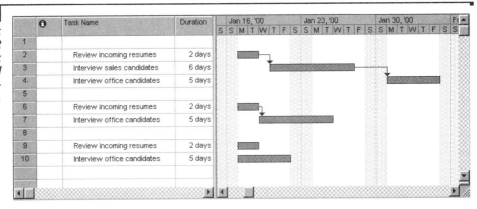

FIGURE 8.15

The effects of Autolink can be seen in the set of tasks. When a task is deleted, the first and third tasks are automatically relinked.

Autolink is an option that is on by default. However, you can choose to turn it off for a specific project, or change the default so that it is always off. To turn Autolink off, follow these steps:

1. Choose Tools ➣ Options.
2. Click the Schedule tab.
3. Click the Autolink Inserted or Moved Tasks checkbox to clear it.
4. If you want Autolink off by default, click the Set as Default button.
5. Click OK to close the Options dialog box and save the changes.

Creating Links in an Outlined Task List

When you create outlined task lists, subtasks are automatically linked to their summary task. This link is inherent in the outlining feature. However, you have several options for how you want to link the summary groups and subtasks within those summary groups together. You can do the following:

- Link subtasks with a summary group and link summary tasks together
- Link subtasks between summary tasks
- Link summary tasks to subtasks in other summary groups

 NOTE For more about outlining tasks, see "Using the Outlining Features," in Chapter 7.

Linking Summary Tasks to Each Other

The most common method of linking in an outlined task list is to link summary tasks together, and to link the subtasks to other subtasks within each summary group. This is the way Project creates links if you select all the tasks and click the Link Task button. This method gives you the flexibility to insert and delete tasks within a summary group, change task durations, and move tasks around without affecting the link with the next group of tasks. Figure 8.16 shows an example of linking summary tasks.

PART

II

Creating a Project
from Start to Finish

FIGURE 8.16

Linking summary tasks gives you the freedom to manipulate subtasks while still retaining the link to the rest of the project.

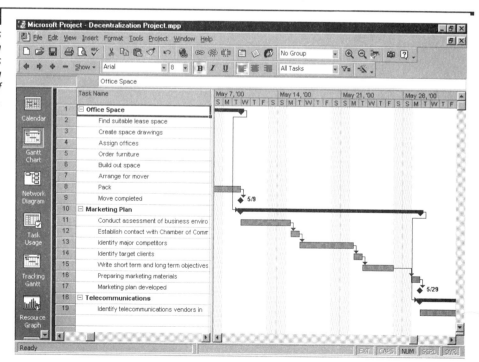

TIP You can easily select all the tasks in a project by clicking in the blank space to the left of the column names and above the task numbers in the Task Entry table.

Linking Subtasks between Summary Groups

Another method of linking tasks in an outline is to link subtasks together between summary groups. In the example in Figure 8.17, the last task in Office Space summary group, the Move completed milestone, becomes the predecessor to the first task in the Marketing Plan summary group, Conduct assessment of business environment.

FIGURE 8.17

Subtasks can be linked directly to subtasks in other groups; in effect, ignoring the summary tasks.

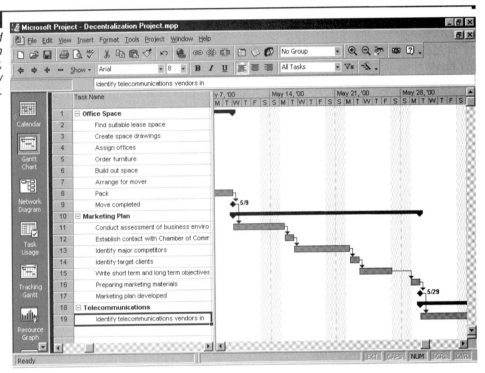

If you choose this method, be very careful if you insert, move, or delete subtasks. You must make sure that the links between groups are maintained even if the original relationship is no longer appropriate.

Linking Summary Tasks to Subtasks

The third method of linking tasks in an outline is to link summary tasks to subtasks in other summary groups. Use this method if you want to link the completion of a summary group to a particular task within another subgroup. In the example in Figure 8.18, the summary task Office Space is linked directly to the third task in the summary group, Marketing Plan, Identify Major Competitors. At the same time, all of the subtasks in the Summary Group are linked together. That creates the equivalent of a lag between the second task, Establish Contact With Chamber Of Commerce, and the third task, Identify Major Competitors, because this third task can't start until the Office Space tasks are all completed.

FIGURE 8.18

Linking summary tasks to subtasks in other groups can impact the overall scheduling of the subtasks.

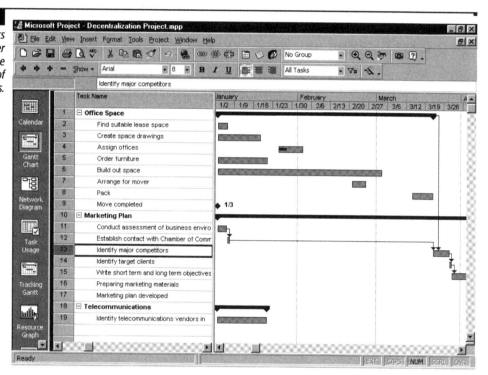

PART

II

Creating a Project from Start to Finish

Allowing for Task Delays and Overlaps

Even though two tasks may be linked, the planned start or finish date of a task may be dependent on a number of other factors. In a finish-to-start relationship, finishing a predecessor task doesn't necessarily mean that you can start the successor task immediately. If you've ever flown on a commercial airline, you have probably experienced this firsthand. Airlines routinely include lag time, a delay between landing and taking off again, in their schedules. This allows time for deboarding, refueling, exchanging baggage, restocking the kitchen, cleaning the cabin, and reboarding. *Lag time* is defined as a delay between any two dependent tasks.

In Figure 8.19, tasks 15 and 16 provide an example of lag time. In this example, the marketing team is planning to request business directories for the local community and then use those materials to identify major competitors. Although the task of requesting directories should take only two days, it may take a few additional days for all of the directories to arrive. By building in a five-day lag time, you can more accurately reflect the expected lag time between requesting the directories and beginning the process of identifying competitors.

 NOTE The scheduled arrival time and the time the airline actually expects a plane to arrive often differs. Even if a plane arrives later than the airline expects, it may be well within the publicized arrival time. "Stretching" the duration to improve the airline's on-time arrival percentage contributes to overall customer satisfaction and standing in the industry.

On the other hand, if a successor task can start before its predecessor is finished, this can be demonstrated through the use of lead time. *Lead time*, then, is the overlap between dependent tasks. Let's say, for example, that one task is to identify target clients of the new regional sales office. Based on the results of this process, the marketing team plans to create marketing materials. As long as you allow some lead time to establish a general sense of the target clients, the marketing team can begin drafting marketing materials. Tasks 18 and 19 in Figure 8.19 show this relationship.

FIGURE 8.19

Task 15 is scheduled to start after a short lag, and task 19 can start after task 18 has a period of lead time.

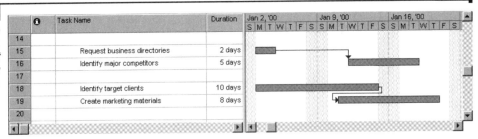

Entering Lags and Lead Time

Lag time and lead time are both entered in the Lag field or in the Predecessors field. Lag time is entered as a positive number and lead time as a negative number. Lag time and lead time can also be entered as a percentage of the predecessor's duration. A 40 percent lead time, for example, means that the successor task would start when the predecessor is 60 percent completed. Use a percentage when you want the lag or lead time to increase or decrease proportionately if the duration changes.

You can enter lag time and lead time by using the Task Information dialog box, using Task Form view, using the Task Entry table, and using the Task Dependency dialog box. To use the Task Information form, follow these steps:

1. Double-click a task to open the Task Information dialog box.

2. Click the Predecessors tab.

3. Select the Lag field.

4. Enter a number or percentage in the cell, or use the spin arrows to increase or decrease the lag or lead time.

5. Click OK to close the Task Information form.

To use Task form view, follow these steps:

1. Click Window ➤ Split in Gantt Chart view to open the Task form.

2. If Predecessors are not visible, right-click on the Task form and choose Resources & Predecessors, Resources & Successors, or Predecessors & Successors.

3. Select the Lag field.

4. Enter a number or percentage in the cell, or use the spin arrows to increase or decrease the lag or lead time.

5. Click OK on the Task form to record the changes.

To use the Task Entry table, follow these steps:

1. Drag the vertical split bar to the right to display the Predecessors field.

2. Select the field, and edit the predecessor to include the lag or lead time information. You must also enter the abbreviation for the relationship type, if it is not already present. Figure 8.20 shows one example of five days of lag time (15FS+5 days) and one example of 40 percent lead time (18FS–40%).

PART

II

Creating a Project
from Start to Finish

FIGURE 8.20

Lag and lead time can be entered directly in the Task Entry table.

	Task Name	Duration	Start	Finish	Predecessors
14					
15	Request business directories	2 days	1/3/00 8:00 AM	1/4/00 5:00 PM	
16	Identify major competitors	5 days	1/12/00 8:00 AM	1/18/00 5:00 PM	15FS+5 days
17					
18	Identify target clients	10 days	1/3/00 8:00 AM	1/14/00 5:00 PM	
19	Create marketing materials	8 days	1/11/00 8:00 AM	1/20/00 5:00 PM	18FS–40%
20					

To use the Task Dependency dialog box, follow these steps:

1. Double-click the connecting line linking two tasks in the Gantt Chart to open the Task Dependency dialog box.

2. Select the Lag field.

3. Enter a number or percentage in the cell, or use the spin arrows to increase or decrease the lag or lead time.

4. Click OK to close the dialog box and save the changes.

Splitting Tasks

As you are planning a project, you may discover that a task will start on particular date, but the person completing the task is going on vacation two weeks into a four-week task. Rather than waiting until she is back at work to start the task, you can split the task so that part of it is completed before she goes on vacation and part of it after. Whether the interruption is planned or comes up unexpectedly as the project is underway, you can split a task to show the interruption in task completion.

To split a task, follow these steps:

1. In Gantt Chart view, click the Split Task button on the Standard toolbar or choose Edit ➤ Split Task from the menu. The Split Task Information box opens and the pointer changes shape, as shown in Figure 8.21.

2. Position the pointer over the task you want to split. As you move the pointer, the Split Task Information task shows you the start date the pointer is over.

3. When you locate the correct date, click the task bar to split the task. Project splits the tasks, separating the two sections by a day. Figure 8.22 shows the split task.

4. You can split a task into as many sections as you want. Repeat Steps 1–3 to split the task into further sections.

After you split a task, you can drag the split section to the desired restart date. Point to the split section and drag with the four-headed arrow pointer.

As you start to drag, the pointer changes shape once again to become a two-headed arrow, and the Task Split Information box reopens. Figure 8.23 shows the process of changing the start date of a split section.

TIP To change the start date of the entire task, drag the first section of the task. This moves all sections of the task. You can also move the start date of the entire task by holding the Shift key down while you drag any section. When you move a task, Project assigns a Start No Earlier Than Constraint to the task. For more about constraints, see "Constraining Tasks," later in this chapter.

FIGURE 8.21

The Split Task Information box gives you information about the start of the task split.

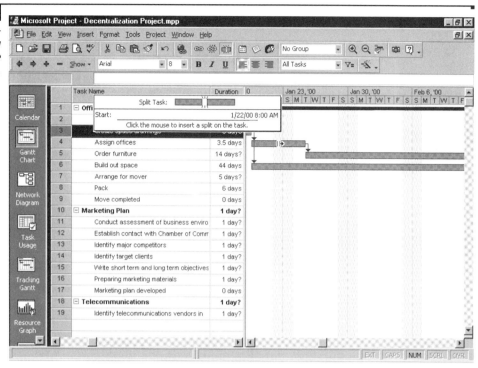

FIGURE 8.22

The task Assign Offices is split into two sections.

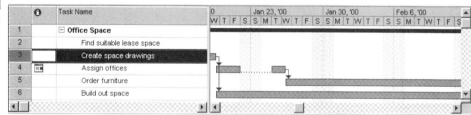

FIGURE 8.23

Change the start date of a section by dragging it to the new start date.

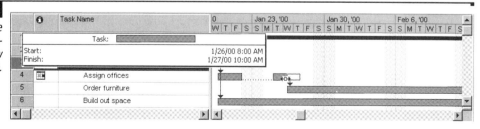

Changing the Duration of a Split Task

 To change the duration of a split task, point to the right side of any task segment. The pointer changes shape to a vertical line with a right arrow. Drag the end of the segment to the new end date, as shown in Figure 8.24. To lengthen a task's duration drag to the right. Drag to the left to shorten it.

FIGURE 8.24

Drag the right end of a task segment to change the task's duration.

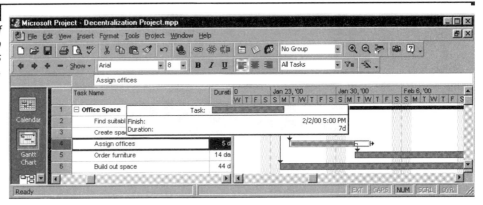

WARNING Be careful that you do not drag the left end of a task when changing a duration. Dragging the left end changes the percent complete rather than the duration.

Removing a Split

To remove a split, drag the section and rejoin it with the previous section of the task.

Constraining Tasks

When you create a project, you can schedule the project to start on a specified date or to finish on a specific date. When you set a project start date, tasks are scheduled to start as soon as possible. When you set a project finish date, tasks are scheduled to start as late as possible. The "as possible" is determined by the relationships (links) that you establish between tasks. As soon or as late as possible is directly related to the start or finish date of a predecessor task.

NOTE To review the project information for the current project, choose Project ➤ Project Information. For more about scheduling the project start or finish date, see "Setting Project Information" in Chapter 6, "Building a New Project."

Other factors, however, may constrain the actual start or finish date of a particular task. For example, if one of the project's tasks is to meet with an individual to review the project and that person is going to be out of town for the period of time you want to meet, the project's schedule can be negatively affected. You can account for this and other scheduling problems by assigning a constraint to the task.

Understanding Constraint Types

In Project, you can choose from eight different constraint options. Table 8.1 describes these options.

TABLE 8.1: CONSTRAINT TYPES

Constraint Type	Description
As Late as Possible	This is the default constraint type when a project is scheduled from the Finish date. Project schedules the task to start as late as it can. The task is scheduled to start as late as it can, based on its relationships and other scheduling parameters.
As Soon As Possible	This is the default constraint type when a project is scheduled from the start date. Project schedules the task to start as early as it can, based on its relationships and other scheduling parameters.
Finish No Earlier Than	The task must be not be completed before the established constraint date.
Finish No Later Than	The task must finish by the established constraint date.
Must Finish On	The task must finish on the established constraint date.
Must Start On	The task must start on the established constraint date.
Start No Earlier Than	The task must not start before the established constraint date.
Start No Later Than	The task must start on or before the established constraint date.

Applying Constraints

To apply a constraint to a task, follow these steps:

 1. Click the Task Information button on the Standard toolbar, or double-click a task to open the Task Information dialog box.

2. Click the Advanced tab.

3. Click the drop-down arrow to open the Constraint type list.

4. Choose the desired constraint from the list.

5. Open the drop-down list in the Constraint Date field to select a date for the constraint (As Soon As Possible and As Late As Possible do not need a Constraint Date).

6. Click OK.

Flexible versus Inflexible Constraints

Inflexible constraints are constraints that restrict scheduling because they require that a task start or finish within specific parameters. Flexible constraints allow Project to calculate the schedule to making appropriate adjustments based on the constraints applied. Table 8.2 shows a list of inflexible and flexible constraints, depending on whether the project is scheduled from the start date or the finish date.

TABLE 8.2: INFLEXIBLE AND FLEXIBLE CONSTRAINTS

| Type | Project Based On | |
	Start Date	Finish Date
Flexible	As Soon as Possible	As Soon as Possible
	As Late as Possible	As Late as Possible
	Finish No Earlier Than	Finish No Later Than
	Start No Earlier Than	Start No Later Than
Inflexible	Must Finish On	Must Finish On
	Must Start On	Must Start On
	Finish No Later Than	Finish No Earlier Than
	Start No Later Than	Start No Earlier Than

When applying constraints, apply inflexible constrains only when they are absolutely necessary. When you apply inflexible constraints, you are restricting Project from establishing a schedule for all the tasks that is consistent with the durations and other scheduling parameters you have assigned to tasks. If, for example, you apply an inflexible constraint to a task, it may be impossible to complete the predecessor or successor tasks within the constraint. If this occurs, Project displays the Planning Wizard message, shown in Figure 8.25, and asks you how you want to handle the conflict.

FIGURE 8.25

If a constraint creates a conflict with the rest of the schedule, Project's Planning Wizard displays this message.

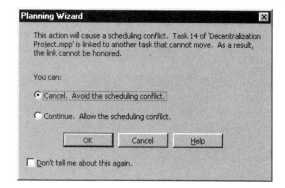

Select Cancel to remove the constraint and avoid the scheduling conflict, or select Continue to save the constraint and allow the scheduling conflict.

 TIP To resolve scheduling conflicts caused by constraints, see "Resolving Scheduling Conflicts," later in this chapter.

Reviewing Constraints

Project indicates that a constraint is applied to a task by adding an Indicators icon to the Indicators field in the Entry table. A blue square on the right side of the calendar icon indicates a flexible task constraint. A red square on the left side indicates an inflexible task constraint. Point to the Constraint indicator to determine what kind of constraint is applied.

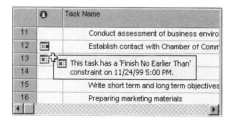

For more about flexible and inflexible tasks constraints, see "Resolving Constraint Conflicts," later in this chapter.

 WARNING You can inadvertently apply a constraint to a task by dragging the task in the Gantt Chart view. Moving a task automatically applies a Start No Earlier Than constraint to the task. Check the Indicators field in the Entry table to see which tasks have constraints applied.

PART

II

Creating a Project
from Start to Finish

Removing Constraints

You can remove a constraint by applying an As Soon as Possible constraint to a task in a project scheduled from the start date or As Late as Possible to a task in a project scheduled from the finish date.

To remove constraints on more than one task, follow these steps:

1. Select the tasks in the Task Entry table by dragging to select successive tasks or by holding Ctrl and clicking to select nonconsecutive tasks.

2. Click the Task Information button on the Standard toolbar or choose Project ➤ Task Information from the menu. The Multiple Task Information dialog box opens.

3. Click the Advanced tab.

4. Click the drop-down arrow to open the Constraint type list.

5. Choose As Soon As Possible in a project scheduled from the start date, or choose As Late as Possible in a project scheduled from the finish date.

6. Click OK to save the new constraint types.

 WARNING Any information you change in the Multiple Task Information dialog box affects all the selected tasks, so be careful to only change things that you want reflected in each of the selected tasks.

Resolving Constraint Conflicts

Constraint conflicts arise when you apply constraints that are in conflict with other parts of the schedule. For example, if you apply a Start No Later Than constraint to a task, such as Order Furniture, and specify a date that actually precedes the finish date of the predecessor, Assign Offices, Project cannot resolve the conflict. You must decide whether the constraint is necessary or whether there is some other way to schedule the tasks to avoid the conflict.

Ask the following questions to determine how to resolve the conflict:

• Is the constraint really necessary? Was the constraint applied intentionally or accidentally? What would have to change in the project plan for it to be possible to remove the constraint?

• Can the finish date of the predecessor task be changed so that it is actually completed by the constraint date?

• Can the duration of the predecessor task be changed so that it can be completed by the constraint date? This may involve having to assign additional resources to the task. For more about using resources to resolve conflicts, see Chapter 9.

- Is it possible to unlink the tasks that are in conflict? Perhaps the task with the constraint would be better linked to a different task or not linked to any task.

- Can the constraint be changed from an inflexible constraint to a flexible one? For example, could the restraint be changed from a Must Start On to a Start No Earlier Than constraint?

Not Honoring Constraint Dates

Another way to resolve constraints is simply to not honor them in the schedule. Project has an option that is turned on by default to always honor constraint dates. You can turn this option off by following these steps:

1. Choose Tools ➤ Options and clicking the Schedule tab.

2. Clear the Tasks Will Always Honor Their Constraint Dates checkbox.

3. Click OK to save the new settings.

When this option is turned off, Project notes the conflicts, but continues to calculate the schedule as if the conflicting constraint weren't applied. Figure 8.26 shows the icon and message that Project displays when a constraint is not being honored.

PART

II

Creating a Project
from Start to Finish

FIGURE 8.26

With the Tasks Will Always Honor Their Constraint Dates checkbox turned off, Project notes the constraint, but doesn't let it create a scheduling conflict.

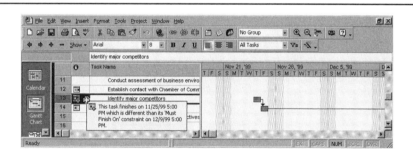

Setting a Deadline

Rather than setting an inflexible constraint, which might negatively affect scheduling, you can now record a deadline date in Project 2000. A deadline is the date you want or need a task to be completed. Setting a deadline does not affect the task schedule in any way. However, if the deadline passes and the task is not completed, Project displays an indicator in the Indicator column.

Project notes a deadline in the Gantt Chart with a downward-pointing arrow.

What's Next

In Chapter 7, you entered tasks and in this chapter you linked tasks to create a project schedule. If you do not plan to assign resources to tasks, your project plan may be near completion. However, if you want to make use of Project's powerful resource scheduling tools, you'll want to spend time reading the next three chapters. In Chapter 9, you'll learn how to enter resources into Project and create budgets. In Chapter 10, you'll learn how Project's scheduling engine works. And in Chapter 11, you'll learn about how to identify over- and underallocations and level resources. These three chapters take you into the real meat of Microsoft Project and give you the tools you need to manage project resources effectively.

CHAPTER <u>9</u>

Defining Project Resources and Costs

I n this chapter, use of Microsoft Project moves into a new and exciting phase. For many small projects, it may be enough to create a simple project plan by setting up the project (Chapter 6), entering project tasks (Chapter 7), and scheduling and linking tasks (Chapter 8). By the time you finish with these activities, you have a solid, workable plan that can serve as an excellent management tool as the project progresses. If this is all you need for the project you are managing, you can skip Chapters 9 and 10, and move right on to Chapter 11, "Preparing Your Project for Publication." However, if your responsibility extends to managing the people, materials, and costs relating to a project, scheduling their time, and making sure the project stays within budget, then you've come to the right place.

Effectively scheduling complex resources is what makes Microsoft Project more than a glorified spreadsheet. Project is not just a tool for listing tasks and entering dates. You can do that in Microsoft Outlook, or even Excel. Project's real power comes in the scheduling engine that runs behind the scenes to take complex information and crunch it down into a realistic road map for project success. Project not only schedules tasks, it schedules the full range of resources needed to complete a project: individuals, teams, facilities, equipment, supplies, and materials. Before you can successfully use Microsoft Project to create a final project schedule, you must understand Project's scheduling rules, why it schedules the way it does, and what it all means to your project.

Resource scheduling in Project is not an area where you want to experiment in ignorance—unless, that is, you want to waste valuable time and end up with a project plan that doesn't work. After you understand the concepts behind the tools and why Project behaves the way it does, you can replace ignorance with confidence as you successfully schedule a project's resources. In this chapter, we'll discuss how to define project resources and costs. Chapter 10, "Assigning and Scheduling Resources and Costs," covers how to assign those resources and costs to tasks to create your project's schedule.

Understanding Resources

As we described earlier, project resources are defined as the individuals, teams, facilities, equipment, supplies, and materials needed to complete a project. Without resources, the tasks outlined in the project could never be accomplished. Some projects may require detailed tracking of all of the resources used in the project. A company that manufactures engine parts, for example, needs to know down to the penny what it costs to produce its parts if it wants to compete successfully as a third-tier vendor to the auto companies. A project to plan the company picnic may not carry the same requirement that every minute of time and costs spent on the project be accounted for.

The amount of investment you put into tracking resources depends on the goal of the project and the expectations of the people ultimately responsible for the project.

To evaluate whether you want to include resources in your project, consider the following:

- Is it important to track the amount of work done by the people involved with the project?

- Is equipment being used in the project, and if so, is it important to know how long it takes the equipment to do its job?

- Is it important that responsibilities for the work of the project be clearly delineated for the people who will be completing the work?

- Do you need a high level of accuracy in scheduling when individual tasks will be completed and how long they will take to complete?

- Do you need to manage work assignments to make sure that people and other resources are not over- or underused?

- Do you need assistance from the resources in other departments, teams, or external sources and have to submit a request for their services?

- Do you need to account for the time and costs spent on the project?

All of these questions can be answered by including resources in the project. If you answered "Yes" to any one of them, you probably want to include some level of resource-tracking in your project.

Estimating Resource Requirements

After you determine that you are going to track resources in the project, you still have a few more questions to answer:

- What kind of resources do you need?

- How much of each resource do you need?

- Where will you get the resources?

Determining Types of Resources

Resources fall into two categories for use in Project: *work resources* and *material resources*. Work resources are the people and equipment assigned to work on a project. Work resources complete tasks by expending time (or work) on the task.

Material resources, on the other hand, are supplies, stock, or other consumable items used to complete tasks in the project. Now, for the first time in Project 2000, you can track material resources and assign them to tasks.

To determine the types of resources you need in the project, review the project scope and task list to see what the project requires. Think about the following questions:

What type of people do you need to complete the tasks?

Will individuals be assigned to the project?

Are teams or departments responsible for certain tasks?

Will you be using outside vendors or contractors?

Are there classes of workers (recruiters or programmers, for example) that can be used interchangeably?

What facilities and equipment do you need?

Does the project require that you schedule certain facilities: a computer lab, conference rooms, or factories, for example?

Will equipment need to be scheduled, such as servers, computers, presses, backhoes, or other industrial machines?

What consumable materials will you use during the course of the project?

Does the project require building products, a special kind of paper, parts to be assembled, or other material goods?

If you are uncertain about the answers to these questions, review the project specifications, consult with others who have completed similar projects, and review old project reports. If similar projects do not exist within your organization, talk with supervisors and other leaders about specific aspects of the project and to hear educated guesses about the types of resources you will need.

 NOTE For more about developing a project scope, refer to "What Is a Project?" in Chapter 1, "Project 2000 Basics."

Mapping Out the Necessary Resource Quantities

After you ascertain the "who" and "what" of the project, you need to consider how much of each resource you need. The quantity of resources, in most cases, is directly related to the desired duration of the task. If the task is to send out marketing materials to prospective clients and the task is estimated to take two days, adding resources (a second person) to the project means that it could be completed in one day. If the assigned resource is only available to work on the task four hours a day instead of full-time, the task will probably take four days. (And maybe longer because of the "gearing up" and "gearing down" that may be associated with work period—getting all the information out, figuring out where people left off, putting everything away at the end of the time, etc.)

Experience and productivity levels of a resource may also influence the duration of a task. A new or inexperienced employee may take longer just because they don't know the computer system with which they are working, or they may be less experienced with completing mail merges used to customize the marketing materials.

In other cases, the quantity of available resources has no relationship to the completion of a task. If you need to rent a computer for the staff member to prepare the mailing materials before the rest of the office equipment is moved to the new facility, renting two computers will not generally make the job go any faster for one person. Conversely, if you have only one computer, adding a second person to the task may not impact the duration.

For the purpose of working in Project 2000, it is valuable to think of work resources in terms of time (such as minutes, hours, days, weeks, months, and years) and to think of material resources in terms of units of measurement (such as pounds, boxes, cubic feet, tons, and dozens).

Defining Max Units   In Project, work resources are assigned a percentage or number to represent the *maximum units* the resource has available to the project. If someone, for example, is available to work on a project full-time, then they would be assigned a maximum unit of 100%. If they were only assigned to your project on a half-time basis, you would assign them a max unit of 50%. Three full-time programmers with similar skills in Visual Basic provide 300% of a VB Programmer resource.

TIP   To change the Max Units field from a percentage to a decimal, choose Tools ➤ Options, and then click the Schedule tab. In the Show Assignment Units As A field, select Decimal from the drop-down list.

Because the Max Units field is a based on a calendar, the Max Units field is not used for material resources. Material resources are measured in assignment units (for example, tons or tons per day) and are set when the assignment is made. For more about assigning assignment units to tasks, see "Assigning Resources to Tasks," later in this chapter.

PART

II

Creating a Project
from Start to Finish

Mastering Max Units and Resource Calendars

The percentage used in Max Units is based on the resource calendar assigned to the resource. If a resource works half-time, you can account for this in two ways: by adjusting the resource's working time or the resource's max units. The first method is the most descriptive because it reflects a person's actual schedule. In this method, assuming that all of a resource's hours are assigned to your project, you would adjust the *resource calendar* to show the resource's actual part-time schedule. The Max Units would show 100% because the resource has 100% of their available 20 hours to work in this project. (For more about adjusting the base calendar, see "Defining the Project Calendar" in Chapter 6, "Building a New Project." For more on setting up custom resource calendars, see "Setting Work Time for Resources," later in this chapter.)

In the second method, you would adjust the *max units* to show the percentage of the Standard (Project) calendar, which is traditionally a 40-hour work week. The resource calendar would reflect a full time schedule, so the Max Units available for this resource to work on the project would be 50%.

Using Consolidated Resource Names   If resources are assigned to complete the same types of tasks, and they share the same working calendar and same rates, you can enter them as one resource by using a consolidated resource name rather than listing each one separately. For example, you can enter programmers, movers, Human Resources, or the name of an organization as the Resource name and then assign them an accumulated percentage for max units. If, for example, you have three full-time programmers working on a project and you list them as a consolidated resource, the max units would be 300%.

In Project 2000, you can use consolidated resource names and assign different work availability to resources within the group. For example, suppose you have a programmer who is assigned to work on another project for the first two weeks of your project, but will then be available full-time on your project along with the other programmers. You can use the Resource Information dialog box to set availability dates for each resource in the consolidated group. To find out more about this feature called Contoured Resource Availability, see "Using the Resource Information Dialog Box," later in this chapter.

Refining Duration Estimates   This point in the project planning is a good time to refine estimates for duration of the tasks. After you have a sense of the resources required, you can adjust task durations to more closely match your newest estimate. To change a duration, follow these steps:

1. Switch to the Gantt Chart view.

2. Select the cell in the Duration field you want to change.

3. Click the Up or Down spin box arrow to the number you want.

4. Select another cell or press Enter to accept the changes.

 TIP In Project 2000, you can now edit directly in a cell by selecting the cell and clicking again in the cell to switch to Edit mode.

 NOTE Entering a **?** after a duration represents an estimate. You can filter the task views to show estimated durations. However, all durations are really estimates at this stage of the project. Enter a **?** if you want to indicate a level of uncertainty about the estimate.

Refining the Task List   When you review the task list with resources in mind, you may find that one task really requires two or more different resources. Even though you can assign more than one resource to a task in Project, when you find that a task needs more than one class of resource (for example, a designer and a programmer) this may indicate that the task should be split up into pieces.

If you find a task that you want to split, insert a new task into the task list. To do this, right-click on a task and choose New Task from the shortcut menu, or click on a task and choose Insert ➢ New Task. The new task is inserted above the selected task.

Obtaining Resources

After you determine the types of resources you need and the approximate quantities, you have to consider where or how you will obtain the resources. Answer these questions to determine where and how you will obtain the resources:

- If you are using staff within your organization, will they be assigned to the project as individuals or as a class of workers? In other words, will you have to consider each individual's work schedule and time commitments, or will you be using a secretarial pool in which all the individuals share a common schedule and work is divided according to availability?

- Will another department or team be handling certain tasks so that you don't have to delineate specific people in the resource list?

- Will you be contracting with external workers for some of the tasks? If so, will you pay them by the hour or on a flat-fee basis? If you are paying them a flat fee, you may be able to identify them as a material resource because you are not concerned about the amount of work it takes them to complete the assigned tasks.

PART

II

Creating a Project
from Start to Finish

- Does your organization own the equipment and facilities you need; or do they need to be purchased, rented, or leased?

- How and from where will you obtain other material resources? Will they be delivered or does one of your resources have to go and pick them up? If you're responsible, you may want to account for the time involved in the pickup and delivery of the materials resources.

Preparing to Enter Resource Information into Your Project   After you determine what kinds of resources you need, how much of each resource you need, and where you will obtain your resources, you are now ready to begin creating a draft resource list for your project. You can enter resources into your project in three ways:

- Create a resource list within your project.

- Share the resource list created in another project.

- Share resources with other projects from a resource pool.

A *shared resource pool* is a master list of resources that is shared among multiple projects in an organization. By using a resource pool, you can schedule work resources across projects while tracking conflicts, over and under allocations and availability.

 TIP Don't assume that resource pools are used only in large organizations with pools of employees. Small companies that have to closely coordinate staff assigned to a variety of projects often use resource pools to communicate information about staff usage between projects.

The rest of this chapter focuses on creating and using a resource list within a project. You can find out more about sharing the resource list created in another project, and creating and accessing a shared resource pool in Chapter 15, "Communicating Project Information."

Entering Resource Information in Project

You can enter work resources into Microsoft Project in several ways:

- Add addresses from an email address book in the Assign Resources dialog box.

- Enter resources directly in a table in the Resource Sheet.

- Add detailed address information using the Resource Information dialog box.

- Enter resources on a form, such as the Resources Form.

- Add addresses automatically as you assign them.

Using the Assign Resources Dialog Box

To quickly enter the names and email addresses of people or groups who are in an email address book, follow these steps:

1. Click the Assign Resource button from the Gantt Chart view to open the Assign Resources dialog box.

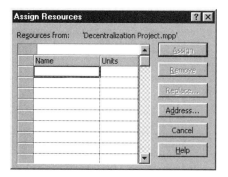

2. Click the Address button.

Project will launch Outlook if it is not already running. You may be prompted to select an Outlook profile.

3. Locate and then double-click the address you want to add, or select multiple addresses and click Add.

If you add a personal distribution group, all members of the group are added to the resource list.

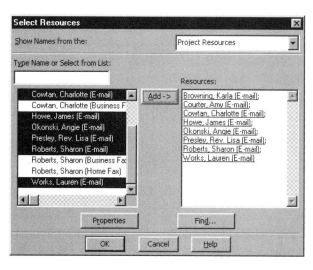

4. When you finish adding all the resources from the address book, click Close in the Assign Resources dialog box.

PART

II

Creating a Project
from Start to Finish

You can add additional information about each resource and add material resources using the Resource Sheet and the Resource Information dialog box.

Using the Resource Sheet

The Resource Sheet is the primary means of entering both work and material resources. As you can see in the Entry view of the Resource Sheet shown in Figure 9.1, you enter a variety of information about resources in the Resource Sheet, including all the fields listed in Table 9.1. Use the Entry view of the Resource Sheet to

- Enter resources for a project
- Set up the pay rates and characteristics of resources
- Group related resources so you can track data by groups

FIGURE 9.1

In the Resource Sheet, you can add work and material resources.

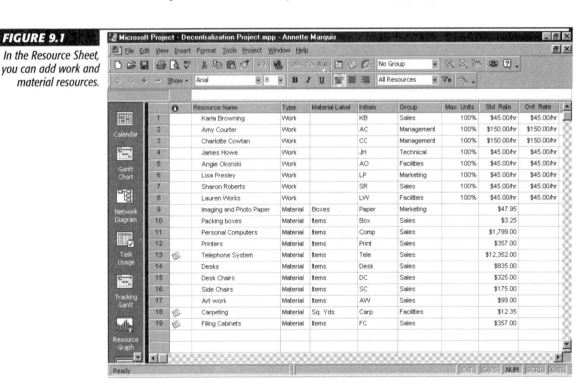

		Resource Name	Type	Material Label	Initials	Group	Max. Units	Std. Rate	Ovt. Rate
1		Karla Browning	Work		KB	Sales	100%	$45.00/hr	$45.00/hr
2		Amy Courter	Work		AC	Management	100%	$150.00/hr	$150.00/hr
3		Charlotte Cowtan	Work		CC	Management	100%	$150.00/hr	$150.00/hr
4		James Howe	Work		JH	Technical	100%	$45.00/hr	$45.00/hr
5		Angie Okonski	Work		AO	Facilities	100%	$45.00/hr	$45.00/hr
6		Lisa Presley	Work		LP	Marketing	100%	$45.00/hr	$45.00/hr
7		Sharon Roberts	Work		SR	Sales	100%	$45.00/hr	$45.00/hr
8		Lauren Works	Work		LW	Facilities	100%	$45.00/hr	$45.00/hr
9		Imaging and Photo Paper	Material	Boxes	Paper	Marketing		$47.95	
10		Packing boxes	Material	Items	Box	Sales		$3.25	
11		Personal Computers	Material	Items	Comp	Sales		$1,799.00	
12		Printers	Material	Items	Print	Sales		$357.00	
13		Telephone System	Material	Items	Tele	Sales		$12,352.00	
14		Desks	Material	Items	Desk	Sales		$835.00	
15		Desk Chairs	Material	Items	DC	Sales		$325.00	
16		Side Chairs	Material	Items	SC	Sales		$175.00	
17		Art work	Material	Items	AW	Sales		$99.00	
18		Carpeting	Material	Sq. Yds	Carp	Facilities		$12.35	
19		Filing Cabinets	Material	Items	FC	Sales		$357.00	

To enter resources using the Resource Sheet or to enter additional information on existing resources, follow these steps:

1. Click View ➤ Resource Sheet, or choose Resource Sheet from the View bar.

2. Choose View ➤ Table ➤ Entry to make sure that the Entry form is displayed.

3. In the Resource Name field, type a resource name.

4. Press Tab to move to the next field.

5. Complete entry in the fields using the field descriptions found in Table 9.1.

TABLE 9.1: RESOURCE SHEET FIELDS

Field	Data Type	Description
ID	Number	The identifier assigned to the resource.
Resource Name	Text	Name of the resource.
Type	Text	What kind of resource is it: Work or Material.
Material Label	Text	The unit of measurement for a material resource: tons, pounds, items, gross, etc.
Initials	Text	Initials to represent the resource name.
Group	Text	Assign a group name that you can give to similar resources to indicate the category of resource (for example: programmer, computer equip., marketing, etc). You can use department names or codes, job titles or job types, or accounting codes for billing. Entering a group allows you to display, sort, filter, or edit resources by the resource group.
Max Units	Percentage/Number	The maximum percentage or number of units that represent the maximum capacity for which a work resource is available to accomplish any tasks during the current time period. For more about Max Units, see "Defining Max Units," earlier in this chapter.
Std. Rate (Standard Rate)	Currency	Rate of pay per time unit for regular nonovertime work. The standard time unit is hour; to enter a different time period, include a forward slash and the unit. For example, $100/d or $1000/w.
Ovt. Rate (Overtime Rate)	Currency	Rate of pay per time unit for overtime hours. Be sure to enter a rate here, even if the rate is the same as the standard rate. Otherwise, Project will calculate overtime hours at $0.00 per hour.
Cost/Use	Currency	Cost that accrues each time you use a resource. For example, if a resource charges a set fee instead of an hourly rate, you would include that fee in this field. Or enter a set delivery charge for delivering a material resource.

Continued ▶

TABLE 9.1 CONTINUED: RESOURCE SHEET FIELDS		
Field	**Data Type**	**Description**
Accrue At	Enumerated	Choose Start, End, or Prorated to show when charges accrue for a resource. The default is Prorated, which applies the costs as the resource is used.
Base Calendar	Enumerated	Choose which calendar—Standard, 24 Hours, or Night Shift—serves as the default calendar for the resource. You can adjust the calendar for the individual resource (see "Set Working Times from Resources," later in this chapter), but it is still related to a base calendar.
Code	Text	An open field to enter any additional code you want to use to classify a resource. It could include a cost center number, a department number, etc. Use it to sort, filter, and report on resources related to a code.

 TIP If many of your resources are paid the same rate, you can set a default standard rate and overtime rate. Go to Tools ➢ Options, and then click the General tab. In the Default Standard Rate field, type the rate. In the Default Overtime Rate field, enter the overtime rate. The default rates are applied to all new resources you created unless you change it.

Displaying or Hiding Fields

If you are not using material resources in your project, you can hide the Material Label column or any other column by following these steps:

1. Select the Material Label column by clicking the Material Label header.

2. Right-click the selected column and choose Hide Column.

 TIP If you right-click directly on the column label, it selects the column and opens the shortcut menu in one step.

To display a column that is not currently displayed, follow these steps:

1. Select the column to the right of where you want the new column to be inserted.

2. Right-click the selected column and choose Insert Column.

3. Select the column you want to display from the Field Name List in the Column Definition dialog box.

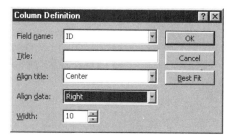

4. Enter the display name you want to use for the field in the Title field.

5. Set the alignment for the title in the field by choosing among Center, Right, or Left from the Align Title field.

6. Set the alignment for the data in the field by choosing among Center, Right, or Left from the Align Data field.

7. Adjust the field width by clicking the spin box arrows on the Width field.

8. Click the Best Fit button if you want Project to determine the best field width, based on the data in the field.

9. Click OK to insert the field.

For more about creating and customizing views, refer to Chapter 17, "Using Views to Evaluate Data."

Using the Resource Information Dialog Box

You can enter additional information about each resource by opening the Resource Information dialog box, shown in Figure 9.2. The dialog box consists of four tabs, described in Table 9.2, in which you can list more detailed data and include exception data, such as availability, about a resource.

PART

II

Creating a Project
from Start to Finish

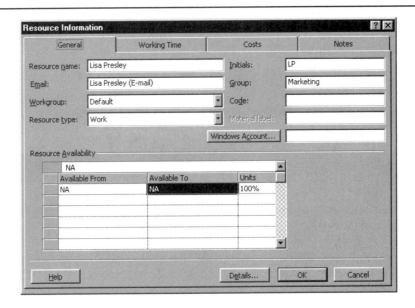

FIGURE 9.2

*The Resource Infor-
mation Dialog box
holds more detailed
information about a
resource.*

TABLE 9.2: RESOURCE INFORMATION DIALOG BOX TABS

Tab Name	Description
General	Basic information about the selected resource and the resource's availability.
Working Time	The active working time calendar for the resource.
Costs	Cost information about the selected resource.
Notes	Notes about the selected resource.

To open the Resource Information dialog box, double-click any resource, or select a resource in any resource view and click the Resource Information button on the Standard toolbar.

Reviewing and Entering General Information about a Resource

The data in the Resource Name, Initials, Group, Resource Type, and Code fields and the Material Label field for material resources are all entered from the Entry view of the Resource Sheet. You can make any desired changes to the data on the Resource Sheet or in the Resource Information dialog box. If you originally selected the resource from an Address book using the Assignment dialog box (see "Using the Assign Resources Dialog Box," earlier in this chapter), the resource's email address also appears here.

About Email Addresses in Project

Even if you don't enter a resource by selecting it from an Address Book, Project still recognizes any name that appears in your Outlook/Exchange Server Address lists. Project does not automatically enter the email address for you, but it will access Outlook contact information if you click the More Details button on the Resource Information dialog box, and it will appropriately address an email message to the resource if you use the Workgroup features. After you have sent a message to a resource using the Workgroup features, Project then adds the email address to the resource information.

Defining Workgroup Type   The Workgroup field on the General page of the Resource Information dialog box defines how you intend to communicate with the resources in the project. You have four choices to select from:

Default   refers to the default setting that governs the entire project.

None   means that this resource will not be involved in workgroup messaging.

Email   uses the default email system to send and receive workgroup messages. For more about using the email system, refer to Chapter 15, "Communicating Project Information."

 Web   uses Microsoft Project Central, Project 2000's new Web-based communication system. Project 2000 must be set up by a system administrator and has a number of other software and system requirements. Chapter 16, "Team Project Management with Project Central 2000," and Chapter 26, "Installing and Administering Project Central 2000," describe the process for installing and using Project Central.

Project automatically assigns the default workgroup type to every resource. Unless you or your system administrator have changed the default workgroup type, it is probably set to the Email option. To review or change the default workgroup setting:

1. Choose Tools ➢ Options.

2. Click the Workgroup tab.

3. Select Email, None, or Web from the Default Workgroup Messages drop-down list.

4. Click the Set as Default button to establish this option as the new default.

5. If you choose Web, enter the URL for the Microsoft Project Central server in the Microsoft Project Central Server URL field and then enter additional preferences for working with Project Central.

6. Click the Set as Default button on the bottom right to establish the Project Central preferences as the default.

7. Click OK to close the dialog box and save the changes.

Entering a Windows User Account   Project Central user accounts can be created from existing Windows NT accounts or as separate Project Central accounts, validated by Project Central. If you are using Microsoft Project Central as the primary workgroup communication method and the resource has an account on your NT network, you can enter the resource's Windows NT account name in the Windows Account field. If you need more information about this setting, see your Project Central administrator or Windows NT Network administrator.

 TIP To learn more about a specific option in any dialog box, click the question mark button in the upper-right corner of the dialog box. When the mouse pointer changes to a question mark, click the option for which you want information. A description of that option appears on the screen. For even more detailed information about each tab in the dialog box, click the Help button at the bottom of each tab.

Entering Resource Availability

The Resource Availability table on the General tab of the Resource Information dialog box can track the Available From date and the Available To date—a start and finish date—for a resource if it differs from the Project Start or Finish Date. By default, the Start and Finish date of the project is designated by *NA* in the Available From and Available To fields.

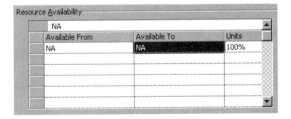

Leave NA in the field to indicate that the resource is available from the Start Date or until the Finish Date of the project. If the resource is available from the start of the project but not until the end, leave NA in the Available From field. If a resource can't start at the beginning of a project but is available to the end of the project after starting, leave NA in the Available To field. Enter specific dates that relate only to the resource, not to the proposed start or finish date for the project. This prevents problems from occurring if the project's start/finish date changes—the dates you entered would no longer correspond to the current start or finish date.

To enter specific dates that a resource is available, follow these steps:

1. Select the Available From field and choose a start date from the drop-down calendar if the resource's start date does not correspond to the project's start date.

2. Select the Available To field and choose an end date from the drop-down calendar if the resource's finish date does not correspond to the project's finish date.

3. Click to adjust the Max Units available to work on a project, if appropriate.

Contouring Resource Availability   With Project 2000, one resource can have several different availability periods during the course of a project and differing amounts of availability (Max Units) during each period. Let's say Lisa is a marketing person who is going to work on the project to help conduct the marketing analysis and prepare marketing materials. When you asked Lisa if she could work on the project, she told you that she has only two weeks of full-time availability at the start of the project and then she can only offer one day a week for the duration. You can enter Lisa's availability, as shown in Figure 9.3. Later, when you assign Lisa to tasks, Project calculates the schedule for the tasks assigned to her, based on her availability at the proposed start date for the task. If you schedule Lisa at 100% when she's only available 20% (one day a week), Project will indicate that Lisa is overallocated.

WARNING   Resource availability isn't related to a resource's rates of pay. If the rate of pay changes during different time periods, you must enter that information in the resource cost table. See "Entering Cost Information," later in this chapter.

FIGURE 9.3

You can contour resource availability in Project 2000 to show when a person is available to work on a project.

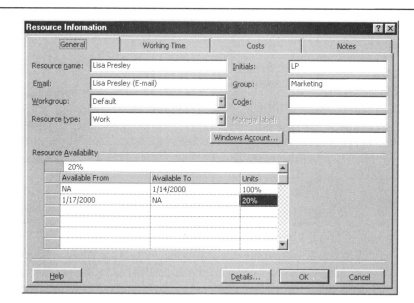

Changing the Working Time for a Resource

When you assign a resource to a task, Microsoft Project uses the resource calendar information to calculate the work for that resource. You must have an accurate working calendar in order for Project to accurately schedule work. When you create a resource, Project assigns the default working calendar to the resource. The Change Working Time dialog box is discussed in detail in "Defining the Project Calendar" in Chapter 6. In this section, we'll review some of the basics and discuss how to make changes to the working calendar for a specific resource.

 NOTE Material resources do not use resource calendars.

You can customize the working calendar for a specific resource on the Working Time tab of the Resource Information dialog box, shown in Figure 9.4, or by selecting the resource in any resource view and choosing Tools ➤ Change Working Time.

If you open the Working Time calendar from the Resource Information dialog box, you have access only to the calendar for the specific resource that you have open. You can make changes to the resource calendar and you can assign a different base calendar to the resource, but you cannot make any changes to the base calendar.

FIGURE 9.4

On the Working Time tab of the Resource Information dialog box, you can make changes to the working time for a specific resource.

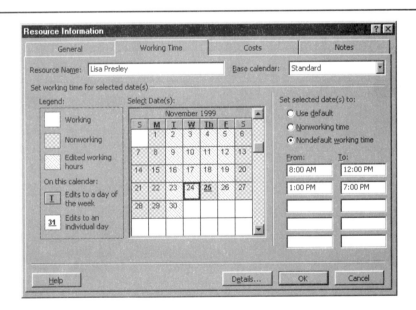

When you open the calendar from the Tools menu, you have access to all the base and resource calendars. Select the calendar you are interested in reviewing from the For drop-down list. Table 9.3 describes where to access a calendar to make changes to it.

TABLE 9.3: CHANGE THE WORKING TIMES

If you want to:	Open the Change Working Time dialog box from:
Edit a base calendar	The Tools ➤ Change Working Times menu option. Select the calendar you want to edit from the For drop-down list.
Assign a base calendar other than the project calendar to a resource	The Resource Information dialog box—switch to a resource view and double-click the resource. Click the Working Time tab.
Edit a resource calendar	The Tools ➤ Change Working Times menu option. Select the calendar you want to edit from the For drop-down list or the Resource Information dialog box—switch to a resource view and double-click the resource. Click the Working Time tab.
Create a new base calendar	The Tools ➤ Change Working Times menu option—click the New button.

 TIP You can distinguish a resource calendar from a base calendar because a resource calendar has the same name as the resource itself.

As a review of the information from Chapter 6, Microsoft Project includes three base calendars:

Standard   Base calendar, shown in Figure 9.5, has a standard work day and work week of Monday through Friday, 8:00 a.m. to 5:00 p.m., with a break from 12:00 p.m. to 1:00 p.m.

PART

II

Creating a Project
from Start to Finish

FIGURE 9.5

The Standard base calendar is a 40-hour work week from 8-5, Monday through Friday.

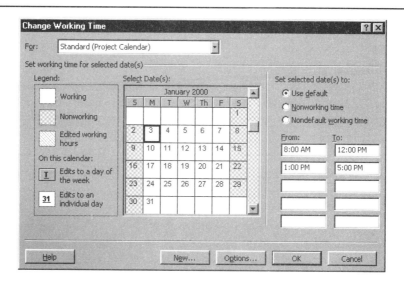

24 Hours Base calendar, shown in Figure 9.6, runs around the clock from Sunday through Saturday, 12:00 a.m. to 12:00 p.m. This calendar is typically assigned to non-human resources such as a press that runs 24 hours a day, or to a resource group such as Security that covers 24 hours a day, 7 days a week.

FIGURE 9.6

The 24 Hours base calendar runs around the clock with no time off.

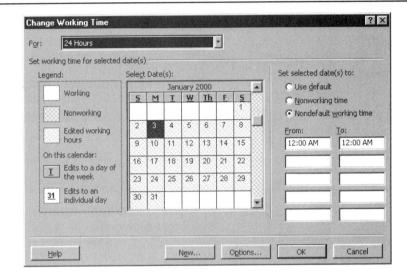

Night Shift Base calendar, shown in Figure 9.7, includes working times from Monday night through Saturday morning, 11:00 p.m. to 8:00 a.m., with a break from 3:00 a.m. to 4:00 a.m.

FIGURE 9.7

The Night-Shift base calendar covers the midnight shift.

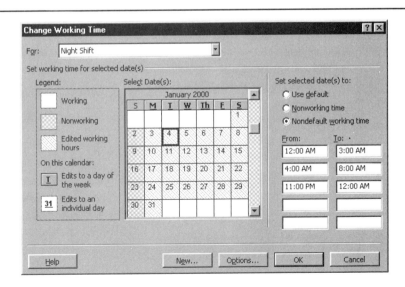

The base calendar that is set as the project default in the Project Information dialog box, (Project ➤ Project Information), shown in Figure 9.8, is designated as the default calendar.

FIGURE 9.8

*Set the default calen-
dar for the project in
the Project Information
dialog box.*

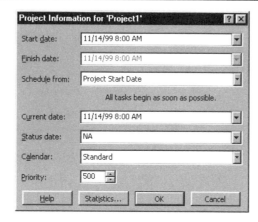

Make any changes that affect multiple resources in the default project base calendar before editing the calendar for individual resources. Refer to Chapter 6 for more about making changes to the base calendar and creating custom calendars.

 TIP If you make changes to the project calendar that affect the number of working hours per day, hours per week, or days per month, you need to manually change the settings on the Calendar tab of the Options dialog box (see "Changing the Default Calendar Options," in Chapter 6). The Working Times calendars control when work is scheduled but the Calendar tab settings affect the way Project converts task durations into work. Chapter 10 discusses in detail how project schedules work.

Setting Work Times for Resources   Whether you access a resource's calendar from the Tools menu or from the Resource Information dialog box, you can use the resource's calendar to enter specific working and nonworking times for the resource. Because it is based on a base calendar, the resource calendar shares the times reflected there. However, the resource may have different work hours, planned days off, or limited availability during the project schedule. Although you can adjust for a resource who is not available on a full-time basis through the assignment of Max Units, you can also adjust their calendar to reflect the available hours and leave the Max Units at 100% (100% of the total available hours reflected in the resource's calendar).

Assigning Calendars to Resources   If you want to assign a different base calendar (for example, the Night Shift calendar) to a resource, open the Resource Information dialog box and click the Working Time tab. Select a new calendar from the Base calendar drop-down list, shown in Figure 9.9.

FIGURE 9.9

Assign a new base calendar to a resource from the Base calendar drop-down list.

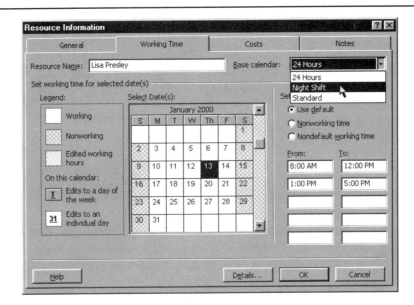

The resource now inherits all of the characteristics of the new base calendar; that is, working and nonworking time, including specified days off.

Making Changes to the Resource Calendar   To change the working times for any of the dates, you must first select the dates you want to change. Table 9.4 reviews the methods for selecting dates.

TABLE 9.4: SELECTING DATES IN THE WORKING TIME CALENDAR

To Select:	Action
A single date	Click the date.
Multiple dates	Hold Ctrl and click each date.
Consecutive dates	Click the first date and hold the Shift key before clicking the last date in the sequence.
Day of the week	Click the column header for that day.
Multiple days of the week	Hold Ctrl and click the column headers or drag across column headers to select consecutive days.

To change a date to a nonworking date, select the date and click the Nonworking Time option.

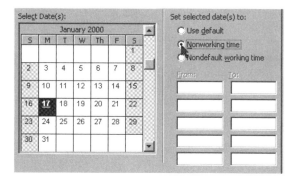

Project shades the date in the Calendar and underlines it to indicate that it deviates from the default calendar.

To change the working hours of a day of the week (for example, all Fridays), select the day by clicking the Day header to select the entire column and click the Nondefault working time option. Enter the scheduled working time in the From and To fields, as shown in Figure 9.10. Pressing Tab to move between the To and From fields automatically selects the contents.

 TIP If times are already entered in the To and From boxes, you can select them by pointing to the left edge of the box and clicking when the pointer changes to a right-pointed arrow.

FIGURE 9.10

To change working time from the default, after selecting the days by clicking and then dragging the day header, click the Nondefault Working Time option and enter the new times.

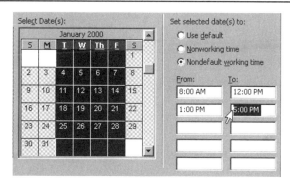

When you have entered new times, Project designates the edited working hours by a lightly shaded pattern.

 TIP To enter a work shift that extends beyond midnight, you must enter the time up to midnight (that is, 11 p.m. to 12 a.m.) on one day and the time after midnight on the next day (12 a.m. to 7 a.m.).

If you want to change any of the calendar dates back to the default working times, select the dates and choose the Use Default option in the Change Working Time dialog box.

 WARNING The Use Default option changes a particular date back to the default for that weekday. If you change the default for that weekday, clicking Use Default changes the day back to the new default, not to the original default for that day. To change an entire weekday back to the original default, select the day column and choose Use Default.

Entering Cost Information

Although Microsoft is very clear about the fact that Project 2000 is not a cost-accounting system, you can still assign and track costs to make projections about project costs and monitor a project's budget. (These are managerial accounting rather than cost accounting functions, after all.) On the Costs tab of the Resource Information dialog box, shown in Figure 9.11, you can record up to five different rates for a selected resource that you can then assign to different tasks. For example, if you have a resource called Technical Writers and the three writers you use have different rates, you can enter each rate separately and still maintain and assign Technical Writers as one resource.

In addition to entering separate rate schedules, you can enter up to twenty-five changes from the established rate in each schedule to account for price changes in material resources and pay-rate changes in work resources. Each of these rates includes an Effective Date, a Standard Rate, an Overtime Rate, and a Per Use Cost.

To enter costs for a resource, follow these steps:

1. Open the Resource Information dialog box and click the Costs tab.

2. If the Effective Date of the cost is the same as the project start date, do not enter an effective date. Otherwise, in Table A, type in a date or click the drop-down arrow in the field and select a date from the calendar.

3. Enter the Standard Rate. For work resources, Project assumes $ per hour ($45.00/h). Type in /**y** for year, /**m** for month and /**d** for day if you want to enter a different type of rate. Material resources use the Material Label you assigned the resource on the General tab in the Material Label field. For example, if you enter **$3** and the Material Label is boxes, the Standard rate would be interpreted as $3 per box ($3/box).

4. Enter the Overtime Rate for work resources, even if the Overtime Rate is the same as the Standard Rate. If a work resource works overtime hours, any additional hours are charged at this rate.

5. Enter any additional Per Use Costs for a resource. For example, include costs for delivery or shipping and handling of material resources, or mileage fees for consultants.

6. If you know when rate increases or decreases will occur, click in the second row, and type in or select an effective date.

7. Enter a Standard Rate or enter a percentage increase or decrease from the rate in the first row. For example, enter **+10%** in the Standard Rate cell.

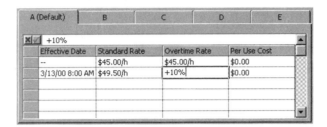

8. Enter the new Overtime Rate and the Per Use Cost.

9. If you want to enter a second rate table, click the B tab and repeat Steps 2-8. Repeat these steps as necessary for tabs C, D, and E.

Assigning a Cost-Accrual Method   The *cost-accrual method* is the way the costs will be paid out once the project starts. You have three accrual choices:

Prorated   is the default choice; it attributes costs to the project as the resources are used.

Start   is the choice you want to make if the costs are due at the beginning of the project.

End   is appropriate if the costs are due as the project is completed.

Because cost accrual cannot be assigned to individual rate tables, you must create a separate resource if the resources within a group have different accrual methods. For example, let's say you have a resource called Conference Rooms that you rent when you need to hold a large meeting. One conference room is owned by a facility that accepts a purchase order for you for payment, whereas another requires payment up front. You would need to list these facilities as separate resources, so you could list the first one with an End accrual method and the second one with a Start accrual method.

To assign a cost-accrual method to the costs, select your choice from the Cost Accrual drop-down list on the Costs tab of the Resource Information dialog box.

Handling Costs That Don't Fit   For many projects in which you are using outside consultants to complete all or part of the project, you may be obligated to pay them upon completing a specific task, reaching a milestone, or beginning work on a subproject. This type of cost arrangement does not lend itself to assigning costs directly to resources. In these cases, you can get a more accurate picture of a project's costs and cash flows by assigning fixed costs to specific tasks in the project. If some of the resources for a project work on a fixed rather than an hourly basis, don't assign costs to those resources. Assign fixed costs directly to the fixed-cost tasks. For more information about assigning fixed costs, see "Entering Fixed Costs," later in this chapter.

Adding Notes about Resources

You can add any additional information you want to store about a resource on the Notes tab of the Resource Information dialog box, shown in Figure 9.12.

FIGURE 9.12

You can enter notes and attach documents on the Notes tab.

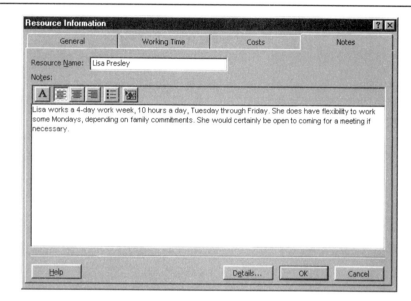

On the Notes tab, you can do the following:

- Enter new notes about a resource
- Revise or add to existing notes
- Format notes
- Insert objects into a note

Table 9.5 provides an overview of the Notes toolbar.

TABLE 9.5: NOTES TAB TOOLBAR OPTIONS

Button	Button Name	Description
A	Format Font	Opens the Font dialog box to change font, font size, font style, underline, color, and script.
≣	Align Left	Aligns paragraphs on the left.
≣	Center	Centers paragraphs.

Continued ▶

PART

II

Creating a Project
from Start to Finish

TABLE 9.5 CONTINUED: NOTES TAB TOOLBAR OPTIONS

Button	Button Name	Description
≣	Align Right	Aligns paragraphs on the right.
≔	Bulleted List	Inserts a bullet and a tab. Bullets stay on until you click the Bulleted List button or press Enter twice.
🖼	Insert Object	Inserts an object created in another application, such as a Word document, an Excel workbook, a graphic, or other object.

Inserting Objects into Notes   When you insert objects into notes, you can insert the contents of the document, as shown in Figure 9.13, or you can include an icon that represents the document.

99 attendence.xls

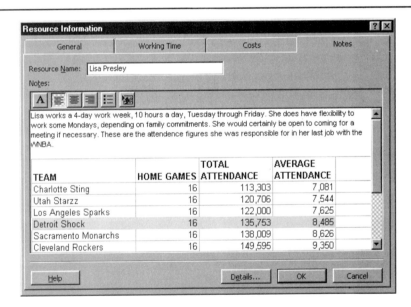

Whether you insert the object as an icon or insert the entire object, you can link the object to the original by clicking Create from File and selecting the Link checkbox on the Insert Object dialog box, shown in Figure 9.14. Any changes made to the original object are immediately reflected in the linked object, as long as the original object and the project continue to be stored in the same file locations.

FIGURE 9.14

You can link an object to its source by select-ing the Link checkbox.

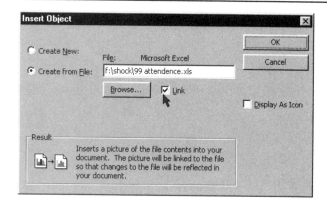

To insert an object into a note, follow these steps:

1. Click the Insert Object button on the Notes tab of the Resource Information dia-log box. It may take a few seconds for the Insert Object dialog box to open.

2. Choose Create New if you want to create a new object from one of the applica-tions listed in the Object Type list, or select Create From File if you want to attach an existing object.

3. If you chose Create New in Step 2, Project launches the application. Create the object and close the application. Project inserts the new object into the Notes tab.

4. If you chose Create From File in Step 2, enter the complete file path or click the Browse button to locate the object file. When you find it, select it and click OK. Project enters the file name in the File box.

5. Choose whether you want to link the file to the original object by clicking the Link checkbox.

6. Click the Display as Icon checkbox if you want to insert an icon and not display the entire document. If you choose this option, you can change the icon by clicking the Change Icon button.

7. Click OK to insert the object.

 NOTE If you do not link the object and choose the Display as Icon option, Project dis-plays the object's type as the name of the icon (for example, Spreadsheet) rather than the actual file name (99 Attendence.xls).

You have now completed entering all of the information in the Resource Informa-tion dialog box. Click OK to close the dialog box.

Much of the information you entered in the Resource Information dialog box is available in the Resource Sheet view. If you added a note to a resource, a Note icon appears in the Indicators column of the Resource Sheet, as you can see in Figure 9.15. Point to the icon to see all or part of the note, or double-click the Notes icon to read the entire note.

FIGURE 9.15

Point to the Notes icon in the Indicators column to read all or part of a note.

	ⓘ	Resource Name	Type	Material Label	Initials	Group	Max. Units	Std. Rate	Ovt. Rate
1		Rianne Anderson	Work		R		100%	$0.00/hr	$0.00/hr
2		Karla Browning	Work		KB	Sales	100%	$45.00/hr	$45.00/hr
3		Amy Courter	Work		AC	Management	100%	$150.00/hr	$150.00/hr
4		Charlotte Cowtan	Work		CC	Management	100%	$150.00/hr	$150.00/hr
5		James Howe	Work		JH	Technical	100%	$45.00/hr	$45.00/hr
6		Angie Okonski	Work		AO	Facilities	100%	$45.00/hr	$45.00/hr
7		Lisa Presley	Work		LP	Marketing	100%	$45.00/hr	$45.00/hr
8					SR	Sales	100%	$45.00/hr	$45.00/hr
9					LW	Facilities	100%	$45.00/hr	$45.00/hr
10				Boxes	Paper	Marketing		$47.95	
11				Items	Box	Sales		$3.25	
12				Items	Comp	Sales		$1,799.00	
13				Items	Print	Sales		$357.00	
14		Telephone System	Material	Items	Tele	Sales		$12,352.00	
15		Desks	Material	Items	Desk	Sales		$835.00	
16		Desk Chairs	Material	Items	DC	Sales		$325.00	
17		Side Chairs	Material	Items	SC	Sales		$175.00	
18		Art work	Material	Items	AW	Sales		$99.00	
19		Carpeting	Material	Sq. Yds	Carp	Facilities		$12.35	
20		Filing Cabinets	Material	Items	FC	Sales		$357.00	

Notes: 'Lisa works a 4-day work week, 10 hours a day, Tuesday through Friday. She does have flexibility to work some Mondays, depending on family commitments. She would certainly be open to coming for a meeting if necessary. These are the attendence figures she w...'

Adding Resources Using Resource Pools

In addition to creating resources for each individual project, Project includes two other methods for using resources:

- Share resources being used in another project.
- Use resources from a resource pool.

Both of these options allow you to create resources once and use them again. In both cases, you are sharing resources. The only difference is whether you are sharing resources with another active project or creating a separate *resource pool*. A resource pool is a project file created solely for the purpose of storing resource information that is shared among multiple projects. Creating a resource pool is generally the preferred method of sharing resources because it makes it easier to manage task assignments between the resources shared in the pool.

For more about resource pools, see "Creating and Using a Resource Pool" in Chapter 14, "Sharing Resources and Tasks among Multiple Projects."

Adding Resources Automatically

When you begin assigning resources to tasks, as you'll do in Chapter 10, you can create resources as you assign them. Any name you enter in the Resource Name field is automatically added to the Resource list. This is an option that you can disable if you prefer. If you enter a resource into the Gantt Chart or other task view, you are warned that this resource is not in the pool and you are given the option to add it.

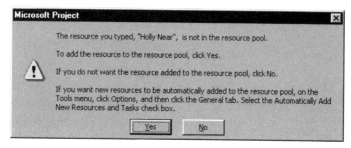

Disabling this option provides protection against inadvertently adding a variation of a resource's name that is already in the pool—Pat Summitt, rather than Patricia Summitt, for example.

Entering Additional Cost Information

In addition to costs related directly to resources, you can plan and track a number of other costs associated with a project. Project supports both fixed and variable costs, which can be related to resources, tasks, and even to entire projects.

Creating cost estimates in a vacuum can be difficult, so it may be helpful to review previous projects' files to which you have access to see how actual costs broke out. In fact, you can even import cost information from other projects and programs into your project.

 NOTE To learn how to import information into a Project file, see Chapter 19, "Importing and Exporting Project Data."

Earlier in this chapter, we discussed how to enter rates and per-use costs for resources. Hourly costs, overtime costs, and per-use costs of work resources and materials assigned to tasks account for all the variable costs you can track in Project.

 TIP Use the Notes tabs of the Resource Information and the Task Information dialog boxes to record information about cost components.

Entering Fixed Costs

A *fixed cost* is a cost that does not change over the life of the project: the cost of a telephone installation, the cost for the movers, work done on a contract basis, or printing costs, for example. You can enter a fixed cost associated with a specific task or summary task in the Fixed Cost column of the Cost Table, shown in Figure 9.16. To display the Cost Table, choose View ➢ Table ➢ Cost. To display additional Cost table fields, such as Fixed Cost Accrual and Total Cost, drag the vertical split bar to the right.

Select a cell and enter the amount of the fixed cost. In the Fixed Cost Accrual column, indicate how the cost should accrue: at the Start, Prorated (over the course of the task), or at the End of the task.

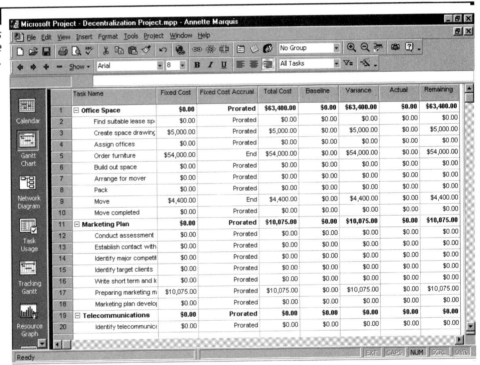

FIGURE 9.16

The Cost Table shows fixed and variable costs for each task.

Understanding Total Costs

When you enter a fixed cost, the Total Cost column changes to include the new cost. The Total Cost column represents the total of standard pay, overtime pay, per-use resource costs, plus fixed costs associated with a task. The Total Cost is calculated based on the actual work completed on the project, the planned work yet to be completed, and the amount of fixed costs. The formula for Total Cost is Actual Cost + Remaining Cost + Fixed Cost. See Chapter 12, "Tracking Project Progress," to see how to use Project to analyze cost variance.

TIP If you want to enter fixed costs for the entire project, display the Project Summary Task. Choose Tools ➤ Options from the menu to display the Options dialog box. Click the View tab. Enable the Project summary task check box, and then click OK. The project summary task is displayed as the first task in the table.

Viewing and Printing Resources and Costs

If you want to print the Resource sheet or the Cost table, set up the Project window to display what you want to print. Project operates on a what-you-see-is-what-you-get approach when it comes to printing. If you want to print the Resource sheet, switch to Resource sheet view before you print. If you want to print the Cost table, switch to the Gantt Chart and open the Cost table. You may want to drag the vertical split bar off to the right to hide the chart and display only the Cost table, as shown in Figure 9.17.

FIGURE 9.17

Drag the vertical split bar off to the right to hide the chart in Gantt Chart view before printing.

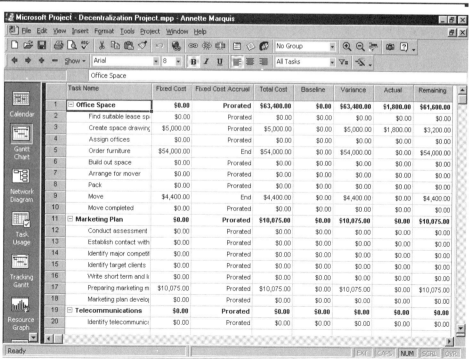

When you have the Project window set up the way you want it, choose File ➤ Print Preview to see how the document looks. If you are satisfied, click Print on the Print Preview toolbar.

If you want to make page setup changes such as changing page orientation and margins, click the Page Setup button on the Print Preview toolbar, or choose File ➤ Page Setup. For more about Page Setup options, see "Printing in Project" in Chapter 5, "Working in Project 2000."

 TIP To include resource notes when you print a resource view, such as the Resource Sheet view, on the File menu, click Page Setup, and then click the View tab. Select the Print Notes check box.

What's Next

Defining resources and costs is the all-important precursor to actually assigning those resources and costs to tasks in the project. You are ready to head into the most critical operation in Project: creating a project schedule based on resources assigned to the project's tasks. It's this scheduling feature that makes Project more than a spiffy Gantt Chart creation tool, and Chapter 10 will help to demystify Project's incredibly sophisticated scheduling engine.

CHAPTER **10**

Assigning and Scheduling Resources and Costs

Assigning resources in Project 2000 does more than add tasks to a lot of peoples' to-do lists. Assigned resources and the sequence and links between project tasks combine to form the project schedule. In this chapter, we'll work with assignments, tasks, and resources to create a schedule that correctly reflects the nature of the work being done in the project before the project starts and as it progresses through the project development.

Working with Duration, Work, and Units

The relationship between time, scope, and cost is called the project triangle. The relationship between *duration*, *work*, and *units* can aptly be described as Project's Bermuda Triangle. Plenty of project managers enter this part of Project and are never heard from or seen again. When we interviewed project managers who had given up on previous versions of Project, a common theme emerged: they had no trouble building their project file until they started assigning resources to tasks and changing resource assignments during the course of the project. Difficulties with setting task type and resource assignment mushroomed when project development started and task durations or work changed in what seemed to be unpredictable ways.

 NOTE Some of these people are still using Project to create stunning Gantt Charts, so they haven't totally abandoned the software. They're just not using it for management, which is where Project can be most helpful.

In this section, we'll demystify duration, work, and units by examining how and when Project calculates each of the three values. When you understand how Project calculates and recalculates, you can set task types and assign resources confidently, knowing that Project will behave as you intend it to as you move into project implementation.

Project 2000 uses the same calculation methods as earlier versions of Project. If you're an experienced Microsoft Project user and understand task types and effort-driven scheduling, you can skim or skip this section. But if you're new to Microsoft Project, or if you're one of the many project managers who've been lost in the Bermuda Triangle, read on. We wrote this section for you.

There are three tables of data used in Project 2000: tasks, resources, and assignments (relationships between tasks and resources). When you assign resources to tasks, Project takes the task's duration (which may be an estimated duration) and multiplies it by the specific percentage or number of units of the resource to arrive at the hours of work that will be done in the task.

NOTE Later in this chapter, you'll see how to change a task's settings so that Project will calculate duration from work and units, or units from duration and work when you assign resources.

The relationship between duration, units, and work is an assignment version of the project triangle, as shown in Figure 10.1.

- *Work* is the assignment version of project *scope*. Work defines what will be accomplished in the assignment: sixteen hours of painting, four hours of shipping, five days of training, and so on.

- Assigning *units* of employees or machinery to a task incurs *cost*.

- *Duration* is time on the project *timeline*: nothing more, nothing less.

The terms are different, but the concept is the same. Just as a change in scope after the project is underway requires the project manager to adjust the budget or timeline, a change in work forces Project 2000 to recalculate units or duration.

FIGURE 10.1

The assignment triangle is a micro version of the project triangle.

Scope

Project

Budget   Timeline

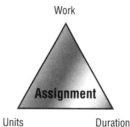

Work

Assignment

Units   Duration

Duration is chronological: the amount of calendar or clock time that will pass between the beginning and end of the task. Changes in duration affect the schedule. If a task's duration is supposed to be one day and it takes three, dependent tasks will have to start two days later than scheduled.

Three people start on a Web design task at the beginning of the day. One person leaves halfway through the day, but is replaced by another person. The task is completed it at the end of the eight-hour workday. The task's duration *is one day.* Work *is the number of person-hours or machine-hours spent on a task.*

The three people work *a total of twenty four hours in their eight-hour day.*

Units are the resources committed to the task and are usually expressed as a percentage (although you can change this setting to use numbers).

The task "used" 100% of two resource units, Amy and Ben, (or 200%) and 50% of two resource units, Carol and Dennis, (100%), for total Web design resource units of 300%. Here's what this task looks like in the Gantt Chart's Entry table:

TIP Don't be distracted by the fact that there are four different individuals assigned to this task. The four people are the equivalent of three resource units assigned 100% of the time.

Duration, work, and units are interdependent, because work is duration multiplied by units: $W=D*U$. If the two part-time workers hadn't been assigned to the task (leaving only 200% *units*), one of two things would have to be different:

- The task *duration* would be longer (2 days rather than 1).

  OR

- Less *work* would be invested in the completed Web design (16 hours rather than 24).

If the total hours of Web design *work* required were 48 hours instead of 24, either of the following would happen:

- It would take 2 days (*duration*) to finish the design.

  OR

- 6 *units* would be assigned to finish the task in one day.

If we had to get the job done in half the time (*duration* of a half day), either of the following would happen:

- Less *work* would be done.

  OR

- The *units* would be increased to 600%.

It isn't always possible to complete a task with less work, to assign more units, or to spend more days or hours completing the task. In just a few pages, you'll see how to change task settings to let Project know which values to calculate and which to leave alone. But first, we'll see how work, duration, and resource units interact when you make an assignment with Project 2000's default task settings.

If you want to see work, duration, and resources in one view, there are two ways to do it: with the Task Form or by inserting columns in a view. Like the Task Information dialog box, the Task Form displays information about one task, as shown in Figure 10.2.

FIGURE 10.2

The Task Form shows information about one task.

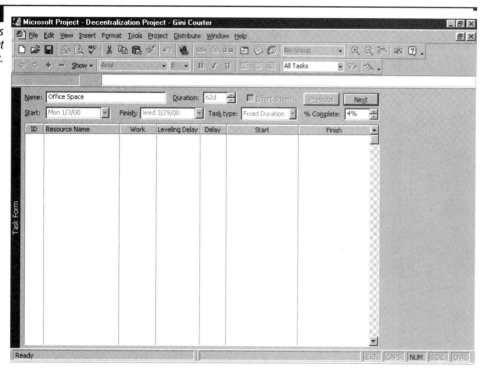

The Task Form can be displayed along with a view such as the Gantt Chart view, and is the best place to set complex assignment information like resource delay. It's also the view many project managers choose when they change task settings as they assign resources to tasks. We'll return to the Task Form later in this chapter when we need that level of detail. For simple resource assignment, however, we find that it is a lot easier to see how Project 2000 calculates work when we use the familiar Gantt Chart view with an Entry table, modified to include a Work column. With the addition of the Assign Resource dialog box, we can see resources, duration, and work. Our Project workspace looks like Figure 10.3 when we're getting ready to assign resources.

PART

II

Creating a Project
from Start to Finish

With the Assign Resources dialog box and Work column displayed, the Gantt Chart view provides the information needed for resource assignment.

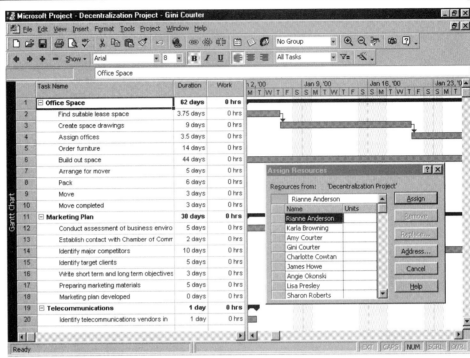

To set up the Project 2000 workspace, as shown in Figure 10.3, follow these steps:

1. Choose View ➤ Gantt Chart to display the Gantt Chart.

2. Choose Views ➤ Table ➤ Entry to display the Entry table in the Tasks area.

3. Adjust the vertical split bar to display the Duration and Start Date columns.

4. Right-click on the Duration column and choose Insert Column from the shortcut menu.

This opens the Column Definition dialog box.

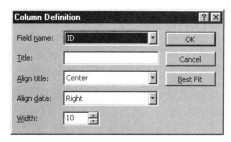

5. Select Work from the Field Name drop-down list, and then click OK.

6. Click the Assign Resources button on the standard toolbar, or choose Tools ➢ Resources ➢ Assign Resources from the menu to display the Assign Resources dialog box.

To examine the way Project calculates duration, work, or units when you assign resources, we created a small project file. Our project has ten tasks with two-day durations (Task 1, Task 2, etc.) and five resources: Amy, Ben, Carol, and Dennis, who have specialized roles; and a pool of non-specialized workers, as shown in Figure 10.4. Each task has an estimated duration, but both work and units (resources) are zero because no resources have been assigned. If you take a couple of minutes and create this simple project, you can play along. (Just sit the book down. We'll wait.)

PART

II

Creating a Project
from Start to Finish

FIGURE 10.4

A simple project with ten tasks and five resources

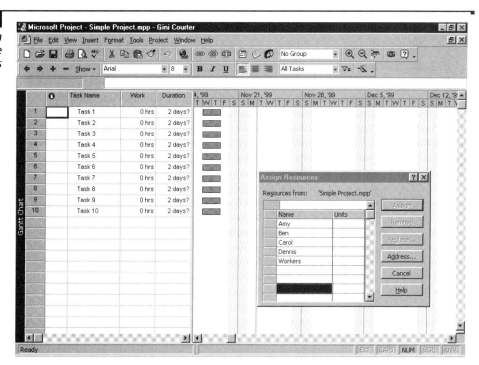

We'll add one resource, Amy, to Task 1 by selecting Task 1 in the Entry table, and then selecting Amy in the Assign Resources dialog box and clicking the Assign button. Project does four things when we make this assignment:

- In the Assign Resources dialog box, Amy's units are set to 100% (100% is Project's default for a resource).

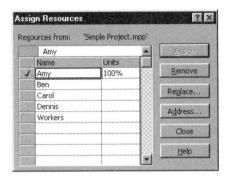

- The task's FinishDate is calculated and used to draw the task bar in the Gantt Chart.

- In the Gantt Chart, Amy's name is added to the task bar.

- In the Work column of the Entry table, work is calculated at 16 hours:

For calculation purposes in Project, a day is 8 hours (unless you previously changed the Hours Per Day Calendar option). If Amy spends 100% of her time for two days working on Task 1, she'll be working 16 hours: 1 unit × 2 days × 8 hours per day = 16 hours of work.

To assign a resource to a task:

1. Open the Gantt Chart (View ➤ Gantt Chart) and Assign Resource dialog box (click the Assign Resources toolbar button).

2. In the Entry table, select the task (or tasks) for which you want to make the assignment.

3. In the Assign Resources dialog box, select the resource (or resources) you want to assign.

4. Click the Assign button.

Now, assign two resources, Ben and Carol, to Task 2. Project calculates that two people assigned for two days will complete 32 hours of work (2 units × 2 days × 8 hours per day):

Using Project to Calculate Required Resources

In Tasks 1 and 2, we knew how many people we could assign (units) and the number of days we could assign them (duration). Project calculated the remaining variable, work, by multiplying units by duration.

Task 3 is different. This task includes 64 hours of work that need to be completed. We don't want Project to calculate work as it did in the first two tasks: we know how much work needs to be done. We need to know how many resources are required or how long the task will take with the resources we assign.

When you enter a value for work before assigning resources, Project calculates the units required to complete the work within the duration:

When we select the Workers resource and click the Assign button, Project divides the work (64 hours) by the duration (2 days), and determines that 4 units of resource (400%) are required to complete the work within the duration:

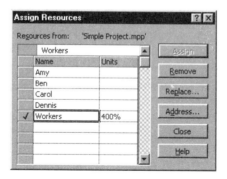

What if we have only three workers available for Task 3? If we reduce the Units available to 300% by using the spin box control or typing a new percentage in the Units field of the Assign Resources dialog box, Project adjusts the task duration rather than the work. The Resource Name at the right end of the task's Gantt Chart bar now reads [300%]. The three workers can complete Task 3, but it will take them more time:

	Task Name	Work	Duration	4, '99 T W T F S S	Nov 21, '99 M T W T F
	Task 1	16 hrs	2 days?		Amy
	Task 2	32 hrs	2 days?		Ben,Carol
	Task 3	64 hrs	2.67 days?		Workers[300%]

 NOTE A resource can be assigned to a task only once. To assign more than one generic resource (worker, painter, production, etc.) assign a larger percentage of the resource: 300% painter for three full-time painters.

Adjusting Assignments

When we changed the resources from 400% to 300% for Task 3, Project didn't calculate work. Instead, it changed duration. When you change the units assigned to a task, Project recalculates duration or work. To determine which of the two values should be recalculated. A task setting determines which value Project will change.

The default setting for tasks is that they are *effort-driven*. With effort-driven tasks, the task's duration is completely dependent on the resources you assign to the task. If you add or remove resources after the initial assignment, Project will recalculate duration, but leave work alone:

- If you add resources, Project decreases duration.
- If you remove resources, Project increases duration.

Adjustments to duration when resources are added or removed are the result of effort-driven scheduling. You can see how Project implements effort-driven scheduling if you assign a resource, and then add another resource to the same task. In Task 4, we'll start by assigning one unit of resource. As with Task 1, Project calculates work at sixteen hours for the two-day duration:

	Task Name	Work	Duration	4, '99 T W T F S S	Nov 21, '99 M T W T F
	Task 1	16 hrs	2 days?		Amy
	Task 2	32 hrs	2 days?		Ben,Carol
	Task 3	64 hrs	2.67 days?		Workers[300%]
	Task 4	16 hrs	2 days?		Amy

In the normal course of events from this point forward, adding or subtracting resources affects only duration because the task's default effort-driven setting forces Project to calculate duration rather than work. To see the recalculation in action, return to the Assign Resources dialog box and add another resource. Project adjusts duration: the two people now assigned can complete the 16 hours of work in 1 day rather than 2:

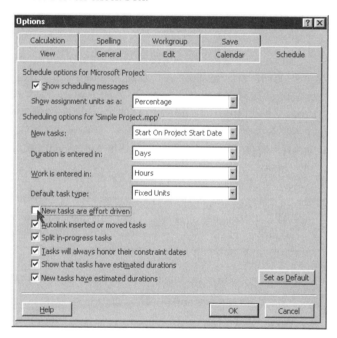

Effort-driven scheduling is the default because in many projects, the bulk of the tasks are effort-driven. Adding resources gets the task completed more quickly. If your project is composed mostly of tasks that are not effort-driven, you'll want to change this default. To change the default for new tasks created in your project file, choose Tools ➤ Options to open the Options dialog box. On the Schedule tab, turn off the New Tasks are Effort Driven check box:

You'll find out how to change the effort-driven setting for existing tasks in the next section.

Changing Task Settings to Change the Way Project Recalculates

A change in work, units, or duration always affects one of the other two variables of the assignment. For tasks created using the default task settings, after the initial assignment,

Project recalculates duration rather than work and work rather than units. There's only one problem with this recalculation paradigm, and at first glance, it's a big one: this isn't necessarily how you want Project to adjust the assignment (and ultimately the budget and schedule) when work, duration, or units change. For some tasks, adjusting duration or work isn't appropriate.

As the project moves into development, you'll do your job as a project manager by adjusting resources, work, and duration. These are typical project management tasks:

- Moving resources from a less-critical task to a more-critical task

- Adding resources to complete a task more quickly

- Changing the amount of work required to complete a task satisfactorily, based on information from team members

- Adjusting the start or finish date for a task to keep the project on schedule

Each time you edit one of the three variables in the assignment triangle, Project will recalculate one of the two remaining variables. To control which of the values is recalculated, you change the task's task type and effort-driven settings.

There are three *task types*—fixed units, fixed work, and fixed duration—that determine which variables Project calculates when you assign resources. The variable you set as fixed is the variable Project will not change. The task types, combined with effort-driven scheduling, determine the variables that Project recalculates when resources are added or removed, or which units, work, or resource variables are edited. By selecting a task type and effort-driven setting, you set Project's calculation method for the selected task.

 NOTE Duration recalculation is limited by task constraints. See Chapter 8, "Scheduling and Linking Project Tasks," for information on constraining tasks.

There are five unique task type/effort-driven combinations:

- fixed-unit, effort-driven (the default setting)

- fixed-unit

- fixed-work, effort-driven

- fixed-duration

- fixed-duration, effort-driven

Fixed means that Project won't recalculate the field's value when values change in either of the other variables. It doesn't mean that the value *can't* change: the project manager can and often will edit the value. Fixed-work tasks are effort-driven. If you select Fixed Work as the task type, Project automatically turns on the effort-driven setting and locks it so you can't change it.

 TIP For each task, you set the task type based on the variable that is constant or that you want to control as the project manager. You choose the effort-driven setting, based on the nature of the task. If adding more units reduces the number of days or hours from the start of the task until completion, then the task is effort-driven. If adding resources doesn't affect duration, the task is not effort-driven.

You change a task's task type and effort-driven setting on the Advanced tab of the Task Information dialog box, shown in Figure 10.5.

FIGURE 10.5

Open the Task Information dialog box to change task type or effort-driven status.

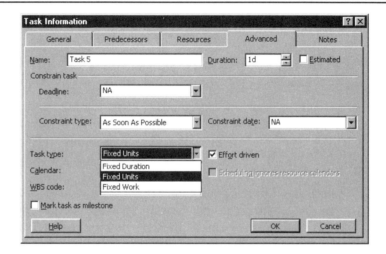

PART

II

Creating a Project from Start to Finish

Each combination is explained in detail in this section.

Fixed-Unit Tasks

With a *fixed-unit* task, the first time you assign resources, Project calculates the amount of work that the resources can do by multiplying duration by units. After the initial assignment, Project holds units constant and adjusts duration when either work or units change. If the duration changes, Project recalculates work. As the project progresses, you'll manage slipping fixed-unit tasks by increasing the units assigned to the task to accomplish the task more quickly.

In a fixed-unit task:

- If you add or remove units, Project recalculates work.
- If you change the percentage of a resource assignment, Project recalculates duration.
- If you adjust duration, Project recalculates work.
- If you change work, Project recalculates duration.

Here is an example of a fixed-unit task. Refer to the previous list to see how Project would handle the task described in the example:

- You assign two gardeners to spend three days restoring the perennial gardens outside the new office building. If you add three more gardeners, more work will be completed in the same three days. If you assign the original two gardeners for six days rather than three, they'll do twice as much work. If you tell the gardeners to do 100 hours of work, it will take them more than twice as long.

For this type of task, change the task's type to fixed unit, turn off effort-driven, and Project will recalculate work and duration, but will not recalculate units:

Fixed-Unit, Effort-Driven Tasks   Project's default task type is both *fixed unit* and *effort driven*. With effort-driven tasks, Project recalculates duration when you add or remove resources to a task. With fixed-unit tasks, Project doesn't recalculate units. With fixed unit, effort-driven tasks, then, there's only one thing left to change—duration. Every change in units assigned or work required affects the schedule. You manage slipping fixed-unit, effort-driven tasks by adding resources to decrease duration.

With a fixed-unit, effort-driven task:

- If you add or remove resource units, Project recalculates duration.
- If you change the percentage of a resource assignment, Project recalculates duration.
- If you change duration, Project recalculates work.
- If you change work, Project recalculates duration.

Here are examples of tasks that should have the default fixed-unit, effort-driven settings:

- Child development specialists are assigned to evaluate children in a preschool. Each evaluation takes an hour, and there are 240 children to evaluate. If you increase the number of specialists from 300% to 500%, the evaluations will be finished sooner. If you decrease the number of children that will be evaluated, duration should decrease.

- Your print shop accepts a large job that will take sixteen hours to print using one offset press. If you assign two presses to the job, you want Project to recalculate duration because the task will be completed in half the time. If the customer doubles the amount of work, Project should double the duration.

When you create a new task with Project's default settings, it will be fixed-unit, effort-driven:

Fixed-Work Tasks

With *fixed-work* tasks, when you make the initial resource assignment, Project calculates the units of resource that are required to complete the task by dividing work by duration. By setting work and duration, you can calculate required resources easily. After the initial assignment, a change in duration affects units; a change in units affects duration. (Project won't, however, remove a resource assignment.) Fixed-work tasks are, by definition, effort-driven. When you choose the Fixed Work task type, Project turns the effort-driven check box on and disables it:

You manage slipping fixed-work tasks by adding resources to complete the task more quickly. If you know how many days you have to finish the task, you can set duration and Project will calculate the resource % required.

You see the difference between fixed-work tasks and the default task settings if you change the task's duration. With fixed unit effort-driven tasks, a change in duration changes work. With fixed-work tasks, a change in duration changes units because Project won't recalculate the amount of work.

With a fixed-work task:

- If you add or remove a resource, Project recalculates duration.
- If you change the percent of units assigned, Project recalculates duration.
- If you change work, Project recalculates duration.
- If you change duration, Project recalculates units.

The following tasks should have their task type set as fixed work:

- Your project includes a Write Scripts task that will take 40 hours. You assign a full-time programmer to work on the scripts for five days. If you add another full-time programmer, the task will be completed in 2.5 days. If you have your programmer work 12-hour days, the work will be done in 3.33 days. If you change the scope of the task and increase work to 56 hours, it will take 7 days rather than 5. If you change duration from 5 days to 1, you'll need 500% of a programmer to complete the task on time.

- You assign painters to prime the walls in an apartment building. The head of your paint crew says it would take 3 painters 5 days (120 hours of work). If you assign more painters, the job gets finished sooner. If painters work overtime, the job gets finished sooner. If you have to get the work done in 3 days, you can shorten the duration, and Project will calculate how many painters you need to assign.

Fixed-Duration Tasks

If a task's type is set to *fixed duration*, when you make the initial assignment, Project 2000 calculates work by multiplying units by duration. After the initial assignment, additional resources will complete more work during the duration, but duration is unaffected by resources or work. If fixed-duration tasks slip, there is no way to get them back on schedule—a two-week fixed-duration task always takes two weeks. When fixed-duration tasks are in the critical path and the project schedule is slipping, you manage the fixed task indirectly by adding resources to its predecessors.

With fixed-duration tasks:

- If you add or remove a resource, Project recalculates work.
- If you change the percent of units, Project recalculates work.
- If you change work, Project recalculates units.
- If you change duration, Project recalculates work.

This task should be created as a fixed-duration task:

- This weekend, your local orchard will let you pick all the apples you want at a very low cost. If you take two friends with you, you can pick three times as many apples. Conversely, if you need to pick three times as many apples as you can pick alone, you'd better invite a couple of your friends.

 TIP When you add subtasks to a task, making it a summary task, Project changes its task type to fixed-duration and disables the task type dialog box, so you can't change the task type. If you subsequently remove the subtasks so that the task is no longer a summary task, Project reinstates the task's original task type.

There is another reason to set a task's type to fixed duration: a task's duration is fixed, and the task is clearly *not* effort-driven. Examples include:

- A floor coating needs 72 hours to set.
- An eight-hour training takes a day. Adding a trainer won't change the duration, but it will double the amount of "work" done during the day.
- A stakeholder has one week to review the proposed logo for a new product.
- The two-day retreat is scheduled as part of the project's start-up.
- Any task being completed by someone outside the project team in a specified duration. You have one person assigned as liaison to the organization completing the task. You can't directly control other resources assigned to the task. For your purposes, and the amount of work, other than that performed by your liaison, is irrelevant.

 TIP You don't have to assign resources to every task in your project. A task can have duration or work values, even if you don't assign any resources.

Fixed-Duration, Effort-Driven Tasks   With *fixed-duration* and *effort-driven* tasks, neither the duration nor the amount of work can increase, so adding resources means that each resource will be assigned at a lower percentage (they'll spend less time working on the task), freeing them for other tasks. If you change the percentage of a unit's assignment, Project recalculates work. You manage fixed-duration, effort-driven tasks by adjusting duration to get work done with fewer resources.

With fixed-duration, effort-driven tasks:

- If you add or remove units, Project recalculates units.
- If you change the percent for assigned units, Project recalculates work.
- If you increase duration, Project recalculates units.
- If you change work, Project recalculates units.

Here are some examples of fixed-duration, effort-driven tasks:

- This weekend, your local orchard will let you pick all the apples you want at a very low cost—but only one person is allowed to pick at a time. If you take a friend with you, each of you will only be able to pick 50% of the time.

If a task requires equipment that is leased for a specific length of time, the tasks may be best described as fixed-duration tasks. If the equipment can be used by only a specified number of people at one time, the task is also effort-driven:

- Your print shop accepts a large job that will take sixteen hours to print using one offset press. You leased excess capacity on another company's press for two days. It takes one person to run an offset press. If you assign two people, each will need to work only 50% of the time (even though they both may try to look really busy).

When you use Project 2000 to manage a project, one of the most important tasks of the project manager is analyzing each task, and then choosing the correct task type and effort-driven setting. Project will recalculate work, duration, and units correctly as you add and remove resources, change durations, or adjust the amount of work that a task requires during the development phase.

To change a task's type or effort-driven setting:

1. Double-click the task, or select the task(s) and click the Task Information button on the standard toolbar to open the Task Information dialog box.
2. Click the Advanced tab.
3. Choose a task type from the Task Type drop-down list.
4. For fixed-unit and fixed-duration tasks, enable or disable the Effort-driven check box.
5. Click OK.

Setting the Default Task Type

The default task type is Fixed Units. To change the task type for new tasks in your project, change the default:

1. Choose Tools ➤ Options from the menu to open the Options dialog box, shown in Figure 10.6.

2. On the Schedule tab, choose Fixed Duration or Fixed Work from the Default Task Type drop-down list.

3. Click OK to close the dialog box.

All new tasks will be created with the new default setting.

FIGURE 10.6

Set the default task type, and enable or disable effort-driven scheduling for new tasks in the Options dialog box.

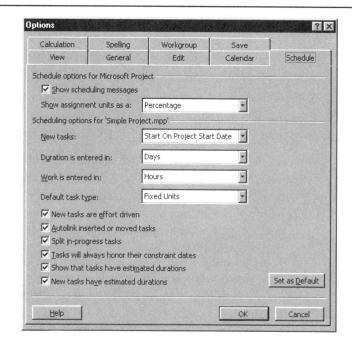

Assigning Resources

We assigned resources to understand how Project 2000 behaves when resources are assigned to a task or an assignment changes. Now, we'll examine different ways to assign work resources and material resources in Project 2000.

An assignment relates a task to the resource responsible for the task. There are many reasons to assign resources. Here are a few:

- Establishing responsibility for the project's task

- Reporting for project management
- Tracking individual and group performance on tasks
- Accurately measuring human and material resources used to complete individual tasks, project phases, and the project as a whole
- Tracking and managing project costs

As we noted earlier in the chapter, you don't have to assign resources to every task in a project. Some tasks, such as product review by customers, have duration but may not consume project resources. If you don't have resources working on a task, don't assign resources to the task.

Assigning a Work Resource from the Assign Resources Dialog Box

To assign resources using the Assign Resources dialog box:

1. Switch to Gantt Chart view (View ➤ Gantt Chart).
2. Select the task(s) that you want to create the assignment for.

3. Click the Assign Resources button on the Standard toolbar.
4. Select a resource name in the Assign Resources dialog box.
5. To assign a resource part-time, use the spin box control or type a percentage less than 100% in the Units field. To assign multiple units of the same resource, use the spin box control or type a percentage greater than 100% in the Units field. To assign more than one resource, select each resource.
6. Click the Assign button to assign the resource.

MASTERING THE OPPORTUNITIES

Assigning a Person from an Address Book

If a person is listed in your email address book and you haven't yet entered them on your project's Resource Sheet, you can assign them directly from the address book. With the task selected in the Gantt Chart, open the Assign Resources dialog box. Click the Addresses button in the dialog box to open your address book. Locate and select the person you want to assign.

When you assign a distribution list or group list, all the members of the list are assigned to the selected task.

Assigning Resources Using the Task Form

When you use the Task Form to enter or view assignments, you usually split the window and display a task view such as Gantt Chart view in one pane and the Task Form in the other. This workspace configuration is shown in Figure 10.7.

FIGURE 10.7

Display the Task Form and the Gantt Chart in a split window.

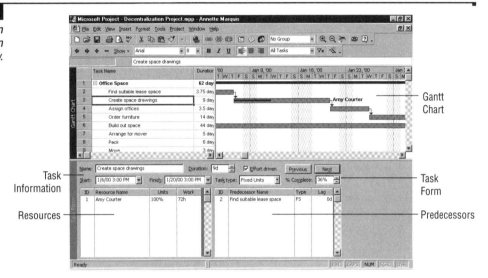

The Task Form provides a wealth of information about the task selected in the Gantt Chart view, and it is the best view to use if you change task type and effort-driven settings as you assign resources to the project tasks. You can see the proposed start and finish dates, the task type and effort-driven settings, as well as the task's predecessors and lag, and resources. To show the Gantt Chart and the Task Form:

1. Choose View ➢ Gantt Chart to switch to the Gantt Chart view.

2. Choose Window ➢ Split Window.

3. Click in the lower pane and choose View ➢ More Views to open the More Views dialog box.

4. Select Task Form and click OK.

To assign resources using the Task Form:

1. In the Gantt Chart, select the task(s) you wish to assign resources to.

2. In the Task Form, select a resource from the Resource Name drop-down list.

3. In the Units and Work columns, use the spin box controls to enter units, work, or both.

4. Repeat Steps 2 and 3 until all resources are chosen for the selected task.

5. Click the OK button in the Task Form to assign the resource(s).

The Task Form gives you a major advantage when you're assigning multiple resources to tasks. In the Assign Resource dialog box, if you change the Units for one resource and then switch to another resource, Project assigns the first resource and calculates work or duration for the entire task, based only on the first resource. In the Task Form, all resources are assigned at the same time, so when you use the Task Form, Project doesn't accidentally calculate work or duration prematurely.

MASTERING THE OPPORTUNITIES

Assigning Resources to Summary Tasks

You can assign resources to project summary tasks. Assign a resource to the summary task if increased duration for the summary task increases their workload (for example, a supervisor or administrative assistant for the team assigned to the tasks rolled up in the summary task). If the resource's workload does not change with the duration of the summary task, assign the resource to a subtask rather than the summary task.

Assigning Resources Using the Workgroup Features

If you use Project 2000's workgroup features, you can assign tasks to people using Team-Assign and Project Central. For information on assigning tasks with TeamAssign, see Chapter 15, "Communicating Project Information." To assign resources using Project Central, see Chapter 16, "Team Project Management with Project Central 2000."

Assigning Material Resources to Tasks

Material resources are materials consumed in the completion of a task, as opposed to equipment used to complete a task. When you assign a material resource, you specify the way the material is consumed. With *variable material consumption*, the quantity of material consumed changes as task duration changes. Examples of variable material consumption include the following:

- Fuel for a generator
- 35mm film in a photo shoot or movie
- Disposable paint rollers
- Bottled gases used in welding
- Antibacterial scrub soap used in a surgical unit

Variable consumption resources are assigned at an amount per time period based on the material label listed for the resource (see Figure 10.8): 10 gallons per day (10 gal/d), 2 packs per hour (2 pk/h), 4 tons per month (4 ton/mo).

PART

II

Creating a Project from Start to Finish

FIGURE 10.8

Specify resource consumption based on the material label from the Resource Sheet.

❶	Resource Name	Type	Material Label	Initials	Group	Max. Units	Std. Rate
◈	**Amy**	**Work**		A		100%	**$0.00/hr**
◈	**Ben**	**Work**		B		100%	**$0.00/hr**
	Carol	Work		C		100%	$0.00/hr
	Dennis	Work		D		100%	$0.00/hr
◈	**Workers**	**Work**		**WK**		100%	**$0.00/hr**
	top soil	Material	yds	TSoil	Soil		$22.00
	fertilizer	Material	lbs	Fert	Chem		$4.75
	grass seed	Material	lbs	grass	Seed		$1.90
	wildflower seed	Material	lbs	wild	Seed		$27.00
	gasoline	Material	gal	gas			$1.50

Choosing the *fixed material consumption* method indicates that the amount of material used is not related to the duration of the task. Examples of fixed material consumption include the following:

- Topsoil in a landscaping project
- Deck boards and wood posts used to build a deck
- Squares of shingles and rolls of roofing nails used on a roof
- Primer, paint, or wallpaper used to paint a room
- 2×4s used to frame a house
- Rivets and steel plate used to build a ship

Materials consumed in a fixed quantity, regardless of duration, are assigned without a time period: 10 gallons (10 gal), 2 packs (2 pk), 4 tons (4 ton). When you assign the material resource, Project calculates work: the total materials used in the task. You can assign material resources from Gantt Chart view with or without the Task Form.

To assign material resources to a task in Gantt Chart view:

1. Switch to Gantt Chart view (View ➣ Gantt Chart).

2. Select the task(s) that you want to create the assignment for.

3. Click the Assign Resources button on the standard toolbar.

4. Select the material resource name in the Assign Resources dialog box.

5. To assign a fixed consumption resource, enter the number of units of the resource that will be used in the task. To assign a variable consumption resource, enter the number of units per unit of duration.

6. Click the Assign button to assign the resource.

Reviewing Assignments

The views you use to assign resources are task views. The Gantt Chart view, for example, displays tasks and the resources assigned to the tasks. Project 2000 also includes resource forms, so you can see resources and their tasks. The forms are used to review assignments from the point of view of the people assigned to them or to see where materials are used in the project. You can't print the resource forms.

The Resource Usage view, which can be printed, combines a timeline with tasks grouped by resource to show the hours that the resource is assigned to tasks each day.

Using the Resource Name Form

The Resource Name form displays limited information about tasks assigned to a resource. To display the Resource Name form, choose View ➣ More Views ➣ Resource Name to open the Resource Name form, shown in Figure 10.9. Double-click a task to open the Task Information form for the task. Use the Previous and Next buttons to move from resource to resource.

Using the Resource Form

The Resource Form, shown in Figure 10.10, includes editable information fields for the resource, including standard, overtime, and per-use rates. Double-click a task to open the Task Information form for the task. Use the Previous and Next buttons to move from resource to resource.

FIGURE 10.9

The Resource Name form shows assignments for the selected resource.

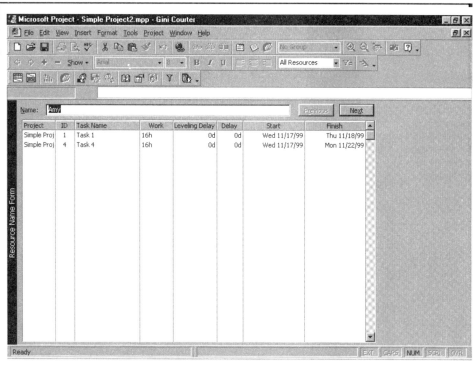

FIGURE 10.10

The Resource form displays resource information and assignments.

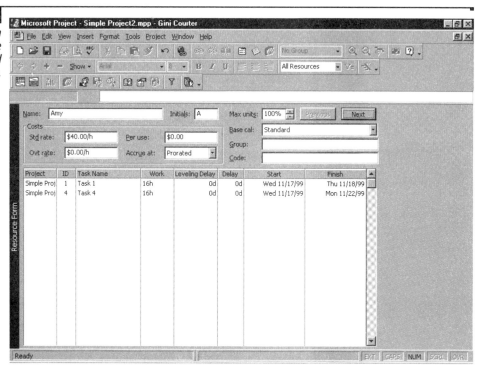

Using the Resource Usage View

The Resource Usage View gives you an easy way to view each resource's scheduled periodic activity. In this view, project tasks are grouped by resource, and resources are listed in alphabetical order. Figure 10.11 shows the Resource Usage view for the Decentralization Project used as an example in previous chapters.

FIGURE 10.11

The Resource Usage View displays tasks grouped by resource.

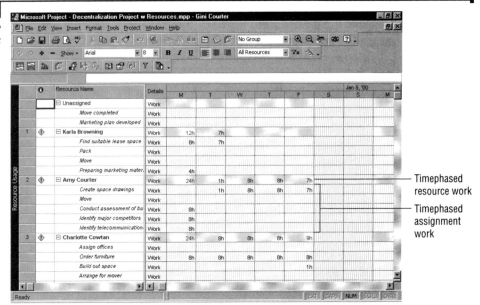

Unassigned tasks, if any, are listed at the top of the view. Click the Collapse button in front of a resource name to hide the list of tasks assigned to the resource. If assignment detail is hidden, click the Expand button to expand the view and display the resource's assignments.

⚠️ **TIP** Overallocated resources and assignments that cause overallocations are formatted with red text in this view. We'll discuss resource allocation in the next chapter.

Adjust the vertical split bar to show the work column, as shown here:

◈	⊟ Karla Browning	**71.8 hrs**
	Find suitable lease space	*15 hrs*
	Pack	*28.8 hrs*
	Move	*24 hrs*
	Preparing marketing materials	*4 hrs*

The total hours shown in the resource's Work column is *resource work*. The total hours of assignment for each time period are shown in the same row of the grid. Assignment hours allocated in the grid are called *timescaled* or *timephased* hours (see Figure 10.11). The resource's assignments are listed under the resource. The total time that the resource is assigned to the work, *assignment* work, is shown in the Work column. Timephased hours for each assignment are displayed in the grid.

Applying a Different Rate Table to an Assignment

In Project 2000, you can enter up to five different rate tables for a resource on the Costs tab of the Resource Information dialog box, shown here:

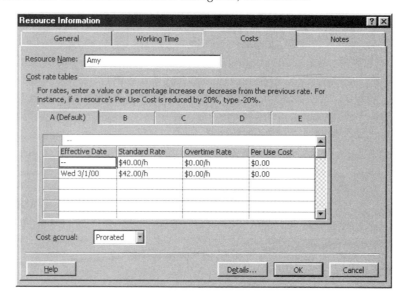

When you assign a resource, Project uses the rate from Cost Rate Table A. To use a rate from a different table for an assignment, double-click the assignment in the Resource Usage view to open the Assignment Information dialog box, as shown in Figure 10.12. On the General tab, select the rate table you want to use from the drop-down list, and then click OK to apply the rate table.

FIGURE 10.12

Apply a different cost table for an assignment in the Assignment Information dialog box.

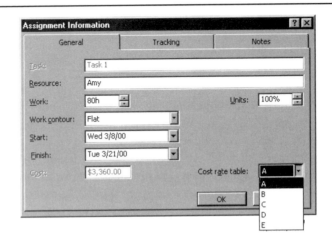

Contouring Assignments

When you make a resource assignment, Project uses the default flat work contour and spreads each unit's effort evenly across the duration of the task. If, for example, a resource is assigned 100% to a 40-hour task with no predecessors, the task will begin immediately with 8 hours of work each day for 5 days. In Gantt Chart view, you can see a task's duration.

However, you can't see the detail showing how many hours of work will be completed each day within the duration. There are two views that show you how the work is distributed within an assignment: the Resource Usage view (refer to Figure 10.11) and the Task Usage view, shown in Figure 10.13.

The shape of the distribution of work within an assignment is the *work contour*. The work contour is not an attribute of the task or the resource; it is an attribute of the assignment. When the work is spread evenly, the contour is flat. The flat contour is appropriate when the same amount of work should be done every day of the assignment. With some assignments, this isn't the case. Writing this book, for example required minimal work at the beginning (preparing an outline), followed by a huge amount of work (writing the text). The project then ramps down as editing continues, but initial writing has been completed.

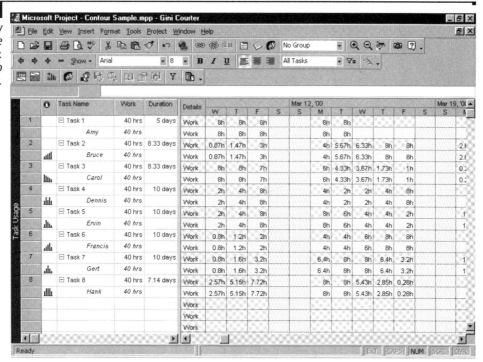

FIGURE 10.13

The Task Usage view is similar to the Resource Usage view. Both are used to contour assignments.

You can change the distribution of an assignment's work by applying a predefined contour. Or, you can edit the existing distribution or the distribution created when you applied a contour to create a custom contour.

Applying a Predesigned Contour

Unlike task type, there is no option to set a contour for the entire project. Every assignment uses the default flat contour until you change it. Project 2000 includes eight predesigned contours:

- Flat (default)—work is distributed evenly.
- Back Loaded—peak activity occurs at the end of the assignment.
- Front Loaded—peak activity occurs at the beginning of the assignment.

- Double Peak—work clusters around two periods of peak activity.
- Early Peak—similar to Front Loaded, but with a ramp up to the peak activity.
- Late Peak—similar to Back Loaded, but with a ramp down from peak activity.
- Bell—a single peak in the middle of the assignment.
- Turtle—a bell with ramp up and ramp down.

To change the work contour for an assignment in either Task Usage or Resource Usage view, double-click an assignment to open the Assignment Information dialog box and choose a contour from the Work Contour drop-down list:

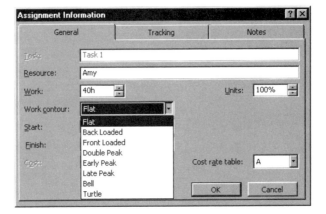

Contours interact with task and resource settings as you manage and adjust assignments during the life of the project. The contour shape is preserved with the assignment when you move the task or the project schedule changes.

 TIP You can add the Work Contour column to the Resource Usage or Task Usage view, and change assignment contours in the view.

When you contour an assignment, Project applies the contour and recalculates work, duration, or units based on the task type of the assignment's task. Before we discuss the effect that task type has on contouring, let's take a look at each of the eight predefined contours, applied to a forty-hour work assignment to a task created with the default fixed units task type.

The Flat Contour

With the Flat contour, work is distributed evenly across the duration of the assignment, as shown in the split window with the Task Usage view on top and the Resource Graph in the bottom window in Figure 10.14. With flat contouring, 50% of the assignment's work is completed in the first half of the assignment duration.

FIGURE 10.14

The default Flat work contour distributes work evenly.

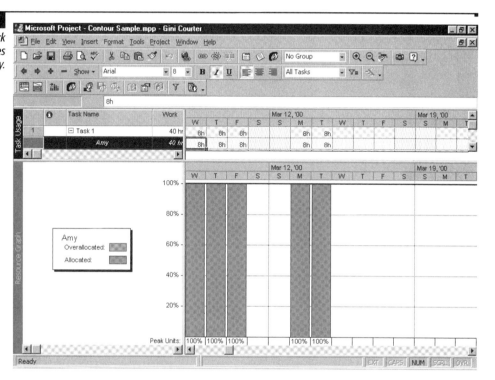

PART

II

Creating a Project from Start to Finish

The Back Loaded Contour

With a back loaded assignment, the majority of the work is undertaken at the end of the assignment. Only 25% of the work is completed in the first half of the assignment's duration. Preparation for an event such as a conference is generally back loaded as work increases when the event approaches. For back loaded assignments, the back loading icon is displayed in the Indicators column. The effect of applying the Back Loaded contour is easily seen in Figure 10.15.

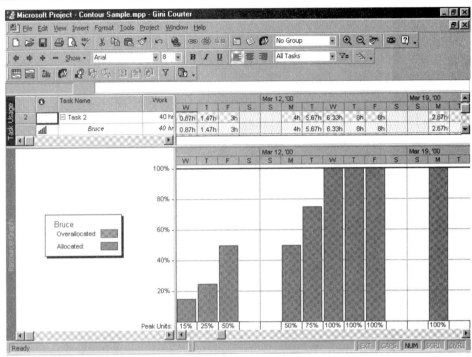

The Front Loaded Contour

Front loading an assignment places the majority of the effort at the beginning of the assignment, as shown in Figure 10.16. Seventy-five percent of the assignment's work is completed halfway through the assignment duration. Select a Front Loaded contour when an assignment involves a significant startup effort and then slowly tapers off.

TIP Contouring stores information that you'd have to track in your head or with a manual system in the assignment. If all assignments used the flat contour, for example, you have to remember to be concerned when a front loaded assignment is only half complete at the 50% duration mark. Contouring assignments so that they reflect the actual workload of the assignment makes it easier for you to track and manage your project.

The Double Peak Contour

Apply the Double Peak contour to assignments that feature two major expenditures of effort, with downtime in between. Halfway through a double-peak contoured assignment, 50% of the work should have been completed, but the assignee is past one of the two hurdles in the assignment. Figure 10.17 shows a forty-hour assignment with double peak contouring.

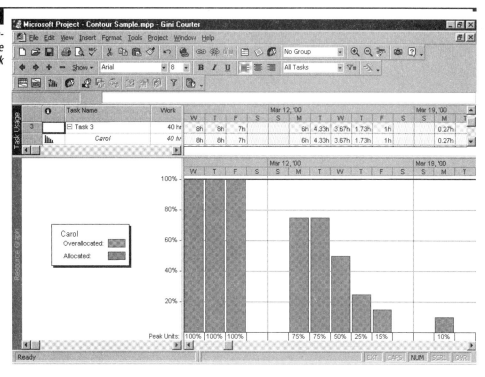

FIGURE 10.16

Front load assign-
ments with extensive
startup work

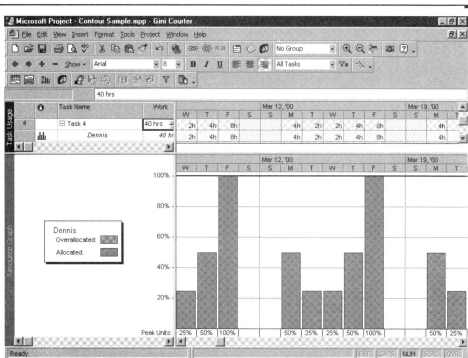

FIGURE 10.17

Double Peak contour-
ing focuses effort at
the 1/3 and 2/3 points
of an assignment.

PART

II

Creating a Project
from Start to Finish

The Early Peak Contour

The Early Peak contour is similar to the Front Loaded contour, but activity starts more slowly. Seventy percent of the work is completed in the first half of the assignment's duration.

FIGURE 10.18

Early peak assignments ramp up to a peak activity level and then taper off slowly.

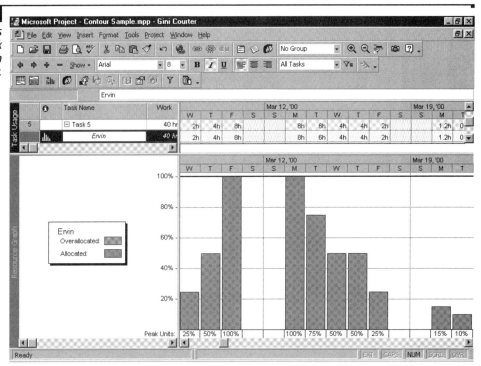

The Late Peak Contour

The Late Peak contour is similar to the Back Loaded contour, but the peak activity is near, not at, the end of the assignment, and is followed by a rapid ramp down. With late peak contouring, only 30% of the work is distributed in the first 50% of the assignment duration. (After the midway point, every day probably seems like Monday.) A 40-hour assignment with Late Peak contouring is shown in Figure 10.19.

The Bell Contour

Use Bell contouring when the assignment requires a rapid ramp up to a large expenditure of effort in a short burst at the midway point, followed by a rapid ramp down, as shown in Figure 10.20.

FIGURE 10.19

Late Peak contouring builds slowly to a peak and then ramps off quickly.

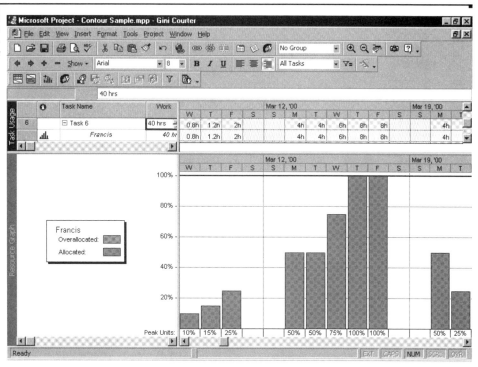

FIGURE 10.20

The Bell contour focuses effort on a peak period in the middle of the assignment duration.

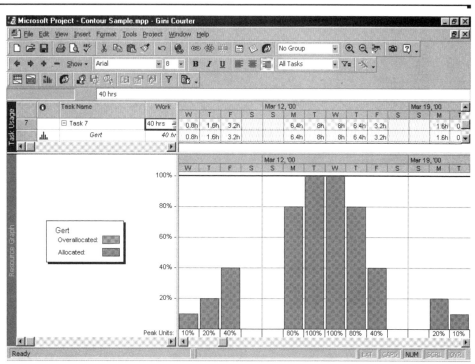

The Turtle Contour

The Turtle contour is like the Bell contour, but with caramel and peanuts. Just kidding. It's actually like the Bell contour, but with faster ramping and a longer period of high activity, as shown in Figure 10.21. With Turtle contouring, the period of peak activity lasts twice as long as with Bell contouring.

FIGURE 10.21

Use the Turtle contour when the peak activity has a longer duration than the Bell contour reflects.

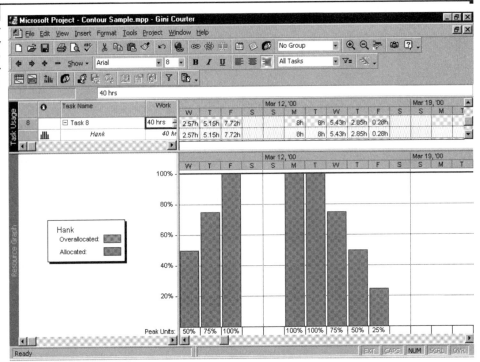

How Task Types and Contours Interact

Each predesigned contour adjusts the amount of work that will be done in each time period. The cumulative result will be a change in duration or work, depending on the task type of the task involved in the assignment. Contouring affects assignments and holds units fixed while contouring. Consequently, contouring never adjusts units. In addition, a task's effort-driven setting is not a factor because effort-driven scheduling applies when resources are added or removed from an assignment.

On the contrary, contouring adjusts the distribution of activity *within* the assignment. To see the effect of task type on contouring, we created three tasks, each of which has a five-day duration, and assigned one full-time resource, Worker B (also known as Buzz).

A section of the Task Usage view with the three assignments, prior to contouring, is shown in Figure 10.22.

FIGURE 10.22

Assignments to fixed-units, fixed-duration, and fixed-work tasks. Work, units, and duration are identical prior to contouring.

10	⊟ Fixed Units	40 hrs	5 days	Work	8h	8h	8h			8h	8h		
	Worker B	*40 hrs*		Work	8h	8h	8h			8h	8h		
11	⊟ Fixed Duration	40 hrs	5 days	Work	8h	8h	8h			8h	8h		
	Worker B	*40 hrs*		Work	8h	8h	8h			8h	8h		
12	⊟ Fixed Work	40 hrs	5 days	Work	8h	8h	8h			8h	8h		
	Worker B	*40 hrs*		Work	8h	8h	8h			8h	8h		

Now, we'll contour each of the three assignments exactly by selecting all three and applying a Double Peak contour. The three contoured assignments are shown in Figure 10.23. For the fixed units and fixed-work task types, contouring the assignment resulted in a change in duration. In the fixed-duration task's assignment, the duration could not be changed, so contouring reduced the hours of work in the assignment.

FIGURE 10.23

The three assignments after applying the double peak contour

	⊟ Fixed Units	40 hrs	10 days	Work	2h	4h	8h			4h	2h	2h	4h	8h
▪▪▪	*Worker B*	*40 hrs*		Work	2h	4h	8h			4h	2h	2h	4h	8h
	⊟ Fixed Duration	20 hrs	5 days	Work	3h	6h	2h			6h	3h			
▪▪▪	*Worker B*	*20 hrs*		Work	3h	6h	2h			6h	3h			
	⊟ Fixed Work	40 hrs	10 days	Work	2h	4h	8h			4h	2h	2h	4h	8h
▪▪▪	*Worker B*	*40 hrs*		Work	2h	4h	8h			4h	2h	2h	4h	8h

Contours are applied to assignments, not to tasks or resources. If you have several resources assigned to a task, you can apply a different contour for each assignment. For an Exhibit at Trade Show task, for example, assignments for staff arriving early to set up could be front loaded, while assignments for staff staying after to break down the display could be back loaded.

MASTERING THE OPPORTUNITIES

The Mathematics of Predefined Contours

When you apply any predesigned contour other than the default contour, Project 2000 determines the duration that will be required after contouring, splits the duration into 10 segments, and then multiplies each segment by a percentage to determine the hours (minutes, days) of work to allocate to the segment. Table 10.1 shows the percentage of work that will be assigned for each segment of the predesigned contours and the average of the work in each segment.

Continued ▮▶

MASTERING THE OPPORTUNITIES CONTINUED

TABLE 10.1: CONTOUR SEGMENT PERCENTAGES

Contour	1	2	3	4	5	6	7	8	9	10	Average
Flat	100%	100%	100%	100%	100%	100%	100%	100%	100%	100%	100%
Back Loaded	10%	15%	25%	50%	50%	75%	75%	100%	100%	100%	60%
Front Loaded	100%	100%	100%	75%	75%	50%	50%	25%	15%	10%	60%
Double Peak	25%	50%	100%	50%	25%	25%	50%	100%	50%	25%	50%
Early Peak	25%	50%	100%	100%	75%	50%	50%	25%	15%	10%	50%
Late Peak	10%	15%	25%	50%	50%	75%	100%	100%	50%	25%	50%
Bell	10%	20%	40%	80%	100%	100%	80%	40%	20%	10%	50%
Turtle	25%	50%	75%	100%	100%	100%	100%	75%	50%	25%	70%

For fixed units and fixed-work tasks, before Project applies the percentages in the contour, it has to perform two additional calculations. First, Project divides the total work in the assignment (40 hours) by the average of the segment percentages for the selected contour (in the case of the Turtle contour, 70%) to determine the new duration for the assignment: 40 hours/0.70 = 57 hours, or 7.14 days (see Figure 10.21).

The additional 2.14 days' duration is the result of assigning less work in the first three and last three segments to contour the task (refer to Table 10.1). Project then divides the duration into ten segments, and allocates the work for each segment based on the percentage shown in the table above.

With fixed-duration tasks, duration can't change, so applying a contour results in a reduction in work.

To quickly calculate the new duration for fixed unit and fixed-work tasks before applying a contour, divide the current duration by the average in the last column of the table. To calculate the new work value for fixed-duration tasks, multiply the current work value by the percentage.

Editing a Contour

When you manually change the work assignments in the Resource Usage or Task Usage view, the result is an edited contour. To edit a contour, switch to Resource Usage view or Task Usage view. In Resource Usage view, you can edit timephased work and the total work for any assignment. You cannot edit timephased or total work for a resource. In Task Usage view, you can edit timephased and total work values for assignments or tasks.

 When you edit a contour, the contour icon shows that it has been edited. If you double-click the assignment to open the Assignment Information dialog box, Contoured is listed as the Work Contour type.

 WARNING Edited contours don't follow the same rules as the predesigned contours. There's nothing to stop you from adding work to an assignment so that the task's Start Date or Finish Date changes. To avoid accidentally changing a task's Start or Finish Date, don't adjust the total work for an assignment in the task table pane on the left. Adjust timephased work only in the timeline pane on the right.

PART

II

Creating a Project
from Start to Finish

Apply the predesigned contour that's most like the contour you wish to create. Click the timephased work cell you wish to edit, and enter a new value. Project distributes the work based on the following rules:

- If the work cell doesn't include the start or finish of the assignment, the work value is distributed over the cell. For example, four hours of work are assigned throughout the day, and units are recalculated at 50%.

- If the work cell includes both the assignment start and finish, work is distributed between the two. If the assignment starts at 8 a.m. and ends at 10 a.m., the four hours will be distributed in that two-hour duration (which means that units will be adjusted to 200%).

- If the work cell includes the start, but not the finish, work is distributed from the start time or date. For example, if an assignment starts at 1 p.m., four hours of work are distributed from 1–5 p.m., and units are calculated at 100%.

- If the work cell includes the assignment's finish, then the work is distributed up to the finish. For example, if the task assignment ends at noon, four hours of work are distributed from 8 a.m. until noon, and units are calculated at 200%.

Whenever you edit a contour, Project distributes the work within the duration and recalculates units. This recalculation isn't obvious in either view. To see the change in units, double-click an assignment to open the Assignment Information dialog box and examine the Units field on the General tab:

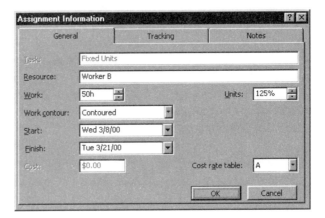

What's Next

In this chapter, you saw how to use task type, effort-driven scheduling, and contouring so that your tasks and task assignments closely resemble the "real-world" behaviors that you'll manage in your project. In the next chapter, we'll make a final pass through the project to ensure that resources aren't overallocated. Then, we'll prepare the project for publication.

CHAPTER <u>11</u>

Preparing
Your Project
for Publication

This chapter focuses on the final phase of the design cycle: checking the project for overallocated resources, correcting overallocations, and using Project 2000 to prepare reports and printed views for the project sign-off meeting. This is both an ending and a beginning: the project design is nearly complete and it's time to get on with the project activities. It's tempting to rush through this final portion of design, but these final steps provide additional insurance that your project will serve as a good guide in the development stage.

Identifying Overallocations

A resource is overallocated when the total of its timephased work for a period exceeds the resource's maximum units. Left uncorrected, overallocated resources pose a serious threat to project success. A resource typically can't work eight hours on one task and eight hours on a second task. When a project includes accidentally overallocated resources, the project manager will have to adjust the schedule or change resource assignments when the overallocation is finally noticed.

Task slippage is a common cause of overallocation as a resource's work from last week moves into this week. If the resource is already scheduled to be working on a different task, the resource may become overallocated. Because you can't tell from the Gantt Chart that you have overallocated resources, check your resources in other views as the project moves into the development phase. In every resource view, overallocated resources are formatted in red so you know immediately that a resource is overallocated. Figure 11.1 shows the Resource Sheet for the XYZ-BOT project that you saw in earlier chapters.

 In the Resource Sheet, Project displays a caution icon in the Indicators column of overallocated resources. Hover over the icon, and Project displays a screen tip that suggests one way to correct the overallocation:

◇ This resource should be leveled based
on a Day by Day setting.

You can choose to delay a task until the assigned resource is available, split the task so only a portion is delayed, or assign additional resources. All three options are valid now, before the project plan is finalized and distributed. If you decide to use Project's leveling feature, discussed later in this chapter, to adjust for the overallocation, you are limited to delaying or splitting tasks. If you prefer to add resources to compensate for the overallocation, you must do so manually—leveling can't add resources to a task.

FIGURE 11.1

Overallocated resources are formatted to stand out in every view.

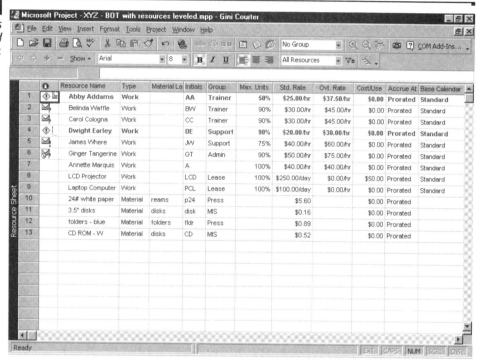

Locating the Overallocated Segments

When you have overallocations, there are several ways to identify the timeframe where the overallocation occurs, and the task or tasks that are causing the overallocation. The Overallocated Resources report lists each of the overallocated resources and the assignments that contribute to the overallocation. To print the Overallocated Resources report:

1. Choose View ➢ Reports to open the Reports dialog box.

2. Click Custom to open the Custom Reports dialog box.

3. Choose Overallocated Resources, and click Print or Print Preview.

The report, shown in preview in Figure 11.2, lists each overallocated resource and all their assignments. It does not identify which assignments result in an overallocation.

There is, unfortunately, no view that shows overallocated assignments, so you have to work on the problem from the point of view of the resource. The Resource Graph (View ➢ Resource Graph), which displays assigned timephased hours for the selected resource, shows when the overallocation occurs. The default Resource Graph for one of our overallocated resources, Abby Addams, is shown in Figure 11.3.

PART

II

Creating a Project from Start to Finish

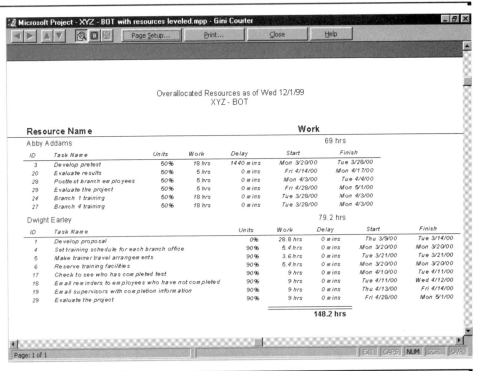

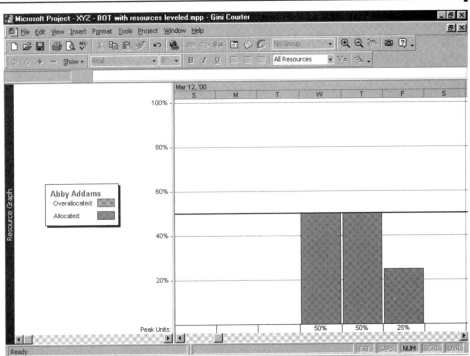

You can spend a long time scrolling the Resource Graph. To make the graph more useful, right-click on the timeline and choose Zoom from the shortcut menu:

Select the Entire Project option to condense the Resource Graph, as shown in Figure 11.4.

PART

II

Creating a Project
from Start to Finish

FIGURE 11.4

Zoom on the timeline to display a resource graph for the entire project.

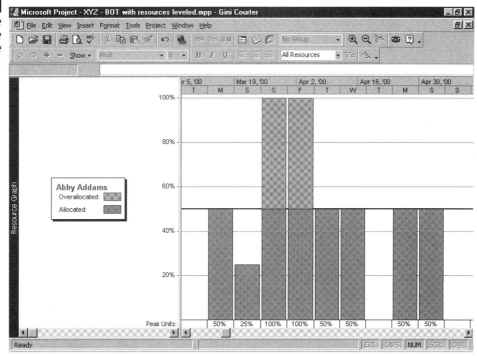

The Resource Graph shows peak hours in each time segment, with overallocated hours in red. To see the resource's tasks, split the window and open the Resource Form (Window ➤ Split) or Resource Name Form (View ➤ More Views ➤ Resource Name Form). The Resource Form and Resource Graph are shown in Figure 11.5. The Resource Form shows the max units for the resource, which may be the problem in this case. The Resource is assigned for 100%, which causes an overallocation because the resource max units are 50%.

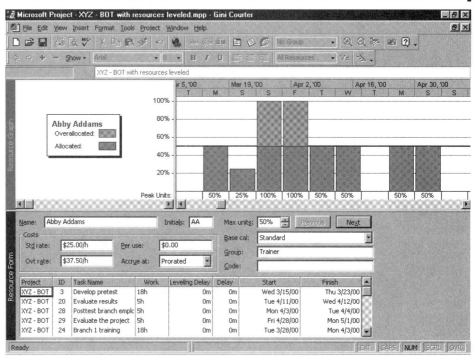

FIGURE 11.5

Combine the Resource Graph with the Resource Form to view assignments and resource information with the resource's schedule.

Viewing Potential Solutions for the Overallocation

This combination of the Resource Graph and Resource Form is the portal to a host of solutions to this overallocation. To view other graphic information, right-click in the graph to open the shortcut menu:

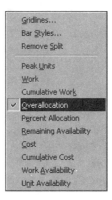

Choose Overallocation to see the periodic overallocation in hours, and then check out some of the other options on this menu. One way to resolve an overallocation is to move an assignment to a point in time when the resource is available. The Remaining Availability option, shown in Figure 11.6, clearly shows that Abby has time available prior to and immediately after her overallocation.

FIGURE 11.6

Display Remaining Availability in the Resource Graph to see when the resource is available.

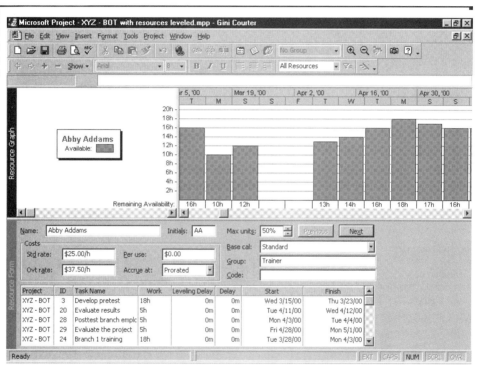

Another way to resolve an overallocation is to assign different or additional resources. The overallocated resource is a member of the Trainers group. (Group information is displayed in the Resource Name Form.) With the Remaining Availability displayed, choose Group from the Filter drop-down list to open the Group dialog box. Enter the group in which you're looking for an available resource:

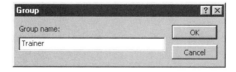

Then, use the horizontal scroll bar under the resource name in the Resource Graph to scroll though the resources in the Trainers group to find a trainer who is available to assign to the task.

PART

II

Creating a Project from Start to Finish

TIP To focus on overallocated resources in any table view that includes resources, choose Overallocated Resources from the Filter list on the formatting toolbar.

Viewing Overallocations by Time Period

The Resource Graph and Resource Form help you locate the overallocations and potential solutions, but it's a difficult place to adjust resource assignments. To see each resource and their assignments in an editable view, display the Resource Usage view (View ➤ Resource Usage). Choose Group from the Group drop-down list on the standard toolbar to arrange resources in groups:

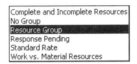

In this view, shown in Figure 11.7, it's easy to see that neither of the other trainers can pick up Abby's tasks that cause the overallocation. Four trainings are scheduled at the same time; with only three trainer resources, this results in an overallocation.

FIGURE 11.7

The cells of the Resource Usage view are editable.

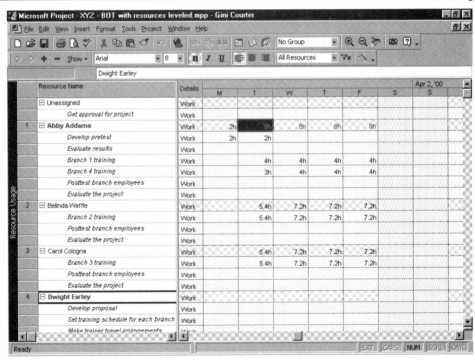

TIP If you're considering changing resource assignments as the project progresses, another useful grouping is Standard Rate, which allows you to see the cost of the current resource and the resource you're considering as a substitute so you can stay within budget.

Choose Format ➤ Details ➤ Overallocation from the menu to add a row for over-allocations, as shown in Figure 11.8. If you have a minor overallocation problem, you can enter new hours for a task in the appropriate cell in the time grid—changing two hours on Monday and five hours on Tuesday to five hours on Monday and two hours on Tuesday, for example. Editing the timephased values in the grid creates a custom contour for the assignment (see Chapter 10, "Assigning and Scheduling Resources and Costs"), which has implications if the assignment is moved later.

FIGURE 11.8

Add a separate row for overallocation detail.

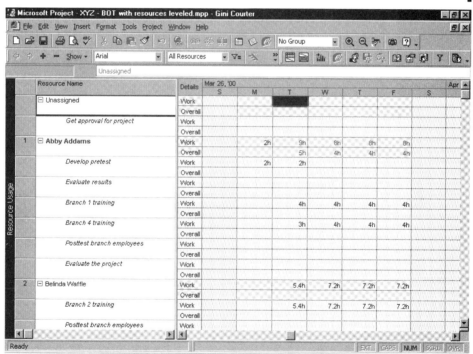

PART

II

Creating a Project from Start to Finish

You *can't* reschedule the start date or finish date of a task in this view: the indented list under each resource is the assignment, not the task. If you double-click an assignment, the Assignment Information dialog box opens:

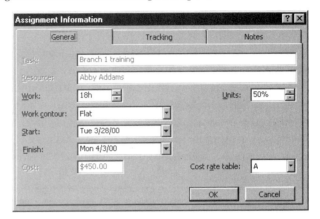

Changing the Start Date in this dialog box changes the *assignment*, not the task start date. The task will appear in the Gantt Chart as scheduled. To change the task to eliminate the overallocation, switch to a task view, such as Task Sheet view or Gantt Chart.

Viewing Tasks with Overallocations

Resources get overallocated, but the possible solutions are constrained by the nature of the tasks involved in the overallocation. The resource overallocation we've been examining until now is the result of too much work in one time period for the available resources in the Trainers group. Our choices are to hire or contract another trainer, or move one of the four trainings. The best place to assign resources to tasks is in a task view such as the Gantt Chart. We can move the training automatically by leveling the resources, which we'll discuss in the next section. Delaying tasks is the way leveling handles overallocations.

To view overallocated tasks, switch to any task view (we'll use the Gantt Chart view) and turn on the Resource Management toolbar (View ➤ Toolbars ➤ Resource Management). Click the Go To Next Overallocation button to move to the next task with an overallocated resource assigned to it. Use the Resource Allocation View button to switch to a combination view with the Resource Usage grid and a Leveling Gantt; the Task Entry view displays a Gantt Chart and the Task Form with the Resource Assignments. In either view, display the Assign Resources dialog box to add or remove resources.

Resource Leveling

Project 2000's leveling feature is used to resolve resource overallocation by delaying or splitting tasks. You can level tasks within a range of dates or level the entire project. Project uses a number of factors to select tasks to delay or split:

- Available slack time
- Task priority, dependencies, and constraints
- Task ID
- Scheduling dates

Before leveling a project, you should make sure that these factors are already set, particularly for critical tasks. See Chapter 8, "Scheduling and Linking Project Tasks," if you need information about any of these task settings. Make a backup copy of the project file before proceeding.

Using Project's Leveling Feature

Select any task. Choose Tools ➢ Resource Leveling to open the Resource Leveling dialog box, shown in Figure 11.9. The settings in the dialog box determine when and how Project 2000 levels resources.

PART

II

Creating a Project
from Start to Finish

FIGURE 11.9

Set options for leveling overallocated resources in the Resource Leveling dialog box.

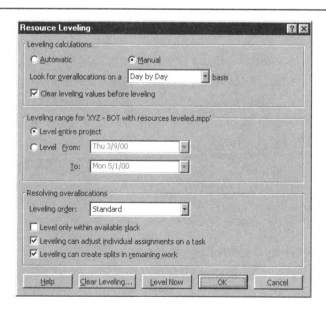

Setting Automatic or Manual Leveling

With Automatic Leveling Calculation enabled, Project will adjust tasks as soon as you change a task or assign a resource that results in an overallocation. Project checks for overallocations after each entry, so with a large project, automatic leveling can slow down overall performance while you're assigning resources or working with the schedule. Also, remember that Project will level by delaying or splitting tasks, so if you're really attached to your project's finish date, don't choose this option.

When you choose the default calculation option, Manual, you control when Project levels resources. *Manual* infers that you'll have to grab a shovel and roll up your sleeves. All the Manual setting really means is that you'll have to open the Resource Leveling dialog box and click Level Now to level resources.

In the Look For Overallocations drop-down list, choose the time period that is an overallocation in this project. Project ignores overallocations with shorter durations than the sensitivity you select. If, for example, you check overallocations on a week-by-week basis, a person can be scheduled to work 16 hours 2 days in a row, and still work fewer than the 40 hours in a week. If you look for overallocations on a day-by-day basis, the person is overallocated on both 16-hour days, so the tasks on those days would be adjusted during leveling. The five resource sensitivity settings are:

- Minute by Minute levels resources that are overallocated by a minute or more.
- Hour by Hour levels resources that are overallocated by an hour or more.
- Day by Day levels resources that are overallocated by a day or more.
- Week by Week levels resources that are overallocated by one week or more.
- Month by Month levels resources that are overallocated by a month or more.

If you turn on Automatic Leveling, disable the Clear Leveling Values Before Leveling checkbox (which is selected by default). When the checkbox is enabled, Project clears delays created by previous leveling operations and the leveling delays that you entered manually, before it levels resources.

Setting a Leveling Range

The default leveling range is the entire project. To level overallocations in a specific time frame, select the Level From/To option and use the drop-down calendar controls in the Resource Leveling dialog box to select the beginning and ending dates between which Project should search for overallocations:

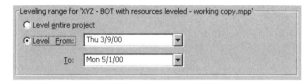

Setting Resolution Options

When Project 2000 levels resources, it makes two passes through the project. On the first pass, it identifies overallocations. On the second pass, it delays tasks based on the leveling order you select. There are some tasks that Project will not delay. Project will not delay tasks that have the following constraints:

- Must Finish On

- Must Start On

- As Late As Possible (for projects scheduled from the start date)

- As Soon As Possible (for projects scheduled from the finish date)

Project won't delay tasks with a priority of 1000, nor will it delay a task that has already started. It will, however, split a task that has an actual start date.

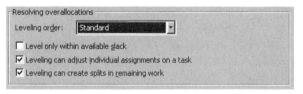

There are three leveling orders: ID Only, Standard (the default), and Priority/Standard. With ID Only, leveling delays tasks with larger ID numbers. If a resource assigned to tasks 27 and 31 is overallocated, Project will delay task 31. If you use ID Only, you'd better be very sure that your tasks were entered in order of importance.

With the Standard leveling order selected, the task(s) to be leveled are chosen based on a number of factors:

- Dependencies: tasks without successors are delayed before tasks with successors.

- Slack: tasks with slack (tasks not on a critical path) are delayed before tasks that have 0 slack.

- Task priority and, if the project includes shared resources, project priority: lower-priority tasks are delayed before higher-priority tasks.

PART

II

Creating a Project
from Start to Finish

- Constraints: constrained tasks are delayed after non-constrained tasks.
- Start Date: tasks with later start dates are delayed before tasks with earlier start dates (which makes the end of the project even more interesting!).

When you select the Priority/Standard leveling order, Project gives primary consideration to the relative priority of two tasks when determining which task to delay. The other factors in the previous list are given secondary consideration. If you haven't assigned priorities to the tasks in your project (other than setting the priority for some tasks at 1000), stick with the Standard leveling order.

TIP Task priority (0 to 1000) is set on the General tab of the Task Information Form. If you don't want Project to delay a task, set the priority to 1000, and use the Standard or Standard/Priority leveling order.

The settings of the three checkboxes in this section of the Resource Leveling dialog box determine what Project can and can't do to level resources. To prevent Project from moving the project finish date, enable the Level Only Within Available Slack checkbox. This checkbox is turned off by default. If you don't have much slack in your project, enabling this checkbox means that Project won't be able to handle many overallocations through leveling.

The Leveling Can Adjust Individual Assignments On a Task checkbox is on by default. When this checkbox is enabled and multiple resources are assigned to a task, Project can delay the start of one resource's assignment without adjusting other resources who are assigned to the task.

Leveling Can Create Splits in Remaining Work is on by default. When this checkbox is enabled, Project can delay a task that's already in progress. Turn this checkbox off to prevent split delays on tasks where completion is greater than 0%.

MASTERING THE OPPORTUNITIES

Mastering Assignment Leveling and Task Splitting

The Leveling Can Adjust Individual Assignments checkbox in the Resource Leveling dialog box enables or disables assignment leveling for the entire project. You can set assignment leveling for specific tasks rather than selecting it here for the entire project. There are some tasks that use resources that work at the same time. The "Play in the World Series" or "Mixed Doubles, second set" tasks, for example, shouldn't assign half of the resources to start hours or days after the others.

Continued

The Level Assignments field is a task property that isn't on the Task Information Form or displayed in any of Project's standard views. To set assignment leveling, switch to a task view such as the Gantt Chart, right-click a column header, and choose Insert Column from the shortcut menu to open the Column Definition dialog box:

Select the Level Assignments column and add it to the view. This is a Yes/No field. Yes allows Project to level individual assignments for the task. No keeps the entire team together for the World Series. Summary tasks allow Assignment Leveling. You can't change this setting for summary tasks.

The Leveling Can Create Splits in Remaining Work field is another Yes/No field available at the task level. Add the Leveling Can Split column to a task view. Choose Yes to enable splitting or No to prevent split delays of tasks that are already in progress.

Launching the Leveling Process

After you set the time period, click the Level Now button, and Project will determine which resources are overallocated, and will then delay or split and delay tasks to reduce or eliminate the overallocation by using the settings you specified in the dialog box. The progress meter in the status bar shows the leveling effort:

Resolving Leveling Conflicts   Some overallocations can't be leveled. If, for example, you allocated a resource to a summary task to track administrative time and the same resource is allocated to one or more of the summary task's subtasks, leveling will pause and you'll be prompted to stop leveling or skip this task.

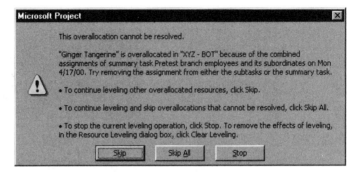

If the summary task assignment was a mistake, note the summary task with the resource assigned, and click Stop to stop the leveling operation. Remove the assignment from the summary task, and start leveling again by choosing Tools ➢ Resource Leveling. Click the Skip button to continue if the summary task assignment was intentional. Click Skip All, and Project won't notify you when other overallocations can't be leveled.

If Project can't resolve an overallocation unrelated to a summary task, a message box lets you know which resource it is unable to level and the date for the overallocation conflict:

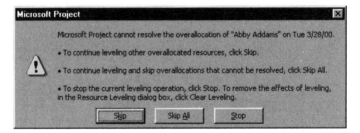

The choices are the same. You can stop, diagnose the problem now and start leveling again, skip over this problem and continue to see reports from Project about conflicts, or skip this conflict and suppress further messages by clicking Skip All.

When there aren't any irresolvable overallocations, leveling only takes a few seconds. After leveling, choose View ➢ More Views ➢ Leveling Gantt to see the changes made by leveling in the Leveling Gantt, shown in Figure 11.10. Green bars indicate the original, preleveled schedule for each task; the gap, if any, between a task's green Gantt bar and the blue Gantt bar is the delay added by leveling.

FIGURE 11.10

The Leveling Gantt shows delays added to eliminate overallocations.

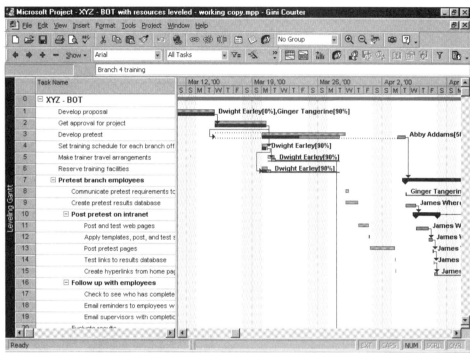

Clearing Leveling Delays

To remove leveling delays, select the tasks you want to remove leveling for and open the Resource Leveling dialog box (Tools ➤ Resource Leveling). Click the Clear Leveling button. Select Entire Project or Selected Tasks, and click OK to remove delays.

NOTE Project will remove *almost* all leveling delays. If you assign a priority of 1000 to a task after leveling, Project won't clear the delay.

Leveling Resources On Your Own

You don't have to rely on Project's leveling feature to level resources. You may want to level some of the overallocated resources one at a time so that you can consider the implications before adding a delay. You can delay a task or an assignment. When you delay a task, the task's start date moves.

Apply *assignment delay* when you want to delay one or more resources, but not all those assigned to a task; or when you want to use different delays for each resource. The view used to assign leveling delays is the Resource Allocation Form with a couple of additions. The Detail Gantt uses the Delay table, and the Resource Usage table includes the Assignment Delay column, as shown in Figure 11.11. You'll set assignment delays in the upper pane and task delays in the table in the lower pane.

FIGURE 11.11

Use the Detail Gantt and Resource Usage Form to add delays manually.

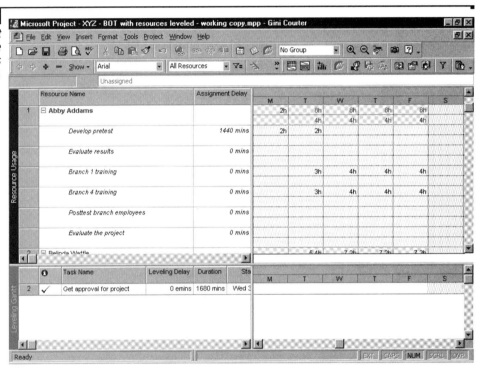

To display the Resource Allocation view with assignment delay and task delay fields visible:

1. Choose View ➤ More Views ➤ Resource Allocation.

2. Click in the Gantt Chart in the lower pane.

3. Choose View ➤ Table ➤ More Tables to open the More Tables dialog box.

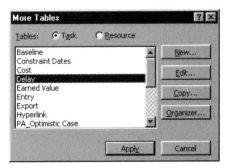

4. Select Delay.

5. Click Apply.

6. In the Resource Usage table in the upper pane, right-click on the Work column heading.

7. Choose Insert Column from the shortcut menu.

8. Select the Assignment Delay column in the Column Definition dialog box.

9. Click OK.

Delaying a task delays all the resource assignments for the task. Clicking the Clear Leveling button in the Resource Leveling dialog box clears task delays. To add delay to a task:

1. In the upper pane, select any assignment for the task you want to delay.

2. In the Leveling Delay field in the lower pane, enter the duration for the delay.

Assignment delay is the amount of time after the task's start date that the resource begins work on the assignment. Resource delay can't be cleared from the Resource Leveling dialog box; you must reverse the delay manually. To delay an assignment:

1. Select the assignment you want to delay in the Resource Usage table.

2. Enter the duration for the delay in the Assignment Delay field.

MASTERING TROUBLESHOOTING

Filtering for Delayed Tasks

To find tasks or assignments with delays, switch to or modify a view to include the delay field you want to see. Then, turn on AutoFilters (Project ≻ Filtered For ≻ AutoFilter) and choose Custom from the field's filter drop-down list. In the Custom AutoFilter dialog box, create a filter to search for any delay greater than 0:

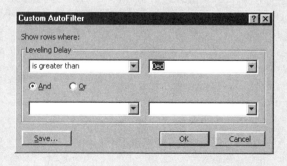

PART II

Creating a Project from Start to Finish

Preparing for Project Sign-Off

The project design is complete, leveled, and ready to present to stakeholders so they can give you the green light to move the project into implementation. The final form of the presentation depends on the relative importance of the project in the life of the organization, the comparative cost of the project, your organization's culture, documentation provided by previous project managers, and other factors too numerous to mention. As the project manager, your task is to make sure that stakeholders understand the proposed project as outlined, and either are in agreement with the plan or provide specific information to help you modify the plan to gain their agreement.

The sign-off meeting is also shaped by corporate culture and your project's position in the organization's life. Sign-off meetings range from a major sales presentation with multimedia and glossy brochures to relatively dull contractual meetings in which the loudest noise is pen-scratching on signature lines. Depending on how involved stakeholders have been in the design process and the amount of momentum and support the project already has, you'll prepare a variety of documents for the sign-off meeting. Materials created with software other than Project 2000 are often included in the project presentation materials for the sign-off meeting, such as:

- Narrative documents: Project Summary, business systems analysis, needs analysis, statement of intent, cover letter, risk/contingency analysis, force-field analysis
- Contractual documents: project contract, project charter, phase charter, letter of understanding, letter of agreement
- Supporting documents: brochures for vendors for contracted phases, references for vendors, comparison charts for material resources
- Electronic documents: electronic slide presentations, Web content
- Project management documents: change request forms
- Product demonstrations: live or video

We'll return to some of the project documents listed here later in this chapter. If you can think of it, it's probably been included in some project's sign-off meeting. For the project team, this can be the occasion for a celebration of a well-constructed plan, as well as the kick-off of a grand new project. We forgot to mention denim shirts with the project's logo, but they're a nice touch. (Feel free to send us a couple. We're also fond of the low-profile baseball caps.)

Project can't embroider shirts yet, but it can provide many of the other documents you may want to include in the presentation materials for the sign-off meeting:

- Summary Reports: Critical Tasks report, summary Gantt Charts, Top Level Tasks report, Milestones report, Project Summary report
- Proposed timelines: Gantt Charts, Calendars

- Budget information: Budget report, Cash Flow report, Crosstab report
- Staffing: Task Usage report, Resource Usage report

In this list, the reports outnumber views. If you don't see information you need to present in a report, you'll usually be able to provide it by customizing and printing a view. Examine the complete list of views and reports in Chapters 17 and 18, where you'll also find help on customizing views to meet your stakeholders' information requirements. Project 2000's reporting capabilities are limited, but its exporting and importing functions are fabulous. If you're comfortable working in Excel, consider exporting tables to Excel to create tables, charts, and summary reports. See Chapter 19 for detailed information on importing and exporting in Project 2000.

Tools to Avoid Scope Creep

Scope management begins with the project definition and continues through the entire project, but it should be a primary consideration as you prepare for the project sign-off. The scope management plan is a tool to help you manage expectations.

The scope management plan has two parts: the change assessment and a description of the change process. The change assessment is an estimate of how likely the project's scope is to change. The scope management plan isn't a list of measurable potential, but management's best guess about how the risk assessment and slack in the plan compare to the changing environment that the project plan operates within. If, for example, you used PERT to estimate durations (see Chapter 13, "Assessing and Managing Risks" for more about using PERT), the plan is less likely to change than if all durations were entered without analysis. If the environment is relatively static during the life of the project, the scope is less likely to change than if business rules are in flux and the organization is trying to respond. If the stakeholders have a clear understanding of the project, scope is also less likely to change.

To complete a change assessment, list the potential sources of scope change during the life of the project. For each source, use a three-point scale to indicate whether change from that source is likely, unlikely, or unknown. As the project progresses, pay close attention to the likely and unknown sources of scope change.

The second section of the scope management plan is the change request process. The process outlines the steps for handling change requests subsequent to the sign-off meeting. Typically, when change requests are received, they are evaluated to determine whether the change falls within the current scope as defined in the project documents provided in the sign-off meeting. If it does not, the project manager determines the following:

- The cost to implement the request
- The amount of delay, if any, if the request is implemented
- Other areas of the project impacted by implementing the request

The process includes an authorization process for requests that don't fall within the project scope. In most organizations, requests that don't increase the budget, extend the timeline, or delay deliverables can be approved by the project manager. The project manager may also have authority within a range. For example, the project manager can approve change requests that delay the project less than one day if the total scope change delay is less than one week or costs less than one thousand dollars to implement, provided that the total project cost overrun is less than ten thousand dollars. The change request process outlines the way requests that exceed the project manager's discretion are handled.

Managing Expectations

Experienced project managers report their secret to avoiding scope creep is to *manage expectations*: specifically, to manage stakeholders' expectations of the project deliverables. Whether your project's deliverables are soft goods, services, or durable goods, the project manager needs to clearly communicate the process for collecting, evaluating, and accepting recommended additions or modifications to the project plan.

The sign-off meeting has three key scope-related deliverables for the project manager. They aren't physical deliverables, so it's harder to know whether you've actually delivered, but the goal is that at the end of the sign-off process, you want stakeholders to understand the following:

- What they're going to get—the deliverables included in the project
- What they're not going to get—the deliverables that are *not* included in the project
- How to get something different—the change request process

At the end of the sign-off meeting, summarize these three items. In the packet of materials for the sign-off meeting, include an outline of the change process and change request forms (or directions for accessing online change forms). Communicate with team members to make sure they understand the process for handling change requests that they receive directly from stakeholders.

 TIP If you use Outlook and Exchange, you can set up a public folder with a simple post form for stakeholders and team members to suggest changes.

Capturing Baseline Data to Track Progress

After the project plan has been finalized—everyone who needs to has signed off and last-minutes adjustments have been made—the project is now ready to go. However, to track progress on the project, you need to have something to compare the actual results to. When you enter actual experience into the plan, Actual Start and Actual

Finish dates for example, Project has nothing to compare it to. To be able to calculate variance from the plan, you first have to save the project plan with a baseline. A *baseline* is a project plan that contains the original estimates for tasks, resources, assignments and costs. A baseline plan includes the data displayed in Table 11.1.

TABLE 11.1: FIELDS CAPTURED IN A BASELINE PLAN	
Data fields	**Type of Data**
Start and Finish Dates	Tasks, Assignments
Duration	Tasks
Splits	Tasks
Work	Tasks, Resources, Assignments
Costs	Tasks, Resources, Assignments
Timephased Work	Tasks, Resources, Assignments
Timephased Costs	Tasks, Resources, Assignments

PART

II

Creating a Project
from Start to Finish

With a baseline, you preserve the plan and use variances to judge your progress. You can compare task, resource, assignment and cost updates to the plan as well as actual information as the project work is completed. These variances are helpful for identifying potential problems in the project and in planning future projects.

When Project saves a baseline, it does not save a separate file. Rather, it saves key project data into Baseline fields within the existing project. The best time to save a baseline is after you have entered all of your estimates for start and finish tasks, duration, and costs; but before anyone has started work on the project.

Saving a Baseline

When you initially save a project, Project's Planning Wizard prompts you to save the project with or without a baseline. In Figure 11.12, you can see the Planning Wizard options. At this point in your project planning, it may be too early to save the project with a baseline. In that case, you have two options:

- Save the project without a baseline and let the Planning Wizard prompt you until you are ready to save the baseline.

- Save the project without a baseline and not be prompted again.

Choose this second option if the project is too small to warrant saving a baseline or if you want to initiate the option to save with a baseline when you are ready.

FIGURE 11.12

FIGURE 11.12

Project's Planning Wizard prompts you to save a plan with or without a baseline.

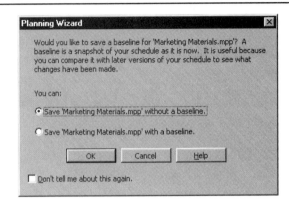

If you are ready to save the plan with the baseline, choose Save [project name] With a Baseline from the Planning Wizard. Project inserts the baseline data and saves the project.

To access the Save Baseline option after you have chosen not to be prompted, click the Tools menu and choose Tracking ➤ Save Baseline. This opens the Save Baseline dialog box shown in Figure 11.13. Click OK to create the baseline. The next time you save the project, Project saves the baseline with the project.

FIGURE 11.13

Use the Save Baseline dialog box to save a baseline without the Planning Wizard's help.

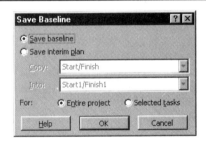

 TIP Before saving a project with a baseline, you may want to save a copy of the plan without the baseline. If you decide that you may have saved the baseline too soon, you can always save a new baseline, but it never hurts to maintain copies of the project prior to major project changes.

Viewing the Baseline

Once you saved the project with a baseline, you can view the baseline data by switching to the Tracking Gantt with the Baseline View, (View ➤ Tracking Gantt and View ➤ Tables ➤ More Tables ➤ Baseline), as shown in Figure 11.14.

FIGURE 11.14

The Tracking Gantt with Baseline view shows baseline and current data in the Gantt Chart and baseline numbers in the table.

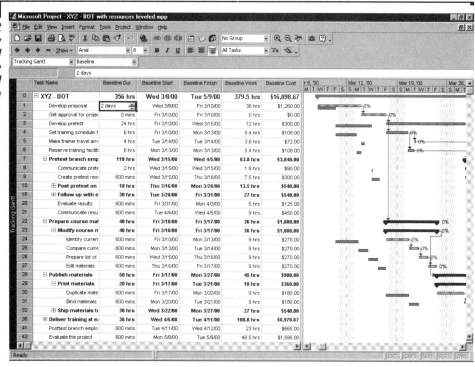

The Tracking Gantt displays gray bars to reflect the baseline. Red bars indicate critical tasks (see "Viewing the Critical Path" in Chapter 13, "Assessing and Managing Risks"), and blue bars show non-critical tasks. The baseline table contains the Baseline Duration, Baseline Start, Baseline Finish, Baseline Work, and Baseline Costs fields.

 TIP The toolbar displayed in Figure 11.14, which shows views and tables, is a custom toolbar designed to make it easier to switch between views and tables. To find out how to create this toolbar, see Chapter 21, "Customizing Project 2000."

Switch to the Variance table (View ➢ Table ➢ Variance) to see how your current plan differs from the saved baseline. If you have just saved the baseline, you should not see any variance. As you make changes to the plan and update actual task, resource, and assignment data, the Variance table is the best place to see how things are going. In Chapter 12, "Tracking Project Progress," we explore tracking project changes in more depth.

Editing the Baseline

After you save a baseline, you may find that you need to update certain data that you want included in the baseline. For example, after you saved a baseline, you find out that a group of tasks that were going to be contracted out can now be handled in-house. To incorporate this change into the project, you need to add some additional subtasks, adjust fixed costs, and add resources. Rather than include the changes as exceptions to the plan, you decide to include them in the baseline.

After you make the required changes to the project, you can follow these steps to revise the baseline for these tasks:

1. Select the changed and added tasks from the Gantt Chart Entry table.

2. Choose Tools ➤ Tracking and choose Save Baseline.

3. Click Selected Tasks.

4. Click OK.

If you decide that the changes to the project are pervasive enough to reset the entire project's baseline, choose Entire Project from the Save Baseline dialog box. This replaces the existing baseline data for the project with the new data.

Clearing a Baseline

To save a copy of a finished project without the baseline or to reverse the action of saving a baseline, you can clear the baseline from the entire project or from selected tasks. To clear the baseline, choose Tools ➤ Tracking ➤ Clear Baseline. Click OK to clear the baseline for the entire project. If you want to clear the baseline data only from some tasks, select the tasks first, choose Tools ➤ Tracking ➤ Clear Baseline, and choose Selected Tasks from the Clear Baseline dialog box shown in Figure 11.15.

FIGURE 11.15

Clear the baseline data only from selected tasks by choosing the Selected Tasks option before clicking OK.

Tracking Interim Plans

When you save a baseline, you save a full set of project estimates that you can use to track changes in your project. After you save a baseline and as your project progresses, you may also want to save interim plans along the way that record changes to the start and finish dates of current tasks.

Let's say, for example, that you have a task in your project that is scheduled to start on 3/15/00. When you save the baseline, the baseline records this as the original start date. You receive a call from your client, who indicates that they cannot release any more funds for this task until the start of the second quarter. Therefore, the start date of the task has to be postponed to 4/3/00. To record this change in the project, you can change the start date of the task to **4/3/00**, which automatically adds a Start No Earlier Than constraint on the task. You can then save an interim plan based on the new start date of 4/3/00. Next week, your client recontacts you and gives you the go-ahead to start the task on 3/20/00. Because the assigned resources have been on hold, you seize the opportunity to get started and enter the actual start date of **3/20/00** in the project. You can now track the history of the task by showing the Baseline (original plan) date of 3/15/00, the interim plan date of 4/3/00, and the actual date of 3/20/00.

 NOTE Because of the Start No Earlier Constraint on the task, you introduce a conflict when you enter the Actual Start Date of 3/20/00. If the Planning Wizard alerts you, you can click Continue to allow the conflict.

Figure 11.16 shows the actual dates (Actual Start/Finish), the current plan (Start/Finish), interim plan dates (Start1/Finish1), and baseline dates (Baseline Start/Finish). See "Viewing Interim Plans," later in this chapter, to set up this view in your project.

FIGURE 11.16

An interim plan allows you to track multiple dates related to a project.

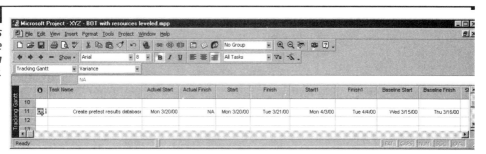

 TIP You may not want to apply the Start No Earlier constraint to the task in every situation. In that case, you can save the interim plan based on the current start/finish dates and then edit the interim start date directly to reflect the desired date. For information about how to do this, see "Updating Interim Plans," later in this chapter.

Saving an Interim Plan   You can save up to ten interim plans during the course of a project, which you can then compare to the project baseline and the current plan. To save an interim plan:

1. Choose Tools ➢ Tracking and choose Save Baseline.

2. Select Save Interim Plan.

3. From the Copy drop-down list, select the fields that contain the start and finish fields you want to save in the interim plan. In our earlier example, you would choose Start/Finish Dates.

4. From the Into drop-down list, select the fields you want to use as the interim plan fields.

5. Select whether you want the plan to apply to the entire project or only to selected tasks.

6. Click OK to save the plan.

Viewing an Interim Plan   To view an interim plan, you must insert the interim start/finish date columns into a sheet view such as the Tracking Gantt view. Follow these steps to view an interim plan:

1. Switch to a sheet view such as Tracking Gantt view—we recommend this view because it already contains all the other start/finish date columns you might want to compare to.

2. Right-click any column head and choose Insert ➢ Column.

3. In the Column Definition dialog box, select the interim plan start field (for example, Start1).

4. Click OK.

5. Repeat Steps 2–4 to add the interim plan finish field.

Updating an Interim Plan   After you have added the interim plan fields to a sheet view such as the Tracking Gantt view, you can edit the dates directly in the interim plan start and finish fields. Click in the interim plan start/finish cell for the task you want to edit.

What's Next

In our experience, this is the point when it's easy for the project manager to wonder why they wanted the job. A huge amount of time has been invested, and the "real project" is just beginning. Here's some good news. Although we can't say that the rest of the project is "all downhill," many of the management tasks in the implementation phase are tasks you're already familiar with from creating the project plan (adjusting the schedule, leveling resource assignments, assigning new resources, and modifying tasks). In Chapter 12, "Tracking Project Progress," we'll look at the day-to-day tasks of project management.

CHAPTER 12

Tracking Project Progress

When you create a project plan in Microsoft Project, the work doesn't end with the approval of the plan. Being an effective project manager means being able to develop a realistic project plan, manage the implementation of the plan, make adjustments to the plan when warranted, and ultimately learn from the process. You must be able to look at the whole project and anticipate the implications of a task that is slipping behind schedule or one that is miraculously completed ahead of schedule. Unfortunately, many project managers spend a lot of time developing the plan and then become too wrapped up in the details of its implementation to manage it effectively. In this chapter, you'll learn how to analyze the progress of a project and make changes to keep the project on track.

Updating Tasks with Actual Data

If you've spent a lot of time in planning a project, nothing is more exciting than seeing the first few project tasks completed. The project is finally underway and all the hard work that went into preparing for the project begins to pay off. In Chapters 15 and 16, we discussed the two most common methods of communicating with project team members about the status of tasks using Microsoft Project's workgroup tools: email and Web communication. With email, discussed in Chapter 15, you can use Project's TeamAssign, TeamUpdate, and TeamStatus tools to send and receive reports from team members. With the Web, discussed in Chapter 16, you can use Microsoft Project Central to keep team members informed about the status of the project, assign them tasks, and receive task reports. Both of these methods automatically update the project with actual work, timephased work, percent complete, and start and finish dates. Refer to Chapters 15 and 16 if you want more information about how to use Project workgroup tools to update project information.

 NOTE Timephased work is work on tasks as it appears on Project's timescale. Team members can report timephased work by using either Project's email or Web workgroup tools.

In the next section, we'll describe each of the data fields that you can use to track project data and then provide an overview of the different ways you can use to update data.

Understanding the Project Update Fields

Some tasks may not have resources assigned to them. Or, for whatever reason, perhaps you can't include some resources in the workgroup communication process. You can record progress on these tasks manually in Project. For tasks that do not have resources assigned to them, you can manually update the following:

- Actual Start and Finish

- Task Status, including Percent Complete, Actual Duration and Remaining Duration
- Costs

For the tasks that you have assigned resources to, you can also update

- Actual Work
- Timephased Work

Actual Start and Finish Dates

Actual Start is the date and time that a task actually begins. Project calculates this date based on entries to the Percent Complete field, Actual Work, or Percent Work Completed fields. You can also manually adjust the Actual Start date, however, if you do the scheduled Start Date field changes to match the Actual Start Date you enter.

Actual Finish is calculated when there is 0 remaining work or when the Percent Complete or Percent Work Complete fields are set to 100%.

 NOTE Both Actual Start and Actual Finish contain NA until it has values to display.

Percent Complete

The % Complete field is the percentage difference between Actual Duration and Duration. The actual formula Project uses is

```
% Complete = Actual Duration / Duration * 100
```

When you enter % Complete, Project automatically calculates Actual Duration and Remaining Duration. If you enter Actual Duration, Remaining Duration, or Actual Work (because it affects Actual Duration), Microsoft Project calculates Percent Complete.

 TIP In addition to the % Complete field, which is based on Actual Duration/Duration, Project also has a % Work Completed field that is based on the amount of actual work completed on the project (Percent Work Complete = (Actual Work/Work) * 100). If you want to enter % Work Completed, switch to any sheet view (for example, Task Sheet/Tracking table) and insert the % Work Completed column into the sheet.

Actual and Remaining Duration

Actual Duration is the total span of working time, regardless of the actual number of hours (amount of work) spent on a task. If a task, for example, starts on Monday and is completed on Friday, the Actual Duration is five days.

PART

II

Creating a Project
from Start to Finish

Remaining Duration is the difference between Scheduled Duration and Actual Duration. Project also calculates Remaining Duration based on the entry in Percent Completed. For example, if the duration of a task is five days and the task is 50% completed, the Remaining Duration is two and a half days.

 WARNING If you assign resources to tasks and use the default, effort-driven scheduling, do not enter Actual Duration. Instead, you should enter Actual Work. If the Actual Duration you enter is greater than the value in the Duration (Scheduled Duration) field, Microsoft Project updates Duration to equal Actual Duration, changes Remaining Duration to 0, and marks the task as 100% complete. For more about effort-driven scheduling, see Chapter 10, "Assigning and Scheduling Resources and Costs."

Actual Costs

Actual Costs include costs incurred by the project to date for resources and fixed costs attached to a task. Project calculates this field based on Actual Work, Actual Overtime Work, Per Use Cost, and Fixed Cost. The formula that Project uses is

```
Actual Cost = (Actual Work * Standard Rate) + (Actual Overtime Work *
Overtime Rate) + Resource Per Use Costs + Task Fixed Cost
```

Because of the complexity of calculating prorated actual costs, we recommend that you generally let Project calculate Actual Cost. However, you can specify whether you enter actual costs or have Microsoft Project automatically calculate them. Follow these steps to calculate Actual Costs manually:

1. Click Tools ➤ Options, and then click the Calculation tab.

2. Clear the Actual Costs Are Always Calculated by Microsoft Project check box.

3. Click OK to close the Options dialog box and save the changes.

If you choose to manually calculate actual costs, any actual costs you already entered will be cleared. If you choose to have Microsoft Project calculate actual costs, you can manually enter additional actual costs after the task is 100% complete.

Actual Work

Project calculates Actual Work based on the amount of work completed by the resources assigned to the project. This field is not available if you do not have resources assigned to a task. When you manually enter Actual Work, Project calculates Percent Work Complete and Remaining Work according to these formulas:

```
Percent Work Complete = Actual Work/Work
Remaining Work = Work-Actual Work
```

When you enter Percent Complete, Percent Work Complete, or Actual Work, Microsoft Project updates Actual Work for the task.

Timephased Actual Work is the actual work broken down into time periods. For more information about entering timephased Actual Work, see "Tracking Timephased Actual Work," later in this chapter.

Entering Task Update Data

You can update most project data by using the Tracking table in Task Sheet view. This view, shown in Figure 12.1, contains the Actual Start (Act. Start) and Finish (Act. Finish), Percent Complete (% Comp.), Actual Duration (Act. Dur.), Remaining Duration (Rem. Dur.), Actual Cost (Act. Cost), and Actual Work (Act. Work) fields. You can enter data into every column except the Actual Costs column. This is, by default, a calculated column. See "Updating Actual Costs," later in the chapter, to see how to enter values in this field.

To switch to the Task Sheet/Tracking Table view, follow these steps:

1. Choose View ➤ More Views ➤ Task Sheet. Click OK.

2. Choose Views ➤ Table ➤ Tracking.

FIGURE 12.1

Use the Task Sheet view of the Tracking table to update task data.

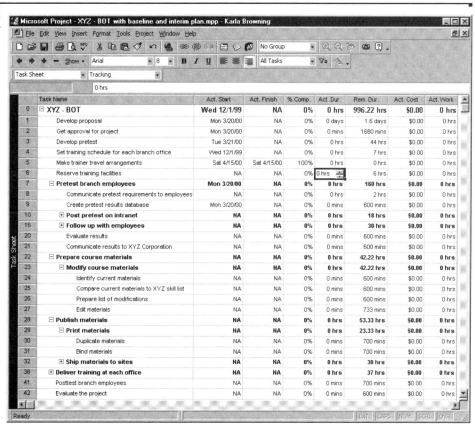

To enter date data into the table, follow these steps:

1. Click the cell you want to enter date data into, such as Act. Start.

2. Click the down arrow to select a date from the drop-down calendar.

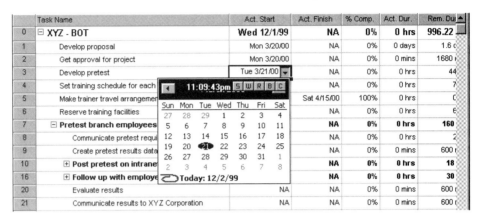

To enter numeric values in fields such as % Completed and Act. Dur., follow these steps:

1. Click the cell you want to enter numeric values into.

2. Use the up and down arrows on the spin box controls to change the values or type a number in the cell.

Using the Tracking Toolbar

The Tracking toolbar, shown in Figure 12.2, is a toolbar filled with useful shortcuts to help you update project information. Table 12.1 describes the function of each toolbar button.

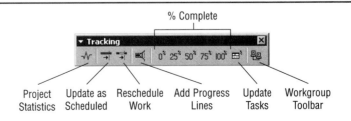

TABLE 12:1: TRACKING TOOLBAR BUTTONS

Button	Description
Project Statistics	Opens a message box, shown in Figure 12.3, that displays current, baseline, actual, and variance for Start, Finish, Duration, Work, and Costs.
Update as Scheduled	Changes the actual start and finish dates of all or selected tasks to match the schedule.
Reschedule Work	Reschedules the remaining duration on all or selected tasks to continue from the Status Date. You can set the Status Date in the Project Information dialog box (Project ➤ Project Information).
Add Progress Lines	Add progress lines to a Gantt Chart view to visually see where the project is ahead and behind schedule. (See "Adding Progress Lines to the Gantt Chart," later in this chapter.)
% Complete	Sets the percent complete on a task—buttons from 0% to 100%.
Update Tasks	Opens the Update Tasks dialog box (see "Using the Update Tasks Dialog Box," later in this chapter).
Workgroup Toolbar	Opens the Workgroup toolbar (see "Using the Workgroup Toolbar" in Chapter 15).

PART

II

Creating a Project
from Start to Finish

FIGURE 12.3

The Project Statistics message box provides a summary of the current project stats.

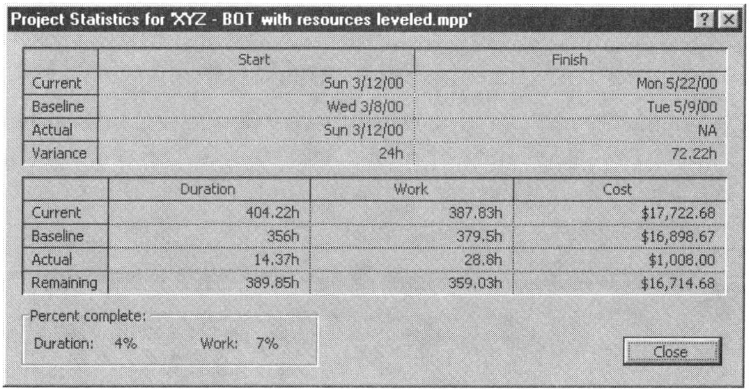

Project Statistics for 'XYZ - BOT with resources leveled.mpp'

	Start		Finish
Current	Sun 3/12/00		Mon 5/22/00
Baseline	Wed 3/8/00		Tue 5/9/00
Actual	Sun 3/12/00		NA
Variance	24h		72.22h

	Duration	Work	Cost
Current	404.22h	387.83h	$17,722.68
Baseline	356h	379.5h	$16,898.67
Actual	14.37h	28.8h	$1,008.00
Remaining	389.85h	359.03h	$16,714.68

Percent complete:

Duration: 4%   Work: 7%

Close

To access the Tracking toolbar, choose View ➤ Toolbars ➤ Tracking.

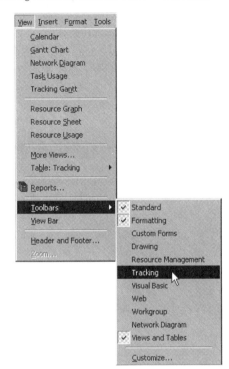

Using the Update Tasks Dialog Box

In the Update Tasks dialog box, shown in Figure 12.4, you can enter % Complete, Actual Duration, Remaining Duration, Actual Start and Finish, and Notes. You can access this dialog box from the Tracking toolbar and from the menu by clicking Tools ➤ Tracking ➤ Update Tasks.

FIGURE 12.4

In the Update Tasks dialog box, you can focus on updating an individual task.

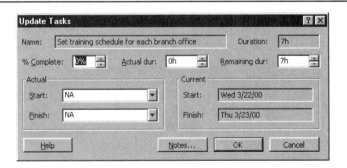

If you are on schedule, you can quickly update the completed tasks in the project to 100% by choosing Tools ➤ Tracking ➤ Update Project. This opens the Update Project dialog box shown in Figure 12.5.

FIGURE 12.5

Use the Update Project dialog box to update a group of on-schedule tasks to 100%.

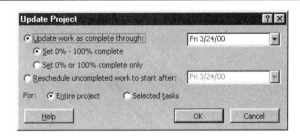

Updating Tasks for the Entire Project

To update tasks for the entire project up through a specified date by using the Update Project dialog box, follow these steps:

1. On the View menu, click Gantt Chart.

2. Click the Tools menu and choose Tracking ➤ Update Project.

3. Click Update Work as Complete Through and then type or select the date through which you want progress updated.

4. Click Set 0% or 100% Complete Only.

5. Select Entire Project.

6. Click OK.

NOTE If you only want to update some tasks in the project, select those tasks before opening the Update Project dialog box.

Entering Percent Complete

In addition to the Update Tasks and Update Projects dialog box, you can update Percent Complete, using the Tracking toolbar, by selecting the tasks you want to update and clicking the appropriate % Complete button (see "Using the Tracking Toolbar," later in this chapter).

Finally, you can update Percent Complete by dragging the left side of the Gantt bar. When you point to the left side of a bar on the Gantt Chart, the pointer changes to a % symbol with a right-pointing arrow. Drag that arrow over the Gantt bar until the correct Complete Through date appears in the information box that opens.

PART

II

Creating a Project
from Start to Finish

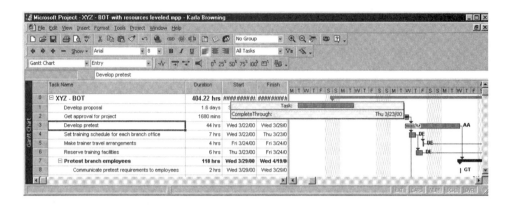

Tracking Timephased Actual Work

You can manually enter timephased actual work, or you can let Project enter it automatically based on data entered by resources in TeamStatus reports. If you want to enter timephased actual work manually, or if you want to review timephased work enter through TeamStatus reports, follow these steps:

1. Switch to Task Usage View (View ➤ Task Usage).

2. Choose the Tracking table (View ➤ Tables ➤Tracking).

3. Click Format ➤ Details, and select Actual Work.

In Figure 12.6, the timephased actual work was entered manually on a daily basis.

FIGURE 12.6

Switch to the Tracking table in Task Usage view to enter time-phased Actual Work.

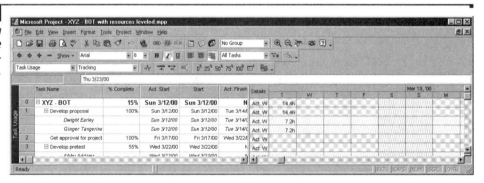

TIP Change the timescale of the Task Usage Tracking table by right-clicking on the gray area that displays the timescale and choosing TimeScale.

Reviewing Variances from the Baseline

Whether you are manually updating task data or using the workgroup tools to have Project update task data based on TeamStatus reports, comparing the actual results with the baseline and interim plan data gives you a lot of information about the status of the project. Project calculates variances to baseline for start and finish dates, duration, work, and costs. You can most easily display these variances by switching to Tracking Gantt view and selecting the Variance table.

The Tracking Gantt view, shown in Figure 12.7, displays gray bars for the baseline start and finish dates, in addition to the blue or red bars for actual or scheduled start and finish dates (red bars indicate critical path tasks).

FIGURE 12.7

The Tracking Gantt shows the difference between baseline dates and actual or scheduled dates.

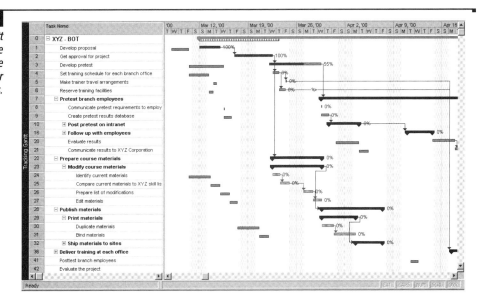

PART

II

Creating a Project from Start to Finish

The Variance table, shown in Figure 12.8, contains fields that show the baseline data and variances, and you can add additional fields to compare actual and scheduled dates and interim plans. For more about baselines, see "Capturing Baseline Data to Track Progress" in Chapter 11.

FIGURE 12.8

Use the Variance table to compare actual results with baseline and interim plan data.

Task Name	Actual Start	Actual Finish	Start	Finish	Start1	Finish1	Baseline Start	Baseline Finish	Start Var
0 ⊟ XYZ - BOT	Sun 3/12/00	NA	#########	Mon 5/22/00	Thu 3/9/00	Wed 5/17/00	Wed 3/8/00	Tue 5/9/00	24 h
1 Develop proposal	Sun 3/12/00	Tue 3/14/00	Sun 3/12/00	Tue 3/14/00	Wed 3/15/00	Fri 3/17/00	Wed 3/8/00	Fri 3/10/00	24 h
2 Get approval for project	Fri 3/17/00	Wed 3/22/00	Fri 3/17/00	Wed 3/22/00	Fri 3/17/00	Wed 3/22/00	Fri 3/10/00	Fri 3/10/00	36 h
3 Develop pretest	Wed 3/22/00	NA	Wed 3/22/00	Wed 3/29/00	Thu 3/30/00	Fri 3/31/00	Fri 3/10/00	Wed 3/15/00	60 h
4 Set training schedule for ea	NA	NA	Wed 3/22/00	Thu 3/23/00	Mon 3/20/00	Mon 3/20/00	Fri 3/10/00	Mon 3/13/00	64 h
5 Make trainer travel arranger	NA	NA	Fri 3/24/00	Fri 3/24/00	Mon 4/17/00	Mon 4/17/00	Tue 3/14/00	Tue 3/14/00	65 h
6 Reserve training facilities	NA	NA	Thu 3/23/00	Fri 3/24/00	Mon 3/20/00	Tue 3/21/00	Mon 3/13/00	Mon 3/13/00	65 h
7 ⊟ Pretest branch employe	**NA**	**NA**	**Wed 3/29/00**	**Wed 4/19/00**	**Fri 3/24/00**	**Thu 4/13/00**	**Wed 3/15/00**	**Wed 4/5/00**	**80 h**
8 Communicate pretest re	NA	NA	Wed 3/29/00	Wed 3/29/00	Fri 3/24/00	Fri 3/24/00	Wed 3/15/00	Wed 3/15/00	80 h

Viewing and Printing Summary Reports

Printing views and reports provide the hard documentation that you sometimes need to evaluate what is going on in a project and communicate information to project stakeholders. At this point in the project, you may be interested in printing some of the project in-progress reports, such as Tasks in Progress, Should Have Started Tasks, and Slipping Tasks. These reports are available from the Reports menu (View ➤ Reports and choose Current Activities).

Costs reports—such as the Cash Flow, Overbudget Tasks, and Overbudget Resources reports—provide invaluable cost information to help you make necessary budget adjustments. The Overallocated Resources reports on the Assignment button and the Task Usage and Resource Usage reports on the Workload button all provide an in-depth look at the status of resource assignments. And, of course, any of the Overview reports give you a snapshot of the project as it stands on a global basis.

You can learn more about printing views and reports in Chapter 17, "Using Views to Evaluate Data," and Chapter 18, "Using Reports to Analyze Data."

Adding Progress Lines to the Gantt Chart

To help you see the status of the project schedule, you may want to add progress lines to the Gantt Chart or Tracking Gantt, as shown in Figure 12.9. When you add progress lines, Microsoft Project draws a line that connects in-progress tasks and tasks that should have started. Peaks pointing to the left represent work that is behind schedule, and peaks pointing to the right represent work that is ahead of schedule.

FIGURE 12.9

Add progress lines to see where the project is ahead of schedule and behind schedule.

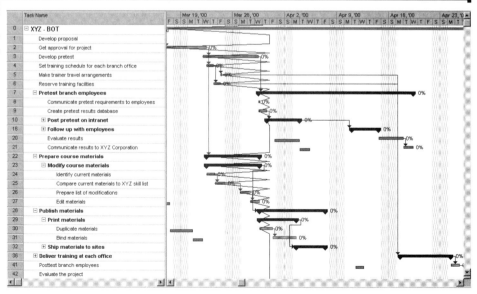

To define progress lines, choose Tools ➤ Tracking ➤ Progress Lines to open the Progress Lines dialog box, shown in Figure 12.10, and follow these steps:

1. Select the Always Display Current Progress Line check box to always display the current progress line.

2. Click At Project Status Date or At Current Date to indicate where you want the progress lines to appear.

3. Select the Display Progress Lines at Recurring Intervals check box; then click Daily, Weekly, or Monthly to specify a time interval to display progress lines at specific time intervals.

4. Indicate whether you want the progress lines to start at the Project Start date or another date that you define.

5. Select the Display Selected Progress Lines check box, and then type or select the dates for which you want progress lines displayed to display a progress line on a specific date. Click the Delete button if you want to remove a date.

6. Choose whether you want to display progress lines in relation to the actual plan or the baseline.

7. Click the Line Styles tab and select progress line type, color, progress point shape, and progress point color for the current and all other progress lines. You can also indicate if you want a date displayed for each progress line.

8. Click OK to close the Progress Lines dialog box and apply the progress lines.

PART

II

Creating a Project
from Start to Finish

FIGURE 12.10

Use the Progress Lines
dialog box to set up
the way you want
progress displayed in
the Gantt Chart.

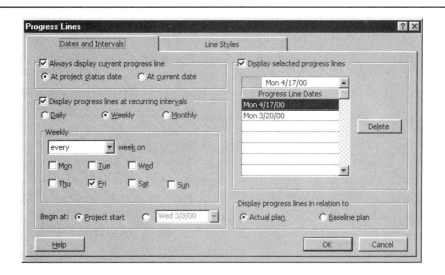

If you want to add additional progress lines to the Gantt Chart, click the Add Progress Lines button on the Tracking toolbar (View ➤ Toolbar ➤ Tracking). When the pointer changes to a tracking line shape, click in the Gantt Chart at the desired date to insert a progress line.

Using Earned Value Analysis to Analyze Project Performance

Real projects don't run precisely on schedule or on budget. When you have tasks starting and finishing ahead of schedule or slipping behind, and costs running over or under budget, it's hard to tell at a glance whether you're under budget because you're behind schedule or under budget because you're spending less than budgeted. (You're just grateful that you're not behind schedule and *over* budget!) It's good to know that you're going to run out of money before you run out. Earned value analysis is a set of simple calculations that separates budget performance from work performance so you can manage costs and work in the midst of the chaos.

Earned value analysis uses three task-related values to calculate variances and ratios that drive project performance analysis and management. There's a bit of arithmetic involved in these values, variances, and ratios, but it's worth examining the formulas so you understand how to apply the values to analyze your project. The task-related values are as follows:

Budgeted Cost of Work Scheduled   BCWS is the cost that would have been incurred for a task from the beginning of the project until the status date if the task were incurring the scheduled costs. BCWS is the baseline budget.

Budgeted Cost of Work Performed   BCWP is the cost that should have been incurred between the beginning of the project and the status date, based on the actual work performed. BCWP is the actual hours calculated at the baseline cost, and is also called *earned value.*

Actual Cost of Work Performed   ACWP is the actual cost incurred for the task between the beginning of the project and the status date. ACWP is actual costs for the task.

BCWS and BCWP are both calculated from the project baseline, so you must save a baseline before you can do earned value analysis. There's another way to describe these three fundamental values. It's overly simplistic, but clearly underlines the differences between the three:

- Budgeted Cost of Work Scheduled is the baseline hourly cost multiplied by the baseline scheduled hours (BCWS = baseline cost * baseline hours).

- Budgeted Cost of Work Performed is the baseline hourly cost multiplied by the actual hours (BCWP = baseline cost * actual hours).
- Actual Cost of Work Performed is the actual hourly cost multiplied by the actual hours (ACWP = actual cost * actual hours).

To see how the three values are calculated, let's look at a task that has 80 hours of work over 10 days duration in the project baseline. The resource assigned to the task in the baseline costs $12.50 an hour, so each day of work was budgeted to cost $100. The project manager had to assign a different resource that costs $16 per hour. At the end of the third day, only 20 hours of work have been performed rather than the 24 hours that were scheduled. Figure 12.11 shows the task's BCWS, BCWP, and ACWP at the end of the third day.

- BCWS: 24 hours were scheduled at $12.50 per hour, so the cost of these three days in the baseline budget is $300 (24* $12.50).
- BCWP: 20 hours of work were performed, so the budgeted cost of the actual work is $250 (20 * $12.50).
- ACWP: 20 hours of actual work were performed at an actual rate of $16, so the actual cost of work performed is $320 (20* $16).

FIGURE 12.11

The Earned Value fundamental values show the difference between budgeted and actual costs.

Task Name	BCWS	BCWP	ACWP	v 28, '99 M T W T F S	Dec 5, '99 S M T W T F S	Dec 12, '99 S M T W T F S
Ten Day Task	$300.00	$250.00	$320.00			Worker 2

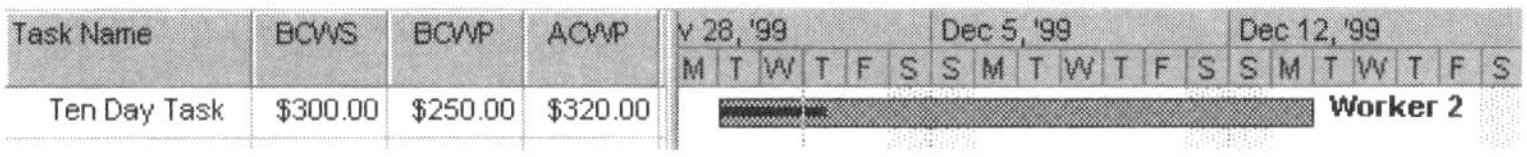

 TIP If you've had a course in managerial accounting, you'll remember these concepts from labor and material variance calculations.

Calculating Earned Value Variances

The three values are used to calculate two variances and two ratios, which is where it really gets interesting. *Schedule variance (SV)* compares BCWS to BCWP (budgeted costs for scheduled and actual work) and isolates the budget difference attributable solely to the difference between scheduled work and actual work. *Cost variance (CV)* compares BCWP and ACWP (budgeted and actual costs for actual work) to isolate the budget difference solely attributable to the difference in resource costs.

$$SV = BCWP–BCWS$$

$$CV = BCWP–ACWP$$

The variances are in dollars. In the example in Figure 12.12, schedule variance (SV) is a negative fifty dollars: –$50. Cost variance (CV) is –$70.

Task Name	BCWS	BCWP	ACWP	v 28, '99 M T W T F S	Dec 5, '99 S M T W T F S	Dec 12, '99 S M T W T F S
Ten Day Task	$300.00	$250.00	$320.00			Worker 2

Calculating Earned Value Ratios

The variance figures reflect the budget for the task, so it's hard to compare the results from one task to another task with a very different workload or hourly cost. A variance of $50 halfway though a one-day task may be worth noticing. A variance of $50 near the end of a yearlong task is chickenfeed, peanuts, or some other cheap livestock food. The two indices use division instead of multiplication, so you can appropriately compare one task to another or one project to another project at the same point in a schedule.

The *Schedule Performance Index (SPI)* is the ratio of actual work performed to the scheduled work (SPI = BCWP/BCWS).

The *Cost Performance Index (CPI)* (not to be confused with the Consumer Price Index, which is clearly not well managed) is the ratio of baseline budget costs to the actual costs incurred for the task (CPI = BCWP/ACWP).

Calculating Cost Estimates

Project 2000 also uses the actual costs and work to estimate the financial future of your project. These estimates aren't strictly part of earned value analysis, but they answer the questions that loom just over the project horizon:

- **Estimate at Completion (EAC)** includes fixed costs, actual costs, plus the remaining costs for a task. Note that this estimate is the estimate if the remainder of a task's work is completed as budgeted.

- **Baseline Cost, or Budget at Completion (BAC)** is as described: fixed costs plus baseline resource costs. BAC includes overtime hours at the overtime rate and standard hours at the standard rate.

- **Variance at Completion (VAC)** is the difference between BAC and EAC (VAC = BAC – EAC).

Now the good news: you're working on a computer with a first-class software package, so you don't have to calculate any of these fundamental values, variances, ratios, or estimates. To see all the earned value variances and cost estimates, display the Earned Value table in any task view. To display earned value columns in a Gantt Chart:

1. Switch to Gantt Chart view (View ➤ Gantt Chart).

2. Choose View ➤ Tables ➤ More Tables to open the More Tables dialog box.

3. Select the Earned Value table and click Apply.

The Gantt Chart with earned value columns for the XYZ-BOT project file is shown in Figure 12.13.

FIGURE 12.13

Project 2000 calculates all the earned values variances.

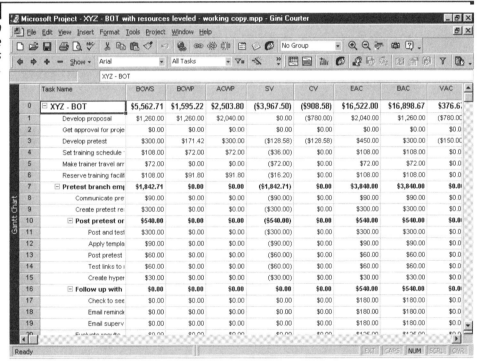

PART

II

Creating a Project
from Start to Finish

 TIP You can add the fundamentals, variances, ratios, and cost estimates to any task view by inserting a column.

Analyzing Variances and Ratios

The three fundamental values (BCWP, BCWS, and ACWP) aren't used directly in analysis. The two variances—schedule variance and cost variance, which can be either positive or negative numbers—are the more important values. The larger the number, the greater the variance between performance and the schedule, or the actual cost and the baseline. When SV or CV are positive, things are looking good. Positive schedule variance means that tasks are ahead of schedule. When cost variance is positive, the project is under budget.

Negative variances are bad news. When schedule variance is negative, the project is behind schedule. If the cost variance is positive, you have some room to add resources to solve the schedule problems. If cost variance is negative, the project is currently over budget.

The earned value indices are small numbers. If there is no schedule variance, then SPI is 1.0. If there's no cost variance, then CPI is 1.0. As with the variances, "negative" numbers (in the case of an index, a number less than 1.0) mean that the project is behind schedule or over budget. Numbers greater than 1 are good. If CPI is greater than 1, the project is ahead of budget. If SPI is greater than 1, the project is ahead of schedule.

 TIP If you want to track your progress when bringing a project back on schedule or within budget, add the CPI and SPI columns to the Gantt Chart, and keep track of changes to the indices at the project or phase level on a weekly or monthly basis.

Analyzing the Cost Estimates

The Estimate at Completion and Baseline at Completion estimates are less important than the Variance at Completion (see Figure 12.12). VAC indicates whether the project will finish over or under budget. If VAC is positive, the project will finish under budget. Negative VAC means that the project will finish over budget. If the budget is constrained, a negative VAC is a call to action if the project is to be completed at all.

Bear in mind that the Variance at Completion estimate is not the result of a trend analysis. If your project is running over budget at the halfway point, VAC reflects the estimate if all remaining tasks are completed within the baseline budget. If you feel the over budget performance will continue for the duration of the project, multiply the VAC by the inverse of the percent of the project completed for an estimate of the true variance at completion. In this example, we'd multiply the VAC by 2 because the project is 50% completed (1 divided by 50% is the inverse of 50%). If the project is 75% completed, and you expect the current budget trends to continue, multiply VAC by the inverse of 75%, 1.33 (1 divided by 0.75 = 1.33).

Applying Earned Value Analysis to Resources and Assignments

Earned value analysis isn't limited to tasks. You can use earned value analysis to analyze resources and assignments to see who or what is over budget and behind schedule. If you're looking for a scapegoat, earned value analysis will help you find at least one. You, of course, would be the other scapegoat because you assigned the resources to the tasks in the first place. But we digress.

 TIP Use earned value analysis in a resource view filtered for materials resources to see variance in materials usage for project tasks.

To see the earned value analysis fields for resources or assignments, switch to an appropriate view, display the Earned Value table by choosing View ➢ More Views, and select Earned Value from the More Tables dialog box. A Resource Usage sheet with the earned value columns is shown in Figure 12.14.

FIGURE 12.14

Use earned value to analyze resource and assignment performance.

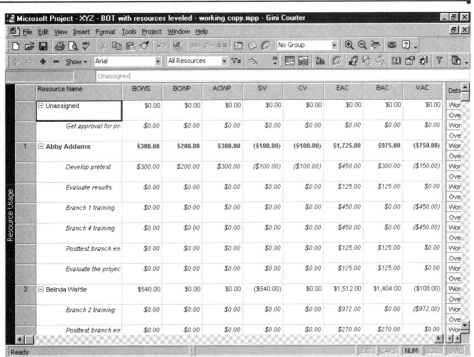

Keeping the Project on Track

After you have analyzed the source of problems with your projects, you can make the necessary adjustments to the project plan to get the project back on track. Although our assumption is, of course, that projects tend to run over budget and behind schedule, believe it or not, some projects may run under budget and ahead of schedule. In both circumstances, you have to decide what to do to correct the variances and bring the project back in line. In Chapter 1, "Project 2000 Basics," we introduced you to the concept of the project triangle: time, money, and scope. Every decision you make about how to adjust the project affects one or more sides of the project triangle and ultimately impacts quality. Notice that we do not say that a change negatively impacts quality. Whether you are ahead or behind your plan, you can make adjustments that have an ultimately positive or negative impact on project quality.

If you find that you are in the enviable position of having more time or money than you anticipated, you can choose to offer your client the option of broadening the scope of the project. Depending on whether your client is an internal or external customer, you may decide it is better to maintain the current scope and save the company some money. If the project is progressing faster than you planned, you might decide to free up some of your project's resources to work on another project.

If, on the other hand, you are running out of time or money, you need to look at ways to reduce scope, streamline tasks, or trim down costs. You might be able to renegotiate the project scope with your clients by dividing the project into phases or by eliminating non-critical tasks. To keep a project on schedule, you might need to add additional resources to regain control of slipping tasks. Whatever choice you make, be sure to review the implications of each decision to scope, time, money, and quality.

What's Next

In Chapter 13, "Assessing and Managing Risks," you'll be introduced to another project management analysis tool, called PERT, and learn how to use PERT and other Project tools to assess and manage risks.

Juggling and Managing Projects

LEARN TO:

- *Assess and Manage Risks*

- *Share Resources and Tasks Among Multiple Project*

- *Communicate Project Information*

- *Manage Team Projects with Project Central 2000*

CHAPTER **13**

Assessing and Managing Risks

Risk refers to events that introduce an element of chance into a project. You can't predict the future, so every project involves risk. Projects that include something innovative and therefore less predictable—for example, a new product design or a development process that you haven't used previously—have a higher chance of failure than a project implementing a procedure that's tried-and-true. In this chapter, we'll discuss strategies to analyze and manage project risk.

Assessing Risk

After a project enters the development phase, events may affect the project timeline, costs, or budget. A difficult aspect of project management is finding ways to complete a project successfully in an environment in which the following occur:

- Contracted resources are suddenly unavailable.
- Members of the project team terminate employment or transfer out of the project team.
- Unseasonably bad weather causes delays for outdoor tasks.
- Customers or stakeholders add deliverables.
- Tasks take more or less time than scheduled.
- Labor disputes delay project activities or increase costs.
- Costs for material resources increase substantially.

Risk management has three components—assessing, planning, and managing risks—that will affect the project timeline, scope, or budget.

Some naïve project managers feel that risk analysis leads to negativity, so they limit the team members' involvement in risk analysis. Other managers feel their personal crisis-management skills will overcome any possible problems, so they skip or give short shrift to the risk analysis. The function of risk analysis is to ensure that your project is only kicked off track by unforeseeable events, as opposed to unexamined events. We recommend a thorough risk analysis and contingency plans to manage or respond to events that can put a project seriously over budget or behind schedule.

When you assess risks, you'll focus on project activities and external factors that increase project uncertainty. Begin by focusing on three types of project tasks:

- Tasks that have estimated durations
- Tasks with external predecessors that are partially or completely outside the project manager's control
- Tasks with long durations

Viewing Tasks with Uncertain Duration

To analyze risks, begin with the unknown aspects of your project. Examine the tasks that have estimated durations, and nail the durations down before the development phase. To view tasks with estimated durations, first turn off AutoFilter if AutoFilter is turned on (Project ➤ Filtered For ➤ AutoFilter). Then, follow these steps:

1. Choose View ➤ Gantt Chart.

2. Choose Project ➤ Filtered For ➤ Tasks with Estimated Durations.

The Gantt Chart will include only tasks with estimated durations. For each task in the Gantt Chart, determine why the duration is estimated. If you can enter the task's duration, do so now. For strategies to analyze task duration, see "Using PERT to Estimate Duration," later in this chapter.

Viewing Tasks with External Dependencies

Tasks that depend on tasks or deliverables from other projects require special consideration. If a task's predecessors are in another project, schedule changes in the other project can impact your project's schedule. For example, one of the deliverables for the marketing project you're managing is a brochure that includes pictures of a product's prototype. Creation of the prototype is a deliverable for another project. The activities to create the prototype are not within your control. The prototype may not be created on time.

The XYZ Branch Office Training project, created in Chapters 2 through 5, was split into two separate projects. Training setup and delivery remain in the original XYZ-BOT project file; curriculum development, printing, and shipping have been placed in a separate project: XYZ Materials. The Materials project is being managed by the training development supervisor.

In the XYZ-BOT project, the final task in the Materials project, Schedule Delivery, appears as a task in the Gantt Chart. The task's bar is gray to indicate that it is an external task, as shown in Figure 13.1. If you double-click an external task in the task table, Project opens the external project file.

PART

III

Juggling and Managing Projects

FIGURE 13.1

External tasks are included in the Gantt Chart.

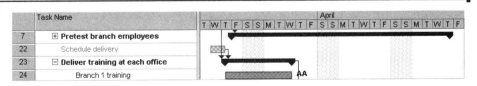

If the external predecessors are being managed in Microsoft Project 2000, you'll get good information about the predecessor. By default, you are notified when information about a task in an externally linked project changes. When you open a file that contains links to another project that has changed, Project 2000 opens the Links Between

Projects dialog box, shown in Figure 13.2, to display the status of external predecessors and successors, and their impact on your project's schedule. In Figure 13.2, the start date for the external linked task has been changed in the XYZ Materials schedule.

FIGURE 13.2

View external predecessors in the Links Between Projects dialog box.

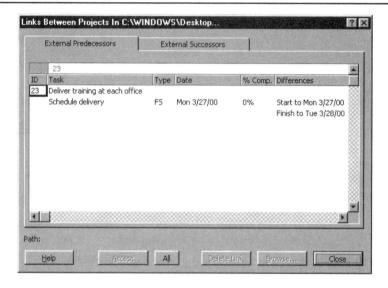

The second tab of the Links Between Projects dialog box shows external successors that rely on your project's tasks. Figure 13.3 shows the XYZ Materials project's external successor, Deliver Training in the XYZ-BOT project file.

FIGURE 13.3

The Links Between Projects dialog box displays external successors that rely on your project's tasks.

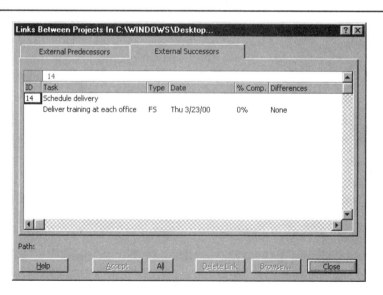

To view the status of external dependencies when your project file is already open, choose Tools ➤ Links Between Projects to open the Links Between Projects dialog box.

 NOTE See Chapter 8, "Scheduling and Linking Project Tasks," for more information about external links.

Flagging Tasks with External Dependencies

Project 2000 makes it easy to communicate about interproject dependencies. When your project depends on external projects that are not managed in Project 2000, you must establish your communication requirements with the other projects' managers. It's a good idea to add visual cues to tasks with external dependencies so they stand out in the Gantt Chart. Select the task and choose Format ➤ Font to open the Font dialog box, and then choose a different font or color for external tasks.

 TIP You can add a custom field to a task to record an external dependency. See Chapter 23, "Customizing Fields and Forms," for information on custom fields.

Viewing Tasks with Long Durations

If a task is scheduled to start on Monday and finish two days later on Wednesday, you'll notice that the task is three days behind when it doesn't finish on schedule. With longer tasks, delays of three days, three weeks, or three months are more easily camouflaged. Even when you use Project 2000's workgroup communication tools to request regular updates, it's sometimes hard to know that a task with a long duration is slipping.

 TIP Longer-duration tasks are less flexible than a series of shorter-duration tasks. When possible, break a task into smaller work packages to increase scheduling flexibility.

It is easy to understand why long-duration tasks often fall behind schedule. Short-duration tasks provide little room to maneuver. Team members realize that a two-day task needs to be started two days before the finish date. There are, after all, only two days when team members can work overtime to make up for a late start. The completion date is only two days away, which makes the deadline very real. After the first day, team members have a good idea of the task's status. They can quantify the number of hours spent on the task, and know how many are left to go.

Team members may report that a task with a distant deadline is on schedule when little or no time has been spent on the task. With longer durations, team members have more days that they can come in early or stay late to play "catch up" before the scheduled finish date. The task deadline is a long way off, whereas other tasks' deadlines (such as that two-day task) are imminent. It may not be practical for the team to work 16 hours tomorrow to get a two-day task back on track, but team members rationalize that they can find eight extra hours sometime in the next month to make up for missing eight hours of work on today's task. When the project team focuses on completing each task by the scheduled finish date, the schedule for longer duration tasks is often compromised so that shorter duration tasks can be completed.

To view tasks with longer duration:

1. Switch to Gantt Chart view (View ➤ Gantt Chart).

2. Display the Entry table (View ➤ Table Entry) or another table that includes Duration.

OR

2. Right-click on the table, choose Insert Column from the shortcut menu, and insert the Duration column.

3. Turn on AutoFilters (Project ➤ Filtered For... ➤ AutoFilter or click the AutoFilter button on the standard toolbar).

4. Click the AutoFilter drop-down arrow in the Duration field.

5. Choose a duration from the drop-down list.

OR

5. Choose Custom to specify a duration in the Custom AutoFilter dialog box, shown next.

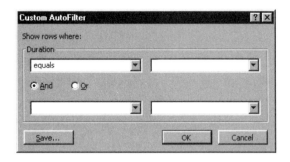

Identifying and Managing Other Risks

Viewing tasks with estimated duration, long duration, or external dependencies focuses on task-based risks. Now that you've examined the trees, step back and look at the entire forest using contingency planning and force-field analysis. With these tools, you'll ask two questions: What can go wrong? What are the forces that support and oppose the project?

Creating a Contingency Plan

A *contingency plan* is a list of events that would impact the project schedule or budget, and plans for handling those events if they occur. For a small project in your area of expertise, you may be able to answer the question: What can go wrong? For larger projects that involve specific technical expertise, assemble members of the project team and brainstorm a list of events that may occur during the life of the project.

Some team members might have difficulty answering the broad question "What can go wrong?" Here are other ways to ask this question that our team members have found helpful:

- What real or potential obstacles would prevent you from performing your assignments as scheduled?
- What guarantees do you need to be able to ensure that you can perform your assignments as scheduled?
- What do you need from the project manager to guarantee your success with this project?
- Do you see any places where you might expect difficulties in the project schedule? If so, where?

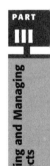

For the XYZ Branch Office Training project, our risk list included the following:

- No training facilities for lease at one or more locations
- Sudden loss of a trainer (personal illness, family illness, or death)
- Incorrect software installed on computers in rented facilities
- Pretests completed too late to be used to drive course content
- Travel problems: cancelled flights, missed connections, weather delays
- Shipped materials don't arrive before training starts

After you identify the risks, develop contingencies to counter each risk. Our risk and contingency analysis is shown in Table 13.1.

TABLE 13.1: XYZ RISK AND CONTINGENCIES

Risk	Contingency
Sudden unavailability of leased lab	Lease laptops and arrange nearby hotel space.
Leased lab is unsuitable	Arrange for branch office director to assign staff to visit and approve leased lab.
Loss of a trainer	Assign backup trainer for each training.
	Make sure that one trainer is unscheduled during each week of training.
Incorrect software installed on computers in rented facilities	Have trainer arrive one day in advance to check facility.
	Provide the trainer with correct software for emergency installation.
Pretests completed too late to be used to drive course content	Develop initial curricula without pretest.
	Increase the delay between pretest release and curricula finalization.
Travel problems: cancelled flights, missed connections, weather delays	Fly the trainer to location one day in advance.
Shipped materials don't arrive before training starts	Provide the trainer with master copy of materials for onsite duplication.
	Verify receipt of shipped materials with each site.

You can't develop a contingency for every risk. If the only airport within 500 miles of the training site is closed for two days because of unusually heavy snowfall, a hurricane, or a bomb threat, travel delay is unavoidable. Brainstorm contingencies where possible, and then decide which contingencies to build into the project plan and which to hold on reserve, based on the likelihood of the risk events and the cost of including the contingency.

NOTE At least one member of every project team can fantasize and defend a list of events that stretch credulity. When someone suggests that "the end of life as we know it" would compromise your project timeline, don't start an exhaustive search for contingencies. Reframe the discussion.

In Table 13.1, for example, having the trainers arrive at the training site one day in advance covers two areas of risk. By arriving a day early, trainers can check to make sure that the software installed at the training site is correct, and they can minimize the risk associated with cancelled flights and missed connections. The costs to implement this contingency include increased expenses for accommodations and trainer pay, but those may be acceptable costs compared to the costs of rescheduling part or all of a training course. Some contingencies have little or no cost: providing trainers with master copies of materials or verifying the receipt of materials shipped to individual sites.

Storing the Contingency Plan

The contingency plan document, which doesn't need to be any more formal than Table 13.1, should be linked to the project summary task. If you need the contingency plan, you probably won't have extra time to search for it! For task-related contingencies such as renting laptops and hotel space, use copy and paste to include the contingency in the task's Notes tab:

Identifying Environmental Risks

Force-field analysis is a tool used by project managers to understand a project's external environment. The results of the analysis are two lists of forces—positive and

negative—that may impact the project. In many organizations, force-field analysis is completed prior to project design. If the negative forces aligned against a project are immense, the project never enters the design phase. See if a force-field analysis has been completed before starting your own analysis.

Unlike the risk/contingency analysis, a force-field analysis is not task-oriented. You may want to complete the force-field analysis on your own, with another project manager, or with your immediate supervisor. The tool is simple: create a two-column list in Word, Excel, or on a sheet of paper. Label one column **Positive**; label the other **Negative**. In the Positive column, list the forces that will support or assist with the project. In the Negative column, list the forces that will oppose or resist the project. The force-field analysis for our sample XZY Branch Office Training project is shown in Table 13.2.

TABLE 13.2: XYZ-BOT FORCE-FIELD ANALYSIS

Positive	Negative
Support from XYZ management	Resistance to training by outsiders.
Solid trainers	Branch offices traditionally oppose or resist "main office initiatives."
XYZ's commitment to professional development	Employees are required to take time from regular tasks to attend training.
Industry-wide interest in training and certification	Trainers' concern about extended time out-of-state.
XYZ involvement in TQM process	Employees' reluctance to participate in workplace tests.

With formal force-field analysis, the next step is to estimate the strength of each positive and each negative force, using a scale of 1 to 10 or 1 to 100. The positive and negative columns are then totaled and compared. If the positive total vastly outweighs the negative total, then the analysis indicates that the project will succeed. If the negative total outweighs the positive total or if the two are close, the project is not likely to succeed. This leaves five possible courses of action:

- Redesign the project to eliminate negative forces.
- Cancel the project.
- Bolster the positive forces so they significantly outweigh the negative forces.
- Weaken the negative forces so positive forces significantly outweigh them.
- Develop strategies that bypass the negative forces.

Many project managers, including your authors, are more comfortable with a less-quantified use of force-field analysis. Accurately naming the forces that impact project success is difficult. The "value" of the strength of the organizational and societal forces identified in the analysis often becomes little more than guesswork. Assigning a numerical importance or strength to each force creates a false sense of precision that can drive poor decisions and wasted effort.

After developing the list of positive and negative forces, we suggest that you view the positives as forces to be maintained and leveraged through the life of the project. The project manager has plenty of opportunities to recognize and strengthen positive forces. For example:

- Project reports can recognize and reinforce the positive forces. In our sample project, one of the positive forces is XYZ Corporation's involvement in Total Quality Management. We could integrate information about our company's TQM efforts in this project into our project reports.

- Information about how this training project reflects the industry-wide movement for training and certification could be easily integrated in a project proposal or project evaluation.

- Informal communications can strengthen and build on the positive forces. We could send personal notes to our trainers to remind them that their expertise is valued and recognized.

Negative forces are often the outgrowth of personal concerns about job security, quality of life, or power within an organization: individual issues can become larger than life as the project progresses. Rather than declare war on negative forces, the project manager can look for ways to downplay or address negative forces without compromising the project plan:

- One of the negative forces is our trainers' concern about extended time out-of-state for training at the branch offices. We could counter this concern by recognizing the concern and asking how we can make the extended time out-of-state more palatable.

- To neutralize the resistance of branch offices to main office initiatives, we could contact each branch office manager to solicit their input about training and training design—and send a handwritten thank-you note after the conversation.

Force-field analysis isn't the most important tool in the project manager's toolkit. Used wisely, though, the analysis identifies the strengths you can build on, and the weaknesses that need to be understood and neutralized as the project progresses.

Using PERT to Estimate Duration

There are two types of estimated duration: deterministic and probabilistic. When the duration for a task isn't likely to vary, the duration is deterministic. It's easy to plan the duration for routine deterministic tasks. You can enter a duration based on the

PART

III

Juggling and Managing Projects

duration the last time the task was completed. Projects, however, aren't largely populated with routine tasks; the nature of projects is non-routine—the new unexplored edge of an organization's operations. Non-routine tasks that are subject to variation are probabilistic.

For example, converting from one accounting software system to another is a project that involves installation, testing, turnover, and evaluation. Although a project may include an accounting component, managing accounts payable or payroll isn't a project—it's an organizational process assigned to a department.

If your organization swaps accounting packages every three years just for fun, you can examine project documentation from the last conversion for guidance on duration. But the last conversion can only serve as a guide. The next conversion—your project—will include different software, different personnel, new vendors, and other variations too numerous to name.

 TIP Past projects are one of the resources that can help you estimate duration. If the project was managed using Microsoft Project, use Project 2000's analysis tools to view baseline durations and the actual time spent on each task. Save projects that include tasks similar to or identical to the tasks in your project into one project database, and use Project's reports and views to glean useful information about project duration.

PERT, the Performance Evaluation and Review Technique, was developed in the early 1960s by the U.S. Navy; Lockheed; and the Booz, Allen & Hamilton consulting firm to manage the Polaris missile project. This was a probabilistic project from wall to wall: More than three thousand contractors completed hundreds of thousands of work packages, many of which were new and unique. PERT has been credited with bringing the Polaris missile project in two years ahead of the original estimates. PERT is a statistical method to estimate duration. At the core of PERT is an understanding that there are some things you can't *know* with precision. If an activity is unique to your project, it makes more sense to think about a range of duration (three to five days) rather than a precise duration (exactly four days).

To implement a PERT analysis, you develop not one, but three task durations: optimistic (best case), pessimistic (worst case), and expected. The three durations are weighted and averaged to determine the task's duration. The default PERT settings give the expected duration four times the weight of either the pessimistic or optimistic duration: PERT duration = (optimistic + 4 * expected + pessimistic)/6.

 NOTE PERT is similar to Critical Path Method, or CPM, which was developed by DuPont. Both CPM and PERT are network methods. CPM relies heavily on historical data; PERT was developed to support duration decisions for tasks without precedent. Project 2000's network views support both methods.

Project 2000 provides tremendous support for PERT. After you enter the three durations for a task, Project calculates the PERT duration. You can change the weights used in PERT calculations. And, unlike many other project-management software packages, Project tracks all three durations for each task, so you can view the optimistic, pessimistic, or expected durations at any point in the project.

Developing PERT Estimates

The PERT estimates are often casually described as worst-case, best-case, and expected (or planned) estimates. "Worst-case" and "best-case" aren't really accurate descriptions, particularly if you have a vivid imagination. The absolute worst-case scenario imaginable has hundreds of hours poured into a twenty-hour task as resources are run over by streetcars, killed in hurricanes, or engaged in acts of sabotage. The best-case scenario includes hiring geniuses who reinvent processes on the fly, shaving fifty percent off of each task duration.

PERT isn't about the worst or best, it's about the likelihood of actual durations within three standard deviations of the mean. You don't need to brush off your probability and statistics textbook to work with PERT. Here are working definitions for each of the three estimates:

- Pessimistic: The task will require this number of hours or fewer 95% of the time (19 out of 20 times).

- Optimistic: The task will require this number of hours or more 95% of the time (19 out of 20 times).

- Expected: The most probable amount of hours the task will require.

With PERT, you can treat one occurrence out of 20 as a fluke (when resources are run over by streetcars, etc.), so you don't have to consider the truly outrageous when you develop your estimates.

There are several good ways to develop estimates, and one truly bad method, which we'll dispense with first. *Don't* develop a single expected estimate, and then add and subtract the same percentage for each task to create pessimistic and optimistic durations. (We've seen this happen in organizations that require a PERT analysis as part of a project proposal.) Here are some methods that are useful:

Historical data For a task that's been completed and documented once or twice before, collect the actual durations and project durations. Use the lowest value as the optimistic, the highest as the pessimistic, and the average of all actual values as the expected duration.

Best guess by experts Find people who've completed similar tasks, and get their best guesses for the three durations for your task.

PART

III

Juggling and Managing Projects

Best guess by experts, version 2　Ask people with expertise in the task area for their estimate of actual time. Use the most frequently guessed value as the expected duration. Use the lowest value as the optimistic, and the highest as the pessimistic duration.

 TIP　Over time, you'll determine which of your colleagues and experts are always pessimistic in their estimates, and which are optimistic. In their areas of expertise, estimates from two or three individuals can consistently represent the entire range of likely values.

You don't have to use PERT to calculate every task in your project. If a task is deterministic, you can enter the same value for all three estimates. To enter PERT estimates, open the PERT Analysis Toolbar and do the following:

1. Choose View ➣ Toolbars ➣ PERT Analysis.

 2. On the toolbar, click PERT Entry Sheet to open the Entry Sheet shown in Figure 13.4.

FIGURE 13.4

Enter durations in the PERT Entry Sheet.

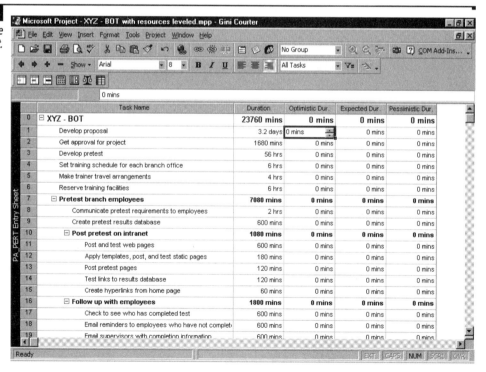

3. Enter the optimistic, expected, and pessimistic durations for each task that you want to calculate a duration for with PERT. For deterministic tasks, enter the same duration in all three fields.

MASTERING TROUBLESHOOTING

Troubleshooting the PERT Analysis Toolbar

The PERT Analysis toolbar is a COM Add-In that should already be enabled. If the PERT Analysis toolbar does not appear on the toolbar list, follow these steps to make it available:

1. From the View menu, click Toolbars; then click Customize.

2. Click the Commands tab in the Customize dialog box.

3. Select the Tools category.

4. Select COM Add-Ins from the Commands section and drag it to a toolbar.

5. Click the Close button to close the Customize dialog box.

6. Click the COM Add-ins button that you placed on a toolbar.

7. In the COM Add-Ins dialog box, click the Add button.

8. Switch to the folder where Winproj.exe (the Project program) resides.

9. Locate a file named `Pertan1.dll`. Select the file and click OK.

10. Click OK again to close the Com Add-Ins dialog box.

11. Choose View ➤ Toolbars ➤ Pert Analysis toolbar to activate.

If you want to enter estimates for one task, click the PERT Entry form button on the PERT Analysis toolbar to open the PERT Entry Form.

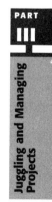

Calculating PERT Estimated Duration

It's a good idea to save your project file just before calculating PERT. When you click the Calculate PERT button, you're prompted to confirm the calculation.

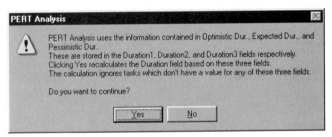

When you click OK to confirm the deletion, only tasks with PERT estimates are calculated. Figure 13.5 shows the Develop Proposal task, before and after PERT Calculation.

FIGURE 13.5

The PERT calculation replaces the value in the Duration column.

	Task Name	Duration	Optimistic Dur.	Expected Dur.	Pessimistic Dur.
0	⊟ XYZ - BOT	23760 mins	0 mins	0 mins	0 mins
1	Develop proposal	3.2 days	2 days	3.2 days	7 days

	Task Name	Duration	Optimistic Dur.	Expected Dur.	Pessimistic Dur.
0	⊟ XYZ - BOT	23760 mins	23760 mins	23760 mins	23760 mins
1	Develop proposal	3.63 days	2 days	3.2 days	7 days

Using the PERT Views

After you enter PERT durations, you can switch between expected, pessimistic, and optimistic views of the project's Gantt Chart, whether or not you calculate durations using PERT. Figures 13.6 and 13.7 contrast the Pessimistic and Optimistic Gantt Charts for a portion of the XYZ-BOT project.

To display the Pessimistic Gantt Chart, make sure that the PERT Analysis Toolbar is displayed (View ➢ Toolbars ➢ PERT Analysis), and click the Pessimistic Gantt button.

To display the Optimistic Gantt Chart, click the Optimistic Gantt button on the PERT Analysis toolbar. In Figure 13.7, the optimistic finish date is eight days before the pessimistic finish date.

FIGURE 13.6

The Pessimistic Gantt Chart shows the latest project finish.

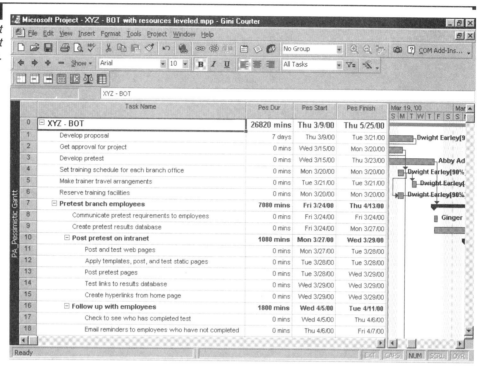

FIGURE 13.7

The Optimistic Gantt Chart shows the earliest reasonable project finish date.

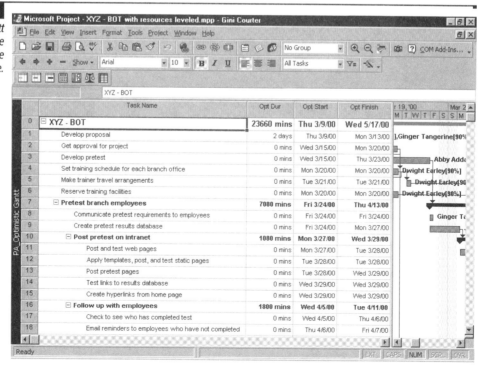

To display the expected project schedule, click the Expected Gantt button on the PERT Analysis toolbar.

MASTERING THE OPPORTUNITIES

The Mathematics of PERT

Imagine twenty projects that include the same task: Task A. In each project, Task A was completed in an actual number of hours. A review of the actual hours for this task in each of the 20 projects looks like this.

Task A: Actual Hours			
Project	Hours	Project	Hours
1	24	11	18
2	24	12	23
3	22	13	23
4	20	14	25
5	32	15	25
6	28	16	28
7	25	17	20
8	25	18	22
9	16	19	24
10	23	20	24

Actual hours range from a low of 16 to a high of 32. The average is 23.55 hours. We created a column chart to show the frequency of each of the actual hours values. The chart is close to the bell curve of a normal distribution that's the result of plotting the frequency of a random variable.

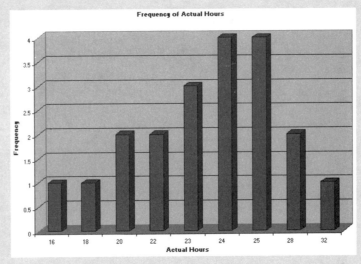

Continued ▌▶

PERT relies on a normal distribution to describe the variability in duration. If we added data from 100 projects that included Task A, we would expect that the shape would become even more normal, clustered around the average time of 23.55 hours, and that it would be four times more likely that the actual hours would be between 23 and 24 than 16 or 32 hours.

PERT analysis assumes that every project task, if repeated enough times, would yield a normal distribution such as the distribution shown previously. The optimistic and pessimistic PERT estimates provide the range of the distribution used to adjust the expected value to determine PERT duration. If you believe that the normal distribution doesn't accurately describe the potential variation in a task's duration, you can change the weights that Project 2000 uses to calculate the PERT duration.

Changing the PERT Weights

The PERT weights assume the normal distribution that's observed with a random variable (see "The Mathematics of PERT" in the previous sidebar). If there is evidence that the distribution of duration for an entire project will not be normal, you can change the weights given to each of the three durations when PERT calculates duration to better reflect the skew in the distribution. The default values are 1 for optimistic, 4 for expected, and 1 for pessimistic. When you change these values, the total must still equal 6. To change the weights, click the Set PERT Weights button to open the Set PERT Weights dialog box:

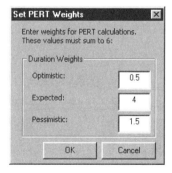

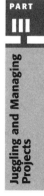

Viewing the Critical Path

Critical Path Method (CPM) and PERT are closely related, and have become intertwined during nearly four decades of use in project management. Originally designed for deterministic projects, the CPM is used to highlight high-risk tasks in a project.

It doesn't matter that the durations for the critical tasks were developed with PERT methods.

CPM is a method used to analyze the relationships between activities in a project. The *critical path* is the series of interrelated tasks that takes the longest time, so it therefore affects the projected finish date. To see the paths in a project file, display a network diagram by choosing View ➤ Network Diagram from the menu. The network diagram is a flowchart of the project activities. Figure 13.8 shows the network diagram for the XYZ-BOT project.

FIGURE 13.8

The network diagram shows the task paths.

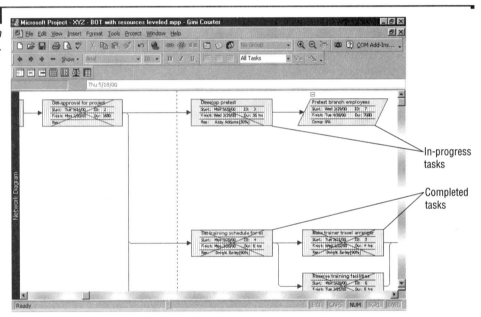

Each task that appears is in an individual box. Summary tasks are parallelograms, whereas tasks are displayed in rectangular boxes. Click the expand or collapse buttons above summary tasks to show or hide summary task's subtasks. Double-click a task box to open the Task Information Form for the task. If you prefer the Network Diagram to the Gantt Chart view, you can create or remove task dependencies and assign resources in this view.

The lines between tasks are the dependencies created by using the Link Tasks button. To display more of the project, choose View ➤ Zoom from the menu to open the Zoom dialog box, shown next.

The smallest zoom is 25%. If you choose Entire Project and your project can't be displayed in its entirety at 25%, you'll be prompted to accept the 25% setting:

The critical path for our project starts in the upper-left corner and continues across the bottom of the application window, as shown in Figure 13.9.

FIGURE 13.9

The critical path is the series of tasks with the longest duration.

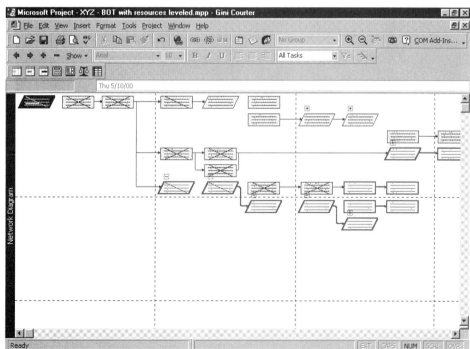

The Network Diagram increases in utility as the project progresses. You can use filters in the Network Diagram as you would in the Gantt Chart view, so you can, for example, display only critical tasks, tasks that are over budget, or slipping tasks. Figure 13.10 shows the XYZ-BOT project's slipping tasks.

FIGURE 13.10

Filter the Network Diagram for slipping tasks.

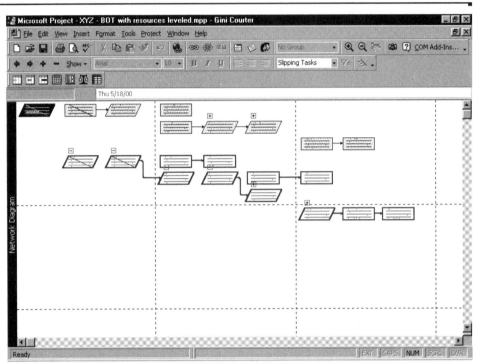

With this filter, you can tell which slipping tasks require your attention—the tasks on the screen that are red and bold because they lie in the critical path.

 TIP For information on customizing the Network Diagram, see Chapter 17, "Using Views to Evaluate Data."

What's Next

No matter how closely you manage risk in your projects, success cannot be achieved without effective communication with and management of the various projects. In Chapter 14, "Sharing Resources and Tasks among Various Projects," we'll explore how to share resources and tasks across multiple projects. In Chapter 15, "Communicating Project Information" and Chapter 16, "Team Project Management with Project Central 2000," we'll show you how to use Project to effectively communicate with your project team.

CHAPTER 14

Sharing Resources and Tasks among Multiple Projects

I n today's high-volume workplace, it is unusual for project managers to have only a single project on their plate. In most cases, project managers have to juggle multiple projects at different stages with different resources—some that relate to each other and some that stand alone. With Project's master and subproject features, you can link related and even unrelated projects to see them all in one place, compare timelines, run consolidated reports, link tasks, and share resources. A department, for example, could have one master project file that shows every project going on in the department, while each project manager has their own subproject file to work with that only shows their projects. In this chapter, you'll learn how to become an even better project manager by keeping your eye on the big picture and still noticing the details.

Working with Multiple Projects at Once

If you are responsible for multiple projects, you can make your life a lot easier if you know a few tricks. With Project, you can have multiple projects open at once, and switch back and forth between them with ease. You can also save the workspace so that rather than opening a several projects individually, you can open a workspace and have them all open at once.

Opening and Viewing Multiple Projects

Project 2000 is designed using a single document interface (SDI). This means that each project has its own application window available to it. The biggest advantage of SDI is that when you open a project, it appears on the Windows taskbar at the bottom of the screen. If you open two projects, they both appear on the taskbar. Although you can still switch between projects using the Window menu command, as shown in Figure 14.1, you now can see every project you have open and switch back and forth by clicking the corresponding taskbar button.

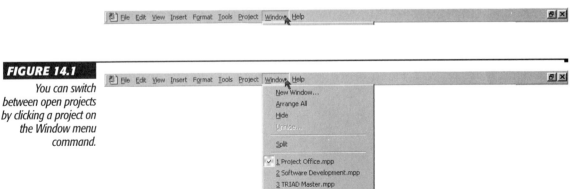

FIGURE 14.1

You can switch between open projects by clicking a project on the Window menu command.

If you would prefer not to have each open project appear on the task bar, you can turn off this feature by choosing Tools ➤ Options and clearing the Windows in Taskbar option on the View tab of the Options dialog box, shown in Figure 14.2

Clear the Windows in Taskbar option to disable SDI.

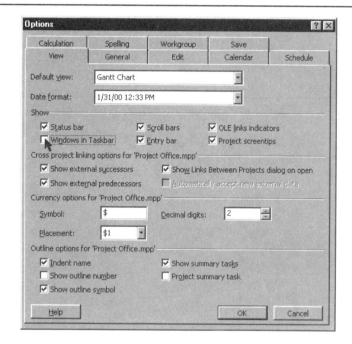

Saving a Workspace

Rather than opening each project you want to work on every time you launch Project, you can save the workspace so the next time you want to open the same files, Project can do it for you. This is particularly helpful when you have projects located on different drives and in different folders. Project remembers the file locations and creates a pointer to them so it can find them again. To save a workspace, follow these steps:

1. Open the projects you want to save in the workspace.

2. Choose File ➤ Save Workspace. The Save Workspace As dialog box opens, as shown in Figure 14.3.

3. Choose a Save In location and enter a file name. Project suggests Resume as the file name, but you can enter any name you like.

4. Click Save.

PART

III

Juggling and
Managing Projects

5. Project prompts you to save the changes to each individual project you have open. Choose Yes to receive a prompt for each file or Yes to All to save them all at once.

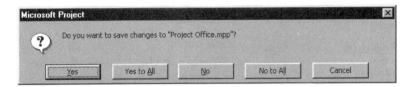

FIGURE 14.3

Save Workspace As dialog box

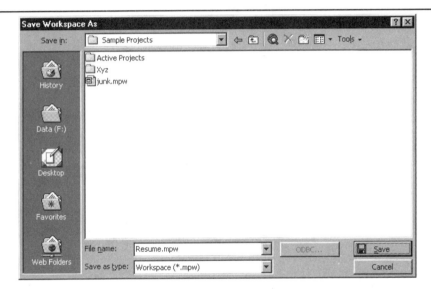

6. If you have not saved a baseline with a project, you may also receive a prompt from the PlanningWizard to save the baseline. You can make a selection and choose OK to be prompted to save the baseline on the next file or OK to All to apply this selection to all the files in the workspace.

After you've saved a workspace, you can close all the individual project files and reopen them at one time. To reopen a workspace:

1. Choose File ➢ Open to open the Open dialog box, shown in Figure 14.4.

2. Locate the folder the workspace is in by default. Project opens the folder you last saved to or if you've closed Project, it defaults to the Save location for projects designated in the Save Options (Tools ➢ Options, Save tab).

3. Select the workspace file from the list. It has a different icon from other project files; if you are displaying file extensions, it has an .mpw extension rather than the .mpp extension of typical Project files.

4. Click the Open button. Project opens each file in the same order in which they were saved.

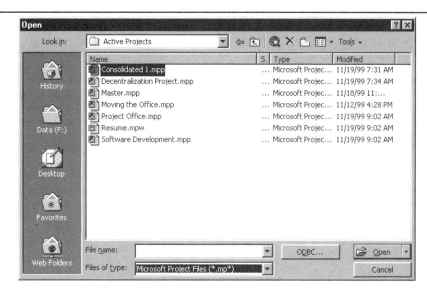

After you've finished working on the workspace files, you can resave them again with the same or different workspace name:

1. Choose File ➤ Save Workspace to reopen the Save Workspace As dialog box—only the workspace files appear in the file list.

2. The workspace should be in the File Name text box. Click Save if you want to use the same name.

3. Click OK to the message box that opens asking you if you want to replace the existing file. Click Cancel if you change your mind and want to give this workspace a new name.

4. You are again prompted to save each individual file and to save baselines (see Steps 5 and 6 on saving a workspace earlier in this section).

When Project saves a workspace, it save all open files in the order in which they were originally opened, not necessarily in the order in which you are currently displaying them. It also saves the current view in each project. However, it does not save open windows such as the Assign Resources dialog box or other open window configurations described in the next section.

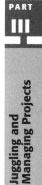

Arranging Open Projects

When you are working with several projects at the same time, you can use the Window menu to make them all visible at once or to hide windows you'd like to run in the background. To make all the open projects visible at once choose Windows ➣ Arrange All. Project resizes the open projects so they can all be displayed, as shown in Figure 14.5.

FIGURE 14.5

Use Window ➣ Arrange All to display all the open projects

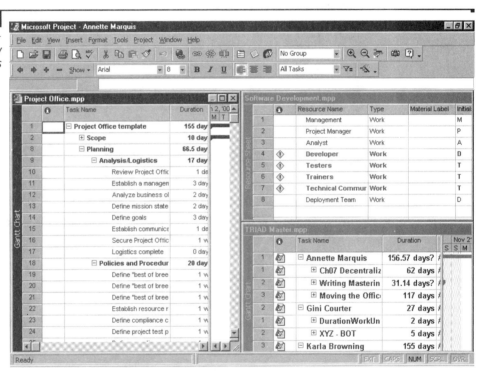

To work in a particular project, click the project to make it active. You can tell the active project because its title bar is blue.

Moving and Copying between Projects

One of the advantages of arranging multiple projects is that you can move and copy tasks, resources, and other text between projects while viewing both projects. You can use the Cut, Copy, and Paste commands, and also drag and drop, to move and copy. Select the text that you want to move or copy and use a standard method to insert the new text into the other project. (For more about moving and copying within Project, see "Moving and Copying Tasks" in Chapter 7, "Entering Project Tasks.")

Hiding and Unhiding Open Projects

Although you may want to have a project open, you may not want it to be included when you use the Arrange All command. You can hide an open project file, by choosing Window ➤ Hide. The project is still open but when you choose Arrange All, the hidden file does not show. The project remains hidden until you exit Project altogether. Even if you close all the other open projects, the hidden project is not visible.

To unhide the project, choose Window ➤ Unhide.

 NOTE If you choose Arrange All before hiding a project, you have to apply Arrange All again after you hide the project to have the visible projects rearrange themselves.

Understanding Master and Subprojects

Projects come in all sizes, from the simplest project with a few tasks to the most complex with thousands of tasks and resources working to complete it. Regardless of the size of the overall project, you may find it useful to work with the project in small digestible portions. With Project, you can divide a large project into small subprojects, and then link them together through one master project. This provides you with the ultimate flexibility of working with a project in its logical divisions while still maintaining a view of the project in its entirety. When considering how to structure your projects, you may want to consider the following:

- A project with distinct phases can be easily divided into subprojects, perhaps even at each milestone, so that each phase or milestone can be managed as a discrete element with its own critical path.

- Complex projects that contain a number of concurrent but clearly delineated task groups can be divided into separate projects, perhaps even with different project managers.

- Tasks that may differ in function but need to be completed on a similar time schedule can be segregated so you can close out parts of a project based on the tasks that are completed by a certain date.

- Tasks that use the same resources throughout a large project can be separated into subprojects so that each resource has a clear idea of their piece of the larger project.

- Projects that involve multiple budgets, cost centers, or discrete billing can be kept as separate projects and then rolled up into a master project to get total project costs.

- A project that involves more than one physical location can be divided into sub-projects that keep all the tasks related to a site in one project for better onsite management and control.

You may find many other reasons to divide projects into logical components. Whatever your reasons, here's how you do it. We'll start by assuming you have one large project you'd like to break up into smaller components and then we'll build it back up again into a master project.

Dividing a Project into Smaller Pieces

Project has no magic wizard or built-in command to divide a project into components so it's up to you to use old-fashioned cut and paste to make it work. Follow these steps to create the subproject projects:

1. Open the large project you want to subdivide.

2. Create a view that puts all the tasks you want to move in consecutive order (see Chapter 17, "Using Views to Evaluate Data," if you need help to do this).

3. Select the tasks you want to move and click the Cut button.

4. Click the New button to create a new project.

5. Click in the first cell of the Gantt Chart and click the Paste button.

6. Save the new project.

7. Repeat Steps 2–6 for additional tasks groups you want to pull out.

 WARNING If you subdivide a fully developed project that contains links between tasks and resource assignments, you may experience dramatic changes in the project's schedule and resource allocation. Be careful to review the schedule and resource allocation before and after you move tasks.

If you want the new projects to become subprojects of the original project, follow the steps in "Creating a New Master Project from Open Projects" below.

Creating a New Master Project from Open Projects

A *master project* is a project that contains other projects. You can consolidate a number of projects into a master project that can be linked to or unlinked from the subprojects. Project gives you three methods of creating master projects:

- You can consolidate multiple projects into a new project file.

- You can insert projects into an existing project file.
- You can open a resource pool and add it and all its sharer files to a master project (see "Creating a Master Project from a Resource Pool and Sharer Files," later in this chapter).

To use the first method, consolidating multiple projects into a new project file, follow these steps:

1. Open or create all the projects you want to consolidate.

2. Choose Window ➤ New Window and hold Ctrl to select each of files you want to be incorporated into the master project from the New Window dialog box, as shown in Figure 14.6.

3. Choose the default view you want all the subprojects to use.

4. Click OK to have Project create a new file and insert the subprojects.

FIGURE 14.6

Select the project files you want to consolidate into a master project.

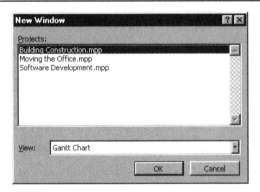

Each project appears in the task list with a project indicator in the Indicator column. If you point to the indicator, a screen tip appears that describes the location of the embedded project (see Figure 14.7).

FIGURE 14.7

A screen tip shows the file location of the embedded project.

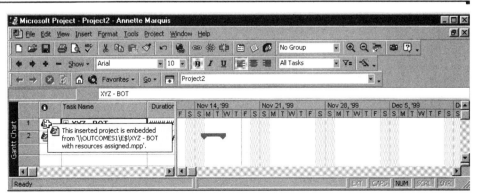

TIP In Gantt Chart view, click the plus and minus symbols in front of the project name to expand or collapse the project's task list.

You can save the new master project and close the subprojects. Any changes you make to the master project are reflected in the linked subprojects. Any changes you make in the subprojects are reflected in the master project.

 MASTERING THE OPPORTUNITIES

Mastering Department-Wide or Organization-Wide Project Management

To get a handle on all the projects within an organization or department, you can create a master project that houses every project you currently have underway. This master project can contain subprojects that serve as master projects for each project manger. These can be further divided into the subprojects that each project manger is responsible for. Figure 14.8 shows an example of a department organized this way. The master project is called [CompanyName] Master. The master project consists of subprojects saved with the project manager's name. Those subprojects each contain the active projects the roll up under that project manager.

To create this department- or organization-wide master, follow these steps:

1. Open all the active projects that one project manager is responsible for.
2. Choose Window ➤ New Window and select all the listed files.
3. Choose the default view you'd like all the subprojects to use.
4. Click OK.
5. Save the new master project using the project manager's name as the file name.
6. Close each of the subprojects but leave the new master project open.
7. Repeat Steps 1–6 for each project manager in your organization.
8. At this point, the only open files should be the master projects named for the project managers. Repeat Steps 2–4 to create the organization-wide master.
9. Save the new organization-wide master, clearly identifying it as the organization-wide master.

You can now create reports, apply views, and analyze data across projects and across project managers. To see the project that a particular task is from, add the Project field to the Gantt Chart. When a project is completed, you can delete it from the master and insert its replacement. Use the Insert ➤ Project command from the menu to insert a project into the master.

IGURE 14.8

*All of the projects in
an entire department
~ organization can be
ked through a single
master project.*

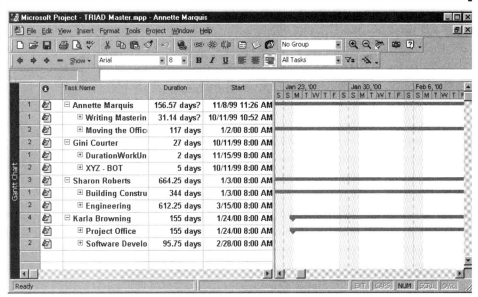

Inserting Projects into an Existing Project File

The second method of consolidating a number of projects into a master project is to insert projects into an existing project file. With this method, you can convert an existing project to a master project. The master project may already contain some tasks of its own, and the subproject you insert becomes one of the tasks. Let's say, for example, that your project includes a group of tasks, such as the tasks involved in preparing a large mailing or installing a network—these tasks are repeated in a number of projects throughout the organization. Rather than re-create them each time you need them, you can set up a project that contains just those tasks. You can then insert the subproject into the larger project and have all the tasks, linking, and task durations already identified.

You can also use this method to insert a project that is not linked to the original project. Use this option if you want to adapt an existing project for your own use without impacting the original project.

 NOTE If you insert a project into an open project, any Outline Level 1 tasks of the original project will be at the same level as the inserted project. Insert both projects into a new project file to put them both at the same level.

PART

III

Juggling and
Managing Projects

To insert a project file into another project, follow these steps:

1. Open the project you want to become the master project.

2. In Gantt Chart view, click in the row below where you want the project inserted.

3. Choose Insert ➤ Project to open the Insert Project dialog box, shown in Figure 14.9.

4. Select the project file you want to insert.

5. If you do not want the inserted project linked to the original file, clear the Link to Project checkbox.

6. If you want to maintain the link between the original project and the master project but do not want the ability to make changes to the subproject from the master, click the drop-down arrow on the Insert button and choose Insert Read-Only. If you make changes in the master project to this subproject, you are asked to save it as a different name when you close the master.

7. Click the Insert button to insert the project.

FIGURE 14.9

Use the Insert Project dialog box to select subprojects to insert into a master project.

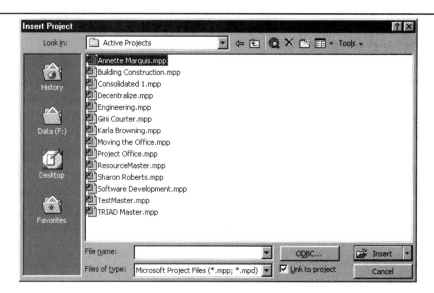

NOTE Summary bars representing inserted projects appear gray rather than black in the Gantt Chart.

MASTERING TROUBLESHOOTING

Why Does the Inserted Project Appear as a Subtask in the Task List?

When you insert a project into a task list in Gantt Chart view, it assumes the outline level of the row above it. If the task above the newly inserted project, is an Outline Level 2 task, then the inserted project will start at Outline Level 2. To force the inserted project to Outline Level 1, select a row directly below an Outline Level 1 task in which to insert the project, or collapse the outline to Level 1 *before* you insert the new project. In either scenario, the newly inserted project becomes an Outline Level 1 task.

Working with Master and Subprojects

One of the biggest advantages of creating a master project is the capability to work with the tasks and schedules of the consolidated project as if it were a single project. You can review all the details of the master project, sort and filter projects, and link tasks between projects. You can also view resource allocation across projects, create reports, and analyze costs. Pretty much anything you can do with a single project you can do with a master project.

PART

III

 NOTE In order to assign resource across projects, you have to share them first. For more about sharing resources between projects and setting up resource pools, see "Using Resources from Another Project or Resource Pool," later in this chapter.

Juggling and Managing Projects

Viewing Inserted Project Information

When you insert a project into another project, you can view information about the project by double-clicking it to open the Inserted Project Information dialog box shown in Figure 14.10.

FIGURE 14.10

The Inserted Project Information dialog box shows information about the inserted project.

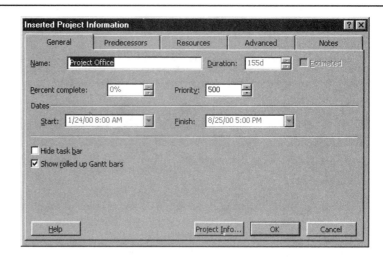

Click the Project Information button on the bottom of the General page of the Inserted Project Information dialog box to see the standard Project Information dialog box you are familiar with from individual projects.

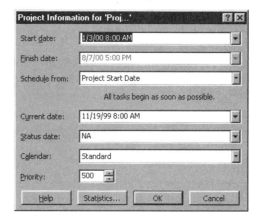

Identifying the Source of the Task or Resource

In working with Master projects, you may find it useful to add the Project column to the Gantt Chart and Resource Sheet. This helps to clearly identify from which project a particular task or resource originated. To insert the Project column:

1. Right-click on the column to the right of where you want the new column to appear.

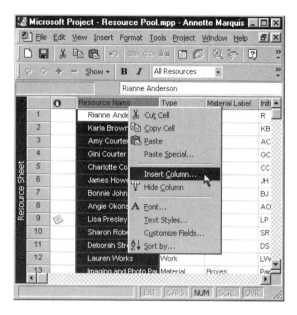

2. Choose Insert Column.

3. Select Project from the Field Name drop-down list. You do not have to enter a Title unless you want the field name to be something other than Project.

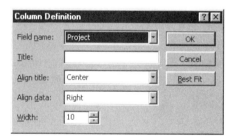

4. Click OK to insert the column. Figure 14.11 shows the results of inserting the Project field in the Resource Sheet.

PART

III

Juggling and
Managing Projects

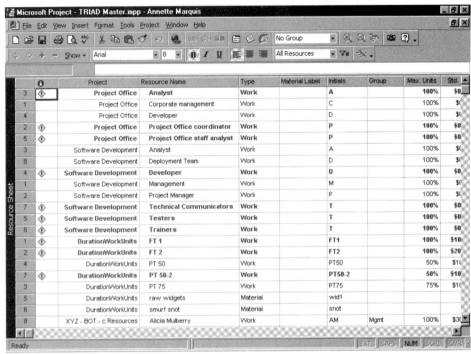

FIGURE 14.11

The Project column
displays the name of
the project from which
the resource or task
originated.

Sorting and Filtering Cross-Project Tasks

In Chapter 17, we describe how to sort and filter Project data to organize and extract the data you want to see. In a master project, you can use those same features to sort and filter data across projects. For example, after inserting all the subprojects into a master project, you can sort the subprojects in the Gantt Chart by Name or by Start Date.

Sorting Projects   When you sort tasks and resources, you have the option of sorting within their projects or summary tasks, or disregarding their current roll-ups and sorting across the entire list. For example, in Figure 14.11, the resources are sorted by project first and then by name. Figure 14.12 shows the same resources sorted without regard to project affiliation.

In the Gantt Chart, you can collapse outline levels to sort subprojects within the master project, or you can expand outline levels to sort all the tasks within all the projects.

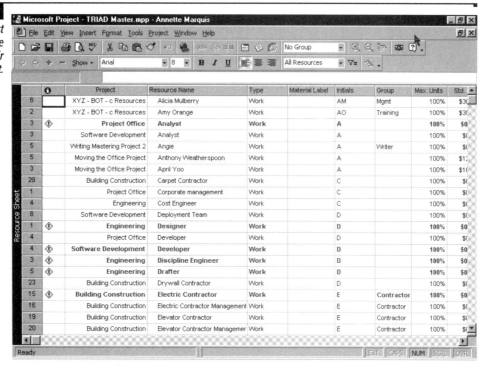

FIGURE 14.12

Resources in this list are sorted by name without regard to their originating project.

To sort the subprojects in a master project, follow these steps:

1. Click the top cell in the ID column to select all the tasks in the Gantt Chart.

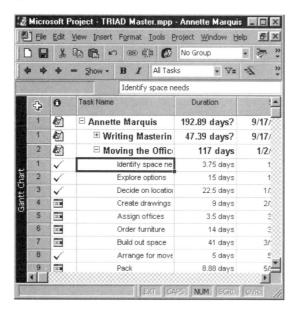

PART

III

Juggling and Managing Projects

2. Select Outline Level 1 from the Outline menu to collapse all the outline levels.

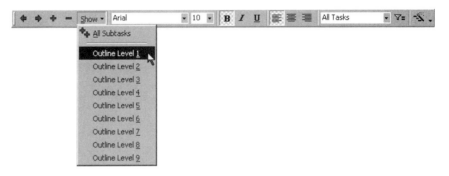

3. Click the Project menu and choose Sort to open a submenu of sort choices.

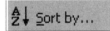

4. Select the Sort criteria you want to apply, or choose Sort By from the submenu to open the Sort dialog box.

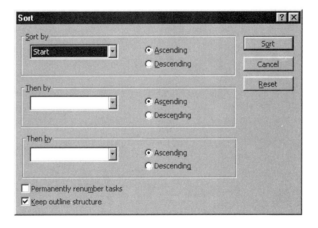

5. Select the fields you want to sort by, and choose Ascending or Descending for each sort level.

6. Click Sort to apply the sort.

 NOTE Because sorting is applied to tasks *within* an outline level, if the task outline is expanded, any sort operation is only applied to the subtasks within each summary task. Tasks are not sorted across projects unless you clear the Keep Outline Structure checkbox in the Sort dialog box.

Sorting between Projects   If you choose to sort tasks *between* projects, by Name or by Start Date for example, you would follow similar steps with some slight variations:

1. Click the top cell in the ID column to select all the tasks in the Gantt Chart.

 2. Select Show All Subtasks from the Outline menu to expand all the outline levels.

3. Click the Project menu and choose Sort to open a submenu of sort choices.

4. Choose Sort By from the submenu to open the Sort dialog box.

5. Select the fields you want to sort by, and choose Ascending or Descending for each sort level.

6. Clear the Keep Outline Structure checkbox.

☑ Keep outline structure

7. Click Sort to apply the sort.

Reversing Sorts and Reapplying Outline Structure   You can reverse a sort by returning to the Sort dialog box (Project ➢ Sort ➢ Sort By) and clicking the Reset button. This restores the outline structure and re-sorts by the ID field within each project.

Applying Filters and Grouping to Tasks and Resources   You can use Filter and AutoFilter to filter data across projects. For example, by turning on AutoFilter in the Gantt Chart, you can show only those tasks that have Start Date of this month. Figure 14.13 shows an AutoFilter being applied to the Start Date field.

 You can also group across projects using the Group By command. Figure 14.14 shows the Group By Critical option. The first group, Critical: No, is collapsed; the second group, Critical: Yes, is expanded to show all the critical path tasks in all the open projects.

PART

III

Juggling and
Managing Projects

FIGURE 14.13

Autofilter can be applied across projects to show all the tasks that are scheduled to start during a certain period.

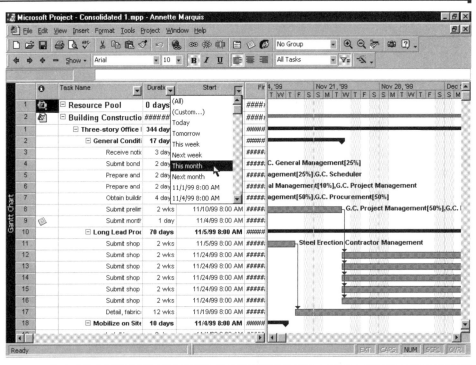

FIGURE 14.14

You can use the Group By command to group across projects in a master project.

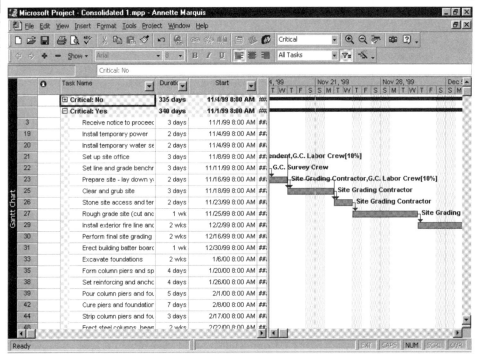

NOTE For more about applying filters and grouping see "Sorting, Filtering, and Grouping" in Chapter 17.

Removing a Subproject from a Master Project

You can remove a subproject from a master project by deleting it just as you would a task: Select the project and press the Del key or choose Edit ➣ Delete Task. The Planning-Wizard warns you that the project is a summary task and deleting it will remove its subtasks as well.

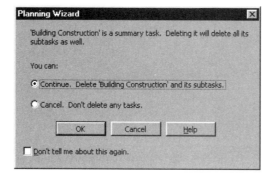

Click Continue to remove the project.

 NOTE Deleting a subproject from a master project does not delete the project file—only the link with the master project is deleted. You can still open each project individually.

Linking Tasks That Cross Projects

You can link tasks between projects, whether or not they are part of a master project. You may, for example, be managing a project that is dependent on the completion of a task in a project for which you are not responsible. You can link to this external project to show how any deviations in that project's schedule affect your project.

Throughout this section, we are using two simple projects to serve as examples for this process. The first project, MOUS Prep, is a project that was agreed-upon by project managers in the MIS department to prepare for and take the Microsoft Office User Specialist (MOUS) exam for Microsoft Project 2000. As a member of the Human Resources Department, you've offered to hold a celebration for everyone who took the exam. You are

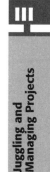

responsible for the party, so you created a project called "MOUS Celebration" to plan the party. You can see the tasks in both projects in Figure 14.15.

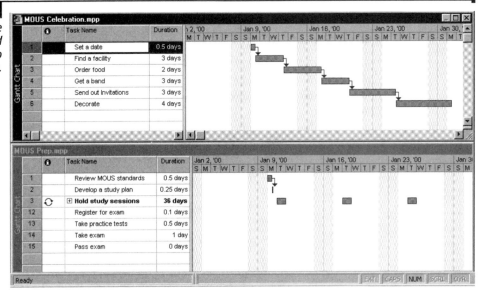

As you outline the tasks of the party plan, you realize that you can't schedule the party until you know the date the project managers are going to take the exam. Although you have no control over the other project, your first task, Set a Date, is dependent upon Task 12, Register for the Exam, in the MOUS Prep project.

To create a link between the tasks, follow these steps:

1. Open both projects that contain the tasks you want to link.

2. Choose Window ➤ Arrange All to see both projects (this step is not required, but makes it easier to see what you are linking).

3. Double-click the task you want to become the successor (dependent) task—this opens the Task Information dialog box. In this example, you'd double-click the Set a Date task in the MOUS Celebration project.

4. Click the Predecessors tab to establish the Register for Exam task in the MOUS Prep project as the predecessor.

5. Select the ID field and type the project name and ID number of the predecessor task using this format: ProjectName\Task ID Number. For example, in this case, you'd enter **MOUS Prep\12** to represent Task 12 in the MOUS Prep project.

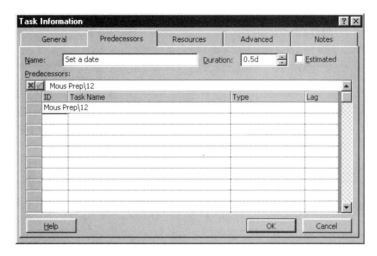

6. Press Enter—Project automatically adds External Project to the Type and Lag fields.

7. Click OK to establish the link.

As you can see in Figure 14.16, Project inserts the linked tasks into each project, displaying them in light gray to represent that they are external to the project. Notice the start date for Set a Date has changed from the original start date of 1/10/00 to 2/23/00 to follow the Register for Exam task.

FIGURE 14.16

The Set a Date task in the MOUS Celebration project is linked to the Register for Exam task in the MOUS Prep project.

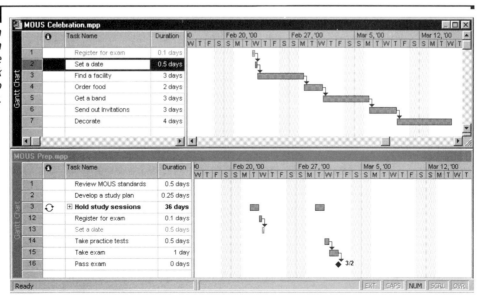

PART

III

Juggling and
Managing Projects

NOTE When you create an external link, the predecessor project file must be open so that Project can establish the path to the project.

If you want to change the link type or add lag/lead time, double-click the successor task again. In the Figure 14.16 example, that would be the Set a Date task in the MOUS Celebration project, and change the link type or add lag/lead time on the Predecessors tab of the Summary Task Information dialog box.

 TIP If you would prefer not to show the ghost (external) tasks in the project, you can turn them off by choosing Tools ➢ Options ➢ View tab and then clearing the Show External Successors and Show External Predecessors checkboxes.

Reviewing and Updating Project Links between Files

Returning to the MOUS Prep project scenario, before starting the MOUS study sessions, project managers in the MIS department decided that there was enough material about Microsoft Project to hold 12 sessions instead of the original 8. As a result, they also changed the Register for Exam task to follow Session 10, instead of Session 7. The Set a Date task in MOUS Celebration is linked to the Register for Exam task in MOUS Prep. Consequently, the Set a Date task is delayed from the original plan.

When projects contain external links, you generally want to know whether changes have been made to the external project that affect your project. Project gives you three alternatives for how to handle changes to externally linked files. These three options are discussed as follows:

- Show the Links Between Projects dialog box on open
- Manually review and update changes to external links without notification
- Automatically accept new external data

Show the Links between Projects Dialog Box on Open

If you choose to show the Links Between Projects dialog box whenever you open a linked file, you can instantly see whether changes have been made that affect the linked tasks. If there are changes, you can review each change that was made to the external project and decide whether you want that change applied to your project. Manually updating changes gives you the most control over the impact of external changes on your project's schedule. If you want to have the Links Between Projects dialog box open automatically when you open a linked project, select the Show Links Between Projects Dialog On Open checkbox on the View tab of the Options dialog box (Tool ➤ Options).

With this option selected, every time you open a linked project, the Links Between Projects dialog box, shown in Figure 14.17, opens.

FIGURE 14.17

The Links Between Projects dialog box shows changes to either of the linked files.

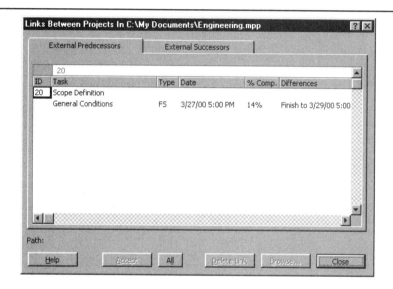

The dialog box has two tabs—External Predecessors and External Successors—and opens automatically to the link in question. The first line shows the task that is linked from the active project—in this case, the Set a Date task from the MOUS Celebration project. When you click the external task, shown in the second line of the dialog box, the path to the external file appears in the Path field at the bottom, and the action buttons on the dialog box become active.

The second line of the External Predecessors tab displays the following information about the conflict:

Task   Displays the externally linked task, e.g. Register for Exam.

Type   Represents the type of dependency between the tasks: (FS:Finish-to-Start, SS:Start-to-Start, SF:Start-to-Finish, or FF:Finish-to-Finish).

Date   The current schedule date of the successor. In this case, the successor, Set a Date, is scheduled to start on 2/23/00.

Juggling and
Managing Projects

% Comp. Shows how much of the predecessor task is complete.

Differences Shows the changes in the external project that is causing the conflict. In the example in Figure 14.17, the Start and Finish Dates of the Register For Exam task have changed.

If additional conflicts are present, they are listed on subsequent rows of the dialog box.

 NOTE If you were to open the project that contained the predecessor task, you could review the same conflict information on the External Successors tab. However, in this case, the Date field would show the current schedule date of the predecessor.

To resolve the conflicts, you can choose to do the following:

Accept the selected changes.

Accept **All** the changes between the active project and external projects.

Delete Link between the projects.

Browse to locate the external file if the link was broken because the file was moved.

Close the dialog box without making changes. If you close the dialog box without making all the changes, the active project is no longer synchronized with the external project. This may be acceptable as long as you are aware of the differences.

 WARNING You cannot undo acceptance of the changes after you accept them.

Manually Review and Update Changes to External Links without Notification

Anytime you are working with a project that has external links, you can manually review and update changes to the external links. With this option, the Links Between Projects dialog box does not open when you open a linked project. However, you can review the links by choosing Tools ➢ Links Between Projects from either the predecessor or successor project. To use this option, make sure that the Automatically Accept New External Data checkbox on the View tab of the Options dialog box (Tool ➢ Options) is cleared.

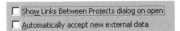

Automatically Process Changes without Notifying You

With this last option for handling changes to external links, you can direct Project to automatically process any changes to your project as a result of external links without notifying you when you open the file. Project handles all the updates behind the scenes. You only become aware if you see an unexpected shift in your project's schedule. To choose this option, click Tool ➢ Options and on the View tab, clear the Show Links Between Projects Dialog On Open checkbox, and click the Automatically Accept New External Data checkbox.

☐ Sho_w Links Between Projects dialog on open
☑ Automatically accept new external data

Deleting Links between Projects

If you want to delete a link between tasks in separate projects, you can choose Remove Link from the Link Between Projects dialog box, shown in Figure 14.17 earlier in this section. You can also select the row that contains the linked task and press the delete key. The task is deleted from the active project but only the link is removed from the external project—the task still remains in the original project file.

MASTERING TROUBLESHOOTING

Mastering Troubleshooting: How Large Can a Project File Be?

If you plan to locate, migrate to, terraform, settle, and develop a viable political system for an asteroid or small planet, then Microsoft Project 2000 is the software you've been looking for. (See Kim Stanley Robinson's *Red Mars, Green Mars, and Blue Mars* for more details.) You can create a project with up to 1,000,000 tasks and assign up to 1,000,000 resources (more than the populations of eight states, including Alaska, Delaware, Montana, and Vermont). You can consolidate 1,000 projects and include up to 65,535 outline levels per project! You can spend up to $999,999,999,999 (that's billions, folks!), and assign 1,666,666,6667 hours of work to a single task. And to top it off, you have only about 49 years to complete the project. The earliest date allowed for calculation is 1/1/1984 and because of the potential Year 2049 problem, the latest date Project can calculate is December 31, 2049. (Yes, the Y2K bug may rear its ugly head in 2049, the date to which much of the recent Y2K problem has been shifted.)

Continued ▶

PART

III

Juggling and
Managing Projects

MASTERING TROUBLESHOOTING CONTINUED

Just so you don't think Microsoft's Project team is completely out of touch with the hardware on the average desktop, the following caveat appears in the Project Help files:

"The following specifications and limits are supported when you run Microsoft Project on Windows 95, Windows 98 or Windows NT, although actual limits and performance speed are greatly dependent on your computer's configuration. Please note that Out of Memory errors may occur before you reach the listed limits."

In actuality, preliminary reports indicate that Project 2000 is spunkier than previous versions. However, be forewarned—if you really find yourself stretching the limits of Microsoft Project, you may also find that you need a much bigger computer.

Using Resources from Another Project or Resource Pool

In many organizations, it may be unusual for an individual resource to be assigned to only one project from now until eternity. Even if a resource is assigned full-time to a long-term project, you can save time and work by including that resource in a resource pool. A *resource pool* is a project file that contains nothing but resource information. This file may be maintained by the Human Resource Department, by your specific department, or by a senior project leader who is overseeing multiple projects. The purpose of a resource pool is to centralize information about resources and to manage resource assignments. In a resource pool, you can monitor availability of each resource and make sure they are not stretched too thinly across multiple projects.

Although you can designate an existing project as a resource pool, we recommend that you create a resource pool in a separate Project file. To create a resource pool, follow these steps:

1. Start a new project file by clicking the New button on the Standard toolbar.
2. Click OK to close the Project Information dialog box.
3. Click the Save button and save the project with a name that describes its resource pool function, such as **MIS Resource Pool** or **Resource Pool 1**.
4. Open the Resource Sheet by choosing View ➣ Resource Sheet.
5. Enter all the resources and basic information about the resources that are available for any project that will be sharing the pool.
6. Save the Project again.

Accessing a Resource Pool from Your Project

After a resource pool is created, you can access it from any open project. A project that uses a resource pool is called a *sharer file*. To access the resource pool from the sharer file, follow these steps:

1. Open the Resource Pool file.

2. Open the project you want to share the resource pool.

3. Choose Tools ➤ Resources and click Share Resources.

4. In the Share Resources dialog box, shown in Figure 14.18, choose Use Resources and select the resource pool file from the list of open projects.

5. Choose whether you want the resource pool to take precedence or whether the sharer should take precedence when conflicts arise. If you choose Pool Take Precedence, changes made to the resource pool overwrite changes made to resources in the shared file. If you choose Sharer Takes Precedence, changes you make to the resource information overwrite the resource pool data and other sharer files. Pool Take Precedence is the recommended method.

6. Click OK to share the resources.

FIGURE 14.18

In the Share Resources dialog box, you choose to share the file that contains the resource pool.

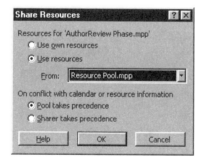

 NOTE   Any resources in the resource pool are added to the active project, and any resources in the active project are added to the resource pool. When sharing a resource pool for the first time, don't include any resources in the sharer file unless you want them added to the pool.

PART

III

Juggling and
Managing Projects

Working with a Resource Pool

After you share a resource pool, the resources from the resource pool are available to you in the sharer file project just as if they were part of the project. You can view the resources on the Resource Sheet (View ➤ Resource Sheet), and you can make assignments using the Assign Resources button on the Standard toolbar or using another resource assignment method you are familiar with from Chapter 10, "Assigning and Scheduling Resources and Costs." However, if you choose to give the resource pool precedence in the Share Resources dialog box, any changes you make to the resource information itself, such as resource name or rate, in the sharer file will not be saved when you close the resource pool.

 NOTE The resource pool project file must be open when you are working with a sharer file.

Closing a Project with a Shared Resource Pool

When you close a project with a shared resource pool, you must close the sharer file and the resource pool separately. If you have made resource assignments in the sharer file, the Planning Wizard brings you a message that asks you if you want to update the resource pool to reflect changes for all the open sharer projects.

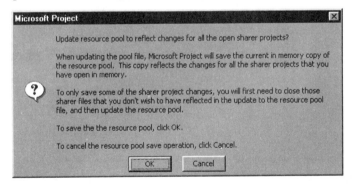

If you want the resource pool to include the new assignment information for the resources you used, click OK. If you don't want to update the resource pool to reflect changes in the sharer file, click Cancel to the message and close the sharer file. Make changes to the resource pool and choose Tools ➤ Resource ➤ Update Resource Pool to update changes to the resource pool.

WARNING If you chose to give the resource pool precedence when you shared the resource pool, all changes you made to the resource information, such as name and rates, in the sharer file will be lost. Resource assignment information, however, will be saved with the resource pool.

Opening a Project with a Shared Resource Pool

When you open a project that uses a shared resource pool, the Planning Wizard asks you whether you want to open the resource pool to see assignments across all sharer files. If you choose this option, Project opens both the sharer file and the resource pool file. This allows you to see all the resources and assignments that are shared across all projects.

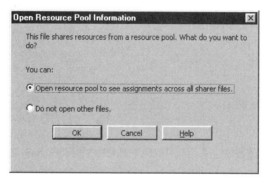

If you choose not to open other files, Project opens only the sharer file and not the resource pool. The only resources available to you in this case are resources you have already assigned to other tasks.

Viewing Resource Assignments

To see resource assignments across multiple projects, switch to the Resource Usage view (View ➤ Resource Usage), shown in Figure 14.19. This view shows resource assignments across all projects that share the resource pool. The tasks are displayed in gray to indicate that they are not native to this project. You can check over- and underallocations by switching to Resource Graph view (View ➤ Resource Graph).

 TIP If you are using a resource pool with your projects, you can hide the resource pool file (Window ➤ Hide) to prevent you from accidentally closing it or to keep the task bar from becoming cluttered. Even with it hidden, you still have access to all the resources in the resource pool.

FIGURE 14.19

Resource Usage view shows all resource assignments across multiple projects.

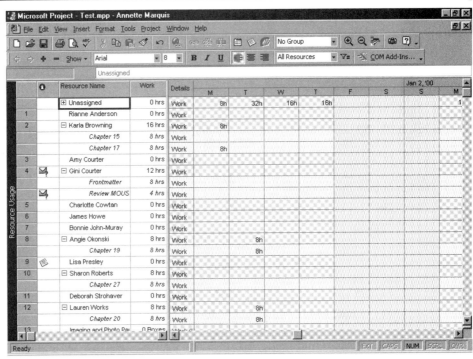

Opening and Editing a Resource Pool

If you want to make changes to a resource pool, you can open that project file directly. When you open a resource pool, Project gives you three options for how you want to open the file.

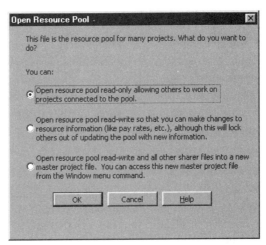

Choose the read-only option if you are opening the resource pool in order to share it with another open project file. Choose the read-write option if you want to make changes to resource pool information such as pay rates. When you use this option, you are locking others out of updating the resource pool with new information. So, before using this option, you might want to make sure that no one else is actively using the resource pool.

Choose the third option if you want to combine the resource pool and all sharer project files into a master project.

Creating a Master Project from a Resource Pool and Sharer Files

The third option on the Open Resource Pool dialog box combines the resource pool and all sharer project files into a new master project file. Using this option, you can see with all the sharer files and the resource pool in one place, making it easier to make decisions about assignments and allocations. This new master project is available from the Window menu. Choose Window and select the unnamed project. Figure 14.20 shows an example of a master project created by using this option.

FIGURE 14.20

Project can create a master project from a resource pool and all the related sharer files.

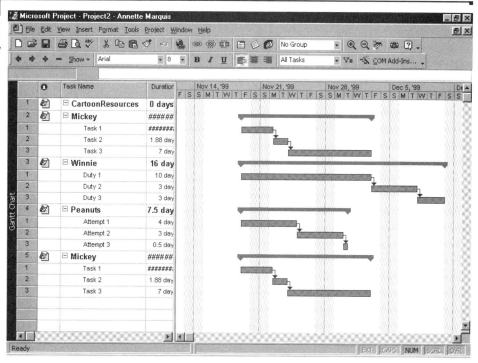

PART

III

Juggling and
Managing Projects

Removing a Shared Resource Pool

If you decide to discontinue using a particular shared resource pool, you can share a project with another resource pool or use the resources from the project file. To switch to another resource pool, open the new resource pool and choose Tools ➢ Resources and click Share Resources from the sharer file. Select another resource from the Use Resource From drop-down list. To stop using a resource pool and return to the resources in the project file, choose Use Own Resources from the Share Resources dialog box.

What's Next

Now that you know how to use Project to manage multiple projects, it becomes even more important to effectively communicate with your project resources about the status of a project's tasks. Chapters 15 and 16 deal exclusively with team communication. In Chapter 15, you'll learn how to communicate using Project's team tools with email. In Chapter 16, we'll introduce you to Project 2000's new Web-based communication system called Microsoft Project Central.

CHAPTER **15**

Communicating Project Information

This chapter is the detailed guide to project communication. We'll begin by examining the role of communication in project management, then look at the methods used to communicate project information: manual, email, and Web-based data collection and feedback.

Understanding Project Communication

We can't overstate the role of communication in a project or its importance to a project manager. Thoughtful, well-planned communication is a significant factor in every successful project. (Well, at least all those we've received communications about!) Inadequate communication can cause even a well-designed project to falter or fail.

Most projects that are worth recording in Project 2000 have a project team—one or more people assigned to work on various project tasks. In addition to the project manager, who is responsible for team communication, team members may include the following:

- The organization's permanent employees
- Temporary employees hired for the project
- Workgroups and their leaders
- Departments and department managers
- Contractors and vendors
- Stakeholders

What needs to be communicated? That depends, in part, on the culture of your organization. Minimally, the project manager needs to communicate direction, expectations, and information required for team members to complete their tasks. The project manager needs to provide management and other shareholders with status reports detailing the progress and health of the project. Team members need to provide the project manager with task status reports so the project manager has accurate information for the project status reports.

In many organizations, particularly those with a less hierarchical structure, team members are encouraged or required to communicate with each other, providing "upstream" feedback about tasks that were completed earlier and "downstream" feedback to team members involved in tasks that occur later in the project. Teams or workgroups engaged in simultaneous tasks share information by email or on a project Web site. The project manager may provide project status reports to shareholders as well as managers.

Whether your organization has a top-down approach to project management or is more workgroup-focused, there's one fundamental truth: the successful project manager accepts responsibility for establishing and disseminating the communication requirements for the project.

Communicating from Microsoft Project

The email and Web communication features of Microsoft Project are collectively known as Project's *workgroup features*. With Microsoft Project 2000, you have two ways to communicate electronically with team members:

- You can use the email message handler to send email with task assignments.
- You can use Microsoft Project Central, Project 2000's new Web client/server system for project communication.

You are not restricted to one choice or the other. Depending on the needs of the resources in your project, you can use either method alone, or you can combine them and communicate with some people via the Web and with others through email. Although many of the workgroup capabilities are the same between the two tools, Project Central allows team members to review all of the project tasks lists and timelines, giving them a much fuller picture of the entire project rather than just their specific tasks.

For the remainder of this chapter, we will focus on using email as your primary communication method. If you're using or plan to use Microsoft Project Central, you will also be interested in Chapter 16, "Team Project Management with Project Central 2000." If you are a network administrator, you will also want to see Chapter 26, "Installing and Administering Project Central 2000."

Using Email to Communicate Project Information

Microsoft Project can freely access email address books available through the messaging application you are using—for example, your Outlook Contact's folder. To use Project's workgroup features and send email messages to a resource, the resource must be listed in one of your active address books or you must enter their Internet email address directly in the Resource Information dialog box. (See Chapter 9, "Defining Project Resources and Costs," for more about the Resource Information dialog box.)

Accessing Email Addresses

To verify that Project can access your email address books, follow these steps:

1. Open your project's Resource Sheet (View ➤ Resource Sheet).
2. Double-click the name of a resource who should be in one of your email address books. This opens the Resource Information dialog box, shown in Figure 15.1.

PART

III

Juggling and
Managing Projects

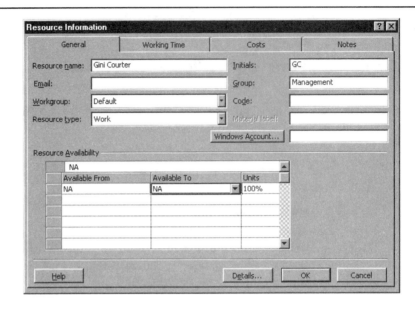

3. Click the Details button on the General tab of the Resource Information dialog box. This opens an Outlook contact form, a Microsoft Exchange Server Properties sheet (like the one shown in Figure 15.2), or the address book form of the MAPI-32 compliant email system you are running. Click OK to close the address book form.

If the message handler does not recognize the name, it asks you to verify the name or enter a new contact according to the process of the email messaging application you are using.

MASTERING TROUBLESHOOTING

Making Your Outlook Contacts Folders Appear As Address Books

Outlook's main Contacts folder does not automatically appear as an email address book. You have to instruct Outlook to make it one. If it is not already set up as an Outlook address book, you can set it up by following these steps:

1. Open Outlook.
2. Right-click on the Contacts icon on the Outlook bar or on Contacts in the folder list.
3. Chose Properties from the shortcut menu.
4. On the Outlook Address Book tab, click the Show This Folder As an Email Address Book checkbox.
5. Enter the name you want to assign to the address book in the Name of the Address Book box.
6. Click OK.

If you want Project to access an additional address book, for example, a subfolder of contacts you create in Outlook to store project resources, you must add it to the list of folders that Outlook checks when it checks a name by doing the following:

1. Choose Tools ➢ Services and click the Addressing tab.
2. Click Add to add the folder to the list of those checked.
3. Select the address book from the list and click Add.

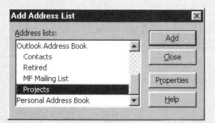

4. Click Add to add another address list or Close to close the Address List dialog box.
5. Click the Move Up and Move Down arrows on the Services dialog box to arrange the order in which you want the address lists checked.
6. Click OK to save the changes.

   The new contacts folder is now available to use in Project.

When Microsoft Outlook Doesn't Recognize a Name

If Microsoft Outlook is your email messaging application, Project turns the reins over to Outlook to manage contact information and addresses. If all the resources you plan to use on a project are available in your Outlook Contact's folder or another address book, Outlook uses that information to respond to requests for information from Project. When you click the Details button of the Resource Information dialog box and Outlook recognizes a name, an Outlook Address book opens. However, if Outlook does not recognize the resource name, a Check Names dialog box opens, asking what you'd like to do.

You can create a new contact or find the name in a current address book for Outlook. To create a new contact:

1. Select Create a New Address For and click OK.

2. Choose New Contact in the New Entry dialog box and click OK.

3. Outlook opens a Contact form for you to complete. When you finish entering the contact information, click Save and Close on the Contact form toolbar to save the contact.

It's possible that Outlook may not recognize a name that is listed in your address book. It might not have been recognized because you spelled it differently, used a nickname, or put the name in a different order (First Name, Last Name versus Last Name, First Name). To find an address that Outlook does not recognize:

1. Click the Show More Names button on the Check Names dialog box to open the Address Book dialog box.

2. Scroll through the list or begin typing the name in the order it appears in the address book.

3. Select the name and click OK to verify the name for Outlook.

MASTERING TROUBLESHOOTING

How Name Order Affects Recognition

When you enter a resource name into Project, Outlook searches for the name as entered. If you enter a name as First Name, Last Name, Outlook looks for that exact name. If Outlook is set to store names in the Address Book as First Name, Last Name, it has no trouble finding the name. However, if you enter a resource name First Name, Last Name and the Outlook Address Book is set up for Last Name, First Name, Outlook

Continued

MASTERING TROUBLESHOOTING CONTINUED

does not recognize the name. You must follow the Check Names procedure outlined earlier in this chapter to locate the name. You can change the order in which Outlook organizes names in the Address Book by following these steps:

1. Open Outlook.
2. Choose Tools ➢ Services.
3. Select Outlook Address Book from the list of available services and click Properties.
4. Choose the Show Names As option you prefer, and click Close.

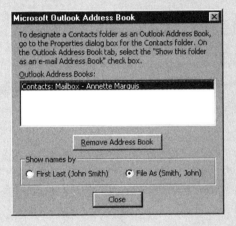

5. Click OK to close the Services dialog box.

Sending and Receiving Workgroup Messages

With Project's workgroup features, a project manager can do the following:

- Send task assignments to team members via email.
- Receive confirmation that the team member has accepted the task.
- Update the project to reflect acceptance of assignments.
- Send updates to team members when task parameters, such as duration, change.
- Request and receive status reports that show how much work the team member has completed on the task.

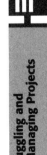

PART

III

Juggling and
Managing Projects

Based on the content of each communication, Project automatically updates the project data to reflect any changes made.

Assigning Tasks to Workgroup Members

The first step in communicating with resources about project tasks is to send Team-Assign messages to the project team. You can send TeamAssign messages from Project as long as you have made email addresses accessible to Project and have installed Project's workgroup features. For more about installing Project's workgroup tools, see the Mastering Troubleshooting sidebar. If you have not yet set up address books, see "Accessing Email Address Books," earlier in this chapter.

MASTERING TROUBLESHOOTING

Installing Microsoft Project's Workgroup Tools

For a project manager to communicate with team members, Project's workgroup tools need to be installed on the project manager's computer and on the computer of each team member. To install the workgroup features on the project manager's computer, run Project's setup program from the CD or network installation point, and choose Install Microsoft Project Workgroup Message Handler from the setup screen. This installs the email team functionality to Project so that the project manager can send team assignments and so that responses and updates are automatically processed by Project. You can verify that the workgroup functionality is installed by launching Project, switching to a task view such as Gantt Chart view, and seeing that the Team options (TeamAssign, TeamUpdate, and TeamStatus) on the Tools ➢ Workgroup menu are active.

Team members do not need to have Microsoft Project on their computers to use the workgroup tools. Team members, however, must be running a MAPI-compliant, 32-bit email system, have a network or Internet mail connection, and have workgroup functionality installed on their computers. Team members can install workgroup functionality by running the application called WGSetup.exe located in a folder called WGSetup on the Microsoft Project CD. To make this easy for team members to access, the network administrator can copy this entire folder to a network drive to which the team members have access. During the installation, team members are asked to identify which email messaging software they use. The answer must correspond to the answer given by the project manager when the project manager installed the workgroup message handler. If a team member is using Microsoft Outlook, they can verify that the workgroup tools have been installed by opening Outlook, switching the Tasks, and finding the menu option New Team Status Report on the Action menu.

You can send TeamAssign messages to a resource, whether or not you have previously assigned a resource to the task. You can use TeamAssign to assign the following:

- Multiple resources to a single task
- The same resources to different tasks
- Different resources to different tasks

When you use TeamAssign, you can choose to send messages for all tasks or selected tasks. If you want to send messages for only specific tasks, switch to the Gantt Chart view and select the tasks you want to assign in the task list. If you want to send messages for all the tasks, you do not need to select them first.

To send messages, follow these steps:

1. Choose Tools ➤ Workgroup to open the Workgroup menu.

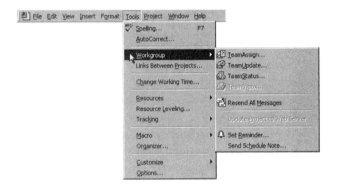

2. Choose TeamAssign from the Workgroup menu.

3. If you have only one task selected, choose whether you want to send messages for all the tasks or only selected tasks. If you have multiple tasks selected, you do not see this dialog box:

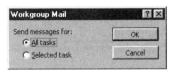

4. If you already have resources assigned to the first task in the list or to the selected tasks, the resource name appears in the To field in the TeamAssign dialog box, shown later in Figure 15.3. You cannot enter addresses directly in this line—wait until you get to Step 7.

5. Click the Subject field text box if you want to enter a different subject for the TeamAssign message.

6. Select the text in the message box to enter a different message to accompany the assignment. Even if you are sending different tasks to different team members, each team member receives the same message.

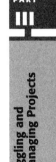

Juggling and
Managing Projects

7. Click the first cell in the To column to enter a resource for the first task.

8. Type the resource's name or click the Address Book button to enter addresses from the current resource pool or the email address book.

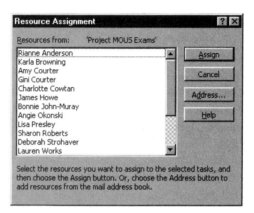

9. If you are using the Resource Assignment dialog box, select the resource you want to assign from the resource pool listed. To select consecutive names, click the first name, hold down the Shift key, and then click the last name you want to assign. To select nonconsecutive names, click the first name and hold down the Ctrl key while you select other names in the list. If you want to add a name from the address book, click the Address button to open the Select Resources dialog box. Select the names you want by clicking Add—click OK when you have selected the resources you want.

WARNING If you select a resource from the address book and that person is not currently in the resource pool, Project automatically adds that name to the pool, even if it's only a variation of the name of someone already in the pool. To prevent Project from automatically adding names to the pool, choose Tools ➢ Options and clear the Automatically Add New Resources and Tasks from the General tab of the Options dialog box.

10. Click Assign to assign the selected resources, and close the Resource Assignment dialog box.

11. If you want to assign resources to additional tasks, click the adjacent cell in the To column (see Figure 15.3) and repeat Steps 7–9.

12. When you have finished making assignments, click the Send button.

NOTE As project manager, you can customize the fields displayed in workgroup messages. See "Customizing Workgroup Messages," later in this chapter.

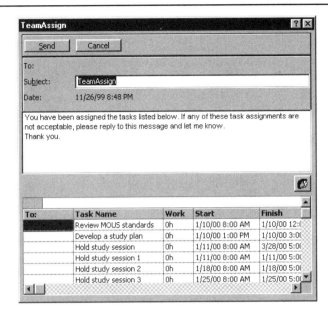

FIGURE 15.3

The TeamAssign dialog box includes a message form with a task list to make task assignments.

Project sends the messages to the team members and adds an icon to the Indicator column next to the task in the project. If you point to the icon, a screen tip indicates the status of the TeamAssign message.

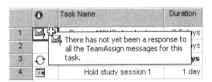

When the team member responds to the message, the icon in the Indicator column disappears.

Responding to Task Assignments

When a team member receives a task assignment, the message appears in their email inbox. If the message arrives through the Internet, the TeamAssign message appears as an attachment to a standard message. The team member opens the message and double-clicks the attachment to open the TeamAssign message. If the message arrives through a network connection, the TeamAssign message appears automatically when the team member opens the message.

The TeamAssign message, like the one shown in Figure 15.4, shows standard message information such as To, Date, From, Subject, and Message and also contains a table at the bottom that lists the tasks that are being assigned. If the team member accepts all the assignments (yes, they can say no!), all they have to do is click the Reply button at the top of the message form. If the team member does not accept one of the assignments, they can click in the Accept? column to change the Yes to No.

FIGURE 15.4

The TeamAssign message gives the team member the option to accept or not accept the task.

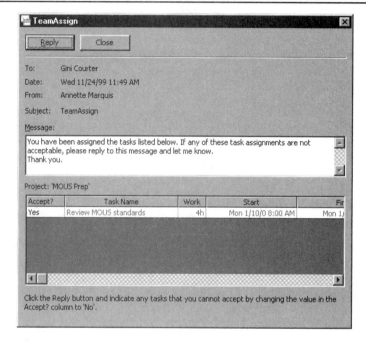

When the Team Member clicks Reply, a new message form opens in which they can enter a message, if desired, or merely click the Send button to send the reply.

If the team member is using Outlook, the Project task is added to the Outlook Task list.

 TIP   If you'd rather not give team members the ability to refuse an assignment, you can remove that option from TeamAssign messages. See "Setting Other Custom Options," later in this chapter.

Updating Responses to Task Assignments

As the project manager, you can open the team member's reply, shown in Figure 15.5, and review the team member's responses to each task assignment.

If you are satisfied with the response, you can click the Update Project button to confirm the team member's acceptance of the task assignments.

If you click the Reply button to reply to the team member before clicking Update Project, Project displays a warning, asking you whether you want to update the project before replying.

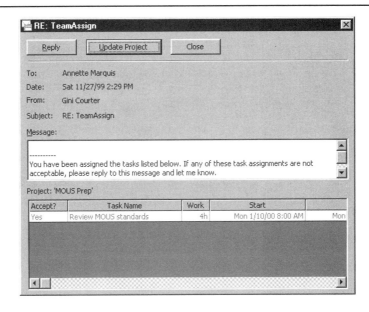

FIGURE 15.5

The project manager an update the project data with the team member's responses.

You may decide, however, that you'd rather send another message to the team member who declined an assignment before updating the project information. That's your prerogative at this step if you click Reply without updating the project first.

MASTERING THE OPPORTUNITIES

Tracking Team Member Responses

Every project contains two fields that are useful for tracking the status of team members' responses to assignments. These fields, Confirmed and Response Pending, are not displayed by default in any view. However, these are valuable fields to add to a task sheet view after you have made team assignments as a way to track the status of those assignments.

		Task Name	Duration	Confirmed	Response Pending
1	✉	Review MOUS standards	0.5 days	No	Yes
2		Develop a study plan	0.25 days	Yes	No
3	↻✉ ⊞ **Hold study session**	**55 days**	**No**	**Yes**
16		Register for exam	0.1 days	Yes	No
17		Set a date	0.5 days	Yes	No
18		Take practice tests	0.5 days	Yes	No
19		Take exam	1 day	Yes	No
20		Pass exam	0 days	Yes	No

Continued ▶

PART

III

Juggling and Managing Projects

MASTERING THE OPPORTUNITIES CONTINUED

To add the fields to the Gantt Chart view, for example, right-click on the column heading where you want the Confirmed field to appear (columns are inserted to the left of the selected field), and choose Insert Column. Choose the Confirmed field from the Field Name drop-down list. Repeat this process to add the Response Pending field.

After a task is accepted by a team member and the project manager updates the project, the Response Pending field changes to No. If a task is declined, the Confirmed field displays No and the Response Pending field also displays No.

The Confirmed field displays Yes to all tasks that have been accepted *and* to all unassigned tasks. The Response Pending field displays No to all tasks that have been declined *and* to all unassigned tasks. We advise not to insert the Confirmed and Response Pending fields until you have assigned every task.

Sending Task Updates

As project manager, when you change the start or finish date or duration of tasks you've assigned to project team members, you can send assignment updates to the appropriate team members. Project notifies that you need to send an update by placing an icon in the Indicator column.

 TIP You can add the Update Needed column to any task sheet as another way to show whether an update should be sent.

To send a TeamUpdate message, such as the one shown in Figure 15.6, do the following:

1. Make the desired changes to the affected tasks.

2. Choose Tools ➤ Workgroup and select TeamUpdate.

3. Click the Subject field text box if you want to enter a different subject for the TeamUpdate message.

4. Select the text in the message box to enter a different message to accompany the update. Even if you are sending different tasks to different team members, each team member receives the same message.

5. Click the Send button to send the update.

Send a TeamUpdate message to notify team members of a change in a task's schedule.

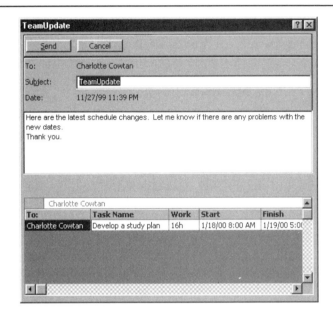

When a team member receives and opens the message, they respond by following these steps:

1. Open the TeamUpdate message.

2. Review the changes and click Reply.

3. Enter a message, if desired, to indicate how the changes affect them.

4. Click Send.

The project manager opens each of the team members' responses and clicks Update Project to document that the team members received information about the change in the project.

Sending and Receiving Status Reports

Status reports from the team members keep the project information up-to-date. Status reports can be initiated by the team members who use Outlook or solicited by the project manager. In a status report, a team member can record the following:

- A message to the project manager
- The actual date they started work on the task

- The amount of work remaining
- The actual work completed on the project task, including dates and number of hours they worked on the task
- The amount of overtime hours they have worked on a task
- Comments about the task

You can include additional fields if you customize workgroup messages before sending the original TeamAssign. For more about how to customize workgroup messages, see "Customizing Workgroup Messages," later in this chapter.

Soliciting Status Reports

As project manager, you can send a request for a status report rather than waiting for team members to submit reports. To request a status report, follow these steps:

1. Select the tasks about which you want to receive status reports; otherwise, you can choose to receive reports on all the tasks in the project.

2. Click Tools ➤ Workgroup and choose TeamStatus.

3. Choose whether you want to send messages for all tasks or only the selected tasks.

4. When the TeamStatus message shown in Figure 15.7 opens, change the subject and the message in the message box, if desired.

5. Enter the start and finish dates of the reporting period in the Ask for Actual Work From drop-down boxes.

6. Click Send to send the TeamStatus message.

FIGURE 15.7

Use the TeamStatus message to request a status report from team members.

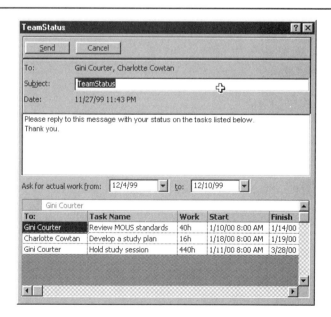

Replying to Status Report Requests

When a team member opens a TeamStatus message, such as the one shown in Figure 15.8, they can click the Reply button and enter actual work completed on the task in the reply form.

FIGURE 15.8

Team members can click Reply and enter the actual hours worked on the task.

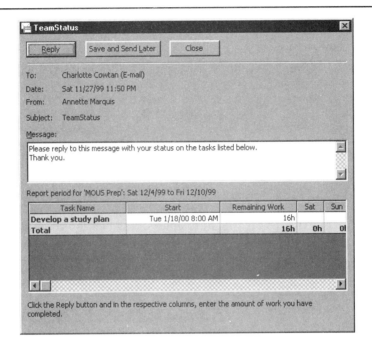

To enter actual work, the team member uses the horizontal scroll bar to see the day they want in the timesheet grid and double-clicks in the corresponding cell of the table. Entries can contain these abbreviations: *m* for minutes and *h* for hours.

Remaining Work	Sat	Sun	Mon	Tue	Wed	Thu	Fri	Comments
0h			2h	3h	5h	7h	120m	
0h	**0h**	**0h**	**2h**	**3h**	**5h**	**7h**	**2h**	

The team member must also enter values in the Start and Remaining Work columns for Project to be able to calculate the percentage of work remaining, to know when work on the task actually started, and to know whether the task is completed (see Figure 15.8).

The team member can choose to Send the report or Save and Send Later. If they choose this second option, the original message moves to their Outbox, showing the team member as the message recipient in the To column. In addition, the message is not italicized, which means that it stays in the Outbox until the team member reopens the message, clicks Reply, and then clicks Send. Even though the team member chooses to send the reply later, all data updated in the timesheet grid appears in the reply that is finally sent.

PART

III

Juggling and
Managing Projects

Once again, when you as project manager receive message replies, you want to open each one of the team members' responses and click Update Project on the message form to integrate the updated information into the project.

Initiating Status Reports by Team Members

A team member who uses Outlook may initiate sending a status report to the project manager at any point in the project. To initiate a status report, the team member follows these steps:

1. Switch to Outlook Tasks and choose Actions ➤ New TeamStatus Report from the menu.

2. The New TeamStatus Report dialog box shown in Figure 15.9 lists the projects for which there are active tasks in the Task list—choose the project or projects to report on.

FIGURE 15.9

The New TeamStatus Report can be generated by a team member whenever they want to report on the status of a project task.

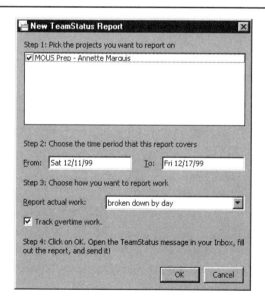

3. Enter a start and finish date for the report in the From and To boxes.

4. Choose how you want to report the work. You can choose Broken Down by Day, As a Total for the Entire Period, or Broken Down by Week.

5. Select the Track Overtime Work checkbox if you want to report overtime hours.

6. Click OK.

7. Open the NewTeam Status Report that Outlook creates in your Inbox.

8. Complete the form by entering the actual start date in the Start column; the amount of work remaining in the Remaining Work column; and, depending on the choice made in Step 4, the actual time spent on the project task. If the team member chose to include Overtime in Step 5, they should enter overtime hours in the Overtime columns and not mix it in with regular time.

9. When all the data is entered, click Reply and then click Send; or click Save and Send Later to have the opportunity to make additional changes.

Updating Project Tasks in Outlook

If a team member makes changes to assigned tasks directly in Outlook, these changes are reflected on the TeamStatus reports about those tasks. Likewise, changes made to tasks in the timesheet grid of the TeamStatus message are reflected on Outlook's Task form. Table 15.1 shows the mappings between Project and Outlook fields.

TABLE 15.1: FIELD MAPPING BETWEEN PROJECT AND OUTLOOK

Project field	Outlook field
Contact	Contacts (only maps the first contact)
Finish	Due Date
Priority	Importance
Project	Categories
Start	Start Date
Task Name	Subject

Other Outlook fields (Status, % Complete, Total Work, and Actual Work) are used by Project to calculate work on tasks. For example, a team member can open a Project task form, shown in Figure 15.10, in Outlook's Tasks module and make changes to any of the work-related fields in the task. The work-related fields are found on the Details tab, shown in Figure 15.11. The next time the team member opens the TeamStatus form, it resynchronizes the work with Outlook so all of these changes are reflected on a task's status report for Project.

PART

III

Juggling and
Managing Projects

FIGURE 15.10

If a team member makes changes to Outlook's Task form, Outlook synchronizes the changes with the TeamStatus form.

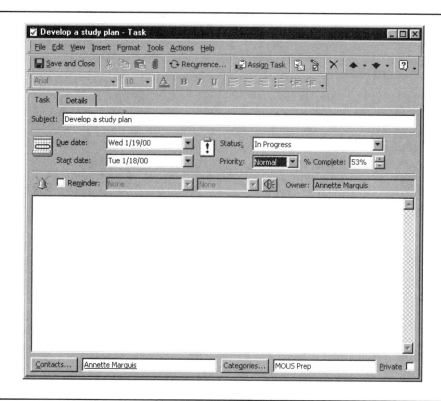

FIGURE 15.11

A team member can make changes to reflect the actual work completed on the task on the Details tab of the Outlook Task form.

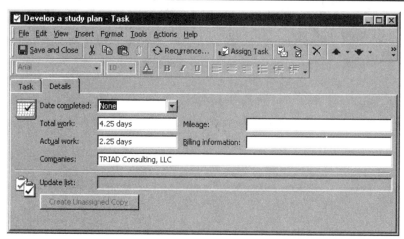

Because Outlook doesn't have a way to record work done by day or week, it evenly distributes the value entered in the Actual Work field on the Task form across the time period for the purposes of the timesheet grid on the TeamStatus message. If you want to record actual work completed on a given day, you must edit the values directly in the TeamStatus message.

Adding and Deleting Tasks

A team member cannot add or delete Project tasks. If a team member adds or deletes an Outlook task, it has no bearing on the project. The project manager must add or delete tasks directly within Project.

Resending All Messages

If you want to resend all workgroup messages related to a task or a project, choose Tools ➤ Workgroup and click Resend All Messages.

Setting Task Reminders

If you are a project manager who is running Outlook, you can have Project attach a reminder to a task. Project copies the tasks to your Outlook task list and activates the reminder. This reminder does not accompany the TeamAssign message—it is for your personal use only. Team members can set their own task reminders within Outlook.

You can set a reminder to appear before the start of the task or before the scheduled finish of a task. You may want to use this option, for example, to remind you to request a status report from team members.

To set a reminder, follow these steps:

1. Select the task or tasks for which you want to send the reminder.

2. Choose Tools ➤ Workgroup and click Set Reminder to open the Set Reminder dialog box.

3. Click the drop-down list to change the time period from minutes to hours, days, weeks, or months.

4. Enter a Set Reminders For value based on the selected time period.

5. Select whether you want the reminder Before the Start of the Selected Tasks or Before the Finish of the Selected Tasks.

6. Click OK to set the reminder.

When the task is sent to a team member who has Outlook, the reminder is set when the task is added to the team member's Outlook task list.

Sending a Schedule Note

A *schedule note* is an email message that another member of the team who has access to Project sends to the project manager, resources and contacts assigned to a task, or to the entire project team. The schedule note can contain a copy of the complete project or an image of whatever view is visible on the screen. You may want to send an image, for example, to a member of the team who is putting together a PowerPoint presentation about the project and wants to include an image showing the Project tasks or Resource Sheet.

 NOTE A *contact* is a person identified as the individual responsible for a task. This may be the resource assigned to the task, or it may be an individual responsible for a team of people working on a task or group of tasks. You can add the Contact field to any Task sheet view and enter a person's name in the field. Although this field is mapped to the Contacts Task field in Outlook, only the first Project contact is mapped in Outlook.

If you want to send a bitmap image of the Gantt Chart or another selected view, switch to that view and select the rows you want to send. To send a schedule note, choose Tools ➤ Workgroup and click Send Schedule Note. This opens the dialog box shown in Figure 15.12.

FIGURE 15.12

You can send a schedule note to the project manager, resources, and contacts.

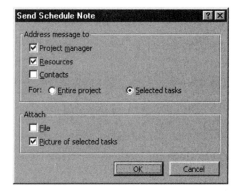

Select the person or people you want the message addressed to (project manager, resources, and contacts), and choose whether to send the entire project or only selected tasks. Click OK to open a pre-addressed message form with the image attached. Enter any message you want to accompany the image. To view the image, double-click it—the image opens in the application on your system that opens bitmap (*.bmp) images. Figure 15.13 shows an image in Microsoft Paint. Close the image and click Send to send the message.

If you want to send a copy of the entire project file, choose Tools ➤ Workgroup, click Send Schedule Note, and select Attach File. This attaches a copy of the project file to the message. Be aware that this is not a linked copy, so any changes made are not reflected in the original project file.

FIGURE 15.13

A picture of the selected tasks opens in Paint.

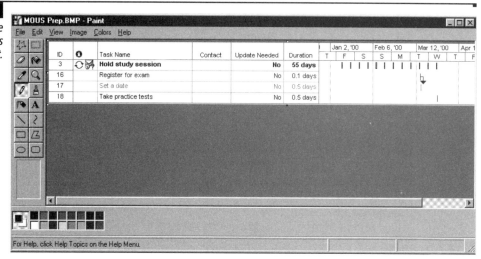

Why Do Schedule Notes Contain Duplicate Email Addresses in the To Field?

In Outlook, you have a choice to display address lists in First Name, Last Name or Last Name, First Name order. You make this selection by choosing Tools ➢ Services, selecting Outlook Address Book (or other address book), and choosing Properties.

Microsoft Outlook cannot reconcile a Project resource or contact that is entered in a different order. So, for example, if you have the address book property set to Last Name, First Name and enter a resource in Project as First Name, Last Name, Outlook sees that entry as two different names and tries to reconcile the First Name and the Last Name as separate entries. To work around this problem, enter Resource and Contact names in Project consistently with the address book properties in Outlook.

Using the Workgroup Toolbar

With Project's Workgroup toolbar, you can access many of the workgroup communication commands you need without using the Tools menu. To activate the Workgroup toolbar, choose View ➢ Toolbars and select Workgroup.

Table 15.2 describes each of the features of the Workgroup toolbar.

PART

III

Juggling and
Managing Projects

	TABLE 15.2: WORKGROUP TOOLBAR BUTTONS	
Button	**Name**	**Description**
	TeamAssign	Sends TeamAssign messages.
	TeamUpdate	Updates changes to the project schedule.
	TeamStatus	Solicits status reports from team members.
	TeamInbox	Used with Project Central to review team messages and update responses.
Resend All Messages	Resend All Messages	Resends all workgroup messages regarding a specific task or group of tasks.
	Set Reminder	Sets a personal reminder in Outlook.
	Send to Mail Recipient	Sends a copy of the project file to a mail recipient.
	Send to Routing Recipient	Routes a project file to several email recipients. (See "Routing Project Files," later in this chapter.)
	Send to Exchange Folder	Posts a project to an Microsoft Exchange public folder. (See "Posting to a Public Folder," later in this chapter.)
	Insert Project	Inserts a copy of another project into the active project.
	Open from Database	Opens a project file that was saved to a Microsoft Access or other database.
	Save to Database As	Saves the active project to a database.

Routing a Project File

When you are finalizing a project plan, it never hurts to solicit comments about the plan from stakeholders in the project. Although you can send each person a copy of the project, you are then faced with the daunting task of consolidating all of the changes into a central project file. If you route the project file instead, each person can make comments and changes to the active copy of the project. It then moves on to the next person on the routing list, and finally returns to you as one project file with all the incorporated changes. All recipients must have Microsoft Project on their systems to review the project file.

You can route a project by using the File menu (File ➤ Send To ➤ Routing Recipient) or by choosing Send to Routing Recipient from the Workgroup toolbar. When you choose this option, a routing slip (like the one shown in Figure 15.14) opens.

FIGURE 15.14

Use a routing slip to send a copy of a file to several recipients in succession.

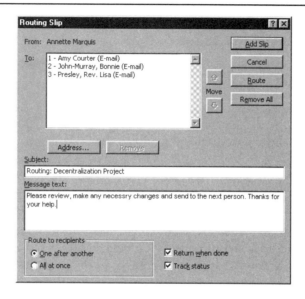

Follow these steps to complete the routing slip:

1. Click the Address button to choose the email addresses of the intended recipients.

2. Select as many recipients as you want from the Address book by double-clicking their name or by clicking once and clicking the To button.

3. Click OK to return to the Routing Slip.

4. Use the up and down Move arrows to change the order of the routing recipients.

5. Edit the subject and enter a message in the Message Text box.

6. Select to route to recipients One After Another or All At Once. The All at Once option sends duplicates to each recipient and should not be used if you want to incorporate changes from multiple recipients.

7. Select Return when Done to have the project file returned when everyone has reviewed it.

8. Select Track Status to receive an email message every time the file is sent on to the next recipient—this helps to know where the project is and whether it has been held up along the way.

9. Click Route to send to the project to the first recipient, or click Add Slip to add the routing slip to the project file but not send it yet. If you choose the Add Slip option, the menu command and toolbar button change to Other Routing Recipient. Choose Other Routing Recipient to add another recipient or to activate the routing by clicking Route. You can remove the routing slip by choosing Remove All.

When a routing recipient receives the message, they can double-click on the attachment to open the project file. When they are ready to send on to the next recipient,

PART

III

Juggling and
Managing Projects

they choose Send To ➤ Next Routing Recipient from the Project File menu. The sender can choose to send the file to the next person on the routing slip or to send a copy of the file to any other mail recipient.

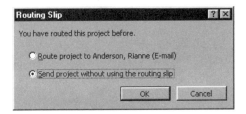

Posting to a Public Folder

To make a project available to multiple stakeholders, the easiest way is to post the project file to a Microsoft Exchange public folder. In a public folder, anyone with permissions to the folder who has Project can open the active project file. To post a project to a public folder, do the following:

1. Click the Send to Exchange Folder button on the Workgroup toolbar, or choose File ➤ Send to ➤ Exchange Folder on the menu.

2. Select the folder to which you want to post the project file from the Send To Exchange Folder dialog box, or click the New Folder button to create a new folder (select the folder you want the new folder to be under before clicking the New Folder button).

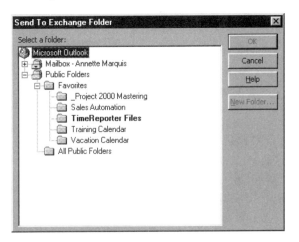

3. Click OK to post the folder.

You can set permissions to the public folder to restrict access to other users. To set permissions to a folder you created, right-click the folder and choose Properties. Click the Permissions tab.

NOTE For more about setting permissions in Exchange public folders, see *Mastering Outlook 2000*, Sybex 1999.

Customizing Workgroup Messages

Before sending the first TeamAssign message in a project, you may want to customize the workgroup messages that Project generates. You can customize the fields that are displayed in the message, as well as the timesheet grid that team members use to report work on the project. To customize workgroup messages, chose Tools ➢ Customize ➢ Workgroup from the menu.

Adding Fields to Workgroup Messages

The Customize Workgroup dialog box, shown in Figure 15.15, displays the list of fields currently in workgroup messages on the right and available fields on the left.

FIGURE 15.15

Use the Customize Workgroup dialog box to add additional fields to workgroup messages.

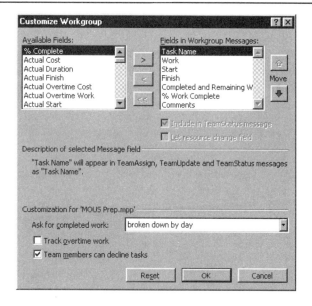

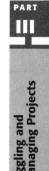

To add a field to the workgroup messages, select the field in the Available Fields column and click the right arrow to move the field into the Fields in Workgroup Messages column. Use the up and down Move arrows to change the order of the fields in the timesheet grid. To remove a field from the message, select the field and click the left arrow to move the field back to the Available Fields column. You can only remove fields that you add—standard fields cannot be removed from the workgroup messages.

If you click on any field, you can see a description of where the field is added.

 NOTE Changing the order of fields affects only email workgroup messages. The order of fields in Project Central is not changed.

Adjusting the Timesheet Grid

Use the Ask for Completed Work field to change the timesheet grid. The default, Broken Down by Day, provides a day-by-day grid for team members to enter daily work on a task. Choose Broken Down By Week if you want team members to enter total hours for each weekly period. Choose As a Total for the Entire Period if you want team members to enter summary totals of only the hours worked for the entire identified period.

Setting Other Custom Options

If you want team members to include overtime work when they enter time in the timesheet grid, select the Track Overtime Work checkbox.

You can give team members the option to decline tasks, or you can restrict that option by selecting or clearing the Task Members Can Decline Tasks checkbox.

To return the field settings to the original default options, click the Reset button.

What's Next

In this chapter, we reviewed the workgroup email tools. In Chapter 16, "Team Project Management with Project Central 2000," you'll have the opportunity to learn about Project Central, Microsoft Project's new Web-based communication tool. With Project, you can use both email and Web based options to manage projects within an intranet and with other external email users.

CHAPTER 16

Team Project Management with Project Central 2000

I n the real world, project managers don't usually have exclusive control over their resources. Most companies share their human resources (and their material resources for that matter) across many projects. In Chapter 14, "Sharing Resources and Tasks among Multiple Projects," you learned how to set up a resource pool or use an existing pool to share resources. In Chapter 15, "Communicating Project Information," you learned how to communicate with team members by using Project 2000 workgroup features. But TeamAssign, TeamUpdate, and TeamStatus don't allow team members to "get the overall picture." Nor do they allow others with interest in a project (such as senior managers and stakeholders) to view project information. That's where Project Central comes in.

Project Central operates within a browser window. In its simplest form, it is a Web site devoted to tracking your company's active projects. At its most complex, Project Central is a database of Project 2000 files and fields with detailed security to control who can access the database and what they see when they do.

Managers post reports, views, and other information for their team members. They can access workgroup features to send the TeamStatus, TeamAssign, and TeamUpdate messages previously discussed in Chapter 15. Stakeholders can log on to see reports and views for which they have permissions. Team members can see their task assignments and deadlines for *all* projects. They can send status updates to their managers and look at certain views from the Project files for which they have assigned tasks.

Setting up, configuring, and administering Project Central requires a bit of time and patience. (See Chapter 26, "Installing and Administering Project Central 2000.") But once it's running, users—including project managers—should find it fairly easy to navigate.

Accessing Project Central

Project Central lives on an intranet. When your administrator configures its settings, she will assign it a URL and communicate that information to you and other users. After you know the URL, you can type it into the address bar of any browser window and press Enter. You'll be prompted for a username and password, as shown in Figure 16.1.

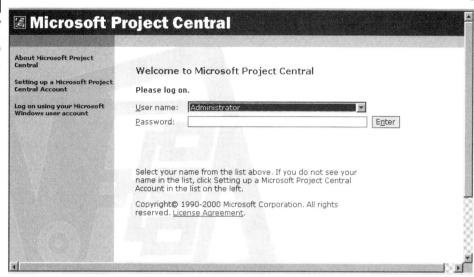

The logon authentication is an essential part of Project Central security. If an employee who is not a member of a project team stumbles across the URL for Project Central (intentionally or unintentionally), they can't get into project information without a user account. (See "Understanding Project Central Permissions" later in this chapter.) Although there are links on the login page that make it look as if anyone can get in, when you click them you won't get far unless you're an authorized user. The About Microsoft Project Central link leads to a text page that introduces the user to Project Central, explaining its purpose and licensing requirements. The Setting up a Microsoft Project Account link brings to mind the "registration" screens you frequently see on the Web. But this link doesn't lead to the "fill-in-the-blank-with-your-personal-information" form you might be thinking of.

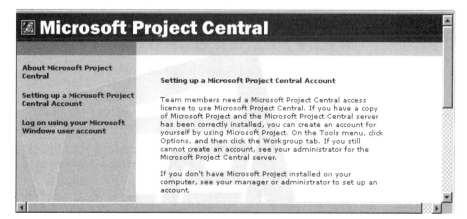

PART

III

Juggling and
Managing Projects

Instead, you'll see another text screen that explains how to create an account from within a Microsoft Project 2000 file. It only works, however, if the Project Central administrator has enabled the feature that allows project managers to create accounts:

The Project Central Administrator can opt to have users log on by using their Windows NT username and password. If that's the case in your organization, click the Log On Using Your Microsoft Windows User Account link and enter that information in the appropriate fields of the Enter Network Password dialog box.

If you're not using your Windows account to log in, use the fields on the Welcome page of Project Central, shown in Figure 16.1. As an authorized user, choose your name from the drop-down list and type in your assigned password. The Project Central Home Page, shown in Figure 16.2, appears.

 NOTE Managers often access Project Central from within their Project 2000 files. Team members may want access from within Outlook. After your administrator has Project Central configured (on a network server and on each workstation that requires access), those options are available. We will discuss them throughout the chapter.

FIGURE 16.2

The Project Central Home Page provides managers, stakeholders, and team members access to information about projects they're working on.

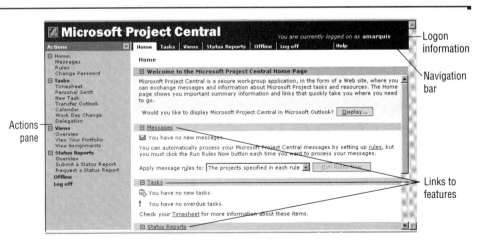

Navigating the Project Central Interface

After logon, Project Central's standard Home Page (refer to Figure 16.2) is loaded. The Home Page provides your "jumping-off" point. You'll see summary information (the number of messages you have waiting, new tasks, status report requests, or responses pending), as well as links to pages containing forms and settings for other Project Central features. During the rest of this chapter, we'll explore those various forms and settings. As an overview, you'll access the following pages most frequently:

Home   For general information, links, password options, email, and email rules.

Tasks   For viewing personal task lists and Gantt Charts, uploading Outlook calendar information, changing scheduled work hours, creating a task request, and delegating tasks (with appropriate permissions).

Views   For looking at task assignments for all projects you're working on and for viewing other resource information for which you've been given permissions.

Status Reports   For requesting and responding to status reports, as well as viewing reports submitted by your team members.

Admin   Only if you have administrative privileges (see "Understanding Project Central Permissions," as follows). Admin settings are for customizing Project Central user settings.

 Project Central is a Web site. Therefore, you can navigate to different pages as you normally would on the Web. (Mouse over the link you want to follow. When the pointer shape changes to a hand, click the link.) Project Central's Home Page provides multiple links to the pages listed above. For instance, if you want to navigate to Tasks, you have at least five choices: click the Tasks link in the middle of the Home Page, click the Timesheet link slightly below the Tasks link just mentioned, click Tasks in the Actions pane (or any of the subtopics listed under the Tasks heading), click Tasks on the Navigation Bar, or mouse over Tasks in the Navigation bar and then choose a subtopic.

Understanding Project Central Permissions

Each person who uses Project Central must have an *account*. Part of each account is the username (to identify a specific person) and password (to authenticate that person's identity). Accounts can be created in a couple of ways. For example, the Project Central administrator will set them up in advance. As a project manager, you can also create accounts for yourself and your team members from within Project 2000 (see "Making Project Data Available to Your Team," as follows), assuming that the administrator has enabled that setting for you. Creating an account isn't as simple as entering a name and password, however. To ensure the security of your company's sensitive project data, each account has certain *permissions* granted to it.

The specific data you see when you log on to Project Central depends on the role, and more specifically the categories, to which your account has been assigned. The assigned role and categories are collectively referred to as *permissions*, and the Project Central administrator usually configures them. For example, those assigned to the Team Member category can usually do the following:

- View their own task assignments and timelines

- Send progress reports to managers

- Delegate tasks to other team members (unless this setting is disabled by an administrator)

- Access views for which they've been given permissions

- Keep managers abreast of changes in their available working time

Users in the Executive Manager category can do all of this, but they may also have access to views on many different projects, even those they are not directly involved in. Two other standard categories are Project Manager and Resource Manager, and, of course, your administrator can create custom categories.

It's conceivable, even likely in many companies, that a person could be an assigned resource (team member) on one project and the project manager on another. As a team member, you can view your tasks, your email messages, and certain views of the project data on Projects X, Y, and Z. As the manager of Project Q, you can see all that, plus you can use the status reports provided by team members to update Project Q. Naturally, as Project Manager, you have access to all views and reports for the project you're managing from within the Project file.

The Project Central administrator has the ability to add and delete accounts and set other users' permissions. The administrator can even provide other users with administrative permissions. Those with administrative accounts have the ability to customize views, allowing users to see certain areas of projects, based on fields and filters. If you're a project manager but not an administrator, you may have to coordinate with the Project Central administrator so that your team members have access to all the information you want them to see.

 NOTE This is just the tip of the very large iceberg surrounding accounts and permissions. Chapter 26 will steer you in the right direction if you're the person setting up user accounts.

Making Project Data Available to Your Team

In theory, anyone with an account and appropriate permissions can see data in Project Central. However, if you as project manager haven't updated the project file to the Web server or sent any workgroup messages since the Project Central accounts were set up, users won't see much when they log on to the Home Page. They'll have no mail messages and no task entries in their timesheets. They won't even be able to see the name of the project unless you configured it for Project Central. So, there are really three general issues controlling what users see: account permissions, Project 2000 file settings, and workgroup messages sent.

Updating a Project to the Web Server

Some administrators prefer to create user accounts and permissions as part of the Project Central setup and configuration. However, the administrator can enable a setting that allows project managers to create accounts for themselves and their team members as they post and update their project file to the Web server. To post a project file, open it in Project 2000, and then follow these steps:

1. Click Tools ➤ Options and select the Workgroup tab.

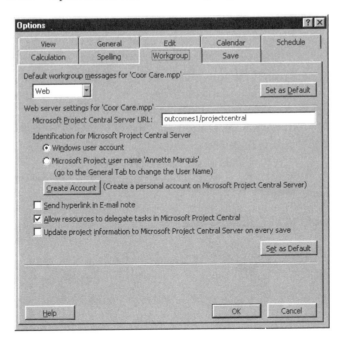

2. Choose Web as the method of communication you want to use for Workgroup messages.

3. Type the URL for Project Central in the Microsoft Project Central URL field.

4. Choose an identification method (see sidebar that follows these steps).

5. Optional! Click Create Account, but only if you don't currently have an account *and* only if you want to work in Project Central (customizing the Home Page or creating views for your team members to see, for instance) *before* you send a workgroup message.

 NOTE You must have an account in order to work on Project Central. However, one is created for you automatically when you send your first workgroup message. Further, the Project Central administrator may have already created one for you. So don't click Create Account if your next action will be to send a workgroup message, or if you already have an account.

6. Enable the Send Hyperlink in E-mail Note feature if you want team members to receive a regular email message, with the URL for Project Central, each time you send workgroup messages. This email is intended to serve as a reminder for resources to log-on to Project Central and retrieve messages. If they're already doing that on a regular enough basis, leave the feature disabled.

7. If you want to allow your resources to delegate tasks to other resources in this project file, enable that checkbox.

8. If you're modifying the Project 2000 file frequently, it's a good idea to enable the Update Project Information checkbox. Project Central displays data from your Project 2000 file, as of the last time you synchronized with the server. If timelines get shifted due to task slippage, the new dates aren't reflected until you sync. If you don't update automatically upon saving, you can do it manually by clicking Tools ➢ Workgroup ➢ Update Project to Web Server.

 MASTERING THE OPPORTUNITIES

Mastering Account ID Methods

If you're a manager creating accounts for yourself and your team members, you are prompted to choose an authentication method for logging on to Project Central. Here are some issues to consider when making that choice:

The Windows NT Account method allows managers and resources to use the same username and password for Project Central as they use for Windows NT. Messages sent through

Continued ▮▶

> ◀ **MASTERING THE OPPORTUNITIES CONTINUED**
>
> Project Central display the NT username in the From field. With this option, you have the advantage of being able to use Windows NT security features.
>
> The Microsoft Project UserName method (for Microsoft Project Server Central authentication) lets you use the name stored on the General tab of Project's Options dialog box. Each Project 2000 user can enter whatever name they like. In small companies, first names often suffice, which lends a personal touch to email messages. Of course, standards must be established, or else you're sure to see messages from the likes of Rich "Wild Man" Steinhoff. Naturally, team members must have Project 2000 installed on their workstations to pull usernames this way. The Project Central administrator can also add users in the Project Central Administrative tools.
>
> If your company is using mixed authentication methods for logging on, switching to strictly NT authentication invalidates all accounts using the Project username. The administrator, as part of the switch, must manually change the authentication method for each of these accounts to make them active again.
>
> If the administrator has set up an account for someone on the team, and has chosen to use the NT account, and then a project manager sets up an account using a Project username, the user will end up with two user accounts. The Project Central administrator can merge the accounts from the Project Central Admin menu. For more about accessing Project Central Admin menu, see Chapter 26.

Initiating Workgroup Messages

Until the project manager sends a workgroup message, team members have no messages and no status reports indicated on the Project Central Home Page (like the one shown in Figure 16.2). If you previously used email workgroup messages, responses to those messages show up in your email inbox. After you make the switch to Project Central, any new TeamAssign, TeamStatus, and TeamUpdate messages you generate as project manager appear in Project Central. Naturally, responses to those messages appear in Project Central as well.

 NOTE If you need a refresher on workgroup features such as TeamAssign, TeamStatus, and TeamUpdate, refer to Chapter 15.

PART

III

Juggling and
Managing Projects

Using the Home Page Features

As mentioned previously, the Home Page provides the starting point for your work in Project Central. Often, users blow by the Home Page with a single click—to features held on other pages. But certain options are accessible only from the Home Page (or most easily accessible from there). These options include email messages, rules features, and password settings.

Sending and Receiving Messages

Project Central is not a substitute for Outlook or another MAPI-compliant email program. You can't generate new email messages from Project Central as you would in a regular email program. You can respond to messages, but only certain types of mail messages appear there. Team Members see the following:

- TeamAssign messages
- TeamStatus messages (not to be confused with status reports that are requested and/or created from within Project Central)
- TeamUpdate messages
- Task delegation messages when other resources transfer their assignments to you
- Responses to these types of messages sent by your manager or other resources

Project Managers also see the following workgroup-related messages:

- Replies to previously sent TeamAssign and TeamStatus messages
- New task requests from team members, stating that they are working on a task that is not currently part of the project file but needs to be
- Requests for task delegation from team members when they have to transfer their own task assignments to another resource

Viewing Messages

Project Central's Home Page indicates when you have new messages. To view them in list format, click an email link (Messages, Microsoft Project Central Inbox, or any of the email links in the Navigation bar or Actions pane). The Project Central Inbox for team member Karla Browning is shown in Figure 16.3.

You can open an individual message a couple different ways. Click the Open Messages link to open the selected message (the one with the square black indicator in the far-left column). Or, you can click the link in the Subject column of the message you want to view.

FIGURE 16.3

The Project Central Inbox holds workgroup messages.

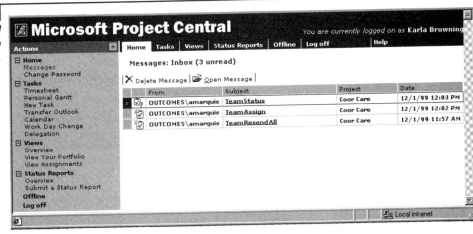

Responding to Messages

Each message type requires a different set of steps to respond. Fortunately, Project Central makes it easy because most messages contain detailed instructions that even your least experienced users can follow. Let's look at an example. We'll open the TeamAssign message from team member Karla Browning's Inbox (shown in Figure 16.3).

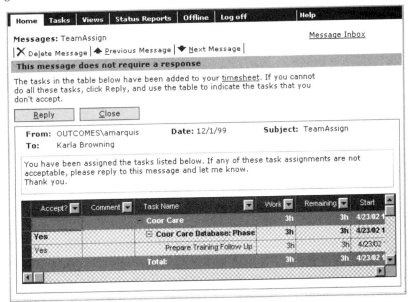

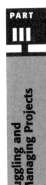

The instructions for this message appear near the top of the page, below the Delete, Next, and Previous message links. One thing that jumps out right away is the banner that instructs the team member that This Message Does Not Require a Response. Although your less-conscientious resources might head directly from the banner to the Delete Message button, hopefully, most will continue reading. Below the banner, Project Central displays text that explains the following:

- Events that have occurred as a result of the email (in this case, tasks were added to the resource's timesheet)

- What the resource should do if this action is unacceptable (click Reply and indicate which tasks cannot be accepted)

Let's say this is an instance in which the resource can't accept the new task. Clicking Reply produces a similar form with another short set of instructions for the user.

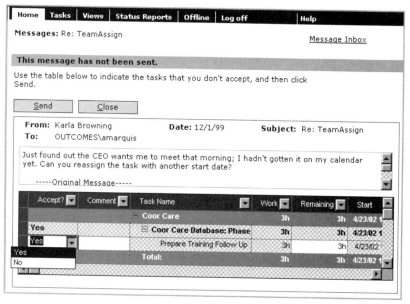

At this point, the user can type a reply message, as shown previously. (Look for an insertion point toward the middle of your message window above the Original Message text.) But the most important thing the user must do is to change the table to reflect the tasks she cannot accept. The Accept? field has a Yes/No drop-down list that defaults to Yes. Changing the Yes to a No declines the task assignment after the message is sent. After the table is updated, the user clicks Send. The message closes and the original TeamAssign message (to which she was replying) is deleted from her Inbox.

TIP As a project manager, you can create rules to automatically process workgroup messages and update your Project 2000 file. See "Using Rules to Automatically Handle Messages," as follows.

Many of the actions required for responding to Project Central messages are similar. Table 16.1 summarizes what team members should do to reply to different types of mail.

TABLE 16.1: RESPONDING TO PROJECT CENTRAL MESSAGES

Message Type	For	Action Required after Opening
TeamStatus	Team Members	Type reply text if desired; enter values in the Actual Work fields for the dates and tasks requested (not Summary Tasks); and then click Send.
TeamAssign	Team Members	Requires a response only if the resource must decline a task. Type reply text, if desired; change the task table Yes fields to No where appropriate; and then click Send.
TeamResend	Team Members	Same as TeamAssign. You're not required to reply unless you must decline a task.
Task Delegation	Team Members	Very similar to TeamAssign messages. You don't have to reply unless you want to decline the delegation.

NOTE Messages that don't require responses stay in your Inbox until they are deleted. Select a message (or open it) and click the Delete Message link to remove it from the Inbox.

Using Rules to Automatically Handle Messages

If the thought of opening and updating dozens of daily messages is overwhelming, you'll be pleased to know that there's an easier way. You can save time and effort by creating rules to automatically process messages that appear in your Inbox. Processing rules automatically updates your Project file. And, if you're already familiar with the Outlook Rules Wizard, you'll be thrilled to learn that Project Central's rules are even easier to set up.

NOTE By default, team members' accounts don't have rules permissions. However, project managers do. If you don't see a Rules link on your Project Central Home Page, contact your administrator.

You can get to the Rules features with a single click on the Rules link in the Messages section of the Home Page. (Or, if you're in the Inbox, you can follow the Rules link there.) In either case, the Rules page shown in Figure 16.4 appears.

FIGURE 16.4

The Rules page allows managers to create rules to automatically process Project Central messages and update Project 2000 files.

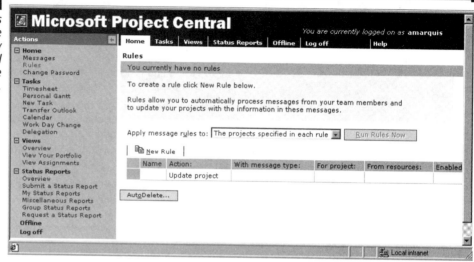

The Rules process requires three steps, the last of which is optional. First, you create one or more rules. Then, when it's time to use the rule(s), you run them. As an optional step, you can set up the AutoDelete options to automatically clean up messages remaining in the Inbox. Rules have to be run (but not created) each time you receive new messages in your Inbox.

Creating Rules

Click the New Rule link on the Rules page shown in Figure 16.4. This opens Step 1 of the Rules Wizard, as follows.

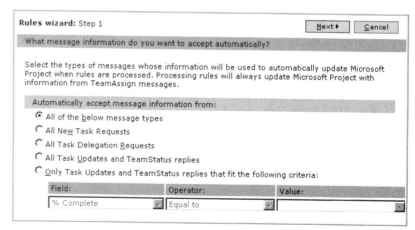

1. You're given five options for selecting the type(s) of message(s) to process automatically. The instructions on this page can be a bit confusing at first because the terms "process" and "accept" are used synonymously here. Also, the first option (All Of The Below Message Types) really only refers to the three message types listed below that option. Select among the following:

   All Of The Below Message Types   If you want all workgroup messages to be processed by Project Central and updated in your Project file. This means that all Task Delegation requests will be approved and all New Task Requests will be granted.

   All New Task Requests, All Task Delegation Requests, or **All Task Updates and TeamStatus Replies**   If you want only the selected message type to be processed automatically. Example: You know you'll always approve Task Delegations, but you want to scrutinize new tasks and status updates. In that case, select the All Task Delegation Requests option.

   Only Task Updates and TeamStatus Replies That Meet the Following Criteria   If you want to create a filter that allows for the automatic processing of some messages but not others. To create a filter, choose a Field and an Operator, and then enter a Value or select a field for the Value by clicking the list button to the right of the Value field (it looks like a gray square with a dot on it.) If you need a bit of help here, Chapter 17, "Using Views to Evaluate Data," contains detailed information about filtering data.

2. Click Next to go to Step 2 of the Wizard.

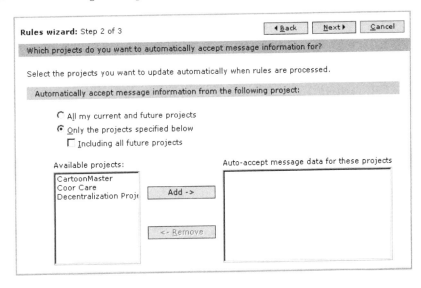

3. At this step of the Wizard, choose whether you want the rule applicable in All Current and Future Projects or Only The Projects Specified Below. If you choose the second option, enable the Including All Future Projects checkbox if you want the rule applied to projects you post in the future. Then, choose the projects you want to select for the rule. Click the one you want from the list on the left and click the Add button to move it to the list on the right. Repeat as necessary. Remove a project from the list on the right by clicking it and then clicking Remove. Click Next when you're ready to proceed.

4. Step 3 of the Wizard offers the same choices as Step 2, but the choices apply to resources, not projects. Choose the resources that you will automatically accept messages from. Click Next.

5. If you chose All Of The Below Message Types or All Task Delegation Requests in Step 1, you're given a fourth step, where you must choose resources to whom tasks may be delegated. Proceed as you did in Step 3 and click Finish when you're through.

You'll see a dialog box, confirming the creation of the new rule and any constraints on applying it to messages already in your Inbox. Note the constraints (if any) and click OK to return to the Rules page, where the banner shows the total number of rules you have created.

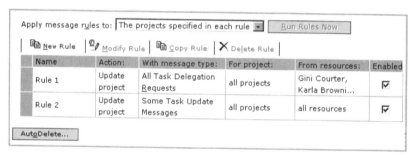

If you want to create a rule that is very similar to an existing rule, select the rule (click the gray rectangle that precedes the rule's name), and click Copy Rule to launch the Wizard and retain all the settings of the selected rule. Proceed through the Wizard, making changes as desired, and then click Finish. The new rule is sequentially numbered and displayed with the others.

Modify an existing rule by selecting and clicking Modify Rule and making changes at appropriate steps of the Wizard. Remove a rule by selecting it and clicking Delete Rule.

Running Rules

Run Rules Now If you have unopened messages, click Run Rules Now to apply the newly created rule, and process existing messages for all projects. The Run Rules Now button appears on the Home Page and on the Rules Page in Project Central. It is disabled when you have no new messages.

It's possible to run some but not all of the rules when you click Run Rules Now. And it's possible to run certain rules on certain projects. The default is to run all rules on all projects. To choose a particular project on which to run rules, select it from the Apply Message Rules To drop-down list. If you want to run only one particular rule, disable the other rules by clearing the checkbox in the Enable field of each one. After you configure the project and rules you want to run, click Run Rules Now.

WARNING Rules don't run automatically for new messages. You must click Run Rules Now each time new messages appear in your Inbox. One exception is for Task Delegation Messages. They are accepted automatically when you log on if you are using a Task Delegation rule.

Using AutoDelete

If you're using rules to process messages automatically, it's usually because you don't need to see each individual message. You didn't want to take the time to open and read each one, or you wouldn't have used a rule in the first place. So, it makes sense to remove these messages from your Inbox after they're processed. That's where AutoDelete is helpful. It allows you to choose which message types are automatically deleted after processing. From the Rules page, click AutoDelete to open the AutoDelete dialog box.

Choose an option for deleting messages. All Of The Below Message Types deletes all four types of messages listed here as checkboxes. If you prefer to have some, but not all, messages types automatically deleted, enable the Messages By Type option and click the message types you do want AutoDeleted. Click OK when you're finished. You can change these settings anytime by clicking the AutoDelete button on the Rules page.

PART

III

Juggling and Managing Projects

Changing Your Project Central Password

From the Home Page, you can access the Change Password link in two places: the Actions pane and the navigation bar. If you're using the navigation bar, mouse over Home and click Change Password to open the Change Your Password page.

Change Your Password

Old Password: _____

New Password: _____

Confirm Password: _____

[Change Password]   [Cancel]

Type your current password in the Old Password field. Press Tab to move to the New Password field. Type your new password there—Project Central requires a minimum of eight characters unless your administrator has designated otherwise. Press Tab to move to the Confirm Password field and type the new password one more time. When you're finished, click Change Password. You'll see a red confirmation message if you've been successful.

 WARNING Don't make the mistake of taking passwords lightly. If you're using family members' names or birth dates, any computer-literate person who knows you can hack your password in about two minutes. Use a minimum of eight characters, and include at least one number or one special character. It's also helpful to miss upper and lower case letters. Bad: *Chelsea*. Better: *#chapter*. Best: *trAck*7q*.

Working with Tasks

Tasks are a critical data component in Project Central. Most, if not all, Project Central communication involves tasks in some way. Tasks are assigned, accepted, declined, delegated, updated, and created here. Understanding task features, therefore, is essential to working effectively in Project Central. We'll begin by exploring tasks from the team members' viewpoint.

Using the Timesheet

Each team member's timesheet shows tasks that have been assigned, updated, or otherwise modified since the project manager began communicating through Project Central. It means that a team member on a two-year project who is just starting out with Project Central won't necessarily see all his tasks on the timesheet. Advise your team to maintain their former task lists until you're sure that Project Central is tracking everything you want tracked.

 NOTE   If your team has been maintaining Outlook task lists, make sure that you read the "Integrating Project Central With Outlook" section, later in this chapter.

As a resource on a project, you can view your own task list (called a *timesheet*) by clicking any of the task links in the Actions pane, on the navigation bar, or within the text of the Home Page itself. Figure 16.5 shows the timesheet for team member Gini Courter.

FIGURE 16.5

Each team member has a Timesheet that lists tasks created or modified since communication through Project Central began.

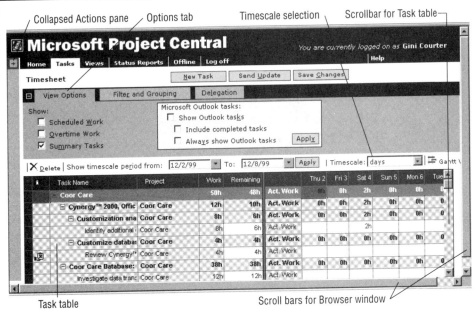

The timesheet has a task field portion (on the left) and a timescale section (on the right). Point to the split between the two and drag the adjustment tool to change the relative size of each section.

Adjust the height of the rows and width of the columns in the timesheet by dragging the appropriate adjustment tool.

Choosing View and Timescale Options

By default, the timesheet displays Summary Tasks with their subtasks and Actual Work in daily increments. You can recognize Summary Tasks because they show up in **bold** unless the Project Manager has applied a different format setting. Click the minus (–) sign in front of any Summary Task to collapse it, thus hiding the subtasks displayed below it. Click the plus sign (+) in front of any collapsed Summary Task to expand it, displaying subtasks. To remove Summary Tasks from the display, leaving only subtasks, clear the Summary Tasks checkbox in the Show list above the timesheet.

To display Scheduled Work in addition to Actual Work for each task, enable the Scheduled Work checkbox. Then, each task shows two timescale rows: one for Actual Work and one for Scheduled Work. Enabling the Overtime Work field adds a third timescale row to each task.

Change dates for which the data is displayed by adjusting the Timescale Period From and To fields. Simply click the drop-down arrow and navigate the calendar to the month you want to use. Click a date to select it. Click Apply when you've chosen both a From and To date.

 TIP   If you click on the year in the Calendar control, you'll get a spin box that allows you to select a year.

By default, the selected period is displayed in Days. But you can choose to show the Timescale in Weeks (which shows data in seven-day, Sunday to Saturday increments). If you select Weeks, and your Period From Date is not a Sunday, the first column in the Timescale portion of the Timesheet shows a "short" week that begins on the Period From date. Selecting Entire Period displays one column that totals all the data during the selected time period.

 WARNING   If you select a relatively long time period, you may not be able to see all your dates. Changing the size of the Timescale portion of the window helps, but you still can't scroll any farther than your browser allows. In general, you'll want to use fairly short time periods to view task data.

Viewing the Personal Gantt

 Gantt View

If you want to see the graphical representation of the Timescale section, click the Gantt View link to the right of the Timescale selection drop-down list. Now, the timesheet shows Gantt bars for tasks scheduled during the selected time period.

Although you can't directly adjust the timescale from Gantt Chart view, you can click Zoom In or Zoom Out to choose smaller and larger time increments, respectively.

 Timesheet

Click the Timesheet link to return to the table view. All timescale settings are as you left them, even if you zoomed the Gantt Chart.

TIP You can also access the Personal Gantt directly from the Actions pane or Navigation bar.

Filtering, Grouping, and Sorting Tasks

Filtering lets you choose which tasks you want to view, based on criteria you specify. (You want to see only tasks that have durations over eight hours.) Tasks that don't meet the filter criteria are hidden. *Grouping* displays like tasks together under a heading you specify. (You're currently working on four projects. You want each project to appear as a heading that you can expand or collapse to display/hide that project's tasks.) *Sorting* tasks allows you to display them in a particular order. (You want to see all tasks in chronological order by start date.) Click the Filter and Grouping tab near the top of the Timesheet page to access those settings.

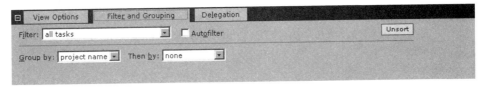

PART III

Juggling and Managing Projects

Applying a Filter After the Filter and Grouping options are displayed, click the drop-down arrow on the Filter field to see filters available for your Timesheet. Most of these list items are self-explanatory: All Incomplete Tasks shows tasks that are less than 100% complete.

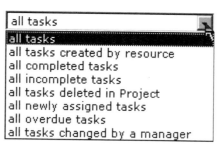

Using AutoFilters Enable the AutoFilter checkbox to activate filter arrows on each of the columns in task portion of the timesheet:

Remember that you can drag the gray bar that splits tasks from timescale in order to see more task fields. AutoFilter features here work just as they do in Excel, and just as they do in other Project 2000 views. You can't save filter settings in Project Central; filters are automatically removed when you switch to another page (but not to another Options tab in the timesheet). If you're not familiar with AutoFilter, here's a quick overview.

When you click the AutoFilter arrow on any field, you'll see three types of items in the list:

All Removes a filter previously applied to that field.

Custom For writing a simple filter query (see "Creating and Saving a Custom Filter" in Chapter 17).

Values The remaining items in the list represent the values displayed in that column.

Choose a value if you want to see tasks that are exactly equal to the value you chose: tasks with four-hour durations; tasks that start February 1, 2000; or just the tasks for Project X. Choose Custom to filter on more than one value, to filter on a numeric or date range, or to filter out a value: all tasks for Projects X and Y; tasks with scheduled start dates between June 1, 2000 and June 30, 2000; or tasks for all projects except Project X.

You can filter on more than one column at once—to see, for example, tasks for Project X with more than five hours of work remaining. Column headers turn blue when a filter is applied. The timesheet is totaled based on the filtered data, as shown here:

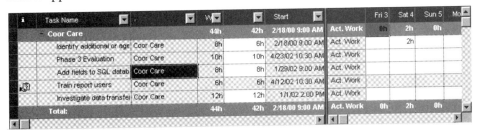

Grouping Tasks on the Timesheet   By default, tasks are grouped by project and all project headers are expanded. Click the minus (–) sign in front of any project headers to collapse the tasks under that header. Click the plus (+) sign to expand them.

To apply a different group setting, select from the Group By and Then By lists on the Filter and Grouping tab of the timesheet. Your group choices are limited to the project name, start date, work, and task name. Figure 16.6 shows part of a timesheet grouped by Project and then by Work, with the 2h, 4h, and 6h groups collapsed and the 8h group expanded.

FIGURE 16.6

Group settings allow you to view tasks under one heading or subheading. Here, we grouped tasks by Project and then by Work.

You can remove the Then By group setting by selecting None from the list. However, Project Central doesn't allow you to remove the primary grouping criteria from the Timesheet. You'll always be grouped by something, but you get four choices for what that something is.

Sorting the Timesheet   There are no sort settings, per se, on the timesheet. There's no list of fields to sort by, and you can't pull up a dialog box to sort by this or that field. Nevertheless, you're always sorted by some criteria, even if you've never sorted your Timesheet. By default, items are displayed in the order you received them.

PART

III

Juggling and
Managing Projects

Click any column header in the task portion of the timesheet to sort tasks in ascending order (A–Z, 1–10) on that field. Click the same header again to sort descending (Z–A, 10–1). An upward pointed triangle indicates that the timesheet is currently sorted in ascending order on the column header displaying the triangle. The downward-pointing triangle signifies a descending sort.

 NOTE You can't sort groups, only tasks within a group. And multi-level sorts aren't supported in the timesheet. Each subsequent sort is a self-contained action.

Remove previously applied sort and list tasks in the order they were received by clicking the Unsort button on the Filter and Grouping tab.

Delegating a Task

As a project manager with a good team behind you, there's little need to micromanage resources. They know when they're falling behind on a task. And your best people will recognize a time crunch before it happens. We hope you're blessed, as we are, with conscientious, forward-thinking staff members who take their assignments and deadlines seriously. In this fortunate situation, a project manager can save hours of reviewing and reassigning tasks by allowing resources to delegate on their own.

NOTE See Chapter 26 to learn about enabling and disabling the delegation option.

Team members click the Delegation tab to see options for delegating tasks. Most of the settings here are for viewing tasks after you've delegated some. The actual delegation process invokes a wizard to walk you through.

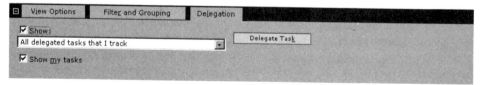

To delegate a task, do the following:

1. Select the task you want to delegate by clicking the dark square at the far left of the task on the timesheet. You can select and delegate multiple tasks at once by holding Ctrl to select additional tasks.

2. Click the Delegate Task button to launch the Wizard.

> Delegated Task 1 of 2: **Investigate data transfer with State of Michigan**, Project: **Coor Care**, Manager: **OUTCOMES\amarquis**
>
> 1) <u>W</u>ho do you want to delegate this task to?
>
> Administrator   ▾
>
> <u>Create a new resource</u> if the person you want to delegate the task to is not in the list above.
>
> 2) Do you want to assume the lead role for this task? By assuming the lead role, you track and approve actuals submitted by the resource.
> ○ <u>Y</u>es   ◉ <u>N</u>o
>
> 3) Do you want to continue to track this task on your My Tasks table?
> ◉ <u>Y</u>es   ○ N<u>o</u>
>
> Co<u>m</u>ments

3. At Step 1 of the Wizard, you'll see text that tells you steps to follow and what happens after you finish your end of the delegation process. Scroll down past these instructions to see the delegation options and a comments field for each task you selected.

   a. Choose the resource to whom you want to delegate the task. If the resource you need isn't listed, click Create a New Resource to open the Create a New User Account dialog box. You need to assign a domain and username for the resource. (See Chapter 26 if you're not sure what to do here.)

   b. Select whether or not you want to assume the lead role on the task you are delegating. If you choose Yes, you still have to send progress reports to the project manager. If you choose No, the person to whom you delegate sends these status updates.

   c. Choose whether or not you want to continue tracking the delegated task. Selecting Yes keeps the task on your timesheet, where you can see whether progress is being made on it or not. Choosing No removes it from the timesheet, so it's difficult to know if the person is working on it. Choose No only if you really trust your delegate! If you chose Yes for assuming the Lead Role, you're forced to continue tracking that task.

   d. Add comments if you want. Comments entered here are visible only to the specific resource you've chosen for this task delegation.

4. Click Next to proceed to Step 2 of the Wizard.

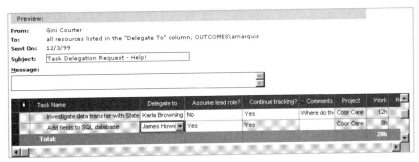

PART

III

Juggling and
Managing Projects

5. Step 2 of the Wizard offers a preview of the message you'll send to the resources you've chosen.

    a. Edit the text in the Subject field, if you want.

    b. Type a message in the Message field if there's text you want all your delegate resources to see.

    c. Change any of the settings in the task fields by clicking in a field and choosing a different setting. Click and type in the comments field or delete text that's already there, if you want.

    d. Change the sort order of the tasks if desired.

6. Click Send when you're finished. You will see a confirmation dialog box. Click OK to return to the timesheet with the View Options tab displayed.

There are certain types of tasks you can't delegate—for example, tasks that have been deleted or tasks that have status requests pending. Project Central displays an explanatory dialog box when you try to delegate tasks that aren't available for delegation.

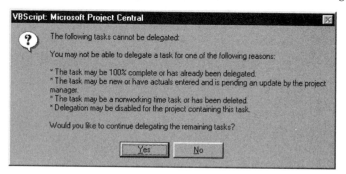

 NOTE All task delegations produce an approval request to the project manager. Tasks aren't officially delegated until the project manager approves the assignment. If you are the project manager, see "Responding to Messages," earlier in this chapter.

Filtering Delegated Tasks   Tasks in the timesheet are shown with various indicators, so you can see at a glance which have been declined, which are pending, and which have been successfully delegated. If you're not sure what an indicator means, mouse over it for an explanation.

When you have at least one delegated task, you have additional options for how to view (and specifically how to filter) the timesheet. Clear the Show checkbox if you don't want to see any of the delegated tasks. Disable the Show My Tasks checkbox if you don't want to see undelegated tasks. Of course, if you disable both checkboxes, you'll see no tasks. If you enabled the Show field, you can choose from the three filter options on the drop-down list.

Requesting Task Status   After the project manager has approved a task delegation, you can request a status report for tasks for which you've assumed the lead. Select the task and click the Request Task Status button to begin this process. Status requests are covered more thoroughly in the "Creating and Sending Status Reports" section, later in this chapter.

Creating a New Task

Project managers aren't omniscient (although you may know some who think they are). There will always be tasks that didn't get thought of during the planning stages. If you're a team member who finds that you are spending a considerable amount of time on a task that isn't listed as part of the project, you'll want to alert your manager to include it.

`New Task`

From the timesheet, click the New Task Button to open the page displayed in Figure 16.7.

FIGURE 16.7

Creating a new task allows a resource to keep his manager apprised of work that needs to be included in the Project file.

New Task		Create Task	Cancel

Create a New Task

You may want to create a new task if you are working on a task that your manager hasn't yet assigned to you.

To create a new task on your timesheet, use the settings below to provide the necessary information for the task, and then click Create Task above. When you send an update for your timesheet, the new task is submitted to the appropriate project manager for approval.

What project do you want the new task to be created in?

Project: `Coor Care`

What outline level do you want to create the new task in?

(•) Create the new task at the top outline level

(○) Make the new task a subtask of: `Customize datat`

Here's a hint!   You can make the new task a subtask of a summary task to which you were assigned.

Task information

Name: `          `
Comment: `          `
Start Date: `12/3/99`
Work: `          `

Fill in the task information as follows:

1. Click the Project drop-down list and choose the project to which the task should be added.

2. Choose an outline-level option. You can make the new task at the highest outline level so that it appears on par with summary tasks. If this is what you want, choose the first option. Or, you can make the new task a subtask of a summary task to which you're currently assigned. In this case, select the second option and choose a summary task from the drop-down list.

3. Type a descriptive name for the task in the Name field. If you want to add additional information, type a short comment in the Comment field. Select a start date for the task and type an estimated task duration in the Work field. Make sure that you indicate whether the duration is in minutes, hours, or days by using this format: 10m, 10h, or 10d.

4. Click Create Task to place the new task on your timesheet.

5. Select the task and click Send Update to notify your manager.

Sending Updates to Your Manager

Fishing for a pat on the back? You can send an unsolicited task update quickly and easily with a couple of clicks in your timesheet.

First, click in the Actual Work field for the date(s) and task(s) you want to update. Type in the number of hours (or minutes or days) you've worked on the task. If the work field currently shows 0h, it's probably best if you update the task in hour increments because that's what your manager is tracking.

> **WARNING** You can't update any numeric fields that are gray on the timesheet. That includes scheduled work fields (because only the project manager can change that setting) and summary task work fields (because they're a calculated field).

Then, select the task(s) you want to update. Click the row selector to the left of the task name. Hold Ctrl to select additional tasks. After the task(s) are selected, click the Send Update button. That's it! The actual work data is sent to your manager and you'll see a confirmation dialog box:

Deleting a Task

If you decide that you really don't want to complete a task, you can delete it from the task list, but only under the following conditions:

- The task is not a delegated task for which you are the lead.
- The task is not a summary task with existing subtasks.
- The task is not a non-working time task.
- The task was not transferred from Microsoft Outlook.

That may not leave a lot of tasks left on your list that you can delete, but if you have one that meets these criteria, you can delete it by selecting it and clicking the Delete button.

Using Views

Project Central lets you view projects in two major ways:

- By project
- By assignment

The By project option is called Your Portfolio. Your Portfolio, shown in Figure 16.8, contains a list of projects that your Project Central administrator has given you permission to see.

FIGURE 16.8

Your Portfolio shows you the projects you have to access, and it lets you view them in a variety of ways.

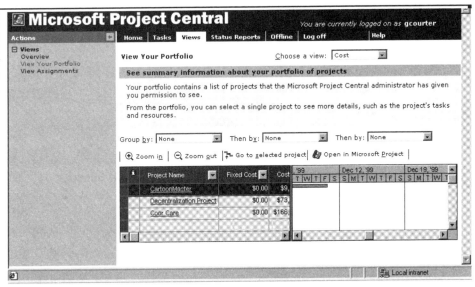

You can choose to view your portfolio in one of five views: Cost, Earned Value, Summary, Tracking, and Work by choosing a view from the View drop-down list. You can also group a view by up to three levels.

To view tasks and other details about a project, click the project and then select a detailed view from the View list. The views available from this list are similar to views available within Project. For a more detailed discussion of views, see Chapter 17.

Choose the field you want to group or click the Unsort button to return the list to the order in which it appears in the project. To filter data, click the down-arrow at the top of any field and select a value to filter on.

Scroll through the Gantt Chart on the right side of the view to see the tasks, or select a task and click the Go to Selected Task button. Use the Zoom In and Zoom Out buttons to change the timescale in the Gantt Chart from fifteen-minute segments up through years.

Go to selected task   Zoom in | Zoom out

Each view represents a table of data. However, only a couple of the table's fields are visible. To see additional fields in the table display, drag the vertical split bar between the table and the Gantt Chart. If you have Microsoft Project available on your system, you can also click Open in Microsoft Project to have all the tools of Microsoft Project at your disposal.

To change the focus of the data to task assignments, click the View Assignments link on the Actions pane. Although View Assignments has only one view available, you can choose to display Summary Tasks, Summary Roll-up, and Non-Working time in the Summary view.

Because this view is assignment-focused, you may be more interested in the timesheet than in a Gantt Chart. You can switch to the Usage view (see Figure 16.9) to show the Usage table in place of the Gantt Chart.

FIGURE 16.9

The Usage table of View Assignments displays a timesheet for each task.

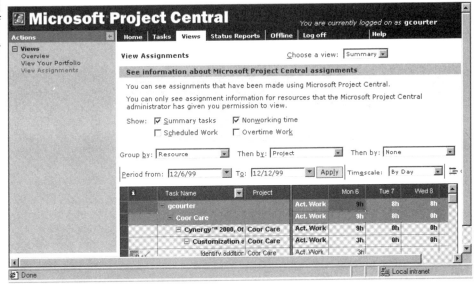

 NOTE You can't make changes to any of the data in the Portfolio or Assignment views—they are only for the purpose of viewing data.

Creating and Sending Status Reports

As a manager, you can design a status report for team members to complete that contains the information you want to receive. You can then combine the responses from several team members in one consolidated status report.

Team members can also design status reports and send them unsolicited to their manager, or they can reply to status reports generated by their manager.

Submitting Status Reports

To request a status report from team members, click the Status Reports menu and choose Send a Status Report. When the Status Reports Overview, shown in Figure 16.10, opens, click Request a Status Report.

PART

III

Juggling and
Managing Projects

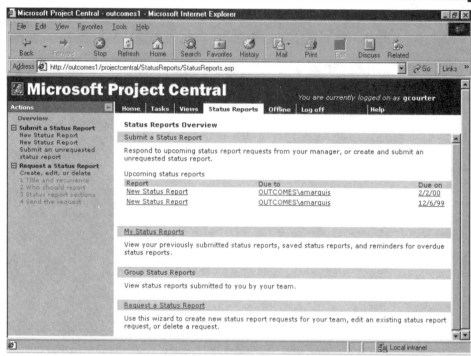

From this page, you can set up a new status report, edit an existing status report, or delete a status report.

To set up a status report, choose the first option and click OK. A four-step wizard walks you through the process of creating a status report. In the first step, shown in Figure 16.11, enter the name of the report, how frequently you want to have the report completed, the recurrence pattern (for example, first Monday of every month), and the date when the report period begins. Click Next to move onto the next step of the wizard.

In the second step, shown in Figure 16.12, select the resources you want to respond to this new report. When you click a resource name and click Add, a checkbox appears in front of their name to indicate that this resource's report will be merged with the other resource reports to create a consolidated report. Clear this checkbox if you want to review the individual reports before consolidating them.

FIGURE 16.11

A four-step wizard walks you through the process of creating a new status report form.

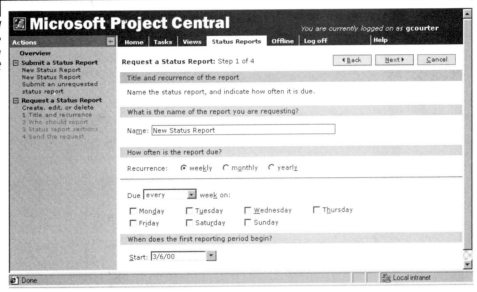

FIGURE 16.12

In the second step, you can identify who should respond to the report.

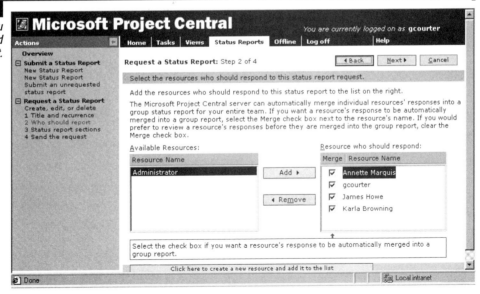

If you want to add a new resource to the resource list, click the button at the bottom. Choose the type of authentication: Windows NT or Project Central, and enter the requested domain and username information. Click Next to move on.

In the third step, enter the sections you want to appear in the report, and include a brief description of each. Project Central offers three suggestions, shown in Figure 16.13. Insert and delete additional items by clicking the Insert Row and Delete Row buttons. Use the Up and Down buttons to change the order of the sections. Click Next to move to the last step.

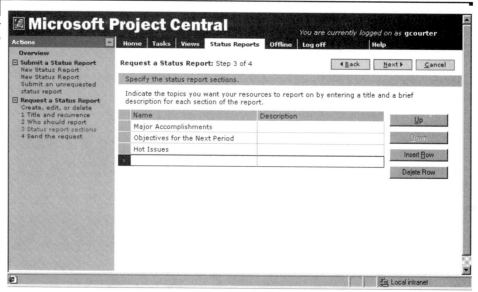

In the fourth and final step of the wizard, you can choose to send the report request to the resources you selected, or save it for later use.

A team member can also create a status report form by choosing Submit an Unre-quested Status Report from the Actions pane. They can enter a report name, name who it is going to, denote the period it covers, and then add whatever sections they want to include. When they are ready to send it, they can click the Send button, or save it and send it later.

Completing a Status Report

When team members receive status reports to complete, they are presented with a form, such as the one shown in Figure 16.14, that contains the sections you included when you set up the report.

Team members can click the Insert Tasks from Timesheet button to select tasks to include in the report. A project task list opens. Changing the No to Yes in the Insert column includes the task in the report. When they have selected all the tasks they want to complete, clicking the Insert Tasks button includes the tasks in the report. Click Done to move back to the report.

FIGURE 16.14

A Status Report form contains the sections that were included by the creator of the report.

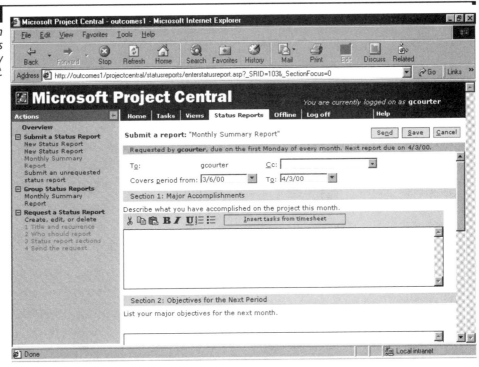

To include their own report sections, team members can click the Click Here to Add Section button at the bottom of the form. Clicking in any of the text boxes activates a formatting toolbar in that section with the Cut, Copy, Paste, Bold, Italic, Underline, Numbered List, and Bulleted List buttons. When they have completed the report, they can click Send to send the report immediately or Save to save it and send it later.

Viewing Status Reports

To view submitted, saved, or late status reports, click the My Status Reports link on the Actions pane. You can filter the list of status reports by choosing a predefined filter from the Filter list:

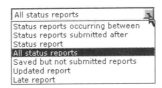

You can also group the reports by Status Report Name, Start Date, and Submitted Reports by choosing a Group By option.

To open a report, click the report in the Report column, or select the report and click Open. Or you may choose to update, forward, or delete the report.

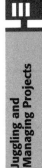

PART

III

Juggling and
Managing Projects

To view a group status report, click the Group Status Reports link in the Actions pane to open the Status Reports Overview, or choose to open a specific group report from the Actions pane. If you opened the Status Reports Overview, you can choose to see a group status report by selecting the report from the list of Group Status Reports. You can then choose whether you want to open an individual team member's report or the team report. A paper icon in the date column indicates a report that is available to view.

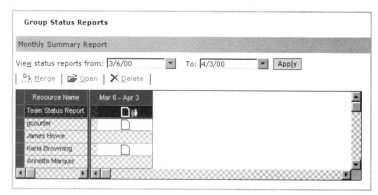

Click the icon in the date column to view that report. The compiled report, shown in Figure 16.15, lists the team member's name in each section before including the comments from that person.

FIGURE 16.15

A compiled team report shows the individual reports from each team member.

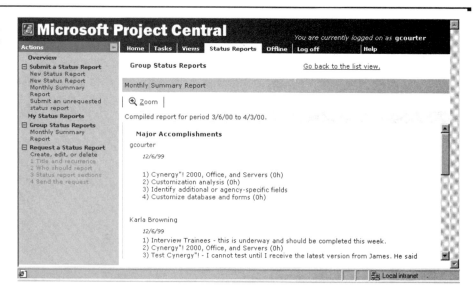

Distributing Status Reports

When everyone's status report is in, you may want to distribute it to other stakeholders in the project. You can do this by emailing it to others, or saving it as HTML and posting it to a Web site. To email a team report, open the team report, and choose File ➤ Send To ➤ Page by Email from the Internet Explorer window. This opens an email form that you can use to send the page.

To save the page as HTML, choose File ➤ Save As, and enter a file location and file name in the Save Web page dialog box that opens.

Sending Updated Project 2000 Data to Project Central

Whether you use the email workgroup tools discussed in Chapter 15 or Microsoft Project Central, you can work inside Project itself to assign tasks, send updates, and solicit status reports. You can use TeamAssign, TeamUpdate, and TeamStatus on the Workgroup toolbar or from the Tools ➤ Workgroup menu to communicate with team members. You can see a more detailed discussion of these workgroup tools in Chapter 15.

 The primary difference when you use Project Central is that you have access to the TeamInbox. You can use the TeamInbox to review workgroup messages from team members within Project Central and then update the project file with the changes that the team members report.

Integrating Project Central with Outlook

In an environment in which team members are already using Microsoft Outlook, you may want to integrate Outlook tasks and non-working time calendar entries into Project Central or integrate Project Central into Outlook. Both options are available for team members who want to coordinate all of their activities into one place.

Consolidating Outlook Data into Project Central

If you want to see how your non–project-specific tasks integrate with your project assignments, you can view them all in Project Central. To show Outlook tasks in Project Central, click Tasks on the Action pane or the navigation bar to open the timesheet. Click the Show Outlook Tasks checkbox. If you want to show active and completed tasks, click the Include Completed Tasks checkbox. Click Apply and then click OK to incorporate Outlook tasks into the timesheet.

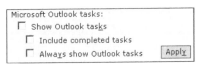

Outlook tasks remain visible in only this session of Project Central. If you log out and log back in again, the Outlook tasks do not display. If you want Outlook tasks to always be visible, click the Always Show Outlook Tasks checkbox, click Apply, and then click OK again.

Although you can view Outlook tasks, you cannot edit them in any way. To remove Outlook tasks, clear the checkboxes and click Apply.

Adding Outlook Calendar Entries to Project Central

Although you can't see your entire calendar in Project Central, you can update your non-working time in Project Central. Non-working time is defined as time marked in your Outlook calendar as Busy or Out of the Office. To add these non-working time entries to Outlook, choose Transfer Outlook Calendar from the Actions pane, or choose Transfer Calendar Entries from Microsoft Outlook from the Tasks menu on the navigation bar. A wizard, shown in Figure 16.16, walks you through the steps of transferring the Outlook calendar data.

FIGURE 16.16

The Transfer Calendar Entries from Microsoft Outlook Wizard walks you through the steps.

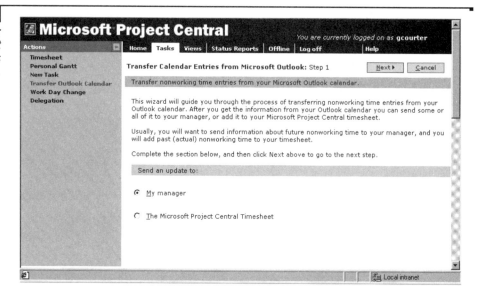

In the first step, you can choose whether you want to send the non-working time data to the timesheet or to the project manager. Project Central recommends sending past (actual) data to the timesheet and future data to the project manager.

Depending on which choice you make in Step 1, Step 2, shown in Figure 16.17, displays default options of future or past data. However, you can enter any time period you prefer.

In the third step, shown in Figure 16.18, you can choose which non-working time entries you want to include. Change the Yes to No in the Send to Project Manager (or Send to Timesheet) column. If you are sending the data to a timesheet, you must also specify for each entry the category set up by the project manager, such as vacation, sick leave, other projects, and so on.

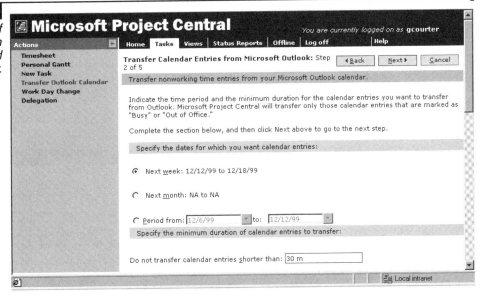

FIGURE 16.17

In the second step of the Wizard, you can choose the time period you want to transfer.

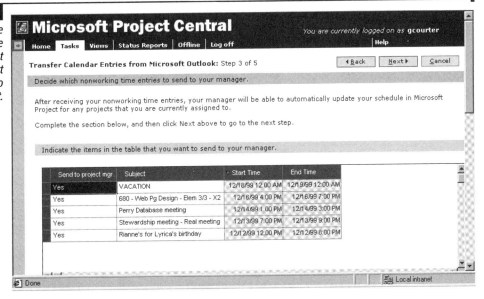

FIGURE 16.18

In the third step of the Wizard, you can choose which tasks you want to send to the project manager or send to the timesheet.

If you chose to send data to the project manager in Step 1, the fourth step of the wizard asks you to select which project manager you want to send the data to. Select the project manager and click Add to address the message to them.

In Step 5, you see a preview of the message to the project manager or a preview of the timesheet data. Click Send to send the data.

PART

III

Juggling and
Managing Projects

Working Offline

Business travel is a fact of life these days, and even if you can't dial into your office server, you can still work with your Microsoft Project Central data. You can do just about everything offline that you can do online, except things that involve viewing, sending, and receiving messages. Table 16.2 outlines the restrictions you have when you are working with Project Central offline.

TABLE 16.2: RESTRICTIONS WITH OFFLINE USE

View/Item	Restriction
Timesheet	Data for only the specified time period is available; cannot send timesheet updates.
Status Reports	Cannot send status reports (you can create and edit); cannot view previously submitted, previously edited, or late status reports. Managers cannot view resource report responses, or create and send new status report requests.
Home Page	Cannot view messages. Managers cannot create or run rules to process messages.

When you are ready to go offline, do the following:

1. Click Offline on the Project Central navigation bar.

2. Enter the time period for which you want project data.

3. Click Go Offline.

To return to online status, click Go Online.

What's Next

If you are a senior project manager who has responsibility for setting up users' access to Project Central, assigning permissions for which projects users' can view and what they can see when they get there, it's important for you to be able to log on to Project Central as an administrator. Although you may not be a system administrator, you know your projects and assignments better than anyone. Work with your systems administrator to set this up and then clearly differentiate your roles. You can find out all about administering projects in Project Central in Chapter 26.

If you are ready to evaluate and analyze your project data, move on to Part IV, "Evaluating and Analyzing Project Data." You'll learn to work with views and reports, import and export Project data, and close a project.

PART IV

Evaluating and Analyzing Project Data

LEARN TO:

- *Use Views to Evaluate Data*

- *Use Reports to Analyze Data*

- *Import and Export Project Data*

- *Close a Project*

CHAPTER 17

Using Views to Evaluate Data

After you've entered tasks, allocated resources, established a timeline, and entered periodic progress data, you'll find that even the smallest project can generate mounds of information! Finding ways to view data that is relevant this minute, while ignoring pieces you don't immediately need, is essential. This chapter focuses on how to look at project data in ways that are meaningful, while avoiding information overload.

Chapter 5, "Working in Project 2000," presented a brief look at views and introduced the two main view categories: Task views and Resource views. Each view can have one or two panes and up to three different elements (worksheet tables, graphical representations, and entry forms). Choosing and customizing views may seem overwhelming at first because there are hundreds of options available in Project 2000. But stick with it and remember, customize only if it helps you interpret your project data more easily. If a default view works for you—leave it be.

Calendar View

Calendar view, a member of the task view category, focuses on task dates and deadlines. Simply click the Calendar button on the View bar to see tasks displayed as bars spanning the days on which they are scheduled. Figure 17.1 shows the March 2000 calendar for the Decentralization project.

FIGURE 17.1

The default Calendar view displays scheduled tasks on a typical monthly calendar.

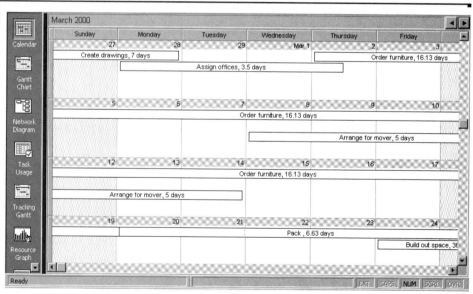

Choosing Dates to Display

Display any month in the Calendar view by clicking the navigation arrows at the top right of the calendar or by using the horizontal scroll bar below. Use the vertical scroll bar to display another set of dates, beginning in one month and ending in another. Notice the screen tip as you scroll; release the mouse button when the tip shows the dates you want to view.

WARNING Most of the view-formatting features in Project 2000 are not subject to the Undo function. You'll want to pay close attention to the formatting changes you make so you can remember the steps to follow if you need to reverse them.

If you wish to see more weeks within the calendar window, drag the horizontal line between each calendar week upward. This allows you to see a larger portion of the project timeline, but some of the tasks may be hidden. You'll see a downward pointed arrow (called the *Overflow Indicator*) on any date when there are tasks you can't see. Double-click the indicator to display a dialog box showing all tasks for that day, their durations, and start and end dates.

For times when you wish to specifically focus on a particular week or two weeks, drag the horizontal week separator downward to display fewer dates, with more detail for each date.

TIP Borrowing once again from Microsoft Excel, Project 2000 has a Make Fit feature for the calendar window. Double-click the adjustment tool and the calendar cells size themselves just tall enough to display all tasks.

You can also choose how to display month, week, and day names; whether you want 5-day or 7-day weeks; and myriad other options. From Calendar view, click Format ➤ Timescale to open the Timescale dialog box.

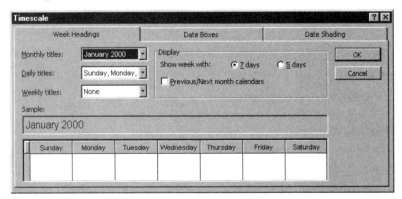

On the Week Headings tab, choose the formats you want to use for Monthly, Daily, and Weekly titles. Then, choose whether to display a 5- or 7-day week. Enable the Previous/Next Month's Calendars feature to see a 30-day thumbnail of the preceding and following months.

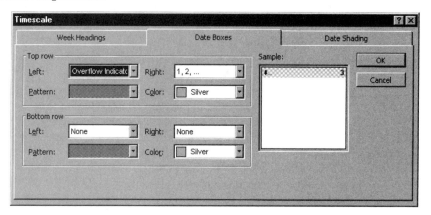

On the Date Boxes tab of the Timescale dialog box, you can format each calendar day to look the way you want it to. Choose the type and style of information you want displayed at the top right and top left of each row. Then, choose a pattern and color to shade the top of each calendar day. You can also format the bottom of each square, but in order to display a pattern and/or color, you must first change one of the Bottom Row (Left or Right) default settings to something other than None.

On the Date Shading tab of this dialog box, you can choose specific patterns and colors for certain types of days. By default, all working days show up white and non-working days are shaded gray. Change the defaults for the standard project calendar, the 24-hour calendar, or any of the resource calendars. (See Chapter 6, "Building a New Project," for more information about different types of calendars.)

Formatting the Calendar

The default Calendar view shows the task names and duration for all types of tasks except summary and milestone tasks. Those task types don't list durations by default. But all the calendar settings are customizable. If there is a certain type of project information you wish to display on the calendar (such as resource names, completion percentages, etc.), you can add it to the task bars. You can also make all tasks of a certain type stand out by changing the default formatting of the bars. From Calendar view, choose Format ➢ Bar Styles to open the Bar Styles dialog box.

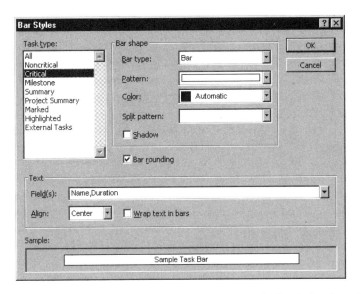

You can see a list of the task types at the left of the Bar Styles dialog box. Choose the task type you want to format and then do the following:

1. Set your shape options by choosing a bar type, pattern, color, and split pattern.

NOTE If there's a task type you don't want to display, choose it and select None as its bar type.

2. If you choose Bar as the bar type, you can enable the Shadow option if you wish.

3. Enable the Bar Rounding feature if you want to show bars across a full day. Enabling or disabling this feature does not affect the actual duration of a task, only the way it is displayed.

4. Using the Fields drop-down list, select the fields you want to appear as text on each bar. To choose more than one field, select the first field, type a comma after the first field name, and select the second field.

5. Position the text within each bar using the Align and Wrap options.

Figure 17.2 shows one week of a project with summary tasks displayed as a line. In this figure, we chose to left-align and wrap the text within each bar.

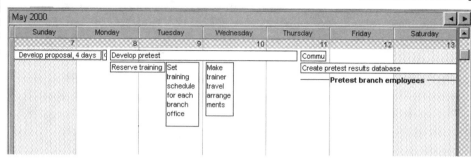

Other Task Views

Task views all have one thing in common: you can use them to enter project tasks. Some of the task views lend themselves to a different level of detail in task entry. For example, you could create a simple project in Calendar view by entering each task and its duration. However, as you learned in Chapter 7, "Entering Project Tasks," more complex projects require additional detail that may be easier to enter in another view. This section focuses on uses and formatting options for other task views.

 TIP In all task views, you can access an entry form for editing the selected task by clicking Window ➤ Split. The entry form appears at the bottom of the window. Drag the horizontal divider to make the entry form smaller or larger.

Gantt Chart View

 Gantt Chart view is the default view you see when you open Project 2000. In this view, you can work with task information in both text and bar graphics format. The left side of the window shows the Project 2000 fields for entering and modifying task names, durations, start and finish dates, and so on. The right side of the window graphically displays each task, its duration, and sequence relative to the other tasks.

Display more of the existing fields in the task list by dragging the window divider to the right, effectively shrinking the size of the Gantt Chart window. Widen the graphical portion of the window by dragging in the opposite direction.

Project 2000 sheet views now allow for variable row height. Use this feature to provide visual space between the rows in the task sheet (and, therefore, the bars in the Gantt Chart). For example, you might want extra space between summary tasks, but no extra space between the subtasks within each summary task. Simply place your mouse pointer below the row header you want to heighten and drag down. Adjust multiple rows by selecting them first (click and drag the row headers) then dragging any selected row.

Gantt Chart view is most typically used for entering tasks and all details associated with a task: duration, priority, assigned resources, predecessors, constraints, percent completed, and more. Chapter 7 has detailed information about entering and editing tasks, and task properties.

 In Project 2000, you can select a particular task by clicking it on the task table portion of the window, or (this is the New part) by clicking its corresponding Gantt bar. No more guesswork trying to determine whether you selected the correct bar.

Customizing Gantt Chart View

Just as you did with the calendar, you can format the bars in Gantt Chart view so that certain types of information stand out. For instance, you might want to highlight bars corresponding to tasks that are behind schedule. Or, maybe you want to italicize all summary tasks in the task list. There are numerous options for formatting both the list and graphical portions of this view.

Formatting the Bars   In this example, we've formatted the Gantt Chart bars so that on Normal tasks, the resource name is displayed inside the bar with the percent completed displayed to the right of the bar. We omitted progress lines and formatted the bars to gray, rather than the default of blue. From Gantt Chart view, click Format ➤ Bar Styles to open the Bar Styles dialog box, shown in Figure 17.3.

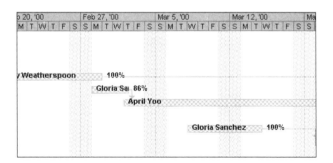

 TIP   You can also double-click any bar in the Gantt Chart to open the Bar Styles dialog box.

FIGURE 17.3

The Bar Styles dialog box for Gantt Chart view offers options for displaying tasks, resources, and other information.

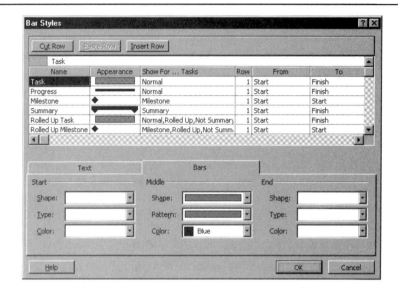

The fields of data displayed are listed in the Name column of the dialog box. To delete information from the Gantt Chart, click one of the fields listed in the Name column, and then click the Cut Row button at the top of the dialog box. Add data fields in the blank rows at the bottom of the list. If you wish to add the field in the middle of the list, click in the row below where you want the new field added and click the Insert Row button. Type the name of the field in the Name column. Then, choose one of the Show For options from the drop-down list that appears when you click in the third column. Choose the bar formatting you want for the field by using the drop-down lists shown on the Bars tab of the dialog box. The Start and End settings are optional; use them if you want to display a symbol at the start or end of the bar, representing the field you're formatting.

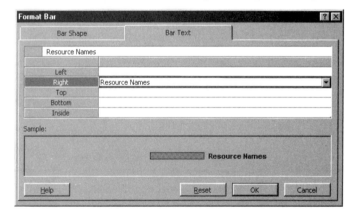

Display any Project 2000 field as text by choosing the field on the Text tab of the Bar Styles dialog box. First, decide where you want the text positioned relative to the bar: left, right, top, bottom, or inside. Click beside that position to activate a drop-down list. Choose a field name from the list.

 TIP If you want to make a number of formatting changes to the Gantt Chart or you want to design your own Gantt Chart, the GanttChartWizard offers up to 13 steps (depending on your choices) that have formatting options for tasks, links, and fields. To access the GanttChartWizard from Gantt Chart view, click Format ➢ Gantt Chart Wizard.

Configuring the Gantt Timescale   Earlier in this chapter, you learned how to format the timescale in Calendar view. Gantt Chart view also contains features to format timescale. Once again, choose Format ➢ Timescale (from Gantt Chart view this time). If you prefer, you can double-click the existing timescale to open this dialog box.

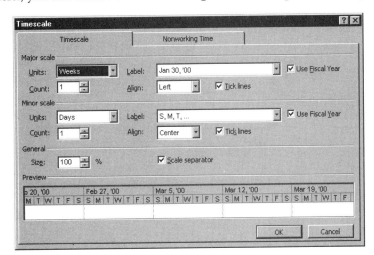

There are two parts to consider when formatting the timescale. The Major scale (usually the larger time increment such as weeks or months) and a Minor scale (smaller than the major unit, such as days or hours). To format the timescale, follow these steps:

1. Choose a unit of time for each scale. Check the Preview pane at the bottom of the dialog box to confirm that you're actually making the modifications you intend to make!

2. Choose a label for each unit.

3. Select an alignment option for the labels of both scales, and disable the Tick Lines feature if you don't want divider lines between each unit on the scale.

4. Adjust the Count spin box to determine the interval between unit labels on each scale. For instance, if the unit is weeks and the count is 2, then you'll see a label every two weeks.

5. Configure the General timescale features. Change the Size spin box to make the scale larger or smaller, thereby showing less or more time in the same amount of

space. Disable the Scale Separator if you don't want to see the horizontal line between the major and minor scales.

6. If you wish to adjust the appearance of the nonworking time on the Gantt Chart, click the Nonworking Time tab of the Timescale dialog box and choose your options there.

7. Click OK when you're finished.

 TIP To hide nonworking time on the Gantt Chart, choose Format ➤ Timescale ➤ Nonworking Time, and choose Do Not Draw from the Formatting Options.

Adjusting Gridline Settings   The appropriate placement of gridlines can be a big help in viewing information displayed across rows and down columns. By default, the Gantt Chart does not show horizontal gridlines (unless you count the horizontal separator between the Major and Minor timescales at the top of the chart). Adjust gridlines for different Gantt Chart components by clicking Format ➤ Gridlines to open the Gridlines dialog box.

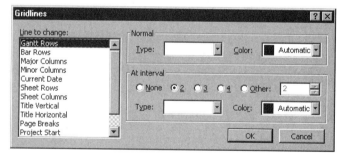

Follow these steps to change the gridlines:

1. Select the line you want to change from the list on the left. Gantt Rows correspond to the numbered rows in the task list. Major Columns correspond to the Major timescale and Minor Columns correspond to the Minor timescale.

2. In the Normal section of the dialog box, select the type and pattern for the gridline. If you want to get rid of an existing gridline, select it from the Line to Change list and click the blank area in the Type drop-down list.

3. Certain gridlines appear repeatedly, so you can apply contrasting gridlines at specific intervals if you wish. Select an interval, line type, and line color. If those options are disabled, it's because you have selected a line type that does not repeat. To skip a gridline at certain intervals, click the blank area on the Type list in the At Interval settings.

Formatting Text in the Task List   It makes sense to spend a few minutes formatting text, even for projects with relatively small task lists. At minimum, you'll want some type of formatting on summary tasks so they stand out from others in the list. For larger projects, you may wish to format milestones, critical tasks, external tasks, or even your timescale. Click Format ➢ Text Styles to open the Text Styles dialog box.

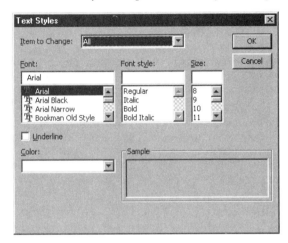

Select the part of the view you wish to format by choosing an item from the Item to Change list. Then, choose a font, font style, font size, and color. Enable the Underline feature if you wish. Repeat the process for each additional item you wish to format. Click OK when you're finished.

Network Diagram View

  Formerly called the PERT Chart, Network Diagram view presents tasks in a flowchart format, with each task displayed in its own node. Tasks are arranged vertically to reflect the hierarchy of tasks in the outline, and arranged horizontally to show relationships between tasks. By default, tasks in progress are displayed with one diagonal line through them, and completed tasks are displayed with crossed diagonal lines. You can enter and edit tasks in Network Diagram view and examine their relationships. Use this view to focus on small groups of tasks while fine-tuning their settings and relationships. Figure 17.4 shows a small portion of Network Diagram view for the XYZ-BOT project.

 NOTE For more about creating and using PERT, see Chapter 13, "Assessing and Managing Risks."

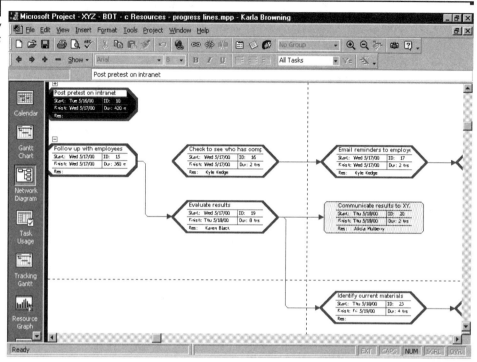

FIGURE 17.4

Network Diagram view allows you to see tasks in flowchart format.

Unless you have a large screen monitor to view the diagram, it's quite possible to become utterly lost while scrolling through the task nodes. To keep from becoming too annoyed, Zoom options can help you find your way around the diagram.

You can zoom way out to see a larger portion of the project. Click the Zoom Out button on the Standard toolbar (the magnifier with the minus sign), or click View ➤ Zoom and choose a setting from the list of options in the Zoom dialog box. The problem is that as soon as you zoom out enough to see a meaningful piece of the project, the task nodes are too small to see the text in them. Did we mention that navigating this view could be annoying? Actually, you can point to any task node, and hover for a minute to enlarge the node and view task information. When you find the tasks you wish to focus on, click to select one of them and zoom back in using the Zoom In button (with the plus sign) or click View ➤ Zoom and select a higher zoom setting.

NOTE You're limited to zoom settings between 25% and 400%. Even if you select the Entire Project setting in the Zoom dialog box, you can't get smaller than 25%, so it's unlikely that you will be able to see all nodes in a project, unless it has only a few tasks.

NOTE Task nodes are attached horizontally to their predecessors, so if you can't find a particular task in this view, find it in the task list (from Gantt Chart view) and determine its predecessor. Look for the predecessor and you'll find the successor task.

Working with Tasks in the Network Diagram

Edit the details of an existing task by double-clicking it to bring up the Task Information dialog box, previously discussed in Chapter 7. Delete a task by selecting its node (with a single click) and pressing Delete on the keyboard. You can also right-click a task node and choose Task Information or Delete Task from the shortcut menu depending, of course, on which action you wish to take.

Use the Outlining symbols (+ and -) adjacent to summary tasks to collapse or expand their subtasks.

As you might expect, you can format the nodes so that certain types of tasks stand out. By default, critical tasks are displayed in nodes bordered in red. Configure the node settings by clicking Format ➤ Box Styles to open the Box Styles dialog box.

 NOTE If you right-click a single task node and choose Format Box from the shortcut menu, you'll have a similar set of formatting options, but they apply to the selected box only.

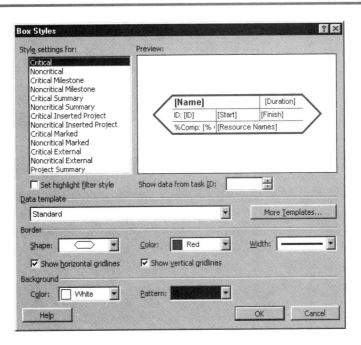

This dialog box works the same way as the Bar Styles dialog boxes we explored in Calendar and Gantt Chart views. Select the type of task from the Style Settings For list on the left. Then configure the Border and Background settings. You'll like the unique preview feature of this dialog box. You can actually choose the task you want to use in the Preview by adjusting the Show Data From Task ID field.

Because each node's formatting is based on a template (called a Box Template), you also have the option for accessing templates for other types of nodes. Project 2000 gives users much more control over the look of Box Templates. If additional templates have been imported or created on your computer, they'll show up on the Data Templates drop-down list.

To create a new template, click the More Templates button and choose New to open the Data Template Definition dialog box shown in Figure 17.5. After you've accessed the dialog box, do the following:

1. Enter a name for the template in the Template Name field.

2. Click the Cell Layout button to choose the number of rows and columns you want in the node. Change the Cell Width setting if you want the cells in the new template to be larger or smaller than the cells of the Standard template. You probably want to keep the Merge Blank Cells With Cells to the Left option. If you didn't, the Task Name displayed in Figure 17.5 would be cut off for no good reason. As long as the cell to the right is blank, why not let the data spill over?

FIGURE 17.5

The Data Template Definition dialog box lets you create a new look for the nodes in Network Diagram view.

Data Template Definition   ? X

Template name: Karla's Data Template

Format cells

Show data from task ID: 5   ▲▼   Cell Layout...

	75%	Set training schedule for each branch office
	NA	AM

Choose cell(s):

% Complete		
% Complete	Name	
Actual Finish		Resource Initials

Font...   Arial 8 pt, Bold   Limit cell text to: 1 line   ▼

Horizontal alignment: Left   ▼   ☐ Show label in cell: % Complete:

Vertical alignment: Center   ▼   Date format: ▼

OK   Cancel

3. After you configure cell layout settings, choose the data fields you want to display in each cell. Click a cell in the Choose Cells area of the dialog box to enable a drop-down list of Project 2000 fields. Select a field from the list.

> **TIP** You don't have to use every cell in each row. In some cases, it makes sense to leave a cell blank so that lengthy data from the cell to the left can spill over, if needed.

4. Choose a font for each cell of the node. When you click the Font button, the settings you choose are applied to the selected cell(s). So it's easy to bold one field (**Percent Complete** in Figure 17.5) and leave the rest of the data in the default font (Arial 8 pt.). To make all cells the same font, select them all from the Choose Fields area of the dialog box, click Font, and choose Settings.

5. Select a Limit Cell Text To setting for each cell. In Figure 17.5, it makes sense to make the Name cell two lines (or more), but you wouldn't need that much space for a field such as Resource Initials.

6. Choose a Horizontal and Vertical alignment setting for each cell. Enable the Show Label in Cell field if you want the field name to precede the data in each cell. (You'll need relatively large cells to do this, or else most of the data winds up out of view.)

7. If the selected cell is a date field, you can choose a date format from the drop-down list of the same name.

8. Click OK to return to the Data Templates dialog box. Click Close to return to Box Styles, click OK, and you're done!

You can apply this new template to any type of task in Network Diagram view. Simply open the Box Styles dialog box (Format ➤ Box Styles), select the type of task from the list at the left and select the template from the Data Template drop-down list. Then, you can change border and background settings for the task type displayed in this template.

Task Usage View

Task Usage view focuses on how much work each resource has completed over time. Use this view to compare actual work and costs to budgeted work and costs. Click the Task Usage View button on the View Bar to display the two-paned window shown in Figure 17.6.

FIGURE 17.6

*Task Usage View lets
you see work
performed by each
resource over time.*

The pane on the left of Figure 17.6 (the *sheet* portion) shows tasks with the assigned resource indented below. The fields displayed on this side of the window focus on the task by default, but you can customize it to display other data by applying a different table. (See "Examining Data with Tables," later in this chapter).

The right portion of the window (the *timeline* pane) displays information related to the resource.

By default, the timeline pane details Work (total person-hours) for each task. Add another Detail field by right-clicking any cell in the Details column or by clicking Format ➤ Details on the menu, and choosing another field.

Right-click again to deselect Detail fields you don't want to view. If the field you want to detail isn't on the menu, you can gain access to additional fields by choosing Detail Styles from the shortcut menu (or by clicking Format ➤ Detail Styles) to open the Detail Styles dialog box.

Fields currently being displayed are shown in the list on the right side of the dialog box. In this example, we're displaying Work and Cost. You'll also notice that All Assignment Rows appears in the Show These Fields list. This simply means that we're looking at data on all tasks that have been assigned to resources as opposed to, say, tasks over 15 hours in duration. (We'll show you how to create this type of constraint in "Sorting, Filtering, and Grouping in Project 2000," later in this chapter.)

Add a field to the Details column by selecting it from the Available Fields list on the left and clicking the Show button. When you add a field to the view, the Show In Menu feature is enabled by default. This allows you to right-click and deselect that field, rather than going all the way into the Detail Styles dialog box. However, once a non-default menu item is removed from the view, it no longer shows up on the menu unless you add it again using the dialog box.

Select any field in the Show These Fields list, and format it by manipulating the Font, Cell Background and Pattern choices in the Detail Styles dialog box. Remove fields from the Details column by selecting them (one at a time or with Ctrl and Shift to select more than one) and clicking the Hide button.

Tracking Gantt View

Tracking Gantt view is similar to the traditional Gantt Chart view, but it compares baseline start and finished dates to scheduled start and finish dates or the percentage of work that has already been completed. As you might expect, you can use this view to do any of the things you would ordinarily do in regular Gantt Chart view: enter tasks and their details, assign resources, and link tasks to name a few. In addition, you can track progress on a task by comparing it to the established baseline of the project.

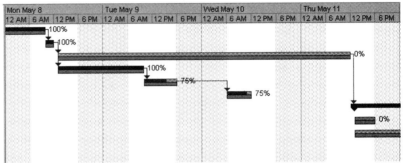

Tracking Gantt view displays two stacked bars for each task. Point to either bar to get a summary of what that bar is showing. The lower bar shows the start and finish dates pulled from the project baseline. The upper bar shows different data, depending on the status of the task. You'll see the following:

- Scheduled start and finish dates if the task hasn't begun yet (that is, the Percent Complete = 0)
- Actual start and completed through dates if the task is in progress
- Actual start and finish dates if the task is complete

When one task *slips* (falls behind schedule), it becomes readily apparent that there's a problem. The upper bar extends past the baseline bar by whatever time increment the task has fallen behind. Naturally, successor tasks are affected by the task slippage, too.

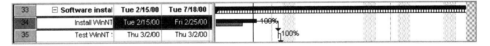

Change the format of Gantt Tracking view just as you would in regular Gantt Chart view: Click Format ➤ Text Styles to change the way tasks are displayed in the task list at the left of the split window. Click Format ➤ Bar Styles to choose a new look for the bars displayed in the graphical portion of the window. Choose Format ➤ Timescale or Format ➤ Gridlines to change those settings in the Gantt Chart.

Resource Views

The resource views all relate to assigning and tracking the use of human resources, materials, and equipment used to complete the project. Remember that a resource can be an individual, a company, a department within a company, a team, a piece of equipment, a room, or any other resource you need for the project. If you want to see data about resources, choose Resource Graph, Resource Sheet, or Resource Usage and you'll see that data spun different ways, depending on which view you select (see specifics as follows).

Many of the Project 2000 views let you see which people you're driving toward premature burnout (politely called *overallocating* in Project). However, resource views tend to make it overtly apparent which resources are being worked past the number of hours available in their calendars.

Resource Graph

To see work, allocation, or cost information about a resource represented graphically, click the Resource Graph button on the View Barbar. Like Network Diagram view, one can easily become lost in the resource graph. It helps to have specific dates in mind when you're viewing work assigned to a particular resource. If the project timeline is scrolled to a time period where the selected resource has no assigned tasks, you'll see nothing in the timeline pane! Figure 17.7 shows assigned work for Amy Orange (on the XYZ-BOT project) during the months of May and June 2000. (Assuming that Amy makes it to June because we're currently planning to abuse her a bit during the week of May 14th.)

NOTE If a resource is overallocated for a particular day but the major timescale shows weeks, you'll see overallocation when the field displayed is Peak Units, but not when the field displayed is Overallocated. For more about resource allocation see, Chapter 11, "Preparing Your Project for Publication."

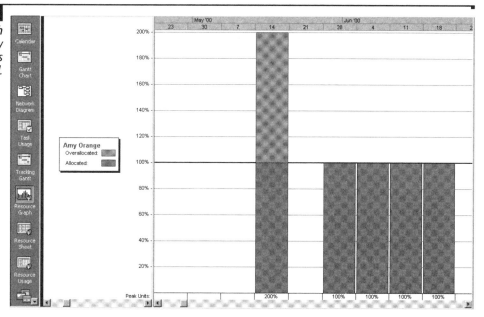

FIGURE 17.7

The Resource Graph makes it readily apparent that resources are overallocated.

Scroll the left pane of the split window to select the resource you want to see in the pane on the right. Scroll the right pane to move the timeline to correspond with the scheduled start and end dates for tasks assigned to the selected resource.

By default, the Detail field shown in the timeline pane is Peak Units (the combined time required for all tasks assigned to that resource at a given point in time). Change the detail by right-clicking in a blank area of the timeline pane and choosing another detail from the shortcut menu. Answer questions such as, "I wonder how much of Karen Black's time we're using during the week of June 1st?" (choose Work Availability or Remaining Availability) and "What is Kyle Kedge's time costing us on May 15?" (choose Cost, and then click the Zoom In button to scale the timeline to days).

Formatting the Resource Graph

As with other views we explored so far, you can format gridlines, timelines, and bars in the resource graph by accessing those features from the Format Menu (or by right-clicking the area of the window you want to format.)

You can also change the type of graph displayed from bar to line, step, step-line, or area graph by right-clicking on the chart and choosing Bar Styles. Select a new type from the Show As field in the Bar Styles dialog box.

Resource Sheet

Resource Sheet view provides a summary of information about resources in a spreadsheet format. In this view, you can enter and review information resources: names, assigned group(s), regular and overtime rates, and so on.

Choose this view to quickly put together a list of resources with details about each. If you want to review information about resources in a non-graphical format, this is also a good view. Compare the number of work hours assigned to each resource or compare resource costs (actual and budgeted).

Add fields to the default table by right-clicking the column header to the right of where you want your new column. Choose Insert Column from the shortcut menu to open the Column Definition dialog box.

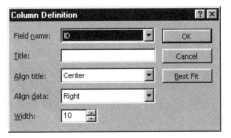

PART

IV

Evaluating and
Analyzing Project Data

Choose the field you want to insert from the Field Name drop-down list. Type a different display name for the field (if you want one) in the Title field. Set Alignment and Width options, and click OK.

You may wish to further customize this view by changing tables (see "Examining Data with Tables," later in this chapter) or by sorting and filtering (also covered later in this chapter).

Resource Usage

 Resource Usage View groups tasks by resources and displays the amount of work, work allocation, and work availability for each resource. (Of course, you can add fields to the table in the left pane by right-clicking a column header, as described in the previous section.)

You can look at some of the same data we saw in Resource Sheet view: costs, scheduled work, or the percentage of capacity a resource is scheduled. Work is displayed by default in the timeline pane on the right, but (as you learned previously) you can right-click in the Details column and choose an additional Detail field.

Customize the timeline, gridlines, and text styles by choosing those options from the Format menu or by right-clicking the portion of the view you wish to format.

More Views

 Understanding and using the standard views described so far can be daunting, especially for a new user. But the Project 2000 expert wants more and Project has more to give! Click the More Views button on the View Bar to see additional view selections. If the available list doesn't contain exactly what you're looking for, you can create your own view. See "Creating and Saving Views," later in this chapter, for more information.

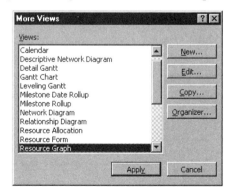

To apply one of these views, simply select it from the list and click Apply.

Examining Data with Tables

By now, we've convinced you that Project 2000's many views present a buffet of options for looking at your data. Most of the views have two (or more) customizable panes, increasing the possibilities for combining different types of data into one split window. Tables offer a quick way to insert multiple data fields (in spreadsheet format) into the currently selected pane of any view. Replace the existing table with another by clicking View ➢ Table: [Current Table] and selecting from the list or by choosing More Tables to open the More Tables dialog box shown in Figure 17.8.

FIGURE 17.8

The More Tables dialog box allows you to choose the type of table you want and insert it in the active view.

Choose from a long list of Task or Resource tables, details of which are discussed more fully as follows.

Task Tables

As the categorization implies, Task tables contain fields that relate to tasks. In the More Tables dialog box (shown in Figure 17.9), choose the Task Option to display Task tables. Select the table you want and click Apply. In most cases, you have to be in a Task-related view in order to insert a Task table into the table pane.

We've worked with many of Project 2000's predefined tables already. Table 17.1 summarizes some of the less frequently used tables.

TABLE 17.1: OTHER TASK TABLES	
Table Name	**Description**
Delay	Displays information needed for resource leveling. Fields include resource names, task duration, delay, scheduled start and finish dates, and successors.

Continued ▌▶

TABLE 17.1 CONTINUED: OTHER TASK TABLES

Table Name	Description
Hyperlink	Shows Web and intranet links assigned to tasks and files in the active project.
PA Optimistic Case	Used in conjunction with Project 2000's PERT Analysis features that assess a best-case scenario for task start and finish dates.
Schedule	Shows typical task information such as start and end dates. Includes a Free Slack field so you'll know the total amount of time that a task can slip before successor tasks are affected.
Variance	Shows the difference between actual start and finish dates compared to the baseline.

Resource Tables

Several table views are also available to assess Resource information. In the More Tables Dialog box (shown in Figure 17.9), select Resource to see a list of prefab Resource tables. Again, we have already seen many of these tables as we've explored Resource views. Table 17.2 lists some of the less frequently used tables, and their purposes.

TABLE 17.2: OTHER RESOURCE TABLES

Table Name	Description
Earned Value	Compares the amount of work completed and actual costs to budgeted work and budgeted costs.
Entry-Material Resources	Displays fields related to material resources, as opposed to human resources. Fields include material label, initials, group, standard rate, and cost-per-use.
Export	Used to save a file in a number of Microsoft Project-compatible file formats.
Usage	Shows resources and the amount of work assigned to each.
Work	Compares each resource's scheduled work against the baseline, against actual completed work, or against remaining work.

Creating and Formatting Your Own Tables

With dozens of tables readily available in Project 2000, you might be wondering why in the world you'd want to make your own! Well, there's always that one extra piece of information you'd like to add, or perhaps there is too much information and you want to delete. Whatever the case, you can make a new table from scratch (lots of work) or create one based on another table that's close to what you want.

As we mentioned in previous sections of this chapter, you can make changes to existing table columns fairly easily, as follows:

- Add or delete a column by right-clicking the column header and selecting the appropriate action from the shortcut menu.
- Change the field name, field title, or text alignment by double-clicking the column header and configuring these options in the Column Definition dialog box.
- Change the size of a column by dragging the column border in either direction, or double-click the column border (on the right) to auto-fit.

These types of changes are permanent for the active project file. That means that the next time you open the file, the tables you've modified will remain as you last left them. However, when you start a new project file, all tables are back to the default column settings.

If you want to change table configurations for the active project, but you also want to leave the original settings intact, open the More Tables dialog box (View ➢ Table ➢ More Tables), select the table you want to modify, and click the Copy button. A working copy of the original table is created and the Table Definition dialog box opens.

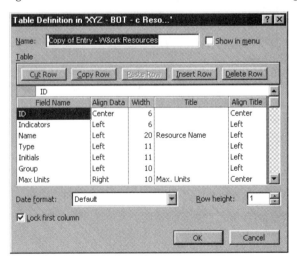

The Table Definition dialog box shows the default fields for the table you've copied. Each field is displayed in its own row along with its properties. Make changes as follows:

1. Enter a table name or leave the default name Copy of [Original Table Name].

2. If you want the table to appear in the menu (and you usually do) enable the Show in Menu check box.

3. Add, delete, copy, or move rows by clicking anywhere in the row and then clicking the appropriate button above. If you want to insert a row, select the row below where you want the new row to appear.

4. For inserted rows, select a field name, alignment, width, and title alignment (using the drop-down lists that appear when you click under that column heading). Type a title if you want to use a more "friendly" name for the field.

5. Change the alignment, width, title, and title alignment for any other fields you want to modify.

6. Enable the Lock First Column feature so it keeps Column 1 in view when you scroll. (You want to make sure Column 1 is some type of identifying field such as ID or Name.)

7. If there are date fields in the table, you can choose a format for those fields.

8. Modify the row height if you want taller rows for data display.

9. Click OK when you finish. The new table appears in the More Tables dialog box, and on the menu (View ➤ Table) if you enabled that feature.

When you create your own table from scratch, you follow most of these steps, too. The only difference is that when you click New in the More Tables dialog box, the Table Definition dialog box opens with no rows displayed. You have to insert rows, and then choose and format the fields you want.

The tables you create are always available in the active project. If you want to make them available in another project (or use a custom table from another project in the active project), use the table Organizer, described in the next section.

 NOTE To delete a table you created, click the Organizer button in the More Tables dialog box, select the table, and click Delete.

 NOTE If you created a custom table in the project file you were working on last month, you can use the Organizer to import the table into this month's projections. See Chapter 21, "Customizing Project 2000," for further information.

Formatting Views

Throughout this chapter, we have discussed ways to customize several of the most popular views.

You also may want to look at the Layout settings for different views. Click Format ➤ Layout to open the Layout dialog box for the view you're in. Figure 17.9 shows the Layout dialog box for Gantt Chart view.

The Layout dialog box in Gantt Chart view allows you to choose how links are displayed, choose bar height, and choose how dates are formatted in the view.

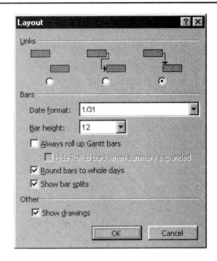

Although specific settings vary, depending on which view you're adjusting, layout changes include the following:

Link Type Choose from the three options to specify whether you want S-shaped links, L-shaped links, or no links displayed.

Date Format Choose how you want date fields to appear in this view.

Roll up Shows subtasks on the same bar as the summary task under which they fall. You can mouse over rolled-up tasks to see the detail of subtasks. In previous versions of Project, you had to enable this setting for each individual bar.

Round Bars Displays the bars as a full day across the entire day whether the task stops mid-day or not.

Bar Splits These show tasks that have been interrupted and restart at a later time. You can choose not to show them.

Show Drawings If you've used the Drawing tools (covered in Chapter 18, "Using Reports to Analyze Data"), you can show or hide the drawn objects you've created.

You'll see additional settings for some of the other view layouts. Figure 17.10 shows the Layout dialog box for Network Diagram view. Here, you can choose to manually position nodes in the diagram. You can also control the Alignment, Spacing, Height, and Width of nodes, as well as the Background Color and Pattern. In Network Diagram view, completed tasks are shown with an X through them and tasks in progress have one diagonal line. Turn these marks off using the check box at the bottom of this dialog box.

FIGURE 17.10

The Layout dialog box for Network Diagram view has most of the standard layout settings, and then some.

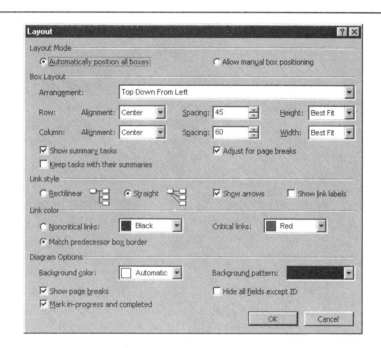

Creating and Saving Views

There are dozens of predefined views available in Project 2000 (as you know). And you can customize any of these views in hundreds of ways, most of which we've discussed in this chapter. But wait…there's more!

Create and save your own views—from scratch or based on an existing view. Here's how:

1. Click the More Views icon on the View Bar to open the More Views dialog box.

2. Click the view you want to use as a basis for your new view, and then click Copy. If you want to create a new view from scratch, simply click the New button. If

you choose copy, the View Definition dialog box opens. If you choose New, you get the Define New View dialog box.

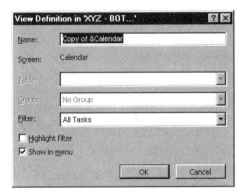

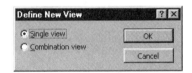

3. If you're starting from scratch, choose whether you want a single pane view or a combination view in the Define New View dialog box, and then click OK. The Single View choice takes you to the View Definition dialog box shown above. The Combination View Choice takes you to a slightly different View Definition dialog box.

4. In the View Definition dialog box, type a name for your new view if you wish to overwrite the default name. For new views from scratch, choose what you want to display in the top and bottom panes, and enable the Show In Menu option. For new views based on another view, choose a different table, group and/or filter for this view. (These settings are discussed more fully in the next section.)

5. Click OK when you're through, and the new view appears along with the others in the More Views dialog box. Click Apply to see your new view. Or click Close to exit the dialog box without changing the current view.

 NOTE You have to use the Organizer to delete a custom view. In the More Views dialog box, click the Organizer button, select the view you want to delete, and click the Delete button. Close the Organizer window.

Using the Organizer with Views

If you want to use a custom view you've created in another project file, the Organizer allows you to "import" it. You can also create a new view by using customized elements (tables, forms, calendars, etc.) stored in another Project file. The Organizer is the tool that makes those elements available in the active project. Open the file(s) that contain the custom elements you want to use. Then click Tools ➤ Organizer, or if you're already in the More Views dialog box, click the Organizer button there.

We first introduced the Organizer earlier in this chapter in connection with customizing tables. So the Tables tab of this window should look familiar. Figure 17.11 shows the Views tab.

FIGURE 17.11

The Views tab of the Organizer window allows you to import a custom view from another Project 2000 file.

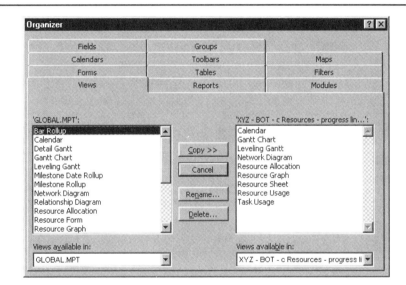

To bring in a custom view from another file:

1. Select the file that contains the custom view using the Views Available In drop-down list on either side of the window.

2. Make sure the active presentation is selected in the other Views Available In drop-down list.

3. Click the view you want to import.

4. Click the Copy button.

5. Close the Organizer. The imported view now appears in the More Views dialog box.

To use a custom element from another project file:

1. Open the Organizer Window.

2. Select the file that contains the custom view using the Views Available In drop-down list.

3. Make sure that the active presentation is selected in the other Views Available In drop-down list.

4. Click the tab for the type of element you want to make available (Tables, Toolbars, Calendars, Forms, etc.).

5. Select the custom element you want to import.

6. Click Copy.

7. Repeat the process for any additional elements you wish to import.

8. Click the Close button to exit the Organizer.

9. The element(s) you imported are now available to apply in a new view. Follow the steps you normally would to create a new view. The imported element(s) will appear on the drop-down lists in the View Definition dialog box.

Sorting, Filtering, and Grouping in Project 2000

The visual elements of a view are easy to recognize. One need only glance at the computer monitor to see, for example, that the bars in the Gantt Chart are formatted blue for regular tasks and red for critical tasks. There are other components, however, that aren't so obvious, but they are still considered part of the view. Examples are as follows:

- The order in which items appear (determined by the last sort settings applied to the view).

- Whether an item is displayed or hidden (this depends on the filter applied).

- Whether an item appears by itself or with like items (depends on the item's grouping).

Sort, filter, and group settings are as important as visual settings in determining how data is displayed in a view. As your project grows, so does the importance of these features.

Sorting a View

Changing the sort order doesn't hide any of your data; it just puts it in a different order. The default sort for most table views is ascending ID order; that is, the lowest ID number appears at the top of the list. Most views, except Network Diagram view, will sort; and some have more fields available to sort by. In general, choose the view you want to sort, click Project ➤ Sort, and choose the field you want to sort by. You'll get ascending (A–Z or 1–10) order if you choose one of the fields on the menu. (One exception to this occurs in resource views. If you sort by cost, the highest cost is shown first.) If you want to sort in a different order or if you wish to use a multilevel sort (resources by last name, then by first name), click Project ➤ Sort ➤ Sort By to open the Sort dialog box.

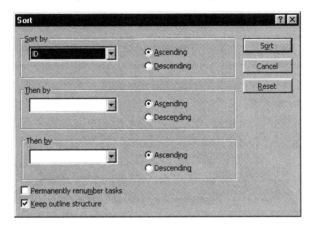

The current sort settings are displayed when the dialog box opens. Choose a different field from the Sort By list. For secondary and tertiary sorts, choose fields from the Then By lists. Then, choose ascending or descending order for each field. If you want items permanently renumbered after the sort, enable that option. For task lists, choose whether to maintain the outline structure.

When you sort a combination view, all panes sort. That means that bars on the Gantt Chart are reordered when you sort the accompanying task list.

 NOTE When you sort a calendar view, you'll only notice minor changes. For time periods when bars overlap, sorting makes a difference. Otherwise, the bars are tied to the calendar date and those, of course, don't move.

Applying a Filter

Too much data? Try on a filter. It's fast and easy, and allows you to see relevant portions of data while hiding the rest. For example, the calendar shows all tasks for any given date. However, you can choose to view one certain type of task by choosing it from the Filter List in the Formatting toolbar.

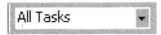

Navigate to the view you want to filter. Then, select a filter from the list on the Formatting toolbar. The default is no filter, so if you haven't applied any filters, task views show All Tasks and resource views show All Resources. If you filtered this view previously, the filter last applied is displayed next to the drop-down list arrow. Show all items in the view by choosing the All option from the top of the filter list.

  TIP You can now apply filters to Network Diagram View.

As you can see, there are more than two dozen filters ready to apply. Many of the filters have names that make it obvious what data gets displayed and what gets hidden. Tables 17.3 and 17.4 identify the functions of several filters that aren't so obviously named.

TABLE 17.3: TASK FILTERS AND THEIR FUNCTIONS

Choose This Filter	To See This...
Confirmed	Tasks that haven't been declined by any of the assigned resources.
Cost Greater Than...	Tasks with dollar amounts above the cost you specify.
Created After...	Tasks you entered into the Project file on or after the date you indicate.
Date Range...	Tasks with start or finish dates after the first date you specify and before the second date you specify.
Late/Overbudget Tasks Assigned To...	You choose a resource and Project displays all tasks assigned to that resource that are over budget or in progress, and destined to finish after the baseline finish date.
Linked Fields	Tasks linked to data in other programs; for example, to a value in Excel.
Task Range	Tasks having ID numbers within a range you specify.
Tasks With Attachments	Tasks with attached objects or note(s).
Tasks With Fixed Dates	Tasks without the As Soon As Possible constraint or for which you have entered an actual start date.
Unconfirmed	Tasks for which at least one assigned resource has declined.

Some filters require input before they can be applied. In those instances, choosing the filter from the list automatically produces a dialog box in which you can provide the parameters for the filter.

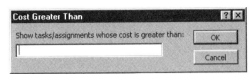

TABLE 17.4: RESOURCE FILTERS AND THEIR FUNCTIONS

Choose This Filter	To See This...
Confirmed Assignments	All tasks a resource has not declined. Only works in Resource Usage view.
Cost Greater Than...	Resources with dollar amounts above the cost you specify.
Cost Overbudget	Resources with scheduled costs greater than the baseline.
Date Range...	Resources and tasks with start or finish dates after the first date you specify and before the second date you specify.
Group	All resources assigned to a group you specify. (More on groups in the next section.)
Linked Fields	Resources to which text from another program has been linked (such as human resources linked to demographic information.)
Resource Range	Resources with IDs between two numbers you specify.
Work Completed	Resources that have completed all their assigned tasks.

Using AutoFilter

AutoFilters provide one of the quickest ways to "pull out" relevant portions of your data for viewing. You want to see all tasks assigned to a particular resource. Or, you want to see all resources with an overtime rate of $30/hr. In any view, click the Auto-Filter button on the Formatting toolbar to turn on the AutoFilters, which appear to the right of column headers.

Figure 17.12 shows the Resource Sheet for the XYZ-BOT project with the AutoFilters turned on. Click the filter arrow for the field you wish to filter on and choose the value you want to display. Project applies a "[Field you filtered on] equals [Value you chose from the list]" test to determine which rows of data to display.

	Resource Name	Type	Material Labe	Initials	Group	Max. Uni	Std. Rati	Ovt. Rati	Cost/Us	Accrue A	Base Calenda
1	Karen Black	Work		KB	Training	100%	$30.00/hr	$45.00/hr	$0.00	Prorated	Standard
2	Amy Orange	Work		AO	Training	100%	$30.00/hr	$45.00/hr	$0.00	Prorated	Standard
3	Julie Maroon	Work		JM	Training	100%	$30.00/hr	$45.00/hr	$0.00	Prorated	Standard
4	Sharon Rouge	Work		SR	Technical	100%	$30.00/hr	$45.00/hr	$0.00	Prorated	Standard
5	William Silver	Work		WS	Technical	100%	$20.00/hr	$30.00/hr	$0.00	Prorated	Standard
6	Kyle Kedge	Work		KK	Support	100%	$20.00/hr	$30.00/hr	$0.00	Prorated	Standard
7	Gerry Chartreuse	Work		GC	Mgmt	100%	$30.00/hr	$30.00/hr	$0.00	Prorated	Standard
8	Alicia Mulberry	Work		AM	Mgmt	100%	$30.00/hr	$30.00/hr	$0.00	Prorated	Standard

Creating and Saving Custom AutoFilters

Let's say you want to see resources with overtime rates between a certain range. Or you want to display all tasks assigned to two different resources. To filter for more than one value at a time or to use a filter condition other than "equals," you need to customize. Click the AutoFilter arrow on the field you wish to filter, and choose Custom from the list. The Custom AutoFilter dialog box opens. This is where you establish the criteria for the filter.

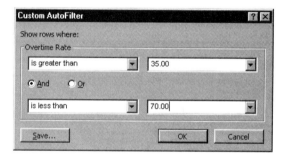

The drop-down lists on the left contain tests: greater than, less than, equals, contains, begins with, etc. The drop-down lists on the right show values for the selected field. You have to select a test from the list, but you can type values if the ones you want to use aren't on the list. For filters that require two tests, you must choose an operator (And or Or):

- Choose "And" if you want both tests to be true in order to display the row.
- Choose "Or" if you want the row displayed when either test is true.

Table 17.5 lists the tests and some information about how to use them.

TABLE 17.5: CUSTOM FILTER TESTS

Test	How It Works
Equals	Rows (in the table) are displayed only if the value in the field you're filtering is exactly the same as the one you select (or type). Can be used for text or numeric values.

Continued ▸

TABLE 17.5 CONTINUED: CUSTOM FILTER TESTS

Test	How It Works
Does Not Equal	Displays rows in the table that don't exactly match the value you select. Used for both text and numeric values.
Is Greater Than	Shows rows in which the field you filtered contains a value greater than the value you specify.
Is Greater Than Or Equal To	Works just like the Greater Than test, except values that are equal to the value you indicate are also displayed.
Is Less Than	Shows rows in which the field you've filtered contains a value less than the value you specify.
Is Less Than Or Equal To	Works just like the Less Than test, except values that are equal to the value you indicate are also displayed.
Is Within	Shows rows in which the field you filtered on contains a value within the range specified by two values you enter (see sidebar that follows).
Is Not Within	Shows rows in which the field you filtered on contains a value outside of the range specified by two values you enter (see sidebar that follows).
Contains	Project displays only the rows in which the field you've selected contains the text string you enter.
Does Not Contain	Project displays only the rows in which the field you've selected contains the text string you enter.
Contains Exactly	Works like Equals, except it can be used for fields such as resources that contain multiple values (see sidebar that follows).

MASTERING TROUBLESHOOTING

Mastering Filter Tests

If you've used filtering in Microsoft Excel or Access, you're probably already familiar with test such as Equals, Do Not Equal, Is Greater Than, and Is Less Than. However, Project introduces three new filter tests that are not quite as intuitive. Specifically, these are Is Within, Is Not Within, and Contains Exactly. Is Within allows you to locate values within a range, such as all tasks with durations that are greater than or equal to 2 days and less than or equal to 5 days. Is Not Within excludes values within the range you identify. The trick is in knowing how to enter the range. To enter a range of values, follow these steps.

   1. Click the AutoFilter button to turn on autofiltering.

Continued

MASTERING TROUBLESHOOTING CONTINUED

2. Click the drop-down arrow in the field on which you want to filter, such as Duration, and choose Custom.

3. In the Custom Filter dialog box, choose Is Within or Is Not Within from the Show Rows Where drop-down list.

4. Enter the range in the Values text box, separated by a comma. For example, to show durations that are greater than or equal to 2 days and less than or equal to 5 days, enter **2,5**.

5. Enter a second test if desired.

6. Click OK to apply the filter.

Project applies the filter and shows rows that are within or not within the designated range.

Contains Exactly is a hybrid of both Equals and Contains. The difference is that Contains Exactly allows you to search for individual values in fields where you have entered multiple values. For example, let's say you have two different resource teams involved with marketing your project. One is called the Project Marketing Team and the other team, which is assigned to other projects in the organization, is called the Marketing Team. Both teams are assigned to work on several tasks jointly. If you want to see all the tasks the company-wide Marketing Team is involved with, Contains Exactly allows you to search each value in a field and see whether it matches. If you instead choose `Equals Marketing Team` as the filter, it ignores the tasks that have more than one resource assigned, and returns only those rows in which the Marketing Team is assigned. If you choose `Contains Marketing Team` as the filter, it returns rows in which the Marketing Team is assigned but also those rows in which the Project Marketing Team is assigned. Only Contains Exactly looks at the individual values within a field and returns the appropriate matches.

Can't find the filter you want to use? Spend a few extra minutes and create your own custom filter. You'll follow the same basic steps as you do when you create your own tables or views. Specifically:

1. Click Project ➤ Filtered For ➤ More Filters.

2. Choose one of the filter options based on what you want to modify: task filters or resource filters.

3. Choose a filter on which to base your new filter and click Copy, or Click New to create a new filter from scratch.

4. Type a name for your new filter and enable the Show In Menu option.

5. Choose new or edit existing operators, fields, tests, and values. When multiple tests are used, Project can apply filter criteria to groups of expressions if you leave a blank line between criteria groups. Within groups of three (or more) expressions, the And statements are evaluated before the Or statements. Between groups, however, expressions are evaluated in the order they appear.

6. Use Cut, Copy, Delete, Paste, and Insert to move, duplicate, remove, or add filter criteria.

7. Click OK when you're finished. The new view now shows up in the More Views list and on the menu if you enabled that option.

 TIP You may have noticed the Highlight button in the More Filters dialog box. Click a filter from the list and click the Highlight button to display the filtered data in blue while still displaying all the other rows in the table.

Grouping Resources

 Project 2000 now allows you to categorize resources by grouping them in ways that make sense to you. For example, in the XYZ-BOT Project, resources are assigned to one of these groups: management, training, technical, or support. Once groups are assigned, you can sort, filter, or edit resources by group.

The Group field is displayed by default in Resource Sheet view. When you're entering resource information, simply type a group name in the field. Resources with the same value in the Group field are, of course, assigned to the same group.

Let's say you want to see the critical tasks assigned to each group, as shown in Figure 17.15. Grouping resources based on multiple criteria requires some additional configuring. First, make sure that all resources are assigned to a primary group. Next, create a custom group as follows:

1. Click Project ➤ Group ➤ More Groups to open the More Groups dialog box. (It should look familiar by now. It looks just like the More Tables, More Views, and More Filters dialog boxes.)

2. Click the New button to open the Group Definition dialog box, or choose an existing grouping on which to base your custom group and click Copy. Make sure that you choose the correct option (task or resource) to get to the fields you want to group by. To create the multiple grouping in Figure 17.13, we chose the Task

PART

IV

Evaluating and
Analyzing Project Data

option and clicked New. If you chose the Resource option, choose Resource Group and click Copy. You can't get to the Critical field because it's task-related.

3. Give your new group a name, and then choose the field you want to group by. Change the order default to descending if you wish. (You might want to do this if you're grouping by a numeric interval, such as cost, so your highest cost appears at the top of the sheet.)

4. Configure formatting options if you want them to be different from the default (we didn't).

5. If you're grouping on a numeric field, the Define Group Interval button will be enabled. Configure an interval for the field in the dialog box that appears when you click the button.

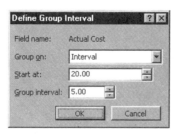

6. Enable the Show Summary Tasks feature, if you wish.

7. Click OK to close the Group Definition dialog box and return to More Groups. Your new group will appear in this list.

FIGURE 17.13

Multiple criteria grouping is new in Project 2000. This example shows critical tasks by resource group.

Task Name	Work	Duration	Start	Finish
⊟ **Resource Group: No Va**	**0 mins**	**12600 mins**	**Thu 5/18/00**	**Fri 6/23/00**
⊟ **Critical: No**	**0 mins**	**240 mins**	**Mon 5/29/00**	**Tue 5/30/00**
Package materials	0 mins	2 hrs	Mon 5/29/00	Mon 5/29/00
Address packages	0 mins	2 hrs	Tue 5/30/00	Tue 5/30/00
⊟ **Critical: Yes**	**0 mins**	**12600 mins**	**Thu 5/18/00**	**Fri 6/23/00**
Identify current ma	0 mins	4 hrs	Thu 5/18/00	Fri 5/19/00
Compare current m	0 mins	2 hrs	Fri 5/19/00	Fri 5/19/00
Prepare list of mod	0 mins	2 hrs	Fri 5/19/00	Fri 5/19/00
Edit materials	0 mins	20 hrs	Fri 5/19/00	Wed 5/24/00
Duplicate materials	0 mins	8 hrs	Fri 5/26/00	Mon 5/29/00
Bind materials	0 mins	4 hrs	Mon 5/29/00	Mon 5/29/00
Schedule delivery	0 mins	2 hrs	Mon 5/29/00	Mon 5/29/00
Posttest branch en	0 mins	16 hrs	Tue 6/20/00	Wed 6/21/00
Evaluate the projec	0 mins	16 hrs	Thu 6/22/00	Fri 6/23/00
⊟ **Resource Group: Mgmt**	**5,640 mins**	**6600 mins**	**Mon 5/1/00**	**Thu 5/18/00**
⊟ **Critical: No**	**5,280 mins**	**6600 mins**	**Mon 5/1/00**	**Thu 5/18/00**
⊟ Develop proposal	4,800 mins	4 days	Mon 5/1/00	Mon 5/8/00
Gerry Charti	*2,400 mins*		*Mon 5/1/00*	*Mon 5/8/00*
Alicia Mulbe	*2,400 mins*		*Mon 5/1/00*	*Mon 5/8/00*
⊟ Get approval for p	120 mins	2 hrs	Mon 5/8/00	Mon 5/8/00
Alicia Mulbe	*120 mins*		*Mon 5/8/00*	*Mon 5/8/00*
⊟ Communicate prete	240 mins	4 hrs	Thu 5/11/00	Thu 5/11/00
Alicia Mulbe	*240 mins*		*Thu 5/11/00*	*Thu 5/11/00*
⊟ Communicate resu	120 mins	2 hrs	Thu 5/18/00	Thu 5/18/00
Alicia Mulbe	*120 mins*		*Thu 5/18/00*	*Thu 5/18/00*
⊟ **Critical: Yes**	**360 mins**	**360 mins**	**Tue 5/9/00**	**Tue 5/9/00**
⊟ Set training schedu	360 mins	6 hrs	Tue 5/9/00	Tue 5/9/00
Alicia Mulbe	*360 mins*		*Tue 5/9/00*	*Tue 5/9/00*

What's Next

Views form the basis for the way you look at project data onscreen. If the project team is small, you can gather the members around the PC monitor to talk about project status. An LCD projector allows you to share this same information with larger groups. But there's always a point when you'll want printed reports for distribution to team members, upper management, board members, stockholders, etc. Chapter 18 walks you through creating reports that display the data you want to share in ways that are understandable to any audience. As an added bonus, you'll learn how to use pictures and drawing tools to add emphasis and "spice up" views and reports.

CHAPTER 18

Using Reports to Analyze Data

To manage a project effectively, you'll communicate with the project partici-pants formally and informally throughout the project cycle. Informal report-ing can be verbal or written. It might require you to take a quick look at your project data, or it might entail sharing information that's already in your head: A team member stops you in the hallway and asks whether the suppliers were able to deliver on time. You run into your boss at the coffee machine and she asks if you're still within budget. You respond to a team member's email, assuring him there is enough slack to cover the extra four hours he's spent on a particular task.

This chapter focuses on the formal reporting required of a project manager. Proj-ect 2000 allows you to create reports to fit most any scenario. And, if you're deliver-ing bad news, at least it will look good!

Printing a View

Chapter 17, "Using Views to Analyze Data," provided extensive information about creating, modifying and applying views. If you can display the information onscreen, you're often one click away from putting it on paper. For example, communicating assignments to team members could be as simple as printing the Gantt Chart.

When you print a view (whether it's a Resource or Task view), the number of columns displayed on the screen is exactly what gets duplicated on paper. Thus, if there are columns in the sheet hidden by the Gantt Chart, they won't show up in the printed view. To print all sheet columns, choose File ➤ Page Setup to open the Page Setup dialog box.

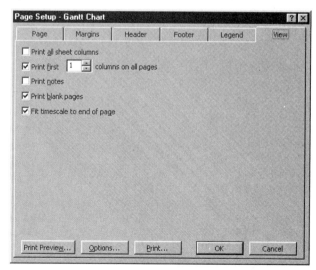

Click the View tab and enable the first option to print all columns. Or, as an alternative, enable the second option and choose the number of sheet columns you wish to print. At any point, you can preview how the printed page will look by clicking the Preview button at the bottom of the dialog box.

Most projects have periodic chunks of "downtime." Although the entire project doesn't come to a screeching halt, certain resources may not be active on your project during a particular time period. If you're printing a Resource view, you'll want to disable the Print Blank Pages feature on the View tab of the Page Setup dialog box so you don't have pages of blank grid for all your effort!

When the view is arranged the way you want it (sorted, filtered, formatted, and so on), click the Print button on the Standard toolbar to print one copy of the view to your default printer. If you're not sure what the printed view will show, click the Print Preview button first.

When you print the Gantt Chart, all expanded tasks print unless you make some adjustments to print settings first. Because a project with more than 50 tasks will be too large to fit on one page, Project prints down and across, left to right, starting in the upper-left corner of the view. Each page is numbered in the sequence it prints. If you're interested only in printing the first few tasks in the project, you might need to print only two of the pages from Gantt Chart view (the sheet with the first few tasks and the corresponding chart bars). Click File ➣ Print to open the Print dialog box.

Enter the pages you want to print in the Page Range section of the Print dialog box.

TIP You can choose to print tasks with start dates that fall within a certain date range. Adjust the dates in the Timescale section of the Print dialog box.

If you're trying to print a very specific portion of the view, try inserting manual page breaks before and after the section you want to print. (Select the task you want to be first on the printed page, and then click Insert ➤ Page Break.) In the Print dialog box, choose the page(s) you want and make sure that the Manual Page Breaks setting is enabled.

 NOTE Delete a page break by selecting the cell below the break and clicking Insert ➤ Remove Page Break.

In most cases, the onscreen view settings are duplicated when you print. That means you can apply a task or resource filter to the view to print just those tasks or resources that meet the filter criteria (see "Sorting, Filtering and Grouping Views" in Chapter 17). Collapse the Outline where you don't need to see the detail behind summary tasks. Expand the Outline in places where detail is important. Format text and bar styles or apply a custom view before you print to see the exact results you want.

Setting Up the Printed Page

Whether you're printing a view or customizing a report, layout settings (margins, orientation, header/footer settings, and so on) are found in the same place. For views, click File ➤ Page Setup or, if you're already in Print Preview, click the Page Setup button on the Print Preview toolbar. For customized reports, click the Setup button in the Custom Reports dialog box. In all cases, the Page Setup dialog box opens, displaying the last tab that was accessed. If you haven't used Page Setup since launching this Project 2000 session, the Page tab displays, as shown in Figure 18.1.

Because most views and reports are quite wide, the default orientation is Landscape. You can change to Portrait, if you wish, on the Page tab of the Page Setup dialog box. Use the scaling controls to shrink or enlarge the image size by a certain percentage (Adjust To), or to force the image to print on a defined number of pages (Fit To). Choose a different paper size if you're not printing on standard $8^1/_2 \times 11$ and enter a First Page Number if you want to start with a number other than 1.

FIGURE 18.1

The Page tab of the
Page Setup dialog box
lets you adjust
orientation, scaling
and paper size.

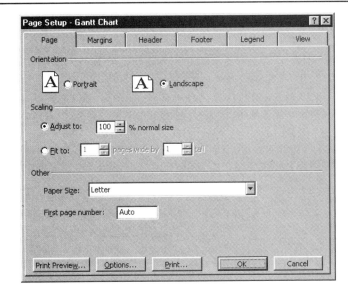

 NOTE The paper sizes displayed in Page Setup are controlled by Windows print settings, not by Project. If you're not seeing a paper size you normally use, check to make sure you're printer is correctly configured with the latest printer driver.

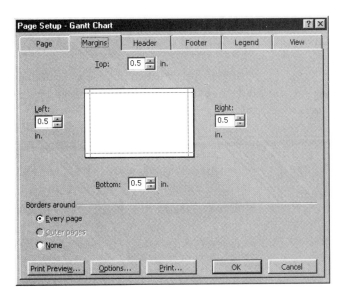

On the Margins tab, you can edit the default settings of $^1/_2$ inch all around, and choose whether and where to print page borders.

Using Headers, Footers, and Legends

Use a header and/or footer to print text and graphics in the top (or bottom) margin area of every page in a view or report. Use a legend to describe information in Gantt Chart, Calendar, or Network Diagram view (but not in reports). The Legend can print on every page of the view or on a page by itself. Click the Header, Footer, or Legend tab of the Page Setup dialog box to configure these settings. If the Page Setup dialog box isn't open, you can click View ➤ Header and Footer from the menu.

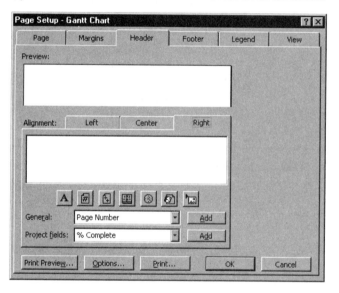

Adjusting settings is the same, whether you're working on a header or footer or legend—just make sure that you're on the right tab of the dialog box before you start. Then, do the following:

1. Choose whether you want the information at the left, center, or right of the page by clicking one of the corresponding tabs below the preview window.

2. Click in the white space below the tab you selected and type information you want to include, and/or

3. Click one of the header/footer shortcut buttons (shown in Figure 18.2) to insert page numbers, current date and time, filename, or pictures, such as a company logo. If you want to format the text, select it and click the Format Text Font button.

4. Insert standard information fields such as manager's name and company name, or select from a list of common Project fields. Choose from the drop-down lists under the shortcut buttons, and then click the Add button to the right of the list.

5. For legends, you must choose whether you want the legend to appear on every page or on a page all its own. Click the Legend Labels Button to format this area of the legend, shown in Figure 18.3.

6. When the preview portion of the dialog box looks like you want it to, click Print to open the Print dialog box and proceed with printing. Alternatively, you can click Print Preview if you want to see the entire printed page, or click OK to close the dialog box and print later.

FIGURE 18.2

The Header, Footer, and Legend tabs of the Page Setup dialog box contain shortcut buttons for inserting and formatting typical information you might put in a header, footer, or legend.

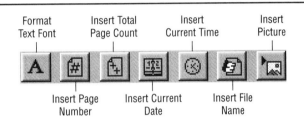

FIGURE 18.3

The legend appears above the footer in Gantt Chart View.

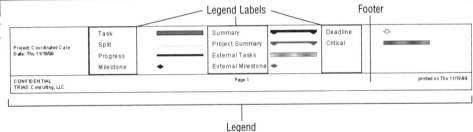

Removing a Header, Footer, or Legend   You cannot "remove" a header or footer from a view—space is always reserved for the header and footer. However, if you delete the text and graphics that appear in the header or footer, the reserved space is blank so nothing prints there. You can choose not to print the Legend by selecting the None option on the Legend tab of the Page Setup dialog box.

NOTE   It's important to note that headers, footers, and legends are specific to the view or report in which they are created. That means, if you've configured a legend in Gantt Chart view, the same legend does not print in Network Diagram view unless you reconfigure it for that view.

TIP You can also embed most views as objects in other applications. For example, you can copy and paste Gantt Chart view into a Word document. See "Using the Copy Picture Button" later in this chapter.

Using Reports

Options for reporting in Project are seemingly endless. Built-in reports exist for each of the situations mentioned above and dozens more. For those rare occasions when Project doesn't have a report to meet the needs of your audience, you can build one from scratch using fields and formatting of your own choice.

In most cases, you'll follow this simple strategy: Navigate to the view or report that is closest to the information you need. Then, customize the view or report by applying filters, grouping, adding or deleting fields, etc. Next, format the report so that information you want to emphasize stands out—change the color of bars in charts, highlight filtered data, add logos, and add pictures and drawn objects where appropriate. Finally, print the view or report you want.

To make it easier to find the report you are looking for, Project categorizes the built-in reports for you. Click View ➤ Reports to open the Reports dialog box. All report categories appear there.

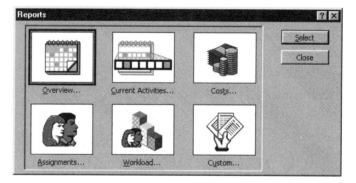

 NOTE The view displayed onscreen at the time the report is generated determines the level and type of detail displayed in the report. For example, if a summary task is collapsed in the outline, the subtasks won't show up in report task lists. Similarly, if you've filtered a view, only the filtered data shows up in the report.

Overview Reports

An overview report provides just that: an overview of an aspect of the project at a fixed point in time. These reports work well with managers, team members, and stakeholders alike. Click the Overview button in the Reports dialog box, and then click Select to see the Overview Reports.

Choose the report that best meets the needs of your audience (you can always customize it later). Click the Select button to display a preview of the report. Table 18.1 offers a brief description of the Overview Reports.

TABLE 18.1: OVERVIEW REPORTS

Report Name	Description
Project Summary	Compares actual dates, durations, work, total costs, and task status with the project baseline.
Top Level Tasks	ID, name, duration, start and finish dates for the highest level tasks and summary tasks, based on the outline.
Critical Tasks	Start and end dates for all critical tasks, including predecessors and successors for each task.
Milestones	Milestone tasks sorted ascending by start date. (Of course, you can change the sort order, and other settings if you customize.)
Working Days	Shows the base calendar in table format, with days of the week in one column and working hours for each day in another column. Exceptions to the base calendar are also shown.

Current Activities Reports

The Current Activities reports are primarily task-focused, but you can add resource information by customizing. (See "Customizing Reports" later in the chapter.) Click the Current Activities button in the Reports dialog box, and then click Select. You'll see the six reports we've summarized in Table 18.2.

TABLE 18.2: CURRENT ACTIVITIES REPORTS

Report Name	Description
Unstarted Tasks	Tasks that haven't begun, listed with their immediate predecessors and related fields.
Tasks Starting Soon	Tasks that are scheduled to start within or finish after a date you choose.

Continued ▶

PART

IV

Evaluating and
Analyzing Project Data

TABLE 18.2 CONTINUED: CURRENT ACTIVITIES REPORTS

Report Name	Description
Tasks in Progress	Tasks that have started, together with the resource information associated with the task.
Completed Tasks	Just like it says—this report shows tasks that have finished with their start and completion dates. The report is sorted by month and then by Task ID.
Should Have Started Tasks	You choose data, and Project lists the tasks that should have started but haven't.
Slipping Tasks	Displays tasks that have been rescheduled past the baseline start date.

Figure 18.4 shows a preview of the Tasks Starting Soon report for a project called Coordinated Care. We adjusted the font size of the report (which you'll learn to do later in the chapter) and the report header (previously covered). All other settings are defaults.

FIGURE 18.4

The Tasks Starting Soon report allows you to display tasks with start and end dates within a range you specify.

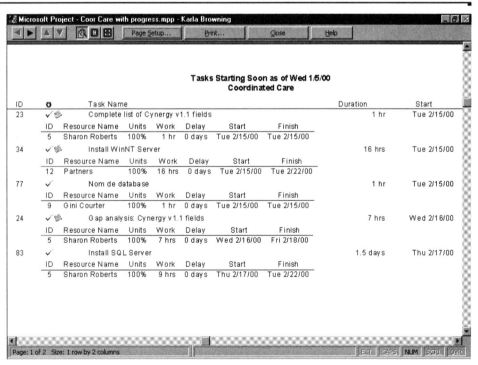

In order to produce the Tasks Starting Soon report, Project requires you to supply two date parameters. In other words, Project needs to know your definition of "soon." Many reports require parameters. You have to define a date range, choose a resource, choose a cost range, and so on. When you select a report that requires one or more parameters, a dialog box displays.

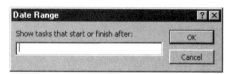

Enter the parameter requested—dates are entered in the mm/dd/yy format—and click OK. If an additional parameter is needed, another dialog box appears.

Cost Reports

In the real world, success or failure of the project is often measured in dollars. You might finish on time with a stellar product. But if you're at double the budget, stakeholders are likely to be displeased.

Cost reports allow you to catch discrepancies early on while there's still a chance of pulling your project back on budget. Project's built-in cost reports are described in Table 18.3.

TABLE 18.3: COST REPORTS

Report Name	Description
Cash Flow	Shows weekly cost by task. Can be customized to show different time units.
Budget	Displays actual vs. budged costs per task. Includes a calculated variance field.
Overbudget Tasks	Tasks with actual costs exceeding baseline costs.
Overbudget Resources	Resources with actual costs exceeding baseline costs.
Earned Value	BCWP (Budget Cost of Work Performed). This report shows how much of the budget should have been spent as of the current date, based on total work and resource costs.

Figure 18.5 previews a Cash Flow report that allows you to see our monthly spending well into the future.

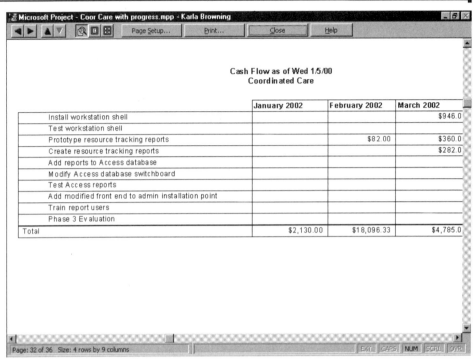

FIGURE 18.5

The Cash Flow report lets you see costs over a certain time period.

Assignment Reports

Resource reporting is the focus of the Assignment Reports group. You can print task lists for the entire team and review them all at once. Or, you can select a resource and print a list of that person's tasks (with completed tasks checked off.) When you click the Assignment Reports button in the Reports dialog box, you'll see four choices, which we've summarized in Table 18.4.

TABLE 18.4: ASSIGNMENT REPORTS

Report Name	Description
Who Does What	Lists each resource and the assigned tasks for that resource. Includes work units, start and finish dates, and a delay field to let resources know whether their work will start on schedule.

Continued ▶

TABLE 18.4 CONTINUED: ASSIGNMENT REPORTS	
Report Name	**Description**
Who Does What When	Resources and their assigned tasks, with a calendar showing daily work assigned for each task. This is a very large report because you get a column for every working day in the project.
To-Do List	You choose a resource, and Project gives you a list of tasks for that resource, along with start and finish dates, duration, predecessor task ID, and other assigned resources. If a task is complete, it's checked off.
Overallocated Resources	Lists overallocated resources with their assigned tasks, including start and finish dates, duration and delay.

Workload Reports

There are two Workload reports. Both provide information on tasks and the resources assigned to them.

The Task Usage Report lists tasks and their assigned in the first column. The rest of the columns are dates (representing one-week increments), with the scheduled work displayed for each task and each resource. Figure 18.6 shows a small portion of one Task Usage Report.

FIGURE 18.6

The Task Usage Report shows when work is scheduled for each resource assigned to a task.

Task Usage as of Thu 11/18/99
Coordinated Care
Gini Courter

	6/25/00	7/2/00	7/9/00	7/16/00	7/23/00	7/30/00	8/6/00	8/13/00	8/20/00	8/27/00
Partners										
Install Office 2000										
Partners										
Test Office install										
Partners										
Reinstall one machine					6 hrs					
Sharon Roberts					6 hrs					
Preparatory Training: Windows and Outlook										
Install remaining Cynergy™ 2000 forms						8 hrs				
James Howe						8 hrs				
Test Cynergy™						4 hrs				
Karla Browning						4 hrs				
Cynergy™ Pilot										
Add Cynergy™ to Office admin install point									7 hrs	
Gini Courter									7 hrs	
Test all pilot machines										4.5 hrs
Karla Browning										4.5 hrs
Train pilot users in Cynergy™										4 hrs
Angie Okonski										2 hrs
Annette Marquis										2 hrs

The Resource Usage report is quite similar to the Who Does What When report (an Assignments report). Resource Usage shows assigned work by week, rather than by day.

Other Reports

If you choose Custom Reports from the Reports dialog box, the Custom Reports dialog box opens, in which you'll find a list of reports available for customization. Several of these reports are different from the ones we've seen in the categories described above. Table 18.5 briefly describes some additional reports you may find useful.

Report Name	Description
TABLE 18.5: CUSTOM REPORTS	
Base Calendar Report	Same as the Working Days report in the Overview section.
Task	A list of tasks, durations, start and finish dates, predecessors, and assigned resources. Similar to the To Do list report, but doesn't prompt for a specific resource.
Crosstab	Very similar to the Task Usage report, except costs are shown in daily increments. (In Task Usage, work is shown in weekly increments.)

Customizing Reports

There are really only two types of customization for reports (and views): You can change the appearance (formatting) and you can change the content. Certain reports (such as the Project Summary) will let you change only appearance. Others offer dozens of options for changing both appearance and content. When you print a view, the content and appearance settings need to be in place before you print. A report can be customized while you're in the process of generating it.

 NOTE Although you can't customize column widths in Project 2000 reports, there is an indirect relationship between the width of the column in the table the report is using and what appears in the report. For example, if the report uses the Entry table and the Name column is set to 80, the column will be much wider in the report than if the column width were set to 20.

Changing the Appearance of a Report

After you've chosen the report you want to produce, click the Edit button to bring up the customization options for that report. If you're working from a resource report, the Resource Report dialog box opens. If you're working from a task report, you'll see the Task Report dialog box.

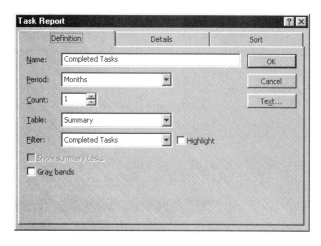

When you're concerned with appearance, rather than content, check the following settings:

1. On the Definition tab, change the Name field if you want the report's title to be something other than the default.

2. Enable the Gray Bands setting if you want to see divisions between major units in the report.

3. On the Details tab, choose whether you want a border around and gridlines between details. Gridlines are the horizontal lines and borders are mostly vertical. (This may be opposite from how you normally think of gridlines and borders.)

4. Click the Text button to choose a font, font style, font size, and color for fields of a certain type.

After you change a report's appearance (or content, for that matter), it's considered "customized" and shows up on the list of reports in the Custom Reports dialog box. If you want to make further changes, select the report from there and click the Edit button.

Changing the Content of a Report

Begin content customization the same way you did with appearance: choose the report you want to produce and click the Edit button. Content customization settings include the following:

Period   Change this setting if you want a different time interval for the selected report.

Count   Determines how many periods to display in one interval. Example: You've selected Month for the Period and 2 for the Count. The report will show two-month time intervals.

Table determines the fields used in the report. To see different report fields, choose a different table, including any custom tables you've created for which the Show in Menu option is enabled. (See Chapter 17 for more on creating and customizing tables.)

Filter Determines the type of task or resource information that gets displayed. For example, the Overallocated Resources report applies the overallocated resource filter so that resources that aren't overallocated do not appear on the report. Enable the Highlight checkbox if you want to see *all* information while highlighting the information that meet the filter criteria. (See Chapter 17 for more on creating and applying filters.)

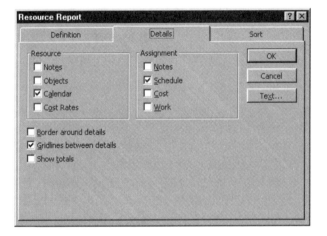

Resource Details (or Task Details) For each field that you enable, except Objects, the information prints once per resource or once per task. Objects work a little differently. (See the Drawing Tools section, later in this chapter.) Example (resource): Enable the Calendar field on the Who Does What report and each resource's calendar prints at the end of the task section for that resource. Example (task): Enable the Predecessor checkbox and each task shows predecessor information.

Assignment Details The choices you make here determine the fields that print for each resource (in Resource reports) or each task (in Task reports). Examples: Choose Schedule to see start and finish dates and delay information; choose Cost to see Baseline Cost, Actual Cost, and Remaining Cost data.

Enable the Show Totals check box (on the Details tab) if you want numeric fields totaled.

Choose a Sort order using the controls on the Sort tab of this dialog box. Chapter 17 covers sorting in views and tables. It works the same when you sort data in reports.

Using Graphic Objects in Views and Reports

Chapter 19, "Importing and Exporting Project Data," describes in detail how you can link or embed objects (such as Word documents, Excel spreadsheets, pictures, and other graphics) to tasks and resources. For example, you can do the following:

- Link a task (such as "Create jingle for new ad campaign") to a Word document that describes in more detail what the task is about. The jingle document might describe the client's feelings about length, type of music, use of lyrics, etc.

- Embed a picture of each resource with its other resource information.

- Insert a text box on the Calendar to remind team members that the network will be down for half a day of reconfiguring.

- Include your company's logo or the client's logo in a view.

- Insert a hyperlink to the client's Web site.

- Attach a brief sound or video clip from each resource, stating its commitment to and goals for the project. (Seems like a lot of extra work for nothing? Think how useful this could be six months from now when that one resource—yes, you know the one—keeps falling behind on scheduled work and seems disillusioned about her role in the project.)

 NOTE Before adding objects to your project, it's a good idea to establish a central location for all project-related files. It could be a shared folder on the network or a Web address on your Intranet. Either way, you'll want links to all the files in one place. That way, the files are easy to locate when you need to link, embed, browse, back up, or edit them.

 The Insert Object button is found on the Notes tab of both the Task Information and Resource Information dialog boxes. When you click it, the Insert Object dialog box, shown in Figure 18.7, opens.

After you open the Insert Object dialog box, you have two choices: You can create a new object from scratch or you can insert an object that already exists.

 NOTE You don't have to attach an object to a task or resource. You can choose Insert ➤ Object from the menu to create the object in the Gantt Chart, for example, as part of the view.

FIGURE 18.7

The Insert Object dialog box lists program and file types compatible with Project 2000.

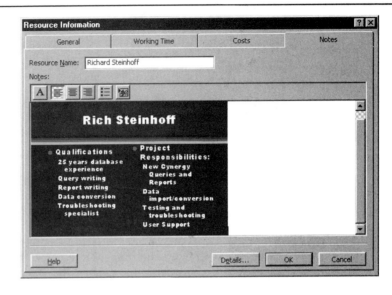

Inserting a New Object

Let's assume that you're attaching this new object to a resource. In the Resource Information dialog box, click the Notes tab. Then, click the Insert Object button to open the Insert Object dialog box. Make sure that the Create New option is selected at the left. Then, scroll the list to choose the type of object you want to create, and click OK.

Project assumes that you know what you're doing with the program you've selected, because once you click OK, the selected program launches. Create the object as you normally would, using the tools of the application you selected. When you're done, close the application and you'll see the new object. Figure 18.8 shows the Resource Information dialog box with a newly created PowerPoint Slide Object.

FIGURE 18.8

Use the Insert Object command to attach items created in other programs to resources, tasks, or views.

Inserting an Existing Object

Click Insert ➤ Object (or click the Insert Object button on the Notes tab of the Task Information or Resource Information dialog boxes) to open the Insert Object dialog box, shown previously in Figure 18.7. Choose the Create From File option, and the dialog box changes to give you browsing options instead of the scroll list of programs.

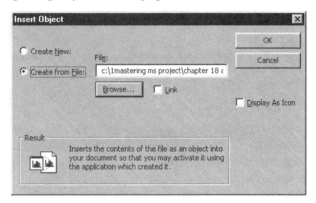

Click Browse to navigate to the folder that contains the object you wish to insert. Select the object file and click OK. The path is inserted in the File field of the Insert Object dialog box. From there, you can choose to link to the file (see Chapter 19 for more on linking), and/or display the file as an icon that users double-click to view. Click OK when you're through and you'll see the object you inserted, or the icon representing that object.

NOTE   You can also attach an object directly to a task or resource, rather than to the Notes for that task or resource. Choose the Task Form or Resource Form view. Right-click the viewer portion and choose Objects. Click Insert ➤ Object and proceed as usual.

Viewing and Printing the Inserted Object

Resource table views display an Indicator column with icons denoting the condition of the resource. When you see the Notes icon in the Indicator column, it indicates that there is something on the Notes tab of the Resource Information dialog box for that resource. Double-click to open the Resource Information dialog box (or right-click the Notes icon and choose Resource Notes from the shortcut menu). You'll see the object or an icon representing the object. If it's an icon, you have to double-click one final time and you're there!

If you want an object you've attached to Notes to appear in a printed report, you have to edit the report to include Notes in the details. From the top, do the following:

1. Click View ➤ Reports to open the Reports dialog box.

2. Choose the type of report you want to print. Let's say you're printing a Who Does What report, and you want to see the pictures you've attached to each resource. Choose Assignments and click Select.

3. Choose Who Does What and click Edit.

4. Click the Details tab and enable Notes. Click OK, and then click Select. You should see the inserted objects at the end of each resource's list of tasks.

MASTERING TROUBLESHOOTING

Working with Objects

Choosing which details to print in a report can be tricky. Your first instinct might be to enable Objects, rather than Notes. But the Objects choice prints only objects you've inserted directly into the view or attached directly to a resource or task, not those you inserted on the Notes tab.

When you insert objects into sheet views, you can't see them to delete them. That's because they're being attached directly to the task (or resource). To see the object, split the window and click in the bottom pane to activate the task form. Then, click Format ➤ Details ➤ Object. The inserted object(s) will print when you enable the Objects option under report details. Unless you spend a good deal of time using the Resource Form (or Task Form), finding an object you previously inserted can be somewhat of a nightmare. It's probably a good idea to attach objects to tasks or resources using the Notes tab, rather than inserting them directly into a sheet view.

Objects cannot be inserted into Network Diagram View, even though that menu choice is available. When you insert an object into the Network Diagram, you're really attaching it directly to a task. Just view the task form (as mentioned previously) to see the inserted object.

Using the Drawing Tools

There's always supplementary information about tasks and resources that you can include in the Notes for that task or resource. However, to highlight this type of information on the Gantt Chart, you might choose to use drawing tools. For example, you could insert a text box with a comment about a task or group of tasks. You can draw lines or arrows to visually relate the text box to a particular task, or you can use the Assign To Task feature to link it for real. Objects created on the Gantt Chart can add information or draw attention to a particular task, as shown in Figure 18.9.

FIGURE 18.9

*Insert a text box and
other drawn objects on
the Gantt Chart to high-
light supplementary
information about the
project.*

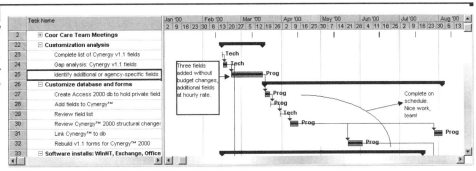

You'll need the Drawing toolbar to create the types of objects shown in Figure 18.9.
Click View ➢ Toolbars ➢ Drawing to turn it on. (You can also right-click an existing
toolbar and choose Drawing.) Project 2000's toolbar (shown in Figure 18.10) uses slightly
different Drawing tools than the other Office 2000 applications. Like the other drawing
tools, there are buttons to create objects and buttons to format existing objects. To
create a drawing object, follow these steps:

1. Click once on the button to select the type of object you want to draw. The
mouse pointer changes to cross-hairs.

2. Click and drag on the Gantt Chart. Release the mouse when the object is the
approximate size you want. If you're creating a polygon, you have to drag a line
for each side of the shape. When you draw the final line that completely
encloses the shape, the polygon tool turns itself off.

3. Move and/or resize the object as needed. To resize, simply point to one of the
object handles. When the pointer changes to a two-headed arrow, drag the object
smaller or larger. (If you're trying to resize a polygon and dragging the handles
only changes its shape, click Draw ➢ Edit Points). To move the object, point at it
(but not on a handle), and then click and drag to the new location.

4. Format the object as desired (see the following section).

FIGURE 18.10

*Project 2000's Drawing
toolbar is specialized
for features you can use
with the Gantt Chart.
This toolbar looks a bit
different from the Draw-
ing toolbar in other
Office 2000 applications.*

Formatting a Drawn Object

Project 2000 objects all have a black line and white fill by default. If all you want to do is change the fill color from white to another solid color, you can select the object and click the Cycle Fill Color button on the Drawing toolbar. Continue clicking until you see the fill color you want.

To change the fill pattern, the border width and color, or to remove the border completely you'll have to adjust the object's properties. Select the object and click Format ➤ Drawing ➤ Properties, or right-click the object and choose Properties from the shortcut menu. The Format Drawing dialog box opens.

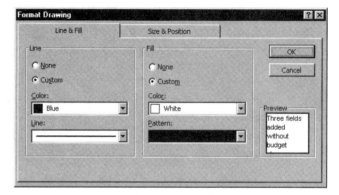

Adjust the line and fill settings until the Preview window displays the look you're aiming for. Then, click the Size and Position tab to see additional settings.

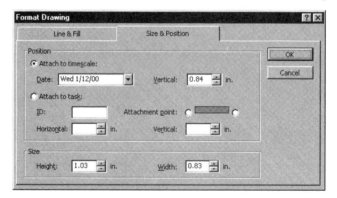

Use the Attach To Timescale option to anchor the drawn object vertically and horizontally, relative to the timescale. The Date control determines where the object is anchored horizontally. The Vertical control reflects the amount of space between the top of the object and the timescale area of the Gantt Chart.

NOTE The Vertical measurement assumes that the Gantt Chart is scrolled to the top.

Use the Attach To Task option to keep the object with the selected task, even if the task gets delayed or scheduled for a different start date. Enter the ID number of the task you're attaching to, and then choose whether you want to attach at the beginning or end of the task bar. Adjust the Vertical and Horizontal spin settings to determine the position of the object relative to the task bar it's attached to.

Here's where it can be a bit tricky. If you're attaching the object to the left end of the task bar, the horizontal spin setting must be a negative number, or the object will still appear to the right of the task bar. If you're attaching to the right end of the task, make sure the horizontal spin setting is a positive number. If both horizontal and vertical settings are set to zero, the object will appear on top of the task bar to which it's attached.

 NOTE You can still drag an object to move it, even if it's anchored to the timescale or attached to a task. The vertical and horizontal settings adjust automatically when you drag to reposition.

You can quickly access the Attach To settings of a selected object by clicking the Attach To Task button on the Drawing toolbar.

Using the Draw Menu

The Draw menu on the Drawing toolbar includes other options for manipulating objects. Drawing objects are placed in separate layers on top of the Gantt Chart. Sometimes, you have to adjust the order of objects so they don't cover up Gantt bars you want to display. For example, the arc we created had to be "sent back" so it didn't cover the Gantt bars. Select the object that's in the way and click Draw ➤ Send To Back. Or, if it's the Gantt Chart that's in the way, click the object and choose Draw ➤ Bring To Front. Bring to Front and Send to Back move the selected object(s) in relation to text and bars of the Gantt Chart itself.

Use the Bring Forward and Send Backward commands when you have more than two object layers on the Gantt Chart. These commands move the selected object one layer at a time.

 TIP Unlike other Office 2000 applications, Project 2000 does not support object grouping. Instead, use the Attach To Task and Attach To Timeline settings to make sure that your graphics stay put.

The Edit Points command on the Draw menu allows you to change the shape of a polygon. When the feature is active, dragging a handle on a polygon changes its shape. When the Edit Points feature is inactive, dragging a handle on a polygon resizes it.

Using the Copy Picture Button

One of the easiest ways to include Project 2000 information in a report is to take a picture of it. The "report" might be a Word document, an Excel spreadsheet, or even a Web page. In Project, navigate to a view that contains the information you need and click the Copy Picture button to display the Copy Picture dialog box.

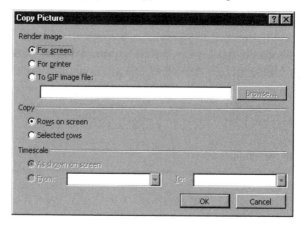

Select a Rendering option. Choose For Screen if you want the picture to display exactly as it looks on your monitor. Choose For Printer if you want the picture to display as it would when printed in Project. Choose To GIF Image File if you're planning to use the picture on a Web page. If you choose this third option, you must specify a file name and location.

Next, choose a Copy option. It's helpful to note that you don't have to print the entire picture. You can select certain portions of your view, click Copy Picture, and choose the Selected Rows option. If you want to use a timescale other than the one shown onscreen, enter the beginning and end dates, and then click OK.

If you chose For Screen or For Printer from the rendering options, switch to the program you want to use to display your Project picture and paste using the appropriate command from that program.

TIP   Ctrl+V works to paste into most Windows-based programs.

NOTE   Copy Picture is not supported in the Relationship Diagram, Resource Form, and Task Form views.

Using Hyperlinks

It is truly the age of "the Net." Almost anyone who uses a computer has surfed the World Wide Web and/or a company intranet. Project 2000, like other Office 2000 programs, supports hyperlinks to document files and to Web sites. When you click the hyperlink, your default browser opens and displays the hyperlinked information.

 NOTE It's helpful to note that hyperlinks do not increase the size of your project file and the linked information is always up to date. However, you may not have access to linked information when you are working offline.

There are several ways you can use hyperlinks in your Project files, as follows:

- Place the hyperlink(s) in a task or resource note.
- Insert a hyperlink into the Hyperlink column in a sheet view.
- Insert the hyperlink into an additional text-based column.

 To insert a hyperlink on the Notes tab of a task or resource, simply type the URL in the open Notes field. It's just too easy!

To insert a hyperlink that appears in the Indicator column of a sheet view, do the following:

1. Switch to a sheet view, and select the task or resource for which you want to include the hyperlink.

2. Click Insert ➤ Hyperlink on the menu, or click the Insert Hyperlink button on the Standard toolbar to open the Insert Hyperlink dialog box.

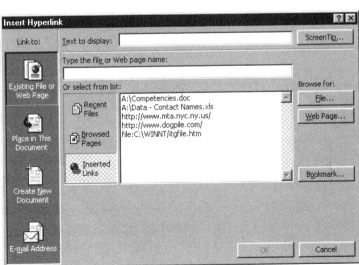

PART

IV

Evaluating and
Analyzing Project Data

3. Select one of the four Link To options displayed on the Places bar at the left side of the dialog box. The choice you make here determines the next few steps in the hyperlink process.

4. If you're Linking To An Existing File Or Web Page, click the appropriate Browse button to find and select the file (or Page) you're linking to. In the Text To Display field at the top of the dialog box, type the text you want to use to indicate the presence of the hyperlink. Click the Screen Tip button and type the text you want to see when you hover the mouse over the Hyperlink icon. Click the Bookmark button to select a specific location within the Web page you're linking to.

OR

If you're linking to a Place In This Document, type some Text To Display and a Screen Tip. Then, enter a task or resource ID and click the view you want displayed when the hyperlink is clicked.

OR

To link to a new document you're about to create, choose that option and then type the Text To Display and Screen Tip. Click the Change button and browse to the folder location where you want to store this new file. Type a file name for the new file and choose a file type from the drop-down list in the Create New Document dialog box, then click OK. Back in the Insert Hyperlink dialog box, choose whether you want to edit the document now (in which case, when you click OK, you're transported to the application for the file type you chose) or choose to Edit the Document Later (to have Project launch the application when you click the hyperlink.)

OR

If you're linking To An Email Address, type the Text To Display and Screen Tip. Then, enter the email address of the person whom you wish to contact, or select it from the list of recently used addresses if it appears there. Enter a subject for the email to have that information in place when you click the hyperlink.

5. Click OK to close the Insert Hyperlink dialog box and create the hyperlink.

The hyperlink icon appears in the Indicators column of the sheet view. When you mouse over the icon, the pointer changes to a hand and you'll see the text you typed in the Screen Tip dialog box. Click the hyperlink to go to the file, Web page, alternative location in the project file, new document, or email address you indicated when you created the hyperlink. To return to the project file, simply close the window that opened when you activated the hyperlink.

You can remove or edit an existing hyperlink by right-clicking the hyperlink icon and choosing Hyperlink ≻ Edit Hyperlink (or Remove Hyperlink).

To link a document on the Notes tab of the Task or Resource Information dialog box, click the Insert Object button and follow the steps you would normally follow to create a new object. (See specific steps under "Inserting A New Object," earlier in this chapter.) Make sure that you enable the Display As Icon checkbox before you click OK. You won't see a hyperlink icon in the Indicators column when you link this way. Instead, you'll see a Note icon. To add a "Tool Tip" for this Note icon, type a short amount of descriptive text anywhere in the blank space around the icon you just inserted.

Creating a New Report

There's not much difference between editing an existing report (which was covered previously in the chapter) and creating a new custom report. The only distinction is the template that gets used. Project 2000 reports are based on one of four templates: Task, Resource, Crosstab, and Monthly Calendar. To create a new report click View ➤ Reports ➤ Custom, and click Select to open the Custom Reports list. Click the New button and you'll see the Define New Report dialog box.

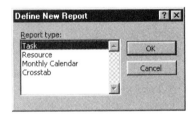

Choose one of the four available report templates to use as a basis for the new report. If you choose Monthly Calendar, you'll see the Monthly Calendar Report Definition dialog box shown in Figure 18.11. All of these settings should be familiar from working with view settings in Chapter 17. (Feel free to revisit the Calendar section of Chapter 17 for a refresher.)

If you choose Resource, Task, or Crosstab, you'll get the same dialog box and setting you use when you edit an existing report of the same type. These configuration settings are discussed at length in the earlier sections of this chapter, "Changing the Appearance of a Report" and "Changing the Content of a Report."

TIP   You can use the Organizer to copy custom reports to other project files. See "Working with the Organizer" in Chapter 21, "Customizing Project 2000," for information about how to copy reports.

What's Next

In this chapter, we've covered some of the basics of inserting objects into your Project files. Chapter 19 addresses other object issues such as converting, linking, and embedding. The next chapter also focuses on moving data into and out of Project files by exploring options for importing and exporting. Exporting project data gives you the option of conducting analysis and developing reports using powerful data-crunching tools such as Microsoft Excel.

CHAPTER 19

Importing and Exporting Project Data

No project takes place in a vacuum. There are reports to produce, presentations to give, budgets to create, and, inevitably, status reports to prepare. In Chapter 14, "Sharing Resources and Tasks among Multiple Projects," you learned how to share information between different projects. In this chapter, you will share Project 2000 data with other applications, as well as enrich your projects by adding objects such as charts, graphics, and video. We'll start by explaining how to import data into Project from several different applications, emphasizing how to make the information work in Project when fields don't quite fit. We will explore the differences between linking and embedding objects in Project 2000, and learn about cutting and pasting. We'll then move on to exporting data from Project and the many possible methods of formatting your data.

Import and Export Basics

Importing moves data into Project from another application. Exporting saves Project data so it can be used in another application. We'll review the file formats, and then learn how to use Project's import tools to determine which data gets imported. Then, we will show you how to apply the tools to specific file formats: for example, how to import a file from Excel or Access.

 TIP If you're importing data into an existing project file, it's a good idea to make a copy of the file first. If you accidentally import data incorrectly, you can discard the project file and use the copy.

Understanding File Formats

Every application has one or more default formats that define the way files are structured. The three-character file extension indicates each file's format. For example, Word documents have the file name extension DOC. The application you use to create a file is the file's native application. There are three file formats that are native to Project. The default file format is MPP, which contains all of the Project data. Project Templates (MPT) and Project Database (MPD) formats are the other two formats supported by Project 2000.

In addition, Project can open files created in other applications, as well as saving in external (non-native) formats: a format other than Project, Project Template, or Project Database. This is extremely useful when sharing Project information throughout your organization, when the other users might not have Project, or are when they are unfamiliar with how to use Project. Table 19.1 contains the native and external file formats supported by Project, as well as their extensions and whether the file type can be imported or exported.

WARNING Earlier versions of Project (4.*x* and below) used the MPX (Project Exchange) format to save files; the MPP format first appeared in Project 98. You can open MPX files using Project 2000 because all the fields defined in MPX are also in MPP. However, there will be "holes" in the data because the MPX file format doesn't support features added in Project 98. See "Importing Earlier Versions of Project" for more information on the limitations of the MPX file format. Project 2000 does *not* let you save data in the MPX format.

TABLE 19.1: FILE FORMATS SUPPORTED IN PROJECT

Extension	Name	Can Import?	Can Export?	Details
MPP	Project	Yes	Yes	Default file format for Project 2000. Contains all project data, including fields, formatting, filters, and embedded objects.
MPT	Project Template	Yes	Yes	Used to create new Project documents using boilerplate data set up by users. The global file (GLOBAL.MPT) is a master template file that can contain formatting information for all projects, but can't store tasks, resources, and assignments.
MPD	Project Database	Yes	Yes	Project Database format is the same as Access 9.0 (2000), and can be processed in Project or Access just like an MDB database file. Can contain multiple projects in a single file.
MPW	Project Workspace	Yes	No	Contains workspace settings for all the open files during a Project session, so all these same files can be opened simply by opening the project workspace.
MPX	Project Exchange	Yes	No	Projects created in Project 4.*x* and earlier used this ASCII format to exchange data between other applications and other versions of Project. Although the MPX format doesn't include new Project fields and functions, you can open projects saved in this format. See the "Exporting Data" section for warnings on saving in this format.

Continued ▶

TABLE 19.1 CONTINUED: FILE FORMATS SUPPORTED IN PROJECT

Extension	Name	Can Import?	Can Export?	Details
MDB	Project 4.*x* Database	Yes	No	Projects created using 4.*x* and earlier used this database structure (Access format).
MDB	Access 9.0 (2000) Database	Yes	Yes	Data saved using this format can be processed by an application that recognizes MDB format as a standard relational database. Queries, reports, and forms can be generated from this type of file. Can contain multiple projects in a single file.
XLS	Excel 97 & 2000 Workbook	Yes	No	Using the Import data maps, Project is able to read in all versions of Excel spreadsheets. However, when Project data is saved in XLS format, an Excel 5.0/95 workbook is created.
XLS	Excel 5.0 & 95 Workbook	Yes	Yes	Excel version 5.0 and newer can open and analyze data exported from Project. Any spreadsheet program that recognizes the XLS format can use this data.
XLS	Excel Pivot Table	No	Yes	Use this format to generate data used in an Excel PivotTable. See the PivotTable Export data map for details.
TXT	Text Files	Yes	Yes	The tab-delimited text file is most useful in exchanging data between platforms and widely disparate applications. Can do only one table at a time–tasks, resources, or assignments.
CSV	Comma Separated Values	Yes	Yes	This file is also useful in exchanging data between platforms and widely disparate applications. Rather than a comma, this format actually uses the default systems list separator. Can only do one table at a time–tasks, resources, or assignments.
HTM HTML	Web Pages	No	Yes	Hypertext Markup Language (HTML) format is used by browser programs. You can export field data to this format, but not an entire project.
Various	ODBC DSNs	Yes	Yes	Can contain multiple projects in a single file.

> **NOTE** MPD and MDB are handled through ODBC, even though Project does not prompt you for an ODBC data source.

Understanding Predefined Data Maps

Anytime you want to import data with an external file format rather than an entire project file created in an earlier version of Project, you must map the data in your external file to the appropriate tables and fields in Project 2000. This is also true when you export part of a project file to a non-native format. The three tables available for import and export mapping are

- Task Table
- Resource Table
- Assignment Table

Combinations of fields in one or more of these tables are collected to form a data map. Data maps list the fields, filters, relationships, sources, and destinations of separate files. Although several of the predefined data maps were developed with a particular application in mind, maps are interchangeable. The main constraint is that some text-based file formats can map only to one table per file, whereas most file formats can map to multiple Project tables. Import/Export Maps are saved in the GLOBAL.MPT file. The global template is shared by all project files, so an import/export map that you create in one project can be used in another project. You can now edit the global template directly in Project also, but care should be taken when making global changes. Before creating a custom data map, check Table 19.2 to see whether Project has a map that includes the list of fields you want to export.

TABLE 19.2: PREDEFINED IMPORT/EXPORT DATA MAPS

Map Name	Table & Fields		Used For
"Who Does What" Report	RESOURCE TABLE:		Resource Scheduling and Tracking; create to-do lists for team members.
	Resource Name	Finish Date	
	Start Date	Total Work	
Compare to Baseline	TASK TABLE:		Evaluate how the work done to date varies from the baseline set when the project was created.
	ID	Baseline Start	
	Task Name	Baseline Finish	
	Duration	Baseline Work	
	Start Date	Baseline Cost	
	Finish Date	Duration Variance	
	Total Work	Work Variance	
	Total Cost	Cost Variance	
	Baseline Duration		

Continued ▶

TABLE 19.2 CONTINUED: PREDEFINED IMPORT/EXPORT DATA MAPS

Map Name	Table & Fields		Used For
Cost Data by Task	**TASK TABLE:**		Financial analysis of the costs associated with each task; budgeting.
	ID	Baseline Cost	
	Task Name	Cost Variance	
	Fixed Cost	Actual Cost	
	Total Cost	Remaining Cost	
Default Task Information	**TASK TABLE:**		Standard data needed to create a task; Pre-decessors and Resource Name fields contain mul-tiple entries separated by commas.
	ID	Finish Date	
	Task Name	Predecessors	
	Duration	Resource Names	
	Start Date		
Earned Value Information	**TASK TABLE:**		To compare how much of your budget you should have spent at a certain period in time compared to how much you actually spent. The snapshot is based on the view applied to the project tasks.
	ID	SV	
	Task Name	CV	
	BCWS	EAC	
	BCWP	BAC	
	ACWP	VAC	
Export to HTML Using Standard Template	**TASK TABLE:**		Publishing project data on an intranet or the World Wide Web; sharing project data with people using non-Windows oper-ating systems.
	ID	Max Units	
	Task Name	Peak Units	
	Duration	ASSIGNMENT	
	State Date	TABLE:	
	Finish Date	Task ID	
	Resource Names	Task Name	
	% Complete	Resource Name	
	RESOURCE TABLE:	Total Work	
	ID	Start Date	
	Name	Finish Date	
	Group	% Work Complete	
Resource Export Table Map	**RESOURCE TABLE:**		Detailed reporting and analysis of Resource information.
	ID	Baseline Cost	
	Unique ID	Actual Cost	
	Resource Name	Scheduled Work	
	Initials	Baseline Work	
	Max Units	Actual Work	
	Standard Rate	Overtime Work	
	Overtime Rate	Group Name	
	Cost per Use	Code	
	Accrue At	Text1–Text5	
	Total Cost	Email Address	

Continued ▶▶

TABLE 19.2 CONTINUED: PREDEFINED IMPORT/EXPORT DATA MAPS

Map Name	Table & Fields		Used For
Task Export Table Map	TASK TABLE:		Even more exhaustive reporting and analysis of task-related information.
	ID	Constraint Date	
	Unique ID	Stop	
	Task Name	Resume	
	Duration	Created	
	Duration Type	Scheduled Work	
	Outline Level	Baseline Work	
	Baseline Duration	Actual Work	
	Predecessors	Cost	
	Start Date	Fixed Cost	
	Finish Date	Baseline Cost	
	Early Start Date	Actual Cost	
	Early Finish Date	Remaining Cost	
	Late Start Date	WBS	
	Late Finish Date	Priority	
	Free Slack	Milestone	
	Total Slack	Summary	
	Leveling Delay	Rollup	
	Percent Complete	Text 1–10	
	Actual Start Date	Cost 1–3	
	Actual Finish Date	Duration 1–3	
	Baseline Start	Flag 1–10	
	Date	Marked	
	Baseline Finish	Number 1–5	
	Date	Subproject File	
	Constraint Type		
Task and Resource PivotTable	TASK TABLE:		Create an Excel Pivot-Table to show Task and Resource relationships. For more information, see "Exporting Data for an Excel PivotTable," later in this chapter.
	Resource Group	RESOURCE TABLE:	
	Resource Names	Resource Group	
	Task Name	Resource Name	
	Start Date	Work	
	Finish Date	Cost	
	Cost		
Task List with Embedded Assignment Rows	TASK TABLE:		Scheduling, status reports, benchmarking, charts and graphs.
	ID	Start Date	
	Task Name	Finish Date	
	Work	% Work Complete	
	Duration		
Top Level Tasks List	TASK TABLE:		Executive summaries; PowerPoint presentations.
	Task Name	Cost	
	Duration	Work	
	Start Date	*Filtered for top-*	
	Finish Date	*level tasks only*	
	% Complete		

Using the Import Tools

Imported data can jump-start your project file. For example, you can import resource lists provided by your Human Resources department and a task list from a workgroup leader rather than manually entering that information in Project 2000. When you import data, you use an import data map to match the fields in the file you're importing to the corresponding fields in your project file.

Importing a file is a three-step process:

1. Select the data to be imported.

2. Map the data's relationship to project data files.

3. Import the data.

To import data into Project from an outside source, you must understand the fields in your input file, and the tables and fields that Project will update so you can map the data correctly. If the data originally was exported from Project for analysis or processing, you might be able to use the same data map used in the original export or modify it slightly. If the source data was created outside of Project, or significantly modified, it is necessary to create a new import data map. Your imported data can be used to create a new project or merged into an existing project.

 TIP All records in your source file will be imported into Project. If you wish to import selected records or fields, you must first modify the source file so that it contains only the data you wish to import into Project.

The same dialog boxes and field selections are used whenever you import files, whether you're importing from an Excel workbook or a comma delimited text file. Excel worksheets are used in this section of the book, but you'll use the same dialog boxes and follow the same steps to create, modify and use import data maps for all file formats.

Selecting the File with Importable Data

When you import data, you begin by opening the file you want to import. Choose File ➢ Open the display the Open dialog box, shown in Figure 19.1. You've seen this dialog box before, so we'll focus on the use of the dialog box when import data. See Chapter 5, "Working in Project 2000," for complete descriptions of the controls in the Open dialog box.

FIGURE 19.1

Launch your import by choosing a file with a non-native format in the Open dialog box.

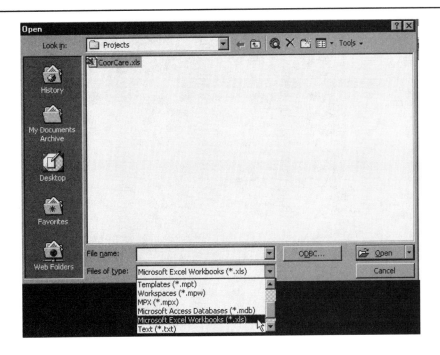

Use the Files of Type, Look In, and ODBC controls to select the file that contains the data you want to import:

- Files Of Type—Select the File Type to import
- Look In or Places bar—Select source file location
- ODBC button—Used to select an ODBC data source

 TIP For information on importing ODBC data sources, see the "Importing from a Database" and "Exporting to a Database" sections in this chapter.

Selecting the Data Source

The Import Mapping dialog box, shown in Figure 19.2, is displayed after you select a file and click the Open button on the Open dialog box.

 The file name in the Import File text box at the top of the Import Mapping dialog box should be the file that you want to import data from. If it is not, click the Back button to return to the Open Dialog Box. Reset the File Type drop-down list, select the file you want to import, and click Open.

FIGURE 19.2

Use the Import Map-
ping dialog box to
choose what data you
want to import by using
an existing data map
or creating a new one.

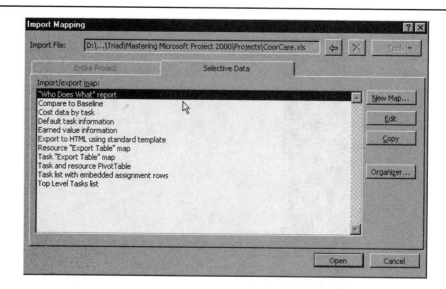

If you click the Back button, the File Type returns to the default MP* (Microsoft Project Files).

The Import Mapping dialog box includes two tabs, which are enabled or disabled, based on the file type you selected to import:

- Import Entire Project—Options on this tab allow you to import an entire project file. Although this tab is always displayed, it is inactive unless you choose a file with a native format for an earlier version of Project: MPP, MPD, MPX, or MDB.

- Import Selective Data tab—This tab is always displayed and enabled. It lists pre-defined import/export data maps included with Project 2000 or created by the user (see Figure 19.2).

NOTE Data maps are stored in the global template file (GLOBAL.MPT), so they can be exchanged between project files.

Creating and Modifying Data Maps

You aren't limited to the existing maps. You can create a new map from scratch, edit an existing map, copy and modify a map, or copy maps from other Microsoft Project files:

- The New Map button creates a new import/export data map.

- The Edit button modifies the current import/export data map.
- The Copy button makes a copy of the current import/export data map.
- The Organizer button copies maps from other projects and templates to this project's list of available import/export data maps. See Chapter 21, "Customizing Project 2000," for more information on the Organizer.

 TIP Click the Edit Button before starting your import so you can preview the mapped data by using the first few rows of your import file.

Specifying Import Settings

Clicking the New Map, Edit, or Copy button opens the Define Import/Export Map dialog box. The Options tab is shown in Figure 19.3.

FIGURE 19.3

Options tab of the Define Import/Export Map dialog box

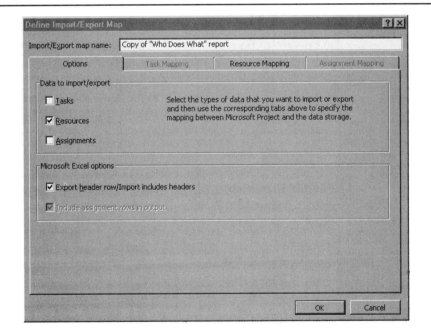

In the Import/Export Map Name text box, enter a name for your new import/export map. Use the Table Selection checkboxes to select the Project tables (Task,

Resource, and/or Assignment) that will receive the imported data. As a table is selected, the tab associated with the table is enabled so you can map imported data to the fields contained in that table.

The second set of options on this tab depends on which file format you're importing. For all file types, check the Import Includes Headers checkbox if the data source includes field names: for example, column headings in an Excel worksheet or a first record with field names in a text delimited file.

 TIP If the data source does not include field names, we recommend that you cancel the import process and add unique field names to the import data source before progressing any further. In the next steps, you'll match Project field names to field names from the import file. If you don't have field names in the import file, it makes it difficult to match field names.

The Include Assignment Rows in Output checkbox is an export-only option. This checkbox is disabled when you import files. There are two other options that appear only when you're importing a text file:

- Text Delimiter drop-down list—Use this to define the character used to separate fields in the import file. The choices are Tab, Space, and Comma.

- File Origin drop-down list—Specifies the system character set of the data to be imported.

 TIP If your import file uses a different delimiter (such as a semicolon or hard return), close the dialog box and use Find and Replace in your import file (or a copy of your import file) to replace the delimiter with a tab, space, or comma. Non-delimited fixed-length field files must be parsed into delimited files before they can be imported by Project 2000.

Mapping Data to Tables

Select any of the enabled mapping tabs to begin mapping the fields in your data source to the fields in the Project tables. The Resource Mapping tab is shown in Figure 19.4.

FIGURE 19.4

The Resource Mapping
tab in the Define Import/
Export Map dialog box

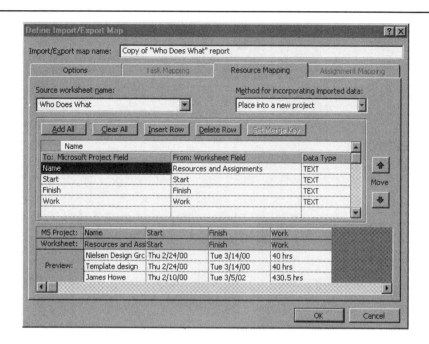

Although the data fields are different for each table, the buttons and selections are the same:

Source Name drop-down list   Depending on the file format of the imported data, this field can be called Source Table Name, Source Database Table Name, or Source Worksheet Name. Some file formats (such as TXT and CSV) don't allow you to choose a Source Name because Project imports the entire file. If you are importing information from Excel, select an option from the box to import data from a specified worksheet.

Method For Incorporating Imported Data drop-down list   Select an option from this drop-down list to import the information in a new project, add it to the end of a current project, or merge the data into the current project using a key field you select. If you are merging data into the current project, the key field you select *must be unique.*

After you set the Source Name and Method, Project reads the field names from the header row of the data source and populates the second column of the mapped fields list, shown in Figure 19.5.

FIGURE 19.5

Project populates the mapped fields list with field names from the import data source.

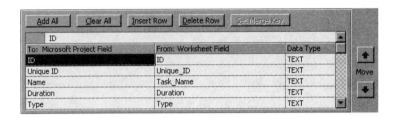

Your goal is to insert, delete, move, and assign fields so that the Project field in the first column matches the field you want to import data from in the second column to create a *mapped field list*. Use the following buttons to create your mapped field list:

Add All   Adds all of the fields from the source file that have a matching name in the selected table to the import/export map.

Clear All   Removes all the fields from the mapped field list.

Insert Row   Inserts a blank row above the selected row in the mapped field list.

Delete Row   Deletes the selected row from the mapped field list.

Set Merge Key   If you are merging the data into an existing project file, select one column in the list common to both files and click Set Merge Key to import the data only into those rows where the merge key fields have common data.

Click the Add button to automatically map fields that have the same name in the import source and Project. Use the drop-down lists in the TO and FROM columns to map the fields that did not have the same name. You can also type in the field name in the cell entry field above the mapped field list, but the name you enter must appear on the list of fields. In the first column (the TO column) of the mapped field list, select field names to specify the fields that you want to be updated, as shown in Figure 19.6. Each field must have a unique name within your project file.

When you select from the TO and FROM field drop-down lists, an item on the Field List, a drop-down box appears, allowing you to select the field name that you want to reference.

In the second (FROM) column, select field names from the data source to specify the fields that you want to import. Each field must have a unique name within the imported file. The third column in the map, Data Type, specifies the format of the data contained in each row. During an import, Project 2000 applies the project table data type to fields being inserted into a project. You can use the Move Up and Move Down buttons to move the selected row up or down in the mapped field list.

For some file formats (such as XLS and TXT), all of the Data Types appear as text, even though they might be numerical in the project table definitions.

FIGURE 19.6

*Select a Project
Table field from the
drop-down list.*

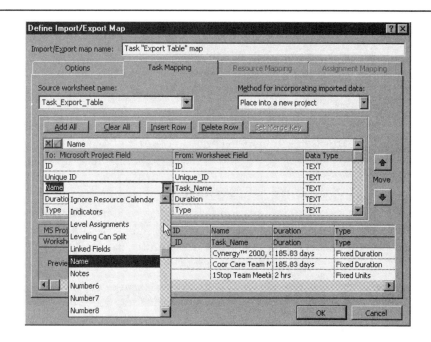

 WARNING If you have chosen the wrong import/export map, the fields will not
match and your mapped table list will look like Figure 19.7. Click the Cancel button and
select a different import/export map or create a new map if your import file doesn't match
any of the currently available import/export maps.

FIGURE 19.7

*Trying to import a file
with the wrong import/
export data map!*

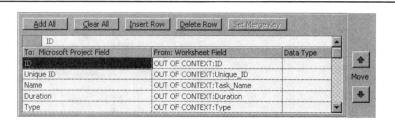

As you map fields, refer to the preview pane at the bottom of the dialog box, shown in
Figure 19.8. The preview includes the field name in Project, the source file field name,
and the first three rows of data from the data source. If there are fields in the import file
that are out of context and cannot be mapped to Project fields, they won't appear in the
preview.

FIGURE 19.8

*Data Preview Pane on
the Define Import/
Export Map dialog box*

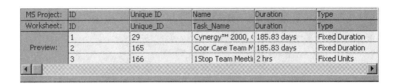

If you're mapping data to more than one table, set up mapped data table on each tab of the Define Import/Export Map dialog box. When you've created the data maps on each tab, click OK to close the Define Import/Export Map dialog box.

Importing the Mapped Data

After you've selected one of Project 2000's predesigned import/export data maps or created your own data map, you're ready to import data. Click the Open button on the Import Mapping dialog box to import the data.

MASTERING TROUBLESHOOTING

Mastering Import Errors

Project 2000 notifies you of mismatch errors that occur during import by displaying a dialog box:

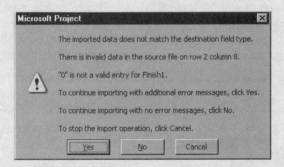

Mismatch errors occur when the data type of the source field conflicts with the data type of the Project field that it's being imported into. For example, if you map a text field such as Employee Name in the import source to a numeric field such as Actual Work, Project can't import the data. When you get import errors, you have three options:

- Click Yes to keep importing. Project displays an error message for each import error.
- Click No to keep importing and suppress further error messages.
- Click Cancel to quit importing.

Continued

MASTERING TROUBLESHOOTING CONTINUED

The best choice depends on two things: the type of project file you're importing the data into and your decision about the source of the problem.

If you click Yes or No, Project continues importing data that leaves holes in the project tables. If you're importing data for a new project file, you can think of this as a trial run. Continue importing data. You can discard the file if there are too many holes. If you click Yes, you'll find out just how many holes there are: Project shows you a message for each data record that can't be imported. If you write these messages down (or turn on screen-capture software and capture the messages in a graphics file), you know what has to be fixed in the import data file. See if Project consistently reports problems in the same column (field) of the import data source. If every record has an error in column 8, which is being imported to the Finish 1 field in your project file, you may have mapped column 8 to the wrong field. After you've received seven or eight messages reporting an error in the same column, you can decide to cancel the import and look at the data map again.

If you click No, you have to examine the project file to find the errors. We never click No because it's more tedious to look for the errors than it is to click Yes and have Project inform us of the errors.

If you're importing data into an existing project, the stakes might be higher. Hopefully, you created a copy of your project file just before opening the import file. If you didn't create a copy of the project file, you should cancel the import and make a backup unless you know that your map is absolutely correct and there are few errors in the import data source. If you decide to continue, click Yes so that Project informs you of each import conflict.

Importing Data from Databases

Earlier versions of Project could export and read the Access file format (MDB). Access 2000 will open the Microsoft Project Database (MPD) files created by Project 2000. Importing data from Access isn't significantly different than importing from Excel or a text file.

Access 2000 is a great database, but some companies and institutions store the bulk of their information on mainframes or large minicomputer databases, not in PC-based databases such as Access. Until recently, that wealth of organizational data was only accessible to mainframe users. If new reports or queries were required, it was time to call in the programmers.

 TIP From Project's point of view, there are three database formats: Project Database, Access, and ODBC-compliant. All other formats are inaccessible.

Improved software and hardware for microcomputer access to mainframe data have radically changed the role of PCs in business, and Project 2000 continues the trend toward greater desktop access to hard-core corporate data with support for the latest version of ODBC (Open Database Connectivity). ODBC is an open standard for database access. ODBC was not developed by Microsoft, but it is often thought of as a Microsoft standard because Windows was the first operating system to support ODBC. Access and SQL Server are both ODBC-compliant, as are many other database programs. Widespread use of the ODBC standard means that you can query data from a variety of sources on your PC, whether or not the data was created on a PC. For example, you might want to import information from a SQL Server or Oracle database by using Project. To do this, you will use a combination of software:

- Project 2000 to map the data and perform the import
- The ODBC Driver Manager, which is part of Windows 95/98/NT/2000
- A specific ODBC driver designed to allow Query to allow access to the SQL Server or Oracle database
- The SQL Server or Oracle database

Importing from an ODBC-compliant database involves one extra step: setting up the ODBC data source, a combination of the database and the appropriate ODBC driver. ODBC-compliant databases usually ship with their own ODBC drivers, and there are third-party drivers available. The ODBC drivers installed on your computer are displayed when you select a data source (see the next section, "Selecting an ODBC Data Source").

MASTERING THE OPPORTUNITIES

Mastering Data Access with ODBC Drivers

Before you can set up a data source, you must have the appropriate ODBC driver. Drivers installed on your computer are listed in the Select Data Source dialog box that's displayed when you click the ODBC button to open the data source. There are two types of ODBC drivers: 16-bit and 32-bit. If you're using Office 2000 or Project 2000 you can use the 32-bit drivers. Use of the 16-bit drivers depends on your operating system. Windows NT Workstation supports both 16- and 32-bit drivers; only 32-bit drivers are supported under Windows 95, 98 and 2000. If you're running Windows and working with vendors to acquire an ODBC driver, make sure that you specify that you require a 32-bit driver.

Continued ▐▶

MASTERING TROUBLESHOOTING CONTINUED

Occasionally, you'll come across a database that doesn't ship with ODBC drivers. It may take some research, but ODBC is such a dominant standard that it's created a market for drivers where none existed five years ago. If the data source you need to connect to is less mainstream and you have to resort to a third-party driver, however, be prepared to pay a hefty price. Drivers for older databases with a relatively small number of PC-based users generally cost more. We recently paid over $700 for an ODBC driver for an obscure database that we really needed to connect PCs to. Get a demo (or a return guarantee) before you buy; there are ODBC drivers that Project 2000 does not support.

The newest ODBC drivers have their own installation programs. Older drivers that required setup through the Control Panel are no longer supported in the version of ODBC that ships with Project 2000 and Office 2000.

Selecting an ODBC Data Source

To import data from an ODBC database, first open the Open dialog box (File ➤ Open). Click the ODBC button in the dialog box to open the Select Data Source dialog box, shown in Figure 19.9. This dialog box is used to connect to file data sources that have ODBC drivers on your machine. File data sources can be shared with other users who have access to the same drivers. Machine data sources are stored on your PC and cannot be shared. Machine data sources are recommended for use with Project 2000, but you can set up a file data source if you prefer.

FIGURE 19.9

*The File DSN tab of
the ODBC dialog box*

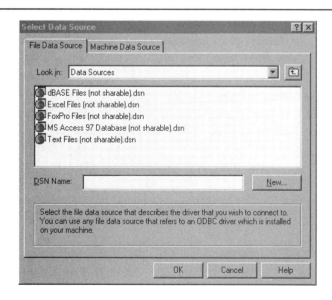

If you want to use Project 2000 to analyze information about a database that is not listed in the File Data Sources list or Machine Data Sources list, first check with the database manufacturer to find out how to get a 32-bit ODBC driver. Often, you'll find that it was included with the software. Also, check the Microsoft Web site (`http://www.microsoft.com`) for additional ODBC drivers. To set up a file data source, set these options in the Select Data Source dialog box:

Look In drop-down list   Displays the current directory for which the sub-directories and file *data source names* (DSNs) are displayed.

File Data Sources list   Displays all file DSNs and subdirectories contained within the directory displayed in the Look In drop-down list. Double-clicking a DSN connects to the data source.

DSN Name   Displays the file DSN name selected in the File Data Sources list (or, you can enter a new file DSN name).

New button   Adds a new file data source. If you click this button, the Create New Data Source dialog box appears with a list of drivers. Choose the driver for which you are adding a file DSN. Click Next, and then specify the keywords for the file DSN.

A machine data source is specific to the machine you are working on and cannot be shared. This is the recommended ODBC data source when working with Project 2000. Click the Machine Data Source tab, shown in Figure 19.10, and set these options to use a machine data source:

Machine Data Sources List   A list of all user and system DSNs that includes the name and type of each DSN. Double-clicking a DSN connects to the data source.

Data Source Name, Type, and Description columns in the Machine Data Sources List   Define the machine data sources available. Type can be User or System. User data sources are specific to a user on your machine, and System data sources can be shared by all users on your machine or by a system-wide service.

New button   Adds a new machine data source. If you click this button, the Create New Data Source dialog box appears with a list of drivers. Choose the driver for which you are adding a user or system DSN. After you click Next, you can verify that the keywords for the DSN are correct.

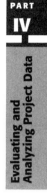

FIGURE 19.10

*Machine Data Source
tab of the ODBC
dialog box*

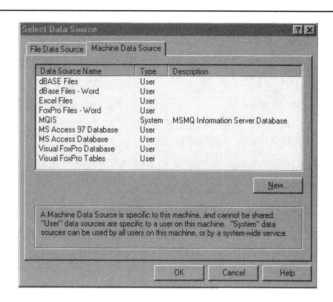

Importing Data from Specific Applications

In this section, you'll find step-by-step instructions and examples for file imports from specific applications. The details of the import process differ because the file formats differ. For example, when importing from Excel, you have to choose the worksheet that the data is stored on. A delimited symbol is required for delimited text files. The overall process is similar, however, regardless of the native format of the import data source. Whether you're importing files from Excel, Access, earlier version of Project, ODBC databases, or text files created by Notepad or a word processor, you'll use the importing tools discussed in the previous section. After you've imported data from a couple of different file formats, you can confidently import data from any format into a Project 2000 file.

Importing from Previous Versions of Project

Project 2000 is backward-compatible and will allow you to open all the file types used in previous Project versions. As Project has matured, however, the number of fields and functions has greatly increased. This means older projects may appear incomplete or may yield unexpected results in Date Scheduling and Duration fields. Carefully check your older project files for completeness and accuracy after importing.

Why Might You Import Data from an Earlier Version of Microsoft Project?

- An ongoing project has spanned multiple releases of Microsoft Project and your organization finally upgraded its software.
- A new project needs historical information contained in an old project.
- Projects are being shared between groups with different versions of Microsoft Project.

Prior versions of Project use these file formats: MPP, MPW, MPX, and MPT.

To open a project file created in a previous version of Project:

1. Select File ➤ Open. The Files of Type List Box default is Microsoft Project Files (MP*) so all Project files in the selected directory location will be listed, with the exception of MDB files (Project Database files created in Project 4.*x* and earlier).

2. Select the location of the file you want to open in the Look In drop-down list.

3. Choose the project file name from the file list and click the Open button. The project opens and displays in your default view.

 TIP   To import MDB files, see "Importing Data from Access," later in this section.

 MASTERING THE OPPORTUNITIES

Mastering Forward Compatibility

Beginning with Project 98, new I/O architecture was designed for extensibility, employing a scheme for installable file serializers (converters). This new architecture provides a way to implement forward-compatibility with future versions of Project. For example, for the next version of Microsoft Project (2002, perhaps?), if the appropriate serializer is available for Project 2000, then a Project 2002 MPP file could be opened in Project 2000. The way that new features from the future version are handled when opening the file in a previous version depends entirely on the designer of the serializer. Note that this forward-compatibility feature begins with Microsoft Project 98. Serializers are not available for Microsoft Project 4.*x*.

Importing Microsoft Excel Workbooks

Files are created in Microsoft Excel with the XLS file suffix. Pivot Tables, which also have the XLS suffix, cannot be imported into Project. Spreadsheet files created using other applications should either be imported into Excel or be saved in either tab-delimited TXT files or comma-separated CSV files, and then imported following the directions for "Importing Text Files," later in this section.

Why Might You Import Data from a Microsoft Excel Workbook?

- Your Human Resources department keeps employee information in Excel that you can import into your project's Resource table.

- Resource hourly rates have changed and need to be adjusted using a complex calculation. Calculate the new rates in Excel and import them into the revised data into Project.

- Data from many applications can be exported in an Excel format file that you can then import into your project file. For example, Outlook contact and task data can be saved as an Excel file and then imported into Project.

- To streamline data entry for a large project. It's much easier to enter repetitive information into a spreadsheet.

Microsoft Excel workbooks use this file format: XLS.

If you wish to import specific records or columns of data, you have to open the file in Excel and modify the data so that it only contains the information to be imported. This can be done by filtering, editing, or grouping; and saving the result as a new file. Because data is mapped by field name, it is not necessary to sort the spreadsheet in the same order as the project. Each column must, however, have a unique name.

 NOTE   Project 2000 does not let you open a Microsoft Excel file that is password-protected. Instead, you get an alert saying that the file cannot be opened. Remove the password in Excel and save the file. After importing, you can restore the password.

Importing Data from Excel Using an Existing Import Data Map

In this example, we will import an Excel spreadsheet (see Figure 19.11) that contains the same fields as the "Who Does What" report import data map.

TIP The complete list of fields included in each Project 2000 import/export map appears in Table 19.2 (near the beginning of this chapter).

FIGURE 19.11

The data in this Excel worksheet will be imported into Project. Note that it contains the same data as the "Who Does What" report input data map.

	A	B	C	D
1	Resources and Assignments	Start	Finish	Work
2	Nielsen Design Group	2/24/00 10:00	3/14/00 11:00	40 hrs
3	Template design	2/24/00 10:00	3/14/00 11:00	40 hrs
4	James Howe	2/10/00 9:00	3/5/02 15:00	430.5 hrs
5	1Stop Team Meetings 1	2/10/00 9:00	2/10/00 11:00	2 hrs
6	1Stop Team Meetings 2	3/9/00 9:00	3/9/00 11:00	2 hrs
7	1Stop Team Meetings 3	4/13/00 9:00	4/13/00 11:00	2 hrs
8	1Stop Team Meetings 4	5/11/00 9:00	5/11/00 11:00	2 hrs
9	1Stop Team Meetings 5	6/15/00 9:00	6/15/00 11:00	2 hrs
10	1Stop Team Meetings 6	7/13/00 9:00	7/13/00 11:00	2 hrs
11	1Stop Team Meetings 7	8/10/00 9:00	8/10/00 11:00	2 hrs
12	1Stop Team Meetings 8	9/14/00 9:00	9/14/00 11:00	2 hrs
13	1Stop Team Meetings 9	10/12/00 9:00	10/12/00 11:00	2 hrs
14	1Stop Team Meetings 10	11/9/00 9:00	11/9/00 11:00	2 hrs

This file may have originally been exported from Project using the "Who Does What" map. Or, you or another thoughtful user may have arranged the worksheet so that it uses the same field names as the map. It takes less time to rearrange columns and change a few headings in an Excel worksheet than it does to create a custom data map.

To import data from Excel using an existing data map:

1. In Project, select File ➤ Open. The File Open dialog box is displayed.

2. Change the Files of Type to Microsoft Excel Workbook (XLS).

3. Use the Look In drop-down list to locate the proper folder and file.

4. Select the file and click the Open button. The Import Mapping dialog box will open. The Selective Data tab will be enabled, as shown in Figure 19.12.

5. Choose the map you want to use and click the Open button. The data is imported into Project.

 TIP Click the Edit Button before clicking Open so that you can see the potential data conflicts between the import file and the Project table fields.

FIGURE 19.12

*The Import Mapping
dialog box for Excel
imports*

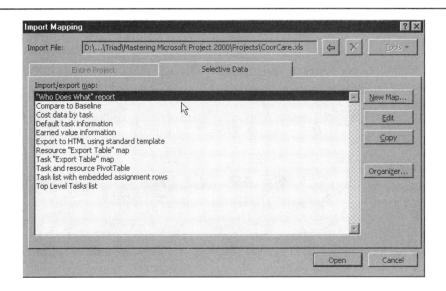

Importing Data from Excel with a Custom Import Data Map

There are two ways to create a customized import data map: by copying and modifying an existing map, or by starting from scratch and adding fields from the import source and then mapping them to their corresponding fields in the Project Resource, Assignment, and Task tables.

Modifying a Copy of an Existing Map   A Notes column has been added to our Excel spreadsheet (see Figure 19.13). We want to import the spreadsheet, including importing data from this column to the Notes field of our project's Resources table. We'll copy and modify the "Who Does What" Report Map to add this field to the import, and save the modified data map as **Annotated Resources and Assignments**.

FIGURE 19.13

*The modified Excel
spreadsheet includes a
Notes column.*

	A	B	C	D	E
1	Resources and Assignments	Notes	Start	Finish	Work
2	Nielsen Design Group	This is the group that will design the templates	2/24/00 10:00	3/14/00 11:00	40 hrs
3	Template design		2/24/00 10:00	3/14/00 11:00	40 hrs
4	James Howe	This is the programmer	2/10/00 9:00	3/5/02 15:00	430.5 hrs
5	1Stop Team Meetings 1	First of 19 Monthly Meetings	2/10/00 9:00	2/10/00 11:00	2 hrs
6	1Stop Team Meetings 2	Second of 19 Monthly Meetings	3/9/00 9:00	3/9/00 11:00	2 hrs
7	1Stop Team Meetings 3	Third of 19 Monthly Meetings	4/13/00 9:00	4/13/00 11:00	2 hrs
8	1Stop Team Meetings 4	Fourth of 19 Monthly Meetings	5/11/00 9:00	5/11/00 11:00	2 hrs
9	1Stop Team Meetings 5		6/15/00 9:00	6/15/00 11:00	2 hrs
10	1Stop Team Meetings 6		7/13/00 9:00	7/13/00 11:00	2 hrs
11	1Stop Team Meetings 7		8/10/00 9:00	8/10/00 11:00	2 hrs
12	1Stop Team Meetings 8		9/14/00 9:00	9/14/00 11:00	2 hrs
13	1Stop Team Meetings 9		10/12/00 9:00	10/12/00 11:00	2 hrs
14	1Stop Team Meetings 10		11/9/00 9:00	11/9/00 11:00	2 hrs
15	1Stop Team Meetings 11		12/14/00 9:00	12/14/00 11:00	2 hrs
16	1Stop Team Meetings 12		1/11/01 9:00	1/11/01 11:00	2 hrs
17	1Stop Team Meetings 13		2/15/01 9:00	2/15/01 11:00	2 hrs
18	1Stop Team Meetings 14		3/15/01 9:00	3/15/01 11:00	2 hrs

1. In Project, open the project file into which you will import the data. (If you do not open a project file, a new project will be created with the imported data.)

2. Choose File ➤ Open. The File Open dialog box is displayed.

3. Change the Files of Type to Microsoft Excel Workbook (XLS).

4. Use the Look In drop-down list to locate the proper folder and file.

5. Select the file and click the Open button. The Import Mapping dialog box is displayed with the Selective Data tab active, as shown in Figure 19.14.

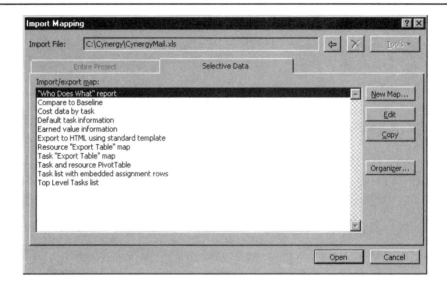

6. Select the report you want to modify and click the Copy button to display the Define Import/Export Map dialog box.

7. Select and replace the Import/Export Map Name Copy of... with the name you'll use for the template.

8. Enable the Export Header Row/Import Includes Headers checkbox.

9. If your spreadsheet contains fields in the Assignment table, click the Include Assignment Rows in Output checkbox. This organizes exported data so that assignment rows appear below tasks or resources, similar to the Task Usage and Resource Usage views.

10. Click OK to return to the Import Mapping dialog box.

11. The map name you entered in step 7 should be selected. If it is not, select it. Click the Edit button.

12. Select the table tab you want to map. The Field Mapping Detail dialog box is displayed. Fields that were included in the predefined import map are already mapped in the Mapped Field List, as shown in Figure 19.15.

FIGURE 19.15

*The Resource Mapping
tab, which contains the
Field Mapping Detail*

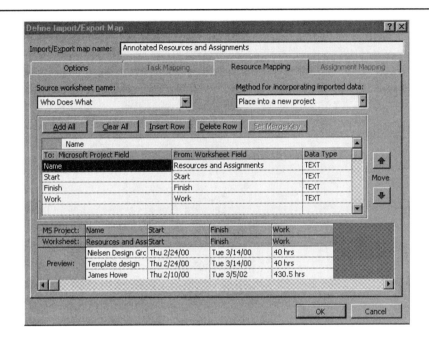

13. If your Excel file has more than one worksheet, select the worksheet you wish to import from the Source Worksheet Name drop-down list.

14. Select the Method for Incorporating Imported Data.

15. Map a field by clicking in the first empty cell in the From: Worksheet Field column. The drop-down list contains unmapped fields from the selected worksheet. Select the field you wish to map.

16. Click on the first empty cell in the To: Microsoft Project Field column. This list contains all the unused fields in the table shown on this dialog box tab. Select the Project field that the data should be imported into.

Repeat Steps 15 and 16 for each field you wish to map.

17. Click OK to save the changes to the Import Map.

18. Click the Open button in the Import Mapping DIALOG BOX to begin the import.

Creating a New Import Map to Update Existing Project Data A spreadsheet, shown in Figure 19.16, contains resource names and new email addresses. We will update the specific project fields with the new email addresses based on a unique merge key: a field with no duplicate values that appears in both the project table and the Excel worksheet. The unique key is used by Project to put the email addresses with the right names, which we think is a good idea.

FIGURE 19.16

The spreadsheet containing resource names and email addresses is used to update the resource information in Project.

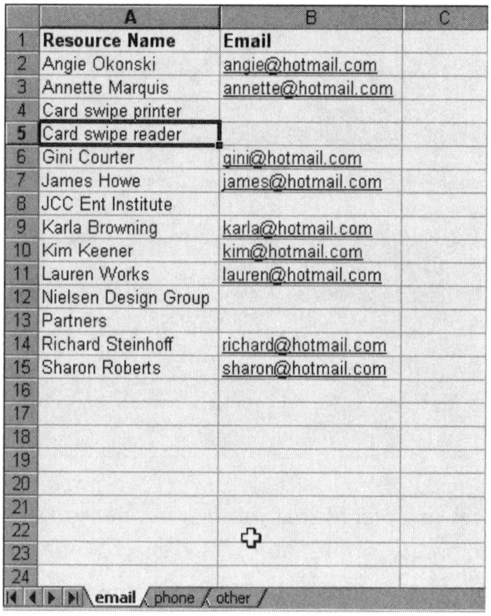

	A	B	C
1	**Resource Name**	**Email**	
2	Angie Okonski	angie@hotmail.com	
3	Annette Marquis	annette@hotmail.com	
4	Card swipe printer		
5	Card swipe reader		
6	Gini Courter	gini@hotmail.com	
7	James Howe	james@hotmail.com	
8	JCC Ent Institute		
9	Karla Browning	karla@hotmail.com	
10	Kim Keener	kim@hotmail.com	
11	Lauren Works	lauren@hotmail.com	
12	Nielsen Design Group		
13	Partners		
14	Richard Steinhoff	richard@hotmail.com	
15	Sharon Roberts	sharon@hotmail.com	
16			
17			
18			
19			
20			
21			
22			
23			
24			

email / phone / other /

In our example, we'll use Resource Name as the unique merge key. The spreadsheet contains each person's name only once, and each resource name in Project must be unique. To facilitate this update, we'll create a new import data map named Resource Email Addresses.

1. In Project 2000, open the project file into which you will import the data. Go to the view that will contain your updated data. Make sure that all fields you want to import to are displayed in the view.

NOTE For our example, we've added a column to the Resource Sheet View to contain email addresses, as shown in Figure 19.17. (See Chapter 17, "Using Views to Evaluate Data," if you want detailed instructions on modifying views.)

FIGURE 19.17

The Resource Sheet View has been modified to contain the Email address field. Now, we will instantly be able to see if the Import was successful.

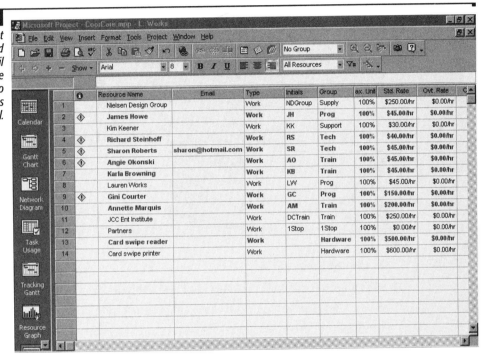

2. When you create the import data map, you need to know the full name of each Project field you want to map to. Often, field names are shortened for use in views and reports. To determine the full correct name for a field, double-click the field heading to open the Column Definition dialog box, shown in Figure 19.18. The field's name appears in the Field Name text box. Note the Name, and then close the Column Definition dialog box without making changes.

FIGURE 19.18

Check the names of fields you want to map in the Column Defini-tion dialog box.

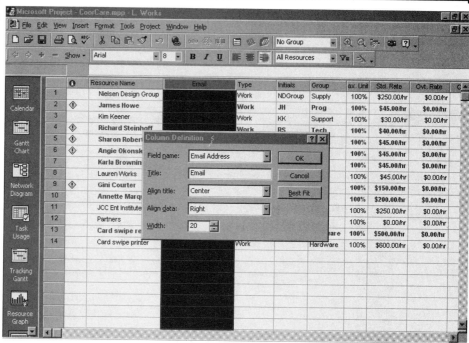

3. Choose File ➤ Open.

4. In the Open dialog box, change the Files of Type to Microsoft Excel Workbook (XLS).

5. Use the Look In drop-down list to locate the proper folder and file.

6. Select the file and click the Open button. The Import Mapping dialog box is displayed with the Selective Data tab activated.

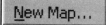

7. Click the New Map Button. The Define Import/Export Map dialog box is displayed. Enter a name for the map.

8. Select the tables you are importing data into in the Data to Import/Export section to activate the table tabs.

9. Enable the Export Header Row/Import Includes Headers checkbox on the Options tab.

10. Select the first table Mapping Tab. The Field Mapping Detail dialog box is displayed, as shown in Figure 19.19.

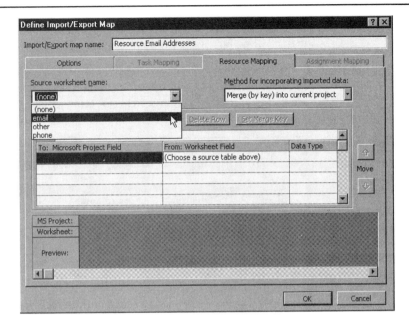

FIGURE 19.19

*The Resource Mapping
dialog box is ready
to create a new
import map.*

11. Select the Source Worksheet Name in the Excel workbook.

12. Select Merge (by key) Into Current Project as the Method for Incorporating
    Imported Data. The Import File header names are now displayed, as shown in
    Figure 19.20. It is time to map the Project Field Names.

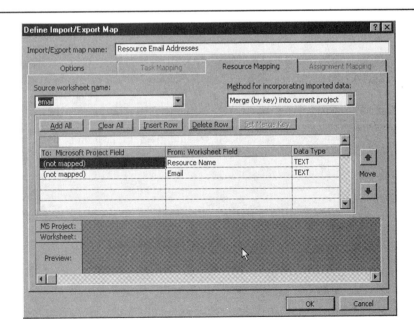

FIGURE 19.20

*Resource Mapping
dialog box now knows
which spreadsheet to
get the fields from.*

13. Click on the first empty cell in the To: Microsoft Project Field column. This list contains all the unused fields in the table. Select the fields you want to import data into and their corresponding worksheet fields.

14. Select the field with unique records in both the project table and the import data source that will be used to find records for the merge process, and click the Set Merge Key button. The merge fields are now set (see Figure 19.21).

FIGURE 19.21

After the Merge Key is set, you can still change it to another field in the field list.

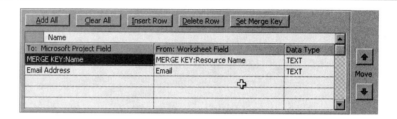

15. Click OK to save the changes to the import map.

16. Make sure that your new map is selected, and then click the Open button in the Import Mapping dialog box to begin the import and update your Project files.

Importing Text Files

Text files are even more common than Excel workbooks. The Windows Notepad application creates text files, but any word processor can export a text file. On Web pages, the submit forms that are used to gather information about visitors, customers, or user logins often save the results in text files.

Why Might You Import Data from a Text File?

- You have access to data created in an application such as Microsoft Word or the Windows Notepad that is needed in your project, and you don't want to retype it all

- You work with an outside source that uses a non-Windows operating system and you need to exchange project information.

- You are plagued with space constraints, and text files are the most compact format.

Text files use these file formats: TXT, CSV.

Before you begin importing a text file, open it and make sure that the file is delimited with either tabs, commas, or spaces between each field. One of the three delimiters has to be used throughout the file. You can't import a file when some fields are separated by spaces and others are separated by commas, for example. In either the TXT or CSV format, a standard carriage return (hard return) separates records.

For word processing documents, open the file in its native application and choose Save As. Select the tab-delimited text file (TXT) or Comma-Separated Values (CSV) file format. If there is not already a header record, enter one at the top of the file with unique descriptive headings for each column. This will greatly ease the import process by displaying import field names to match against the Project field names.

MASTERING THE OPPORTUNITIES

Manipulating Text Files

You can't always dictate the quality of the data you receive. You often have to take what you get. You request a list of materials to add to your project's Resource Sheet and someone saves the contents of a Word document, including the materials table, into a text file. Then, they add some data separated by spaces or commas from another Word

document. Or, an Excel worksheet that includes commas within cells (such as 512 West Elm Street, Apt. 2) is saved as a CSV file. The commas within the record act as delimiters, which means that Apt.2 becomes the City, the city name is used for a State field, and so on. In both of these examples the file has the data you need, but not in a format you can import. Does this happen? Absolutely. When it does, here are the strategies we use to "shake and bake" the data into a usable form:

Determine what the data really looks like. Open the text file in Word, and click the Show/Hide button on the standard toolbar. With the non-printing characters displayed, data separated by tabs looks very different than data separated by hitting the space bar a few times:

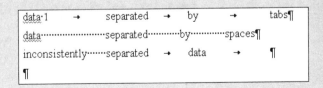

Continued

If the file appears to be largely tab-delimited, use Word's Convert Text To Table feature (Table ➤ Convert ➤ Text to Table) to pour the text into a table. Records that are formatted differently from the first record stand out because they don't fill all the cells in a table row. Use copy and paste to put data in the correct columns of the table. When the data is consistent, use Convert Table to Text (Table ➤ Convert ➤ Table to Text) to convert the table to tab-delimited text or comma-delimited text:

If a file has more than one field's value in a column (for example, the resource's group name is followed by its full name) or if it uses more than one field for a single Project field (for example, separate first name and last name fields when Project uses a single field, Resource Name), open the file in Excel. You may be required to complete some minimal mapping before Excel will open the file, but it's worth your time. Excel is the best place to deal with data that is consistent, but it needs to be split or combined. Use Excel's Text to Columns feature (Data ➤ Text to Columns) to separate a single field into multiple columns.

To combine two columns (first name and last name) into a single column, create a formula. If, for example, the first names are in column A and the last names are in B, this formula will combine cells A5 and B5, including a space between the two to produce a full name that can be imported into the Resource Name field in Project 2000:

```
=A5&" "&B5
```

When you're finished parsing the data into the fields you need, choose File ➤ Save As and save the document as a text file, or save the document in Excel and import the Excel workbook.

Importing a Text File Using an Existing Import Map

Follow these steps to use a predefined import data map to import data from a delimited text file:

1. In Project 2000, choose File ➤ Open to display the Open dialog box.

2. Change the Files of Type to Text (TXT) or Comma-Separated Values (CSV).

3. Use the Look In drop-down list to locate the proper folder and file.

4. Select the file and click the Open button. Select Open. The Import Mapping dialog box is displayed.

5. Select the correct Import Map and click the Edit button. The Define Import/ Export Map dialog box will be displayed, as shown in Figure 19.22.

The Define Import/ Export Map dialog box is used to map data from text files.

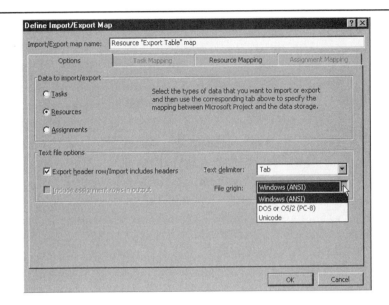

6. Select the text delimiter (Tab, Space, or Comma) used in your file.

7. Select the File Origin: Windows, DOS or OS/2, or Unicode.

8. Click OK to close the dialog box.

9. Click Open on the Import Mapping dialog box to import your data into Project.

Creating a New Import Map for a Text File

1. In Project 2000, open the project file into which you will import the data. Go to the view that will contain your updated data. Make sure that all fields you want to import to are displayed in the view.

TIP When you create the import data map, you need to know the full name of each field you want to map to. To determine the full correct name for a field, double-click the field heading to open the Column Definition dialog box. The field's name appears in the Field Name text box.

2. Choose File ➤ Open.

3. In the Open dialog box, change the Files of Type to TXT or CSV.

4. Use the Look In drop-down list to locate the proper folder and file.

5. Select the file and click the Open button. The Import Mapping dialog box is displayed with the Selective Data tab activated.

6. Click the New Map Button. The Define Import/Export Map dialog box is displayed. Enter a name for the map.

7. Select the type of data you are importing: Tasks, Resources, or Assignments. The corresponding tab in the dialog box is activated based on your choice.

8. Enable the Export Header Row/Import Includes Headers checkbox.

9. Select the appropriate mapping tab: Task Mapping, Resource Mapping, or Assignment Mapping.

10. Select a Method for Incorporating Imported Data. Project will display the header names from the import file.

11. Click on the first empty cell in the To: Microsoft Project Field column. Select the fields you want to import data into.

12. In the From: Text file, select the corresponding fields from the text file.

13. If you're updating existing records, select the field with unique records in both the project table and the import data source that will be used to find records for the merge process, and click the Set Merge Key button.

14. Click OK to save the changes to the Import Map.

15. Make sure that your new map is selected, and then click the Open button in the Import Mapping dialog box to begin the import.

Importing Data from Databases

In large and mid-sized organizations, much of the data project that managers would deem worth importing is housed in databases. The departments that own information you want to include in your project file—Personnel, Materials Management, Manufacturing, and Purchasing, for example—are big-time database users. Database applications give them a place to store all the excellent information that project managers like you and I covet.

Why Might You Import Data from a Database?

- You work for a behemoth and the only databases that can hold all of your employee data are on a mainframe.
- You have specific Access applications that team members use for reporting progress.
- Resource or materials information is stored in an Access database.
- You ran queries on multiple project files in a database and have updated them accordingly. Now you need to put the data back in Project 2000.
- You need to open a project created in Project 4 and stored in an Access database (MDB) file.

Database files use these file formats: MPD, MDB, and various ODBC formats.

Upgrading Project Databases

If you saved Microsoft Project 98 projects in a database, you can upgrade the entire database to the Microsoft Project 2000 database format, whether the databases were saved in a Project, Access, or another ODBC format. You can upgrade the existing databases to the original database or another database.

The database upgrade utility uses Visual Basic code, so you must set the macro security level to low before you can use the utility. To set the security level, choose Tools ➢ Macro ➢ Security to open the Security dialog box. On the Security Level tab, choose the Low option, then click OK to close the dialog box. (After running the utility, it's a good idea to reset the security level to Medium.) Close all open database files, then display the Database Upgrade toolbar (View ➢ Toolbars ➢ Database Upgrade Utility). This toolbar has only one button. Click it to open the Database Upgrade Utility dialog box, shown in Figure 19.23.

In the left pane, choose the database file that contains the projects you wish to upgrade. Click to select individual projects in the file, or click the Select All button to select all projects. In the right pane, choose a target type and location. Select the same location as in the left pane to upgrade the existing database or DSN; click the New button to create a new DSN or database file. After setting the source and target information, click Upgrade to create the target database or DSN.

FIGURE 19.23

Upgrade project
databases from a
variety of ODBC
compatible formats
with the Database
Upgrade Utility.

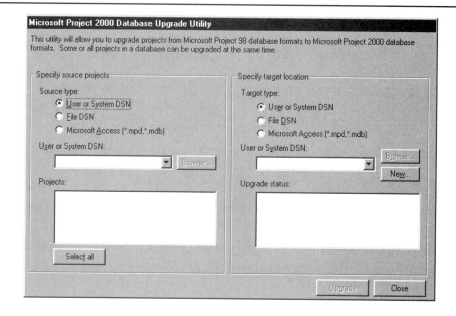

Importing a Project from a Project Database

Microsoft Project Database (MPD) is a proprietary file format for an Access database. It contains all project data for one or many projects. Project Database is the preferred method of exchanging project data, replacing the MPX format used in Project 4.

To import a complete project from a Project Database:

1. Start Project.

2. Choose File ➤ Open.

TIP   The Files of Type default is All Project Files (MP*), so file lists can get quite long if you're a busy project manager. (Is there any other type?) Change the Files of Type to Project Database (MPD) to limit your search.

3. Use the Look In drop-down list to locate the proper folder and file.

4. Select the database and click the Open button. The Open From Database dialog box is displayed.

5. On the Entire Project tab (see Figure 19.24), select the project you want to import.

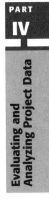

IGURE 19.24

*The Entire Project tab
ntains a list of all the
projects contained in
the database.*

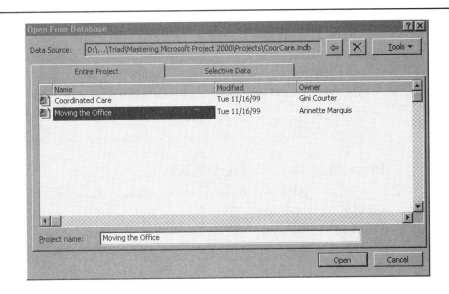

6. Click Open in the Import Mapping dialog box to import your data into Project.

 WARNING If project data in the MPD file has been changed by using an application other than Project, it may no longer be compatible with Project's table and field definitions. If any inconsistencies are encountered during an import, Project generates an Error Log so you can make corrections to the file.

Importing Data from an Access Database

Follow the procedure listed as follows to import an entire project from an Access database or to use a predefined data map. To edit or create a data map, see "Creating a New Import Map" in "Importing Data from Excel," earlier in this chapter.

1. Start Project.

2. Choose File ➢ Open.

3. The Files of Type to Microsoft Access Databases (MDB).

4. Use the Look In drop-down list to locate the proper folder and database file.

5. Select the file and click the Open button to open the Import Mapping dialog box.

6. You can import Entire Projects or Selective Data from Access. If the database you selected contains complete project files, both tabs will be enabled. If not, only the Selective Data tab will be active.

7. To import an entire project, select the project from the list on the Entire Projects Tab and click Open to begin importing data.

   OR

   To import selected data, select an import map on the Selective Data tab.

8. Click the Edit button to open the Define Import/Export Map dialog box.

9. Ensure that the data fields correctly map to the Project Table fields. Click OK.

10. Click Open on the Import Mapping dialog box to import your database into Project.

Importing Data Using ODBC

Importing with ODBC is a two-step process: setting up the ODBC connection and importing the data as you would from other file types. Follow the procedure listed as follows to link to an ODBC data source:

1. In Project 2000, choose File ➤ Open to display the Open dialog box.

2. Click the ODBC button. The Select Data Source dialog box, shown in Figure 19.25, opens.

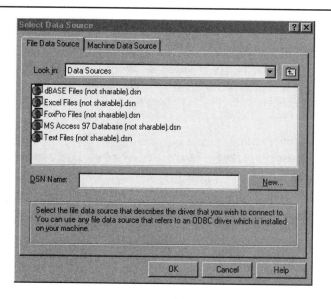

3. Select the tab (File Data Source or Machine Data Source) that lists the data source you want to open. Machine Data Source, the recommended choice, creates a data source that can be used by any user on this computer.

4. Choose the data source and click OK. The Select Database dialog box, shown in Figure 19.26, is displayed.

FIGURE 19.26

the Select Database
dialog box, you can
lect the database file
you want to import.

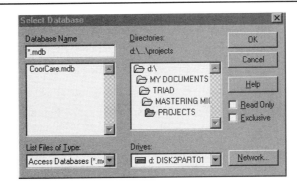

5. Select the database file you want to import and click OK. After you've selected your data source, you can select a database, and then set up your import. Follow these steps to import an entire project or selected data using an existing Import data map. To edit or create a new import data map, see "Creating a New Import Map" in "Importing Data from Excel," earlier in this chapter.

6. The Open From Database dialog box is displayed:

- To import an entire project, select a project from the list on the Entire Projects Tab and click Open.

- To import selected data, select the correct Import Map on the Selective Data Tab and click the Edit button. The Define Import/Export Map dialog box will be displayed. Ensure that the data fields correctly map to the Project Table fields. Click OK .

7. Click Open on the Import Mapping dialog box to import your database into Project.

Moving a Microsoft Outlook Task List to Microsoft Project

Project and Outlook support two common file formats: Access and Excel. We'll export data from Outlook to Excel, create a custom data map, and import the data from Excel into Project. To play along, you need to have Outlook 98 or 2000; and Excel 95, 97, or 2000 installed on your computer. This is a multi-step process, but well worth the effort if your team uses Outlook as its Personal Information Management software.

Step 1: Exporting Tasks from Outlook to Excel

1. Open Microsoft Outlook and switch to the Tasks view.

2. Select File ➤ Import and Export to open the Import/Export Wizard. If the Wizard doesn't open or if the Import and Export menu item is disabled, run Outlook or Office Setup to install the Import/Export Wizard. (While you're at it, you may want to see what else wasn't installed the first time.)

3. In the first step of the Wizard, choose Export to a File. Click Next.

4. In the Create a File Of Type list, select Microsoft Excel. Click Next.

5. In the Select a Folder To Export From list, accept the default selection, Tasks. Click Next.

6. In the Save Exported File as text box, type a name for the Excel file you're creating. Click Next.

7. Click Map Custom Fields to display the Map Custom Fields dialog box (see Figure 19.27) so you can verify the fields you want to export.

FIGURE 19.27

In the Map Custom Fields dialog box, you can select and verify the fields you want to export.

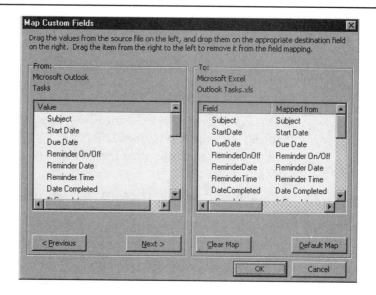

8. You can remove Outlook fields from the export list now if you know you won't want to import particular fields into Microsoft Project. When you have finished removing fields from the export list, click OK to return to the Export to a File dialog box.

9. Click Finish to create the Microsoft Excel file.

Step 2: Massaging the Imported Data in Microsoft Excel

1. In Microsoft Excel, open the file you just created.

2. Delete any thick bars—or open squares—in the Notes column or any other column. (These are symbols for non-printing characters.) If you leave these symbols in the file, they'll cause import errors in Project. The symbols are more of an issue in Outlook 98 than in Outlook 2000, but it doesn't hurt to check! (Think of it as a symbolic gesture.)

3. If your export includes the Priority column, use Excel's Replace feature (Edit ➤ Replace) to replace the word **Normal** with **Medium** to translate Outlook's middle-priority setting into Project-speak.

4. Check the values in the TotalWork and ActualWork columns against the task information in your Outlook task list. These columns map to Duration and Actual Work in Microsoft Project. In some cases, Excel imports the Outlook values and converts them to minutes, and in others, into hours. You should adjust all values to days or fractions of days before importing the file into Microsoft Project.

5. Save your file. Close Excel if you wish.

Step 3: Importing the Excel Data into Microsoft Project

1. Open the XLS file in Project. Select File ➤ Open. Select XLS in the Files of Type list, locate your Excel spreadsheet file, and then click Open to display the Import Mapping dialog box.

2. Click the New Map button to open the Define Import/Export Map dialog box.

3. Type a name for the new map, such as **Outlook Tasks From Excel,** in the Import/Export Map Name text box. Select the Import Includes Headers checkbox, and choose Tasks in the Data to Import/Export area.

4. Click the Task Mapping tab and map the fields you want to import. You do not have to map every field on the spreadsheet. See Table 19.4 for frequently exported Outlook task fields and their corresponding Project fields. (For information on fields that aren't included in the table, see the topic "About standard fields in Microsoft Outlook in Microsoft Outlook Help" and the "Task Fields topic in Microsoft Project 2000 Help.")

5. When your map is complete, click OK to return to the Import Mapping dialog box. Select your map and click Open to begin importing your Outlook Tasks into Project.

PART

IV

Evaluating and
Analyzing Project Data

TABLE 19.4: OUTLOOK AND PROJECT TASK FIELDS MAP

Outlook field	Project field	Comment
Start Date	Start (scheduled start), Actual Start	Outlook tasks don't have to have a start date, but Microsoft Project tasks do. If you have many blank start dates in Outlook, don't map Start Date; otherwise, the empty cells will default to today's date.
		Tasks that do have a start date in Outlook will be imported with the Start No Earlier Than constraint applied (or Start No Later Than if the project is scheduled from the finish date).
Due Date	Finish	There is no corresponding field in Microsoft Project to Outlook's Due Date. The closest field is the Finish field, which shows the date and time that a task is scheduled to be completed.
		Tasks that do have a due date in Outlook will be imported with the Finish No Earlier Than constraint applied (or Finish No Later Than if the project is scheduled from the finish date).
Total Work	Duration	Outlook stores Total Work in minutes. (Outlook assumes an 8-hour workday.) Convert to days in Excel before importing.
Priority	Priority	Must change Outlook's default priority, Normal, to **Medium**.
Subject	Name	(this is the task name)
% Complete	% Complete	(field name exports as "_Complete")
Date Completed	Actual Finish	
Actual Work	Actual Work	
Notes	Notes	
Contacts	Contact	
Categories	Project, Text1–Text30	
Billing Information, Mileage, Status, etc.	Text1–Text30, or Number1–Number20.	Microsoft Project provides 30 blank text fields and 20 blank number fields you can re-title and use for miscellaneous information.

Exporting Data from Project

The knowledge amassed in a typical project can benefit the entire organization. But the best way to share this information is not always a Gantt Chart. You can create reports, publications and presentations. You can send selected project data to a spreadsheet for some serious financial analyses. You can also, using Microsoft Project Central, send information to Outlook Task folders. When you're starting a project, you'll be very motivated to import data because it saves time for you and your team. At the end of the project, export critical data to provide a jumpstart for the next project—you might be the project manager!

Using the Export Tools

As with the Import section of this chapter, we'll begin with a quick review of the dialog boxes and controls you'll use to export files. You'll use the same tools to map fields. Although Excel worksheets are used in this illustration, the dialog boxes displayed and the steps taken to Create, Modify and Use Export data maps are the same for all Project file formats.

When you save a project file in a non-native file format, you're exporting the file. Choose File ➤ Save As to open the Save As dialog box.

Use the controls to choose a file type and location:

Save As Type   Select the format of your new file.

Look In or Places bar   Select the destination of your saved file.

ODBC button   Used to select an ODBC data source, this button opens the Select Data source dialog box. You'll find information about data sources in the "Importing from a Database" section, earlier in this chapter.

If you're exporting to any destination other than an ODBC database, click the Save button to open the Export Mapping dialog box, and select or create a data map for use in the export.

Defining the Data to Export

From the Save As dialog box, the next stop is the Export Mapping dialog box (see Figure 19.28), which looks amazingly like the Import Mapping dialog box. (We think they were identical twins, separated at birth.) The file name in the Export File text box at the top of the dialog box should be the file that you want to export data to. If it is not, click the Back button to return to the Open dialog box.

FIGURE 19.28

Define the data you
want to export in
the Export Mapping
dialog box.

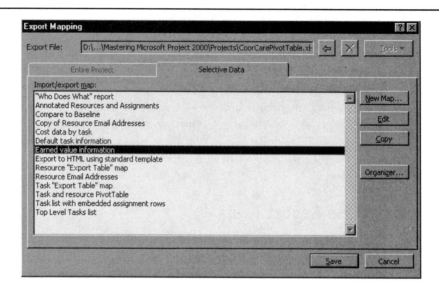

The Export Mapping dialog box includes two tabs, which are enabled or disabled based on the file type you chose to export to:

Export Entire Project tab   Options on this tab allow you to export an entire project file. Although this tab is always displayed, it is inactive unless you choose to export to a native format for an earlier version of Project: MPP, MPD, MPX, or MDB.

Export Selective Data tab   This tab is always displayed and enabled. It lists predefined data maps included with Project 2000 or created by the user (see Figure 19.28).

NOTE   Data maps are stored in the global template file (GLOBAL.MPT) so they can be exchanged between project files by using the Organizer.

Creating and Modifying Data Maps   You aren't limited to the existing maps. You can create a new map from scratch, edit an existing map, copy and modify a map, or copy maps from other Microsoft Project files:

New Map button   Create a new data map.

Edit button   Modify the current data map.

Copy button   Make a copy of the current data map.

Organizer button   Copy maps from other projects and templates to this project's list of available data maps. (See Chapter 21, "Customizing Project 2000," for more information on the Organizer.)

Setting Options for the Exported Data File   Selecting the New Map, Edit, or Copy Button opens the Define Import/Export Map dialog box, shown in Figure 19.29.

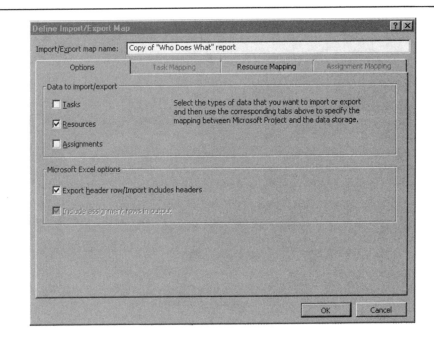

If you've imported data from external file formats into Project 2000, you're probably familiar with this dialog box. The controls on the Options tab include

Import/Export Map Name   Contains the current Map name; type in the name of your new Import/Export Map.

Table Selection   You are given the option to select which tables in Project contain the data you will be exporting (Task, Resource, Assignment). As a table is selected, the tab associated with it becomes active and you can map the fields contained on that table.

Export Header Row/Import Include Headers   Selecting this option sends descriptive header fields, along with the data being exported.

Include Assignment Rows in Output   Project organizes exported data so that assignment rows appear below tasks or resources, similar to the Task Usage and Resource Usage views.

Text Delimiter (text files only)   Defines the character used to indicate that a field has ended. The choices are Tab, Space, and Comma. Tab is the default for TXT files and Comma is the default for CSV files.

File Origin (text files only)   Specifies the system character set of the data to be exported. This is Windows (ANSI) for all Project files.

Set options for your exported file, and then move to the tabs for each of the tables you checked in the Table Selection checkboxes to map the export fields.

Mapping Exported Data on the Mapping Tabs   Selecting the Task, Resource, or Assignment Table Mapping tabs opens the Table Mapping dialog box, as shown in Figure 19.30.

FIGURE 19.30

Use the Table Mapping dialog box to map Project fields to the export file.

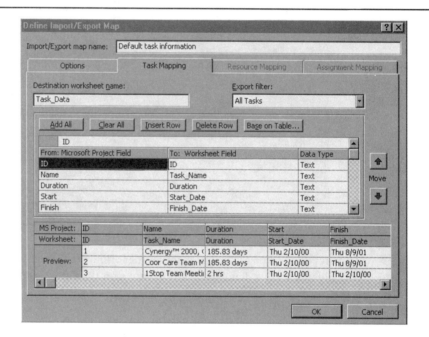

Although different data fields are available on each table's tab, the same dialog box opens. Use the dialog box controls to select the location for exported data within the export file and, if you wish, a filter for the exported data.

Destination Worksheet Name   Type a name in the box for the database table, worksheet, or HTML table title. This field is not available for text files (TXT and CSV).

Export Filter drop-down list   Select an option from the Export filter box to select only certain tasks or resources to be exported. This contains all the filtering options available in Project.

Add All button   Adds all of the fields from the source file to import to the import/export map.

Clear All button   Removes all the mapped fields from Mapped Field List.

Insert Row button   Inserts a blank row above the selected row in the Mapped Field List.

Delete Row button   Deletes the selected row from the Mapped Field List.

Base on Table button   Adds all of the fields contained in a task or resource table to the map.

FROM: Microsoft Project Field column   Choose field names from the drop-down list in each row to specify the fields that you want to export, as shown in Figure 19.31.

FIGURE 19.31

Select the fields you want to export from the Project Field drop-down list.

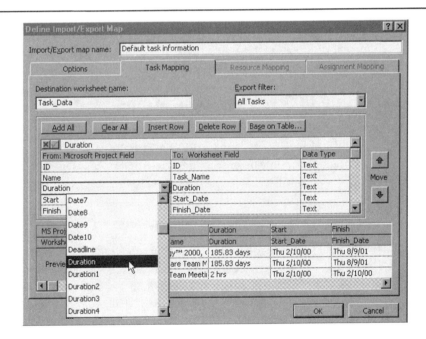

TO: Worksheet/Database/Table/Text Field column   Enter field names in the rows to specify the fields that you want to create. Each field must have a unique name within the imported file.

Data Type column   Format of the data contained in each row. For some file formats (such as XLS and TXT), all of the Data Types will appear as text, even though they might be numerical in the project table definitions.

Move Up and Move Down buttons   Use these buttons to move the selected row up or down in the Mapped Field List.

The preview pane at the bottom of the dialog box changes to reflect the data map you're creating. Each column contains the field name from Microsoft Project, the field name in the export file, and a preview of the first three rows of data from the selected Project table, as shown in Figure 19.32.

MS Project:	ID		Name	Duration	Start	Finish
Worksheet:	ID		Task_Name	Duration	Start_Date	Finish_Date
Preview:	1		Cynergy™ 2000, (	185.83 days	Thu 2/10/00	Thu 8/9/01
	2		Coor Care Team M	185.83 days	Thu 2/10/00	Thu 8/9/01
	3		1Stop Team Meeti	2 hrs	Thu 2/10/00	Thu 2/10/00

If you're exporting data from more than one table, map the fields on each table's mapping tab. Click OK to close the Table Mapping dialog box and return to the Export Mapping dialog box. Click the OK tab to begin exporting your file.

Exporting to Specific Applications

In this section, you'll find step-by-step instructions and examples for exporting Project 2000 files to specific applications. As with importing, the export routines for each application vary only because of the different file formats used by applications. Whether you're exporting Excel, Access, Project, ODBC databases, or text files, you use the same tools.

Exporting to Project 98

You could import files from all the prior versions of Project, but this is a one-way street for Project 4 files. Project 2000 doesn't export to the MPX format. This means that, unless you save your project as a Project 98 MPP and then open Microsoft Project 98 and save your file as a previous version, you can't export a project file to earlier versions of Project such as Project 4.

Why Might You Export Data to a Project 98 File?

- An ongoing project has spanned multiple releases of Microsoft Project and your organization was the first to upgrade.
- Projects are being shared between groups with different versions of Microsoft Project.

Project 98 uses these file formats: MPP, MPT.

To save a project file as a Project 98 MPP:

1. Open the project that you want to save.
2. Select File ➤ Save As to open the Save As dialog box.
3. Select Microsoft Project 98 (*.mpp) in the Save as Type drop-down list.
4. Select the destination for the new file the Look In drop-down list or Places bar.
5. Choose a destination file name from the file list, or type in a new name.
6. Click the Save button. Your file will be exported.

Exporting to Microsoft Excel Workbooks and Pivot Tables

You can export Project field data to Microsoft Excel either as a spreadsheet or as a pivot table (two worksheets in a workbook). Because Excel data is not stored relationally, Assignment records that are associated with resources and tasks can be exported to Excel, but they will not be formatted (outlined and indented) as in Project. Assignment rows will appear below their corresponding Task or Resource rows, but will be indistinguishable. Create a new Import/Export Data map that contains the Assignment flag (yes/no) from the task or resource table will give you a column to filter on or use in formulas.

Why Might You Export Data to an Excel Workbook?

- It's time for some serious number-crunching.
- You want to run some "what if?" scenarios using Excel's Solver to support your project-management decisions.
- Pivot tables are the best way to graphically show relationships.

Microsoft Excel uses this file format: XLS.

Exporting to a Workbook Follow these steps to use an existing import/export map to export project data to an Excel Workbook. If you need to create or modify an import/export map, see "Creating a New Import Map to Update Existing Project Data" in the "Importing Microsoft Excel Workbooks" section, earlier in this chapter.

1. Open the project you want to export.
2. Select File ➢ Save As. The File Save dialog box is displayed.
3. Select Microsoft Excel Workbook.xls in the Save as Type drop-down list.
4. Select the destination for the file in the Look In drop-down list or Places bar.
5. Choose a destination file name from the file list or type in a new name.
6. Click the Save button. The Selective Data tab of the Export Mapping dialog box is displayed.
7. Click the Export Header Row/Import Includes Headers checkbox so that columns will be named in the Excel file.
8. If you wish to export the Assignment rows to Excel, click the Include Assignment Rows In Output checkbox.
9. Select the Import/Export Map you want to use and click the Save button. Your Project data will be exported to an Excel workbook.

When you open the new Excel file, there is a separate worksheet for each of the tables defined in the Export Map you used, as shown in Figure 19.33. In addition, the assignment rows are listed under their corresponding Resource or Task rows.

FIGURE 19.33

An exported Excel file. Note that there are three worksheets, one for each of the Project tables in the Export Map. The highlighted rows are a task and its embedded assignments. Hard to tell the difference, isn't it?

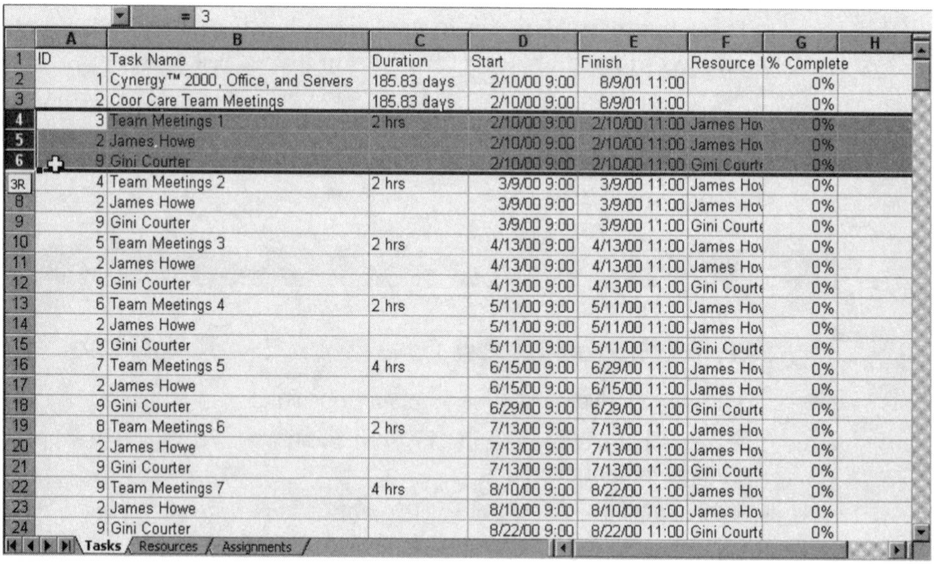

	A	B	C	D	E	F	G	H
1	ID	Task Name	Duration	Start	Finish	Resource I	% Complete	
2	1	Cynergy™ 2000, Office, and Servers	185.83 days	2/10/00 9:00	8/9/01 11:00		0%	
3	2	Coor Care Team Meetings	185.83 days	2/10/00 9:00	8/9/01 11:00		0%	
4	3	Team Meetings 1	2 hrs	2/10/00 9:00	2/10/00 11:00	James Hov	0%	
5	2	James Howe		2/10/00 9:00	2/10/00 11:00	James Hov	0%	
6	9	Gini Courter		2/10/00 9:00	2/10/00 11:00	Gini Court	0%	
3R	4	Team Meetings 2	2 hrs	3/9/00 9:00	3/9/00 11:00	James Hov	0%	
8	2	James Howe		3/9/00 9:00	3/9/00 11:00	James Hov	0%	
9	9	Gini Courter		3/9/00 9:00	3/9/00 11:00	Gini Court	0%	
10	5	Team Meetings 3	2 hrs	4/13/00 9:00	4/13/00 11:00	James Hov	0%	
11	2	James Howe		4/13/00 9:00	4/13/00 11:00	James Hov	0%	
12	9	Gini Courter		4/13/00 9:00	4/13/00 11:00	Gini Court	0%	
13	6	Team Meetings 4	2 hrs	5/11/00 9:00	5/11/00 11:00	James Hov	0%	
14	2	James Howe		5/11/00 9:00	5/11/00 11:00	James Hov	0%	
15	9	Gini Courter		5/11/00 9:00	5/11/00 11:00	Gini Court	0%	
16	7	Team Meetings 5	4 hrs	6/15/00 9:00	6/29/00 11:00	James Hov	0%	
17	2	James Howe		6/15/00 9:00	6/15/00 11:00	James Hov	0%	
18	9	Gini Courter		6/29/00 9:00	6/29/00 11:00	Gini Court	0%	
19	8	Team Meetings 6	2 hrs	7/13/00 9:00	7/13/00 11:00	James Hov	0%	
20	2	James Howe		7/13/00 9:00	7/13/00 11:00	James Hov	0%	
21	9	Gini Courter		7/13/00 9:00	7/13/00 11:00	Gini Court	0%	
22	9	Team Meetings 7	4 hrs	8/10/00 9:00	8/22/00 11:00	James Hov	0%	
23	2	James Howe		8/10/00 9:00	8/10/00 11:00	James Hov	0%	
24	9	Gini Courter		8/22/00 9:00	8/22/00 11:00	Gini Court	0%	

Exporting Data for an Excel PivotTable   A pivot table is a powerful tool for data analysis. Pivot tables summarize the columns of information in a database in relationship to each other. You will need to work with the pivot table, however, to make it beautiful, and to adjust the layout and tweak the data being charted. See your Excel documentation for more information on working with pivot tables.

The Task and Resource PivotTable Export Map comes predefined in Project 2000. (You can also create your own export data map using the steps described earlier in this chapter.) To export Project data to an Excel PivotTable, simply open your project file and do the following:

1. Choose File ➢ Save As from the menu.

2. In the Save As dialog box, select Excel PivotTable.xls from the Files of Type list.

3. Select a file location and enter a file name, and then click the Save button.

4. In the Export Mapping dialog box, select the Task and Resource PivotTable Export Map.

    If you click the Edit button, you will see the Define Import/Export Map dialog box. The Microsoft Excel Options pane has been replaced with the following message: "Exporting to Microsoft Excel PivotTable creates two sheets for each type of data you choose to export. One sheet contains the data used for the PivotTable and the other contains a default PivotTable. The last field in each map is used as the default data field for the PivotTable. All other fields are used as row fields in the Pivot Table."

5. Click Save to create your PivotTable file.

WARNING   Even if you use an Export Map specifically designed for a pivot table, you must select Excel PivotTable from the File of Type drop-down list. If you choose Excel Spreadsheet, you will have the same data exported, but the PivotTable worksheets will not be created.

Use the Analyze Timescaled Data Wizard to Export to Excel   The Analyze Timescaled Data Wizard exports cost data to Excel so that you can analyze costs and cost variances (including the PERT variances) by the day, month, or other period. Data exported from the XYZ-BOT project file is shown in Figure 19.34.

The Analyze Timescaled Data Wizard is launched from the Analysis toolbar (choose View ➢ Toolbars ➢ Analysis from the menu or right-click on any toolbar and choose Analysis).

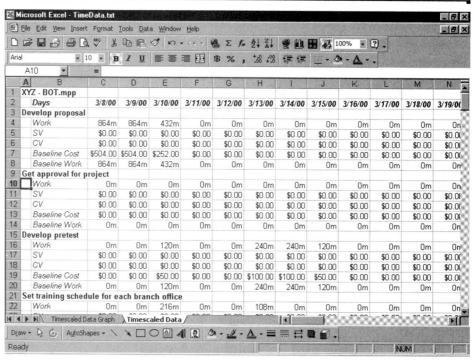

 TIP Like the PERT Analysis Toolbar in Chapter 13, "Assessing and Managing Risks," the Timescaled Data Wizard is a COM Add-In. If the Analysis toolbar does not appear on your toolbar list or if the Analysis toolbar does not include an Analyze Timescaled Data in Excel button, follow the steps in the Mastering Troubleshooting sidebar in Chapter 13 to install Anlyzts.dll.

You can export the entire project, or selected tasks. To export data using the wizard:

1. Switch to Gantt Chart view and display the Analysis toolbar (View ➢ Toolbars ➢ Analysis).

2. Select the tasks for which you want to export cost information.

3. Click the Analyze Timescaled Data in Excel button on the toolbar to launch the wizard.

4. In the first step of the wizard, choose Entire Project or Selected Tasks to export. Click Next.

5. In the second step of the wizard, shown in Figure 19.35, use the Add and Remove buttons to create the list of fields to export. In Excel, the fields will appear in the order they're listed in the Field to Export list. It's difficult to rearrange the fields in Excel (see Figure 19.34), so make sure they appear in the order you want before clicking Next.

6. In the third step of the wizard, shown in Figure 19.36, enter starting and ending dates for the export.

7. Choose a time unit from the Units drop-down list. Click Next.

8. In the fourth step, use the option buttons to indicate whether Excel should chart the exported data. Click Next.

9. In the final step, click the Export Data button to launch Excel and begin the export.

FIGURE 19.35

Use the Add and Remove buttons to create the export field list.

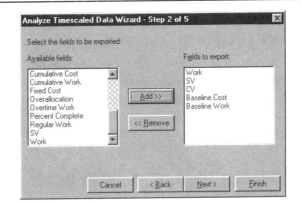

FIGURE 19.36

Choose a date range and reporting unit in the Analyze Time-scaled Data Wizard.

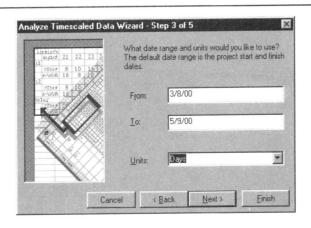

The exported data (refer to Figure 19.35) lists each task, followed by the timephased data for the fields you selected in the wizard. The final rows of the spreadsheet list totals for each field.

The wizard does not create row totals. To determine, for example, the total cost variance for the selected tasks, add totals in the first blank column in the Excel worksheet.

NOTE Why is Excel data stored in such an OLD format? Considering Project's structure and data requirements, nothing would be gained by saving XLS files to a later format. By saving to the earlier format, however, it is more compatible with the various versions of Excel still floating about. This ensures that Project can work with most versions of Excel without having to select explicit Save As choices for the version you're using.

Exporting Data to Text Files

Project 2000 allows you to export ASCII text in three different formats: comma-separated values (CVS), tab-delimited text (TXT), and space-delimited text (TXT). The Import/Export mapping process differs only in that only one Project table can be exported at a time. If you need to combine data from multiple tables, consider using the XLS or MDB formats. You could then further convert the data to a text format in Excel or Access.

Why Might You Export Data to a Text File?

- Text files are the most basically formatted and easily shared–especially with users who have older machines or software.
- Text files can be read by nearly all applications.
- Text files are small, so you can email data using a slower modem and not suffer too much.

Text files use these file formats: TXT, CSV.

Follow the procedure listed below to use a predefined export map. If you need to create or modify an import/export map, see "Creating a New Import Map to Update

Existing Project Data" in the "Importing Microsoft Excel Workbooks" section, earlier in this chapter.

1. Open the project file you wish to export.

2. Choose File ➤ Save As to open the Save As dialog box.

3. Change the Files of Type to Text (TXT) for tab or space-delimited files or CSV to create comma-delimited files.

4. Use the Look In drop-down list or Places bar to select your text file destination.

5. Select the file or type a file name, and click the Save button. The Export Mapping dialog box is displayed.

6. On the Selective Data tab, choose an Export Map and click the Edit button. The Define Import/Export Map dialog box will be displayed, as shown in Figure 19.37.

7. Select the text delimiter to use in your file. The choices are tab, space, and comma. Note the File Origin defaults to Windows and cannot be modified.

8. Click OK to accept the text file specifications.

9. Click Open on the Export Mapping dialog box to export your data into a text file.

FIGURE 19.37

You can designate the text delimiter to use in your file in the Define Import/Export Map dialog box for text files.

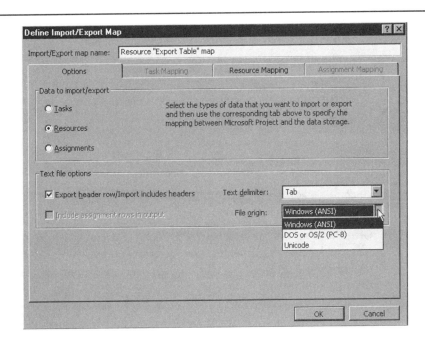

Exporting Data to Databases

Why Might You Export Data to a Database?

- To send project data for analysis on heavy-duty mainframe or mini-computer-based databases
- To query Project 2000 data using SQL and OLAP tools

Databases use these file formats: MPD, MDB, various ODBC formats.

Save an Entire Project as a Project Database (MPD) or Access Database (MDB)

This format saves your whole project into an Access database. The proprietary file extension for Project Database is MPD, and this is the preferable format to use when exchanging project data. An MPD file can contain multiple projects and be queried just like an Access Database (MDB).

1. Open the project you want to save as a Project Database file.
2. Choose File ➢ Save As.
3. In the Save As dialog box, select the destination for the database file.
4. Select MPD or MDB in the Save As Type drop-down list.
5. Type or select the file name for your exported database. Remember that database files can contain multiple projects when choosing a file name.
6. Click Save.
7. The Save to Database dialog box is displayed, as shown in Figure 19.38.
8. Choose to save the entire project file or export Selective Data.
9. Click Save to export your project database.

For an MPD file, Entire Project is the only export option available. Enter the Name To Give The Project In The Database. If your project has already been saved as a file, its file name will appear in the field. We recommend that you use descriptive names whenever possible—for instance, if you had a project database containing historical project data (the same project file at different times used for trend analysis), you would need to differentiate between projects that will likely have the same file name. Queries and reports that compare results of multiple projects are easily run against a Project database.

FIGURE 19.38

*Select or enter a
project name in the
Save to Database
dialog box.*

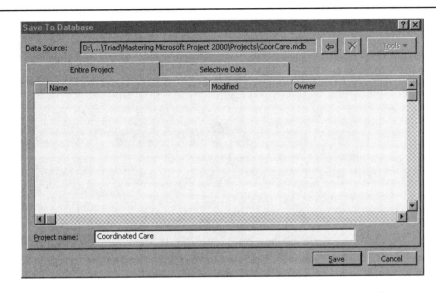

With an Access database, if the database file already exists, you will see the message
box shown in Figure 19.39. You have three choices: appending the data you are saving
onto the end of the existing database, overwriting the database with the data you're
exporting, or canceling and renaming your destination file. Appending your project file
will allow multiple projects to be stored in the same database.

FIGURE 19.39

*You see this message
when you attempt to
export your project to
a database file that
already exists.*

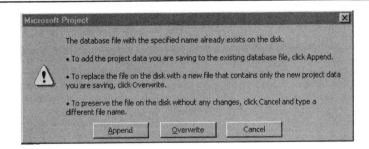

NOTE If you want to export data to an ODBC database, speak with your database
administrator, and then refer to "Importing Data from an ODBC Database," earlier in this
chapter.

Exporting Data as HTML

Hypertext markup language, or HTML, is the language of the Web, and is fast becoming the universal language for data presentation. HTML pages can be published on your Web server, and viewed in a browser by users, regardless of the type of computer they use.

Why Might You Export Data to an HTML File?

- To publish data on your intranet or the Internet.
- To share data with users on Unix systems.
- To take "snapshots" of project data for posterity.

HTML files use these file formats: HTM, HTML.

Project uses import/export maps to determine which fields are exported to HTML, and may use a template to determine how and where the information is displayed in the HTML file. You can create or edit both the HTML import/export maps and the HTML templates.

1. Select File ➢ Save As.

2. In the Save As dialog box, select Web Page (HTML) from the Save As Type dropdown list. Type the name of your destination file and click Save.

3. In the Import/Export Map dialog box, select the name of the map you want to use for exporting your data; or click New, Edit, or Copy to define a new map or edit an existing map. (See "Creating, Copying, and Modifying an Import Map," earlier in this chapter.)

4. Click Save.

 TIP You can also choose "Save as Web Page" from the File menu to export a project to HTML.

You can edit the sample templates that Microsoft Project provides for creating formatted HTML files from exported data, or you can create your own templates. If you're exporting project data based on a template, make sure that the template includes Microsoft Project template tags for all of the data being exported by the map, and make sure that all the tags have the correct spelling and syntax.

MASTERING TROUBLESHOOTING

Why Isn't My Image File In the Project Data I Exported to HTML Format?

When you export project data and images to HTML format, it's best to keep all your exported files in the same directory, so there are no paths in the HTML output. If you move the resulting files, move them together and keep the relative paths the same in the destination directories.

If you find that the image file is not showing after exporting to HTML format, check the following possibilities:

- If you export Microsoft Project data to HTML format and then move the resulting HTML file, be sure to move all the associated image files as well. If you don't move image files, they will not display when you open the HTML file in the new location.
- If you export Microsoft Project data to HTML format and then move the resulting HTML file, make sure that the destination directories have the same relative relationship as the source directories because only relative paths are stored in the HTML output.
- If you're using an HTML template, the image tag could be missing or incorrect.
- If you specify an image file with an HTTP or FTP address, Microsoft Project will not verify the access to or the existence of the image file. Make sure that you can access the image file at the specified address.

Converting, Linking, and Embedding with Project

Object Linking and Embedding, or OLE (pronounced "o-lay"), is a protocol that allows applications to communicate with each other to create or update objects; data that can be embedded or linked in another applications. Word documents, Excel worksheets and charts, Access tables, and PowerPoint slides are all examples of objects you can insert (embed or link) in Project 2000. You can also insert graphics, sounds, video, and virtually anything else you can select and copy to the Clipboard.

OLE requires an application that can create OLE objects (an OLE server) and an application that can accept OLE objects (an OLE client). Project 2000 is an OLE client, but it is not a fully compliant OLE 2.0 server, so Project 2000 data cannot be shared in the same manner with all applications. (You can link or embed Project data in Excel. See "Copying Data Objects from Project" at the end of this chapter.)

NOTE Which objects can you link or embed into Project 2000 files? The list is long and keeps growing. Select Insert ➤ Object from the menu to see the list of OLE servers installed on your computer.

The alternative to OLE is to convert data or objects. When you convert a selection, it is translated from its native format (the format used by the application it was created in) to a format that can be used directly by the application you place the selection into. Importing and exporting both use conversion rather than OLE. Converting creates a copy. After the selection is converted, you use the tools in the destination application to work with it. You can change the converted data without affecting the original because the converted data is, after all, only a copy.

The easiest way to convert (and embed or link) data in Project is to copy and paste. This is especially useful if you just need a few values, rather than an entire file. Open Project and the other application (called the source application if objects will be copied FROM; open the destination application if objects will be pasted INTO). Select the object in the source document and copy it to the Clipboard. You can close the source application if you wish; with some programs you'll be asked if you want to retain the contents of the Clipboard. Choose Yes or you'll have to reopen the source application and copy again.

Understanding Converted Objects

Switch to the destination document and place the insertion point where you want to paste the selection. To convert the data, simply paste it into the document. Of course, copying data into Project is more complex than simply converting values from an Excel spreadsheet into a Word table, although the conversion of fields takes place automatically. But, when copying into Project, it is important that the correct fields receive the data. Without an Import/Export Map to guide you, a custom Table view will need to be created in order to allow a block of data to be inserted into your project. See the section "Copying Data into Project" for step-by-step instructions.

 NOTE If you're moving large chunks of data or entire files from a supported file format into Project 2000, use importing rather than copy-and-paste.

Understanding Linking and Embedding Objects

When you embed an object, a copy of the object that retains its native format is placed in the destination document. The Excel object is still "in" Excel, but it appears in the Project document. If you change the object pasted in Project, the original selection in Excel remains unchanged because it is, after all, a copy.

With a link, a relationship is established between the selection in the native application and the pasted entry in the destination document. When you open your project file, Project reloads the Excel selection directly from the worksheet. When you begin to edit the object, Project launches Excel and you make your changes there. This ensures that the original data and the linked copy are synchronized; changes to the original data are reflected in the linked object. Linking has two advantages: it saves disk space, and, more importantly, linking is dynamic. If the source for the object changes, the change is reflected in all linked objects because a linked object is not a copy.

Understanding Hyperlinks

A *hyperlink*, a connection between two areas of a document or two different documents, is commonly used in Internet sites and other documents that are to be viewed online. When users click a hyperlink, they move to the destination location in the same document, a different file, or even an address on the World Wide Web. For example, you can insert a hyperlink in a project that opens a PowerPoint presentation or a Web page.

 MASTERING THE OPPORTUNITIES

Attaching Information to a Project File

Ignoring importing for a moment, you have four ways to attach external information to a project file. Here's an FAQ to help you choose a method and find objects after you attach them.

> *What are the methods for attaching information or objects to a project file and when should I use them?*

Create a hyperlink A hyperlink does not increase the size of your project file, and updates to the linked information are immediately available. However, when you are working offline, you may not be able to access hyperlinked information.

Copy and paste it Use the copy-and-paste method for small amounts of text and graphics that won't be frequently updated, for example, a company logo pasted into a header.

Embed it An embedded object becomes part of your project file, so the information in your project file will not change if someone modifies the source file.

Link an object using OLE Because linked data is stored in the source file, a linked object does not increase the size of your project file, and the linked object is dynamically updated.

Continued ▐▶

MASTERING THE OPPORTUNITIES CONTINUED

Where can I attach different objects?

Hyperlinks   You can insert a single hyperlink that will be shown in the Indicators field in a sheet view. You can place any number of hyperlinks in a note. You can also use additional text columns in your project for hyperlinks.

Pasted objects   You can paste objects into a graphics area in Microsoft Project.

Embedded or linked objects   You can place objects in a graphics area or a sheet view.

Entire files that are linked or embedded   You can link or embed entire files or sections of files into a graphics area.

Okay, it's in my project, now how do I find it?

• In sheet views, hyperlink icons and note icons appear in the Indicator field.

• If you've used the Hyperlink field, or an additional field, these hyperlinks are visible in sheet views, as well.

• To see where a hyperlink leads or what a note contains, you can hover over the icon.

• Information added to a header, footer, or legend appears on the printed page.

• Hyperlinks in the Objects box can be displayed on forms. You can use the Tasks with Attachments filter to quickly locate them.

Embedding in Project

There are three ways to embed data or an object in a Project 2000 project file: embedding data using copy and paste, embedding an object using copy and paste, and creating a new object in Project. When you create an object in an application, it's automatically embedded. (It can't be linked—it doesn't exist anywhere else.)

TIP   Embedding, linking, and converting data sets begins with copying data or an object. Use any of these methods to copy selected data or objects in the source application:

• Right-click and choose Copy from the shortcut menu.

• Choose Edit ➣ Copy from the menu.

• Click the Copy button on the Standard toolbar.

• Hold Ctrl and press C on the keyboard.

Copying and Pasting Data from Another Application

To copy and paste data from another application into Project, follow these steps:

1. Open the source application. Select the data to be embedded in Project and copy it.

2. Open your project file. Select Edit ➤ Paste Special to open the Paste Special dialog box, shown in Figure 19.40.

3. Select the Paste option button.

4. Select the Text Data format in the As list. Text and numbers will be embedded in the selected data or graphical area of Project.

FIGURE 19.40

*Use the Paste Special
dialog box to convert,
link, embed, or create
a hyperlink to an
object.*

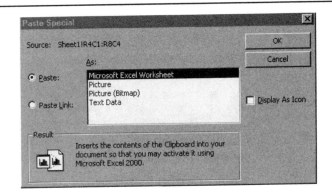

Embedding an Object Using Copy and Paste

To embed an object into Project by using copy and paste, follow these steps:

1. Open the source application. Select the data to be embedded in Project and copy it.

2. Open your project file. Choose Edit ➤ Paste Special to open the Paste Special dialog box.

3. Select the description in the As list that includes the term object (for example, Microsoft Excel Worksheet Object) and click OK.

You can tell an object because it has handles when selected. If you double-click the object to edit it, the native application will open with your file as the active document. From the computer's point of view, OLE is a complex operation. Give Project a moment to accept and place the new object.

Creating a New Embedded Object in Project

To create a new object and embed it into a Project file, follow these steps:

1. Select Insert ➤ Object.

2. Click the Create New option button.

3. Select the type of object you would like to insert.

4. If you want your embedded object to be displayed as an icon, check the Display as Icon box.

5. Click OK, and your object will be created and the associated application will open for you to work with the object.

Embedding an Entire File in Project

If you want to embed an entire file into a Project file, follow these steps:

1. Select Insert ➤ Object.

2. Select the Create from File option button.

3. Type in the file name or click the Browse button to search.

4. Clear the Link checkbox.

5. If you want your embedded object to be displayed as an icon, check the Display as Icon box.

6. Click OK to embed the object.

Embedding Data in a Task, Resource, or Assignment Note

Pasting information into a task, resource, or assignment note is a convenient way to keep track of information related to your schedule. You can copy information from, for example, an e-mail message, a word processing document, a spreadsheet, or a Web page and paste it into a note.

To paste information from another application, follow these steps:

1. Open the program containing the information you want to copy and then copy it.

2. In Microsoft Project, select the task, resource, or assignment to which you want to add a note.

3. Click the Notes button on the Standard toolbar. In the Notes area, press Ctrl+V, or right-click and choose Paste from the shortcut menu to paste the information into the note.

Linking Data to a Project

Copy and Link Data from Another Application

If you want to copy data into a Project file and maintain a dynamic link to the source file, follow these steps:

1. Open the source application. Select the data to be embedded in Project and copy it.
2. Open your project file. Choose Edit ➢ Paste Special to open the Paste Special dialog box.
3. Select the Paste Link option button (refer to Figure 19.40).
4. Select the Text Data format in the As list. Text and numbers will be embedded in the selected data or graphical area of Project.

Inserting a Link to a File

If you're creating a link to an infrequently used reference file, create the link as an icon. Users click the icon to open the linked file. Follow these steps to insert a link to a file:

1. In your project file, select Insert ➢ Object from the menu.
2. Choose the Create from File option button.
3. Type in the file name or click the Browse button to search.
4. Enable the Link checkbox.
5. If you want your linked object to be displayed as an icon, check the Display as Icon box.

Updating Linked Objects in the Project File

When you insert text or a picture as an object and link it to another file, automatic link updating is enabled. If you add a number of links to files that change frequently, or if you occasionally want to report on the current status of the project before links are updated, you can change the updating method so you control when links are updated. To change to manual link updating:

1. Select Edit ➢ Links to open the Links dialog box, shown in Figure 19.41.
2. Select the link for which you want to control updates from the source program.
3. Click the Manual Update option button to suspend updates from the source document.

 TIP The Link commands are not available for linked objects contained in a task, resource, or assignment note.

FIGURE 19.41

Change the update method to manual and then update links when you wish in the Links dialog box.

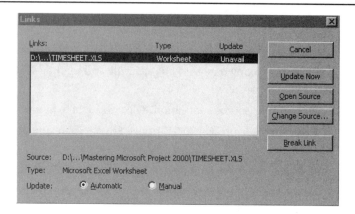

When you are ready to update links in the your project, open the Links dialog box again and click the Update Now button. You can also change the file that is linked by clicking the Change Source button, or edit the data in the source application by clicking the Open Source button.

 WARNING If you use manual linking, adopt a consistent method for updating so you don't pass off last month's information as the latest data.

Breaking an Object's Link

When you break an object's link to information in a source file, the information remains in your project file as an embedded static picture that cannot be edited. Canceling an object's link can be useful if you don't plan to change the object or you need to send the project file to someone who may not have access to the source program or file that is the OLE server for the object. To break an object's link:

1. Select Edit ➢ Links.

2. Select the link you wish to delete.

3. Click the Break Link button.

Moving or Copying an Object within Project

After you insert an object into your project, you can copy or move it to a different location within your project file. If you copy or move a linked object, it will retain its link to the source program.

1. Select the object you want to copy or move.

2. Copy the object by using any one of the following methods:

   • Choose Edit ➢ Copy from the menu

- Click the Copy button on the Standard toolbar
- Right-click and choose Copy from the shortcut menu
- Hold Ctrl and pressing C on the keyboard

OR

To move an object, cut it by doing the following:

- Choose Edit ➢ Cut from the menu
- Click the Cut button on the standard toolbar
- Right-click and choose Cut from the shortcut menu
- Hold Ctrl and press X on the keyboard

3. Select the new location for the object.

4. Paste the object in the new location by doing the following:

- Select Edit ➢ Paste
- Click the Paste button on the standard toolbar
- Right-click and choose Paste from the shortcut menu
- Hold Ctrl and press V on the keyboard

MASTERING TROUBLESHOOTING

Displaying Link Information for a Linked Object in a Note

The link information for an OLE object that was inserted from a file into a note is not directly visible, so you may find yourself wondering, "What file is this linked to?" You can check the link information by making a temporary copy of the object and pasting it into the Gantt Chart:

1. In Project 2000, choose View ➢ Gantt Chart.

2. Display the note containing the object you want to review.

3. Select the object inside the note and click Copy.

4. Close the note, and then click Paste to paste the object in the Gantt Chart.

5. Select Edit ➢ Links to open the Links dialog box and view the link information.

To remove the temporary copy of the object, select it in the Gantt Chart, and then press the Delete key on your keyboard.

Displaying Project 2000 Graphics Areas

Many objects can only be inserted into specific areas called graphics areas. These objects aren't all graphics. Word document objects, for example, can be inserted only in graphics areas. Table 19.5 lists these areas and how to display them. For many of the graphics areas (such as the bar area of a Gantt Chart), you can simply click in the area to paste or paste link a graphic object.

TABLE 19.5: PROJECT 2000 GRAPHICS AREAS

Graphics Area	How to Display
Notes Tab	Task View—Select a task and click Task Notes.
	Resource View—Select a resource and click Resource Notes.
	Resource Usage View—Select a task and click Assignment Notes.
	Task Usage View—a Resource and click Assignment Notes.
Page header, footer, or legend	File ➢ Page Setup. Click the Header, Footer or Legend tab.
Report header or footer	View ➢ Reports. Choose a report type and click Select. Click Page Setup, and then click the Header or Footer tab.
Gantt Chart	On the View Bar, click the Gantt Chart icon.
Objects box	Select a task or resource view. Window ➢ Split. Click the form view in the bottom pane. On the Format menu, point to Details, and then click Objects.

Inserting Specific Objects in a Project File

In this section, we'll show you how to insert files commonly attached to project files:

- Supporting documents created with programs in Microsoft Word such as the Project Summary, Business Systems Analysis, Project Proposals, task-related memos to vendors, or team members

- Excel worksheets, tables, and charts: including vendor quotes, supplemental budget materials, project analyses, pivot table reports, and charts used in stakeholder meetings

- PowerPoint presentations and slides from team meetings and project status reports

- Graphics used in reports and printed views, such as your organization's logo, a project or product logo, or client graphics; and supporting graphics including product sketches, site plans, and digital photos

- Hyperlinks to documents and Web resources such as vendor Web sites, client documents posted on the Web, and internal project documents posted on your organization's intranet
- Multimedia files, including video and sound files such as site videos and digital recordings of design meetings
- Organization chart objects that illustrate the organization of the project team or customer organization

Inserting Documents

A document file (created in Microsoft Word, for example) inserted as an object is interpreted by Microsoft Project as graphics information and can therefore be placed in any of the graphics areas listed in Table 19.5. You can also insert more than one object for a selected task or resource, with the succeeding objects displayed adjacent to the previously inserted objects. You can move and size an object in a Gantt Chart or a Note:

1. Open a Microsoft Project file and select the graphics area into which you want to insert a document.
2. Select Object ➢ Insert to open the Insert Object dialog box shown in Figure 19.42.
3. Select the Create from File option.

FIGURE 19.42

Insert entire files in graphic areas with the Insert Object dialog box.

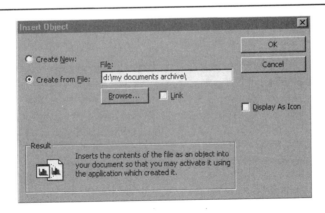

4. Type the path and file name of the document you want to insert, or click Browse to locate and select the file.
5. To embed the document in your project, clear the Link checkbox. To link the document to your project, select the Link checkbox.
6. To display the object as an icon, select the Display As Icon checkbox. The default is to display the contents of the file you insert.
7. Click OK to link or embed the document file.

Inserting Excel Worksheets, Tables, and Charts

Project, like Excel, is a table. You can use copy and paste to copy single values or small sections of data from and Excel worksheet directly into a Project 2000 table. Make sure that the data you are pasting is formatted correctly, and the converters will do the rest.

WARNING Pasting blocks of data (multiple columns and rows) from Excel into Project can be tricky. Unlike in an Import operation, there are no field names to match, and no safeguards to stop you from overwriting the wrong fields if your source and destination data groupings are different. See the next section for how to safely negotiate this danger zone.

Copying and Pasting Excel Text or Numbers into Project Data Tables   Pasting text or numbers from another program into a Microsoft Project view helps you avoid the extra work of retyping information. It does, however, require a little preparation because the type of information pasted into your project file must be organized in the same way as the Microsoft Project table.

We will use our earlier example of updating resources with their email addresses, but rather than using an import data map, we will copy the cells we need from the Excel worksheet, and paste them directly into the Resource Sheet. There are no keys to match resource names in this process, so we must be diligent in setting up the data in Excel, and selecting or modifying the view in Project. The data columns *and rows* must be in the same order in the Excel worksheet and the Project view.

NOTE   If you paste information into fields that already contain information, Microsoft Project replaces the information in those fields with the pasted information. If you paste text into blank rows, Microsoft Project treats the information as new tasks or resources. You cannot paste into fields that contain calculated values, such as calculated values in a cost table.

To copy data from Excel to a Project table, follow these steps:

1. Open your source document in Excel and examine the columns. Switch to Project 2000 and find the View/Table combination that most closely matches the Excel columns. Determine whether any changes must be made to column order in Excel or to the columns displayed in the Project view.

2. Insert columns in Project or rearrange columns in Excel so that the columns you want to copy data from and to are side by side, in the same order.

3. If you are adding columns of data to existing tasks, resources, or assignments in Project, sort the Project data (Project ➤ Sort) or the Excel data (Data ➤ Sort), or both so that records are displayed in the same order.

 TIP This is a great time to save your Project file.

4. In Excel, select the data you will use by pasting it into Project and copying it (see Figure 19.43).

5. Select the field where you want to paste the information. The cell may be blank or may contain text that will be replaced with the copied information.

6. Select Edit ➤ Paste (or click the Paste button, etc). The existing data, if any, is replaced by the pasted data.

FIGURE 19.43

Select the data in your Excel spreadsheet. The order of the columns and rows must match your current Project view.

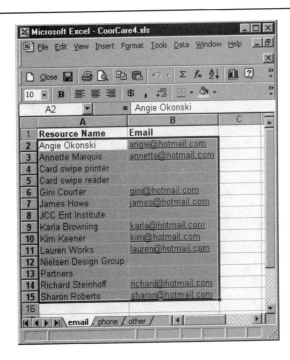

MASTERING THE OPPORTUNITIES

Creating a New View for Pasted Data

Sometimes, it's easier to create a new view that includes the fields you want to paste, along with the Project key field you need to display to know how to sort the Excel file. In this example, we will add a new column to the Resource Sheet view for email address and sort the view by Resource Name so that it matches the data in Excel. You could also manipulate the data in Excel to match the order in Project...but that's another book! (We recommend *Mastering Excel 2000* from Sybex, in case you wondered.)

To create a new view in Project, select View ➢ Tables ➢ More Tables and click the New button to display the Table Definition dialog box. Enter a table name and add the fields as you would when creating a data map.

We've created a table with two fields: Resource Name and Email Address:

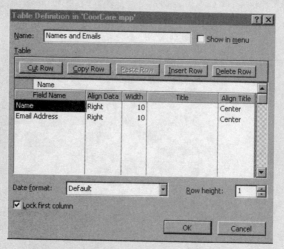

After you create the table, you may need to sort it to match the Excel worksheet data. Choose the table from the Tables list (View ➢ Tables) and examine the data. To set a sort for a table, select the column you want to sort by, right-click, and choose Sort By on the shortcut menu:

Linking Or Embedding Microsoft Excel Data as an Object   You can also paste data from Excel into Project as an object. You can embed the data as an object independent of its original file, or link it for dynamic updates from the Excel source file. You can also link or embed fields, cells, records, or rows into any Project table. Why would you do this? Another person or department updates the Excel file, and your project file needs to reflect the current data.

To paste data from Excel as an object, follow these steps:

1. Open Excel and select the information you want to link or embed.

2. Copy the data, chart, or table to the Clipboard.

3. In Project, select an appropriate view.

4. Select a location for the object.

5. On the Edit menu, choose Paste Special.

6. To embed the object, select the Paste option. To link the object to the source document, select Paste Link.

7. Click Display as Icon to display an Excel icon rather than the actual data. Double-clicking the icon will display the data.

8. Select the format of the data to be pasted. The choices for Excel are Excel Worksheet, Picture, Bitmap, and Text.

9. Click OK to attach the object to your project file.

 TIP   You can embed or link an entire Microsoft Excel file into a graphics area of your project. Follow the instructions for "Inserting Documents," earlier in this section.

Inserting a PowerPoint Slide or Presentation

You can copy and paste text or graphics from PowerPoint into Project, but you can also insert individual slides or an entire presentation as a linked or embedded object. The choice of locations is limited, but appropriate. The Gantt Chart view can include links to a slide or a presentation. Notes can include embedded slides, links to presentations, or static pictures of slides.

 TIP   Don't be bothered by this limitation. You can export files or selected slides from PowerPoint to Word, and Word documents work in any graphics area.

To embed or link one or more individual slides in a graphics area:

1. In PowerPoint, select the slide or slides you want to insert into Project, and copy it to the Clipboard.

2. In Project, display the view into which you will be inserting the slide. Click in the graphics area or note, and then choose Edit ➢ Paste Special from the menu or shortcut menu.

3. To embed, choose Paste; to link, choose the Paste Link option and choose Microsoft PowerPoint slide object in the As box.

4. Select the Display As Icon checkbox to display the linked slide as an icon.

5. To paste the slide into a note, click OK.

To embed or link an entire presentation, insert the file:

1. Activate the graphics area where you want to embed or link the presentation.

2. Choose Insert ➢ Object from the menu.

3. In the Insert Object dialog box, choose Create from File.

4. Select the file.

5. Choose the Paste Link option to link or the Paste option to embed the Microsoft PowerPoint Presentation object.

6. Enable the Display as Icon checkbox to have an icon represent the presentation. If you don't enable this checkbox, the first slide will be displayed in the graphics area.

7. Click OK to embed or link the object.

When you create an embedded or linked object from multiple slides or an entire presentation, only the first slide is displayed in the graphics area, as shown in Figure 19.44. To view the other slides, double-click the embedded object to start the slide show.

FIGURE 19.44

Double-clicking the slide object in this Task Note launches the full screen PowerPoint presentation.

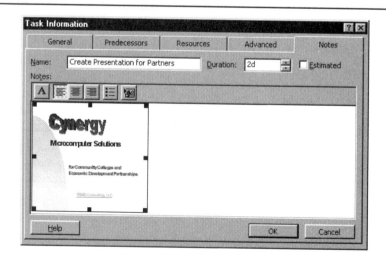

Embedding and Linking Graphic Images with Copy and Paste

You can copy a graphics image created in another program and paste it into Microsoft Project as a linked object that will be updated whenever the original image changes. Linked graphics images can be placed only in the Gantt Chart or the Objects box. If you paste an image into any other Microsoft Project graphics area, it will be converted to a static picture. The source application for your graphic must be an OLE 2.0 server to create a linked graphic.

1. Open your graphic's source program and copy the image.

2. Open a Project file and select the graphics area into which you want to paste the image as a linked object.

3. Select Edit ➤ Paste Special to open the Paste Special dialog box.

4. Select the Paste Link option to link to the graphic. Select Paste to embed the graphic object.

5. If you want to change the image type, click a different type in the As list.

6. If you want to display the image as an icon instead of its original form, select the Display As Icon checkbox.

7. Click OK.

Inserting a Graphics File as an Object

You can add an entire graphics file as a linked object that will be updated whenever the original image changes. You can create a new graphic image or chart within Project 2000 using the Insert Object dialog box. Linked graphics files can be placed in any of Project's graphics areas except headers, footers, and legends.

NOTE   We'll show you how to place graphics in these areas in "Jazzing Up Headers, Footers and Legends" in the next section.

To insert a graphics file as an object:

1. Open a Microsoft Project file and select the graphics area where you want to place the graphics file as a linked object.

2. Display the Insert Object dialog box by clicking on the Insert Object icon in a Note, or by selecting Insert ➤ Object from a Gantt Chart or Objects box.

3. To insert an existing image, choose Create from File. To create a new image, choose the Create New option and select the type of object to create from the Object Type list.

4. In the File box, type the path and file name of the picture or chart you want to insert, or click Browse to locate and select the file.

5. Select the Link checkbox if you wish to link the existing graphics file. Clearing the Link checkbox will embed the graphic. New images can only be embedded.

6. To display the image as an icon instead of its original form, select the Display As Icon checkbox.

7. Click OK to embed or link the image.

Inserting Video and Sound Files

To work with video files within Project, you must have Microsoft Media Player installed. The Media Player is included on the Windows CD. Your computer should have a sound card and speakers to play sound. As with graphics files, you can link or embed video and sound files:

1. In Project, select Insert ➢ Object.

2. In the Insert Object dialog box choose Create From File.

3. Select your video or sound file.

4. Select the Link checkbox if you wish to link rather than embed the file.

5. Click OK.

To play the video or sound file, double-click on the icon.

 TIP   You can also use copy and paste to embed a video or sound file. Open the file in the Microsoft Media Player. Select Edit ➢ Copy to place the file on the Clipboard. In Project, click in the graphics area where you want to paste the file, and then select Edit ➢ Paste.

Inserting an Organization Chart

The Organization Chart object is included with Office and also available for free from the Microsoft Web site (www.microsoft.com). To insert an organizational chart object:

1. Open your project file and select the graphics area where you want to insert the Organization Chart.

  • In a task, resource, or assignment note, click the Insert Object button.
  • In the Gantt Chart view or Objects box, select Insert ➢ Object from the menu.

2. Click Create New and select MS Organization Chart 2.0 from the Object Type list. If you cannot find Organization Chart 2.0 on the list, run the Microsoft Office Setup program and install it or download from the Microsoft Web site.

3. Click OK. An organization chart will be inserted into your graphics area and the MS Organization Chart application will open in a separate window, as shown in Figure 19.45.

FIGURE 19.45

The MS Organization Chart Window will open so you can create an Organization Chart Object in Project 2000.

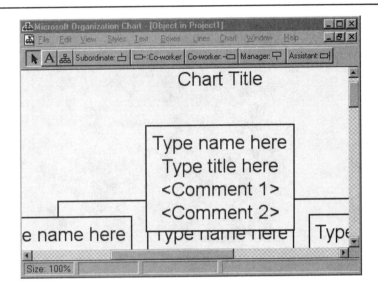

4. Update your chart in the Organization Chart 2.0 application window. When you are finished, close the window to return to Project. You will be prompted to save changes to the object. Click Yes.

TIP There are many other objects that you can insert into Project. To see what objects are available on your machine, switch to Gantt Chart view in a project and click in the graphic area. Select Insert ➤ Object to see the list of objects you can create.

Inserting Hyperlinks in a Project File

Although you can insert a wide variety of objects in your project file, it isn't always wise to do so. If your project includes twenty to thirty embedded files, it takes longer to open and uses an increased percentage of your system resources. Embedded files, in particular, create another problem: because embedded files are copies of the originals, your project may not always include the latest version of critical files. Hyperlinks pointing to documents on your computer, network, or the Internet provide clear links and easy accessibility without burdening the project file itself.

To insert a hyperlink to a document or Web site:

1. Open the project file and select the view where you want to create the hyperlink.

2. Select a task, resource or assignment you want to create the link in and click the Insert Hyperlink Button or select Insert ➤ Hyperlink from the menu to open the Insert Hyperlink dialog box shown in Figure 19.46.

FIGURE 19.46

Create links to documents on your network or the Internet in the Insert Hyperlink dialog box.

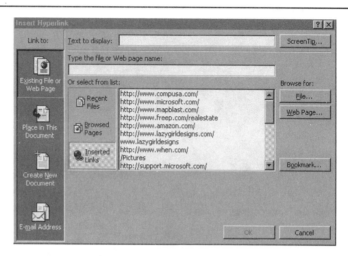

3. Click Existing File or Web Page in the Link To bar.

4. Specify the following options for the destination:

- Type the path to the file or the address of the Web page in the Type The File Or Web Page Name text box. Alternatively, select one of the files or Web pages that appear in the Or Select From List box. The addresses in the list box change, depending on whether Recent Files, Browsed Pages, or Inserted Links is selected to the left of the list box.

- Choose File to display the Link To File dialog box when you want to browse for a file. Then, select the name of the file and choose OK to place its exact path in the Type The File Or Web Page Name text box.

- Choose Web Page to open your default browser. Then, select one of the Web addresses in the Address drop-down list, and press Enter to place that address in the Type The File Or Web Page Name text box. If necessary, close or minimize your browser to return to the Insert Hyperlink dialog box.

- Choose Bookmark to display the Select Place in Document dialog box. Then, select the name of a heading or a bookmark of one of the locations listed in the Select An Existing Place In The Document list box, and choose OK to place that location's address in the Type The File Or Web Page Name text box.

5. The address that is placed in the Type The File Or Web Page Name list box appears in the Text To Display text box. To have descriptive text appear as the hyperlink in your document, type it in the Text To Display text box.

6. By default, the address in the Type The File Or Web Page Name text box appear as the ScreenTip for the hyperlink. Choose ScreenTip to display the Set Hyperlink ScreenTip dialog box, type the descriptive text that will appear in the ScreenTip when you point to the hyperlink in the ScreenTip text box, and then choose OK.

7. Choose OK to insert the hyperlink in the selected task or resource.

The Hyperlink icon will appear in the Indicator column of the task or resource. Click the hyperlink icon to move to the hyperlink location. You can also create a hyperlink to the following:

- A view in the current project
- A specific resource or task in a view in the current project
- A new document
- An email address

You'll be asked to set the following options in the Insert Hyperlink dialog box:

Place In This Document   Enter text to represent the hyperlink. Select a view and, optionally, enter a task or resource ID within the current project.

Create New Document   Type a name for the new document in the Name Of New Document text box. Alternatively, choose Change to display the Create New Document dialog box, select the folder for the new document, type its name in the File Name text box, and then choose OK. Choose Edit The New Document Later or Edit The New Document Now in the When To Edit area.

Email Address   Type the email address in the Email Address text box, and then type the subject of the email message in the subject text box. Alternatively, select one of the email addresses listed in the Recently Used Email Addresses box to enter it in the Email Address text box.

MASTERING THE OPPORTUNITIES

Setting Up Hyperlinks

Before adding hyperlinks to your project, create a folder on your computer or network, or a Web site on your company's intranet that has links to all the project-related files. If the information will reside on a computer, the main folder will contain all the supporting project files. If the information will reside on an intranet, the Web site will contain links to all the supporting project files.

Collecting your files in one place helps you because of the following:

- Files are in one location and that location can easily be communicated.
- Fewer hyperlinks are required because a single hyperlink can provide access to a folder of related files.
- Placing the files on the intranet or Web allows easy access to information for team members who are distance workers or have different applications on their computers.
- Archiving and backing up your files is easier.

Jazzing Up Headers, Footers, and Legends with Graphics

You can insert a graphic file as a static picture in Headers, Footers and Legends. This is a similar process to copying and pasting a picture into these areas. In this example, we will use the Gantt Chart view, but this process works in most views.

1. Open Project and go to a Gantt Chart view. Select File ➤ Page Setup. The Page Setup dialog box is displayed, as shown in Figure 19.47.

FIGURE 19.47

The Header tab of the Page Setup dialog box for a Gantt Chart

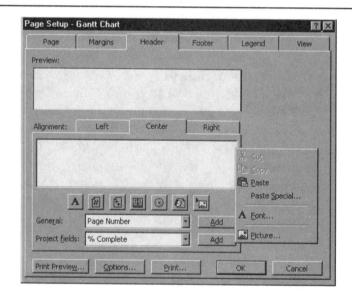

2. Click the Header, Footer, or Legend tab.

3. Click the Left, Center, or Right tab.

4. Click in the text box and then click the Insert Picture icon, or right-click and select Picture from the shortcut menu.

5. In the folder list, open the folder that contains the picture you want.

6. Select the picture you want then click Insert to close the dialog box and insert the picture.

Size a picture by selecting the picture and dragging its border. Move a picture by selecting the picture and dragging it.

You can cut or copy a picture from any Microsoft Windows program and paste it into a Microsoft Project header, footer, or legend. Once copied, you can paste the picture before, between, or after existing header, footer, or legend text.

1. Open the application that contains your picture. Select and copy the image.

2. In Project, select File ➤ Page Setup to open the Page Setup dialog box.

3. Click the Header, Footer, or Legend tab.

4. Click the Left, Center, or Right tab.

5. Click in the text box and paste the image from the Clipboard to embed the image.

Improving Headers and Footers of Reports with Graphics

You can insert a graphic file in the header or footer of a report using Insert Picture, or copy and paste. To insert a picture from a file, follow these steps:

1. Select View ➤ Reports to open the Report dialog box. Select the category and report you want to open in Print Preview.

2. Click the Page Setup button to open the Page Setup dialog box, shown in Figure 19.48.

FIGURE 19.48

The Footer tab of the "Who Does What" report

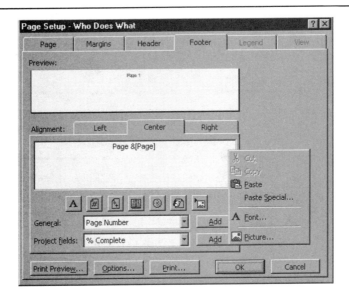

3. Click the Header or Footer tab.

4. Click the Left, Center, or Right tab.

5. Click in the text box and then click the Insert Picture icon, or right-click and select Picture from the shortcut menu.

6. In the folder list, open the folder that contains the picture you want.

7. Select the picture you want then click Insert.

To insert a picture using copy and paste, select the picture in the source application and copy it to the Clipboard. Follow Steps 1–4 to move to the area of the report where you want to paste the image. Choose Edit ➤ Paste, or right-click and choose Paste from the shortcut menu to paste the image from the Clipboard.

 WARNING Headers, footers and legends cannot always be customized. For example, the Project Summary Report does not allow any modifications to its Header and Footer area.

Copying and Pasting Data and Objects from Project

You can copy and paste existing Project information, even an entire view, into a file created in another program by including the information as an object. You can either embed or link Project objects in Excel worksheets. Project data cannot be embedded or linked in applications such as Word. You can copy data to paste as an object or convert to an external format from any Microsoft Project view.

 TIP To determine whether another program on your computer can accept Microsoft Project objects, open the application and choose Insert ➤ Object or its equivalent. Look in the list of object types for Microsoft Project objects.

Embedding and Linking Project Data in Excel

To embed or link project data into an Excel Worksheet, follow these steps:

1. Open Project. Select the view that contains data to be embedded or linked in an Excel workbook.

2. Select the data and copy it.

3. Switch to Excel and choose Edit ➤ Paste Special.

4. In the Paste Special dialog box, choose Paste to embed the object or Paste Link to dynamically link the object.

Figure 19.49 shows a Project Gantt Chart embedded in an Excel worksheet.

FIGURE 19.49

*Project views can be
linked or embedded in
Excel files.*

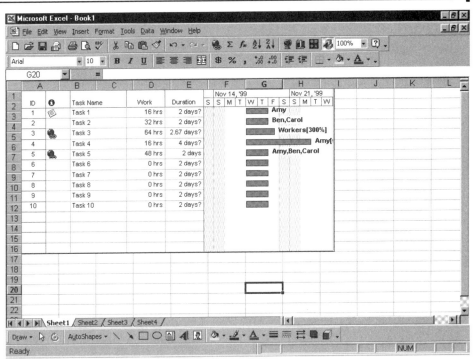

Copying a Project View into Another Application

You can copy information as a static picture from any active Microsoft Project view and
paste it into any program capable of displaying graphics as images. You can also save
the picture in a Web-compatible file format. You can copy a picture of the entire view,
or select and copy a portion of any view except the Relationship Diagram, Task Form,
and Resource Form views. Pictures of Gantt Charts often find their way into project
summaries created in Word. To include a Project view in a document created in another
application, select the data you want to include in your picture and copy the data to the
Clipboard. To include all visible portions of the view, choose Edit ➤ Copy Picture from
the menu to display the Copy Picture dialog box, shown in Figure 19.50.

Specify how you want your image rendered:

- To copy the information as displayed on a screen with all formatting intact,
  choose For Screen.

- To copy the information as it would be printed, choose For Printer.

- To copy the information as a GIF to use in a Web page, choose To GIF Image
  File, and specify the path and file name.

FIGURE 19.50

Use the Copy Picture dialog box to render images of views for use in print documents or Web pages.

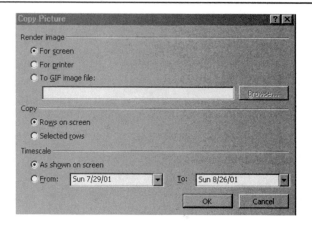

To copy information for a range of dates other than those currently displayed in the timescale, type or select starting and ending dates in the From and To boxes. When you selected a format and range, click OK if you clicked For Screen or For Printer, switch to the program into which you want to paste the Microsoft Project information, and then paste the picture using the program's Paste command.

 NOTE If your picture's dimensions exceed 22 inches by 22 inches, you will be prompted to make the necessary size adjustments before displaying it in another program.

Copying Microsoft Project Cells

You can copy task or resource text in Microsoft Project and paste it into another program. When copying cells, copy the field information from the table portion of a view. You can also copy the text of a task note, resource note, or assignment note.

Select the fields you want to copy and then click the Copy button, or choose Edit ➤ Copy Cell from the menu. Open the destination document and select the area where you will insert the cells, and then paste the information into the application.

What's Next

You designed, implemented, managed, viewed, and reported on your project, and you know all the ways and places you can move data for analysis. In Chapter 20, "Closing a Project," you'll use these reporting and exporting skills and some new strategies and methods to close your project.

CHAPTER <u>20</u>

Closing a Project

Many projects are never really completed; they just fizzle out and fade away. You are probably familiar with the excitement that goes into launching many new projects. Depending on the size of the organization and the environment in which you work, you may be involved in projects that are announced with great fanfare. Even a project that is announced behind the closed doors of your supervisor's office generally starts out with a certain momentum. The single most effective trait of an effective project manager is the ability to close a project with the same level of enthusiasm as when it is started. Closing a project can be the easiest and the hardest part of project management—it involves a rigorous evaluation and review of the decisions, processes, and effort that went into making a project a success or doomed it to failure. It's not always pleasant, but it is always educational. In this chapter, we'll look at how Microsoft Project 2000 can help you and your organization to get the most from closing a project.

To Close or Not to Close

Project managers list a host of reasons why they might never officially close a project. In some cases, "scope creep" has caused the project to mutate and grow in a thousand different directions, so much so that the original project may no longer even be recognizable. In other cases, the project may have failed to reach its objectives and the key players would rather not draw too much attention to that fact. Perhaps, political factors in the organization make it imprudent to evaluate and close some projects. And in all too many cases, other priorities get in the way. Although the primary objectives of the project may have been met, no one takes the time to evaluate the process and learn how it could be done even more effectively next time.

 NOTE For more about how scope creep affects a project, see "What Is a Project?" in Chapter 1, "Project 2000 Basics."

The process involved in closing a project can be as critical as the process involved in defining and designing the project at the outset. If your goal is continuous quality improvement, it is imperative that every project success or failure be carried through to its conclusion—you cannot improve if you don't know what it is you are improving.

Closing a Project

One of the most important factors in setting up a project is defining when a project can be deemed complete. If the deliverables and milestones are clearly spelled out, then it becomes clear when the project has met them, or when it is no longer possible or desirable to meet its objectives. So, the first step in closing a project actually happens before the project even starts. In the early stages of the project development, you must decide what the project will look like when it is done—what determines success? Obviously, if the project involves building a piece of machinery, it is a little more obvious when you have reached your objective than if the project is designed to raise awareness about the importance of exercise in maintaining good physical health. In either case, however, a clear definition of success at the outset goes a long way toward determining whether you have made it.

What Is Success?

Success is often defined in a very limited way: Did you build this machine or produce this publication? However, success may come in many different and surprising forms. Perhaps in failing to produce the item you set out to produce, you discover something totally unexpected. Perhaps the process did not work in this project, but it became clear how the same process could be successful in another project. Or maybe the team came together for the first time and now, knowing what to expect from each other, it will be successful the next time around. Although you can reach some conclusions about a project, keep yourself open to other ways a project may have succeeded or failed despite the project's objectives.

After you decide that a project has met its objectives or that it will *not* reach its objectives, you can proceed with the other steps involved in closing a project. These steps include the following:

- Conducting a project review, including a review of the processes used in the project
- Evaluating project results
- Communicating information about the project results to all the stakeholders
- Preparing for future projects

If the project is the result of a contract for your services, you may also have to finalize contract-related issues as part of closing a project. The contract may include an inspection or sign-off before the final invoice is paid. If that's the case, you certainly want to take care of those issues so you can submit the final invoice for payment. All of these items should be listed in the original project planning materials—it's always a good idea to go back and review everything you agreed to at the beginning to make sure you are not missing anything. When you are sure you know what you need to wrap up the project, you are ready to move on to the project review meeting.

Conducting a Project Review

One person rarely accomplishes a project in its entirety. That's not to say that a person working alone couldn't use Microsoft Project to help guide them through a complicated project. Project has all the tools you need to manage tasks and schedules in a project, even if you are the only resource available to the project. However, most projects are the result of a team effort. We're using the word team in its loosest sense—teams do not necessarily require cohesiveness—only the effective ones do!

Assuming that you are working on a project with a group of people, one of the most beneficial ways to begin the process of closing a project is to hold a final project review meeting. This meeting, sometimes referred to as a post-implementation review or post-mortem, should include as many of the key players involved in the project as possible, regardless of how insignificant their role. The meeting should be designed to minimize intimidation and encourage open and honest participation. If a team member anticipates that he is going to be hung out to dry, you can be certain that the review will be of limited value to the continuous quality-improvement process.

In preparing for the project review meeting, you may want to make several end-of-project reports available to the review team. Microsoft Project 2000 can create many of these reports for you, giving you the data you need to support any conclusions that come from the review and providing information that could open doors to discussion of other factors that might have been overlooked. You can find out more about creating these end-of-project reports in Project in "Creating Final Reports," later in this chapter.

During the review meeting, someone should be designated as the recorder to keep a record of the key points that come from the review. At the end of the review meeting, these key points can be written up to be included in the final project report.

Reviewing the Project Constraints

One definition of project management is to efficiently use resources to complete a project as designed, on time, at the desired level of performance, and within budget. When conducting a project review, this definition is often a good place to start a general discussion about the project. Using the criteria listed in this definition, how did you do? Did you use resources efficiently? Was the project completed as designed? Was it completed on time? Do the results meet the standards of quality and performance? How do actual costs compare to budgeted costs? This discussion often evokes the need to dig deeper, and perhaps more scientifically, as you break down the project lifecycle.

Problem Identification: Was the Problem Accurately Identified?

Accurate identification of the problem is the only way to solve it. As you look back on the entire project, could you have done a better job identifying the problem? Did you identify the real problem, or did you mistake a symptom for the actual problem?

Definition: Was the Problem Clearly Defined?

After the problem was identified, did you research the causes of the problem thoroughly? Did you consider all the possible causes of a problem? Is there anything you missed?

It's All a Matter of Perspective

A young man was visiting with his grandmother in the garden behind her old farmhouse. His grandmother commented how good it was to be out in the yard where she could see the pristine lake that bordered her property. She told her grandson that she didn't get outside much anymore and missed the lake, which she couldn't see from the house. The grandson looked at the overgrown hedgerow that ran between the house and the garden, and vowed to himself that next weekend he'd come over and cut the hedgerow back so his grandmother could see the lake. So, the following Saturday morning, he traveled out to his grandmother's house and, using an electric trimmer, had that hedgerow cut back to size in no time at all. When his grandmother answered his knock at her door, the young man smiled proudly and said, "Grandma, I trimmed that overgrown hedgerow for you, so now you'll be able to see the lake from the house." His grandmother let out a hearty laugh and said, "Silly boy, I still can't see the lake—there are no windows on that side of the house."

Project Design: Did the Project's Design Fit the Problem Definition?

You may have developed a fantastic product as a result of your project but if it's the solution to the wrong problem, you've missed the boat. In this stage of the review, you want to look at each step in the entire design process:

Define the Project's Objectives   Were the objectives measurable and achievable?

Finalize the Project Scope   Was the project scope inclusive and exclusive enough? Was it wide enough to accomplish the objectives and narrow enough to stay on target?

Identify Project Tasks   Did the tasks fit the job? Were they consistent with the project scope? Were some tasks unnecessary, and did any tasks get missed?

Break Each Task into Logical Components   Were the tasks defined logically? Were they broken down sufficiently enough to be understandable to the team members?

Assign Resources   Were the right resources involved in the project? Were the right material resources identified? Were any needed resources missed?

Create Estimates   Were the cost estimates accurate? Were the correct rates used for work resources? Were any fixed costs missed in the cost estimates? Were any estimated fixed costs found to be unnecessary.

As part of the design review, you may also want to find out if team members and other stakeholders had enough input into the design. Were their ideas and concerns heard as the project was designed? What other methods could be used to solicit appropriate input into the design phase?

Development: How Did the Project Unfold?

The development phase is where the real fun begins. Initial planning is complete and the actual work starts. During this part of the review, you want to find out what it was like to be doing the work of the project. Certainly, it's important to document if the project stayed on schedule, but even more importantly, you want to find out what happened that took it off schedule. Was it poor planning or did something interfere with the process? If some tasks finished ahead of schedule, how did that affect the rest of the schedule? Were schedules realistic to begin with? Were resource assignments realistic? Did the plan include enough material resources as well as work resources. How were over- or underallocations handled?

At this stage of the review, you also want to look at how the project team functioned. Examine the communication methods you used—did everyone feel like they were in the loop? Email, telephone, face-to-face meetings, written correspondence, and the Web are all valid forms of project communication. Which methods worked best? What could be done to improve communication next time? Should additional methods of communication be tried?

Implementation: Could the Results of the Project Be Implemented?

Projects are generally designed to create something new, whether it is something as concrete as an airplane or as intangible as a method to develop high morale within a company. When a project is completed, you should be able to implement the results in some way: use the object you created, sell the product, implement the policy. If the results can't be implemented, what went wrong along the way? Was it something intrinsic to the project or are external factors influencing its implementation? For example, if the project's objective was to develop a prototype for a new software product, is there money available to finance the production of the software? What factors are outside of your control? What, if anything, could you and the project team have done differently to carry the project through implementation? Does the product work or is a lot of rework required?

Evaluation: Are You Happy with the Results?

The final stage of the review is the formal evaluation stage. After all is said and done, did you accomplish your objectives? Are the stakeholders satisfied with the results? Do team members have other process concerns about things that impacted the project? If you do this project again, what will you do differently? How would you rate the overall success of this project?

Creating Final Reports

Although the review meeting is as much focused on process as it is on performance, Microsoft Project 2000 can help you prepare reports that are useful in conducting the review. These reports give you the facts and figures to fuel the discussion, and make sure that everyone is working from the same data. The reports can also show problems and successes that you might have otherwise overlooked.

Project has two vehicles for directly reporting project data: reports and views. Chapter 17, "Using Views to Evaluate Data," provides details about how to create custom views in Project 2000, how to add and remove columns, and how to sort and filter views to see just the data you want to see. Chapter 18, "Using Reports to Analyze Data," covers how to use the built-in reports and how to build custom reports that focus on particular data. You might also want to review Chapter 19, "Importing and Exporting Project Data," to learn how to export data from Project into Microsoft Excel and other applications to conduct even further analysis.

In this section, we'll discuss the predefined reports and views that can give you the data you need to conduct the postmortem and prepare a final project report.

To create a Project report, choose View ➤ Reports and select the appropriate report category from the Reports dialog box, shown in Figure 20.1.

FIGURE 20.1

Select a report category to view the reports in each category.

Using Project's Predefined End-of-Project Reports

Project has seven predefined reports that offer valuable data in preparing a final project report. There are three overview reports: Project Summary, Milestone, and Top-Level Tasks; and four cost reports: Budget, Earned Value, Overbudget Tasks, and Overbudget Resources.

The Project Summary report, shown in Figure 20.2, is found by clicking the Overview category of the Reports dialog box and then clicking the Project Summary Report button. The Project Summary report provides an overview of the following:

Dates including start and finish dates, baseline start and baseline finish, actual start and actual finish, and start variance and finish variance.

Duration including scheduled and remaining duration, baseline and actual duration, and variance and percent complete.

Work including scheduled and remaining work, baseline and actual work , and variance and percent complete.

Costs including scheduled and remaining costs, baseline and actual costs, and variance.

Task Status including the number of tasks not yet started, tasks in progress, tasks completed, and total tasks.

Resource Status including the number of work resources, overallocated work resources, material resources, and total resources.

FIGURE 20.2

The Summary Report shows the key project statistics in a summary report style.

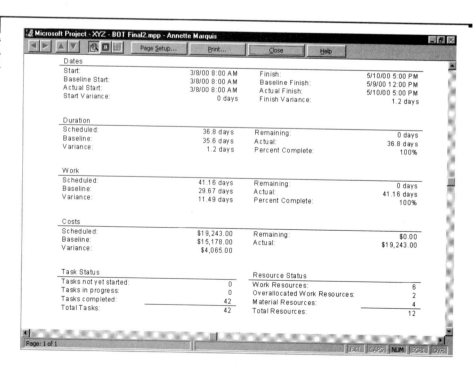

TIP The default Project Summary reports data in minutes. You can change the report to reflect hours, days, weeks, or months by resetting the Schedule options for Duration and Work. Choose Tools ➢ Options and click the Schedule tab. Change the Duration Is Entered In and Work Is Entered In fields to reflect the desired measure.

The Milestone report, shown in Figure 20.3, and also found by clicking the Overview category of the Reports dialog box, gives a summary of the project's milestones. It includes Task ID, Task Name, Duration (0), Start and Finish Dates, and Predecessors.

FIGURE 20.3

The Milestone Report focuses on the Project's milestones and shows when they were actually achieved.

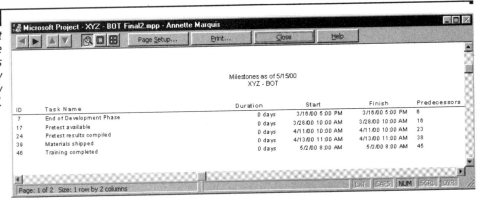

The Top-Level Tasks report, shown in Figure 20.4, is an overview report that shows the Task ID; Task Name; and actual figures for Duration, Start, Finish, % Comp (Percent Complete), Cost, and Work. This report shows only Level One tasks on the outline, so you can focus in on the major activities of the project without getting lost in the details.

FIGURE 20.4

The Top-Level Tasks report shows actual schedule and cost figures for the project.

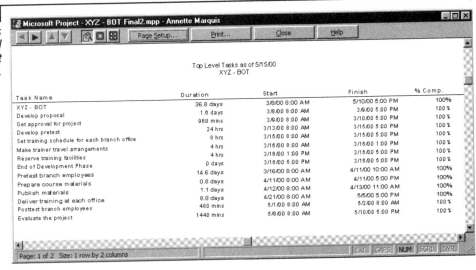

The Budget report, shown in Figure 20.5, is found in the Costs category of the Reports dialog box. The Budget report includes columns for Task ID, TaskName, Fixed Cost, Fixed Cost Accrual (method), Total Cost, Baseline (costs), Variance, Actual and Remaining. You can use this report to see how actual costs compare to budgeted (baseline) tasks and how much money, if any, is remaining in any of the task budgets.

FIGURE 20.5

Use the Budget Report to view budgeted versus actual costs.

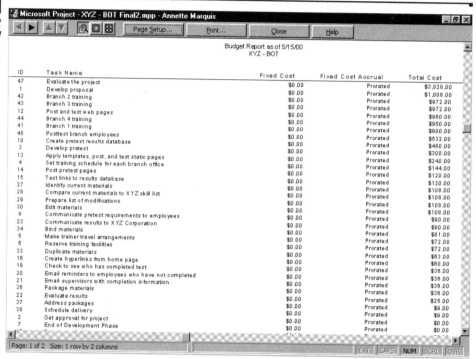

 TIP If you find the Budget report a little limited, you can switch to the Cost table in Gantt Chart view to see all the data from the report. Print the table, or save the table as an Excel workbook or pivot table in which you can manipulate the data to your heart's content. Choose File ➤ Save As and choose Microsoft Excel Workbook (*.xls) or Microsoft Excel PivotTable (*.xls) as the Save As Type at the bottom of the dialog box.

The Earned Value report, shown in Figure 20.6, is a standard project-management report, designed to show how a project's budgeted costs compare to actual costs. The Earned Value report shows the budget cost of work scheduled (BCWS), budgeted cost of work preformed (BCWP), actual cost of work performed (ACWP), scheduled variance (SV), cost variance (CV), estimate at completion (EAC), budget at completion (BAC), and variance at completion (VAC). Earned value can be monitored all throughout a project's lifecycle to measure the cost of work performed up to the status date or the date of the report. At the end of a project, the EAC, BAC, and VAC provide final summary data about the project. EAC is equivalent to the Cost field in Project; on this report, it shows the total scheduled or projected cost for a task. BAC is equivalent to the Baseline Cost field in Project. VAC is the difference between EAC and BAC.

FIGURE 20.6

Use the Earned Value Analysis report to show the variance between actual costs and baseline costs.

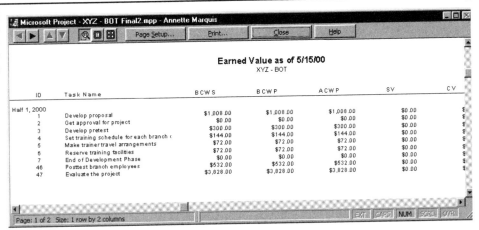

NOTE For more about earned value analysis, see "Using Earned Value Analysis to Analyze Project Performance," in Chapter 12, "Tracking Project Progress."

The Overbudget Tasks report, shown in Figure 20.7, contains the same fields as the Budget report, but displays only tasks that are over budget when compared to the baseline.

FIGURE 20.7

Use the Overbudget Tasks report to focus on tasks that have exceeded their cost budget.

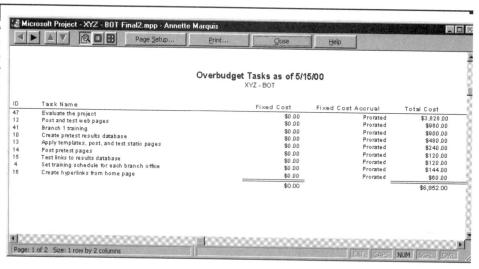

The Overbudget Resources report, shown in Figure 20.8, identifies variances in the cost of resources. The report includes columns for ID, Resource Name, Cost, Baseline Cost, Variance, Actual Cost, and Remaining. You can use this report to see how you managed your work and material resources.

FIGURE 20.8

The Overbudget Resources report lists resources that cost more than originally planned.

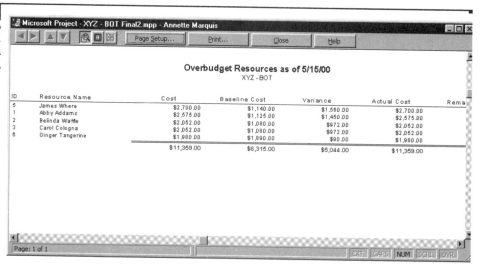

Creating End-of-Project Views to Analyze Results

In addition to Project's standard reports, you can print views that contain data you want to incorporate into the end-of-project review. Views are much more flexible than reports—you can add the columns you want and remove columns that don't provide valuable information.

NOTE For more about working with and customizing views, see Chapter 17.

Several views are particularly informative at the end of a project. The Gantt Chart is certainly a good place to start. By applying different tables to the Gantt Chart, you can focus on variances, cost, work, etc. For example, Figure 20.9 shows the Gantt Chart with the Tracking table, and Figure 20.10 shows the Gantt Chart with the Cost table. In both cases, we've dragged the vertical split bar off to the right, so only the table is displayed.

FIGURE 20.9

The Gantt Chart view with the Tracking table provides a summary of the project's schedule data.

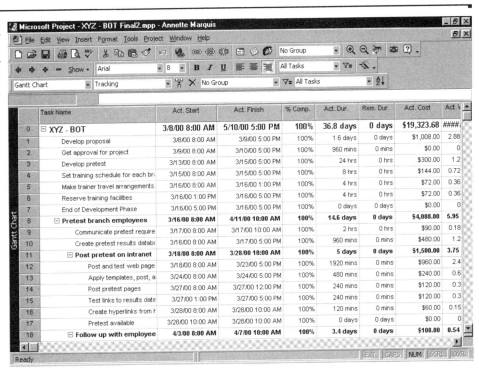

 NOTE The third toolbar shown in Figures 20.9 and 20.10 is a custom toolbar called Tables and Views. If you want to create this toolbar for your own use, see the Mastering the Opportunities sidebar in Chapter 21, "Customizing Project 2000."

When you want a more graphical representation of schedule variances, switch to the Tracking Gantt view. This version of the Gantt Chart shows both the baseline schedule and the actual schedule. The baseline schedule appears as light gray bars, and the actual schedule appears as solid blue bars. In Figure 20.11, you can easily see where the slippages in the project occurred.

FIGURE 20.10

The Gantt Chart view with the Cost table provides a summary of the project's cost data.

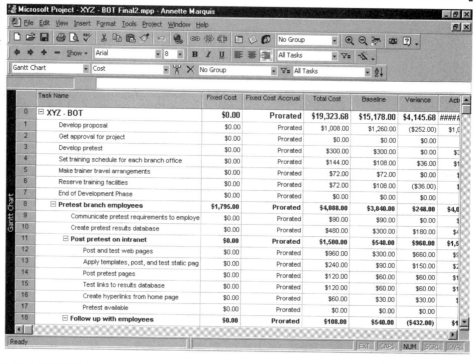

FIGURE 20.11

Switch to Tracking Gantt view if you want a graphical illustration of the schedule variances.

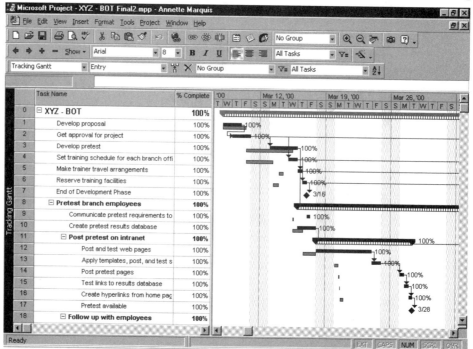

Communicating Project Results

After preparing all the project reports and conducting the project review meeting, it's time to make the project results public. Depending on your organization, on the project itself, and on the politics within the organization, communicating project results can mean very different things. For some projects in some organizations, it may mean that you prepare a written report, submit it to your supervisor, and that's that. Other situations may call for a more dramatic report of project results. You may be asked to post a report to the company intranet or perhaps give a presentation at the next company-wide teleconference.

In addition to the wealth of data you can print directly from Project, you can use Project's export features to respond to just about any request for information that you receive. Table 20.1 lists common requests for information and a recommended method for responding to each request. Chapter 19 gives you more details about how to accomplish any of the methods that involve saving, copying, or using other export methods.

TABLE 20.1: REQUESTS FOR INFORMATION AND RECOMMENDED REPORT METHODS

Information Request	Report Method
Produce a printed report	Create and print Project's reports and views.
Post results to a Web page	Determine what fields you want to export to a Web page from the task, resource, and assignment fields. See "Exporting Data as HTML" in Chapter 19 to learn how to save as a Web page.
Create charts to show cost data	Save the project as a Microsoft Excel workbook and create the chart from the data in Excel.
Give a live presentation	Prepare a Microsoft PowerPoint presentation. You can copy data into Word, convert it to a table (Table ➢ Convert ➢ Text to Table), and copy it into a PowerPoint slide.
Provide easy access to the project file for others to review	Post the project to a public Microsoft Exchange folder (File ➢ Send To ➢ Exchange Folder) or to a Web folder (File ➢ Save As, and click Web Folders on the Places bar).

Whether you choose one of these methods of communication or all of them, other people in your organization will generally benefit from hearing about your team's experience with a project. This is your opportunity to raise expectations in your organization about what quality project management is all about. Wow them with the quality of your analysis about the project's successes and failures and you'll set yourself apart from the masses, whose projects generally fade away into nothingness.

Preparing for the Next Project

Project management is a science of experience. Estimating durations is not nearly as hard the second time you plan the same type of activities. Assigning resources becomes much easier after you are familiar with the resource pool and have a sense of the quality and quantity of an individual or team's work. When you finish a project, try to identify those things that might be useable in future projects. Keep a summary of each project you manage, so you can go back and review the things you learned and the mistakes you don't want to repeat. Use your experience with prior projects to guide your decision-making about new projects you are undertaking.

If you anticipate that you may manage a similar project in the future, you can save the project file as a template (see "Creating and Using Custom Project Templates" in Chapter 21). When you begin planning the new project, you can open the project template, and a big piece of your work will already be done.

What's Next

This chapter ends Part V: Evaluating and Analyzing Project Data, the last part of the book that is directly focused on the project life cycle. Part VI takes you behind the scenes of Microsoft Project 2000 to teach you how to customize and automate Project to do what you want it to do. Chapter 21 begins with showing you how to set Project's options to reflect your needs, customize toolbar and menu bars, create and use templates, and work with Project's Organizer to copy virtually anything in Project to another project file.

PART V

Customizing and Automating Project 2000

LEARN TO:

- Customize Project 2000

- Create Project 2000 Macros

- Customize Fields and Forms

- Automate Project 2000 with VBA

- Use Advanced Programming in Project 2000

- Install and Administer Project Central 2000

CHAPTER **21**

Customizing Project 2000

Microsoft Project 2000 makes it easy to customize the Project environment so that it acts just the way you want it to. You can set options that affect that global template and some that affect only the currently active project. You can customize toolbars and menu bars so they display the buttons and menu features you use most frequently. In addition, you can base your project on one of the nine templates included with Project 2000 or you can create your own user templates for use with future projects. After you get everything the way you like it, Project's Organizer can then help you share your customized project setting with other projects.

Setting Project Options

Options control Project's overall application appearance and behavior. All of Project's options are organized into categories and can be found in Project's Options dialog box. You can access them by choosing Tools ➤ Options from the menu.

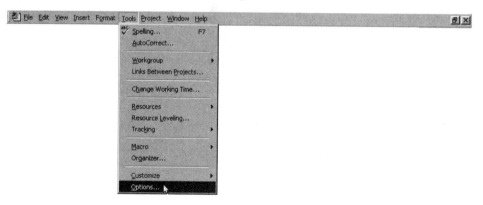

Option Setting Types

Options in Microsoft Project can be global or project-specific. *Global settings* pertain to projects that have already been created, the current project, and any new projects that you create. *Project-specific settings* pertain only to the current project.

Figure 21.1 shows three examples of project-specific settings on the View tab of the Options dialog box in the sections titled Cross Project Linking Options, Currency Options, and Outline Options. You can see the project, Coor Care.mpp, listed next to each of these options. This makes it easy to identify that those options are project-specific. If there is not a project name next to the option, you can assume that the setting applies to all projects, and is a default or global setting.

Some options give you the choice to apply them to the current project or apply them globally to all projects. Anywhere you see the Set As Default button on the Options dialog box, you have this choice. The Set As Default button applies only to the specific settings in close proximity to and generally directly above or to the right of the button—all the settings on a tab are not necessarily affected.

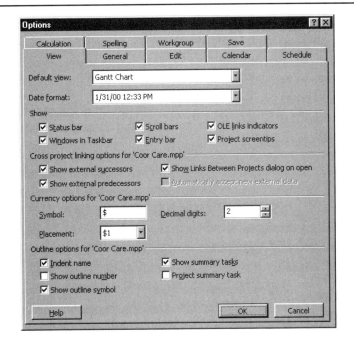

PART

V

Customizing and
Automating Project 2000

FIGURE 21.1

Options available on the View tab of the Options dialog box affect Project's displays and field formats for dates and times.

View Options

The View tab, shown in Figure 21.1, lets you specify the Default view, the view that appears when you open a project. You can also specify the date format you want to use in your projects. You can do this by choosing from the available options in the Date Format drop-down list. Depending on the nature of the majority of your projects, you can choose a date setting that also includes the time. The View tab lets you specify such additional things as the number of decimal places you want to display for currency and what symbol, if any, you would like to use for currency.

TIP You can get a quick definition of each option in the Options dialog box by clicking the question mark button in the upper-right corner of the title bar. After clicking the question mark button, the mouse pointer turns to a question mark. Move the question mark to the particular field and click.

Outline Options

The outline options at the bottom of the View tab, shown in Figure 21.1, relate to the open project and designate how you want the outlining features to function. Some of these options may be dimmed, depending on which view you are in. To access all the options, you must be in a task view (such as Gantt Chart view). With these options, you can choose to indent subtasks, show an outline number, and show an outline symbol next to each task. If you want to hide summary tasks so only tasks that require action are displayed, clear the Show Summary Tasks checkbox.

If you want to display a project summary task, click the Project Summary Task checkbox. This feature is most commonly used in master projects, but it can also be used to roll up an entire project into one task.

TIP You can change the name of a project summary task and enter other information about the task by double-clicking the task and editing the data in the Summary Task Information dialog box.

General Options

On the General tab of the Options dialog box, shown in Figure 21.2, you can set general options for Microsoft Project and some options specific to the open project. The first section allows you to determine whether you want Microsoft Project Help to display on startup or the last open file to open automatically the next time you start Project (Open Last File On Startup). It also allows you to set your Recently Used File List on the File menu to whatever number of entries between 0 and 9 you want to see.

Make sure your name is listed in the User Name text box because this field is used to identify who the project author is and who last saved the project—both properties that are invaluable when working on a team project.

The Microsoft Project Planning Wizard is a help system that notifies you when your project is developing conflicts in scheduling or other errors that could affect the accuracy of the project. You can turn off the Planning Wizard or reduce the amount of advice it gives you by clearing any of the four Planning Wizard checkboxes.

PART

V

Customizing and
Automating Project 2000

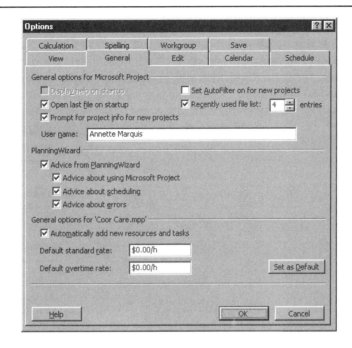

FIGURE 21.2

*Options available
under the General
tab of the Options
dialog box control
how Project handles
your project files.*

The General Options at the bottom of the General tab relate specifically to the currently active project, in this case Coor Care.mpp. The Automatically Add New Resources and Tasks checkbox is enabled by default, allowing you to add resources to the pool and tasks to the project implicitly. For example, you can create a new resource simply by assigning the resource to a task. When the checkbox is disabled, you're prompted to confirm the addition of each resource assigned that doesn't already exist in the resource so you don't accidentally create resources by misspelling the name of an existing resource.

You can also set a Default Standard Rate and a Default Overtime Rate for resources you add to the project. This is a timesaver if you use a lot of resources that share the same rate. Be sure to click the Set as Default button if you want these rates to appear in all the projects you create.

 NOTE The Default Standard Rate and Default Overtime Rate fields do not affect resources already included in the project, only the new ones you add.

Edit Options

The Edit tab, shown in Figure 21.3, contains general editing options that determine how Project allows you to edit and view information on your projects. Once again, remember that the settings displaying the open project's name apply only to that project.

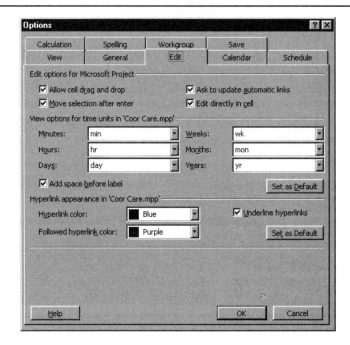

Table 21.1 describes the general Edit options available on the Edit tab.

TABLE 21.1: GENERAL EDIT OPTIONS FOR MICROSOFT PROJECT

Option	Description
Allow Cell Drag And Drop	This option allows you to point to the border of a selected cell and move it to another cell by dragging.
Move Selection After Enter	Pressing Enter moves the cell pointer down one row.
Ask To Update Automatic Links	Project displays a message, asking whether you want Project to update links to OLE objects whose source has changed rather than updating these links automatically.
Edit Directly In Cell	A new feature of Microsoft Project 2000; you can now edit directly in a cell by selecting a cell and then clicking in the cell. You can turn this feature off by clearing this checkbox.

Calendar Option

The Calendar tab contains critical settings that determine how Microsoft Project interprets the days and weeks of the current project. These settings should be set according to your organization's working environment. Figure 21.4 displays the default calendar settings that are used unless you manually change them.

FIGURE 21.4

The Calendar tab contains options critical to how Project calculates the schedule for projects.

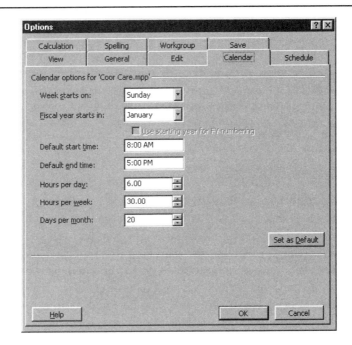

The first settings on the Calendar tab let you define what day your week starts and what month your Fiscal year starts. These selections affect displays and reports that have to do with weekly, annual, and quarterly amounts.

The default start and end times should be set as the same as the start and end time hours in the Standard Project calendar (Tools ➤ Change Working Time). These settings are used in several places and should be set based on the working hours of your organization.

Microsoft Project calculates project schedules by reducing all time parameters, such as Hours per day and Hours per week to minutes. These time fields need to be set up correctly in order to ensure that task durations, amount of work, and resource units required are calculated correctly.

A new field on the Calendar tab for Microsoft Project 2000 is the Days per Month field. Project 2000 now recognizes months as a valid unit of duration, allowing you to enter **1 mo, 1 mon,** or **1 month** in the duration field. Project interprets this based on how many days you've defined as constituting a month. The default is 20 days because that's the typical number of working days per month. This new feature helps to define task durations that span over a month or more.

WARNING The Calendar settings do not automatically apply to all projects, and therefore need to be set each time a project is created unless you click the Set as Default button to establish them as the default setting for all projects. For more about the Calendar options, see "Defining the Project Calendar" in Chapter 6, "Building a New Project."

NOTE Some settings that have to do with dates and times are set through the Microsoft Control Panel (for example, the time format and date separator). Refer to your Microsoft Windows documentation for more information.

Schedule Options

On the Schedule tab of the Options dialog box, shown in Figure 21.5, you can find options related to how Microsoft Project schedules task durations. The general schedule options at the top of the tab, which pertain to all your projects, include options for identifying whether you want Project to provide messages about scheduling conflicts and how you want to show assignments: as a percentage or as a decimal figure.

The next section of the dialog box pertains to various scheduling options for the current project. You have the option here to determine how you want all New Tasks to be scheduled. The available options are as follows:

- Start on Project Start Date
- Start on Current Date

The setting, Start on Current Date, is useful if you are adding new tasks after the actual project start date.

By default, Project enters Duration in days and Work in hours. You can change either of these settings to Minutes, Hours, Days, Weeks, and Months to affect how Project interprets an entry when you do not specify a unit of time. For example, in Figure 21.5, the Duration is set to Days. If you enter a task and enter a **2** in the Duration column, Project automatically sets the duration to 2 Days, based on this setting.

The checkboxes at the bottom of the Schedule tab clarify how you want other scheduling issues handled. Table 21.2 describes these options.

FIGURE 21.5

*On the Schedule tab
of the Options dialog
box, you can tell
Project how you want
tasks to be scheduled
and the default units
of time Project uses.*

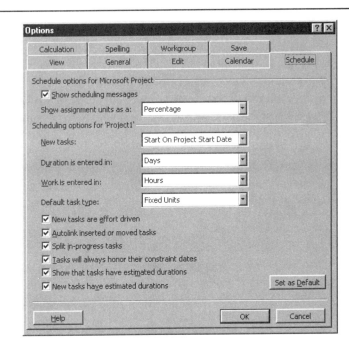

TABLE 21.2: SCHEDULE OPTIONS AVAILABLE IN PROJECT 2000

Option	Description
New Tasks Are Effort-Driven	Tasks are defined as effort-driven unless you change the setting for a specific task.
Autolink Inserted Or Moved Tasks	Automatically creates links when you move, delete, or insert tasks.
Split In-Progress Tasks	Allows you to split tasks even if they are already in progress.
Tasks Will Always Honor Their Constraint Dates	If a constraint is placed on a task, the constraint takes precedence over other scheduling changes.
Show That Tasks Have Estimated Durations	Task durations followed by a question mark are designated as estimated.
New Tasks Have Estimated Durations	All new tasks are given an estimated duration of 1 day (unless you've changed the Duration Is Entered In default).

Calculation Options

The Calculation tab, shown in Figure 21.6, determines various calculation settings, including whether you want Project to calculate the Project schedule and costs automatically, or whether you want to prompt it to calculate them. This option is helpful when you are working with very large projects and the project is running slow because of the calculations involved. However, you must remember to come back to the Calculation tab of the Options dialog box and click Calculate to have Project calculate the project.

Other settings on this tab include options related to how you want Project to calculate the schedule and costs in the open project. You may want to change the Actual Costs Are Always Calculated By Microsoft Project option if want to be able to enter your own total cost figures rather than have Project calculate them. Clear this checkbox to enter your own total cost figures.

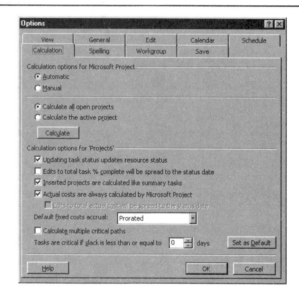

Spelling Options

Microsoft Project uses the same Spelling tools found in other Microsoft Office products, including the AutoCorrect features, which automatically fix commonly misspelled and mistyped words. To see a complete list of AutoCorrect options, close the Options dialog box and choose Tools ➢ AutoCorrect.

On the Spelling tab, shown in Figure 21.7, you can choose which fields contain data that you want Project to check when you run the Spelling feature from the toolbar. You may find it useful to turn spell-check off for fields that have names in them, such as Name-Resource and Code-Resource because names often come up as spelling errors. To turn off a particular field, select the Yes cell and click the drop-down list to choose No.

FIGURE 21.7

Using the Spelling options of the Options dialog box, you can prevent Project from checking the spelling in some fields.

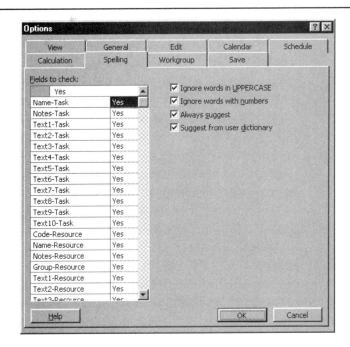

PART

V

Customizing and Automating Project 2000

Workgroup Options

When you are managing a project, you can use email and the Web to communicate with others on the project team. On the Workgroup tab of the Options dialog box, shown in Figure 21.8, you can set up the method of communication. If you are using Microsoft Project Central 2000, you can enter server and account information for the Project Central server (see Chapter 26, "Installing and Administering Project Central 2000" for more information about Project Central server and account information).

Save Options

The Save tab of the Options dialog box, shown in Figure 21.9, contains settings that pertain to how and where your Microsoft projects are saved. This dialog box allows you to change the file locations and save Project 2000 files as database files, Project templates, or Project 98 files.

FIGURE 21.8

Use the Workgroup options to specify a method of communicating with a project team.

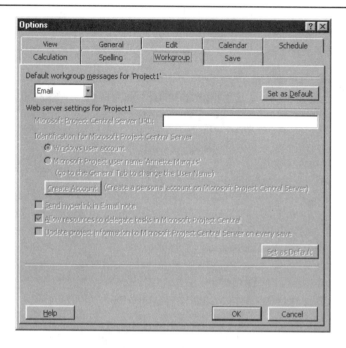

FIGURE 21.9

Use the Save options to specify where you would like Project to save files by default.

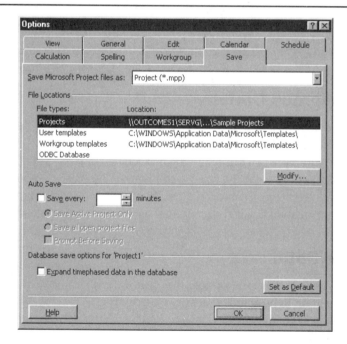

For the first time, with Project 2000, you can set a default save location for projects. Select Projects under File Types and click the Modify button to set the desired location. You can also set AutoSave options so that Project saves the active project or all open projects for you automatically every so many minutes.

WARNING Project's AutoSave feature is not the same as the AutoRecover feature in Microsoft Word. Word's AutoRecover recovers documents when the application terminates unexpectedly. Project's AutoSave resaves the open project.

Customizing Toolbars and Menu Bars

Microsoft Project 2000 is designed to create an environment that supports the way you use Project. When you initially launch Project 2000, it displays a personal toolbar, default command bars with "frequently used" menus and buttons. As you use menu selections and toolbar buttons, they are added to the menu or toolbar. When an entire toolbar cannot be displayed, the buttons you have used most recently are displayed, and others are hidden. For many users, this helps weed out commands that are rarely used, making the ones you do use easily available. And, for some of us, however, spontaneously regenerating toolbars are a bit too much customization. In this section, we'll show you how to turn off the personal toolbars feature.

As you work in Microsoft Project 2000, you'll develop your own approach to routine project tasks, and you may find a need to control which menu options and toolbar buttons are visible. You can customize all of the Menu bars, toolbars, and shortcut menus within Project 2000.

Changing Command Bar Options

To access options for command bars, right-click any Microsoft Project toolbar or Menu bar, and choose Customize from the shortcut menu to open the Customize dialog box. Click the Options tab to view the options for menus and toolbars (see Figure 21.10).

PART

V

Customizing and
Automating Project 2000

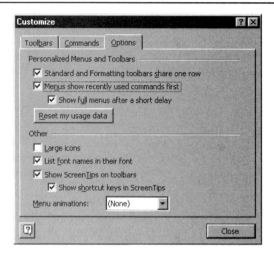

The available options are the following:

Standard and Formatting Toolbars Share One Row   Enabled by default. Turn off the check box to stack the toolbars, resulting in more room to display buttons.

Menus Show Recently Used Commands First   With this option (enabled by default), each application shows you a personalized menu (short menu) with the commands you use frequently. Turn this off, and you'll see full menus in Project and all Microsoft Office applications.

Show Full Menus After A Short Delay   If you like personalized menus, you will generally want to leave this turned on, or you'll never get to see the items you don't selected without customizing the menu to add items. This option also affects all Microsoft Office applications.

Reset My Usage Data   For menus to be personalized, there has to be a mechanism for tracking how often you use different menu options and toolbar buttons. Office tracks and saves your *usage data* when you close each application. This button resets the buttons displayed when a toolbar is not wide enough to display all the buttons and the menu commands shown in the personalized menu.

Large Icons   Intended for users with restricted vision, these icons are truly large. Just turn them on for a moment, and you'll either love them or rush to return them to their normal size.

List Font Names In Their Font   This option affects only the Font drop-down list on the Formatting toolbar. It makes it easier to choose a font, but you take a bit of performance hit, particularly if you have a large number of fonts installed on your computer.

Show ScreenTips On Toolbars   Formerly called ToolTips, ScreenTips are enabled by default; turning them off here turns them off throughout Microsoft Office.

Menu Animations   Although interesting initially, these effects (Unfold, Slide, and Random) can get cloying rather quickly. Animation is disabled by default.

After you've changed the options, click OK to close the Customize dialog box and apply the options you chose.

 TIP   To make command bars appear and behave as they did in Microsoft Office 97, disable the Standard and Formatting Toolbars Share One Row and Menus Show Recently Used Commands First checkboxes.

Customizing Command Bars

While the Customize dialog box is open, all displayed command bars are open for editing. Drag menu items or buttons to new locations to rearrange them, or drop them in the document window to delete them. To add a toolbar button or menu command, click the Commands page of the Customize dialog box. The Commands page from Microsoft Project is shown in Figure 21.11.

FIGURE 21.11

Drag commands from the Commands page to a toolbar or menu.

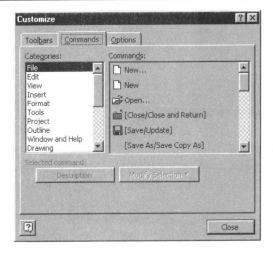

Commands are grouped into categories. Choose a category in the Categories pane, and then locate the command you want to add in the Commands pane. (Click the

Description button to see a brief description of the selected command.) Drag the command onto a toolbar or the Menu bar. To add a command to an existing menu, point to the menu and then place the command in the appropriate place when the menu opens.

You can rearrange, delete, or display toolbar buttons and menu items without opening the Customize dialog box. Simply hold the Alt key while you drag the command.

Each toolbar has its own set of built-in buttons. To quickly add or remove built-in buttons on a toolbar, click the More Buttons drop-down arrow on the right end of any toolbar, and choose Add or Remove Buttons from the menu. Buttons displayed on the menu have a check mark. Click the button name to add or remove the button from the toolbar.

TIP The default settings for an application's built-in menu and toolbars are retained even after you customize the menu or toolbar. To return a command bar to its original settings, switch to the Toolbars page of the Customize dialog box, check the Toolbar(s) you want to change to its original setting, and then click Reset.

You aren't limited to the built-in toolbars. Creating a new toolbar gives you the opportunity to gather all the toolbar buttons you frequently use in one place. To create an entirely new toolbar, click the New button on the Toolbar page of the Customize dialog box. You are prompted for a new toolbar name. Enter the name and click OK to create an empty toolbar. To populate the toolbar, drag buttons onto the toolbar from the Commands list. To copy a button from an existing toolbar, hold Ctrl while dragging the button.

Creating and Using Custom Project Templates

Every project is based on a *template*, which can be defined as a predefined set of project information. When you create a new blank project, you are using the default Global project template, GLOBAL.MPT. The Global template is blank, but does contain some very general default project settings.

Similar to other Microsoft applications, Project 2000 comes with a number of predefined templates, specifically nine different project templates. In addition, you can create your own templates or modify an already existing template to meet your needs. By default, the Project templates are stored in C:\Program Files\Microsoft Office\Templates\1033.

Project's templates are a good place to start building a project because they create the project up for you and provide a set of already-defined tasks that pertain to a particular type of project. Templates are designed to allow for consistency and help to ensure that critical steps are not missed when creating a project plan. Essentially, they provide a guide to help you create your project plans.

Opening Templates

Opening a template is as easy as opening a file. When you open a project template, you are opening up a copy of the project file based on a particular template, not the actual template.

Follow these steps to open one of the nine templates provided by Microsoft Project:

1. Choose File ➤ New to display the New dialog box.

2. Click on the tab labeled Project Templates.

3. Select the template icon that you want to use to create a new project.

4. Choose OK to open the new Project Information dialog box.

5. Enter the appropriate data in the Project Information dialog box. At minimum, enter the project's Start Date and verify that the current date is correct.

You are now working in a project file based on the template you chose. The project is named after the template until you save it the first time and specify a different file name. If you need more information on how to save a file, refer to "Saving Project Files" in Chapter 5, "Working in Project 2000."

Using the Sample Templates

The templates that come with Microsoft Project 2000 provide a framework for several different types of common projects. Each template can be modified to meet the specific needs of you and your organization. Table 21.3 lists the Microsoft Project templates and gives a brief description of each. For more detailed descriptions of the templates, review Bonus Chapter B, "Getting a Head Start with Project 2000 Templates," on the Downloads page of the Sybex Web site (http://www.Sybex.com).

TABLE 21.3: MICROSOFT PROJECT SAMPLE TEMPLATES

Project Template Name	Description
Commercial Construction	This template provides the tasks necessary to construct a commercial building. Providing a model of the builder's plan for the project, this template uses a Critical Path Method schedule.
Engineering	Provides a template that includes the steps and relationships that are necessary to scope, evaluate, and design a $5 to $25 million capital cost project. The project template is centered on the manufacturing process.

Continued

TABLE 21.3 CONTINUED: MICROSOFT PROJECT SAMPLE TEMPLATES	
Project Template Name	**Description**
Infrastructure Deployment	This template is designed to identify the required steps and processes to initiate, design, and deploy a new infrastructure. The template is based on a phased methodology, which uses milestone-completion phases as a means for reporting.
Microsoft Solutions Framework	This template is based on a Process Model for Application Development, and is a combination of a milestone-planning model and an iterative development process.
New Business	Thinking about starting a new business? This template is designed to identify those tasks necessary to properly evaluate a potential business opportunity.
New Product	This template provides the framework for developing a new product using a structured approach that should allow for successful new product development.
Project Office	This template is designed to provide the steps necessary to create an enterprise project office. It provides the steps necessary for the entire project life cycle, from conceptualization to the creation a project office. The template is based on a phased methodology and uses phase-completion milestones as a means for reporting.
Residential Construction	Like the Commercial Construction template, this template provides a model of the builder's plan for the project and uses a Critical Path Method schedule.
Software Development	Provides a template that can be used to manage the activities involved in the software-development process. The template is based on a phased methodology and uses phase-completion milestones for reporting.

Creating a New Template

When one of the pre-existing project templates doesn't meet your needs, you can create your own template for your organization, division, or department's use. Many companies, for example, that utilize a quality methodology have a set of project tasks that must be completed throughout every project lifecycle. It is necessary to complete these tasks in order to ensure that the quality methodology is being adhered to. This can easily be achieved by creating a new project template.

Follow these steps for creating your own template:

1. Create a project with all the necessary information that you want to be contained in the template.

2. Choose File ➢ Save As.

3. Enter the name of the template in the File Name text box.

4. Choose Template from the Save as Type drop down list.

5. Click the Save button.

6. Choose any type of data you do not want to save with the template by clicking the checkboxes in the Save As Template dialog box that opens.

7. Click Save.

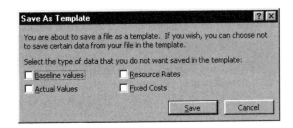

To base a project on the template you created, select New from the File menu. Your new template appears among all the predefined project templates.

Modifying Template Files

To modify a template, open a copy of the template by choosing the template, making the changes, and saving the file as a template. You can either save over the original template by giving it the same name or save it with a different name.

Making Changes to the Global Template

In Word, new documents are based on NORMAL.DOT, Word's default template. New Project 2000 files are based on GLOBAL.MPT, which is called the *global template*. Some of the settings in the Options dialog box (for example, the Effort Driven setting) affect the global template. Other changes are made in the Organizer.

 WARNING Changes you make to the Global template affect all new project files.

Working with the Organizer

The Organizer allows you to save customized project settings. You can easily share these customizations with your other projects. You can use this feature to utilize specific, defined customizations for your organization, division, or department workgroups; or you may find that you just want to use it for your own purpose to save time when creating your own individual project plans.

The Organizer can be used to copy customized items from one project file to another. You can also use the Organizer to rename items or delete an item that you no longer need.

Figure 21.12 displays the Organizer dialog box, and Table 21.3 lists the different types of objects you can change in the Organizer. To access the Organizer, choose Tools ➤ Organizer from the Menu bar.

Organizer dialog box, showing the various groupings

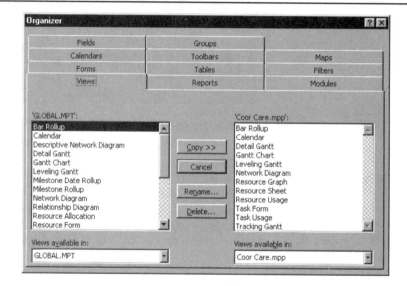

TABLE 21.3: ITEMS IN THE ORGANIZER

Object Groupings	Description
Views	Sheets, forms, and graphs such as Gantt Charts and Resource Sheets used to display project information.
Modules	One or more procedures, functions, or subroutines created with the Macro Recorder or in the Visual Basic IDE.
Reports	Print-ready reports, such as the Overallocated Resources and Slipping Tasks reports, as well as custom reports you create.

Continued ▶

Object Groupings	**Description**
Forms	Standard and user-customized dialog boxes, designed to display detail about a single item such as the Task Information Form or Resource Information Form.
Tables	Information about Resources, Costs, Tasks, or Assignments, often displayed as part of a view. For example, the Gantt Chart with Entry Table is a combination view/table.
Filters	Used to display a subset of information for a table, view, or report. Project 2000 includes filters for tasks (such as the critical task filter) and resources (such as the resource name and group filters).
Calendars	Base calendars for the project, including the Standard calendar and calendars created by the user.
Toolbars	The command bar collection, including all the predesigned toolbars, the Menu bar, and custom toolbars you've created. There are twelve toolbars that can be customized.
Maps	Specifications for how data is imported from or exported to other applications.
Fields	Standard and user-definable-fields (Cost1, Cost2, etc.) that are included in Project (this feature is new in Project 2000).
Groups	Sorting and filtering specifications for fields.

TABLE 21.3 CONTINUED: ITEMS IN THE ORGANIZER

Copying Items from One Project to Another

The Organizer is the ideal place to copy items from one project to another. The following example copies a calendar from the Global template to the Coor care project file. You can pull calendars from other sources by choosing different project files from the drop-down lists located at the bottom of the calendar tab. In the example shown in Figure 21.13, the two fields are labeled Calendars Available In because the Calendar tab is displayed. Other tabs in the Organizer have similar fields.

Follow these steps to copy an item:

1. When copying an item to another file, you need to make sure that the target file is open.

2. Choose Tools ➢ Organizer.

3. In the Organizer dialog box, choose the tab that contains the item you want to copy. Figure 21.13 shows the Calendars tab.

PART

V

Customizing and
Automating Project 2000

FIGURE 21.13

Use the Calendars tab grouping in Organizer to copy calendars from one project to another.

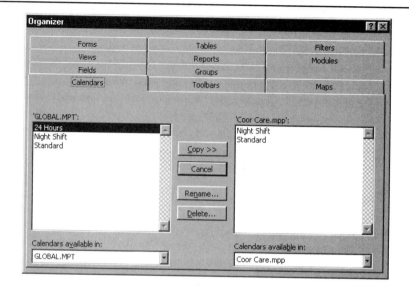

4. Choose the item you want to copy from in the dialog box. Copy the 24 hours setting by selecting it from the left side of the screen.

5. Click the Copy button. If there is already an item with the same name in the target file, a message appears that asks you to confirm that you want to overwrite the existing item (see Figure 21.14). Choose Yes to replace the item in the target file or use Rename to save it to the target file with a different name.

6. Click the Close button located in the middle of the dialog box to close the Organizer.

 NOTE These same steps can be used to copy any item that is managed by the Organizer.

FIGURE 21.14

A warning message appears if an item already exists.

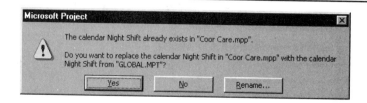

TIP Items can be copied to the Global Template from other Project Templates, as described in the previous section. You can also use these steps to copy items from any of the pre-existing Project templates to the Global template.

Renaming Items with the Organizer

If you want to rename an item, such as a calendar that exists in a project file, you must use the Organizer.

Follow these steps to rename items:

1. Choose Tools ➢ Organizer.
2. In the Organizer dialog box, choose the tab that contains the item you want to rename.
3. Choose the Item you wish to rename.
4. Click the Rename button. The Rename dialog box opens.
5. Type the new name for the item.
6. Click the OK button.
7. Click the Close button located in the middle of the dialog box to close the Organizer.

Deleting Items

The Organizer is also the only way to delete customized items.

Follow these steps to delete an item:

1. Choose Tools ➢ Organizer.
2. In the Organizer dialog box, choose the tab that contains the item you want to delete.
3. Choose the Item you wish to delete.
4. Click the Delete button. The Delete confirmation box appears.

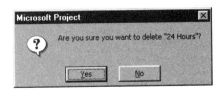

5. Click the Yes button to complete the deletion of the item.
6. Click the Close button located in the middle of the dialog box.

PART

V

Customizing and
Automating Project 2000

What's Next

Setting options, designing toolbars, and using templates are all valuable ways to adapt Project to the way you work. In Chapter 22, "Creating Project 2000 Macros," you'll learn how to use macros to automate Project so that it not only adapts to the way you work but actually makes your work easier.

CHAPTER <u>22</u>

Creating Project 2000 Macros

Project 2000 is more than just the application and templates you install from a CD. In earlier chapters, you saw some of the flexibility built into Project 2000. You can customize reports, views, and the application interface. This chapter is an introduction to the most powerful Project 2000 customization tool of all—its programmability. As with the Office 2000 applications, with Project 2000, you can create your own software by telling Project exactly how you want it to work.

You'll use Visual Basic for Applications (VBA) to program in Project 2000. There are essentially two ways to create VBA programs. The simplest method available in Project (as well as in Office applications such as Word, Excel, and PowerPoint) is to record *macros*—VB programs that run within a host application—using a Macro Recorder. Or, if you're already familiar with Visual Basic, you can create Project macros by opening a programming module and typing line after line of code. You'll learn about Visual Basic and Visual Basic for Applications in Chapter 24, "Automating Project 2000 with VBA," and Chapter 25, "Advanced Programming in Project 2000." But you don't have to know how to program in Visual Basic (or even desire that knowledge) to be able to create macros in Project 2000. We'll begin our work with VBA using the Macro Recorder and sneak up on the programming stuff in later chapters.

Creating a Macro

There are three reasons why users create macros: to automate infrequent complex tasks, to efficiently complete frequent tasks, and to make applications accessible for less experienced users.

Managing infrequent complex tasks   You have to perform a task that you perform infrequently, and it includes a series of steps that aren't intuitive. If this were a physical task (such as replacing your car's timing belt or making tapioca pudding), you'd have a manual or recipe to follow. Some computer users would save the list of steps in a Word document, and then open or print the document each time they need to perform the task. A macro is a superior alternative to the Word doc because the macro stores and executes the instructions.

Efficiently completing frequent tasks   As you use Project, you'll find yourself changing the same settings in each new project file. For example, you always change the text on the Gantt Chart bars to resource initials rather than resource names, so your Gantt Charts have a consistent, easy-to-read layout. It takes very little time to change the settings in the view, but it takes only a minute longer to record a macro that you can run each time you start a new project file.

Making Project easier to use You learned the steps to print the five project documents that you circulate at the end of each month, but your administrative assistant could easily print and distribute them. You could send him to Project classes or even buy him his own copy of this excellent book, but learning Project isn't the priority. Printing reports is. Adding a few macros and putting them on a toolbar makes Project 2000 accessible for a user.

In Project 2000, you create macros by using the Macro Recorder. The Macro Recorder is like a VCR (but easier to use): you record a series of actions, and then play back the recording at some future time. To record a macro, you turn on the Macro Recorder, complete the steps you want to record, and then save the macro. The next time you need to execute the same steps, you run the macro.

Getting Ready to Record a Macro

Before recording a macro, you should practice the steps you want to record because once you begin recording, all your actions are recorded, mistakes included. Take note of the conditions your macro will operate under and set up those conditions. Will you always use the macro in a specific document? If so, open the document. Will the macro be used to change or format selected text or numbers? Then, have the text or numbers selected before you begin recording the macro, just as you will when you run the macro at a later time.

When you have practiced the steps and set up the same conditions the macro will run under, select Tools ➢ Macro ➢ Record New Macro to open the Record New Macro dialog box, shown in Figure 22.1.

FIGURE 22.1

The Record Macro dialog box in Project.

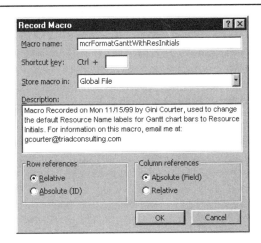

The suggested name is "Macro1." (Microsoft didn't use a lot of imagination here.) Enter a more descriptive name, rather than a functional name, for the macro, as shown in Figure 22.1. For example, "CorporateHeaderFooter" is better than "ChangeHeader-Footer" because the name provides a clue as to what gets changed in the header and footer. Visual Basic names, including macro names, can be up to 255 characters long. The names can contain numbers, letters, and underscores, but not spaces or other punctuation; and they must begin with a letter. You can enter uppercase and lowercase letters in a name; whereas Visual Basic preserves your capitalization style, it is not case-sensitive (that is, "FormatGanttChartWithInitials" and "formatganttchartwithinitials" are the same name, but one is more difficult to read).

NOTE If you really miss having spaces between words, use underscores, but the Initial Caps case used in the previous examples is preferred by many programmers.

If your organization uses a naming convention, you'll probably prefix the macro name with mcr for macro or bas for Visual Basic code. (Some companies use only the bas prefix, whether or not you create the macro with a macro recorder. Check the standards for your organization if you're not sure.) Enter a new description. If other users will have access to the macro—which ultimately happens unless it you add code to have the macro self-destruct if you go on vacation—include your name and contact information (extension or email address) in the description, as shown in Figure 22.1.

To be able to run the macro by pressing a keyboard shortcut key, enter a letter in the Shortcut key box. You can use Ctrl and a letter for lowercase letters, or hold Shift and enter a letter for uppercase letters. You can't use numbers or punctuation marks, or any key combination that is already used in Microsoft Project 2000. If, for example, you try to assign the letter P, Project will notify you that the letter is already used for another function (printing).

Actually, most of the "best" letters are already used, and the Ctrl+Shift combinations invite problems. Users easily forget to hold Shift, so they end up printing the Gantt Chart instead of formatting Gantt Chart bars. Later in this chapter, we'll show you how to attach macros to command bars, which is our preferred method. You can include shortcut keys for menu selections if you or the people you're creating macros for prefer the keyboard to the mouse.

Storing a Macro

In the Store Macro In drop-down list, select the document you want the macro stored in. A macro's storage location determines how you'll be able to access and run it later.

If you select the current project, the macro will be available only in this project. If you want the same macro somewhere else, you have to copy it to the other project (in the Visual Basic editor or the Organizer) or re-create it. Macros that are stored in a project, including a template, are called local macros. Storing a Project macro in the Global file creates a global macro, available to all project files created in Project 2000.

From the description, you might think that you should save every macro as a global macro, but all the global macros load each time you launch Project 2000; they take up space in memory; and any macro names you use globally can't be reused in individual projects. Unless a macro is going to receive wide usage, it's best to store it in the current project.

MASTERING THE OPPORTUNITIES

Macro Storage and the User Interface

The decisions about where to store Project macros, and where to place toolbar buttons or menu commands that let users run the macros are directly related. Users should always be able to find the buttons for macros that they need to run. And they should be able to see buttons only if the macros are available. Clicking a button for a macro that Project can't find results in an error message.

For example, let's say you're creating macros to automate a project file that will be distributed to workgroup members in a variety of locations. In this case, you should store the macros locally in the project file you'll distribute. The buttons that users click to run the macros should be displayed in the distributed project, and they should not be visible if your client switches from your project to another open project file. To achieve this, you can create a custom toolbar that will be turned on when the workbook opens and off when it closes. (See Chapter 25 for information on displaying and hiding custom toolbars with VBA.)

You may create other macros that everyone in your workgroup uses for project files. For example, you might create a macro that adds a custom footer including the date, time, filename, and the text "© All rights reserved" with the year and your department name. This is a good candidate for a global macro. For information on customizing or creating Project 2000 toolbars, see Chapter 21, "Customizing Project 2000."

Absolute and Relative References

If you select cells while recording your macro, when you run the macro, it selects the same column (field) each time it is run, regardless of which cell is first selected. The Macro

Recorder records an absolute reference to the column ("go to column 4," as opposed to "move one column to the right"). It would be nice if it worked the same way for rows, but it doesn't. By default, the Macro Recorder records movement between rows as a relative reference ("move down 2 rows" rather than "go to row 3"):

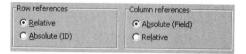

If you want a macro to select columns or move to a column relative to the position of the active cell, choose the Relative Column References option. If you want your macro to select the same row, regardless of the position of the cell pointer when you run the macro (for example, row 3), choose the Absolute (ID) option in the Row References options. You don't have the same relative/absolute flexibility here that you have in Excel; the entire macro is recorded with the settings you choose in the Record Macro dialog box. (You can change the settings for the next macro you record. The default settings are restored each time you start Project 2000.)

Recording Your Actions

After you set the options in the dialog box, click the OK button to begin macro recording. The message Recording displays at the left end of the status bar to show that you are recording a macro. The Stop Recording toolbar also opens. The macro recorder records the actions you take, but not the delay between actions, so take your time. If you want the macro to enter text, enter the text now. To include menu commands in the macro, just make menu selections as you normally would. To record the mcrFormatGanttWithResInitials macro, follow these steps:

1. Right-click in an empty area of the Gantt Chart and choose Bar Styles from the shortcut menu:

2. In the Bar Styles dialog box, click the Text tab.

3. Choose the Resource Initials from the Right drop-down list:

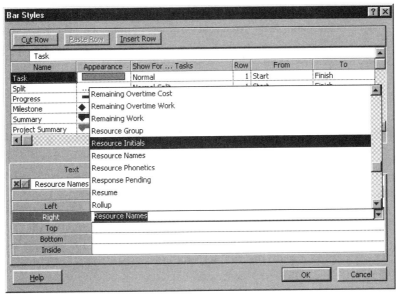

4. Close the Bar Styles dialog box.

5. Choose Tools ➢ Macros to open the Macros menu. The Stop Recorder button on the menu is enabled:

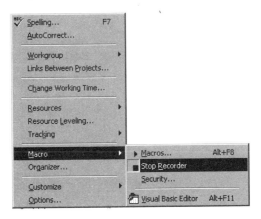

6. Choose Stop Recorder to stop recording.

You don't need to do anything special to save the macro now. Local macros are saved when you save the current project. Global macros are automatically saved when you close Project 2000.

TIP If you want to format text in a macro, choose the formatting options from the Format Font dialog box rather than clicking toolbar buttons to select font, font style, size, and alignment. If you use the buttons, the results when you run the macro will be unpredictable because the toolbar buttons are toggles. For example, if selected text is already italicized, clicking the Italics button turns Italics off.

Running Macros from the Macros Dialog Box

It's always a good idea to save your project file before you run a new macro. If you've made a mistake during recording, the playback results may not be what you expected. To run a macro, choose Tools ➤ Macro ➤ Macros to open the Macros dialog box, shown in Figure 22.2. By default, macros from all open project files, including the global file, are displayed. Change the selection in the Macros In drop-down list to view only the macros in the current file. Select the macro from the scroll list and click the Run button to execute the macro. You can't enter text or choose menu options while the macro is executing. When the macro is finished running, Project returns control to you.

FIGURE 22.2

Run your macros directly from the Macros dialog box.

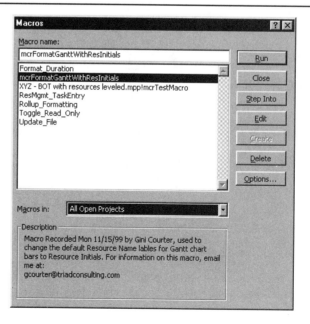

In our project file, one resource name didn't change to initials when we recorded the macro or when we played it back. It would have been easy to blame the macro, but there's an easier (and more logical) explanation: that task bar had been changed individually earlier in the project, and the local setting takes precedence over the setting for all bars in the Gantt Chart. To fix this, we double-clicked on the bar, switched to the Text tab, selected the Right text box, and clicked the Reset button. When we tested the macro again, the text on all task bars, including our "problem" bar, changed to resource initials.

This may seem obvious, but the only way to know whether the macro really works is to reverse the changes you made when recording the macro before playing it back. Change the Bar Style text to Resource Names, and then run the macro to make sure that names are changed to initials.

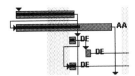

MASTERING TROUBLESHOOTING

Pulling the Plug: Terminating a Macro During Execution

You can accidentally create a macro that won't be able to run to completion because it gets caught in a loop. Often, this will happen when you make a logical error or a typing error creating a macro in Visual Basic rather than with the Macro Recorder.

When a macro won't stop on its own, you need to be able to terminate it. If you need to stop a macro during execution, press Ctrl+Break. A Visual Basic dialog box opens, allowing you to End program execution or Debug the macro in the Visual Basic Editor.

If Ctrl+Break doesn't stop macro execution, press Ctrl+Alt+Del once to open the Close Program dialog box. Select the application that contains the macro, and click the End Task button. When you reopen the application, you probably need to revert to the copy of the document that you saved before running the macro.

Deleting Macros

Until there's a "Biggest Macro Bloopers" show in prime time on MSNBC, there's no need to save macros that include mistakes and their corrections, or that don't perform as intended. There are two ways to delete a macro. If you need to improve the way a recorded macro executes, you can record the macro again, using the same name. You are asked if you want to overwrite the existing macro with the new one.

If you no longer need a macro, choose Tools ➤ Macro ➤ Macros to open the Macros dialog box, select the macro from the macro list, and click the Delete button to delete the macro from the project, template, or global file.

Opening a Project File That Contains Macros

If you can add code to a Project 2000 file, so can the people who write viruses. Viruses are self-replicating programs. When you open a file that contains a virus, the virus copies its code into the application's default template, effectively becoming a global virus. From that point forward, every project you save in the application will be infected, which means that every file you give to someone else on a disk or via the Internet will also contain the virus—not the best way to improve your popularity at work or home.

Macro viruses are a recent phenomenon because powerful application programming languages are relatively new. If an application isn't programmable, there's no way to create a macro; application programming languages that can create or save files open the door for code that can replicate itself. Put the two together, and you have an environment suitable for macro viruses. The first macro virus was created in 1994 for demonstration purposes. Within a year, macro viruses created for other purposes were found "in the wild." Early macro viruses were designed to embarrass and were, in the world of viruses, relatively benign. They'd ship humorous or nasty messages to a few of your Outlook contacts, or change the header or footer in a file to something you wouldn't want to distribute at a meeting.

The damage a virus is designed to do is referred to as its *payload*. Some recent macro viruses have a heftier payload. Viruses that modify the Windows registry, for example, or delete some or all folders from the default drive make us yearn for those good old days a few years ago when the typical macro virus payload was repeated display of a happy birthday message for someone you'd never heard of.

Project 2000 does not include virus-detection software, but you should install some unless you never receive email or files from another computer by disk, network, or Internet connection. (That means you won't be using Project 2000's workgroup or Project Central features, right?) Project does, however, scan every project file you open to see whether it contains macros. When it finds macros in a file, the response depends on the security settings on your computer and the documentation provided with the macro.

Security and Digital Signatures

Windows 98 and NT support *digital certificates* (also called *digital signatures*) issued by companies like VeriSign for use by software developers and individuals to certify the authenticity of the contents of a file, program, or email message. Although anyone can obtain a digital certificate, a certain amount of information (such as a credit card number and verifiable email address) changes hands during the application process. The company or organization issuing the certificate tracks the certificates, and can contact the certificate owner if software or files with their certificate include viruses.

This isn't foolproof—we have certificates and could, on a lark, send a few digitally signed files with nasty macros to our friends and loved ones just before disappearing into the wilderness. We'd write virus macros that ran automatically when users opened the project file so we didn't have to count on our recipients running them for us. This wouldn't be fun for long, though (if it ever was). The recipients would know with certainty that we sent the files. We'd need to stay in the wilderness for a long time.

A digital certificate isn't enough by itself to guarantee safety. A layer of security is added when the user controls which digital certificates they're willing to accept. The security settings are maintained in Internet Explorer. When a new valid certificate is presented, you can choose to accept the individual certificate, reject the certificate, or indicate that you always trust content from the certificate's provider (for example, InstallShield, Beyond.com, or Microsoft).

If you open a file that contains macros but has no digital signature, Project displays this message box:

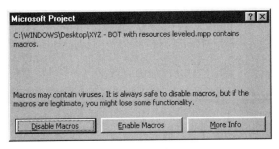

It never hurts to choose Disable Macros. Disabling the macros gives you an opportunity to look at them in the Visual Basic Editor without risk of infection. After disabling macros, you can look at the macros in the Visual Basic Editor (see Chapter 25). Check the macro's description (refer to Figure 22.1) and see whether it was written by you or a coworker. If you know that the file is from a trusted source (with good virus-detection software on their system); or if you've just examined the macros, judged them satisfactory, and closed the file, click the Enable Macros button to load the project file and enable the macros.

 TIP This raises yet another good reason to always enter your name and contact information when creating a macro: It gives other users less reason to delete the macro, and gives a way to reach you if they're still not sure.

When you open a file with a digital signature that's not already on your list of trusted sources, Project displays this dialog box:

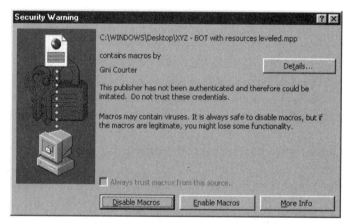

The dialog box shows the owner of the certificate, which may be enough, particularly if the owner is a coworker or team member. If you feel you need more information, click the Details button to view certificate details. This lets you see whether the certificate comes from the person's employer or is a personal ID obtained from a digital signature provider. Ultimately, though, you have the same choices as in the prior message box: Disable or Enable Macros.

 MASTERING THE OPPORTUNITIES

Managing Project File Risk

You've probably figured out by now that we take viruses seriously. We run virus-detection software all day, every day; and scan every floppy disk and Zip disk that leaves our office. Twice. We're computer consultants, and we can't afford to be remembered as the company that gave you a virus that wiped out your hard drive.

Continued

PART

V

Customizing and
Automating Project 2000

> ## MASTERING THE OPPORTUNITIES CONTINUED
>
> As a project manager, you'll be sending email and document files to communicate project information on a regular basis, which increases your exposure to viruses and the costs associated with spreading viruses to other users. Most organizations include some anti-virus software on their workstations. If you have software, check with your network administrator to see how often the software is updated. Virus-detection software that hasn't been updated in six months is relatively useless. Over one hundred new macro virus strains are found in the wild (on desktops like yours and mine) each month. As of October 31, 1999, the Virus Test Center at the University of Hamburg (keepers of one of the best non-commercial lists of viruses: http://agn-www.informatik.uni-hamburg .de/vtc/) had identified 4,593 macro viruses. Nearly 80% of the reported macro viruses use Microsoft Word as a host. This isn't because Word is easier to write viruses for, but because it has such a large number of users that it's a natural target. The first virus designed specifically for Project was reported in October 1999. It's a low-risk, relatively harmless virus that moves back and forth between Word and Project. The next virus, of course, may reassign resources and change task durations.
>
> There are a number of good virus-detection software companies that regularly update their virus files. Some even email virus alerts to registered users. We use McAfee software; you can download time-limited demos from its Web site, www.mcafee.com.

Adding Macros to Command Bars

At the beginning of this chapter, we noted three reasons to create macros. When you create macros for the third reason, making Project easier to use for a novice, you should also think about customizing command bars. Rather than giving the administrative assistant a list of reports with instructions, you can create a report menu that prints each report he needs to create and distribute. In the next few pages, we'll create a menu for the external reports we distribute monthly to various stakeholders. These reports include the following:

Tasks in Progress

Tasks Completed

Slipping Tasks

Cash Flow

Overbudget Tasks

Gantt Chart with Cost Table

Tracking Gantt

Before we can customize the Menu bar, we need to record macros that create these reports and views. Jot down your list of periodic reports and create your macros so you can add them to the command bar. We use the same group of reports in all our projects, so we'll create global macros. If the reporting requirements vary with each of your projects, you may want to create local macros or a core set of global macros for the reports and views printed in most projects.

MASTERING TROUBLESHOOTING

Print and Display Issues in Macros

When you print a view or report, focus passes from Project into the Print Preview window. This window, you may notice, doesn't have a Project menu (or toolbars), so you can't access the Stop Recording button. It doesn't matter whether or not you print the preview. The Macro Recorder pauses when you reach the Print Preview window, and doesn't start again until after you close the Reports dialog box.

If you set a print range or number of copies, the Macro Recorder won't catch it.

To stop recording, close the Preview window, and then close the Reports dialog box (if you were printing a report rather than a view). Then, choose Tools ➢ Macro ➢ Stop Recorder. When you run the macro, it will finish executing with the report displayed in the Print Preview window.

When you record the macros to print views, choose the view from the View menu, even if it is already displayed. Return to the View menu and choose the Table. Double-click the right edge of each column to adjust the column width to best fit, even if the columns are already adjusted. Move the split bar into the last column you want to display, and then double-click the split bar to adjust the split. When the macro runs, it will select the view and table, and adjust the columns before opening the Print Preview window.

Adding macros to command bars isn't substantially different from the command bar customization in Chapter 21. Right-click on any toolbar and choose Customize from the shortcut menu, or choose View ➢ Toolbars ➢ Customize from the Menu bar to open the Customize dialog box. Before you start dragging and dropping, decide where your macros should appear on the toolbar or Menu bar. There are a few possibilities, including the following:

- You can add buttons to the standard or formatting toolbar.
- You can create a custom toolbar.

Good custom toolbars are a lot of work. We have to use text on the buttons or spend days creating icons that are meaningful enough to serve as the primary means of identifying the action that will occur when the user clicks the button. Another approach is to have our assistant memorize the frowning face icon as the Overbudget Tasks and the little telephone as the Tasks in Progress, but the goal is to make the interface friendlier for our assistant, not introduce new memorization tasks. The Save button looks like a floppy disk. The Print button has a printer on it. What icon will deliver that level of meaning for the Tracking Gantt? How will it differ from the Gantt Chart with Cost Table? If we need to display text for our users, we may as well use Menu bars rather than toolbars. For example, we could either add the individual macros to the Macros menu (Tools ➤ Macros) or create a menu item on the Macros menu called Reports (Tools ➤ Macros ➤ Reports), and then add the macros to what would be a sub-sub-submenu.

Both these options assume, however, that our administrative assistant knows or cares that this functionality is provided by macros. Right now, we'd like to keep her away from the other Macros options, not draw her towards them. There's no incredibly logical menu to put these macros on with the possible exception of the View menu. The problem with the View menu is that it already has Reports, Gantt Chart, and Tracking Gantt on the menu, which will cause confusion. Fortunately, we're not constrained by the existing options on the Menu bar:

- Create a new menu item like File and Edit. Each macro would be a separate menu command on the menu.

If we're going to create a new "main menu" item, there are a couple of standards to bear in mind. In Windows applications, choices on the Menu bar are one-word choices. The fact that lots of program menus look like this isn't coincidence—it's part of the design standard that programs have to meet to have the Windows seal on their software box. We probably won't be applying for Microsoft approval, but it's good to follow the standards anyway because users know how to interact with programs that conform to these standards. Applications that demonstrate disregard for standards give even novice users the impression that they were created by people who weren't paying attention.

You can add a new menu option almost anywhere, but the left-most menu choice should be File (if it appears on the menu) and the choices at the right end are Window and Help. A term should appear only once in the entire menu system, so we should avoid naming our menu **Reports** because Reports appears on the View menu. We'll name our menu item **Distribute,** and then place it between Project and Window on the menu.

On the Command tab of the Customize dialog box, shown in Figure 22.3, choose the New Menu option at the end of the Categories list. Drag the New Menu item Command from the right pane and drop it in place on the Menu bar.

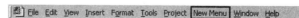

Right-click on the command to open the shortcut menu. Enter the name that should appear on the menu. Type an ampersand (**&**) in front of the letter that serves as the shortcut key for the command (we chose D because it isn't used anywhere else on this level of the menu).

You can hold Alt and press D to open this menu, just as you can hold Alt and press F to open the File menu.

Now, we'll add macros to the Distribute menu. In the Customize dialog box, choose the All Macros category to display the local macros for this workbook and global macros, as shown in Figure 22.3.

FIGURE 22.3

Customize toolbars and the Menu bar in the Customize dialog box.

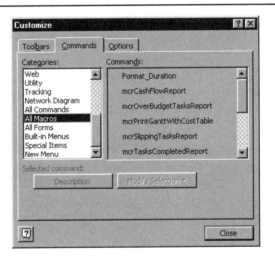

Drag the first macro you want to place on the menu from the command pane onto the Distribute command. Pause while the Distribute menu opens. Drop the command onto the menu. Continue dragging and dropping macros until they're all on the menu:

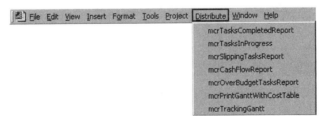

Right-click on the first menu item to open the shortcut menu. Change the name from the macro name to the name you'll want the user to see. Use the ampersand to create a shortcut key for the user:

Commands on the highest level of the menu, the Menu bar, are represented only by text. Commands on the drop-down menus can have text and buttons. If you're ever going to put these macros on a toolbar, you can start training users in advance by assigning icons and text to the menu commands. The button image set has more than twice as many images as the image set in Office 2000. To display an image, right-click on the menu command to open the shortcut menu, and choose Change Button Image. Project automatically changes the display setting on the shortcut menu to Image and Text.

Change the name, display, and button image settings for the remaining menu items. Drag and drop menu items to rearrange them if you want. When you are finished, click Close to close the Customize dialog box. Here's what our finished Distribute menu looks like:

PART

V

Customizing and
Automating Project 2000

What's Next

Macros and command bars are just the tip of Project's customization iceberg. In the next chapter, you'll learn how to add customized Project fields and add custom fields to the standard input forms so you can collect different kinds of cost, task, and resource information. It's new. It's epic. It's a lot like *Titanic*, but without Kate, Leonardo, the boat, and the great soundtrack (and hopefully, the "crash" at the end!).

CHAPTER 23

Customizing Fields and Forms

t's hard to believe, but there might be times when Project just doesn't do everything you need. For example, you may need to track information that Project doesn't have a field for, or want to view or enter information in a way that doesn't match any of the forms predefined in Project 2000. Fear not, Project comes packaged with nearly 400 custom fields and the tools to create your own custom forms. In this chapter, we'll look at how to create, modify, and manage custom fields and custom forms in Project. We'll begin by defining and locating Project's custom fields and forms. We'll show you ways that custom fields and forms can enhance your work in Project, and then customize fields and include the fields on custom forms. Finally, we'll look at managing your forms using the Organizer.

Introducing Custom Fields and Custom Forms

A field contains one kind of information and is either part of a table, a form view, or the time-phased area of the usage views. In Microsoft Project 2000, there are several categories of fields: task and time-phased task fields, resource and time-phased resource fields, and assignment and time-phased assignment fields.

 Project 2000 isn't a database management tool, such as Access, so you can't create new tables and add new fields at will. To allow customization, Project includes groups of predefined fields that are assigned. The fields are already assigned to the task, resource, and assignment tables. Each field in a group has a similar placeholder name, such as TaskCost1, TaskCost2, through TaskCost10, to allow up to 10 custom Task Cost fields. When you customize one of the fields, you change its placeholder name and set the field's properties. You can't, however, add fields to the tables—customization is limited to the predefined fields. Tables 23.1 through 23.3 show the custom fields included in the Task, Resource, and Assignment tables.

Custom Task Fields

The task fields are used in the task views, such as the Gantt Chart, Task Sheet, and Network Diagram views, to display specific information for each task. Table 23.1 shows each custom field located in the task tables, the field type, and an example of how you might use the fields in the group.

TABLE 23.1: CUSTOM TASK FIELDS

Field Name	Field Type	Examples of Uses
TaskCost1–TaskCost10	Currency	Track high and low historical task costs in your project. Enter the highest reported historical cost for a task in the Cost1 field and rename it **HighPastCost**. Enter the lowest historical cost in the Cost2 field and rename the field **LowPastCost**.
TaskDate1–TaskDate10	Date	Include an estimated completion date for the work on a milestone phase. Add the DateX field to the table. Then, for all milestone assignments, enter the estimated completion date in this field.
TaskFinish1–TaskFinish10	Date	Include interim finish dates in a task sheet. Add the FinishX field and call it "Interim Finish." Or, add a custom finish field and enter a projected milestone finish date for the task.
TaskStart1–TaskStart10	Date	Record interim start dates in a task sheet. Add the StartX field and call it **Interim Start**.
TaskDuration1– TaskDuration10	Duration	Enter the longest estimated duration for a task in the Duration1 field and the shortest estimated duration in the Duration2 field.
TaskOutlineCode1– TaskOutlineCode10	Enumerated	The project accountant refers to the project plan to obtain information about task costs. She wants to see tasks grouped by cost centers and to obtain summarized information based on these cost centers. She creates a custom outline code field called **Task Cost Code**, along with a lookup table with the list of codes. She then applies the appropriate cost codes to the applicable tasks. She gets the hierarchical and summarized information she needs when grouping by the custom Task Cost Code outline code field.
TaskNumber1– TaskNumber20	Percent and Number	Use to show which department is responsible for a task. Add a NumberX field to the Task Sheet view, rename it **Dept Code**, and then enter the appropriate data. You can sort on the Dept Code field to show how tasks are grouped by department, or show the organizational structure of a project.
TaskText1–TaskText30	Text	Use to show which department is responsible for each task. Add a TextX field to the Task Sheet view, rename it **Dept Name**, and enter the appropriate data. Use it the same way as the Dept Code field described previously.
TaskFlag1–TaskFlag20	Yes/No	Use to identify certain tasks for which you need to track specialized accounting information. Add a Flag field and click Yes in the field for each task that needs the special tracking. Filter for that Flag field to view and work with only those tasks marked Yes.

PART

V

Customizing and
Automating Project 2000

Custom Resource Fields

The resource fields are all the custom fields you can use in the resource views, such as the Resource Sheet and Resource Usage views. These fields show summarized information for each resource (but not individual assignment information). Table 23.2 shows each custom field located on the resource tables, the field type, and an example of how it might be used.

TABLE 23.2: CUSTOM RESOURCE FIELDS

Field Name	Field Type	Examples of Uses
ResourceCost1–ResourceCost10	Currency	Use to track high and low estimated resource costs in your project. Rename Cost1 **High Est. Cost**, and enter the highest estimated resource cost for a task. Rename Cost2 **Low Est. Cost**, and enter the lowest estimated resource cost.
ResourceDate1–ResourceDate10	Date	Use to add birthdays to your resource information. Add the Date1 field to the Resource Sheet, and call it **Birthday**.
ResourceFinish1–ResourceFinish10	Date	Use to store additional baseline finish and start dates. To save pairs of start and finish dates as interim baseline plans, point to Tracking on the Tools menu, click Save Baseline, and then click Save Interim Plan. Click the custom start and finish fields you want to use.
ResourceStart1–ResourceStart10	Date	Use to store additional baseline finish and start dates. To save pairs of start and finish dates as interim baseline plans, point to Tracking on the Tools menu, click Save Baseline, and then click Save interim plan. Click the custom start and finish fields you want to use.
ResourceDuration1–ResourceDuration10	Duration	Enter the longest estimated duration for a resource in the Duration1 field and the shortest estimated duration in the Duration2 field.

Continued

TABLE 23.2 CONTINUED: CUSTOM RESOURCE FIELDS		
Field Name	**Field Type**	**Examples of Uses**
ResourceOutlineCode1– ResourceOutlineCode10	Enumerated	The project resource manager refers to the project plan to obtain organizational information about resources. He wants to see resources grouped according to the organizational breakdown structure, and to obtain summarized information based on this structure. He creates a custom outline code field called *Organization*, along with a lookup table with the list of codes. He applies the appropriate organization codes to the applicable resources. He sees the hierarchical and summarized information he needs when grouping by the custom Organization outline code field.
ResourceNumber1–ResourceNumber20	Percent & Number	Use to show the department to which each resource belongs. Add a NumberX field to the Resource Sheet view, rename it **Dept Code**, and then enter the appropriate data. You can sort the resources using the department name field to show how the resources are distributed by department or to show the organizational participation in a project.
ResourceText1–ResourceText30	Text	Use to show the department to which each resource belongs. Add a TextX field to the sheet portion of the Resource Sheet view, rename it **Dept Name**, and enter the appropriate data. Use it the same way as the Dept Code field described previously.
ResourceFlag1–ResourceFlag20	Yes/No	Use to review contract resources residing in a variety of groups. Add a Flag field and click Yes in the field for each contractor. You can then filter for that Flag field to view only those resources marked Yes.

PART

V

Customizing and
Automating Project 2000

Custom Assignment Fields

The assignment fields can be viewed only at the bottom of the Task Form and Resource Form and in the Task Usage and Resource Usage views. They show information about each assignment. You can change the assignment field that appears at the bottom of the Task Form or Resource Form view by pointing to Details on the Format menu, and then clicking a command. Each command shows a different set of assignment fields. Table 23.3 shows each custom field located on the assignment tables, the field type, and an example of how it might be used.

 NOTE You can't type information in the customized assignment fields like you can with customized task and resource fields. You can import or export data into and out of the assignment fields, display them in views and reports, and update them with VB code.

TABLE 23.3: CUSTOM ASSIGNMENT FIELDS

Field Name	Field Type	Examples of uses
AssignmentCost1– AssignmentCost10	Currency	Use to track high and low estimated costs in your project. Enter the highest estimated cost for an assignment in the Cost1 field and the lowest estimated cost in Cost2.
AssignmentDate1– AssignmentDate10	Date	Use to define interim start and stop dates if work on the assignment is interrupted before an interim finish point is reached.
AssignmentFinish1– AssignmentFinish10	Date	Use to include interim finish dates for multistep assignments, or finish dates based on percent complete.
AssignmentStart1– AssignmentStart10	Date	Use to include interim start dates for multi-step assignments.
AssignmentDuration1– AssignmentDuration10	Duration	Use to compare estimates. Enter the longest estimated duration for an assignment in the Duration1 field and the shortest estimated duration in the Duration2 field.
AssignmentNumber1– AssignmentNumber20	Percent & Number	Use to show which department is responsible for an assignment. Add a NumberX field to the Task Usage view, rename it **Dept Code**, and then enter the appropriate data. You can sort on the Dept Code field to show how assignments are grouped by department, or to show the organizational structure of a project.
AssignmentText1– AssignmentText30	Text	Use to show which department is responsible for each assignment. Add a TextX field to the sheet portion of the Task Usage view, rename it **Dept Name**, and enter the appropriate data. Use it the same way as the Dept Code field described above.

Continued ▶

TABLE 23.3 CONTINUED: CUSTOM ASSIGNMENT FIELDS

Field Name	Field Type	Examples of Uses
AssignmentFlag1– AssignmentFlag20	Yes/No	Use to separate work done by employees versus contractors. Add a Contractor field and click Yes in the field for each assignment to a contractor. You can then filter on the Contractor field to view only those assignments marked Yes.

Where to Use Custom Fields

Custom fields can be inserted and displayed in any sheet view. In addition, you can use custom fields in the dialog boxes listed in Table 23.4.

TABLE 23.4: WHERE CUSTOM FIELDS CAN BE INSERTED

Dialog box	To Display
Column Definition	Double-click the column heading to display.
Filter Definition	Select Project ➢ Filtered For ➢ More Filters. Choose a filter name, and then click Edit.
Customize AutoFilter	On the Formatting toolbar, click the AutoFilter button. In a column heading, open the drop-down list, and choose Custom.
Crosstab Report	Select View ➢ Reports ➢ Custom and select a Crosstab Report. Before previewing the report, click the Edit button, and then click the Sort tab.
Box Styles	Choose View ➢ Network Diagram. Select Format ➢ Box Styles ➢ More Templates. Select a template and click Edit.
Replace	Select Edit ➢ Replace
Table Definition	Select View ➢ Tables ➢ More Tables. Select a table name, and then click Edit.
Bar Styles, Text tab	Select Format ➢ Bar Styles and click the Text tab.
Bar Styles	Choose View ➢ Calendar, and then choose Format ➢ Bar Styles.
Sort	Select Project ➢ Sort ➢ Sort By.
Find	Select Edit ➢ Find.
Define Import/Export Map	Select File ➢ Save As. In the Save As Type drop-down list, choose Text (Tab delimited). Select Save ➢ New Map.

PART

V

Customizing and
Automating Project 2000

Creating Custom Fields

Creating a custom field is actually "customizing a custom field" by renaming an existing Project field. You can insert a custom field, as in any sheet view, by inserting a column. Custom fields can be part of a calendar bar, Gantt Chart, or Network Diagram task box. You can also sort and search on custom fields. Follow these steps to create a custom field. The attributes, calculation method, and display options are discussed in depth in the text that follows the steps.

Follow these steps:

1. Select Tools ➤ Customize ➤ Fields. The Customize Fields dialog box is displayed, as shown in Figure 23.1.

FIGURE 23.1

Set field name and properties in the Customize Fields dialog box.

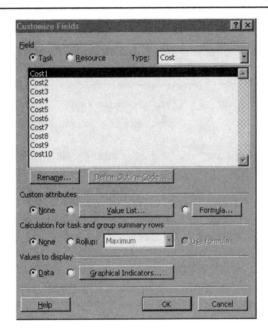

2. Select Task or Resource to choose the table in which you want to customize a field.

3. Select the field type from the Type drop-down list.

4. Select the field you want to customize.

5. Click the Rename button to rename the field.

TIP Don't skip this step, even if you're customizing only one field in a project file. A descriptive name serves two purposes: It reminds you of the field's contents. But perhaps more importantly, changing the placeholder name lets other users know that this field is already being used.

6. Select the Custom Attributes, Calculation method, and Values display options. Click OK when you're finished customizing the field.

Setting Custom Attributes for a Custom Field

The custom attributes specify the way values are entered in the custom field. You can specify a list of values or construct a formula used to calculate the field value. The custom attribute choices are as follows:

- None
- Value List
- Formula

You'll often select None to create a text box in which a user types data. This is the type of field used for Task Name, Resource Name, and other open text fields.

Creating a Value List   Use Value List to create a drop-down list of values that users select from. The Resource Type field in the Resource Sheet and the Task Type field on the Advanced tab of the Task Information dialog box are two of Project's many value list fields. Users appreciate the convenience of selecting from a drop-down list if the following situations are true:

- Choosing from the list is faster than typing the full entry.
- The list is organized in a logical way so users can locate their item.

If the list of values is too long or users have to hunt for the entry they want to select, the value list is an impediment rather than an aid. (As the project manager and person responsible for summary reporting, you might, however, choose to include a list that other users view as cumbersome.)

Consistency may be the hobgoblin of small minds, but it vastly improves the usefulness of reports and views that are sorted, grouped, or filtered. Lists improve reporting, sorting, and filtering because they standardize the data entered in a field: Human Resources is always entered as Human Resources rather than HR, Human Res., or Personnel. If the entire universe of values that can appear on the list is known, you can limit users to values that appear on the list.

For greater flexibility with lists that may change, you can allow users to enter new items, and add the new items to the list automatically or with the user's confirmation.

PART

V

Customizing and
Automating Project 2000

To create a value list for the custom field, click the Value List button in the Customize Fields dialog box to open the Value List dialog box shown in Figure 23.2.

FIGURE 23.2

Use the Value List dialog box to define values for a drop-down list for the custom field.

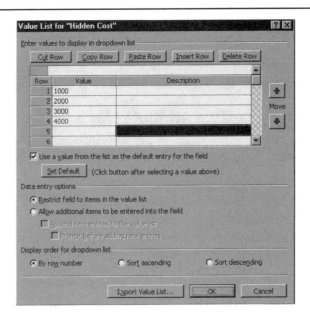

Click the Import Value List button to import a value list already defined for another field into this custom field. To create a new list, enter the values and optional descriptions in the value table. Set the default value by enabling the Use A Value From The List As A Default Entry For The Field check box, selecting the default field, and clicking the Set Default button. The field you set as the default is displayed in red.

If you limit the entries to the values already defined in the value list, you'll see this warning:

The message box appears, even if there are no existing entries in this field. Click OK to proceed. Click Cancel if you want to verify the Value List. Click the Allow Additional Items To Be Entered Into The Field checkbox to not restrict the field to only those items on the list.

Finally, choose the order in which the value list drop-down list will be displayed.

MASTERING THE OPPORTUNITIES

How Value Lists Behave

The type of value list used in Project allows users to choose an item from a value list by typing. The user can click the drop-down arrow to open the list, and then type the first character to move to the first entry that begins with that character. Typing additional characters moves you to the first entry that begins with the string of characters the user has entered. In a value list of state abbreviations, for example, typing an **M** moves to MA, the abbreviation for Massachusetts; typing an **N** moves to MN, Minnesota (rather than to NM for New Mexico).

This is somewhat helpful because before typing any characters the user must click the drop-down arrow to open the list. In a limited list, if the user simply types **M** and presses Enter or Tab to choose Massachusetts, Project displays an error message:

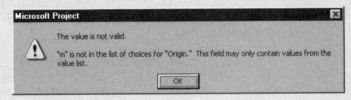

If the list is not limited, M is accepted as a valid entry, which makes it difficult to accurately report on the contents of this field.

Creating a Calculated Field Calculated fields display results based on a formula. Some of the fields in Project 2000 (such as those listed below) use code to simulate calculated fields, but the results of the calculation can be overwritten by the user:

- Task Start Date, Finish Date, Total Cost
- Duration, Work, Units Assigned

Custom calculated fields are read-only—you can't overwrite a value in a custom calculated field.

In the Customize Fields dialog box, select the Formula option to open the Formula dialog box shown in Figure 23.3. Enter the formula you want to use to calculate the custom field. You can type in a formula *a la* Microsoft Excel. Or, Project will build a formula as you select fields from the Field drop-down list, functions from the Function drop-down list, and operations using the operator buttons. Click the Import Formula button to import a formula already defined for another field into this custom field.

FIGURE 23.3

The Formula dialog box defines the formula used to calculate the value of a custom field.

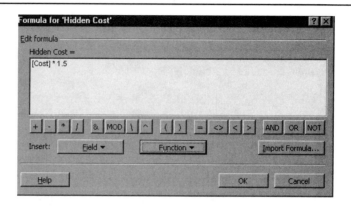

Setting Calculations for Summarization

Number and date fields can be summarized. (This option is disabled for text fields.) In the Customized Fields dialog box, select a calculation method to be used when the field is placed in summary reports:

None   The field is not part of any summary rows.

Rollup   Rolls the value of your field up into the summary rows based on the method you select. The choices are Average, Average First Sublevel, Maximum, Minimum, and Sum.

Use Formula   This choice is enabled only when you have selected a formula to be used for calculating the value of the custom field. With this option, Project applies the formula to the data in the summary row just as it does for an individual task, resource, or assignment item.

Setting the Field's Display Options

For all fields, set the Values to Display option in the Customize Fields dialog box to indicate how the field should be displayed.

Use the following to specify how the field will actually appear in views—with data or a graphical indicator:

Data   The actual values will be displayed.

Graphical Indicators   Displays a selected graphical indicator in place of the actual data values.

Choosing the Graphical Indicators option opens the Graphical Indicators dialog box:

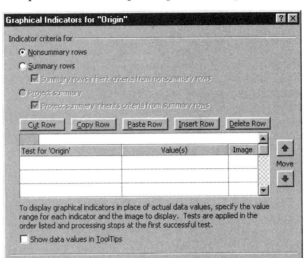

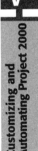

To set a graphical indicator, select whether the indicators will be displayed for non-summary rows, summary rows, or the project summary. Then use the three columns in the grid to set criteria for each value or range of valid values for the field, as follows:

1. In the Test column, choose an appropriate logical test for each value.

2. In the Value column, enter a value (a text string, number, date) or choose a field from the drop-down list.

3. In the Image column, choose a graphic indicator from the drop-down list of colorful little symbols.

Click the Import Indicator Criteria button to import a criteria list from another field. If you want users to be able to see the data on demand, enable the Show Data Value in ToolTips check box.

For example, we have created a custom field called Maximum Overtime Cost Allowed. We want to display a red flag when the Actual Overtime Cost field on the Task Table is greater than or equal to the Maximum Overtime Cost Allowed. The settings in the Graphical Indicators dialog box are shown in Figure 23.4.

After you create a custom field, insert the field as a column in a view as you would insert any other column. The field appears in alphabetical order in the field list.

In the graphical Indicators dialog box, you can choose to display a red flag when maximum overtime costs have been exceeded.

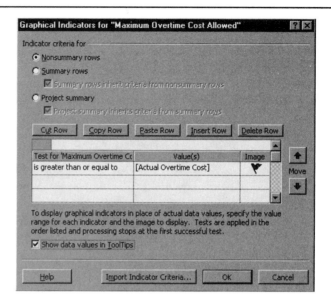

Deleting Custom Fields

You can delete only the *attributes* of a custom field: the custom field existed before you customized it, and will exist after you reset its attributes. For example, if you have created a new custom field by renaming Cost7 to **Maximum Cost**, deleting Maximum Cost deleted any attributes you gave the field, such as the name or the valid values associated with it. However, you cannot delete the Cost1 field.

To delete a custom field from the current project or the global template, do the following:

1. Select Tools ➤ Organizer to open the Organizer.

2. Click the Fields tab.

3. Select the custom field you want to delete in the global template, Global.mpt, or the active project's list.

4. Click the Delete button.

5. Click OK to close the Organizer.

Your custom field's attributes are removed and the field can be customized for another purpose.

Practice with Custom Fields

In Chapter 22, "Creating Project 2000 Macros," we invited you to create macros and a menu bar to get a hands-on feeling for Project 2000 programming features without altering one of your own very important project files. In this chapter, we'll create two custom fields and a custom form that will include the fields. The fields and custom form will become part of the Travel Application developed in Chapter 24, "Automating Project 2000 with VBA," and Chapter 25, "Advanced Programming in Project 2000."

Here are the two fields we need to create. We'll walk you through the first field. You can create the second field on your own:

In the Task table, we need a text field named Location. In the Task table, we also need a cost field, Travel Cost, with a Sum rollup method. To create the Location field:

1. Select Tools ➢ Customize ➢ Fields to open the Customize Fields dialog box.
2. Select Task to choose the Task table.
3. Select the field type, Text, from the Type drop-down list.
4. Select the field you want to customize, Text1.
5. Click the Rename button to rename the field.
6. Enter Location in the Rename Field dialog box and click OK.
7. Click OK to close the Customize Fields dialog box.

Creating Custom Forms in Project 2000

A *form* is a window or container for working with information within Project 2000. Forms are used for data entry, and allow access and updating of fields not displayed in the current view. Forms make data entry easier and reduce the chance of data entry error by placing fields consecutively in the order they are generally entered.

Each form contains a number of *controls*—interface elements such as text boxes, option buttons, and command buttons—that you use to interact with the form. You'll be familiar with most (if not all) of these controls from your work with other Windows applications and with the default dialog boxes and forms used in Project. In addition to the Task Information and Resource Information dialog boxes, there are twelve built-in forms used for specialized data entry, described in Table 23.5.

TABLE 23.5: BUILT-IN FORMS

Form Name	Type	Description
Cost Tracking	By Task	A snapshot view that compares costs and percentage of work and duration completed.
Earned Value	By Task	Displays calculations of Schedule Variance, Cost Variance, and Variance at Completion. You can enter only the Percent Complete in this form.
Task Entry	By Task	Allows users to enter the Task Name, Duration, Dates fields and Rollup indicator.
PERT Entry	By Task	Allows users to enter the Optimistic, Expected, and Pessimistic duration estimates.
Schedule Tracking	By Task	Displays the Start and Finish Dates baseline, actual, and calculates the duration. You can change the Percent Complete.
Task Relationships	By Task	Displays the list of predecessors and successors for the task you select.
Tracking	By Task	Displays the duration and dates for the selected task. You can change the Percent Complete.
Work Tracking	By Task	Allows users to update the Actual and Baseline Work fields, along with the Work Percent Complete and Task Percent Complete.
Cost Tracking	By Resource	Displays the total work and costs for a resource for all tasks, as well as total percent complete.
Entry	By Resource	Basic entry for a resource: name, initials, group, standard rate, and max available units.
Summary	By Resource	Displays overall cost and work information. You can update the Maximum Available Units or add Notes.
Work Tracking	By Resource	Compares the percent of work completed to the baseline.

Any custom form you create or change is saved in your active project file unless you use the Organizer to move the form to Global.mpt.

Why Create Custom Forms?

Project 2000's built-in forms provide a great deal of flexibility and functionality straight out of the box. For many business purposes, however, you will need to extend or modify their functionality. For example, if you are managing a project where the team members travel, you might wish to track the travel dates and costs. By using custom forms, you can do this easily. Likewise, you might be able to speed up the creation of frequent task changes or assignment additions by creating custom forms that already contain or automatically enter part of the information for you.

You can customize a form in several ways, as follows:

- Present the information on the form so that you don't have to fill it in each time you create an item based on the form. For example, if you regularly need to create new tasks for "Implementing a Product" at different locations, you can create a custom form that contains all information except the Location Name and Date.

- Add fields to or remove them from an existing form. For example, you might choose to add one or two extra fields to the standard Resource Entry form so you could enter their contact information (phone number and email address) at the same time you enter a resource.

- Create a new form with text, group boxes, buttons and/or fields.

- Change how the controls on the form work.

As with Microsoft Outlook, the primary method of creating a custom form in Project is by basing it on one of the existing forms. For minor customizations, you can simply extend the existing functionality of a form by adding custom fields and features. For more radical customizations, you can remove most of the existing components for a form, providing yourself with an almost clean slate for designing your own form. You can also build a custom form from scratch.

Opening a Custom Form

Before you start with a brand new form, check the predefined forms in Project. You can see all the custom forms from any view, but you can only apply custom forms from a view of the correct associated table. For example, you must go to a view based on the Resource table, such as Resource Sheet, Resource Graph, or Resource Usage view to apply a custom resource form.

To open a custom form, do the following:

1. Select Tools ➢ Customize ➢ Forms. The Custom Forms dialog box opens, as shown in Figure 23.5.

PART

V

Customizing and
Automating Project 2000

FIGURE 23.5

The Customize Forms dialog box contains a list of all the custom forms you can display.

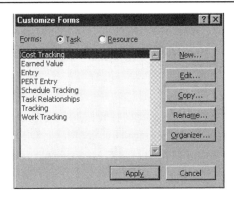

2. Choose Tasks or Resources to choose the type of form you want to display.

3. Select a form from the Forms List.

4. Click the Apply button to view the custom form.

MASTERING THE OPPORTUNITIES

Improving Access to Custom Forms

The multi-step method for opening a custom form is cumbersome, especially if you frequently use a particular custom form. To simplify matters, you can assign a shortcut key to your favorite custom form or add a command to open the form to a toolbar or menu bar.

To assign a shortcut key, select a form from the list in the Custom Forms dialog box and click the Rename button. In the Key box, type the letter you want to use to activate the custom form. Make sure that your selected letter isn't already being used in Project. If you choose a letter that is reserved (such as Ctrl+C for copy), you will be warned of the conflict and instructed to choose another character.

You can also assign the Form Open command to a button. Simply select Tools ➤ Customize ➤ Toolbars. Select the All Forms category and choose the form you want to appear on your toolbar. You can drag and drop the Form Name to the top of your screen. Most of the forms already have a graphic assigned (Cost Tracking), but you can further customize the button by adding a graphic for those poor forms that are text only (PERT Entry). Add the button to your toolbar, right-click on the button, and select Change Button Image from the shortcut menu.

If you record a macro (Tools ➤ Macros ➤ Record New Macro) that includes opening a custom form, you have to close the custom form before you can stop recording (Tools ➤ Macros ➤ Stop Recording). Close the form by clicking the OK button. If you click Cancel, Project assumes that you didn't mean to open the dialog box, so it doesn't record the action. Information on creating macros and adding macros to command bars is in Chapter 22.

Creating a Custom Form

If you have created custom fields in your project, or just need to enter or view information in ways not covered by the predefined custom forms, you can create your own custom form or modify an existing form. We will be using the Custom Form Editor to create a new custom form. This form, called Travel Information, contains the two custom fields we added in the last section—Location and Travel Cost—as well as the Task Name.

Working with the Custom Form Editor is similar to creating a form in Access, but the editor is less sophisticated. You select the table that contains the information you want to display, format the information, add labels and text, and assign actions to be performed.

You have following three choices when making a custom form:

Edit an Existing Form   From the Custom Forms dialog box, you can select an existing form and press the Edit button. This displays the Custom Form Editor with the selected form open for editing. Any changes you make and save to the selected form will change the predefined custom form in this project only.

Copy an Existing Form   You can use an existing form as a template when making a new custom form. Clicking the Copy button in the Custom Forms dialog box opens a dialog box where you can name your new form and assign it a shortcut key. After you click OK, the Custom Forms dialog box opens the selected form for editing, as shown in Figure 23.6.

PART

V

Customizing and
Automating Project 2000

FIGURE 23.6

You can use the Custom Form Editor to edit a copy of an existing custom form.

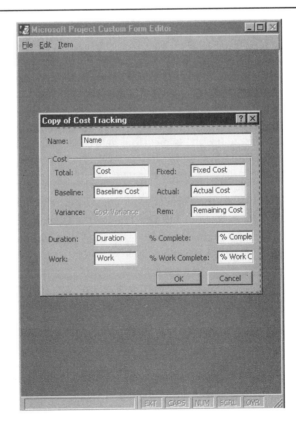

Create a New Form When you click the New button in the Custom Forms dialog box, the Custom Form Editor opens with a small empty dialog box open for editing. The only buttons that are on the new form are the OK and Cancel buttons.

 NOTE The Custom Form Editor is an application invoked by Project. The Editor doesn't have toolbars, so use the File, Edit, and Item menus to work on custom forms. To exit the application, select File ➤ Exit. The Close button on the title bar of the custom form is disabled while you are working in the Custom Form Editor.

Working in the Custom Forms Editor

After you select a custom form to edit or copy, or choose to create a new form, name the form in the Define Custom Form dialog box and then enter the Custom Form Editor. Here's a step-by-step walkthrough of the process required to create a new form called **Travel Information**.

 NOTE This form uses the two custom fields created earlier in this chapter. Information entered in the form is used in the VBA application created in Chapter 25. For some hands-on practice with Project's Custom Form Editor, launch Project 2000 and open the project file that contains the two custom fields, Travel Cost and Location, created earlier (see "Practice with Custom Fields"), or create the two custom fields in a new project file now.

From the Custom Forms dialog box, select the Task radio button on the Forms area, and click the New button. The Define Custom Form dialog box is displayed. Enter the data, as shown in Figure 23.7. When you press the OK button, the Custom Forms Editor is displayed.

Name your new forms or rename old forms with the Define Custom Form dialog box. You can also assign shortcut keys from here.

Adding Fields to a Custom Form

The first thing we will do is add the required fields to our Travel Information form. Fields come from your project and Project displays the most current data. Fields can be defined as display-only or updateable. We'll add three fields to this form: Task Name, and two custom fields created for this form, Travel Cost (Cost1), and Location (Text1).

To add fields to a custom form, follow these steps:

1. In the Custom Form Editor, select Item ➤ Fields. The Item Information dialog box, shown in Figure 23.8, is displayed.

PART

V

Customizing and
Automating Project 2000

FIGURE 23.8

The Item Information
dialog box lets you
determine what fields
will be on your form,
their location and size,
and whether or not
they can be updated.

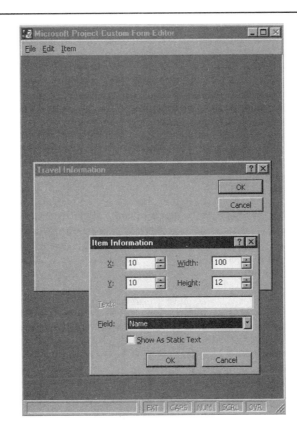

2. Complete the information on the Item Information dialog box for each field you wish to place on your form:

Field Select the field (Name for the Task Name field) from the drop-down list.

X and Y   Select the horizontal and vertical offsets from the upper-left corner of the new form. It's easier to move the field after it has been created, rather than entering values for X and Y, so we'll leave the default settings.

Width and Height   Specify the width and height (in pixels) of the field you are adding to the form. This can also be adjusted by sizing the field once it has been created, so we'll leave the defaults.

Show as Static Text check box   When checked, the field displays as read-only text rather than as an editable field. We want users to be able to enter data in this field, so we'll leave the default Off setting.

3. Click the OK button to place the Name field on the Travel Information form.

Repeat steps 2 and 3 for the custom fields Travel Cost and Location.

 TIP   Use the X and Y offset, width, and height settings when you want to place fields precisely so that a custom form resembles other custom forms in the same set. You can open any custom form in the Editor, double-click on a control, and see its offset and size properties.

Figure 23.9 shows the Travel Information custom form with these three fields added.

FIGURE 23.9

The Travel Information form with fields added

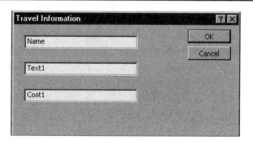

The fields have been added, but this form needs more customization. Now we'll add text to label the fields.

 NOTE   Although you can create a drop-down list to modify a custom field on an existing form, you cannot create a drop-down list box to add to a custom form.

Adding Text to a Custom Form

You add text to a form to identify the fields and controls on the form, to describe the actions a user can take, or to provide additional information that is not obvious from the data fields. We will add a text box to describe what information should be entered on the Travel Information form, and labels for the two custom fields.

To add text to a custom form, follow these steps:

1. In the Custom Form Editor, select Item ➤ Text. A text box appears on the Travel Information form. Double-click on the text box to display the Item Information dialog box, shown in Figure 23.10.

2. In the Item Information dialog box, enter the following information:

    Text Type in the text you want displayed in your form.

    X and Y Select the horizontal and vertical offsets from the upper-left corner of the new form, or leave the defaults and move the text box in the Editor.

    Width and Height Specify the width and height (in pixels) of the text box you are adding to the form, or leave the defaults and adjust the field after it has been created.

3. Click OK to close the Item Information dialog box.

PART

V

Customizing and
Automating Project 2000

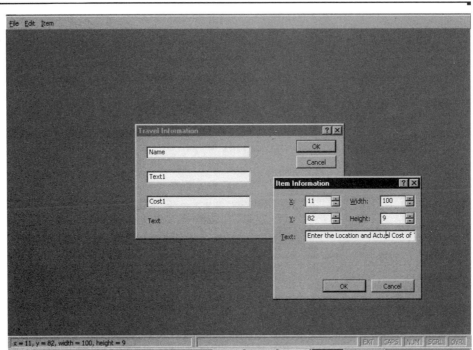

FIGURE 23.10

Use the Item Information dialog box to input the text for your custom forms as well as position the text boxes.

To resize or move a control, first select it. Point to the center of the control and drag the control to move it, or drag one of the handles to resize the control.

We followed the previous instructions to create three text boxes. One contains instructions for users, one is the label for the custom field Location, and the last is the label for the custom field Travel Cost. Figure 23.11 shows the Travel Information form with the three text boxes added, and the following position and size adjustments:

- The two field labels have been moved to be next to their respective fields.

- The instruction box has been resized so that all the information is visible.

- Text1 and Cost1 have been moved to the right.

- The Task Name field has been expanded so long task names will display fully.

The Travel Information custom form contains all the fields and labels it needs to be used by team members entering their travel costs.

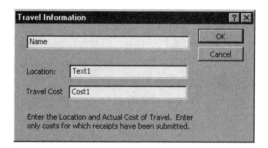

Adding a Group Box to a Custom Form

Group boxes are used to create sections in a custom form. Related information can be visually differentiated and complex forms seem simpler when fields are placed in logical group boxes. As an example, see the Define Import/Export map dialog box. Importing is such a complex process that there are four tabs of data and within each tab there are one or more group boxes to clarify the data that needs to be entered.

NOTE Forms like the Define Import/Export dialog box can't be created in the Custom Form Editor. Complex tabbed forms are created using the Visual Basic UserForm editor, which you'll see in Chapter 25.

On our custom form, the process is much simpler, as follows:

1. In the Custom Form Editor, select Item ➤ Group Box. A group box appears on the Travel Information form. Double-click on the group box, and the Item Information dialog box for group boxes is displayed. This is the same as the Item Information dialog box for text.

2. In the Item Information dialog box, enter the following information:

Text   Type in the name of your group box.

X and Y   Select the horizontal and vertical offsets from the upper-left corner of the new form. You can simply move the group box, rather than entering values for X and Y.

Width and Height   Specify the width and height (in pixels) of the group box you are adding to the form. This can also be adjusted by sizing the field after it has been created.

Figure 23.12 shows our custom form with the group box added to improve clarity.

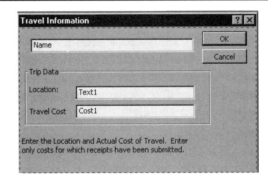

FIGURE 23.12

The trip data has been separated from the rest of the fields on the Travel Information form by adding a group box around the Trip Cost and Location fields.

Adding Buttons to a Custom Form

You can add only two buttons to a custom form: OK and Cancel. (This is because custom forms are built on a dialog box "chassis.") To add a button in the Custom Form Editor, select Item ➤ Button. Select the OK or Cancel button to place it on your custom form.

TIP   You can resize and move the buttons after they have been created, but we don't recommend resizing them, nor do we recommend placing them in new and unique locations. The buttons are created in the standard size used in Project 2000 forms. If you move the buttons, make sure that the OK button is to the left of the Cancel button in a horizontal layout, or above the Cancel button in a vertical layout to conform to the Windows standard and minimize user error.

Change the Position of a Custom Form

You can set the size of your custom form when it opens, as well as its location in the current window. For example, if you will always be opening your custom form from the Gantt Chart view and don't want to cover up the Task Names, you would move your dialog box toward the right side of the window. To change the position or size of your custom form when it opens, do the following:

1. From the Customize Forms dialog box (Tools ➤ Customize ➤ Forms), select your form and click Edit. The Custom Form Editor is displayed.

2. Select Edit ➤ Select Dialog to select the whole form, or click on the background of the custom form.

3. Select Edit ➤ Information or double-click on the form to display the Form Information dialog box.

4. Type in the X and Y coordinates for your form (1,1 is the upper-left of your screen) and increase the value in either field to move the dialog box to the right (for X) or down (for Y) one pixel. Clicking Auto for X and Y will center your dialog box on the user's screen. The X and Y coordinates will be automatically updated when you move your form around within the Custom Form Editor screen.

5. Type in the Width and Height of your custom form. Changes to the size of the form using the mouse automatically update these fields.

6. Choose File ➤ Save to save your form.

7. Choose File ➤ Exit to close the editor and return to Project 2000.

Using the Organizer to Manage Custom Forms

So, now you've made this wonderful Travel Information form and you want to use it in other projects. How do you make the custom form available outside your project? By using the Organizer to move the custom form definition to Global.mpt.

Select Tools ➤ Organizer to display the Organizer dialog box. Select the Forms tab, shown in Figure 23.13. The left pane shows forms in the global template. The right pane shows forms in the current project. (See Chapter 21, "Customizing Project 2000," for information on using the Organizer.)

To copy a form to the global template, follow these steps:

1. Select the form in the current project.

2. Click the Copy button to copy the form to the global template.

3. Click OK to close the Organizer.

FIGURE 23.13

The Forms Organizer is used to manage custom forms.

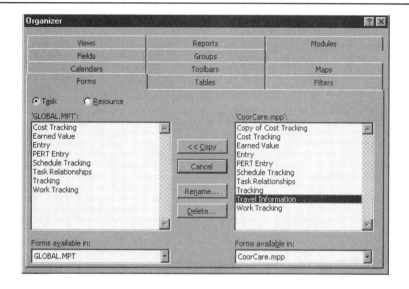

You also might need to delete a custom form in order to replace it with a newer form. Use the Organizer to perform this task also.

To delete a form, follow these steps:

1. Choose Tools ➤ Organizer to display the Organizer.

2. Click the Forms tab.

3. Select the form you want to delete.

4. Click the Delete button. You'll be prompted to confirm the deletion.

5. Click OK to close the Organizer.

What's Next

Macros, discussed in Chapter 22, and custom fields and forms, discussed in this chapter, provide a lot of tools for customizing Project to suit your needs. If you need to go even further, Visual Basic gives you the maximum flexibility for making Project do exactly what you want it to do. In the next two chapters, you'll learn how to customize Project 2000 extensively with Visual Basic.

PART

V

Customizing and Automating Project 2000

CHAPTER **24**

Automating Project 2000 with VBA

Automation has always been the great promise of the computer age—get more work done or lounge in your recliner as the computer toils away at repetitive tasks. In order to have your computer perform a series of actions at the click of a button, you need to tell the computer what to do in words that it understands. What if your company has a need for a specialized contact sheet, wants to speed up the budget approval system, or wishes to collect disparate versions of a Word document and create a report on the changes as quickly as possible? Clippit is cool, but you can't simply tell your computer to "go do" these things, as you would tell a human assistant. You need to write a program.

This is where Visual Basic and Visual Basic for Applications (VBA) come in. Computers are perfectly literal, so when writing a program, you have to tell the computer exactly what to do, where to find things, and what to do if something unexpected happens.

Microsoft has worked hard to make programming with VB and VBA relatively easy, using English language terms strung together to tell your computer what to do. If you've programmed in the past, you should find Visual Basic fairly easy to learn. If you haven't programmed before, the learning curve will be a little steeper because you also have to learn to think like a computer. But the hardest part about using VB to automate Project 2000 is learning Project 2000, not learning VB. If you're working in this chapter, chances are you already have Project 2000 under your belt.

In the next two chapters, we will discuss Visual Basic and its offspring, VBA. There is yet another child of Visual Basic, called VBScript, that is used in Microsoft Outlook and is fine-tuned for Internet and communication tasks, but that's a different application!

 NOTE   VB and VBA are identical in syntax: the commands and command structures you use to create programs. Microsoft created VBA with a trimmed-down version of the VB programming interface, called the Integrated Development Environment (IDE), which focuses more on augmenting the capabilities of a host application (in this case, Project) rather than creating freestanding applications.

What Is Visual Basic?

To understand what VB is, we need to understand what it does. Within the scope of its capabilities, VB performs the tasks you request. VB cannot be used to tell your computer to tape tonight's WNBA game unless your computer is actually capable of controlling a video-recording device. If it can, taping tonight's game is a slam-dunk with VB.

However, you will probably not be seeking video recording help from VB. You'll use the application-based version of VB, VBA, to automate tasks and extend the capabilities of Project 2000. Project is an accomplished assistant for a number of project management tasks, but Microsoft realized that there was no way it could anticipate the exact needs of all its users, so it enabled you to enhance Project 2000 by using programming code and forms.

Introducing the Integrated Development Environment

When you add a resource, record progress on a task, or map data for import, you are using a form. As shown in Chapter 23, "Customizing Fields and Forms," you can use the Microsoft Form Editor to create and modify Project's custom forms. Working in the Visual Basic Integrated Development Environment to create code or a form is not much different from creating a Project custom form—except that the IDE is more powerful and easier to use than the Custom Form Editor! As you'll see, the "visual" part of Visual Basic comes from the fact that most of the code is generated by drawing the controls onto a virtual canvas, the aforementioned forms. To open the VBA IDE, start up your computer and follow these steps:

1. Open Project and select Tools ➤ Macro ➤ Visual Basic Editor. You can also open this window by holding Alt and pressing F11.

   The Visual Basic environment is displayed. If this is the first time you've opened the IDE, it's a blank sheet. Now, we will open the windows we need to begin working in the IDE.

2. Select View ➤ Project Explorer. The Project Explorer window is displayed.

   This window is used like the Windows Explorer to select the project and the Objects, Forms, or Modules with which to work.

3. Select View ➤ Properties Window.

   The Properties window contains the properties for the selected object. If you have worked with Microsoft Access, you already have experience with Properties Windows. If not, browse through the properties for your currently active project and you will see that display, prioritization, and function defaults are defined in this window. Changes you might have made to your project defaults will appear in the Properties window.

You now have a large blank area in which to work, and two open windows, Project Explorer and Properties, with which to begin. This pristine IDE is shown in Figure 24.1.

PART

V

Customizing and
Automating Project 2000

FIGURE 24.1

The Visual Basic environment includes several windows.

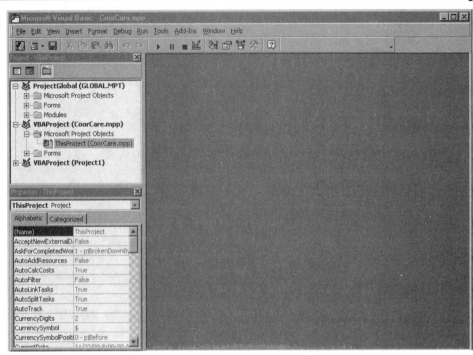

Understanding Objects and Events

We'll create a simple UserForm to introduce the different parts of the VBA IDE and some VB concepts. Select Insert ➢ User Form, or click the Insert User Form button on the toolbar. A new User Form window opens in your workspace, along with a VB toolbar called the Toolbox, which contains form controls.

A *control* is an object, such as a button or a text field, that you add to a form and that can modify the form's behavior. For example, the OK buttons that show up in most dialog boxes are controls.

 NOTE If you ask five programmers "What's an object?" you'll get five different answers, ranging perhaps from "Huh?" to a formal definition of an object from the world of object oriented programming: an object is a self-contained entity that includes both code and data. This formal definition is not only more useful than the first, it's also arguably true for VB objects. Here's a more approachable definition: an *object* is a component or a collection of components. Objects can contain other objects. The Project 2000 application is an object, which includes a Project object, which includes a Calendar object.

Attached to (or "behind") each control, you create code that makes the control do what you wish. If the control you placed on your form was a CommandButton control, you could, for example, program the button to open a Save dialog box to automatically let you choose a folder and save the current document. Or, you could have the button print the current view, close the application window, or any other task within VB's universe of programmability. The CommandButton is just a button to which you can attach code.

An *event* is a user- or system-generated action, such as the user clicking on a button or a CD-ROM activating the AutoPlay software. Visual Basic is called an event-driven programming language because it responds to events. You place control objects on your forms and then program them to activate in response to specific events. In the case of a command button, you would program it to respond to a Click event: the event that happens when a user mouses over to and clicks the button.

Each control on a form has its own capabilities and can be coded to operate independently of everything else on the form. As an example, we'll look at the OK button that you find in almost every dialog box. To create an OK button in VB you would simply click the CommandButton tool in the Toolbox, drag the cursor to the form, and drop. This procedure creates a button called **CommandButton1**, as shown in Figure 24.2. Note that the Project Explorer window is now set to your new UserForm, and the Properties window is displaying properties for the CommandButton you have just added.

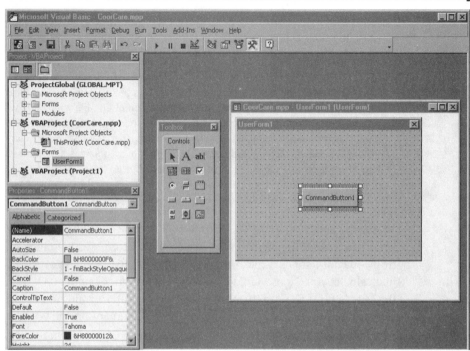

FIGURE 24.2

A new Command-Button on a form

Understanding Controls and Properties

Each control has a set of properties that defines how the control works. The properties for the CommandButton control are simple, and you use them to define the way the control looks and behaves. In Figure 24.3, the Default property of CommandButton1 is set to True. This means that if you open this form in an application and press the Enter key, the button will "click" as if you'd clicked the button with the mouse. In Windows applications, almost all dialog boxes have a default button that responds this way when you press the Enter key. The default button is enabled when the dialog box opens.

Another of the control's properties is its Name. Each control receives a unique name when it is created so it can be individually identified later. You can rename your controls anything you like as long as each name is unique. It is also a good idea to make the names easily recognizable so that you can readily recognize their purpose when you reuse or edit the code next year.

TIP In the naming convention used by most VB programmers, command button names are prefixed with cmd: for example, cmdOK, cmdPrintReport, and cmdCancel.

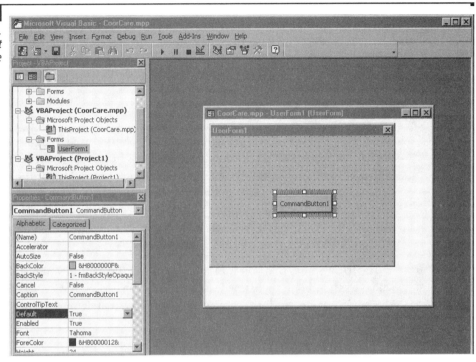

FIGURE 24.3

CommandButton, showing the Default property set to True

When you choose a control to place on a form, your choice is based largely on the properties the control needs to have and the events the control needs to be able to respond to. If you want a control that responds to a user mouse click, then a command button will do fine. It's not the control you'd choose, however, if you want a control that a user can enter text in.

If we create a simple form, place a CommandButton control and a TextBox control on it, and program the form to put something in the TextBox control when the CommandButton is clicked, we have a simple example of programming in action:

If, on the other hand, we include the controls and omit the code, we'll have an example of programming "inaction." The form will look the same, but without code to tell the button control what to do, it won't do anything. When you click the button, nothing happens. It's safe to say that users don't appreciate this type of form very much, regardless of how nice it looks or how many hours you spent creating it.

Understanding Visual Basic Code

You can think of writing code as writing a list of instructions for the computer to use. In the IDE, we would begin creating the instructions by double-clicking the Command-Button control to open the Code Editor, which automatically adds the following code (which, in the world of programmers, is called a *snippet* or a *stub*):

```
Private Sub CommandButton1_click()


End Sub
```

The IDE assumes that you want to add code to the control you just double-clicked, which was automatically named CommandButton1 when it was placed on the form. This snippet is a procedural framework, a structure that defines the beginning and the end of a Visual Basic procedure.

 NOTE In the code snippet (no relation to Clippit), `Private` tells the control that this code will only be available in the form that it is being constructed in.

Sub is short for subroutine. The terms subroutine and function both refer to types of procedures in VB. Independent blocks of VB code are called *procedures*. There are three kinds of procedures in VBA: functions, subroutines, and property procedures. You probably already know what a function is from your work with Excel functions (such as AVERAGE and SUM) or Project calculated fields: a *function* is code that returns a value as the result of one or more calculations, comparisons, or other operations. For example, when you SUM a column of numbers in Excel, the result (a total) is returned to the cell containing the SUM formula. A *subroutine* is code that performs an operation, but doesn't return a value. For example, a subroutine can open or close a form or report, launch an application, or write values in a table.

 NOTE Property procedures are beyond the scope of this book—but please don't confuse them with plain old properties, which you'll be working with a lot in this chapter.

CommandButton1_Click identifies the CommandButton by name and indicates what event will trigger the procedure: a click. End Sub indicates the close of the procedure.

 NOTE If you define a name for the control in the control's Name property, such as cmdOK, before opening the code window, that name is used in the click event procedure in the code.

To get the command button to close the window when it is clicked, we just need to add one command between the Private Sub and End Sub lines: Unload Me. The whole completed procedure looks like this:

```
Private Sub CommandButton1_click()
    Unload Me
End Sub
```

 Now that we've added a command in language that VB can understand, it will perform the action we ask of it. Clicking the small blue arrow button on the toolbar that looks like the Play button of a CD or DVD player (or pressing F5) causes the form to run. This is the same as selecting Run ➤ Run Sub/UserForms. If you click the Command button on the form, the form disappears.

 NOTE You can create code without first creating a button: it's called a macro. See Chapter 22, "Creating Project 2000 Macros," to learn how to create macros using the Macro Recorder. To create a new macro in the VBA IDE, choose Tools ➤ Macro ➤ Macros and type a name for the macro. The Create button will be enabled. Click the Create button to open the Visual Basic Editor.

Making Use of Visual Basic

In the previous section, we took a quick look at what VB is and the parts of the VBA IDE. Now, we're going to examine what VB can be used for. To begin, let's further examine what VB can do as a language.

VB is a complete and powerful event-driven language, which means that each component, like our example button, can operate independently of the rest of the program. When an event occurs, VB responds by running the procedure that was defined for that specific event, if any. If no procedure was defined for the event, nothing happens. These event procedures are tied to the controls that you place on your forms for user interaction or to use Project 2000 or Windows features: for example, the Common Dialogs control adds the capability to use system-based Open and Save dialog boxes with only a few lines of code.

In our example in the previous section, we told CommandButton1 to execute the code related to it when it was clicked. The click was the event and the code executed is the event procedure.

 NOTE Event-driven programming should not be confused with object-oriented programming languages. A programming language can be event-driven, object-oriented, or both. For example, programs such as Visual C++ and Delphi are both event-driven and object oriented. These languages (which are more complicated to understand and use than VBA) allow objects to define the parameters of children objects through inheritance. VBA doesn't support this level of object-oriented inheritance, but it is nevertheless a very powerful programming environment. The full version of Visual Basic, used to create commercial applications, supports the development of COM components (ActiveX DLLs and EXEs), which can be used in multiple applications. If you have the Microsoft Office Developer's version of Office 2000, you can create COM Add-Ins for Project 2000 in the VBA IDE.

Generally, VB is considered a Rapid Application Development (RAD) tool, with which custom solutions can be prototyped, debugged, and built in a much shorter period of time than with other languages. One of the more common reasons VB is deployed is to provide fast development of database front-end applications. Here are three uses that specifically relate to Project:

- You can automate forms and data handling, create new data, or access existing data in a project file from another application.
- You can launch and use other Office 2000 applications from within Project.
- You can customize Project to better meet your needs by creating customized forms and personalized applications.

We will now revisit the Visual Basic IDE in greater detail, so you can more completely take advantage of the programming capabilities of Project 2000.

Introducing the Visual Basic IDE

Project 2000 macros are stored in Visual Basic *modules*. So, the macros you've already created with the Macro Recorder are written in VB. To examine or edit a macro, choose Tools ➤ Macros to open the Macros dialog box, select the macro you want to examine, and then click the Edit button to open the Visual Basic Integrated Development Environment (IDE), also referred to as the VB Editor. To go directly to the VB Editor from Project, choose Tools ➤ Macro ➤ Visual Basic Editor.

FIGURE 24.4

The Visual Basic IDE includes a Code window, Project Explorer, and Properties window.

Object list   Code window   Procedure list

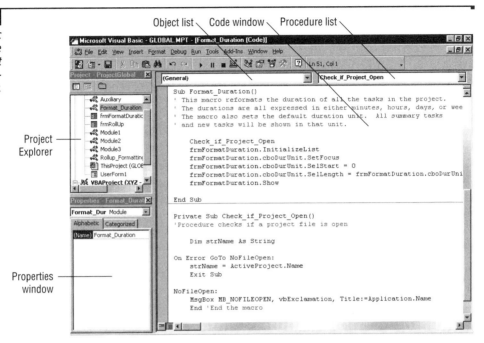

Project Explorer

Properties window

In Figure 24.4, the Project Explorer and Properties window are open to the left of the Code window. The Project Explorer shows all the open VBA projects. Every document can have one project associated with it; the project is stored with the document. The project in Figure 24.4 has three types of project components: project objects, forms and modules. A *module* is a container for VB code. Each macro you create with the Macro Recorder is placed in a new module, so this project contains three macros created with the recorder. Projects can include two other types of project components: classes and references to templates or other documents.

 TIP   If you have a lot of macros, the Project Explorer will quickly fill up with modules. Use cut-and-paste to move the macros to one module window, or use two or three modules to organize your macros by functionality, and then delete the empty modules. To delete a module, right-click it in the Project Explorer and choose Remove Module *n* from the shortcut menu. In addition, you can use the Organizer to work with modules and macros, and decide which should reside only in your own project and which should be copied to Global.mpt (see Chapter 21, "Customizing Project 2000," for information about how to use the Organizer).

PART

V

Customizing and Automating Project 2000

The Properties window displays the properties for the object selected in the Project Explorer. The Code window displays code from the active component in the Project Explorer. Double-click a module, or select the module and click the View Code button in the Project Explorer to display the module's code in the Code window. If there are a number of macros in a module, select the macro name from the Procedure list at the top of the Code window.

Code lines that begin with an apostrophe (') are *comments* that explain the code. In the Visual Basic Editor, remarks are color-coded green. The code itself is displayed in the default text color, black.

The following code (which also appears in Figure 24.4) is a portion of a Project macro that reformats the duration of all your Project tasks. We created the macro by recording our actions with the Macro Recorder, then we added a subroutine, Check_if_Project_ Open, to see whether the project is actually open before running the macro. Here's the code generated by the Macro Recorder with our one-line addition:

```
Sub Format_Duration()
' This macro reformats the duration of all the tasks in the project. The
durations are all expressed in either minutes, hours, days, or weeks. The
macro also sets the default duration unit. All summary tasks and new tasks
will be shown in that unit.

Check_if_Project_Open

  frmFormatDuration.InitializeList
  frmFormatDuration.cboDurUnit.SetFocus
  frmFormatDuration.cboDurUnit.SelStart = 0
  frmFormatDuration.cboDurUnit.SelLength =  frmFormatDuration
.cboDurUnit.TextLength
  frmFormatDuration.Show

End Sub
```

If you want to learn about Visual Basic, recording macros and studying the resulting code is a good way to begin.

TIP When you are ready to go farther with Visual Basic, you may want to refer to *Mastering VBA 6* (Guy Hart-Davis, ISBN 0-7821-2636-7) and *The Visual Basic Language Developer's Handbook* (Ken Getz et. al, ISBN 0-7821-2162-4).

The previous code begins with the word Sub because it's a subroutine. Following Sub is the macro name we entered in the Record Macro dialog box and a set of parentheses. In a function, the parentheses surround the names of the argument variables that are used by the function, just as they do in Excel and Access. Most macros don't have input variables, so the parentheses are empty. The user name, the date recorded, and other remarks are from the Description in the Record Macro dialog box.

The `Check_If_Project_Open` function does exactly what its name implies, as you'll see later in this chapter. Five lines of code follow. The second line sets the focus on the Combo box "Duration Unit" in the Format Duration form. Setting the Focus means that the control is received by the Combo box for the upcoming actions.

```
frmFormatDuration.cboDurUnit.SetFocus
```

`frmFormatDuration.cboDurUnit` identifies the object within its parent object: `cboDurUnit` is a combination box object on the form `frmFormatDuration`. `SetFocus` is a method of the object. Methods are actions for objects. Methods are discussed later in this chapter.

When the VB interpreter hits the `End Sub` line, it's finished running the macro. It returns focus (control) to the host application, Project 2000.

Creating a Procedure in the VBA IDE

An event procedure is tied to an object event (such as a button's click event), and automatically runs when that event occurs. The `Format_Duration` macro is a *general procedure*. The code isn't tied to any particular button or control, and runs only on demand. General procedures are very useful. You can fire this macro by assigning it to a toolbar button, a command button, the macro menu, a menu bar, or all of the above.

To create a general procedure without the Macro Recorder, follow these steps:

1. Insert a new module (Insert ➤ Module) in the project or open an existing module.

2. Choose Insert ➤ Procedure from the menu to open the Add Procedure dialog box, shown in Figure 24.5.

3. Enter a name for the procedure in the text box. The naming convention for procedures is to use the bas prefix.

4. Choose the Type of procedure you're creating: subroutine, function, or property.

5. Select a scope. The Scope is a procedure's range: Private procedures can be called only by other procedures in the same module; Public procedures can be called by any procedure in the same application.

6. Click OK to add the procedure's snippet to the Code window.

Begin documenting your procedure. Type an apostrophe, hit the space bar, and then enter at least your name and the current date. Feel free to add more descriptive information if you wish, beginning each line with an apostrophe. In the next section, we'll begin entering code to create a procedure.

PART

V

Customizing and
Automating Project 2000

FIGURE 24.5

FIGURE 24.5

Use the Add Procedure dialog box to create new procedures.

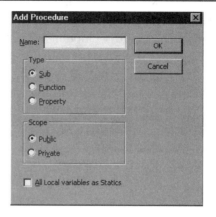

MASTERING TROUBLESHOOTING

Getting Help with VBA and Project 2000 Objects

When you enter code, you need to know which objects are available, and what properties and methods the object has. For a list of objects, use the VBA libraries, which are just a click away in the Object Browser. Click the Object Browser button (or choose View ➢ Object Browser) to open the browser, shown here:

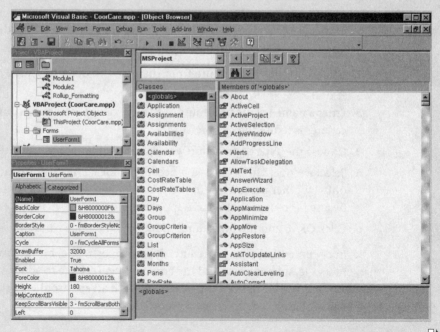

Continued

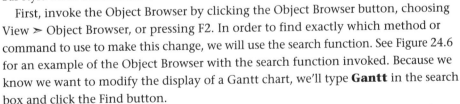

MASTERING TROUBLESHOOTING CONTINUED

The library for the current application should already be selected, but you can choose other libraries from the Project/Library drop-down list. To search for an object, enter part or all of the object's name in the Search Text box and click the Search button. When you choose an object in the Class pane, you'll see a list of properties and methods for the object in the right (Member) pane of the browser. If you want more information about the selected object, click the Help button in the Object Browser.

For a more global view of application objects, browse the object model, the map of all the objects in an application. The model shows each object and how it relates hierarchically to other objects in the application. To access the object model for an application, open the application, launch Help, and search on the word *object*.

Select any object or collection in the model to get more information on the object, including samples of code using the object.

The model uses different colors for objects and *collections*, which are groups of objects. For example, there is a collection of paragraphs in a document and a collection of documents in an application. Collections are important application features from a programming point of view. You can iterate through a collection if you want to count the number of paragraphs or save all open documents, but you also have the ability to affect one item in the collection. Select any object or collection in the model to get more information on the object, including samples of code using the object.

We will now create a simple procedure to format the bars of a Gantt chart for a Milestone task to be blue rather than their default color of black. We will then use this new bar style when a Milestone is Overdue.

First, invoke the Object Browser by clicking the Object Browser button, choosing View ➤ Object Browser, or pressing F2. In order to find exactly which method or command to use to make this change, we will use the search function. See Figure 24.6 for an example of the Object Browser with the search function invoked. Because we know we want to modify the display of a Gantt chart, we'll type **Gantt** in the search box and click the Find button.

FIGURE 24.6

*The Object Browser in
the VBA IDE, with the
results of a search for
the word Gantt*

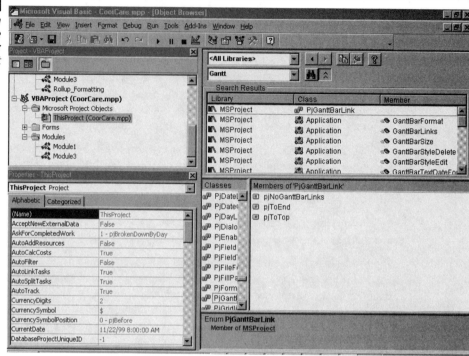

The results of this search include the function Gantt Bar Style Edit. We will use this function to create a new Gantt Bar Style. This function has a lot of arguments. Select the Gantt Bar Style Edit function and click the Help button to open the VBA Help page for this function. Briefly, the syntax for GanttBarStyleEdit is this:

```
expression.GanttBarStyleEdit(Item, Create, Name, StartShape, StartType,
StartColor, MiddleShape, MiddleColor, MiddlePattern, EndShape, EndType,
EndColor, ShowFor, Row, From, To, BottomText, TopText, LeftText, RightText,
InsideText)
```

NOTE If the VBA Help files were not installed as part of your original Microsoft Project 2000 installation, you will be prompted to install them. If you click Yes, make sure that you have the Microsoft Project 2000 CD-ROM available or that Project was installed from a network installation point so the Installer can find the files it needs.

In order to create a new Gantt Chart Bar Style, we need to know the following information:

Argument	Definition
Item Number	For a new style, the Item is always –1
Create	Yes
Name	Overdue Milestone
ShowFor	Milestone
StartShape	Diamond
StartColor	Blue
MiddleShape	None

The code to create the style looks like this:

```
Sub CreateGanttBar()
  GanttBarStyleEdit Item:=-1, Create:=True, Name:="Overdue Milestone",
  ShowFor:="Milestone", StartShape:=pjDiamond, StartColor:=pjBlue,
MiddleShape:=pjNone
```

Now that the Overdue Milestone Gantt Bar Style exists, you can assign it to all milestones in the Gantt chart that are overdue. A Milestone is overdue if it is not completed and the Finish Date is less than (prior to) today. If these two conditions are true, you will use the GanttBarFormat function to assign the Overdue Milestone Gantt Bar Style to your milestones.

```
If Task.Milestone = Yes Then
If Task.ActualFinish > Today Or Empty Then GanttBarFormat GanttStyle:=15
End IfEnd
```

 MASTERING TROUBLESHOOTING

Troubleshooting Simple Code Problems

What can go wrong? Visual Basic is expecting very specific kinds of information. If you forget, for example, to put = True for the Create property, VB will stop executing in the middle of your code and open a message box:

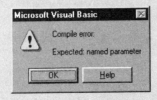

Continued

PART

V

Customizing and
Automating Project 2000

MASTERING TROUBLESHOOTING CONTINUED

When you click the OK button, you'll switch to the VBA IDE. The name of the faulty procedure will be highlighted, and the property that brought VB to a halt will be selected. If the problem isn't obvious, right click-on the code line and choose Quick Info from the menu to see the syntax, required arguments, and optional arguments for the current line of code. Refer to the VB Help files for more in-depth information and examples for objects and properties. Fix the problem, and then click the Run Sub button to try again.

Understanding Parts and Functions of VBA Code

To work with VB, you need to know more about the syntax of the language—the rules that govern how the language works. Just as most human languages have widely recognized parts (such as nouns, verbs, adjectives, and so on), programming languages break down into a number of parts that you put together in *statements*: arrangements defined by the syntax of the language.

You put together statements by using combinations of keywords, objects, properties, methods, constants, and variables, with required arguments and optional arguments specifying information. In the next sections, we'll look at what each of these terms mean and how you work with them.

Keywords

A *keyword* is a word defined as having a meaning in Visual Basic. Keywords include object names, properties, methods, and argument names. It's possible to create variables, constants, and procedures that have the same names as Visual Basic keywords. This is called *shadowing* a keyword, and isn't usually a good idea because it becomes easy to get confused. For example, there's an object called `BaselineCost`, so it's a bad idea to create a variable, constant, or procedure named `BaselineCost`.

As we'll see in a little while, you can name your variables, constants, and procedures pretty much anything that strikes your fancy, so there's no real reason to shadow a keyword—but there are so many keywords in Project 2000 that it's surprisingly easy to shadow a keyword accidentally.

Collections

Groups of objects are organized into collections, which provide an easy way to access the objects. For example, the `ResourceGroups` collection contains a collection of `Group` objects, each of which represents a "group" of resources. The collection `TaskGroups` also contains a collection of Group objects, each of which represents a "group" of tasks. Usually, the name of a collection is the plural of the object, Calendars is the collection of Calendar. The Group collection objects example is an exception, however, where the same object can be collected into two different collections (confused yet?). Collections themselves are objects, too. To reduce confusion, from now on, we'll refer to any collection as a *collection* rather than a *collection object*.

Methods

A *method* is a built-in action that you can perform on an object; more technically, a method is a *procedure* (a set of instructions) for an object. For example, the `Group` object that we met a moment ago has a `Delete` method that deletes the specified group and a `Copy` method that makes a copy of the specified group. The `Calendar` object has methods including `Period` (for representing a period of time) and `Reset` (for resetting base calendar properties to their default values).

Like a property, a method appears after the name of the item it refers to, separated by a period. For example, the `Delete` method appears like this:

```
Item.Delete
```

Most methods take one or more *arguments*: parameters that supply pieces of information necessary to the method. Some arguments are required, while others are optional.

Other methods take no arguments. For example, the `Delete` method takes no arguments, because none is needed—Project is deleting the specified item, and that's all the information it needs to do so.

Constants

A *constant* is an item in memory that keeps an unchanging piece of information while a program is executing. You can specify the appropriate constant in your code instead of the corresponding value, because it provides an easy way of handling complex information or information that may change from computer to computer, such as the location of a particular Project file. Project uses constants to signify frequently used information, such as the month of the year (for example, the constant `pjApril` in the `pjMonth` group of constants represents April) and the options available while performing actions (for example, `pjDateFormat` contains more ways to format the date on Project views and reports than you could possibly use). Each constant has a numeric value associated with it; for example, the constant `pjDate_mm_dd_yyyy` in the `pjDateFormat` group has the numeric value 20 associated with it. When using VBA to automate Project procedures, you can use either the descriptive constants or the numeric values to specify the constant you wish to assign.

Variables

A *variable* is a location in memory that you set aside for storing a piece of information while a procedure is running. You can create as many variables as you need, and you can give them any name that meets Visual Basic's naming rules. As we mentioned before, it's a bad idea to shadow a keyword by giving a variable the same name.

The rules for creating names for variables in Visual Basic and VBA are simple:

- A name can be up to 40 characters long.
- A name must begin with a letter.
- A name can include letters, numbers, and underscores.
- A name cannot include spaces or symbols other than the underscore.
- A name must be unique within its scope.

Scope is discussed in "Creating Variables" later in this chapter.

MASTERING THE OPPORTUNITIES

Naming Variables

When you name a variable, you can include a prefix so that the variable name clearly indicates the type of data the variable is designed to hold. Following this convention from the beginning really pays off when you need to change or troubleshoot your code. Here are the prefixes for the commonly used data types with examples of each prefix used in a variable name:

Boolean: bln (blnOverEstimate)

Currency: cur (curVendorEstimate)

Date: dte (dteEstimatedComplDate)

Integer: int (intDaysPastEst)

Object: obj (objExcelChart)

Single: sng (sngProjInterestRate)

String: str (strLocation)

Try to make your variables names short enough to type accurately, but descriptive.

Data Types

Visual Basic and VBA include a range of variable types, called *datatypes*, designed for particular kinds of data. For example, you would store a string of text such as a word or phrase in a string variable, whereas you would store an integer (whole number) value in an integer variable. Table 24.1 lists the data types available in VBA, and the range of values available for each type. You can also create user-defined types by using the Type statement in VBA. See the Visual Basic help files for more information on creating user-defined data types.

TABLE 24.1: VBA DATA TYPES

Data type	Storage size	Range
Byte	1 byte	0 to 255.
Boolean	2 bytes	True or False.
Integer	2 bytes	-32,768 to 32,767.
Long (long integer)	4 bytes	-2,147,483,648 to 2,147,483,647.
Single (single-precision floating-point)	4 bytes	-3.402823E38 to -1.401298E-45 for negative values; 1.401298E-45 to 3.402823E38 for positive values.
Double (double-precision floating-point)	8 bytes	-1.79769313486231E308 to -4.94065645841247E-324 for negative values; 4.94065645841247E-324 to 1.79769313486232E308 for positive values.
Currency (scaled integer)	8 bytes	-922,337,203,685,477.5808 to 922,337,203,685,477.5807.
Decimal	14 bytes	+/-79,228,162,514,264,337,593,543,950,335 with no decimal point; +/-7.9228162514264337593543950335 with 28 places to the right of the decimal; smallest non-zero number is +/-0.0000000000000000000000000001.
Date	8 bytes	January 1, 100 to December 31, 9999.
Object	4 bytes	Any Object reference.
String (variable-length)	10 bytes + string length	0 to approximately 2 billion.
	Length of string	1 to approximately 65,400.
Variant (with numbers)	16 bytes	Any numeric value up to the range of a Double.
Variant (with characters)	22 bytes + string length	Same range as for variable-length String.
User-defined (using Type)	Number required by elements	The range of each element is the same as the range of its data type.

The Variant data type is the default data type, so it is automatically used if you don't specify a data type when you declare a constant, variable, or argument. Variables declared as the Variant data type can contain string, date, time, Boolean, or numeric values. Variant data types take up more storage space than other types, and should be avoided unless the data type is unknown.

MASTERING THE OPPORTUNITIES

Converting a Variable to a Different Type

In a procedure, you might need to convert data to a different type in order to process it or modify it. The following table lists the functions used to convert data in VBA.

Function	Returns
Abs	Absolute value of the number or expression
Asc	ASCII value of the first character in the specified string
Chr	Character representing the ASCII value entered
Cbool	True if the expression is nonzero, otherwise False
Cdate	Date representation of the expression or number
DateSerial	Date variable of the date specified by year, month, and day
DateValue	Date variable from a text expression or a string
TimeSerial	Date variable of the time specified in hours, minutes, and seconds
TimeValue	Date variable from a text expression or a string
CByte	Byte representation of the expression or number
CInt	Integer representation of the expression or number
CLng	Long representation of the expression or number
CSng	Single-precision representation of the expression or number
CDbl	Double-precision representation of the expression or number
CStr	String representation of the number; also returns a string from a Boolean, Date, or error value
Fix	For positive values: next lower whole number; for negative values: next lower whole negative number
Int	For positive values: next lower whole number; for negative values: next higher whole negative number
Sgn	1 for positive value, -1 for negative value (the sign of the expression or number)
Hex	String containing hexadecimal representation of the expression or number
Oct	String containing octal representation of the expression or number

Continued

MASTERING THE OPPORTUNITIES CONTINUED

Here are several examples using these conversion functions:

- `Asc(strCity)` returns the ASCII value of the first character in the string `strCity`.
- `CBool(1000-900)` returns `True`.
- `DateSerial(1998, 10, 31) - DateSerial(1998, 9, 19)` returns **42**, the number of days between the two dates.
- `Hex(16)` returns **10**, the hexadecimal representation of the decimal number 16.

You can use all the conversion functions in calculated custom fields, too.

Creating a Variable

You can create a variable in two ways: by declaring it *explicitly* (listing it at the beginning of a procedure) or by creating it *implicitly* (by simply using it in your code).

Declaring a Variable Explicitly   When you declare a variable explicitly, you can also set the variable's scope, which determines where the variable will be available. There are three types of scope:

- Procedure level: the variable is only used in the procedure.
- Private level: the variable can be used by any procedure in the same module.
- Public level: the procedure can be used by any project open at the same time as the module that contains the procedure.

To declare a variable explicitly, use a `Dim` statement, a `Private` statement, or a `Public` statement. Variable declarations are usually listed at the top of a subroutine, immediately following the opening Sub line and any user documentation, so they're available when needed in the procedure.

To declare a variable with procedure-level scope, use a `Dim` statement within the procedure. The following procedure asks the user for an estimate date. The second line of code declares a procedure-level variable called `dteEstDate` (a date variable). The third statement displays an input box and assigns its result to the `dteEstDate` variable.

```
Sub InputEstDate()
   Dim dteEstDate as Date
   dteEstDate = InputBox("Enter the date for this estimate.")
End Sub
```

Private and Public scope variables are declared at the *module level*: code at the beginning of the module prior to any procedures. All private and public variables must be declared explicitly with module level code.

To declare a variable with Private scope, use a `Private` statement prior to the procedure at the beginning of the module. The following statement creates an integer variable named `intDaysPastEst` with Private scope:

```
Private intDaysPastEst As Integer
```

To declare a variable with Public scope, use a `Public` statement prior to the procedure at the beginning of the module:

```
Public objExcelChart As Object
```

Creating a Variable Implicitly   Instead of declaring a variable explicitly, you can create it implicitly by typing the variable's name in code. The following statement implicitly creates the variable `intMyValue` by assigning the value **123** to it:

```
intMyValue = 123
```

When you create a variable implicitly, it has procedure-level scope only, and is assigned the Variant datatype.

MASTERING THE OPPORTUNITIES

Declaring Variables

If you're creating variables with procedural scope, it's still a good idea to declare them explicitly. When you declare variables implicitly, every typo becomes a new variable. It's easy, for example, to mistype `intExprDate` as `intExpDate`. With implicit variable creation, you now have two variables. You can spend a long time trying to determine why your code isn't working as designed.

There's another reason to use explicit declaration: your code is easier to change or troubleshoot when you can easily see the variables used in a procedure at the top of the procedure's code.

Continued

To make sure that every variable used in a procedure is declared, set the Require Variable Declaration option on the Editor page of the Visual Basic Editor's Options dialog box (Tools ➤ Options):

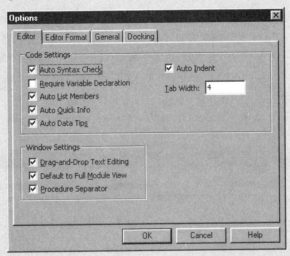

You can also require explicit declaration on a procedure-by-procedure basis by entering **Option Explicit** as a module-level command prior to the first procedure at the beginning of the module.

PART

V

Customizing and
Automating Project 2000

Assigning a Value to a Variable

To assign a value to a variable, use an equal sign after the variable name, followed by the value. The following statement assigns the value 55 to the variable intDaysExpired:

```
intDaysExpired = 55
```

The following statement assigns the value "Ferndale" to the variable strLocation:

```
strLocation = "Ferndale"
```

 TIP To assign an object to a variable, you need to use a Visual Basic Set statement rather than the equal sign.

VBA Operators

VBA provides a full complement of *operators*—items used for comparing, combining, and otherwise working with values. The operators fall into four categories:

- Arithmetic operators (such as + for addition and / for division) for mathematical operations
- Logical operators (such as Or) for building logical structures
- Comparison operators (such as = and >=) for comparing values
- String operators (such as & for joining two strings)

Table 24.2 lists the operators in their categories, with brief examples of each and comments on the operators that are not self-explanatory.

TABLE 24.2: VBA OPERATORS

Operator	Meaning	Example	Comments
		Arithmetic Operators	
–	Subtraction	x = y–1	
–	Negation	–x	
+	Addition	x = y + 1	
*	Multiplication	x = y * 2	
/	Division	x = y / 2	
\	Integer division (Div)	x = y \ 2	Integer division truncates the remainder.
^	Exponentiation	x = y ^ 2	
Mod	Modulo	53 Mod 12	Modulo returns the "remainder" part of a division operation.
And	Conjunction	If x>1 And x<2	Both conditions must be True for a True result.
Not	Negation	If not x>1	
Or	Disjunction	If x>100 Or X<20	If either condition is True, the result is True.
XOr	Exclusion	If x>100 XOr y>100	If one condition is True and the other is False, the result is True; the result is False if both conditions are True or both are False.
Eqv	Equivalence	If x Eqv y	If both are True or both are False, the result is True.

Continued ▶

Operator	Meaning	Example	Comments
TABLE 24.2 CONTINUED: VBA OPERATORS			
		Logical Operators	
Imp	Implication	If x Imp y	True if both values are True or the second comparison is True.
		Comparison Operators	
=	Equality	If x = y	
<>	Inequality	If intTest <> 55	
<	Less than	If x < 10	
>	Greater than	If x > 20	
<=	Less than or equal to	If x <= 9	
>=	Greater than or equal to	If x >= 19	
Is	Object equivalence	If x is y	
		String Operators	
&	Concatenation	strA&strB	
+	Concatenation	strA+strB	Less-often used due to potential confusion with addition.

PART

V

Customizing and
Automating Project 2000

Structures Used in VB Code

In this section, we'll briefly discuss some of the programming structures that you can use in Visual Basic code. These structures fall into three major categories:

- Sequential structures, in which one command follows another and all commands are executed.
- Conditional structures, in which a decision is made to execute one set of commands based on the value of a variable.
- Looping structures, in which one or more commands are repeated.

Sequential Structures

Sequential structures are the simplest structures. The procedure executes each command, in order, until it hits the End Sub command. The sample statements that have appeared in this chapter and the macros we created in Chapter 22 used a sequential structure.

Using Conditional Structures

Conditional structures are used to direct program flow based on one or more conditions. There are two major types of conditional structures: If (in a variety of flavors) and Select Case.

If Statements

VBA supports three types of If statements:

- If/Then
- If/Then/Else
- If/Then, ElseIf/Else

VBA also supports the IIF (immediate if) statement used in Microsoft Access.

The If/Then Statement   The If/Then statement is the simplest If statement, and is the same statement used in Excel, Access, and a variety of programming languages. Here's the syntax of the If/Then statement:

```
If condition Then
   (commands executed when condition = True)
End If
```

The condition is a test constructed using operators and variables or constants. If the condition is true, the lines of code between the If and End If statements is executed once. If the condition is false, VB skips to the command line that follows the End If statement.

If/Then/Else Statements   With the If/Then/Else statement, you can execute one of two sections of code, depending on the condition. The syntax is as follows:

```
If condition Then
   (commands to be executed when condition = True)
Else
   (commands to be executed when condition = False)
End If
```

If/Then... ElseIf/Else Statements   The third type of If statement is the If/Then...ElseIf/Else statement. This structure lets you test more than one condition. The syntax for the basic If/Then...ElseIf/Else statement is as follows:

```
If condition1 Then
   (commands to be executed when condition1 = True)
ElseIf condition2 Then
   (commands to be executed when condition2 = True)
Else
   (commands to be executed when neither condition = True)
End If
```

With this version of If, VB executes the first group of commands if the first condition is true. If the first condition is false, it checks to see whether the second condition is true. If it is, it executes the second group of commands. You don't have to stop here. You can use ElseIf again and test a third condition, a fourth condition, and so on. If none of the conditions is true, VB executes the commands following the Else statement and prior to the End If.

As soon VB tests a condition that is True, it executes the commands following the condition, then skips to the command following the End If statement. No other conditions are tested.

Select Case Statements

Select Case is much like If/Then...ElseIf/Else, and is used to execute one or more commands based on one value. Here's the syntax for Select Case:

```
Select Case expression
  Case expression1
    [commands]
  Case expression2
    [commands]
  Case Else
    [commands]
End Select
```

The Select Case structure begins with a Select Case statement and ends with an End Select statement. *Expression* is a value or phrase used to determine which case gets executed. VB evaluates each Case statement in turn. As soon as finds a matching case, it executes the commands for that case, then skips to the command line following the End Select statement.

Looping Structures

VBA supports a bevy of looping structures used to repeat a set of commands. The two families of looping structures are For loops and Do loops. For loops execute a series of commands a set number of times based on the value of a counter that's incremented by VB. Do loops rely on a condition and check to see whether it's true or still true before the commands in the loop are executed. We'll discuss four different looping structures commonly used in VBA:

- For/Next
- Do While
- Do/Loop While
- Do Until

For/Next Loops

A For/Next loop repeats for a specified number of times, controlled by a counter variable. The syntax for a For/Next loop is:

```
For counter = start To end [optional Step stepvalue]
    (commands to be executed if counter < end)
Next counter
```

The counter is a numeric variable. When VB hits the For line, it checks the value of the counter and compares it to the End value:

- If the current value of counter is less than or equal to the end value, VBA executes the statements in the loop. When it hits the Next line, it increments the counter and loops back to the For command.

- If the current value of counter is more than the end value, VBA skips to the command line following the Next command.

By default, the counter value is incremented by 1. To have VB increment by a different positive or negative value, include the optional Step keyword, followed by the increment you want to use:

```
For intTaskCount = 10 to 50 Step 5
```

If the Step increment is a negative number, VB subtracts the increment from the counter and continues executing the commands in the loop until the counter value is less than the end value:

```
For intTaskCount = 50 to 10 Step -5
```

There are four types of Do loops: Do While... Loop loops, Do... Loop While loops, Do Until... Loop loops, and Do... Loop Until loops. In the following sections, we'll look at each type in turn.

Do While Loops   The Do While loop tests a condition, and executes the commands in the loop as long as the condition is true:

```
Do While condition
    (commands executed if the condition is true)
Loop
```

The first time VB hits the Do While command, it evaluates the condition. If the condition is true, VB executes the commands in the loop. The Loop command returns execution to the Do While line, where VB evaluates the condition again.

Do/Loop While Loops   With Do While, if the condition is false the first time through, the commands between Do While and Loop are never executed. If you need the commands to execute at least once, use the Do Loop While command structure:

```
Do
    (commands executed if condition is true)
Loop While condition
```

With this structure, the condition isn't tested until the commands in the loop have been executed once.

Do Until Loops   The Do Until structure is the opposite of the Do While structure. With Do Until, commands in the loop are executed until the condition is met:

```
Do Until condition
    (commands to be executed if condition is not true)
Loop
```

NOTE   There's also a Do/Until loop structure that tests the condition after the first time through the loop.

PART

V

Customizing and
Automating Project 2000

Using Message Boxes and Input Boxes

In your programs and macros, you can use message boxes to display information or ask for confirmation of a task. By using an If structure or Select Case structure linked to the value that the message box returns, you can determine which button in the message box the user has chosen. You can use this value to direct the program flow appropriately.

The syntax for displaying a message box with VBA is as follows:

```
MsgBox(Prompt[, Buttons] [, Title] [, Helpfile], [, HelpContext])
```

Prompt is the only required argument for the MsgBox statement. Prompt is a string that is displayed as the text in the message box.

Buttons is an optional argument that specifies the buttons that the message box displays, the icons that the message box displays, the default button, and the modality of the message box. Each of these four elements can be specified with either a value or a constant. You use the + operator to join the values or constants together.

Your first choice is the buttons the message should display. Your options are shown in Table 24.3.

TABLE 24.3: COMMAND BUTTON CONSTANTS

Value	Constant	Buttons
0	vbOKOnly	OK (the default if you omit the Buttons argument)
1	vbOKCancel	OK, Cancel
2	VbAbortRetryIgnore	Abort, Retry, Ignore
3	vbYesNoCancel	Yes, No, Cancel
4	vbYesNo	Yes, No
5	vbRetryCancel	Retry, Cancel

Next, you can choose which (if any) of the standard four message box icons to display. The choices are shown in Table 24.4.

TABLE 24.4: STANDARD MESSAGE BOX ICONS

Value	Constant	Displays
16	vbCritical	Stop icon
32	vbQuestion	Question mark icon
48	VbExclamation	Exclamation point icon
64	VbInformation	Information icon

Next, you can set a default button for the message box. If you choose not to set a default button, VBA makes the first (leftmost) button in the message box the default—the Yes button in a vbYesNo message box, the OK button in a vbOKCancel message box, and so on. Table 24.5 gives you the choices of default buttons for a message box.

TABLE 24.5: MESSAGE BOX DEFAULT BUTTONS

Value	Constant	Default Button
0	vbDefaultButton1	The first button
256	vbDefaultButton2	The second button
512	vbDefaultButton3	The third button
768	vbDefaultButton4	The fourth button

In theory, you can choose whether to make the message box application modal (the default) or system modal. Application modality means that you can take no further actions in the application until you dismiss the message box; system modality means you can take no further actions on your computer until you dismiss the message box. In practice, this system modality does not work—even if you use the vbSystemModal argument, the resulting message box will be application modal. (See Table 24.6.)

TABLE 24.6: MESSAGE BOX MODALITIES

Value	Constant	Modality
0	vbApplicationModal	Application modal
4096	vbSystemModal	System modal

Finally, you can now specify some new information for your message box. The Help button can now be automatically added, the message box window can be set in the foreground, and two options that are most useful when working with Project in a language that reads from right to left. Text can be right-aligned, and text can read from right to left. (See Table 24.7.)

TABLE 24.7: MESSAGE BOX OPTIONS

Value	Constant	Displays
16384	vbMsgBoxHelpButton	Adds Help button to the message box
65536	VbMsgBoxSetForeground	Specifies the message box window as the foreground window
524288	vbMsgBoxRight	Text is right aligned
1048576	vbMsgBoxRtlReading	Specifies text should appear as right-to-left reading on Hebrew and Arabic systems

Title is an optional string argument specifying the text to appear in the title bar of the message box. In most cases, it's a good idea to specify a Title argument to make it clear which procedure has caused the message box to appear. If you do not specify a Title argument for the message box, VBA will display **Visual Basic** in the title bar, which is singularly uninformative.

Helpfile is an optional argument, specifying the Help file to invoke if the user summons help while the message box is displayed.

Context is an optional argument, specifying the topic to display in the Help file. If you use the Helpfile argument, you must use a corresponding Context argument.

For example, the following statement specifies the message box shown in Figure 24.7. This message box has Yes, No, and Help buttons, with the No button the default, and displays the question mark icon.

```
MsgBox "Delete all selected tasks?", vbYesNo + vbDefaultButton2 + vbQuestion +
vbMsgBoxHelpButton, "Delete Selected Tasks"
```

FIGURE 24.7

A custom message box, using a vbDefault-Button2 setting and a question mark icon

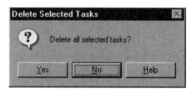

The previous statements simply display the message boxes described. They don't let you know which button the user clicked. To return a value from a message box, declare a variable for the value and set the value of the variable to the result of the message box:

```
Dim intResponse as Integer
intResponse = MsgBox "Delete all selected tasks?", vbYesNo
```

VBA stores the user's choice of button as a value in the Response variable. Table 24.8 shows the values and their corresponding constants.

TABLE 24.8: MESSAGE BOX RESPONSE VALUES

Value	Constant	Button Selected
1	vbOK	OK
2	vbCancel	Cancel
3	vbAbort	Abort
4	vbRetry	Retry
5	vbIgnore	Ignore
6	vbYes	Yes
7	vbNo	No

The following statements use a Select Case structure to establish which button the user chooses in an Abort/Retry/Ignore message box:

```
Dim AbortRetryIgnore
AbortRetryIgnore = MsgBox("Abort, retry, or ignore?", vbAbortRetryIgnore +
vbCritical
Select Case AbortRetryIgnore
Case vbAbort
  'Abort the procedure
Case vbRetry
  'Retry the procedure
Case vbIgnore
  'Ignore
Case Else
  'Nothing should produce a Case Else here
End Select
```

For simple Yes/No or OK/Cancel message boxes, you can use a straightforward If statement:

```
If MsgBox("Is it raining?", vbYesNo + vbQuestion, "Weather Check") Then
  MsgBox "It's raining."
Else
  MsgBox "It's not raining"
End If
```

PART

V

Customizing and
Automating Project 2000

Use the Buttons Arguments in Order for Easy Reading

The Buttons arguments do not have to be in the order discussed here—they will work in any order. For example, VBScript is smart enough to work out that the 1 in the following statement, rather than either of the 0s, refers to the type of message box:

```
MsgBox "Proceed?", 0 + 16 + 1 + 0, "Bad Value"
```

Better yet, you can mix values and constants if you wish. So the following three statements are functionally equivalent:

```
MsgBox "Proceed?", 1 + 32 + 256 + 4096, "Bad Value"
MsgBox "Proceed?", vbOKCancel + vbQuestion + vbDefaultButton2 +
vbSystemModal, "Bad Value"
MsgBox "Proceed?", 4096 + 32 + vbOKCancel + 256, "Bad Value"
```

Continued

CONTINUED

That said, your code will be easier to read if you use the standard order: type of message box, icon, default button, and then modality. It will also be easier to read—though a little longer—if you use the constants rather than the values.

Using Input Boxes

You can use input boxes to gather single pieces of information from the user. By using an If structure linked to the value the input box returns, you can determine whether the user has entered valid information and direct program flow appropriately.

The syntax for an input box is as follows:

```
InputBox(Prompt, Title, Default, XPos, YPos, Helpfile, HelpContext)
```

Prompt is a required string argument that specifies the text prompt to be displayed in the input box.

Title is an optional string argument that specifies the text for the title bar of the input box. As with MsgBox, if you don't specify a Title argument, VBA will display **Visual Basic** in the title bar of the input box.

Default is an optional string argument that specifies the default text to display in the text box inside the input box. Often, you'll want to omit the Default argument. At other times, you may want to use a Default argument to provide text likely to be suitable for the user (for example, the current user name in an input box asking for the user's name) or text that may need adjustment.

XPos and YPos are measurements in *twips* (a twip is 1/1440") that specify the horizontal and vertical positioning of the input box on the screen. It's usually best to omit these arguments and have VBA use the default positioning for the input box, which is centered horizontally and one-third of the way down the screen.

As for MsgBox, Helpfile, and Context are optional arguments specifying the Help file and topic to use. When you specify Helpfile and Context, VBA adds a Help button to the input box.

To display an input box and return the text string that the user enters, declare a variable for it and set the value of the variable to the result of the input box:

```
Dim strUserName as String
strUserName = InputBox("Enter your name.", "User Name")
```

You can then check the value of the variable (here, strUserName) to make sure that it is not an empty string (""), which will result if the user either clicks the Cancel button in the input box or clicks the OK button without entering any text in the text box. Figure 24.8 shows this input box.

FIGURE 24.8

Use an input box to get one piece of information from the user.

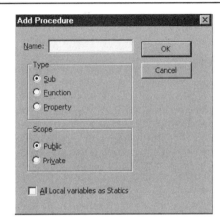

PART

V

Customizing and
Automating Project 2000

What's Next

This chapter introduced you to essential VBA concepts so you can begin writing your own VBA code. In the next chapter, you'll apply the information from this chapter to create a custom VBA application in Project 2000.

Advanced Programming in Project 2000

For the bulk of this book, you've been learning how to do things yourself in Project 2000. In Chapter 22, "Creating Project 2000 Macros," you started learning to teach Project to complete tasks using the Macro Recorder. The Macro Recorder is teaching *by example*. Programming is teaching *by instruction*. In this chapter, you will spend less time *showing* Project how to do it and more time *telling* Project how to do it. Before you can explain things to Project/VBA, you will need to learn about the way VBA views Project.

In this chapter, you'll have the opportunity to create two applications: a Charged Cost Application and a Linked Expenses application. Project is not an accounting program, so it doesn't have built-in support for job costing and estimating for external customers. The rate and fixed cost information entered in a Project 2000 project file can reflect our internal cost for a project or the prices that we'd charge to customers, but not both.

The Charged Cost application allows you to track two sets of costs within one project so you can generate reports for internal and external use. To do this, we'll use two rate tables and some code that switches between the two. Although we built (and actually use) this application to track internal and external costs, this is not the limit of its use. The Charged Cost application could also be used for testing different scenarios when planning a project: "Should we build our new line of widgets in our Kalamazoo plant or in our Springfield plant?"

The Linked Expenses application demonstrates linking Project 2000 task fields to external sources. The Linked Expenses application was designed to link the Fixed Cost field of a task to a cell in an Excel workbook to look up distance information. After you examine the application, you can create similar applications to retrieve information from Excel, Access, and other data sources for use in Project 2000.

 NOTE In Chapter 23, "Customizing Fields and Forms", we created two custom fields for the Linked Expenses application. If you skipped this activity, go back to the "Practice with Custom Fields" sidebar in Chapter 23 and create these fields now.

Understanding the Project Object Model

Every application that can be automated with Visual Basic has an object model. The *object model* is a road map to the objects in the application that have been *exposed*—that can be used in VB automation. By now, you should understand the Project object model fairly well: you have been reading about it and working with it for the last 24 chapters. The structure of the Project object model mirrors the structure of Project 2000.

You know, for example, that before you can create a task, you need to have a project opened. Likewise, in VB you will need a Project object before you can create a Task object. There's a term for the relationship between the two: the Project object is the *parent object* for the Task object.

Project 2000 is built on the concept of the Component object model (COM). Simply put, COM is the idea that an application has built-in components, with each component responsible for providing a specific functionality. The application is built by linking together the individual components. COM allows existing components to be reused for other applications. New components can be introduced or existing components replaced without requiring an update to the entire application.

COM is not a new idea in software, but what is significant about Microsoft's implementation of COM, ActiveX, is that it is a widely used standard. Prior to ActiveX, there were a number of company-specific standards for developing COM components. If a product were built on one standard, it could not share components with or utilize components from another standard.

ActiveX, developed by Microsoft but currently administered by the Open Group, is a standard set of technologies that allows applications such as COM components to work together, even if they were created using different programming languages. Object model ActiveX is based on abstracting code into objects that have properties, methods, and events. These objects are exposed so they can be manipulated with Visual Basic code.

 NOTE Like most applications, Project 2000 has objects that aren't exposed, so they can't be directly manipulated programmatically.

Project 2000 exposes many more objects than prior versions of Project. Exposed objects can be used in a VBA module attached to a project document or called from other programs such as Excel, Word, and Visual Basic to automate actions within Project. An application's ActiveX object model is your reference guide to the objects that you can use in programming code. The ActiveX object model is hierarchical in structure like the Windows folder structure. For example, the Project Object contains collections of task objects and resource objects because a project file can contain tasks and resources. The Project Object is the parent object of both the Task Object and the Resource Object. Figure 25.1 details the hierarchy of the Project object model.

PART

V

Customizing and
Automating Project 2000

FIGURE 25.1

The Project Object Model, as shown in the Project Help file

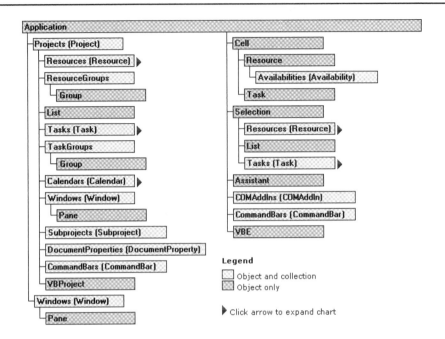

Two objects in the structure (the Application Object and the Project Object) are publicly creatable; the others are not. A *publicly creatable object* can be created outside the native application. When Project 2000 is automated from another application, such as an Excel VBA Project, new instances of the application and project objects can be created using the CreateObject function. You can also create new instances of the Application and Project objects from within Project 2000 using the New keyword in the variable declaration or a Set statement. From Excel or any other VB-aware application, you can create a new Project 2000 Application Object or Project Object or work with existing items in a project file. You can't create a new task, however, using the CreateObject function. Project 2000 objects, other than the Application Object and Project Object (such as task and resource objects) have to be created by using methods of a parent object. For example, to create a task, you rely on the parent Project Object and use the Add method of the Tasks collection of the Project object.

 NOTE The file that contains VB code modules and UserForms attached to an application file is called a VBA Project (not to be confused with Project 2000 or a project file).

The Project object model generally has two types of objects: objects that represent items and objects that represent collections of items.

We're assuming that you're fairly familiar with the terminology that Project 2000 uses to refer to items and fields. If you think of the way that you normally use the application, the object model should be easy to understand. For example, a project has a number of tasks. On a task's dialog box, there is a tab where a number of resources have been assigned to the task and a tab that lists the task's predecessors (tasks that the task depends on). Here's how these relationships are reflected in the Project object model:

- A `Project` object has a `Tasks` collection filled with `Task` objects.
- A `Task` object has an `Assigments` collection with `Assignment` objects.
- The `Task` also has a `DependencyTasks` collection with `DependencyTask` objects.

As we noted in Chapter 23, the hard part about automating Project 2000 or any other application isn't understanding Visual Basic—it's understanding the application. In the next section, we'll examine the objects in the Project object model and their events in detail. As you read through this section, you'll find that the object model directly reflects the way Project 2000 operates.

The Application Object

At the top of the object model is the `Application` object, which provides access to Project 2000 itself. One of the primary roles of the `Application` object is to provide access to other top-level objects that you will manipulate through code, just as you fire up the Project 2000 application to get to a project's tasks and resources. The `Application` object is a very versatile object and in theory, any action in Project 2000 can be accomplished through the use of methods of the `Application` object. However, using the `Application` object to manipulate tasks and other items is often the least efficient way to accomplish the job. Furthermore, although you can change the value of any field for an item with the `Application` object, the `Application` object provides no methods for examining the *current* value of a field in an item.

 NOTE The `Application` object has several hundred methods. In fact, it has one method for each command that appears on a menu bar or toolbar. All the commands that appear in a macro created with the Macro Recorder are actually methods of the `Application` object.

The publicly createable `Application` object also has public events, which can be automated from applications other than Project 2000. Table 25.1 lists the public events of the `Application` object.

TABLE 25.1: APPLICATION OBJECT EVENTS

Event	Condition when event occurs
NewProject	Occurs after a new project is created. (Cannot be canceled.)
ProjectBeforeAssignmentChange	Occurs before the user changes the value of an assignment field.
ProjectBeforeAssignmentDelete	Occurs before an assignment is deleted or replaced.
ProjectBeforeAssignmentNew	Occurs before one or more assignments are created.
ProjectBeforeClose	Occurs before a project is closed.
ProjectBeforePrint	Occurs before a project is printed.
ProjectBeforeResourceChange	Occurs before the user changes the value of a Resource field.
ProjectBeforeResourceDelete	Occurs before a resource is deleted or replaced.
ProjectBeforeResourceNew	Occurs before one or more resources are created.
ProjectBeforeSave	Occurs before a project is saved.
ProjectBeforeTaskChange	Occurs before the user changes the value of a Task field.
ProjectBeforeTaskDelete	Occurs before a task is deleted or replaced.
ProjectBeforeTaskNew	Occurs before one or more tasks are created.
ProjectCalculate	Occurs after a project is calculated. (Cannot be canceled.)

All Application events have a Cancel parameter, with the exception of the NewProject and ProjectCalculate events. If you set the Cancel parameter to True, Visual Basic will abort the pending event. This is consistent with your experience in Project 2000. With only two exceptions, you can cancel any event, just as you can click the Cancel button in the Save As dialog box to cancel Project's pending Save event. The events that you can't cancel with code can't be canceled from the user interface, either. When you click the New button on the toolbar, you can't change your mind and cancel the request.

To use Application events, you need to declare a module-level Application object variable. (Module-level declarations appear before any procedures in a module. See Chapter 24, "Automating Project 2000 with VBA," for information on declaring variables.) Then, you use the WithEvents keyword to inform VBA that this object has events that you are going to write event procedures for. You cannot use both the WithEvents and New keywords in the same declaration statement, nor can you use WithEvents for a Variant or generic Object variable; the object type must be explicitly declared. Here's the declaration statement for the Application object:

```
Dim WithEvents pjApplication As MSProject.Application
```

After you declare an object variable WithEvents, you need to set it to an object. The Set statement should be placed with the code that handles the initialization of the module. The following code samples show the placement of the Set statement for a `ThisProject` module and a `UserForm` module. We will be covering these types of modules a little later in the chapter.

```
'Setting the Application object in a ThisProject Module
Private Sub Project_Open(ByVal pj As Project)
  Set pjApplication = pj.Application
End Sub


'Setting the Application Object in a UserForm Module
Private Sub UserForm_Initialize()
  Set pjApplication = Application
End Sub
```

 TIP In the last chapter, we discussed types of modules: User Forms, Class Modules, and modules, also known as standard modules. There's a fourth type of application-created module specifically called the `ThisProject` module, which is in scope (open) for the duration of a project. You can use `WithEvents` in User Forms, `ThisProject` modules, and Class modules, but you can't use it in standard modules. For more information on module types, refer to Chapter 24.

The Project Object

The `Project` object represents an opened project document. The `Projects` collection of the `Application` object contains all project files that are currently open—the same collection of objects you see if you open Project's Window menu. To create a new Project you can use the Add method of the `Projects` collection or the `FileNew` method of the `Application` object.

To open an existing project file, you use the `FileOpen` method of the `Application` object. The opened project document is automatically appended to the Projects collection, just as it automatically appears in the list of files on the Window menu. The documentation for the `FileOpen` method may seem a little overwhelming. The `FileOpen` method has a number of optional parameters to tell Project how to open a file if it is not a project document. The `Activate` method of the `Project` is used to set the project as the active project.

The Project Object is the other object in Project's object model that has public events. (Table 25.2 lists the public events of the Project object.) You'll write event procedures for the Project Object's events in the `ThisProject` module. When you use the `ThisProject` module, you do not need to declare and set an object variable as you do for the `Application` object. The `ThisProject` module is already pointed at the current project.

TABLE 25.2: PROJECT OBJECT EVENTS

Event	Condition when event occurs
Activate	Occurs when the project is switched to the active project in the application.
BeforeClose	Occurs before the project is closed.
BeforePrint	Occurs before the project is printed.
BeforeSave	Occurs before the project is saved.
Calculate	Occurs after the project has been calculated.
Change	Occurs when any information in the project is changed, but not if the user simply switches views or filters.
Deactivate	Occurs when the project is switched from the active project in the application (i.e., another project is activated.)
Open	Occurs when a project is opened.

Using the Task Object

The Task object represents a task within a project. This object allows the fields of a task to be examined or changed programmatically. Task objects are not top-level objects, and must be created or accessed by using the Tasks collection of a top-level object. The Tasks collection contains the tasks associated with the collection's parent object. This is usually a Project object, a Selection object, or a Cell object. To add a new Task to the Parent object, you use the Add method of the Task collection.

```
Dim objProject As MSProject.Project
Dim objTask As MSProject.Task

Set objProject = Application.ActiveProject
Set objTask = objProject.Tasks.Add()
```

FIGURE 25.2

The Task Branch of the Project object model, as shown in the Project 2000 VB Help file

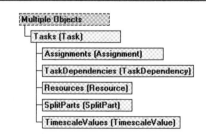

Using the Resource Object

Resources are handled similarly to tasks within the object model, as shown in Figure 25.3. The `Resource` object represents a resource within a project.

FIGURE 25.3

The Resource Branch of the object model as shown in the Project Help file

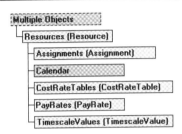

Like Task objects, a `Resource` object must be accessed through the `Resources` collection:

```
Dim objResource As MSProject.Resource
Dim objProject As MSProject.Project


Set objProject = Application.ActiveProject
Set objTask = objProject.Resources.Add()
```

Using the Assignment Object

The `Assignment` object represents the link between a Task and a Resource: the assignment of the resource to the task. Assignments are created using the Add method of the Assignments collection. The Add method of the Assignments collection has three optional named parameters: `TaskID`, `ResourceID`, and `Units`, which are identical to the ResourceID, TaskID, and Units fields in the Assignments dialog box.

```
'Adding an Assignment from a Task
ActiveProject.Tasks(1).Assignments.Add ResourceID:=1, Units:=100
```

or

```
ActiveProject.Tasks(1).Assignments.Add ,1, 100
```

```
'Adding an Assignment from a Resource
ActiveProject.Resources(2).Assignments.Add ResourceID:=2, Units:=100
```

or

```
ActiveProject.Resources(2).Assignments.Add, 2 , 100
```

Using the Cell and Selection Objects

The Cell object and Selection object represent selected items within the Project application. Neither of these objects belongs to a collection, nor can new instances of the objects be created. To access these objects, properties of the Application object must be used. The ActiveCell property of the Application returns a Cell object, and the ActiveSelection property returns a Selection object.

The Cell object represents the active cell selected in the table view. The FieldID and FieldName properties of the Cell object represent the column in the table. The FieldID property is a long integer, Long, that contains the internal code Project uses for the field. FieldID is useful when you need to use the GetField or SetField methods of a Task object or Resource object. FieldID works fine when passing field identifiers between functions, but FieldID 188743687 is not very significant to users. The FieldName property returns the full name of the Field as a string: if the active cell is the Actual Work field in the Task table, the FieldName property does not return "Actual Work"; it returns "Task Actual Work".

MASTERING TROUBLESHOOTING

Implementing the Cell Object

The Cell object, returned by the ActiveCell property of the application object, is not as simple to use as one would think. There are a few quirks about this object. The Cell object has a Resource property to return a Resource object if the cell refers to a field in a resource, and a Task property to return a Task object if the cell refers to a field in a task. The Cell object does not, however, have a property to inform you which type of object the Cell refers to. When you call the Cell object, you need to know which property to call or an error will occur, so you need a method to determine the type of item the active cell refers to. There is an unused type in the model PjFieldType that can be either pjTask or pjResource, which we'll use to get this information. The function that follows makes use of pjFieldType:

```
Public Function ActiveCellType() As PjFieldType

    Dim pjCell As MSProject.Cell
    Dim ReturnValue As PjFieldType

    Set pjCell = Application.ActiveCell

    If InStr(1, pjCell.FieldName, "Task", vbTextCompare) = 1 Then
        ActiveCellType = pjTask
```

Continued ▐▶

MASTERING TROUBLESHOOTING CONTINUED

```
    Else
        ActiveCellType = pjResource
    End If
End Function
```

If you want to examine only the text in the active cell, you can simply use the Text
property of the Cell object. However, if you wish to alter the value in the active cell
programmatically, it becomes a little trickier. The Text property of the Cell object is read-
only, so you will have to use a property of the appropriate Resource or Task object:

```
Sub SetActiveCellTo(Value As String)
    Dim pjCell As MSProject.Cell
    Dim lngFieldId As Long

      On Error Resume Next
    Set pjCell = Application.ActiveCell
    lngFieldId = pjCell.FieldID
    If Not (pjCell.Resource Is Nothing) Then
        pjCell.Resource.SetField lngFieldId, Value
    ElseIf Not (pjCell.Task Is Nothing) Then
        pjCell.Task.SetField lngFieldId, Value
    Else ' Cell does not belong to an item
    End If
End Sub
```

Project has defined constants for all the FieldID numbers. These constants are the
full name of the field, prefixed with pj. The FieldID constant for Task Actual Work
would be pjTaskActualWork. This also works for custom fields, but you must use Project's actual name for the field (Task1, Cost7, and so on). Thus, the FieldID constant
for the Task1 custom field would be pjTask1.

 WARNING The Cell object always returns a FieldName and FieldID, but the
Resource and Task properties are only valid if the active cell is in a row corresponding to
an item. If you call the Resource or Task property when it does not apply, a trappable
error will occur. Routines that use these methods need to have appropriate error-handling.

The Selection object represents a selected range of cells within the table view. The methods of the Selection object are very similar to the methods of the Cell object. The Tasks property returns a Tasks collection if the selection is in a tasks table. Likewise the Resources property returns a Resources collection if the selection is in a resource table. A selection can include multiple columns in the table, so List objects are used to return the field IDs and field names of the selected columns. The FieldIDList property is used to retrieve a List of field IDs for the column. In a similar fashion the FieldNamesList property is used to retrieve a List of field names. The List object has two main properties: the Count, which returns the number of items in the list and the Item property, which returns the value of the item as a string. The following example would display the names of all selected columns in a message box.

```
Dim pjSelection As MSProject.Selection
Dim pjListNames As MSProject.List
Dim strMsgText As String
Dim i As Integer

Set pjSelection = Application.ActiveSelection
Set pjListNames = pjSelection.FieldNameList

If pjListNames.Count > 0 Then
  For i = 1 To pjListNames.Count
    strMsgText = strMsgText & " " & pjListNames(i)
  Next i
Else
  strMsgText = "No Cells Selected"
End If

MsgBox strMsgText
```

 WARNING The Item property of a List always returns a string value. If you use a string for the FieldID parameter of the GetField or SetField methods, however, an error will occur. To prevent this error you can use the CLng function to convert the string to a long integer as follows: CLng(ActiveSelection.FieldIDList(i)).

Creating User Forms

A UserForm, which is a form module in VBA, should not be confused with a Project 2000 Custom form. Like Outlook 2000, Project 2000 has two types of forms, each with its own capabilities and creation methods. It is important to differentiate between the two types. Project 2000 custom forms, created by using Project's Custom Form Editor, were discussed in Chapter 23. This chapter discusses the second type of form you can use in Project, the UserForm.

For simplicity, we can say that a UserForm is a VBA form. It is created using the Visual Basic Editor. Technically, that is not entirely accurate, but it will serve our purposes. Most of the programming done in VB (as opposed to VBA) is built on forms. Without the application interface provided by Project 2000 or Office 2000, programmers have to use forms to develop an interface to hang their code on. You'll find uses for forms in VBA, too: when you want to collect information from users, provide structured choices, or give feedback.

To create a UserForm, just open Project and create a new project. Choose Tools ➤ Macros ➤ Visual Basic Editor to open the IDE. Choose Insert ➤ UserForm from the IDE menu to open a new form.

PART

V

Customizing and
Automating Project 2000

 NOTE When we were planning the applications we wanted to illustrate in this book, the idea foremost on our minds was a Travel Cost Calculator. The form described here is taken from this application. It is a fairly simple form that introduces the basics of building a dialog box and demonstrates a method used to add custom fields directly to a project. If you are curious about the ultimate fate of our Travel Cost Calculator, see our note at the end of the chapter.

Selecting Controls

Our form will be used to collect two pieces of information from the user. There are several spreadsheets that include travel information. Users can select any of the spreadsheets to grab location data. First, the user will select a location in which an Excel spreadsheet is stored. Second, the user will select a rate per mile traveled. We also need a way for the user to let us know they have finished entering the data, or to discard the data they entered. To create our user interface, we'll use form controls from the Toolbox.

The Control Toolbox is similar to the tool palette of a paint program. When you click a control's button on the Toolbox, the mouse pointer turns into an icon for that type of control. After you have selected the type of control you want to use, draw it onto the form as you would draw a shape in a paint program.

To move, resize, or modify the properties of a control, first select the control. The selection tool is used to select one or more controls. If you hold down the Ctrl key, you can select or unselect multiple controls. Occasionally, the pointer does not change back to the selection control after you paint a control. If this happens, click on the Selection tool to get your normal mouse pointer back.

The CommandButton control should be used for actions that happen immediately, such as canceling a dialog box, opening another form, or printing a report. You use the Click event of the CommandButton control to respond to the users' actions.

The TextBox control provides users with an area where they can edit or input text. You use this control to collect information from the user.

The ListBox control allows you to display a list of predefined options to the user. This control can be set to accept a single option from the list or allow the user to make multiple selections. ListBox controls are useful by providing the user with a list of items from which to choose.

The ComboBox control is a combination of a TextBox and a ListBox control. When you want users to select one item from a list or enter an item that doesn't appear on the list, use a ComboBox. You also can set a ComboBox to function like a drop-down list. In Dropdown list mode, the ComboBox functions as a ListBox that allows the user only one choice. Drop-down list boxes are useful on forms that have many controls because they require less room.

The Label control allows you to place text on the form that a user cannot edit. You use this control to place labels for your TextBox and other controls. Users are used to labels not doing anything, so you should avoid placing event procedures on labels.

The Image control allows you to place images in the form. You can use this control to add your company's logo to the form or to add an image that represents the purpose of the form.

The OptionButton control is used to provide the user with a list of pre-defined options, from which they can select a single option. OptionButtons should be grouped so that a user can select only a single option. There are two ways to create an option group in VB: place OptionButton controls in a frame, or assign the same GroupName property to each OptionButton control.

Both the OptionButton and the CheckBox controls have a GroupName property. If you set this property when the user selects a button or clicks on the button, any other buttons in the group are unselected. Although you can set a Group for a CheckBox, you should avoid this. By convention, OptionButton controls should be used if the Buttons are grouped and CheckBox controls should be used if the buttons are not grouped.

The ToggleButton control is similar in function to a CheckBox, and provides an alternate graphical appearance to the CheckBox for yes/no controls. Normally, the CheckBox is used on UserForms for data entry or UserForms that could be paper forms, and ToggleButtons appear on forms that function like control panels.

The Frame control is a container control. It allows you to group controls together. Users are accustomed to frames, so frames make your form more understandable. The more controls you add to an application, the longer it takes to load and the less responsive it is, so some programmers avoid frames.

The MultiPage control is a container control with tabs for each page. Each tab is a separate page that you can place controls on. When the user switches tabs, the control automatically hides the controls from other pages and shows the controls on the active page.

The TabStrip control allows you to place a row of tabs on a control, similar to those in a property sheet. This control is not a container control, and is normally only used when tabs are used to change the view or filter options of a forms control. Under most circumstances, the MultiPage control will be more useful.

The SpinButton control allows users to select a numeric value. You can set a Min and Max range for the value. You can also set the SmallChange property of the control to determine how much the value changes with each click from the user. This control provides no indication to the user of its current value, so it is usually paired with another control, such as a label or textbox, to display the value.

The ScrollBar control is similar to the SpinButton control, except that it has a graphical slider that indicates the relative position of the control's current value in its range. In addition to the Min, Max and SmallChange properties, the ScrollBar has a LargeChange property, which determines the value change if the user click in the slider region.

Placing Controls on a UserForm

We can begin work on the UserForm by placing two command buttons: one that saves the data, and one that cancels the action by closing the UserForm. To place a command button, select the button in the toolbox, and then click in the UserForm to place a button of the default size. Drag instead of clicking to create a larger or smaller button (or simply click to place the default button and then resize it).

To change the appearance of the button, you change the button's properties. Select the first button and look at the Properties window, shown here:

For more information about a property, click its name in the Properties window and press F1. To change a property, click its name in the Properties window, and then type a value or choose a value from a drop-down list. For example, you would change the button's name by clicking on the Name property and typing text. The properties you'll want to change on the first button are shown in the following table.

Property	Value	Description
(Name)	cmdSaveSettings	Name used to refer to the button in code; cmd is the command button prefix.
Caption	Ok	Text for button face.
Default	True	User can "click" on this button by pressing Enter key.

Select the other button and change these properties to create a Cancel button:

Property	Value	Description
(Name)	cmdCancel	Name used to refer to the button in code.
Cancel	True	User can "click" this button by pressing Esc key or closing form.
Caption	Cancel	Text for button face.

Then, select the UserForm by clicking anywhere on the form's background and change its properties:

Property	Value	Description
(Name)	dlgTravelCostSettings	Name used to refer to the form; dlg is the prefix for a dialog box.
Caption	Travel Cost Settings	Text for form title bar.

Each form can have only one button where the Default property is True and one button with a Cancel property that's True, but they can be the same button. You set the Cancel button's Default property to True when confirming an action that's often selected by mistake, and when not canceling results in an irreversible action such as deleting a file.

Next, you need to add two TextBox controls and two Label controls. The only properties that need to be changed for the text boxes are the Name properties, so we can refer to the controls easily in our code. The first control is named txtXlsLocation, and the second text box is named txtMileageRate.

The Label controls really do not need to have their Name properties changed; they are just labels and won't be referred to programmatically. We'd label them anyway, just for consistency, using the lbl prefix: lblMileageRate and lblXlsLocation. The Caption property is the critical property for a label. Set the lblXlsLocation (label1) Caption property to "Location Worksheet:" and the lblMileageRate (Label2) caption property to "Mileage Rate:" to label the UserForm controls as shown here:

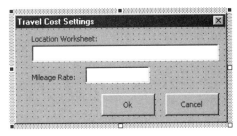

PART

V

Customizing and
Automating Project 2000

TIP You may be tempted to change the background of the UserForm or switch to an extremely conspicuous font for the option button labels. Don't. Users know what a good interface looks and acts like. For example, if the user changes the system colors in the Control Panel, the colors used in your application should change, too. If you lock in a specific background, your users may not complain, but you've already planted the seeds of doubt. All experienced Windows users know, if only subconsciously, that "real" programs use the system colors set in Windows.

Adding Code to the Form

The procedures you wrote earlier by using the VB Editor or the Macro Recorder have been general procedures that can be run from a toolbar, menu bar, shortcut key, Macros dialog box, or the VB IDE. *Event procedures* are blocks of code attached to an object's events that run in response to an event: a mouse click, a key press on the keyboard, or a system event.

In this form, there are three events to care about. You need events to handle a user clicking either of the two command buttons. And you will need a procedure attached to one of the `UserForm`'s events to do a little setup when the form loads. You may be asking: "But what about my text boxes?" You really don't care *when* a user types an entry in the text boxes; you just care what the text is when they click the `cmdSaveSettings` button (captioned `Ok`). If the user clicks the `cmdCancel` button (captioned `Cancel`), the contents of the text boxes won't matter. But as soon as either command button is clicked, it's time for action, so we'll create code attached to events on these two command buttons.

Coding the Cancel Button   The Cancel button doesn't need to do too much, so let's create that event code first. Select the `Cancel` button, right-click, and choose View Code or double-click the command button to open the module attached to the `UserForm`. You won't find this module in the Project Explorer; it's only accessible when you're editing the `UserForm`. You'll notice that the snippets for the command buttons have already been created. There's an underscore before `Click` in the subroutine names because the code is assigned to a button's Click event:

If the user clicks the `Cancel` button (or presses Esc), the appropriate response is to close the form. This code does the trick:

```
Private Sub cmdCancel_Click()
    dlgTravelCostSettings.Hide
    Unload dlgTravelCostSettings
End Sub
```

After you create an object, it's added to the VBA Project's Object list. You'll find your form `dlgTravelCostSettings` and all of its controls on the Objects list. To add the object name, just type enough unique letters of the name (such as `dlg`), hold Ctrl, and press the space bar to fill in the remainder. Type the period after the object name, and you'll see the VB Editor's Auto List Members feature, which opens a list of events and objects to choose from:

You can test the procedure by clicking the Run Macro button. The form will appear; clicking the Cancel button should close the form and return you to the VB IDE.

TIP You don't have to use the form's name explicitly, as we do in our examples. You can omit the name of an active object and jump straight to methods; so, if the form is active, the Hide command hides the active form. If you prefer, you can use the pronoun Me to refer to the active object: Me.Hide hides the object that currently has focus. Including the form name increases the amount of code, but it also provides documentation and makes debugging easier, so we generally list objects explicitly in our code.

  Use the View Object and View Code buttons at the top of the Project Explorer to switch back and forth between the form and code windows.

Coding the OK Button When a user clicks the cmdSaveSettings button, you want to store the location of the Excel worksheet and the rate that the user entered in the TextBox controls. You need to store this information in a way that we can recall it when the user reopens the project file. A simple variable will not work because, regardless of scope, variables are removed from memory when you unload the application they're created in. To keep a value from one Project 2000 session to another, you need to use a document property.

A *document property* is a custom property or piece of information that has been assigned to a document in Microsoft Office. To see the custom properties for a file, choose File ➤ Properties from the application menu and click the Custom tab. The properties for a Project 2000 file are shown here:

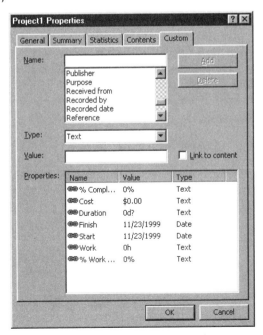

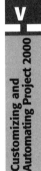

PART

V

Customizing and
Automating Project 2000

You use the custom documents to store information that applies to the project as a whole. Here are the properties in the Project Object Browser:

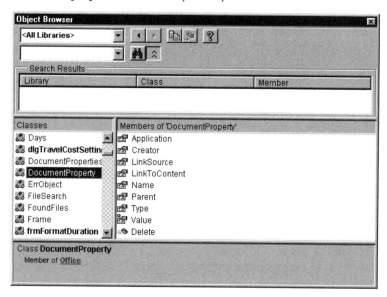

The `DocumentProperties` collection contains all the `DocumentProperty` objects for a project document, `Project` object.

 TIP Custom `DocumentProperties` is a standard object in Microsoft Office Products. In Project 2000, the Project object is the document of the application, but other office products also have documents with custom properties. Excel workbooks and Word documents, for example, have `DocumentProperties` collections to store custom information.

Creating and Using a DocumentProperty First, we'll declare a `DocumentProperties` object:

```
Dim objDocProps As DocumentProperties
```

Then, we'll use the `Set` command to set the object to the current project document's collection of document properties:

```
Set objDocProps = _ ActiveProject.CustomDocumentProperties
```

We'll add a new property named `TravelCostWorksheet` to the collection and set the value of the property in one line of code.

```
objDocProps.Add "TravelCostWorksheet", False, _
        msoPropertyTypeString, _
        txtXlsLocation.Text
```

The new property, an object of the Project object, contains the user-entered value in (the Text property of) the txtXlsLocation text box. We'll create a similar line of code to store the text entered in the txtMileageRate control.

MASTERING THE OPPORTUNITIES

Handling Run-Time Errors

Following the Procedure Declaration, there's a line of code that redirects program flow in case of an error while the procedure is running. The command is part of an error-handler:

```
On Error Resume Next
```

Error-handling allows you to plan for potential errors. Within your error routines you write code to correct problems, if possible, or at least to report the problem to the user and exit cleanly. In this case, you are telling the program to go to the next line if an error is encountered. This assumes that the next line will check for an error and correct it if one should arise.

In addition to run-time errors, your error-handlers will also need to handle validation errors. Validation errors are errors that will not cause run-time errors, at least not at their origin, but produce invalid results.

Another part of error-handling is validation. Validation attempts to catch errors before they actually become a problem. The first step in this procedure is to make sure that both textboxes contain values. If the data entered by the user is invalid, the procedure notifies the user and exits without taking any further action. This allows the user to correct the data and resubmit it.

After the appropriate information has been stored, we'll use the same code as the Cancel button to hide and unload the UserForm. Here's the complete procedure for the cmdSaveSettings button:

```
Private Sub cmdSaveSettings_Click()
    Dim objDocProps As DocumentProperties
    Dim objPropLocation As DocumentProperty
    Dim objPropRate As DocumentProperty

    On Error Resume Next

    If (Len(txtXlsLocation.Text) = 0) Or _
      (Len(txtMileageRate.Text) = 0) Then
        MsgBox "You need to enter both a location " &_
            "And a rate to proceed."
```

PART

V

Customizing and
Automating Project 2000

```
      Else
        Set objDocProps = _
    ActiveProject.CustomDocumentProperties

        Set objPropLoctaion = objDocProps("TravelCostWorksheet")

        If objPropLocation Is Nothing Then
          objDocProps.Add "TravelCostWorksheet", False, _
                msoPropertyTypeString, _
                txtXlsLocation.Text
      Else
        ObjPropLocation = txtXlsLocation.Text
      End If

        Set objPropRate = objDocProps("TravelCostRatePerMile")

        If objPropRate Is Nothing Then
          objDocProps.Add "TravelCostRatePerMile", _
                False, _
                msoPropertyTypeString, _
                txtMileageRate.Text
      Else
        ObjPropRate = txtMileageRate.Text
      End If
      dlgTravelCostSettings.Hide
      Unload dlgTravelCostSettings
    End If

    Set objDocProps = Nothing
    Set objPropLocation = Nothing
    Set objPropRate = Nothing
    End Sub
```

TIP Before a form can be displayed, it must be loaded in memory. If you loaded the form with code, you'd use a command line such as Load *formname*. However, if you forget to load the form and just display it by invoking the form's Show method (*formname*.Show), VB loads the form and then displays it. When you don't want to display the form, you can hide it with its Hide method (*formname*.Hide), but the form is still in memory. To close the form, you must also unload it: Unload *formname*.

You also want the form to see whether settings have already been saved for these properties. If the settings have been saved, then they should be displayed when the form opens. The event in this case would be the startup or Initialize event of the UserForm itself. For this procedure, you will need to use the drop-down lists at the top of the Code window. Select UserForm for the Object (left) drop-down list. Then select Initialize from the Event (right) drop-down list (see Figure 25.4). Here's the procedure:

```
Private Sub UserForm_Initialize()
  Dim objDocProps As DocumentProperties
  Dim objDocProp As DocumentProperty

  On Error Resume Next
  Set objDocProps = ActiveProject.CustomDocumentProperties

  Set objDocProp = objDocProps.Item("TravelCostWorksheet")

  If Err.Number = 0 Then
    txtXlsLocation.Text = objDocProp.Value
  End If

  Set objDocProp = objDocProps.Item("TravelCostRatePerMile")
  If Err.Number = 0 Then
    txtMileageRate.Text = objDocProp.Value
  End If
End Sub
```

PART
V

Customizing and
Automating Project 2000

FIGURE 25.4

Selecting the Initializing Event procedure

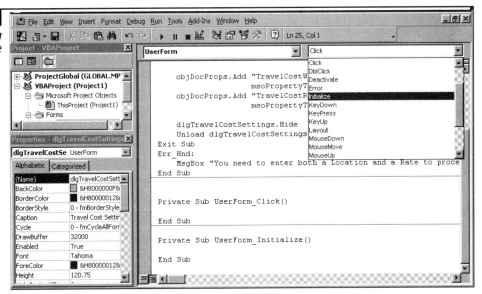

Test the procedure to ensure that it works. Open the Properties of the Project document from the File menu of Project 2000 (File ➢ Properties) to make sure that the document properties were saved:

Some basic error-handling has been added in these procedures, but it is far from thorough. See the VBA Help file for more information on error-handling.

Opening the UserForm   We still need one more procedure—a global procedure to open the UserForm. This procedure will allow you to assign the form to a command bar button. In the Project Explorer, activate Module1 and create the following code to display the UserForm:

```
Public Sub ShowTravelCostSettings()
    dlgTravelCostSettings.Show
End Sub
```

This user form isn't used in any application yet. In our completed Travel Cost application, we will display the form by calling it with a macro or program code.

Creating Project Applications

The term *application* is generally applied to any software that requires one or more external modules to function. Applications are not self-contained software programs, but an application of code modules to achieve a specific goal. It has long been debated whether there is such a thing as a true program in the Windows environment or whether all Windows programs are actually applications. Project itself is often referred to as an application, but if it is an application, it is an *executable application* because, aside from Windows, it doesn't require external modules to run.

A Project application is simply a collection of customized objects—toolbars, custom Project forms, and VBA modules—designed to work together to achieve a common objective. Applications created in Project 2000 are *macro applications*, as opposed to *executable applications* (programs) because Project applications require external modules from Project 2000. Project applications must be stored within a project document and run from within Project 2000. The only real distinguishing feature between a simple macro (or any of the individual custom components that you have worked with so far) and a macro application is numbers. If you bring all the individual pieces together properly, their worth is greater than the sum of their individual parts.

Managing Project Applications

In Project 2000, you will work with two types of applications: template-based applications and global applications.

Template-based applications contain customized functionality that applies only to a given template. Template-based applications often rely on views and custom fields that only exist within a template. The customized components for macros are placed in the template file.

Global applications are far more generalized applications. These applications are designed to extend the functionality of Project 2000 itself. A properly constructed global application should be able to run on any Project document. Global applications cannot rely on specific items (tasks, resources, or assignments) that exist within the project file. Likewise, they are far more constrained in the use of custom fields.

All the customizations that make up the application need to be saved in the same place. If not, your project will not run correctly. After you have finished your application, use the Organizer to make sure that all the components of your project are stored together. The Organizer, discussed in Chapter 21, "Customizing Project 2000," can also be used to distribute Visual Basic components between projects.

 TIP UserForms are a type of Visual Basic module and are listed on the Modules tab of the Organizer, not on the Forms tab. The Forms tab lists Project custom forms.

Global applications are stored in a special project document, GLOBAL.MPT. When Project starts, it automatically loads this file, giving users access to all applications placed within it. Although most objects default to being created in the GLOBAL.MPT, VBA modules created with the IDE default to being created in whichever project is the currently selected, active VBA project in the IDE.

Public subroutines created in other standard modules can be used as macros, but the Macros dialog box always returns to the same module to create new macros. Even if you add standard modules to a project or rename the module, the Macro Recorder will still return to this module when you create new macros. By default, the first module created in the VBA project is named Module1. Because this module is used to store macros, you should rename the module to reflect its special status. By convention, standard module names are prefixed with 'bas' to denote the type of module; basMacros would be a

PART

V

Customizing and
Automating Project 2000

suitable name. To rename Module1, select Module1 in the Project Explorer and change the module's Name property in the Properties window:

 TIP Even if an application is a global application, you should save a copy of your application independently in a project document. If you ever need to need to reinstall the application (for example, after the accidental deletion of GLOBAL.MPT) or distribute it to someone else, you will have a clean copy to work with.

Automating Other Applications from Project

VBA is not limited to Project. You can automate any application that supports automation (also referred to as OLE automation, ActiveX automation, or OLE Inprocess serving) from within Project 2000. If you have been following along with the examples, you have already used ActiveX automation. VBA procedures, including macros, control Project through ActiveX automation. There is not much difference to automating other programs in VBA; you simply need to have access to the objects of the application. There are two ways to access an object, just as there are two ways to declare VB variables. Late binding, also called weak typing, is analogous to implicit declaration; early binding (strong typing) resembles explicit declaration.

Accessing an Object with Late Binding

The simplest way of accessing an object is through a process called late binding. In *late binding*, you use the `CreateObject` or `GetObject` functions to retrieve an object. The following example opens the Excel workbook `'C:\My Documents\Employees.xls'`. It then reads rows 2 through 11 of the Excel spreadsheet and creates a Project resource for each line, setting the standard rate and the overtime rates for the default pay rate table. Of course you could do the same thing using an import map (see Chapter 19, "Importing and Exporting Project Data"), but in a few pages, we'll create a similar procedure to link rather than import Excel data from Project 2000.

```
Dim pjResource As Resource
Dim xlSheet As Object
Dim i As Integer

Set xlSheet = GetObject("C:\My Documents\Employees.xls")

For i = 2 To 11
  Set pjResource = Resources.Add(xlSheet.Cells(i, 1).Value)
  pjResource.StandardRate = xlSheet.Cells(i, 2).Value
  pjResource.OvertimeRate = xlSheet.Cells(i, 3).Value
Next I
```

Accessing an Object with Early Binding

Alternately, you can use *early binding*, which is analogous to explicit variable declaration. With early binding, you declare the type of application that an object comes from before using it:

```
Dim xlApp as Excel.Application
```

Then, you can refer to specific objects within the Excel Application object in your procedure. Early binding has two major advantages:

- Applications run more quickly and efficiently because part of the work is handled at compile time.

- You can use the Object browser and the Auto List Members feature of VBA to create the code.

Early binding also has one huge disadvantage. If the object library that includes the object isn't installed on the machine, your application won't run, even if the application does not need the object at the time. To use early binding, you need to add a reference to the object library for the program you wish to automate. Whether or not you use early binding, the error-checking and Auto List help you get from adding the library reference makes it worthwhile, as follows:

1. In the Visual Basic IDE, choose Tools ➤ References to open the References dialog box:

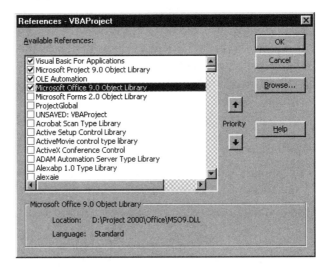

The References dialog box lists all the object libraries installed on your system. If you use Microsoft Office, you'll see libraries for familiar applications such as Excel, Outlook, and Word. Libraries that are currently loaded are listed at the top of the list (with check marks). The Visual Basic for Applications, Microsoft Project 9.0, and OLE Automation libraries are automatically referenced when you work with the VB IDE from Project 2000.

2. Scroll down the list and select the library(ies) you want to use in your application. For our application, we need to add the Excel object library.

3. Click OK to close the References dialog box.

Now, you can access all the objects in the Excel object model. The VB Editor will correctly highlight code that uses incorrect methods or events.

 TIP Don't include library references that aren't required in the current application; libraries use system resources whenever the project file is opened.

Creating the Charged Cost Budget Application

Project 2000 is primarily designed for internal project management. The budget features are not equipped to handle many of the needs of contractors. Project managers for contractors or consulting firms will actually want to track two budgets: an actual cost budget and the charged cost budget. The need to track two sets of costs is not unique to contractors. Departments often charge a fixed rate for work done for other departments, but need to track and manage internal costs as a project progresses.

One solution is to create two projects with different rates, but this involves double entry as you receive status reports. We're assuming that you have other, more pressing project management tasks to occupy your time.

Our approach takes advantage of a new feature in Project 2000: multiple rate tables. Project 2000 provides five rate tables for resources. The rate tables appear on the Costs tab of the Resource Information form:

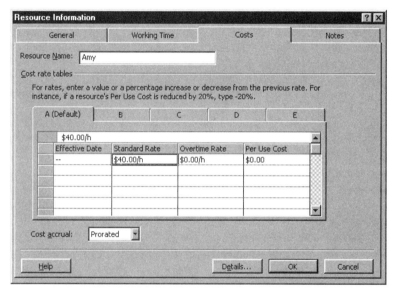

If we place internal costs in Table A and charged costs in Table B, switching the rate table for the all the assignments in a project will switch budgets.

This simple application automates the process of switching between rate tables. For this application, you really need only a command bar with two macros. One sets all the assignments to Rate Table A and the other sets all assignments to Rate Table B. Although you could build this macro application by recording a find and replace action, you would have to record changing to a view with assignments in it. If you build this application using Assignment objects, you will not need to alter the view.

Because this project will require a number of private procedures, we'll create a new module. Open the Visual Basic Editor and add a new module to your VBProject (GLOBAL.MPT).

1. In the Project Explorer, choose the Global.MPT VB project.

2. Choose Insert ➤ Module from the menu.

3. Select the new module in the Project Explorer.

4. In the Properties window, name the module `basChangeCostTable`.

The first step is to build the subroutine that will actually do the work. For a procedure to run as a macro, it must be declared as a public subroutine without parameters. Any procedure that meets these requirements will be listed as an available macro, even if it was not created by using the Macro Recorder. You can add the macro to a command bar if you wish. A public subroutine without parameters begins with the familiar snippet you saw beginning in Chapter 24. Here's an example from earlier in this chapter:

```
Public Sub ShowTravelCostSettings()
```

We don't want our procedure to appear on the list of macros in the Macros dialog box, but we don't have to worry in this instance. We're creating a private subroutine that includes parameters.

 TIP If you do not want a procedure to be listed for users as an available macro, you should declare it either as a private subroutine, as a function, or as a subroutine with parameters.

The method for changing the tables is identical, so it makes sense to build the method as a subroutine and pass it the table identifier as a table. This procedure uses a nested loop structure, discussed in Chapter 24, to change the `CostRateTable` property of all the assignments in the project.

The Assignments collection is not directly accessible from the Project object; each Task has its own collection. The outer loop iterates (moves) through each Task object in the Project to get that task's Assignments collection. The inner loop then iterates through each Assignment object in the collection and changes the `CostRateTable`.

```
Private Sub ChangeAssignedRateTable(TableId As Integer)
  Dim colTasks As MSProject.Tasks
  Dim objTask As MSProject.Task
  Dim objAssign As MSProject.Assignment
  Dim colAssigns As MSProject.Assignments

  Set colTasks = ActiveProject.Tasks
'start outer loop to iterate through tasks in the task collection
  For Each objTask In colTasks
'start inner loop to iterate through assignments for this task
    Set colAssigns = objTask.Assignments
```

```
     For Each objAssign In colAssigns
        objAssign.CostRateTable = TableId
     Next objAssign
'end of inner loop
  Next objTask
'end of outer loop
Set colTasks = Nothing
Set objTask = Nothing
Set objAssign = Nothing
Set colAssigns = Nothing


End Sub
```

 TIP The last four Set commands in the code aren't truly required. When an object drops from scope, its value is set to Nothing. However, it's better form (and minimizes the chance for error) to actually set these objects to Nothing in code.

Because the subroutine has a parameter (the name of the rate table), we need to create procedures that can be run as macros to front-end the actual workings of the application. The two procedures listed below simply call the subroutine that does the work and pass the appropriate constant value for the macro. These two public subroutines without parameters will be included in the Macros dialog box and can be placed on a command bar button.

```
Public Sub Use_Rate_Table_A()
  Call ChangeAssignedRateTable(0)
End Sub


Public Sub Use_Rate_Table_B()
  Call ChangeAssignedRateTable(1)
End Sub
```

At this point, you have a simple yet functional application. To make the application user friendly, you'll need to create a command bar for your application (refer to Chapter 22).

Further Suggestions for the Charged Cost Budget Application

As the application stands, there are still limitations. Although only one of the two budgets can be baselined, this should be a minor limitation in most cases. The work, duration, and date baseline values will be identical. The actual and total costs will be accurate, with the exception of fixed costs, mentioned as follows. You will be able to calculate variances on only one budget, however.

This simple application does not adjust fixed costs. Fixed costs are not dependent on a rate table. This is a problem if the charged cost for fixed costs is different from the internal value for fixed costs. A possible solution would be to create two custom Cost fields for tasks. One is for fixed cost to be used in Table A and the other for fixed cost in Table B. You could then add code to the procedure so that when it executes, it copies the current value out of the Fixed Cost field and places the appropriate value into the table.

Creating the Linked Expense Application

Your company has a beautiful Excel workbook template for calculating the fixed costs of a project. Currently, you enter or copy and paste values from the workbook into the appropriate cell of the project's Task table. Values in the workbook change occasionally, so importing the workbook's contents into a project isn't a one-time solution. It would be nice if you could link the value of a Fixed Cost cell in a Project 2000 file to a specific cell in an Excel workbook. Unlike Word and Excel, however, Project 2000 does not support a field links feature.

Though it is doubtful that the degree of field linking that is offered in Word or Excel can be achieved in a VBA project, the potential benefits of even limited field linking are too good to pass up. Double entry is not only inefficient, it also increase your chances of data-entry errors. This application implements a basic linked field. This application falls far short of plumbing the potential VBA offers for creating linked fields, but it provides a good starting point for understanding linking, using automation outside Project 2000, and creating a neat application, all at the same time.

This application has several requirements. To accomplish the linking task, it's not enough to simply create a link. The application needs to be able to do the following:

- Select the Excel workbook that contains budget information that is linked to the project.
- Edit and remove the file link.
- Link the specified cell in Excel to the Project Fixed Cost field.
- Remove these links.
- Update the project file when the information in the Excel workbook changes.
- Release Excel.

It takes a fair amount of time to open up Excel. To prevent unnecessary opening and closing of Excel, the macros will be designed to see whether the workbook is already open. If not, they will open the workbook. When the macro is done, it will leave the workbook open so other macros can use it.

Issues in the Linked Expense Application

That covers the minimum steps that you need to implement this Project application. However, you can add other features as well. It would be nice, for example, to be able to open up the Excel workbook from Project. Adding this feature requires one additional macro, so we'll include it in the application.

Before we begin coding, we need to make some other decisions that affect how the application functions. For example, we must decide whether we want this application to be globally available or part of a template. The application as designed has one critical limitation: because it holds a reference to the Excel workbook in a public object variable, the macro will work for only one project at a time. If this application is placed in GLOBAL.MPT, the user will have to close the budget of one project before opening the budget of another project document. This can be corrected by adding one line at the end of each macro:

```
Set xlWorkbook = Nothing
```

However, doing this will cause Excel to open and close every time one of the macros is called. This might get rather tedious when a user is initially linking fields to the workbook.

Creating the Custom Field

You will need to have one custom field to store link information. (See Chapter 23 for detailed information on creating and using custom fields.) Rename the custom Task field Text30 **"Budget Link Source"**. You could use any field you want, but our macros are written for the field Text30. This field was chosen because it is unlikely that it has been customized for other use. To rename a custom field in Project 2000, follow these steps:

1. In Project, choose Tools ➤ Customize ➤ Fields to open the Customize Fields dialog box.

2. Use the option buttons to choose Task or Resource, then select the Type of field you want to customize from the drop-down list.

3. Select a field from the field list and click the Rename button.

4. In the Rename dialog box, type a new name for the field and click OK.

5. Click OK to close the Customize Fields dialog box.

Renaming a custom field in the Customize Fields dialog box has no effect on the object model. For example, you renamed the custom Task field Finish1 as SubmitToAccounting. To access your custom field from VB, you would still use the Finish1 property, not the SubmitToAccounting property.

WARNING Although Project allows you to use custom fields for tasks and resources you should avoid using them in VBA whenever possible. In Project 2000, you can't really create custom fields for tasks and resource items. When you create a custom field, you're really changing the Display name of a predefined extra field in Project. Conflicts in your applications can occur if two macros use the same custom field to store macro-specific information. Having said that, we'll be using a custom field in this application.

Creating the Application Code

Open the Visual Basic Editor, select the project you want to create the application in, and create a new Module. Name the module `Excel_Budget`. The following paragraphs describe the forms and procedures that handle the application requirements listed at the beginning of this section. The descriptions are followed by the code for the application. You can download this code, and a sample Excel workbook, from the Mastering Project 2000 page on the Sybex Web site (`http:\\www.sybex.com`), but you'll learn more about the objects used in this application if you create one or more of the procedures in the VB Editor.

Selecting the Excel Workbook To select the Excel workbook, you could use a User-Form like the form we created earlier in this chapter. Because we need to collect only one text value, a macro with an input box will suffice. The macro `Excel_Budget_Workbook_Link` collects the information and stores it in a custom document property.

Removing Current Document Properties The macro `Excel_Budget_Workbook_UnLink` clears the document property and all the custom link fields.

Linking the Excel Cell to Project Linking an Excel cell reference to a Task Fixed Cost field requires more than just a simple button on a tool bar. We need a `UserForm` to collect the linking information from the user. The `UserForm` `dlgLinkExcelCell`, which we'll create in a few pages, also handles storing the information to link the cell to the Fixed Cost cell in Project. As with any `UserForm`, we'll need a way to display the form, so we'll create the macro `Excel_Budget_Add_Link` to show this form.

Breaking the Link Unlinking a cell does not require a `UserForm`; a simple button on a toolbar will do. This will be handled by the macro `Excel_Budget_Remove_Link`. This macro will unlink only the task for the active cell.

 TIP This is all our application needs. For example, if you want to redesign this macro to unlink all selected tasks, review the information on Selection object in Chapter 24 or the Object Browser.

Updating the Links   When an item is initially linked, the current value stored in Excel will be copied to the fixed cost. However, like linked fields in Word or Excel, the links in this application will not automatically be updated. Your application will need a method to refresh the links. This is accomplished by the macro `Excel_Budget_Update_Links`.

Closing Excel After You Finish   We decided that the individual macros for managing links would open Excel if it were not already opened, but would not close Excel. The user wouldn't appreciate this application closing an Excel session they were using. The Object Variable that refers to Excel is placed in a standard module in the Global template. After Excel is opened, the reference will be held until project closes. Though Excel is opened invisibly, it is still loaded into memory. Once the user is done with Excel there is no reason to continue using system resources to run it.

Because your application cannot tell when the user is finished with Excel, you need to provide the user with a way of informing your application that they are finished. This can be handled through a command bar button. The macro `Excel_Budget_Deactivate` contains the code for this command button.

Showing Excel from Project   Unlike many applications, Excel opens invisibly when it is called through automation. To open Excel so the user can edit the linked workbook, you merely have to make Excel visible. The macro `Excel_Budget_Show` handles the settings to make the workbook visible to the user.

Private Procedures   There are three additional procedures that the application will need. These procedures should be called only by this application so they will be private. The first two procedures handle reading and writing the workbook path to a custom document property. The other procedure opens Excel and the workbook if they are not already opened.

The completed code for module `Excel_Budget` is as follows:

Completed Code for VBA Module `Excel_Budget`

```
'Way of refering to the Excel workbook (for macro procedures)
Public xlWorkBook As Object


'String to hold error Message for Connection to Excel Error.
Const strConnectErrMsg = "Error Connecting to Linked Worksheet. " & _
          "Check Budget Settings, to verify " &_
   "workbook location is correct."
```

```
Public Sub Excel_Budget_Add_Link()
  If ActivateExcel Then
    dlgLinkExcelCell.Show
  Else
    'Report error if can not connect
    MsgBox strConnectErrMsg, vbCritical
  End If
End Sub


Public Sub Excel_Budget_Remove_Link()
  'Clear link information
  ActiveCell.Task.Text30 = ""
End Sub


Public Sub Excel_Budget_Show()
  If ActivateExcel Then
    'Excel Starts invisible show it now
    xlWorkBook.Application.Visible = True
    xlWorkBook.Activate
  Else
    'Report error if can not connect
    MsgBox strConnectErrMsg, vbCritical
  End If
End Sub


Public Sub Excel_Budget_Update_Links()
  Dim objTasks As Tasks
  Dim objTask As Task
  Dim strField As String
  Dim strMsg As String

  On Error Resume Next

  'Check that we can access Workbook before update
  If ActivateExcel Then
    Set objTasks = ActiveProject.Tasks
    'Iterate through list and
```

```
    For Each objTask In objTasks
      strField = objTask.Text30
      If Len(strField) > 0 Then
        objTask.FixedCost = xlWorkBook.Names(strField).RefersToRange.Value
        If Err.Number <> 0 Then
          strMsg = "An Error occured while attempting to update Task:" & _
              objTask.ID & ")" & objTask.Name & "From Excel Cell:" & _
              strField & vbCrLf & "Error " & Err.Number & ":" & _
              Err.Description
          Err.Clear
          'Report error
          MsgBox strMsg, vbCritical
        End If
      End If
    Next objTask
    'Report Update done
    MsgBox "Update Complete", vbInformation
  Else
    'Report error if can not connect
    MsgBox strConnectErrMsg, vbCritical
  End If

End Sub

  Set objTask = Nothing
  Set objTasks = Nothing
Public Sub Excel_Budget_Workbook_Link()
  Dim strPath As String

  strPath = GetXlsBudgetPath
  strPath = InputBox("Enter Full Path to Excel Workbook:", strPath)

  'Input box Returns "" if user clicks cancel.
  If Not (strPath = "") Then
    'If user did not update path
    SetXlsBudgetPath strPath
```

```
'If the user was connected then we need to disconnect from old workbook and
connect to new workbook.
    If (xlWorkBook Is Nothing) Then
        'Disconnect from old workbook
        Set xlWorkBook = Nothing
        'Connect to new workbook.
        If Not ActivateExcel Then
            'Report error if can not connect
            MsgBox strConnectErrMsg, vbCritical
        End If
    End If
  End If
End Sub


Public Sub Excel_Budget_Workbook_Unlink()

    'Errors will occur if attempt to set values in
    'Summary tasks-this just ignores these errors.
    On Error Resume Next
    Dim intResult As Integer
    Dim objTasks As Tasks
    Dim objTask As Task

    'Display confirmation message
    intResult = MsgBox("Are you sure you want to unlink the Excel Workbook and
all linked fields?", vbYesNo)
    If intResult = vbYes Then
        Set objTasks = ActiveProject.Tasks
        'Remove any links to Excel cells
        For Each objTask In objTasks
            objTask.Text30 = ""
        Next objTask
        'Clear path
        SetXlsBudgetPath ""
    End If
    Set objTask = Nothing
    Set objTasks = Nothing

End Sub
```

```
Public Sub Excel_Budget_Deactivate()
  'Disconnect from workbook
  Set xlWorkBook = Nothing
End Sub

Private Function GetXlsBudgetPath() As String
  Dim objDocProps As DocumentProperties
  Dim objDocProp As DocumentProperty

  On Error Resume Next
  Set objDocProps = ActiveProject.CustomDocumentProperties

  'If Doc Prop not found will return error
  Set objDocProp = objDocProps.Item("ExcelBudgetWorkbook")
  If Err.Number = 0 Then  'error 0 is no error
    GetXlsBudgetPath = objDocProp.Value
  Else
    'Return no path
    GetXlsBudgetPath = ""
  End If

  Set objDocProps = Nothing
  Set objDocProp = Nothing

End Function

Private Sub SetXlsBudgetPath(Path As String)
  Dim objDocProps As DocumentProperties
  Dim objPropLocation as DocumentProperties

  Set objDocProps = ActiveProject.CustomDocumentProperties

  If Len(Path) > 0 Then
    Set objPropLocaion = objDocProps("ExcelBudgetWorkbook")

    If objPropLocation Is Nothing Then
      objDocProps.Add "ExcelBudgetWorkbook", False, _
              msoPropertyTypeString, Path
    Else
```

PART

V

Customizing and
Automating Project 2000

```
        End If
    Else
      Set objPropLocation = objDocProps("ExcelBudgetWorkbook")
      If Not (objPropLocation Is Nothing) Then
        objPropsLocation("ExcelBudgetWorkbook").Delete
      End If
    End If
    Set objDocProps = Nothing
  End Sub


  Private Function ActivateExcel() As Boolean
    Dim strPath As String

    On Error GoTo Err_Hnd

      'If The Object Variable points to nothing attempt to Get workbook object
    If Not (xlWorkBook Is Nothing) Then
        'Lookup stored Path
      strPath = GetXlsBudgetPath

        'Check to see we have a path, before opening workbook
      If strPath <> "" Then
          'Attempt to get object
        Set xlWorkBook = GetObject(strPath)
      End If
      'Else: Already Connected to workbook
    End If
    ActivateExcel = True
  Exit Function
  Err_Hnd:
    Set xlWorkBook = Nothing
    ActivateExcel = False
  End Function
```

Creating the UserForm

The next step is to create a new UserForm in the same VBA project that contains the module Excel_Budget. Change the name of the form to dlgLinkExcelCell.

This form is very similar to the form you built in the introduction to UserForms earlier in this chapter. The form will have three controls. You will need to add a CommandButton, Label and a ComboBox:

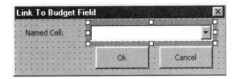

Add the controls and set these properties for dlgLinkExcelCell:

Control	Property	Value
Commandbuton1	(Name)	CmdApplyLink
	Caption	Ok
	Default	True
CommandButton2	(Name)	CmdCancel
	Cancel	True
	Caption	Cancel
Label1	(Name)	LblCellNames
	Caption	Named Cell:
Combobox1	(Name)	CmbCellNames
	MatchRequired	True
UserForm	(Name)	dlgExcelCellLink
	Caption	Link to Budget Field

Adding Code to Respond to UserForm Events

After you have set the properties and arranged the controls on the form, switch to the code window for the form. There are only three events that we care deeply about (or even care minimally about) in this form. They are the following:

- When the user Clicks on cmdCancel
- When the user Clicks on cmdApplyLink
- When the form loads

Sound familiar? You will find that most normal dialog boxes need only these three events.

The Update macro relies on cells that are named. Excel has a collection object of all the names in the workbook. The ComboBox will list all the names that the Update macro will accept as valid. The main purpose of the Initialize event procedure is to load the names from the names collection into the cmbCellNames list. The event procedure

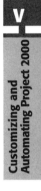

cmdCancel_Click is identical to that used in the UserForm you designed earlier. The last event will link an Excel cell to the fixed cost field of the currently selected task. The completed code for the user form follows:

Completed Code for VBA UserForm dlgLinkExcelCell

```
Private Sub cmdCancel_Click()
  Me.Hide
  Unload Me
End Sub

Private Sub cmdApplyLink_Click()
 'Link Cell
  ActiveCell.Task.Text30 = cmbCellNames.Value
  ActiveCell.Task.FixedCost = xlWorkBook.Names(cmbCellNames
.Value).RefersToRange.Value
 'Close Form
  Me.Hide
  Unload Me
End Sub

Private Sub UserForm_Initialize()
  Dim colNames As Object 'Names
  Dim objName As Object 'Name

  Set colNames = xlWorkBook.Names
 'Exit Sub
'Clear List
  cmbCellNames.Clear
'Add items to list
  For Each objName In colNames
    cmbCellNames.AddItem objName.Name
  Next objName

Set colNames = Nothing
Set objName = Nothing

End Sub
```

Before you release the application, you would create a custom command bar with menu items or buttons for the seven macros. See Chapter 22 for examples and instructions. You will need to create a command bar with a button or menu item to run each of the following macros, which were discussed earlier in the chapter:

- `Excel_Budget_Workbook_Link` to establish the link to the Excel spreadsheet
- `Excel_Budget_Workbook_UnLink` to clear the document property and the link fields
- `Excel_Budget_Add_Link` to show the user form
- `Excel_Budget_Remove_Link` to break the link
- `Excel_Budget_Update_Links` to refresh the links to the Excel worksheet
- `Excel_Budget_Show` to make the workbook visible
- `Excel_Budget_Deactivate` to close the Excel session

You'll also need to display the custom fields and fixed cost fields in a task view (such as the Gantt Sheet). Refer to Chapter 16 for information on displaying fields.

Further Suggestions for the Linked Expense Application

With the current macros, you are limited to pulling cells from a single Excel workbook. It would be nice if you could determine the workbook on a per field basis. Obviously this would require some modifications to the UserForm, but it will also require some additional custom fields or a method of parsing the information from a single field.

A true Open File dialog box would be superior to the input box. However, this is not a feature built into VBA. To get access to standard dialog boxes, you would need to make Windows API calls or use an ActiveX control such as the Microsoft Common Dialog Control.

 TIP   See the VBA Help files for information on API calls from DLLs and adding ActiveX controls. We also recommend the *VBA Developer's Handbook* published by Sybex (Ken Getz and Mike Gilbert: 0-7821-1951-4).

This application does not bind to summary tasks because summary tasks have calculated values. Like other costs, the fixed cost of a summary task is the sum of the fixed cost of all its subtasks.

PART

V

**Customizing and
Automating Project 2000**

MASTERING THE OPPORTUNITIES

Using the *TimeScaledValues* Collection

Project does not include travel time or travel costs in the budget unless you include them as fixed costs or per-use costs, either of which must be hand calculated when a project task requires more than one trip. When we were initially brainstorming project ideas for this chapter, we considered creating a travel-cost calculator, which is a Project application that we'd use on a regular basis. The functionality that we desire includes the following:

- Calculating the total travel cost for a particular task, based on mileage to and from the work site and the number of days a resource is assigned to the site
- Calculating mean travel time for tasks completed at remote work sites
- Calculating duration, work, and units in a manner that accurately reflects mean travel time for project scheduling and cost analysis

The first two are easy. The last, however, is really nasty. In our spare time, we're still working on the application…and working and working. It didn't take us long to discover that calculating travel costs for a project is a little trickier then it would first appear, so this is an application that's still in development. But as part of our work, we've spent a considerable amount of time with a new collection in Project 2000, the TimeScaledValues collection. The TimeScaledValues collection provides a means for examining time-phased information on a field of an item (Task, Resource or Assignment). The TimeScaledData Method of an item returns a TimeScaledValues collection.

The following lines of code create a collection of time-phased values for the work field of objTask. Then, it iterates through the values and counts the days within work scheduled.

```
Function TaskDaysScheduled(objTask As Task) as Integer
Dim objTSVs As TimeScaleValues ' Holds all days for Task
Dim objTSV As TimeScaleValue ' Holds a single day
Dim intCount As Integer ' Count of Days with work
Dim sngWork As Single ' The Number of hours in the TSV

Set objTSVs = objTask.TimeScaleData(objTask.Start, objTask.Finish,
pjTaskTimescaledWork, pjTimescaleDays)
```

Continued ▐▶

MASTERING THE OPPORTUNITIES CONTINUED

```
For Each objTSV In objTSVs
  If IsNumeric(objTSV.Value) Then
    sngWork = CSng(objTSV.Value)
    If (sngWork > 0) Then intCount = intCount + 1
  End If
Next objTSV
TaskDaysScheduled = intCount
End Function
```

A nested loop such as the one used in the Charged Cost Budget application would be even better then the previous code. In this case, you would call the `TimeScaledData` of the Assignment, not the Task. For an accurate travel-cost application, custom information will need to be stored with the assignments, not with tasks or resources. Project does support custom fields for assignments; however, these fields can only be accessed programmatically. `UserForms` will be needed to fill in information for these fields. You will not be able to add these custom fields to views, so you will likely need custom fields in tasks and resources to store summaries and macros to roll the information into those custom fields. Finally, you will need a method of rolling the custom costs into the budget.

Some final advice on creating applications: Don't become discouraged if it does not do everything you want it to immediately; the first version does not need to do it all. Build your applications in phases. If you tackle too much at once, you'll never finish the application. (But you're already a master at project management, so you knew that.)

VBA is a very powerful tool that will let you build incredibly sophisticated applications. Developing a large Project application is, itself, a project. Project 2000 is an excellent tool for project management; use it to manage your application development as well.

What's Next

From this point forward, you're on your own. Unlike using VBA with Excel, Word, and Access, you won't find hundreds or even dozens of articles in developers' magazines on how to automate Project or a score of downloadable applications on the Microsoft Web

PART

V

Customizing and
Automating Project 2000

site. If you like what you've seen in this chapter and want to create more Project 2000 applications, here are some resources that might be helpful:

Mastering Visual Basic for Applications by Guy Hart-Davis is the premiere guide for the Visual Basic for Applications programming language. Most VB books spend 90 to 95% of their content on creating standalone applications. This book focuses precisely on VB for automation with programs such as Project and the Office suite.

Every application that can be automated with VB includes the application's object model. With most applications, you can access the model by firing up VB. If that doesn't work, open the VB IDE in any application (for example, Project 2000) and load the application's library. Use the Object Browser to examine the model.

For detailed information about automating to and from a specific Office application, we use the *VBA Developer's Handbook* written for that software:

- *Mastering VBA 6* (Guy Hart-Davis: 0-7821-2636-7)

- *Word 2000 Developer's Handbook* (Guy Hart-Davis: 0-7821-2329-5)

- *Excel 2000 Developer's Handbook* (Marion Cottingham: 0-7821-2328-7)

CHAPTER **26**

Installing and Administering Microsoft Project Central 2000

Microsoft Project Central is a Web-based messaging system that pulls single or multiple Project summaries together in one central location. It allows for collaborative planning and tracking among project managers and resources, and easy Web-based reporting. By providing access to project data, Microsoft Project Central extends project management organizationally, even to users who do not have Microsoft Project installed on their desktops. Project Central provides enterprise-wide, one-stop shopping for project information.

Although there are some installation tasks that require network administrator's skills, most Project Central administrative tasks are better handled by someone, such as a senior project manager, who is familiar with Microsoft Project 2000 and with the actual projects about which the teams will be communicating. This chapter focuses on installing and administering Project Central and assumes that the person doing the installation is already familiar with server installations. For information on using Project Central to manage your projects or work on a project, see Chapter 16, "Team Project Management with Project Central 2000."

Understanding Microsoft Project Central

Microsoft Project Central consists of two applications: a client and a server. Team members can plan, deliver, and view their work through the Project Central client interface, shown in Figure 26.1. With proper permissions they can add and delegate tasks. Project managers can review up-to-date information and request status reports. Senior project managers can get concise, action-oriented views and project summary information. The client requires a Web browser, either Internet Explorer 4 or greater, or the Browser Module for Microsoft Project Central (a 32-bit Windows client) for those who do not use Microsoft Internet Explorer.

Project Central Server is installed on a Windows NT OS–based machine. It supports Microsoft SQL Server 7, Oracle, or MSDE (Microsoft Data Engine), a scaled-down version of SQL Server that is included with Project Central. The setup program makes the necessary connection between Internet Information Server, Microsoft Project Central, and the selected database.

Microsoft Project files and databases are not stored in Microsoft Project Central. You must, however, save your Microsoft Project to a shared network location in order to make information available to Microsoft Project Central. If you store your project on your desktop, the project will not be available unless the folder is shared and your computer is turned on.

Only summary information and configuration options are stored in the Project Central database. If you uninstall Project Central or delete items from the database, you still retain your entire Microsoft Project 2000 file or database.

FIGURE 26.1

Microsoft Project Central's Web-based interface takes project communication to a whole new level.

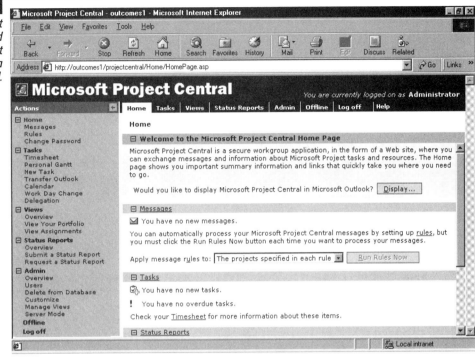

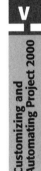

PART

V

Customizing and
Automating Project 2000

NOTE Some administrative tasks need to be performed after the initial installation, but after these are completed, any project manager may begin using Microsoft Project Central by entering the URL of the Microsoft Project Central Web server on the Workgroup page of the Options dialog box (Tools ➢ Options).

Enhancements, such as personal Gantt Charts, filtering, sorting, grouping, task delegation, reports, reporting mechanisms, the ability to work offline, set message rules, and much more make Project Central a necessary tool in project management.

Web Server Requirements

Microsoft Project Central Server takes advantage of a full-scale Windows NT or Windows 2000 server. It integrates well with the applications and services installed. However, it can be installed on a Windows NT workstation if no more than 10 users—project managers, administrators, and workgroup members—need to work on the projects in Project

Central. Before continuing, you may want to check the server that will host Microsoft Project Central and note the following:

- Memory
- Available disk space on shared drives
- Operating system (some flavor of Windows)
- Internet Information Server (Web-hosting software)
- Database server (SQL Server, Oracle, or MSDE)

For the operating system, Internet Information Server, and database, note their version numbers and any installed service packs. You can compare your server's information to the tables that follow, and make sure that you have the correct hardware and software to begin your install. Table 26.1 shows the system hardware requirements for a default installation of Microsoft Project Central. The table shows the minimum requirements for Project Central to run at all; your system requirements will undoubtedly be greater and may vary, depending on the configuration options you choose.

TABLE 26.1: PROJECT CENTRAL SERVER HARDWARE REQUIREMENTS

Hardware	Minimum
Hard Disk space	100MB
Processor	Intel Pentium 200Mhz or equivalent
Memory	128MB RAM

Software requirements vary greatly, depending on your operating system. Please read the following carefully and note which software is required for each operating system. It is important that the correct versions are installed for each operating system. Table 26.2 lists the server software requirements.

TABLE 26.2: PROJECT CENTRAL SERVER SOFTWARE REQUIREMENTS

Software	Requirement
Windows and IIS	Windows Server NT 4.0 with Service Pack 4 or greater and Internet Information Server (IIS) 4.0. IIS 4.0 is included with Windows NT Option Pack 4, or
	Microsoft Windows 2000 (Advanced Server or Professional) and IIS 5.0. IIS 5.0 ships with Windows 2000, or
	Option Pack 4 with Windows NT 4.0 Workstation, Service Pack 4 and IIS 4.0, but you will be limited to 10 simultaneous connections.
Database	Microsoft SQL Server 7,
	Oracle Server 8, or
	Microsoft Database Engine

You can obtain Option Pack 4 from the Microsoft Web site: `http://www.microsoft`
`.com/NTServer/all/downloads.asp`. Microsoft Database Engine is included on the
Project Central CD.

Workstation Client Requirements

The browse client-side interface runs on any Pentium computer operating with Windows 95 or greater, but, as with any Web software, more memory and a faster network
connection are nice things to have. To use Microsoft Project Central, a user must have a
browser installed on their workstation. Internet Explorer 5.0 is included on the Microsoft
Project Central CD. If your organization does not use Internet Explorer, you must install
the browser module included on the Microsoft Project Central CD. Table 26.3 lists the
hardware and software requirements for the Project Central client.

TABLE 26.3: PROJECT CENTRAL WORKSTATION REQUIREMENTS	
Hardware/Software	**Minimum**
Processor	Intel Pentium 75Mhz or equivalent
Available drive space	10–20MB
Operating system	Windows 95 or 98, or Windows NT Workstation 4.0 with Service Pack 3 or later
Browser	Microsoft Internet Explorer 4.01 or later, or the Browser Module for Microsoft Project Central

Preparing for Server Installation

After you've checked your server installation against the information in Table 26.2
and added or updated server software, the next step is to set up the database. Carefully read the description for the database you wish to install before proceeding.

Using MSSQL7

There are two installation methods for Microsoft SQL Server 7.0: you can use the
default installation of the database or you can create your own database. To use
the default method, you run three scripts from the command prompt: `crttable.sql`,
`insdefsq.sql`, `insdefsi.sql`. The first script creates the database and builds the tables:

```
[CD_ROM drive]:\pjcntrl\Isapi\1033 (or the appropriate language folder)
\osql –U <account name> -P <password> -I Crttable.sql [shouldn't be indented
in 2nd line]
```

The second script inserts default records for the tables:

```
[CD_ROM drive]:\pjcntrl\Isapi\1033 (or the appropriate language folder)
\osql -U <account name> -P <password> -d Project_CentralDB -I Insdefsq.sql
```

CD-ROM drive is the drive where SQL can find the Project Central installation CD. Account Name and Password are the account name and password for the SQL Server 7 database administrator. You must use Project_CentralDB for the -d parameter.

```
Command Prompt                                              _ □ X
C:\PJCNTRL\ISAPI\1033>osql -U sa -P ppj -d Project_CentralDB -i Insdefsq.sql_
```

NOTE For information on how to create your own database, see the Sybex Web site at www.sybex.com.

WARNING If you do not give the correct account name and password, the scripts will not be able to execute and you will receive a warning message.

Using Oracle

You cannot run a default installation when using an Oracle database. See the help file on the Microsoft Project 2000 [CD-ROM Drive] \Pjcntrl\help\1033\Svrsetup.htm for information on how to create the database to be used with Oracle.

Using MSDE

Microsoft Database Engine is only a viable option if you have 10 or fewer users (and with some systems, you may find that more than 5 results in serious performance degradation). If MSDE is not installed on your system, the Install Now option from Microsoft Project Central setup will automatically install MSDE, create the database, and run the SQL scripts. After you reboot your system, you are ready to continue the Microsoft Project Central installation. If MSDE is installed on your system, Microsoft Project Central setup does not reinstall the database.

Installing Microsoft Project Central Server

After the preceding specifications have been met, you can begin installing Microsoft Project Central Server. If you have chosen to use MSSQL or Oracle, you must use a Custom Installation. If you are using MSDE, then choose the Install Now option.

NOTE Although you should install Microsoft Project Central Server on a drive formatted with the NTFS file system to secure your Web site, it is not a requirement.

Starting Microsoft Project Central Server Setup

To install Microsoft Project Central on the server, follow these steps:

1. Insert your Microsoft Project 2000 CD into your CD-ROM drive. The setup program should run automatically.

   OR

   If autorun is disabled, choose Run from the Start menu and enter the following command: **[CD-ROM Drive]:\autorun\autorun**.

2. Select Microsoft Project Central Server from the Microsoft Project setup window, as shown in Figure 26.2.

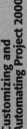

Select Microsoft Project Central Server from the Microsoft Project 2000 setup window.

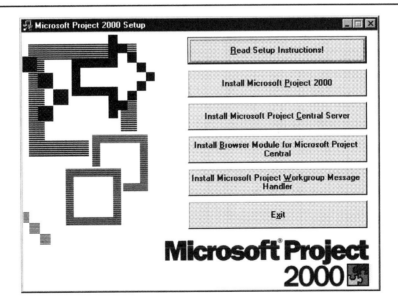

3. Read the End User License Agreement (EULA) and click Next.

4. If none of the three databases listed are installed on your server, choose Install Now. If SQL Server, Oracle, or MSDE are installed, select Customize, as shown in Figure 26.3.

FIGURE 26.3

Select your installation options from the Microsoft Project Central Server installation dialog box.

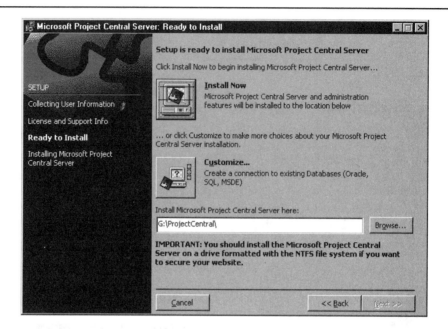

5. Select the shared drive where you want Microsoft Project Central installed (refer to Figure 26.3). The installer defaults to the drive with the most available space.

Installing with No Existing Database

Click Install Now if you're not using MSSQL7 or if Oracle and Microsoft Data Engine are not already installed on the server that will house Microsoft Project Central.

WARNING If you have one of these database engines installed on this server, and you click Install Now to choose the default installation, Microsoft Project Central will not function properly. You (and your users) will receive an error message when trying to view Microsoft Project Central from a browser. You have to use Customize if you have any of these database engines installed.

Installing with an Existing Database

Choose Customize if you are using MSSQL7 or Oracle or have MSDE installed on the server that will house Microsoft Project Central. Complete the following steps in the Microsoft Project Central Server Connect to Database window (shown in Figure 26.4):

1. Select whether you want to use MSDE, MSSQL, or Oracle.

2. Enter the name of the server that hosts your database.

3. Enter your logon information for the named database server.

4. Enter the name of the database you created to hold your Project information.

5. Click on the Test Connection button to validate the information you just entered. If you receive the message "Test connection failed," go back and check your information. If you receive the message "Test connection completed successfully," click OK.

6. Click the Install Now button.

FIGURE 26.4

*Enter information
to connect Micro-
soft Project Central
Server to an existing
database.*

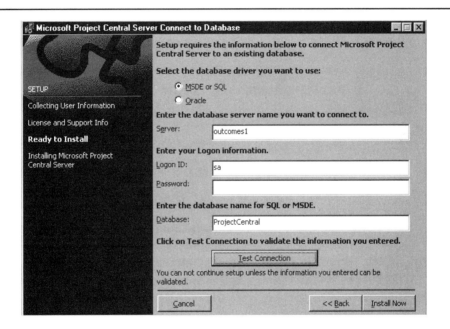

When installation is complete, you are asked to restart the server. After the server reboots, you can configure the server for your project managers.

Installing Project Central Clients

A Web browser is needed to use Microsoft Project Central. A whole new outlook on Microsoft Project begins when you open this interface. You may use Internet Explorer 4.*x*, 5.0, or the Browser Module. The Browser Module and IE 5.0 are included on the Microsoft Project 2000 CD.

NOTE To comply with licensing requirements, every user account created in Microsoft Project Central must have a valid copy of Microsoft Project installed on their desktop or a Microsoft Project Central client access license.

Installing Internet Explorer 5

To install Internet Explorer 5, follow these steps:

1. Insert the Microsoft Project 2000 CD into the CD-ROM drive.

2. Exit the Installation window if it appears.

3. Choose Run from the Windows Start menu.

4. Type the following command: **[CD-ROM drive]:\IE5\EN\ie5setup.exe**.

5. Click OK. The setup for IE 5 begins.

6. When prompted, restart your system.

 TIP If you need to install IE 5 on a number of user workstations, you'll save time if you use the Internet Explorer Administration Kit (IEAK), available for free download on the Microsoft Web site. IEAK is a tool to create custom installations from a single server point or a CD.

Installing Windows Browser

The Windows Browser module is an IE 5 substitute that works with Project Central. To install the Windows Browser, follow these steps:

1. Insert the Microsoft Project 2000 CD into the CD-ROM drive.

2. The Installation Window should automatically appear. If it does not, choose Run from the Start menu and type the following command: **[CD-ROM Drive]:\autorun\autorun** and click OK.

3. Select Install Browser Module for Microsoft Project Central from the installation menu.

4. Follow the directions for each step until you reach the Ready to Install window.

5. Select either Install Now, which installs the browser to the default location with default features, or Customize, which allows you to select where and how you want the browser installed.

When setup concludes, you'll be prompted to restart your system.

Administering and Customizing Microsoft Project Central Server

The Microsoft Project Central Administrator has permission to add, modify, deactivate, and remove user accounts; set database options; clean up the Microsoft Project Central database; and control access to the Microsoft Project Central site. The administrator can also customize the appearance of Microsoft Project Central Web pages by adding a company logo, hyperlinks to other Web sites, or hyperlinks to other files on the network. The administrator defines roles, which limit available functionality, and categories, which limit views of project data.

It is in the Administration Module, shown in Figure 26.5, where non-project time categories such as vacation, sick leave, or work not related to the project are defined. After the definitions are set, nonworking time can be tracked along with project time. The result: a complete timesheet solution for project managers. Gantt bar formatting is done from this module, along with setting the Authentication security options. It is at this point in the process that the senior project manager or appropriate supervisory personnel may want to be involved to set up the project management and human resource aspects of Project Central.

PART

V

Customizing and
Automating Project 2000

FIGURE 26.5

The Overview page of the Administration module contains information on areas waiting to be configured.

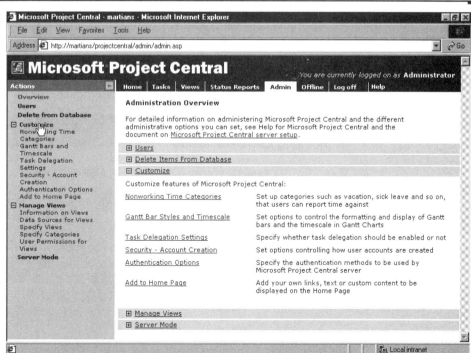

Understanding Server Mode

Microsoft Project Central Server runs in two modes: normal and single user. Single user mode is used for administrative tasks that lock database objects or change security settings.

Normal Mode

Normal mode is the Microsoft Project Central Server run mode that allows users to access project data. If the server is not in normal mode, users other than the administrator cannot log on and projects cannot be updated.

Single User Mode

Some administrative tasks can be performed only in single user mode, including the following:

- Deleting items from the database
- Merging user accounts
- Changing authentication options
- Changing nonworking time

It is important for data integrity that you make sure that there are no users connected to the database before you change modes. The database must be locked to prevent accidental corruption:

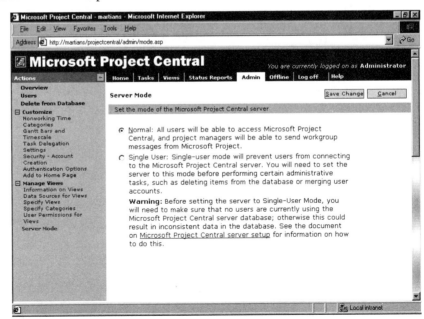

Before switching to single user mode, send an email to all users, warning them to stop using the server, either directly through a browser or through Microsoft Project, at a specified time. After all users have logged off, you can safely change modes. To change modes select Admin ➤ Server Mode from the top menu or select Server Mode in the Actions menu.

WARNING When you finish your administrative tasks, make sure you switch Microsoft Project Central back to normal mode.

Logging On to Microsoft Project Central

Open a browser, either locally on the server or from a remote machine. Enter the following URL including the server name (the name of the computer where Project Central is installed):

`http://[servername]/projectcentral`

When you open this site for the first time, you will see a Security Warning. Click Yes to continue. If you click the No button, you cannot access the Microsoft Project Central site.

The Microsoft Project Central setup program creates a default user named Administrator. This user has a blank password. The first time you logon, type **administrator** in the username box and leave the password box blank. A dialog box appears, asking you to change your password. (This is highly recommended.) To change your password, click Yes. You will be asked for your old password, to enter a new password, and to confirm your new password. Leave the Old Password box blank and after you enter your new password twice, click the Change Password button or press Enter:

Change Your Password

O̲ld Password:	
N̲ew Password:	********
Confir̲m Password:	********

[Change P̲assword]   [C̲ancel]

NOTE   When you initially set your password, it must be at least eight characters long. After you have logged in, you can change that parameter in the Authentication section of the Customize menu.

Using the Administrative Functions

The Admin tab and all administrative functions, shown in Figure 26.6, are available only to the user accounts that have administrative permissions.

FIGURE 26.6

The Admin menu is only visible if you have administrative permissions.

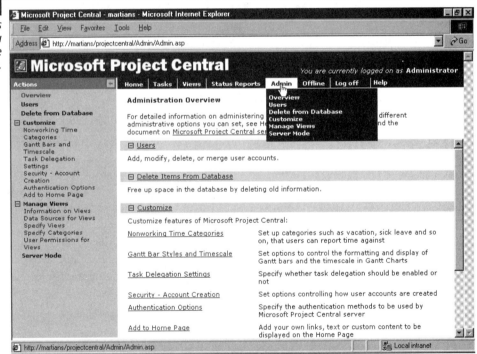

Creating Users Accounts

Microsoft Project Central automatically creates an administrative account with a blank password when you install Project Central. All other accounts must be created by an account with administrative permissions. Accounts can also be created by project managers if you set appropriate security options. You can find out more about this method in "Setting Security and Account Creation Permissions" later in this chapter (it is also discussed in Chapter 16).

The Users view displays a list of users, how each account is authenticated, its role, and its status. You can use the drop-down arrows to filter any of the columns in the user table.

Selecting a User Role

There are three roles in Microsoft Project Central: Administrator, Manager, and Resource. Table 26.4 describes each role.

TABLE 26.4: PROJECT CENTRAL USER ROLES

Role	Permissions	Default Category
Administrator	Full Administrative	None
Manager	Inherited and Allocated	Project Managers
Resource	Allocated	Team Members

You add, modify existing users, and merge or delete user accounts by choosing Admin ➢ Users from the Microsoft Project Central Menu bar or by clicking on Users in the Actions frame on the left side of the Microsoft Project Central window (see Figure 26.6). To create a new user, follow these steps:

1. Expand the Users section of the Administration window.

2. Click Add User.

3. Select the desired authentication method. If you chose Microsoft Project Central server authentication, the dialog box also asks for a password and password confirmation.

4. Enter the user name. If you are using Windows NT authentication, you must enter the domain name with the user name.

Add a New User

Authenticate new user by	⦿ Windows NT Authentication, using the Windows User Account
	○ Microsoft Project Central server authentication, using a logon ID and password
Windows User Account:	amarquis\Outcomes
Email:	amarquis@triadconsulting.com
Role:	Resource ▾

5. Enter the email address of the new user.

6. Select the role of the new user.

7. Scroll back to the top of the page.

8. Click the Save Changes button.

Modifying a User Account

To modify a user account or reset the password for an account, follow these steps:

1. Select the account you wish to modify.

2. Click Modify Account Options.

The account properties appear below the User List.

3. Change the account option or click Reset Password.

4. Scroll up to the top and click the Save Changes button.

Deleting a User Account

When you delete a user account, you are deactivating the account. It still appears in the User List, but the status is inactive. To delete a user account, follow these steps:

1. Select the account to delete.

2. Click the Delete User menu option. A message box confirms the deletion:

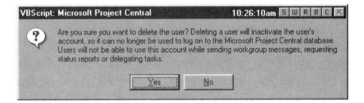

3. Click Yes.

Another message box appears, confirming the update. The user still appears on the User list, but is inactive.

Merging User Accounts

By default, project managers and resources can create Microsoft Project Central user accounts. Project managers can create accounts by sending workgroup messages to project resources and by specifying Windows user accounts when they enter information in the Resource Information dialog box. Resources can create user accounts by delegating tasks to other resources. If project managers and resources do not use a standard naming convention when they create accounts, a single resource might end up with multiple Project Central accounts.

 TIP As a Project Central administrator, you can restrict project managers and resources from creating user accounts by choosing Admin ➢ Users ➢ Security-Account Creation from within Project Central and clearing the two checkboxes. See "Setting Security and Account Creation Permissions" later in this chapter.

When a person has more than one resource account, you can consolidate these accounts to prevent this person from having to log in several times to retrieve all their information. If more than one account has actually been used for a resource, before you merge the accounts, the project managers must make the required changes to their project files and resend corresponding workgroup messages. Only after this has been accomplished in all active projects should you merge the two user accounts or these assignments will be lost.

 NOTE You must set Microsoft Project Central server to Single Server Mode before you can merge user accounts.

To merge two user accounts, follow these steps:

1. Click on Merge Users.

2. Select the two users you want to merge from the drop-down box. After the merge operation, the new account will be the user account in the text box on the left.

3. Scroll to the top and click Save Changes.

4. Reset the Server Mode to Normal.

Deleting Items from the Database

You may need to delete items from the Microsoft Project Central Database to free up space, to process a merge account request, or to remove data that is no longer needed.

Point to the Admin tab on the Microsoft Project Central menu and select Deleting Items from the Database, or select Deleting Items from the Database on the Actions frame. You must set Microsoft Project Central server to Single User mode before you can delete any data. If you are not in Single User mode, you see this error message:

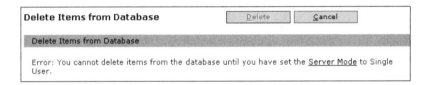

You can choose to delete Tasks, Messages, Status Reports, and entire Project summaries for all users or selected users. You may also select the parameters for which of the preceding data you want deleted. After the options are set, scroll back to the top and click the Delete button. You're asked to confirm your action.

 WARNING This action is irreversible. After data is deleted from the Microsoft Project Central database, there is no way to retrieve it.

After you complete this action, make sure you reset the Server Mode to Normal.

Customizing Project Central

Microsoft Project Central gives you the ability to control many aspects of your projects, from who can create user accounts to how users log in, from what color your Gantt bars are to a personalized home page featuring your company logo. Figure 26.7 shows the customizable settings for Project Central.

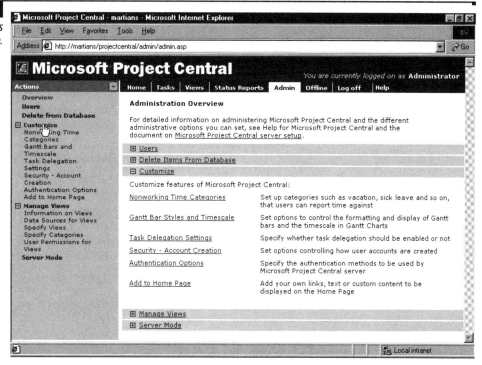

FIGURE 26.7

Project Central is customizable.

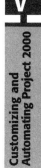

PART

V

Customizing and
Automating Project 2000

Nonworking Time Categories

You can set up and specify categories of nonworking or non-project time. These categories are displayed in users' timesheets, in a special Nonworking Time section, and users are able to report time against these categories.

Figure 26.8 shows the nonworking time for a Microsoft Project Central Server. Sick Leave and Vacation are the two default entries. You can keep or delete these entries and/ or create your own. For each category, you can associate a code that can be in numeric, text, or Microsoft Project outline code format. Microsoft Project Central server does not use these codes, and users do not see them, but they are stored in the Microsoft Project Central server database, so you can use them for your own reference.

 WARNING You must be in Single User mode to edit Nonworking Time Categories.

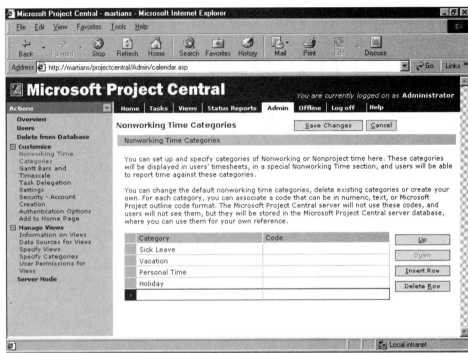

Customizing Gantt Bars and Timescales

On this page, you can customize the color, size, style, and name of nineteen different Gantt Charts. You can also designate the beginning day of each chart. Giving each Gantt Chart a unique name allows Project Managers and Team Members to quickly choose the correct chart from a drop-down list.

Customizing Gantt Charts

To customize a Gantt Chart, select Gantt Bar Styles and Timescales from the Customize menu shown in Figure 26.9. From the Gantt Chart drop-down box at the top of the page, select the chart you want to customize. Click in the cell that contains the information you want to change.

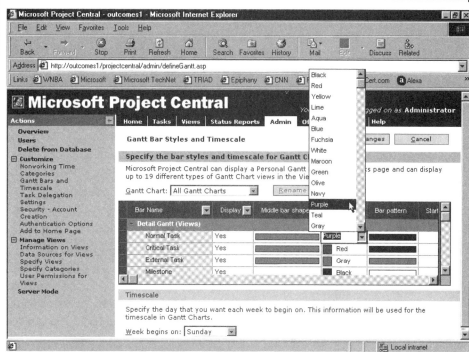

FIGURE 26.9

Setting Gantt Chart options in Project Central

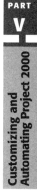

At the bottom of the page, select which day you want the week to begin on from the drop-down box. Click on the Save Changes button at the top of the page. After you have made changes, give the chart a descriptive name. Click the Rename button and enter the name. Click the Accept button to save the new name:

Changing the Task Delegation Setting

There are times when resources need to delegate tasks to other resources. For example, a project manager assigns tasks to a team leader. The team leader in turn assigns those tasks to other members of the team. If one team member becomes overloaded with work, becomes ill, goes on vacation, or just has a better plan for how to spend next week, that team member could delegate some of their tasks to another team member. (It's this last reason that creates a need for the ability to disable the Task Delegation feature.) Specify whether you want the Task Delegation feature to be enabled or disabled for Microsoft Project Central by choosing Task Delegation Settings from the Actions pane. If the feature is enabled, resources can delegate tasks to other resources.

Setting Security and Account Creation Permissions

The features in this section determine who can create accounts. Both options—to allow managers to create accounts and to allow resources to create accounts—are enabled by default. If you need tighter security for creating accounts, you may want to disable one or both of these options.

Setting Authentication Options

Microsoft Project Central users are authenticated in one of two ways. The first is the Windows NT user account authentication; the second is Microsoft Project Central authentication. Choose which way your want your users to be authenticated by clicking the Authentication Options in the Actions pane. By default, the Mixed option is enabled, allowing you to use either authentication method. You can also change the password length for Microsoft Project Central on this page.

 NOTE You must set Microsoft Project Central server to Single User mode before you can change the authentication mode.

To set authentication options:

1. Choose Authentication Options from the Customize menu or from the Actions menu.

2. Select which method you want to use for authentication. If you chose Windows NT authentication only, all current Microsoft Project Central accounts will be disabled; if you chose Microsoft Project Central authentication, all current Windows NT user accounts will be disabled.

3. Click the Save Changes button.

4. Reset the server mode to Normal.

TIP To change the password length for Microsoft Project Central server authentications, enter a number in the Minimum Length That Users Must Set Their Passwords To textbox, and then click the Save Changes button at the top of the page. This only changes the length for any new accounts. It does not disable current accounts and it does not affect users whose accounts are authenticated by Windows NT Server.

Customizing the Project Central Home Page

You can add your own links and content to the Microsoft Project Central Home Page. They will appear in special sections at the bottom of all users' home pages. This is one way to provide organization-specific information to all users conveniently, saving users from browsing or searching for the project information that you want them to have on hand. Figure 26.10 shows a customized home page that includes a page from a Web site.

PART

V

Customizing and Automating Project 2000

FIGURE 26.10

Customize the home page to deliver information to all users.

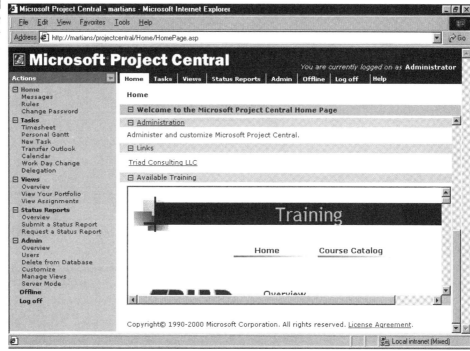

Adding Links

To add links to the Microsoft Project Central Home Page, click on Add to Home Page in the Customize menu or on the Actions frame. Type in the name of the link as you want it to appear on the Home Page. Next, type in the complete URL address in the next column including the http or file prefix. Figure 26.11 shows the content needed for the Home page to appear as it does in Figure 26.10.

FIGURE 26.11

You can customize the Home page by entering links and adding them to the page.

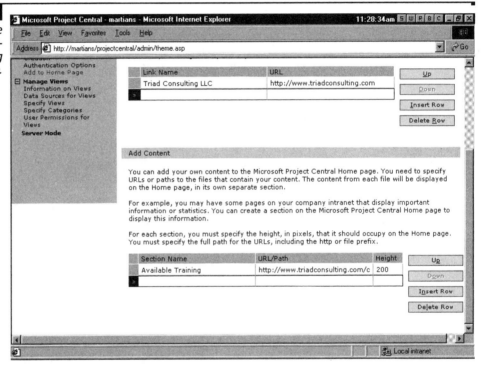

Scroll up to the top of the page and click Save Changes.

Adding Content

You can create a section on the Microsoft Project Central Home Page to display other information that may be important to users. This information must already be included on an intranet or Internet Web page. You must specify the height, in pixels, that it should occupy on the Home Page. You also must specify the full path for the URLs, including the http or file prefix. The content from each file will be displayed on the Home Page, in its own separate section.

For each section, fill in the information in the Add Content table, including how you want the section name to appear (see Figure 26.11).

After you finish, scroll up to the top and click Save Changes.

Managing Views

In this area, you define what Microsoft Project Central users can see in their Views section. This requires you to follow specific procedures. Make sure that you read each section before continuing. If you are not familiar with Microsoft Project 2000, you may want to seek the knowledge of a senior project manager in your organization (or read the earlier chapters in this book!)

Data Sources for Views

The Data Sources for Views page lists all the data source names (DSNs) used by projects in Microsoft Project Central.

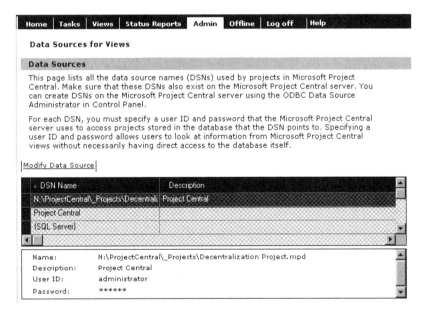

The DSNs must exist on both the Microsoft Project Central Server and the computer on which the project resides. You can create DSNs on any computer by using the ODBC Data Source Administrator in the Control Panel. Ideally, the server administrator should set up the needed DSNs and make them available to project managers.

Specify Views

Views are composed of a set of fields and filters that allows the user to focus on only certain areas of a project. (For more information on views, see Chapter 17, "Using Views to Evaluate Data.") As the administrator, you can create and define views to see Microsoft Project Central assignment information, a collection of projects, or to see details of an individual project. Point to Admin on the menu and choose Manage Views. Choose Specify Views in the Actions pane.

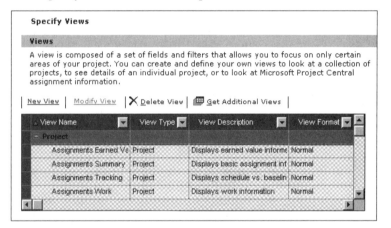

Defining a New View

Choosing New View from the menu opens the Define Views page. It presents all the options available to create a new view. Make your selection in each section and fill in the tables. A drop-down box appears when you click on a cell in a table.

Click the OK button at the top of the page when you are finished. The new view is now available for your users.

Modifying a View

Select a view to modify and click Modify View on the menu. The Modify View page looks exactly like the Define Views page. You can change any of the options except the View Type. When you are finished making changes, click the OK button at the top of the page.

Deleting a View

Use this menu item with caution. Select the view you want to delete and click Delete View on the menu. This action is completed without any confirmation. The Specify View's page resets and the view you deleted is no longer in the Views table.

WARNING After a view has been selected and you click Delete View, the view is deleted immediately. You will not have an opportunity to confirm or cancel the deletion.

Importing Additional Views

You can import HTML, data access, and ASP pages you create in other applications. For example, you can import HTML pages created in Word, Excel, PowerPoint, FrontPage, or Outlook and Data Access Pages are created in Access 2000. Save the pages in the \\[servername]\projectcentral\root\views folder. Choose Get Additional Views on the menu, and new pages in this folder are added to your Views table. When the views are added, a message box appears to let you know the pages were imported successfully:

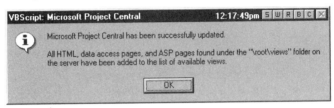

Specify Categories

A category can contain a single user or a group of users. Microsoft Project Central creates four default categories during installation. They categories are as follows:

Executive Manager   No default users

Project Managers   All users with the role of manager

Resource Manager   No default users

Team Members   All users with the role of resource

You can't delete the Project Managers and Team Managers categories, but you can remove the Executive Manager and Resource Manager categories if you wish.

With the exception of the default assignment of Resources and Managers, the Microsoft Project Central administrator specifies the users, projects, views, or portfolio and assignment information for each category. You might add new categories for specific projects or modify existing categories to allow specific team members like supervisors or team leaders to view more details about the project they are working with.

When you select Add Category you are directed to the Define Category page shown in Figure 26.12; when you select Modify Category, you are directed to the Modify Category page. The only difference in the two pages, other than the title, is that some selections are already made in the Modify View page.

PART

V

Customizing and
Automating Project 2000

FIGURE 26.12

Add categories to give groups of users different views.

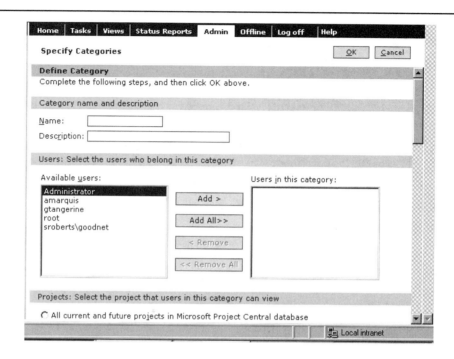

To add or modify a category, point to the Admin tab and select Manage Views. Choose Specify Categories. When the Specify Categories page opens from the Actions pane, click the appropriate menu item (to modify a category, you must have it selected in the table).

The following is a list of options you can set:

Users   Select the users who belong in this category

Projects   Select the project that users in this category can view

Portfolio Views   Select views for displaying the portfolio of projects

Project Views   Select views for displaying individual projects

Assignment Views   Select views for displaying Microsoft Project Central assignment information

 WARNING   Before you can see any data in the Assignment view, you must set permissions to control which assignments can be seen by users in this category. To set these permissions, see the following section.

After you finish making your selections and setting the options, scroll back to the top of the page and click the OK button.

Setting User Permissions for Views

You can change a user's permissions by assigning them to one or more categories and specifying which assignments they can view. To modify these permissions:

1. Choose Admin ➤ Manage Views.

2. Select User Permissions for Views from the Action frame.

3. Select the user whose permissions you want to modify.

4. Click Modify User Permissions.

5. Select the options you wish to use.

6. Enable or disable the Allow This User To See All Assignments Of All Users He Has Sent A Workgroup Message To check box.

7. Click the OK button at the top of the page.

Views are an important part of the user's experience with Project Central, and they provide the security and control that project managers require. When creating and managing views, it's essential to receive input from the project managers. Those who are knowledgeable about all the active projects in the organization are in the best position to make decisions about what views are available to which users.

PART

V

Customizing and
Automating Project 2000

INDEX

Note to the Reader: Page numbers in **bold** indicate the principal discussion of a topic or the definition of a term. Page numbers in *italic* indicate illustrations.

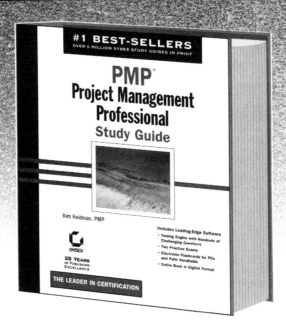

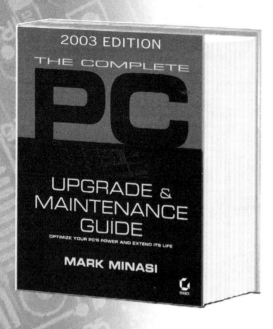

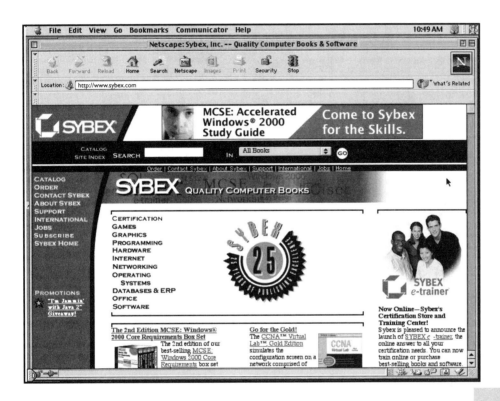